The Polarized Presidency of George W. Bush

The Polarized Presidency of George W. Bush

Edited by
George C. Edwards III and Desmond S. King

OXFORD
UNIVERSITY PRESS

OXFORD

UNIVERSITY PRESS

Great Clarendon Street, Oxford ox2 6DP

Oxford University Press is a department of the University of Oxford.
It furthers the University's objective of excellence in research, scholarship,
and education by publishing worldwide in

Oxford New York

Auckland Cape Town Dar es Salaam Hong Kong Karachi
Kuala Lumpur Madrid Melbourne Mexico City Nairobi
New Delhi Shanghai Taipei Toronto

With offices in

Argentina Austria Brazil Chile Czech Republic France Greece
Guatemala Hungary Italy Japan Poland Portugal Singapore
South Korea Switzerland Thailand Turkey Ukraine Vietnam

Published in the United States
by Oxford University Press Inc., New York

© The several contributors 2007

The moral rights of the authors have been asserted
Database right Oxford University Press (maker)

First published 2007

British Library Cataloguing in Publication Data
Data available

Library of Congress Cataloging in Publication Data
Data available

Typeset by SPI Publisher Services, Pondicherry, India
Printed in Great Britain
on acid-free paper by
Biddles Ltd., King's Lynn, Norfolk

ISBN 978–0–19–921797–7

10 9 8 7 6 5 4 3 2 1

To Jeffrey and Samuel
'Son, thou art ever with me' (Luke 15: 31)

Contents

Contents

List of Figures

List of Figures

List of Tables

Notes on Contributors

Scott B. Blinder is a post-doctoral fellow in Comparative Government, specializing in US politics, at the University of Oxford, Nuffield College. In addition to work on public opinion and the Iraq War, his research has focused on political psychology, political socialization, and attitudes toward issues of race and ethnicity in various contexts, including US public opinion and European immigration policy.

John P. Burke is Professor of Political Science at the University of Vermont. He is the author of a number of books, including *Becoming President: The Bush Transition 2000–2003*, *The Institutional Presidency: Organizing and Managing the White House from FDR to Bill Clinton*, *Advising Ike: The Memoirs of Attorney General Herbert Brownell*, *The Institutional Presidency*, *How Presidents Test Reality: Decisions on Vietnam 1954 and 1965*, and *Bureaucratic Responsibility*.

George C. Edwards III is Distinguished Professor of Political Science and Jordan Chair in Presidential Studies at Texas A&M University. He has authored dozens of articles and has written or edited twenty-one books on American politics and public policy making. He is also editor of *Presidential Studies Quarterly*. His latest books include *On Deaf Ears: The Limits of the Bully Pulpit*, *Why the Electoral College Is Bad for America*, and *Governing by Campaigning*.

Louis Fisher is a specialist in constitutional law with the Law Library of the Library of Congress and previously worked for the Congressional Research Service as a specialist on separation of powers. His books include *In the Name of National Security* (2006), *Military Tribunals and Presidential Power* (2005), *The Politics of Executive Privilege* (2004), *Nazi Saboteurs on Trial* (2003), and *American Constitutional Law*.

William G. Howell is Associate Professor at the Harris School of Public Policy at the University of Chicago. He has written widely on separation-of-powers issues and American political institutions, especially the presidency. He is the co-author (with Jon Pevehouse) of *While Dangers Gather: Congressional Checks on Presidential War Powers* (2007); and author of *Power without Persuasion: The Politics of Direct Presidential Action* (2003), and many articles.

Lawrence R. Jacobs is Professor of Political Science, Mondale Chair for Political Studies, and Director of the Center for the Study of Politics and Governance in the Humphrey Institute at the University of Minnesota. He has authored or co-authored numerous articles in leading journals and five books, including *Healthy, Wealthy, and Fair, Inequality and American Democracy, Politicians Don't Pander: Political Manipulation and the Loss of Democratic Responsiveness*, and *The Health of Nations*.

Gary C. Jacobson is Professor of Political Science at the University of California, San Diego. He is the author of *The Politics of Congressional Elections, Money in Congressional Elections, The Electoral Origins of Divided Government, Competition in U.S. House Elections, 1946–1988*, and, most recently, *A Divider, Not a Uniter: George W. Bush and the American People*. He is also co-author of *Strategy and Choice in Congressional Elections*.

Charles O. Jones is Professor Emeritus of Political Science, University of Wisconsin-Madison and a Non-Resident Senior Fellow at The Brookings Institution and The Miller Center of Public Affairs, University of Virginia. He is a former editor of the *American Political Science Review* and a former president of the American Political Science Association. His recent books include *The Presidency in a Separated System*, 2nd edn., and *Passages to the Presidency: From Campaigning to Governing*.

Desmond S. King is the Andrew W. Mellon Professor of American Government and Professorial Fellow of Nuffield College at the University of Oxford, and a Fellow of the British Academy. His research deals with US politics and comparative welfare policy, and race and American political development. He is the author and editor of numerous books, including *In the Name of Liberalism* and *Making Americans: Immigration, Race and the Origins of the Diverse Democracy*.

Douglas L. Kriner is assistant Professor of Political Science at Boston University. His research interests center on American political institutions, with a specific focus on the influence of inter-branch politics on the conduct of military affairs. He has published in *Public Opinion Quarterly*.

Martha Joynt Kumar is Professor of Political Science at Towson University. She has published numerous articles on presidential–press relations, White House communications operations, and transitions into the White House, and written or edited *Portraying the President: The White House and the News Media, White House World: Transitions, Organization, and Office Operations*, and *Wired for Sound and Pictures: Communicating From the White House*.

Thomas S. Langston is Professor of Political Science at Tulane University. He is the author of several books on the presidency, including *Ideologues and Presidents: From the New Deal to the Reagan Revolution, With Reverence and*

Contempt: How Americans Think about Their President, and *The Cold War Presidency.* He also authored *Uneasy Balance: Civil–Military Relations in Peacetime America since 1783,* and is at work on a book about presidential ineptitude and malfeasance.

James P. Pfiffner is University Professor in the School of Public Policy at George Mason University, and his research focuses on the presidency, American national government, and public management. He has published many articles and book chapters and written or edited ten books on the presidency, including *The Strategic Presidency: Hitting the Ground Running, The Modern Presidency,* and *The Character Factor: How We Judge America's Presidents.*

Richard M. Pious is Adolph and Effie Ochs Professor of American Studies in the Department of Political Science, Barnard College, and is Professor in the Graduate School of Arts and Sciences, Columbia University. He is the author of *The American Presidency* (1979), co-author of *The President, Congress and the Constitution* (1984), and author of *The War on Terrorism and the Rule of Law* (2006).

Fiona Ross is a senior lecturer in Politics at the University of Bristol. She is currently completing a monograph on the partisan politics of welfare restructuring in America and Britain, which investigates how party-specific effects manifest themselves during the policy process. She has also published numerous journal articles and book chapters on the politics of restructuring in post-industrial societies.

1

Introduction

George C. Edwards III and Desmond S. King

George W. Bush already has a distinctive legacy. Beginning with the protracted denouement of his election in 2000 and punctuated by the 9/11 terrorist attacks, wars in Afghanistan and Iraq, the devastation of Hurricane Katrina, and major changes in domestic policy, his presidency has polarized American politics and left durable impressions on public policy (Hacker and Pierson 2005). Elected in 2000 on what seemed to be a moderate platform in domestic policy and a cautious approach to international relations, George W. Bush has transformed policy in each. The administration's response to the 9/11 terrorist attacks, its desire to reorient fundamental aspects of domestic policy, and its efforts to build a lasting Republican majority are some of the most important political developments in the past generation.

As befits a president who has sought to reconfigure public policy and build a lasting governing coalition, there are two widely held and divergent views of his performance. To his detractors, Bush is a parochial, intellectually shallow, close-minded, hard-right cultural warrior who combines smug ideological certitude with a stunning indifference to facts and evidence. Opponents dismiss the president as unequal to the demands of the office, incapable of thoughtful reflection, an intellectually passive ignoramus robotically repeating platitudes. They see him as impervious to lessons of experience, unwilling to admit or correct mistakes, and unable to adapt his preconceptions to inconvenient realities. They complain that he suppresses dissent among his advisers and uses them as an ideological echo chamber rather than a source of competing views.

There is also a positive view. In this perspective, Bush is a mature and confident leader who is comfortable with himself and in wielding power. He is a president who is willing to tackle the large—and difficult—issues such as Social Security and the war on terrorism, with decisiveness and serene resolution. Moreover, an ideological coherence drives this administration, which, at least in the first term, often pursued its goals in an effective strategic manner. In the final analysis, his supporters argue, Bush is a president in tune with the mainstream of the American public and one who has brought about substantial and much-needed changes in public policy.

How can Americans have such contrasting views of the president? Why is the country so divided while it fights a war on terrorism?

Policy and Polarization

The extraordinary divergence in views of the president and his performance are reflected in an apparent paradox in American politics. In one important sense, Bush has moved the Republican Party to the left, espousing compassionate conservatism. Bush is not antigovernment in the tradition of Goldwater, Reagan, and Gingrich. He believes that Americans do not want to reduce government radically. Instead, they expect it to assuage two of life's greatest fears—illness and old age. Thus, we spend nearly 40 per cent of the federal budget on Social Security and health care. People also want help at the other end of the life cycle with improved education—and thus a better life—for their children. This is the record of a strong centralized state, comparable to other advanced democracies (Pontusson 2005), that mobilizes and allocates national resources to achieve national aims defined by the preferences of the governing party. It is not the sign of a weak and fragmented center incapable of exercising centralized authority, the conventional account of the US federal government (King 2007).

Central to Bush's electoral strategy has been pre-empting traditional Democratic issues such as education and health care. The size of both the federal budget and the national debt has grown substantially during his tenure. The very large deficits run up by the administration have certainly angered a number of traditional conservatives. Only a decade ago, led by Newt Gingrich, Republicans moved into ascendancy in Congress by promoting traditional conservatism, including smaller government, lower budgets, and reduced public services. In the 'Contract with America' they vowed to abolish four cabinet-level departments, including the Department of Education. Bush, however, supported adding a prescription drug entitlement to Medicare and substantially increasing federal aid to education. In this sense, then, the president has tried to capture the center for Republicans by advocating more liberal policies than did his Republican predecessors, thereby weakening the Democrats' hold on a traditionally Democrat Party issue.

On the other hand, Bush is the most polarizing president in polling history.[1] The first Gallup poll of Bush's tenure found that he had the highest level of *disapproval* of any new president since polling began (Gallup Poll 2001). Similarly, Gary C. Jacobson reported that the public's initial reception of

Bush found the widest partisan differences for any newly elected president in polling history. In the 28 Gallup and CBS/*New York Times* polls taken before September 11, 2001, Bush's approval ratings averaged 88 per cent among self-identified Republicans but only 31 per cent among Democrats (Independents averaged 50 per cent). This 57-point difference indicates an extraordinary degree of polarization (Jacobson 2003). Yet this gap between the assessments of Democrats and Republicans was just the beginning. In the 21–3 May 2004 Gallup poll, the difference between his approval among Republicans (89 per cent) and Democrats (12 per cent), was an astounding 77 percentage points! That gap of 70 points or higher has been common since Bush's fourth year in office (see, for example, Jones 2004*a*).

These are extreme and unprecedented levels of polarization (Jacobson 2006, ch. 1). No president, dating back to Harry Truman, has had a partisan gap above 70 points in any Gallup poll in a re-election year. Moreover, Gallup had never before found such a high proportion of partisans with such strongly opposing views of a president. In the 21–3 May 2004 poll, 64 per cent of Republicans said they strongly approved of the job Bush was doing as president, while 66 per cent of Democrats strongly disapproved. As Gallup put it, "Bush is the only president who has had more than 6 in 10 of his party's identifiers strongly approving of him at the same time that more than 6 in 10 of the other party's identifiers strongly disapprove of him." The only other president to have more than 60 per cent of a partisan group disapproving of him was Richard Nixon in the year of his resignation, when 61 per cent of Democrats strongly disapproved of him. At that time, Nixon had overall job approval ratings below 30 per cent (Jones 2004*b*).

Gallup found that 95 per cent of Republicans voted for Bush in 2004—but only 7 per cent of Democrats did so (Jones 2004*b*). Jacobson's analysis of the National Election Studies found the highest level of party line voting in the 52-year history of the National Election Studies. With partisan leaners (those who say they "lean" toward identifying with one party or the other) included, 89 per cent of Democrats and 91 per cent of Republicans voted for their party's candidates. If we exclude the leaners, 92 per cent of Democrats voted for Kerry while 94 per cent of Republicans voted for Bush (Jacobson 2006, 190). Although Bush received a modest 5-point bounce in his approval rating after his election in 2004, his 53 per cent rating was actually the lowest of any of the last seven presidents who won election while serving as president in the first poll conducted after their elections.

The war in Iraq has been the most important policy of the Bush Administration. Although the president enjoyed majority support for going to war in the spring of 2003, by 2005 the public's evaluations of both the war, the postwar US occupation of Iraq, and the president's management of it split along party lines. This division was much greater than it had been for any other US military engagement since World War II including the Vietnam

War, widening the partisan gap in overall evaluations of the president in the process (Jacobson 2006, ch. 6).

At least part of the explanation of the antipathy to Bush among Democrats is the president's basic strategy of placing strong government in the service of conservative values. The central value for Bush appears to be freedom (both as a domestic priority and as a plank of foreign policy). He is much less concerned with equality, especially equality of outcome, which is at the heart of traditional liberalism (Barry 1996). Bush aims to expand individual choice and empower individuals—and increase their responsibility for themselves. Thus, the president's reforms offer opportunities and incentives for individuals to become more self-sufficient (see Edwards 2006).

Bush argues that government curtails freedom not by being large or active but by making choices that should be left to people, undermining their individual responsibility in the process. Thus he is flexible, willing to support expanding, reforming, or shrinking government, as long as it increases people's choices. He wants to change the structure of government, not its size. He is less concerned with how much government spends than with how it spends it. He wants to reduce the demand for government rather than, as traditional conservatives do, the supply of it. And he wants to accomplish this by, in his words, "empowering people."

Bush has attempted to shift decision-making responsibilities from government to individuals through providing education vouchers to parents and the option of health savings accounts for everyone, and through partially privatizing Social Security (individual investment accounts) and Medicare prescription drug benefits (competing insurance plans). Government would still provide or safeguard resources devoted to these programs, but much of the decision making about them would center on individual choice. Similarly, low taxes expand each earner's freedom by enlarging discretionary income.

This is an ideologically driven agenda, just as the president depicts the war against terrorism in his speeches as an ideological struggle analogous to the Cold War. It seems reasonable to argue that Democratic opposition to Bush's domestic policies such as school standards and choice, medical savings accounts, partial privatization of Social Security, and cuts in individual income taxes reflects a basic fight over the classic goals of equality and freedom. Lowering income taxes, which fall mainly on the wealthy, increases inequality. Tax savings cannot help the poorest Americans, who pay no income tax now. Creating options in public schools, Medicare, and Social Security threatens their comprehensive coverage of the population—and also everyone with a stake in maintaining the status quo. Thus, Democrats fear that the true intention of the president's proposals is to relieve government of its responsibilities and replace public programs with a free market that values efficiency more than the equality of a social safety net.

Bush wants to rewrite the social contract, initiated in Franklin D. Roosevelt's New Deal enacted in the 1930s, that has defined the past four generations of Americans. The current system broadly spreads the financial risks of the vicissitudes of life over most of the population. Expanding freedom increases risk for the less well off. Their lack of slack resources puts them at greater risk from downturns in the stock market (affecting personal accounts in Social Security) or mistakes in evaluating their health care needs or an unexpected inability to save for them. Health accounts could also leave the sick in more traditional plans with higher costs as healthier people opt out of sharing the risk of illness. In addition, individual retirement accounts and health savings accounts make it more difficult for the wealthy to subsidize the poor under Social Security, Medicare, and Medicaid (which covers much of nursing home care).

Conservatives argue that inequalities of outcomes are manifestations of freedom and prerequisites for progress (Micklethwait and Wooldridge 2004). They believe that Democratic policies produce a culture of dependency by diminishing individual competence and dignity and thwart the benefits that result from competing alternatives (Mead and Beem 2005). Liberals, in contrast, argue that only by emphasizing equality can society protect its weakest members and guarantee every American a basic dignity of lifestyle. Moreover, they say the evidence is clear that America has prospered in the post-New Deal era and see no reason to change what they view as successful policies; if anything, enduring inequalities of race and class require their expansion (Jacobs and Skocpol 2005; Massey and Denton 1993). We cannot resolve these differences in outlook here, but we can understand that the stakes are high for the outcome of battles over Bush's policies.

Polarization and Enhanced Government Power

Freedom is not the president's only value, of course. The president also supports big government—a big federal government, the administrative state (Aberbach and Peterson 2005, Johnson 2006, Kettl 2002, Skowronek 1982, Stears 2002)—where it will help him achieve his goals, pre-empting the 50 states on policy issues in the process. He supported limiting personal injury lawsuits or removing class action lawsuits from state courts, limiting the discretion of school administrators and teachers, limiting states issuing drivers' licenses to illegal immigrants, and allowing off-duty and retired police officers to carry concealed firearms wherever they travel. Interestingly, the president had a policy outcome in mind when he proposed shifting class action lawsuits from state to federal courts and away from sympathetic judges and juries. He presumed that federal judges and juries would be less generous to plaintiffs. Similarly, he anticipated that federal judges would order the reinsertion of

Terri Schiavo's feeding tube, in contrast to state judges. In essence, he is asking federal judges to make decisions based on political predilections—exactly what he has denounced in other settings.

Equally importantly, Bush has supported some strong governmental constraints on individual freedom. The president is willing to use federal power aggressively to achieve moral and cultural goals, including limiting abortion and stem cell research and prohibiting gay marriage. Some feel his proposals to use tax revenues to support faith-based schools and social programs violate their protections under the Establishment Clause of the First Amendment. There is an increasingly strong relationship between religiosity and party identification in the United States. As white, southern evangelicals have moved to the Republican Party, the Christian Right has become more central to its success. The Democratic Party, on the other hand, has become more assertively secular. It is not surprising, then, that Democrats have disdain for Bush.

Enhanced executive power features in foreign policy, where the administration sees itself at war (Rudalevige 2005). As the president declared in the opening sentence of his 2006 National Security Strategy doctrine: "America is at war. This is a wartime national security strategy required by the grave challenge we face—the rise of terrorism fueled by an aggressive ideology of hatred and murder" (NSS 2006: i). At the core of foreign policy now is the fight against terrorism, and the most significant aspect of this fight has been the war in Iraq.

For a substantial period following 9/11, the president was at historic highs in the polls, and there was a wide public consensus supporting his efforts to combat terrorism. Yet by the time of the Iraq war, the country was divided and this cleavage deepened as first chaos and then prolonged violence characterized the aftermath of the war. The expenditure of lives and treasure without signs of visible progress certainly contributed to the nation's polarization. More broadly, however, the Bush Administration's projection of a muscular foreign policy and its willingness to act without traditional allies raised concerns among a substantial segment of the public. At the core of this group were those who initially responded so enthusiastically to Howard Dean's antiwar candidacy for the Democratic nomination in 2004 and defeated Democrat Senator Joseph Lieberman's race in the 2006 Connecticut primary. In addition, the White House's arguments on behalf of the war and its claims of progress soon rang hollow to all but Republican ears in the public electorate (Edwards 2006, chs. 3–4).

In addition to exercising the broad investigatory powers authorized under the USA Patriot Act, President Bush has claimed wide executive powers and authorized the creation of military tribunals for non-US citizens, ordered US citizens held indefinitely without charging them with crimes or providing legal counsel, permitted warrantless eavesdropping by the National Security

Agency (NSA) despite the terms of the 1978 Foreign Intelligence Surveillance Act, and resorted to "extraordinary rendition" to transfer suspects out of the United States to countries that practiced torture. President Bush's statements when signing bills passed by Congress also reflect his aggressive view of executive power. The president had vetoed no bills prior to July 2006, when, partially to appease many of his core Republican supporters, he vetoed a bill permitting broader federal support for stem cell research. In essence, rather then vetoing bills, he has issued written statements about how the executive interprets the law, often in a way contradictory to the legislation's essence (Cooper 2005). It is no wonder that commentary on the new "Imperial Presidency" is common.

Bush's expansive claims of inherent prerogative powers, especially when acting as commander in chief, are one of the most distinctive aspects of the Bush presidency. This is an administration inclined toward a broad view of the president's inherent powers, but also one that faces severe critics. Thus, unilateral powers that avoid the usual checks and balances of the separation of powers system are convenient. At the same time, however, the president's use of executive power has contributed to the nation's political polarization. Although the administration argues that the president's goal is to protect Americans' freedom, many critics view his extensive use of executive power as a fundamental threat to civil liberties and balanced government.

Louis Fisher examines the scope of inherent powers and argues that constitutional law does not support the president's claims for them and that his efforts to exercise such powers pose a substantial risk of doing fundamental damage to the US's constitutional framework, individual rights, and personal liberties. The regular invocation of inherent powers threatens the Constitution because it concentrates political power within a single branch that insists it may exercise exclusive powers unchecked by Congress, the judiciary, or the public. The exercise of inherent powers necessarily undermines legislative deliberation, political accountability, and public participation. Acquiescence to such claims by the president leads to the type of government that the framers feared and thought they had put behind them.

Richard Pious focuses on the president's use of prerogative powers and the treatment of detainees in the war on terror. President Bush asserted his prerogative power in interpreting and reinterpreting conventions and customary international law obligations, and in interpreting the obligations of government officials to execute faithfully statute law, the *Uniform Code of Military Justice*, and various directives. Pious finds that officials at the highest levels of government made decisions based on the constitutional authority of the president (as administration lawyers defined it) that left open the probability that detainees would be subjected to inhuman treatment and torture as defined by international law. The author also explores why the issue of the treatment of prisoners has not risen to the level of an Iran-Contra affair and what the reaction tells us about the politics of prerogative power.

William Howell and Douglas Kriner continue the discussion of the politics of unilateral power, arguing that such power is not absolute; rather, it is fundamentally limited by the capacity and willingness of Congress to amend or overturn an order once given. However, during the first six years of the administration, Congress did little legislatively to rein in the president. The authors argue, however that it is important not to overlook the more subtle, yet tangible, ways through which Congress can affect the president's strategic calculus. By holding hearings, raising criticisms, and issuing public appeals for a change of course, members of Congress can, and have, materially raised the political costs of unilaterally creating public policy. When the political costs of either advancing or merely defending an especially controversial unilateral action have become prohibitive, Bush has often given ground. Through a series of case studies and new experimental survey data, they show that congressional opposition to the president systematically influences the willingness of average citizens to support the president's military campaigns abroad; and, moreover, that such opposition has induced the president to back off from his preferred policies. Thus, the authors demonstrate that congressional checks on presidential war powers, though certainly diminished, remain a core feature of unilateral politics.

As a window into the Bush Administration, foreign policy offers understanding of some core aspects of this presidency and its use of executive power as these have emerged in response to particular crises. First, the ideological commitments of the Bush presidency have been set out starkly—the transfer of the promotion of freedom from domestic into foreign policy, increasingly coupled with the promotion of democracy. Bush (2005*b*) told an audience at Riga, Latvia on 7 May 2005 (the sixtieth anniversary of the allied victory in Europe) that "the advance of freedom is the great story of our age," and that "we seek democracy in [the Middle East] for the same reasons we spent decades working for democracy in Europe—because freedom is the only reliable path to peace." President Bush places this ideological struggle increasingly as the contemporary equivalent of the ideological struggle demarcated by his predecessor Harry Truman, which became the Cold War. Giving the commencement address at West Point, Bush proclaimed,

like the Cold War, we are fighting the followers of a murderous ideology that despises freedom, crushes all dissent, has territorial ambitions, and pursue totalitarian aims. Like the Cold War, our enemies are dismissive of free peoples, claiming that men and women who live in liberty are weak and lack the resolve to defend our way of life. And like the Cold War, they are seeking weapons of mass murder that would allow them to deliver catastrophic destruction to our country. If our enemies succeed in acquiring such weapons, they will not hesitate to use them, which means they would pose a threat to America as great as the Soviet Union.

Speaking to another student audience, President Bush (2005*a*) reiterated the theme: "see, we're in an ideological struggle. It's very important for the students here to understand that there is an enemy which has an ideology, and they're driven by an ideology." The recent National Security Strategy document underlines that this is an engagement for the long term: "the United States is in the early years of a long struggle, similar to what out country faced in the early years of the Cold War" (2006: 1).

Second, foreign policy mirrors the Bush presidency's willingness in domestic policy to deploy an expanded bureaucratic apparatus in the service of policy ends. The Bush Administration has demonstrated a remarkable openness to an enlarged federal administrative state. We have noted already changes in domestic policy. In the interests of a more robust effort in the war on terrorism, the federal government has undergone significant reorganization (a strategy also with precedent in the early years of the Cold War struggle (Grossman 2001)). A new Department of Homeland Security is in place under whose rubric 22 government organizations and agencies have been integrated into a single department.[2] A new post of director of national intelligence has been created to oversee the intelligence acquired separately by the FBI and the CIA. The Department of Justice has been reorganized to focus more on terrorism, as has the FBI. The Patriot Act authorizes measures compelling law enforcement and intelligence agencies to cooperate. The Defense Department has been revamped with the creation of a new Northern Command focused on homeland security and the expansion of the Special Operations Command. The federal budget allocation for covert operations has grown.

One might argue that any presidential administration would have overseen comparable extensions of the federal bureaucratic structure, but this argument overlooks two significant issues. First, these structures will remain in place beyond the Bush Administration, thereby offering opportunities for additional refashioning of the federal government. Second, in the setting of exceptional polarization and partisan divisions, the spoils of office-holding accrue overwhelmingly to the party controlling all the three branches, as the Bush's Republican Party did for most of his tenure, enabling nontrivial exercises of State power. The Supreme Court has exercised some limited control on the executive—most notably, in *Rasul* v. *Bush* (2004) and *Hamdan* v. *Rumsfeld* (2006) concerning the rights of detainees at Guantanamo Bay. Nevertheless, many other new powers have been left unchecked, including the rendition of prisoners and warrantless surveillance of phone calls; and although the administration conceded in July 2006, after the *Hamdan* ruling, that terror suspects held by the United States had rights under the Geneva Convention and international law (reversing the position taken by the White House after the 9/11 attacks), it lobbied Congress to pass legislation that would limit the rights granted to detainees.

One important reason for the Bush Administration's success in enlarging executive power and the federal administrative state is that despite the historic levels of polarization, Americans remained overwhelmingly patriotic. This quality gives stability to the US polity independent of individual presidencies and therefore policy-making opportunities.

Polarization and Patriotism

How does a political movement capable of polarizing the electorate deploy and refine the common values of Americanism despite deep polarization in public opinion and voting? The answer is by making a common tradition serve the new agenda.

President Bush has been skillful in this task, especially in citing the US's checkered history of racial and ethnic conflicts as a model for new nations. Furthermore, far from aping the commonplace alarmist populist cries (Huntington 2004) about the threat posed to the US's integration and stability by racial and ethnic diversity, the Bush team has chosen mostly to celebrate this quality.

President Bush (2005a) warned his Latvian audience about the struggles confronting new democracies addressing historical injustices, finding a redemptive parable in American history:

for my own country, the process of becoming a mature, multi-ethnic democracy was lengthy and violent. Our journey from national independence to equal justice included the enslavement of millions and a four-year civil war. Even after slavery ended, a century passed before an oppressed minority was guaranteed equal rights. Americans found that racial division almost destroyed us, and the false doctrine of "separate but equal" was no basis for a strong and unified country. The only way we found to rise above the injustices of our history was to reject segregation, to move beyond mere tolerance, and to affirm the brotherhood of everyone in our land.   (Bush 2006)

This language and historical narrative buys into what we may term America's "post-multicultural settlement," that is, public acknowledgement of racial and ethnic group distinctions combined with federal policy designed to ensure that public policies reduce rather than accentuate divisions among groups based on race, ethnicity, or national background. This task is resonant with historical connotations. It no longer presumes a teleological narrative toward a melting-pot identity: Americans embrace diversity and shared values as equal aspects of their national identity (King 2005, 167; and see Hollinger 1995).

In public opinion surveys polling Americans' levels of patriotism, there has been some decline during the Bush years in those who feel "extremely proud" to be American (peaking in 2003). Nevertheless, a Gallup poll on 4 July 2006 found 57 per cent of respondents to be "extremely proud," 25 per cent "very proud," and a mere 3 per cent "not at all proud." There is a partisan division here with 74 per cent of Republicans compared with 47 per cent of Democrats fitting the "extremely proud" category. Gallup has posed this question eight times since January 2001, when the figure for "extremely proud" was 55 per cent (and 32 per cent "very proud"), enjoying a peak in the middle of 2003 (70 per cent declared as "extremely" and 20 per cent "very" proud of being American).

Thus, polarization has not significantly dented aggregate levels of patriotism, but attitudes to patriotism do show some of the same features of polarized views found elsewhere in the political system: 47 per cent of Democrats, 40 per cent of liberals, 46 per cent of 18–29 year olds, and 46 per cent of those earning less than $20,000 a year respond as "extremely proud" of their national identity. Majorities of these groups did not offer the "extremely proud" response. In addition, although potentially a powerful resource for the president, strong patriotism did not translate blindly into steady or uncritical support for the president's war in Iraq. By September 2005, two-thirds of the public disapproved of his competence in this task, down from 76 per cent support in April 2003 (Edwards 2006, 102–3).

The embrace of diversity pervades foreign policy and national security rhetoric. President Bush's first National Security Strategy doctrine, issued post-9/11, declared that "America's experience as a great multiethnic democracy affirms our conviction that people of many heritages and faiths can live and prosper in peace. Our own history is a long struggle to live up to our ideals" (NSS 2002, 4). And many commentators remarked upon Americans' response to the terrorist attacks on the Pentagon and New York City as one that transcended existing divisions, especially that between white Americans and African Americans.

Predictably, however, new group divisions did emerge, as some Arab and Muslim Americans discovered. Although consistent with a post-multiculturalism, their expression has been modest compared to previous wartime reactions—such as the treatment of German Americans in World War I or of Japanese Americans in World War II. The use of Guantanamo Bay to incarcerate but not charge alleged combatants in the terror war is the modern equivalent. But it has not been a policy success, in that some Americans consider it an inappropriate action for a democratic state committed to the rule of law and habeas corpus rights for its citizens.

There are at least two difficulties with the Bush style of patriotism within a setting of political polarization. First, some commentators and analysts challenge the extent to which racism has declined, and find in the post-multiculturalist rhetoric a lip-service to diversity that camouflages enduring inequality (Singh 2004). Second, there is a marked difference in public opinion for President Bush between white and non-white Americans. Over

80 per cent of African Americans and over two-thirds of Latinos disapprove of his performance and report an intention to vote for Democrats. A Gallup poll in June 2006 found just 15 per cent of African Americans approved of the job Bush was doing, compared with almost 80 per cent who disapproved. Some writers maintain that such political divisions by racial and ethnic group reflect how embedded these categories are in the language of US politics and that they should therefore be made explicit, since they reveal fissures in the ideology and practices of American nationhood (Ellis 2005; Singh 2004; Smith 1997, 2003; though see Berns 2001). Accounts of the persistence of racial inequalities in the US illustrate this claim (see essays in Jacobs and Skocpol 2005), and some critics of the Bush Administration's foreign policy argue that US policy makers do not view populations in the Middle East as equals (Little 2002, p. xx). Partly to address this unpopularity among black voters President Bush spoke at the annual meeting of the NAACP in July 2006.

These concerns about the endurance of racial and ethnic sources of divisions point to a second problem. Polarization is a divisive configuration politically, yet patriotism around the idea of one nation—which is the response evoked during wartime—is in danger of clashing with the embrace of diversity. Visiting China in February 2002, President Bush (2002) used his live television broadcast to proselytize freedom to the Chinese people: "life in America shows that liberty, paired with law, is not to be feared. In a free society, diversity is not disorder. Debate is not strife. And dissent is not revolution. A free society trusts its citizens to seek greatness in themselves and their country."

Balancing the value of individual freedom with a powerful conception of one-people nationhood is challenging. As a political force, the United States is undoubtedly strengthened by the ability of its leaders to mobilize a united people around the one-nation theme. Beneath the veneer of this one-people nation, however, lie group divisions that have historically proved fissiparous. Although the sources of group divisions have changed over time in response to new demands for political inclusion and unanticipated international pressures, they have not dissipated. Polarization of the depth now observable is potentially a nontrivial threat to this nationhood rhetoric, severely exacerbated by the Iraq war. It took at least a generation to excise and heal the damage to America's civic nationhood values done by the Vietnam War (McCriskin 2003: ch. 3), but the nation was less polarized during that conflict than it is at present.

In sum, balancing patriotism as an integrating national value during a period of polarization is a challenge consistently faced by the presidency of George W. Bush. There are other important dimensions of his presidency that contribute to the polarized nature of American politics in the first decade of the twenty-first century, however. One of these is the view of his critics that the way he determines policy, his decision-making process, is fundamentally flawed.

Making Decisions

The essence of the president's job is making decisions—about foreign affairs, economic policy, and literally hundreds of other important matters. Decision making involves designing policy, selecting and motivating personnel, obtaining appropriate advice, and managing crises. The task is a difficult one. Presidents need to ensure that they have a full set of options and the appropriate information necessary for evaluating them. They also require a working relationship with subordinates and an organization in the White House that serves presidential decision-making needs. George W. Bush does not dissent from this view. Asked by students in Kansas how best to describe his job he opined, "if I had to give you a job description, it would be a decision-maker. I make a lot of decisions. I make some that you see that obviously affect people's lives, not only here, but around the world. I make a lot of small ones you never see, but have got consequence. Decision-maker is the job description" (Bush 2006).

There are many influences on the decisions presidents make. In the broadest sense, the parameters set by prior commitments of the government that obligate it to spend money, defend allies, maintain services, or protect rights constrain all presidents, the type of factors analyzed by historical institutionalism and path-dependence arguments (Steinmo et al. 1992). The diverse obligations of the president and his top aides impose severe limitations on the amount of time they can devote to generating and evaluating options and information.

Each president is unique, however. What kind of a decision maker is George W. Bush? Most of the common criticisms of his performance focus on the quality of his decisions. Is such criticism the result of disagreement with the decisions themselves, or is there a basis for the claim that the first MBA president is not competent at what is perhaps the core task of a chief executive?

Two of the most important events of the past generation have been the September 11, 2001 terrorist attacks on the United States and the US invasion of Iraq in 2003. The terrorist attacks caught the country by surprise. The United States invaded Iraq on the premise that it possessed substantial stocks of weapons of mass destruction. In both cases there were serious problems with the information the president received. The Bush White House has portrayed the president and his top advisers as consumers of imprecise intelligence, making the best decisions they could in a murky world of secret plots and illicit programs.

There is another view, however, one that emerges from studies of the president's decision-making process. On the one hand we find a president who raises important questions and occasionally asks for more data, but on the other hand we see a president who at crucial moments failed to press for critical details. When the CIA briefed the president on 6 August 2001 about the threat from al-Qaeda, he did not follow up with questions, instructions, or discussions with his top advisers (see *9/11 Commission Report* 2004, 260–2; Woodward 2004, 80). When the president expressed dismay at the CIA's information regarding Iraq's possession of weapons of mass destruction following a briefing on 21 December 2002, CIA Director George Tenent replied that the case was a "slam dunk." There is no evidence the president pushed the CIA for more information (Woodward 2004, 249).

President Bush often describes himself as an instinctual decision maker (ibid. 136–7, 145, 168, 342; see also Suskind 2004, 165–6). Potential drawbacks to relying on instincts are investing too little time in soliciting and cultivating the views of others, and not pushing advisers as hard as one should. Some also describe the president as intellectually passive. To the extent that this is an accurate description, it also discourages tough questioning (for contrasting views see Suskind 2004, 57–60, 107–9, 126, 148–9, 153, 295–306; and Hughes 2004, 93, 282).

Each president brings to office a distinctive world-view, psychological needs, routines of processing information, intellectual curiosity, energy, and rigor, and manner of making decisions. The contribution of personality and personal style to presidential decision making will perhaps always be a topic of some controversy among political scientists. Personality and style, elusive as concepts, are frighteningly subjective as variables. Every once in a while, however, a president comes along whose personality and style are so distinctive, and whose major decisions are so consequential and daring, that scholars are forced to confront the possibility that, in addition to such major factors as organizational structure and decisional processes, the personal qualities of the American chief executive are in fact having the most profound consequence for the nation and the world.

That, Thomas Langston argues, is the situation we observe today. George W. Bush did not have to lead the nation to war in Iraq; many other leaders in his position would not have done so. His decision for war is not fully explicable without reference to his personality and his personal style. In exploring Bush's decision making he identifies key personality traits and elements of the president's world-view and traces their consequences. For example, because of the president's impulsive personality he was prone to act on instinct; because of his assertiveness and fondness for decisive action he was apt to choose, when following his instincts, more over less belligerent alternatives. And because of his fatalism he was not inclined to ask a lot of questions about consequences. Once Bush fixed upon a policy, or began down a path to which he had publicly committed himself, he did not tolerate doubt. In addition, Langston shows how the decision for war against Iraq was actually the product of six smaller decisions, often rashly made, prior to the ultimate decision for invasion, with each progressively narrowing the president's options.

Every president has broad discretion in structuring his decision making in the White House. There are many ways to do this, and each has consequences for the effectiveness of the advisory system. Virtually all observers of the presidency agree that there is no ideal organization for the White House that is appropriate for every president. The organization of the White House inevitably reflects the personality and work habits of the incumbent. Moreover, the chief executive's personal style dominates any organizational scheme, no matter what the organizational charts may say. If presidents have a penchant for acting without adequate deliberation, they will defeat any advisory system they have established in the White House.

On the other hand, organization does indeed make a difference. Presidents need their staff to give them time to focus on priorities and reflect on questions of basic strategy. The president's staff also needs to screen issues so that the president deals only with those requiring direct involvement by the chief executive. In addition, the staff should promote the thorough evaluation of options without aggravating the proclivity toward isolation that White Houses usually evidence over time and distorting information and insulating the president from diverse—and critical—points of view.

Quality decision making requires more than simply presenting the president with a diversity of views. There are differences among advisers in persuasive skills, intellectual ability, policy expertise, power, status, standing with the president, and analytical staff support. These disparities may distort the decision-making process by giving some viewpoints an undue advantage.

In his influential study of presidential power, Richard Neustadt (1990, chs. 6–7) alerted future presidents that they would need information, including tangible details, to construct a necessary frame of reference for decision making. Presidents cannot assume that any person or advisory system will provide them with the options and information they require, and thus they must reach out widely. If a president fails to do so and is not able actively to oversee the decision-making system, the consequences may be profound.

John Burke focuses on understanding decision making in the Bush presidency through first analyzing its formal organizational processes, including the structure of the advisory process, the access of advisers to the president, the coordination and management of the advisory process, and the president's penchant for delegation, his emphasis on loyalty, and his willingness to impose organizational discipline on top advisers. On each dimension he finds the process wanting. Next, the author focuses on the administration's collegial deliberation, raising troubling questions about the president's failure to press critical questions (such as the reliability of evidence regarding weapons of mass destruction in Iraq and the premises on which the administration planned for postwar Iraq) and his tendency to focus on how to accomplish something rather than *whether* to accomplish it. He also addresses the issues of diversity of *whom* Bush chose to engage and the imbalance of power and influence among the principals.

The bureaucracy is a primary source of options and information for the president. Yet the bureaucracy is not a neutral instrument. Individuals and the agencies they represent have interests of their own to advance and protect and may not view issues from the president's perspective. The structure of the flow of information and the development of options in the White House may also hinder decision making. The demands of the White House itself may distort the information it receives from below.

Presidents and their aides bring to office sets of beliefs about politics, policy, human nature, and social causality—in other words, beliefs about how and why the world works as it does. These beliefs structure their frame of reference for evaluating policy options, for filtering information and giving it meaning, and for establishing potential boundaries of action. Beliefs also help busy officials cope with complex decisions to which they can devote limited time, and they predispose people to act in certain directions. Although sets of beliefs are inevitable and help to simplify the world, they can be dysfunctional as well.

James Pfiffner continues the examination of decision making in the Bush presidency, focusing on the use of intelligence before the war in Iraq. Like Langston, he concludes that the decision to go to war was fragmented and serial, and neither deliberative nor comprehensive. He finds that although bureaucratic pathologies may have been at work, in the case of Iraq the main problem was a rigid mindset on the part of administration policy makers. Their commitment to regime change in Iraq led them to neglect the lessons of past policy failures and blinded them to contrary evidence and reservations developed through the intelligence process. In its search for evidence and analysis to corroborate its preconceptions about Iraq the administration also politicized the advisory process by creating separate bureaucratic units to provide alternative analyses of evidence, "stovepiping" these analyses directly to policy makers without standard vetting, and intimidating intelligence analysts.

Although presidents have substantial discretionary authority, much of the time they must build coalitions to govern. This task is always a challenge for chief executives, but it is especially difficult in periods of high polarization.

Governing in Polarized Times

George W. Bush has broken from the incremental, fiscally prudent, and moderate approaches that characterized the presidencies of both his father and Bill Clinton. Instead, he took office with an ambitious agenda and has boldly re-examined and challenged the basic tenets of decades of foreign, economic, and domestic policy. Yet the president was first elected without even a plurality of the vote, the country is closely divided politically, and partisan polarization is at its highest level in modern times. Thus the president's base is firm, but it is also narrow. Revolutions are usually not built on such modest foundations.

How has the president attempted to make sweeping changes in public policy without broad support for doing so? One response is to make greater use of unilateral powers, a topic we introduced earlier. Yet even the most expansive view of presidential prerogatives does not encompass making substantial and permanent changes in domestic policy. Achieving the president's domestic policy goals such as cutting taxes and reforming Social Security would depend on building coalitions.

The US is a large, diverse nation in which political power is fragmented both vertically and horizontally. This environment forces every president who wishes to have a significant influence on public policy to invest substantial time and energy in building supporting coalitions. Most of this effort focuses on marshaling public opinion and coalescing support in Congress.

Governing by Campaigning

Without a mandate for change, with close party divisions in Congress, and with substantial hostility to his efforts to transform policy and create a lasting Republican majority, the White House concluded that it was unlikely to pass the president's program without increasing its political capital. As a result, George W. Bush chose to govern by campaigning, relying on taking his case to the people and counting on public opinion to move Congress to support his policies. This strategic decision surprised many observers, who thought that for Bush, English was a second language. Nevertheless, the president has taken his case to the public in an unprecedented fashion. Soon after taking office, he launched a massive public relations campaign on behalf of his priority initiatives. At the core of this effort was the most extensive domestic travel schedule of any new president in American history. The White House never looked back and continued in a permanent campaign for the hearts and minds of the American public.

Bush's approach is not unique, of course. The president's relations with the public sit at the core of the modern presidency. Both politics and policy revolve around presidents' attempts to garner public support, for both themselves and their policies. Three fundamental and widely shared premises about the relationship between public opinion and presidential leadership underlie this mode of governance: that public support is a crucial political resource for the president; that the president must not only earn public support with his performance in office, but also must actively take his case to the people; and that through the permanent campaign the White House *can* successfully

17

persuade or even mobilize the public exploiting the bully "pulpit" (Edwards 2003).

How has the public responded to the president? Gary Jacobson shows that not only is the public more widely divided by party in their evaluations of Bush's performance than they have been about any president since pollsters began asking about presidential approval, but they are also more widely divided by party about the wisdom and necessity of the war in Iraq than they have been about any major US military action during the same time span—even including Vietnam. The public's unusually wide partisan divisions over evaluations of President Bush and his decision to force a regime change in Iraq are closely connected. Republicans' initial high regard for the president and trust in his honesty, especially among Christian conservatives, encouraged acceptance of his original case for war. When the premises of his argument proved faulty, Republicans either missed the story or decided it was irrelevant and continued to support the war, accepting the administration's claim that it was integral to the war on terrorism and thus to the security of the US. Democrats, on the other hand, tended neither to trust Bush nor to appreciate his performance as president, so their support for the war depended crucially on belief in its necessity. The failure to find weapons of mass destruction or evidence of Saddam's complicity in 9/11 confirmed their distrust and as a result, their support for going to war collapsed and their opinion of the president's performance and integrity became overwhelmingly negative. Partisan differences in reactions to events and revelations in Iraq thus reinforced partisan differences in prior beliefs about the president.

It is one thing to go public. It is something quite different to succeed in moving public opinion. How successful has George W. Bush been in his efforts to govern through a permanent campaign? It is one of the most interesting ironies about the Bush Administration that despite investing extraordinary time and energy attempting to obtain the public's support and demonstrating both skill and discipline in its efforts, the public has been largely unresponsive to the White House (Edwards 2006, chs. 3–4, 7).

Lawrence Jacobs examines the rise of presidential promotional activity and its impact on White House strategy by tracing changes in the White House's institutional capacity for reaching the public, the nature of public appeals, and changes since the era before the permanent campaign. He argues that the norm of accommodation that marked Roosevelt's and Johnson's monumental legislative programs has given way to an expectation of presidential domination. The development of the promotional presidency and the inflated expectations of presidential dominance on which it is based seduced George W. Bush (as they did Bill Clinton) into squandering striking opportunities for policy change and placed him in a weakened political position. Even the White House's impressive institutional capacity to shape public opinion is restricted by the public's predispositions, its reliance on alternative sources of information, and the avalanche of messages from political rivals and the media that contradict and challenge the president's presentations. In addition, party activists, contributors, lobbyists, wealthy Americans, and other vocal and well-organized groups may have more influence on legislators and other policy makers than general public opinion.

There may be other pay-offs of going public, however. Scott Blinder asks why, in light of the evidence that the president's going public has little impact on the public's political preferences and judgments, would a savvy political administration undertake a public relations campaign regarding the war in Iraq? In an innovative study, he shows that Bush's campaign for war in Iraq was successful not through persuasion but through making the issue more salient to voters. By repeatedly discussing the threat of Saddam Hussein's possession of nuclear weapons and his links to al-Qaeda, the Bush Administration was able to force Iraq toward the top of voters' lists of concerns by the fall of 2002. The prominence of Iraq on the agenda heightened the electoral concerns for members of Congress who were considering voting against the resolution authorizing the use of force against Iraq. They were reluctant to oppose a popular president on a prominent issue on which the public evaluated him positively. Congressional Democrats were more likely to vote to authorize military force if they had reason to feel vulnerable in the midterm election and had reason to believe that their electoral constituency was likely to be hawkish toward Iraq.

Despite all their efforts to lead public opinion, presidents do not directly reach the American people on a day-to-day basis. It is the news media, or press, that provides people with most of what they know about chief executives, their policies, and their policies' consequences. The media also interpret and analyze presidential activities, including even the president's direct appeals to the public. The media act as the principal intermediary between the president and the public, and relations with the press are an important aspect of the president's efforts to lead public opinion.

Martha Kumar examines the Bush White House's communications operation, including its basic functions and the staff requirements of each. She devotes special attention to the need for both long-term planning and coordination for offensive efforts and for an organization capable of quick-response defensive moves. In the first term, the White House was able to set priorities, plan ahead, coordinate among government units, and stick with the plan, making news on the president's terms. The administration has been less successful, however, in handling unanticipated situations and criticisms of the president, and in responding to what others wanted to talk about. At the same time, the author points out that there are natural limits to what communications operations can do that depend upon the president himself, the difficulties in most administrations of admitting communications problems, and the troubles that come with promoting unpopular policies.

Leading Congress

The Bush White House's core governing strategy has been to go public, with the goal of winning public support to persuade Congress to support its initiatives. Without a mandate and with a substantial minority of the public viewing his election as illegitimate, the George W. Bush presidency commenced under difficult circumstances. In his first term, however, the president surprised many observers, who underestimated both his resolution and his political skills. The White House made unusually focused efforts to govern strategically and effectively exploited the context in which it was attempting to govern by focusing on priorities, moving rapidly to exploit opportunities, setting the national agenda, and displaying tactical flexibility.

Despite sensitivity to strategy and a disciplined approach to implementing it, the administration faced the familiar frustrations of contemporary presidents. The public was unresponsive to the president's pleas for support, and Congress was unimpressed with the president's historic 9/11-induced approval ratings. As a result, the president relied heavily on his party's congressional leadership, which effectively delivered at least the House for his legislative proposals.

One reason for the lack of public response to the president is that he and his Republican allies in Congress have opted to "seize the day." Hacker and Pierson (2005, 2) argue that the Republican majority has shown "little inclination to tack to the political center. It has strayed dramatically from the moderate middle of public opinion." For Republicans, polarization constitutes a viable strategy because it delivered electoral and legislative success in 2000, 2002, and 2004. Such a strategy dictates sticking with policies attractive to the electoral base and consequently an insular decision-making style that responds to a relatively narrow support base within the electorate.

Charles O. Jones focuses on the big picture of the president's relations with Congress. He argues that George W. Bush brought a "chief executive" style of leadership to the White House in 2001, based on the president's disposition and experience. The 9/11 attacks and wars in Afghanistan and Iraq, the attendant involvement in Middle Eastern governing and politics, and a natural disaster of epic proportions reinforced the president's orientation. At the same time, congressional Republicans have had their longest period of party control since the 1920s. This juxtaposition of the "legislative" Republican Congress and the "chief executive" Republican president created a relationship that was very demanding on the president's party in Congress. Jones explores how an experienced Republican Congress interacted with a "chief executive" president. His comparisons with other newly elected presidents enrich his conclusions regarding the Bush presidency.

In the heady days after his re-election, the president announced an ambitious agenda to avoid the traditional pitfalls of second-term presidents, including the domestic policy priorities of reforming Social Security, revising the tax code, limiting litigation, and easing immigration rules. In retrospect, it is clear that he substantially overestimated his political capital and over-reached with his bold and aggressive program of reform. When he could rely on his party or buy Democratic votes with pork-barrel expenditures, he met with success. When he had to persuade a skeptical public or Republicans in Congress, however, he had more difficulty. At the end of the year, only some litigation limits had passed, and Social Security, tax, and immigration plans were dead or comatose. Lawmakers also rebuffed Bush's call to make perma-nent his first-term tax cuts. Things did not improve in 2006, as Republicans openly rebelled against the White House in the area of national security, forcing the president to accept changes in the USA Patriot Act, challenging the administration's domestic wiretapping program, and moving quickly to overturn the approval of an Arab company's takeover of terminals at major American ports.

Fiona Ross focuses on the president's efforts to reform the nation's most expensive policy: Social Security. She begins with the premise that achieving a major reform with thin congressional majorities and vocal and committed opponents would be difficult, and she identifies the necessary, if insufficient, conditions for path-breaking change in Social Security. Then she argues that the partisan image of the chief executive is a critical explanation of presiden-tial success in the legislative arena. Parties incur unequal risk in attempting to reform social programs, because voters and organized elites react asym-metrically to social policy reform by the Democrats and Republicans. The analysis situates these two variables within the confluence of contextual and congressional-centered variables thought to condition presidential policy leadership and argues that the odds are stacked against Social Security reform even under conditions of unified government, but that they are overwhelm-ing for a Republican administration.

Patterns of the Past

The presidency of George W. Bush has been a turbulent one. It is only natural therefore that we focus on what appear to be its most distinctive aspects. We should not forget, however, that this presidency—and especially what appear to be its greatest failures—has followed common patterns.

An obvious example of this enduring commonality is President Bush's aggressive use of unilateral executive power. Just as President Franklin D. Roosevelt used an executive order during wartime to intern Japanese Amer-icans, most of whom were US citizens, so President Bush declared consti-tutional authority under the commander in chief powers to detain indefi-nitely non-combatant enemies. This strategy succeeded for five years, until the Supreme Court concluded that such an expansive and unilateral view of executive authority violated the Constitution's strictures about separated powers and defendants' rights. Thirty-two years earlier, in 1974, the Supreme Court denied President Nixon's claim to "executive privilege" as grounds for withholding tape recordings of conversations in the Oval Office, which the special prosecutor investigating the Watergate affair had subpoenaed. It was the job of the Court—not the president—to define executive privilege.

President Bush's expansive approach to executive power has not been confined to foreign and security policy. He has sought to exploit the advantages of partisan strength and re-election to the White House to reformulate "foundational ideas" in US politics (Ceaser 2006), such as the extent to which officials measure school performance using indicators established by Washington rather than state indicators. He also wishes to revitalize the religious dimension in those foundational ideas as in promoting federal funding for faith-based programs (Smith 2006).

How does President Bush's use of unilateral powers sit historically with other presidents' use of this authority? It is not entirely inconsistent. Famously or notoriously, President Richard Nixon defended one of his executive orders—authorizing warrantless wiretapping of Americans—bluntly: "when the President does it, that means that it is not illegal." This stance provoked the Foreign Intelligence Surveillance Act establishing the FISC system of special courts and review for wiretapping requests. Nixon's governing style of disregarding constitutional norms also prompted Congress to enact the War Powers Resolution designed to place some congressional controls on executive war powers.

These examples illustrate a recurring theme of presidential and American politics. National electorates select the president. Presidents interpret their elections as mandates making them the primary centers of political authority and imparting to them a special legitimacy, especially when managing crises. The patriotic outrage engendered by the attacks on New York and the Pentagon in September 2001 enhanced President Bush's ability to exercise unilateral power. The polarized partisan environment of contemporary American politics has contributed as well, as the Republicans majority in Congress has weakened legislative oversight of the executive. So in the enduring struggle between executive and legislature to shape political development and policy choices, President Bush is willing to test significantly the potential of unilateral executive power and has done so in a highly favorable political context. But the content of this expanded unilateral executive power has unsurprisingly provoked antithetic responses.

We can speculate about two aspects of these likely responses. First, the expansion of executive power by presidents in the past has led to congressional initiatives to retrieve and enlarge the legislature's oversight powers. Separate partisan control of the executive and legislature would provide an obvious context for such a restoration. We have already cited the Nixon presidency in this respect. Second, all policy and institutional restructurings have unintended and unanticipated effects. Thus President Bush's willing strengthening of the powers and interventionist capacities of the American administrative state constitute a set of institutional resources that may well be used in ways quite unforeseen by the current administration. Franklin D. Roosevelt hoped that his response to the demands of the African-American-led March on Washington movement in 1941—the creation by executive order of a temporary Fair Employment Practice Committee to enforce nondiscrimination among employers benefiting from federal contracts—would excise the steam from this social demand. In fact, it proved the irresistible trajectory to the modern affirmative action in employment regime.

Post-mortems of the war in Vietnam find significant failures in the White House's decision making (see e.g. Burke and Greenstein 1989; McNamara 1995). President Lyndon Johnson was insensitive to the impact of advisory structures, so, frequently, options were neither coherently assembled nor carefully considered, and there was a lack of broad strategic debate in which the underlying assumptions of policy could be questioned. Policy differences at all levels were typically not lucidly stated or directly analyzed, and there was a lack of forums in which contradictory views could be clarified, studied, and debated. In addition, Johnson failed to press for additional alternatives or to question incisively the options presented to him.

Similarly, the premises shared by top decision makers trammeled effective analysis of options. These beliefs included the views that a Vietnam free of Communism was important to the security and credibility of the United States, that the war-torn country was a critical testing ground for the ability of the United States to counter communist support for wars of national liberation, that Communism was a world conspiracy, that South Vietnam would fall to the North without American aid, and that if South Vietnam did fall to the communists, the rest of Southeast Asia would follow. Defining doctrine in terms of necessity foreclosed policy options, rendering US intervention a foregone conclusion. It was difficult to challenge such a doctrinal consensus. As a result, "no comprehensive and systematic examination of Vietnam's importance to the United States was ever undertaken within the executive branch. Debates revolved around how to do things better and whether they could be done, not whether they were worth doing" (Gelb and Betts 1979, 190, 353–4, 365–7; see also McNamara 1995).

The similarities to the Bush Administration's policy toward Iraq are clear. The belief that Iraq possessed weapons of mass destruction and had links with terrorists caused officials to misread—and sometimes influence—intelligence data to support their assumptions of the need for an invasion. The view that liberating Iraqis from a brutal dictatorship and establishing Iraq as a democratic model for the Middle East led the administration to conclude that the American military would be welcomed as liberators. These premises constrained officials anticipating mass resistance to the occupation. Consequently, they did not plan for it (Packer 2005; Gordon and Trainor 2006). Like Lyndon Johnson, George W. Bush focused on how and when to invade Iraq rather than on the more important question of whether he should do it.

The environment in which the president operates is complex and uncertain, characteristics with which the human mind is not comfortable. Humans have cognitive needs and prefer stable views to a continuous evaluation and re-evaluation of options. Presidents have to find a level of consistency with which they are comfortable and that is compatible with their intellectual capacities and psychological needs. They often depend on developing clear-cut (some would say "simplistic") cognitive frameworks for making decisions. Once Ronald Reagan came to an "understanding" of an event, he did not want to deal with facts that challenged his understanding. As Secretary of State George Schultz put it, "no fact, no argument, no plea for reconsideration would change his mind" (1993, 263, 819).

Richard Clarke, an antiterrorism adviser to George W. Bush, observed that the president "looked for the simple solution, the bumper sticker description of the problem" (2004, 243–4). Former treasury secretary Paul O'Neill was even more critical, telling author Ron Suskind that he never heard George W. Bush "analyze a complex issue, parse opposing positions, and settle on a judicious path." He described the president in meetings as silent and expressionless, uninformed and unengaged: "The only way I can describe it is that, well, the President is like a blind man in a room of deaf people" (Suskind 2004, 114, 149).

Another means of reducing inconsistency and thereby decreasing the pressure to consider alternatives is similar to what we commonly term "wishful thinking." Secretary of State George Schultz (1993, 263, 1133) has described his boss, Ronald Reagan, as engaging in wishful thinking regarding issues and events, sometimes rearranging facts and allowing himself to be deceived—for example, when he insisted that he had not traded arms for hostages in the Iran-Contra affair. Wishful thinking also played a prominent role in decision making about the ill-fated invasion of Cuba at the Bay of Pigs at the beginning of the Kennedy Administration and the lack of adequate planning for the US peacekeeping operation in Iraq.

The Bush Administration's attempts to influence Congress by obtaining public support is another common pattern in the contemporary presidency. Going public has been the typical governing strategy for the White House over the past three decades. Failing in these efforts is also typical (Edwards 2003). In his memoirs, Ronald Reagan—the "Great Communicator"—reflected on his efforts to ignite concern among the American people about the threat of communism in Central America and to mobilize them behind his program of support for the Contras. "For eight years the press called me the 'Great Communicator.' Well, one of my greatest frustrations during those eight years was my inability to communicate to the American people and to Congress the seriousness of the threat we faced in Central America" (Reagan 1990, 471).

Bill Clinton also based his strategy of governing on moving the public to support his policy initiatives. Despite his impressive political and communications skills, the evidence is clear that the president typically failed to obtain public support. He did succeed in defending the status quo against radical departures proposed by his Republican opponents, but he could not rally the public behind his own initiatives. Summing up the health care reform debacle, Jacobs and Shapiro (2000, 115) conclude that the "fundamental political mistake committed by Bill Clinton and his aides was in grossly overestimating the capacity of a president to 'win' public opinion and to use public support as leverage to overcome known political obstacles—from an ideologically divided Congress to hostile interest groups." Scholars will be writing similar statements about George W. Bush's efforts to reform Social Security.

Richard Neustadt felt tying scholarship to governing was important, because governing is the primary reason we study politics. One reason for studying the presidency is improving our capacity to govern effectively. Although we recognize that officials repeat common mistakes, we nevertheless hope that the experiences of the Bush presidency will help future administrations as they seek to govern in the American polity.

References

The 9/11 Commission Report. 2004. New York: Norton.

Aberbach, Joel D., and Peterson, Mark A. (eds.) 2005. *The Executive Branch.* New York: Oxford University Press.

Barry, Brian. 1996. "Political Theory, Old and New," in Robert E. Goodin and Hans Klingemann (eds.), *A New Handbook of Political Science.* Oxford: Oxford University Press.

Berns, Walter. 2001. *Making Patriots.* Chicago: University of Chicago Press.

Burke, John P., and Greenstein, Fred I. 1989. *How Presidents Test Reality: Decisions on Vietnam, 1954 and 1965.* New York: Russell Sage Foundation.

Bush, George W. 2002. "President Bush Speaks at Tsinghua University, Beijing." 22 February. White House website.

—— 2005a. "President Discusses Global War on Terror at Kansas State University." 23 January. Accessible at White House website.

—— 2005b. "President Discusses Freedom and Democracy in Latvia." 7 May. Accessible at White House website.

Bush, George W. 2005*c*. "President Delivers Commencement Address at the US Military Academy at West Point." 27 May. Accessible at White House website.

—— 2006. "President Discusses Global War on Terror at Kansas State University, January 23, 2006." Accessible at White House website.

Ceaser, James W. 2006. *Nature and History in American Political Development*. Cambridge Mass.: Harvard University Press.

Clarke, Richard A. 2004. *Against All Enemies*. New York: Free Press.

Cooper, Phillip J. 2005. "George W. Bush, Edgar Allen Poe, and the Use and Abuse of Presidential Signing Statements." *Presidential Studies Quarterly* 35 (September): 515–32.

Edwards, George C., III. 2003. *On Deaf Ears: The Limits of the Bully Pulpit*. New Haven: Yale University Press.

—— 2006. *Governing by Campaigning: The Politics of the Bush Presidency*. New York: Longman.

Ellis, Richard J. 2005. *To the Flag: The Unlikely History of the Pledge of Allegiance*. Lawrence, Kan.: University Press of Kansas.

Gallup Poll. 2001. *News Release*. 5 January.

Gelb, Leslie H., with Betts, Richard K. 1979. *The Irony of Vietnam: The System Worked*. Washington, DC: Brookings Institution.

Gordon, Michael R., and Trainor, Bernard E. 2006. *Cobra II: The Inside Story of the Invasion and Occupation of Iraq*. New York: Pantheon Books.

Grossman, Andrew D. 2001. *Neither Dead nor Red: Civilian Defense and American Political Development during the Early Cold War*. New York: Routledge.

Hacker, Jacob S., and Pierson, Paul. 2005. *Off Center: The Republican Revolution & the Erosion of American Democracy*. New Haven: Yale University Press.

Hollinger, David A. 1995. *Postethnic America*. New York: Basic Books.

Hughes, Karen. 2004. *Ten Minutes from Normal*. New York: Viking.

Huntington, Samuel. 2004. *Who Are We? The Challenge to America's National Identity*. New York: Simon & Schuster.

Jacobs, Lawrence R., and Shapiro, Robert Y. 2000. *Politicians Don't Pander*. Chicago: University of Chicago Press.

—— and Skocpol, Theda (eds.) 2005. *Inequality and American Democracy*. New York: Russell Sage Foundation.

Jacobson, Gary C. 2003. "The Bush Presidency and the American Electorate." *Presidential Studies Quarterly* 33 (December): 701–29.

—— 2006. *A Divider, Not a Uniter: George W. Bush and the American Public*. New York: Longman.

Johnson, Kimberley S. 2006. *Governing the American State*. Princeton: Princeton University Press.

Jones, Jeffrey M. 2004*a*. "Bush Ratings Show Historical Levels of Polarization." *Gallup News Service*. 4 June.

—— 2004*b*. "How Americans Voted." *Gallup News Service*. 5 November.

Kettl, Donald F. 2002. *The Transformation of Governance*. Baltimore: Johns Hopkins University Press.

King, Desmond. 2005. *The Liberty of Strangers: Making the American Nation*. New York: Oxford University Press.

_____ 2007. "The American State and Social Engineering." *Governance*, vol. 20: 109–26.

Little, Douglas. 2002. *American Orientalism: The US and the Middle East since 1945*. Chapel Hill, NC: University of North Carolina Press.

Massey, Douglas, and Denton, Nancy A. 1993. *American Apartheid*. Cambridge Mass.: Harvard University Press.

McCriskin, Trevor. 2003. *American Exceptionalism and the Legacy of Vietnam*. Basingstoke: Palgrave.

McNamara, Robert S. 1995. *In Retrospect: The Tragedy and Lessons of Vietnam*. New York: Times Books.

Mead, Lawrence M., and Beem, Christopher (eds.) 2005. *Welfare Reform and Political Theory*. New York: Russell Sage Foundation.

Micklethwait, John, and Wooldridge, Adrian. 2004. *The Right Nation: Conservative Power in America*. New York: Penguin.

National Security Strategy. 2006. *National Security for Combating Terrorism*. Washington, DC: Executive Office of the President.

Neustadt, Richard E. 1990. *Presidential Power and the Modern Presidents*. New York: Free Press.

Packer, George. 2005. *The Assassin's Gate: America in Iraq*. New York: Farrar, Straus & Giroux.

Pontusson, Jonas. 2005. *Inequality and Prosperity: Social Europe v. Liberal America*. Ithaca: Cornell University Press.

Reagan, Ronald. 1990. *An American Life*. New York: Simon & Schuster.

Robinson, Greg. 2001. *By Order of the President: FDR and the Internment of Japanese Americans*. Cambridge, Mass.: Harvard University Press.

Rudalevige, Andrew. 2005. *The New Imperial Presidency: Renewing Presidential Power after Watergate*. Ann Arbor: University of Michigan Press.

Schultz, George P. 1993. *Turmoil and Triumph*. New York: Scribner's.

Singh, Nikhil Pal. 2004. *Black is a Country: Race and the Unfinished Struggle for Democracy*. Cambridge, Mass.: Harvard University Press.

Skowronek, Stephen. 1982. *Building a New American State*. New York: Cambridge University Press.

Smith, Rogers M. 1997. *Civic Ideals: Conflicting Visions of Citizenship in U.S. History*. New Haven: Yale University Press.

_____ 2003. *Stories of Peoplehood*. Cambridge: Cambridge University Press.

_____ 2006. "What if God was One of Us? The Challenges of Studying Foundational Political Concepts." In James W. Ceaser, *Nature and History in American Political Development*. Cambridge, Mass.: Harvard University Press.

Stears, Marc. 2002. *Progressives, Pluralists and the Problems of the State*. Oxford: Oxford University Press.

Steinmo, Sven, Thelen, Kathleen, and Longstreth, Frank (eds.) 1992. *Structuring Politics: Historical Institutionalism in Comparative Analysis*. New York: Cambridge University Press.

Suskind, Ron. 2004. *The Price of Loyalty*. New York: Simon & Schuster.

Woodward, Bob. 2002. *Bush at War*. New York: Simon & Schuster.

_____ 2004. *Plan of Attack*. New York: Simon & Schuster.

Notes

1. Our use of 'polarization' concerns public opinion and voting, not income inequalities, which is how the term is employed by scholars of comparative political economy (Jacobs and Skocpol 2004; Pontusson 2005).
2. They are: the US Customs Services, the Immigration and Naturalization Service, the Federal Protective Service, the Transportation Security Administration, Federal Law Enforcement Training Center, Animal and Plant Health Inspection Service, Office for Domestic Preparedness, the Federal Emergency Management Agency, Strategic National Stockpile and the National Disaster Medical System, Nuclear Incident Response Team, Domestic Emergency Support Teams, National Domestic Preparedness Office, CBRN Countermeasures Programs, Environment Measurements Laboratory, National BW Defense Analysis Center, Plum Island Animal Disease Center, Federal Computer Incident Response Center, National Communications System, National Infrastructure Protection Center, Energy Security and Assurance Program, the Secret Service, and the Coast Guard.

Part I

Exercising Power

2

The Scope of Inherent Powers

Louis Fisher

Immediately after the terrorist actions of 9/11, President George W. Bush came to Congress for statutory authority to act militarily first against the Taliban and al-Qaeda in Afghanistan and later against Iraq. He also obtained statutory authority for the USA Patriot Act. Increasingly, however, he began to act pursuant to what he considered to be exclusive, independent, and inherent powers, not subject to congressional or judicial constraints. Through these powers he authorized the creation of military tribunals for non-US citizens, held US citizens indefinitely without charging them with crimes or providing counsel, permitted eavesdropping by the National Security Agency (NSA), and resorted to "extraordinary rendition" to transfer suspects out of the United States to countries that practiced torture.

The purpose of this chapter is to explore the constitutional source of "inherent powers." The first step is to analyze what is meant by express, implied, and emergency powers. One can read the US Constitution to see powers expressly stated. There are also powers legitimately implied in the Constitution, and even, on extraordinary occasions, emergency powers. But where does one find inherent powers and what would be their limits? The next step is closely to examine the 1936 Supreme Court case, *Curtiss-Wright*, that is most often cited for supporting inherent and extra-constitutional powers for the president. The chapter then moves to the use of inherent powers by President Harry Truman in 1952 to seize steel mills to prosecute the war in Korea, and the reliance on inherent powers by President George W. Bush to accomplish a range of war-related actions. Truman's initiative was repudiated by the Supreme Court in the *Youngstown* case, but the legal and political limits of Bush's actions are still being played out.

From Express to Emergency Powers

The Supreme Court regularly informs the public that the US Constitution "creates a Federal Government of enumerated powers."[1] In its continuing effort to educate citizens on fundamental principles, it announces: "Under our Constitution, the Federal Government is one of enumerated powers."[2] Of course that is false. Why would the Court choose to speak in such a simplistic and misleading fashion? If the three branches of government were confined to enumerated powers, the Court could not exercise judicial review, which is not expressly stated in the Constitution. Nor could the president remove certain executive officials, withhold documents from Congress, and enter into executive agreements, all of which are done on a regular basis and subject to various limitations. Similarly, Congress exercises a number of powers that are not enumerated, including the power to investigate, issue subpoenas, and hold executive officials in contempt (Fisher 1997, 2004a). Clearly, the federal government is one of enumerated powers plus implied powers and the Constitution is none the worse off for it. Implied powers can be exercised consistently with the spirit of the Constitution, republican government, separation of powers, and the system of checks and balances.

Under extraordinary conditions there is also room for the exercise of emergency powers, provided they follow prescribed procedures. At the start of the Civil War, President Abraham Lincoln took actions that were beyond his Article II powers, including suspending the writ of habeas corpus, removing funds from the Treasury Department without an appropriation, and raising troops. He preserved constitutional government because he never pretended to govern solely on his own powers as president or as commander in chief. He conceded that he exercised some of the powers reserved to the legislative branch under Article I. When Congress returned to session he reported to the lawmakers what he had done, and why. He explained that his actions, "whether strictly legal or not, were ventured upon under what appeared to be a popular demand and a public necessity, trusting then, as now, that Congress would readily ratify them" (Richardson 1897, vii. 3225).

In this manner, Lincoln never claimed that he was free to act outside the Constitution, even in the midst of the greatest crisis the United States has ever faced. He acted under what he called the "war power," which combined what was available to Congress under Article I and to the president under Article II. He believed that his actions, especially suspending the writ of habeas corpus, were not "beyond the constitutional competency of Congress" (ibid.). Through these actions and statements, Lincoln recognized that the superior lawmaking body was Congress, not the president. For that reason he asked Senators and Representatives to authorize what he had done. That is not the behavior of a dictator. Congress debated his request at length, with members supporting him on the explicit understanding that his acts were

illegal and required statutory authority. Congress passed legislation "approving, legalizing, and making valid all the acts, proclamations, and orders of the president, etc., as if they had been issued and done under the previous express authority and direction of the Congress of the United States" (12 Stat. 326 (1861)). Lincoln based some of his actions on statutes enacted in 1795 and 1807, which authorized the president to use military force to suppress insurrections.[3]

Advocates of independent and inherent presidential power often cite the Supreme Court's decision in *The Prize Cases* (1863), which upheld President Lincoln's blockade in the southern states. But the Justices did not sanction open-ended, unchecked presidential action in time of war or emergency. Justice Robert Grier ruled that the president as commander in chief had no power to initiate war, but in the event of foreign invasion (a defensive power) the president was not only authorized "but bound to resist force by force. He does not initiate the war, but is bound to accept the challenge without waiting for the special legislative authority."[4] In such situations the president had no choice but to meet the crisis in the shape it presented itself "without waiting for Congress to baptize it with a name; and no name given to it by him or them could change the fact."[5]

Nothing in this language opens the door to any and all presidential actions in time of war. Grier carefully limited the president's discretion to defensive actions, noting that he "has no power to initiate or declare a war against either a foreign nation or a domestic State."[6] The executive branch took exactly the same position in court. During oral argument, Richard Henry Dana, Jr., who was representing the president, acknowledged that Lincoln's actions had nothing to do with "the right *to initiate a war, as a voluntary act of sovereignty*. That is vested only in Congress."[7]

There are other examples of presidents taking extraordinary actions while still respecting and maintaining the constitutional system. President Thomas Jefferson went beyond congressional instructions in entering into the Louisiana Purchase, but he disclosed what he did and never manufactured legal doctrines of inherent power to justify his actions. He knew he needed the support of both Houses of Congress and was willing to submit the documents required to build legislative understanding and assure statutory sanction (Fisher 2004*a*: 39–40). Whatever corners he cut he never invoked extraconstitutional powers.

The "Sole Organ" Doctrine

From 1789 to 1950, the Federal Government operated on the basis of enumerated, implied, and—on rare occasions—emergency powers. The year 1950 marked the first time that a president (Harry S. Truman) took the country to war without coming to Congress, either before or after, and he later tried to invoke "inherent power" to seize steel mills to prosecute the war in Korea. More on that later. The concept of inherent or extraconstitutional power poked its head up in the famous case of *United States* v. *Curtiss-Wright* (1936), written by Justice George Sutherland. His opinion brims with soaring claims about the freedom of presidents to act without statutory authority in the field of foreign affairs. Although these assertions are plainly dicta, so often is the language quoted by academics and courts that even extraneous utterances, over time, have a way of appearing to be the holding of the Court. Not only is much of the Sutherland opinion dicta, it is erroneous dicta, resting on fundamental misconceptions and misrepresentations. Nowhere is that more evident than in Sutherland's reliance on a speech by John Marshall in 1800, describing the president as "the sole organ of the nation in its external relations, and its representative with foreign nations."[8] The sole organ doctrine is of current interest because it was cited by the Bush Administration in 2006 as part of the legal grounds for justifying NSA eavesdropping. I will turn to that argument later.

When read in context, Marshall's speech did not support independent, inherent, exclusive, or extraconstitutional powers for the president in foreign relations. Marshall's objective was to defend the authority and constitutional duty of President John Adams to carry out an extradition treaty. The president was not the "sole organ" in formulating the treaty. He was the sole organ in *implementing* it. That and nothing more.

During the legislative debate in 1800 (an election year for president), opponents of President Adams insisted that he should be impeached or censured for turning over to England someone charged with murder. Because the case was already pending in an American court, some lawmakers urged that action be taken against Adams for encroaching upon the judiciary and thus violating the doctrine of separation of powers. Adams had operated under the extradition article (Article 27) of the Jay Treaty, which provided that the United States and Great Britain would deliver up to each other "all persons" charged with murder or forgery (8 Stat. 129, Art. 27).

The debate began with a member of the House requesting President Adams to provide documents "relative to, the apprehension and delivering of Jonathan Robbins, under the twenty-seventh article" of the treaty (10 *Annals of Cong.* 511 (1800)). Although critics of Adams claimed that Robbins was "a citizen of the United States" (ibid. statement by Rep. Livington), the State Department regarded Robbins as an assumed name for Thomas Nash, a native Irishman (ibid.). US District Judge Thomas Bee, who was asked to turn the prisoner over to the British, considered the individual to be Thomas Nash.[9]

Five months before the House debate began, Marshall had written an article for the *Virginia Federalist* (Richmond) on 7 September 1799, setting forth his analysis of the dispute over what he called "the case of Robbins"

(Cullen 1984, iv. 23). He explained that on matters of extradition nations communicate with each other "through the channel of their governments," and the "natural, and obvious and the proper mode is an application on the part of the government (requiring the fugitive) to the executive of the nation to which he has fled, to secure and cause him to be delivered up" (ibid. 25). The concept of "sole organ," then, included this capacity of the president to act as the channel of communication with other nations. By implementing Article 27 of the Jay Treaty, President Adams had "executed[d] one of the supreme laws of the land, which he was bound to observe and have carried into effect" (ibid. 28).

Having honed his major arguments, Marshall was well prepared to respond to the House resolutions leading to possible censure or impeachment. He argued that there were no grounds to rebuke President Adams. In matters such as carrying out an extradition provision in a treaty, "a case like that of Thomas Nash is a case for Executive and not Judicial decision" (10 *Annals of Cong*. 611 (1800)). Here is the "sole organ" comment in full context:

The President is the sole organ of the nation in its external relations, and its sole representative with foreign nations. Of consequence, the demand of a foreign nation can only be made on him.

He possesses the whole Executive power. He holds and directs the force of the nation. Of consequence, any act to be performed by the force of the nation is to be performed through him.

He is charged to execute the laws. A treaty is declared to be a law. He must then execute a treaty, where he, and he alone, possesses the means of executing it.

The treaty, which is a law, enjoins the performance of a particular object. The person who is to perform this object is marked out by the Constitution, since the person is named who conducts the foreign intercourse, and is to take care that the laws be faithfully executed. The means by which it is to be performed, the force of the nation, are in the hands of this person. Ought not this person to perform the object, although the particular mode of using the means has not been prescribed? Congress, unquestionably, may prescribe the mode, and Congress may devolve on others the whole execution of the contract; but, till this be done, it seems the duty of the Executive department to execute the contract by any means it possesses.   (10 *Annals of Cong*. 613–14)

Marshall emphasized that President Adams had not attempted to make foreign policy single-handedly. He was carrying out a policy made jointly by the president and the Senate (for treaties). Only after the policy had been formulated through the collective effort of the executive and legislative branches, either by treaty or by statute, did the president emerge as the "sole organ" in implementing national policy. Marshall also recognized that there were limits on the president's authority to make law where Congress had not provided it: "And although the Executive cannot supply a total Legislative omission, yet it is not admitted or believed that there is such a total omission in this case" (ibid. 614).

What if Thomas Nash had been an American and pressed into service on the British ship *Hermione*, where he committed murder? Could he have been transferred to England and tried and executed there? Marshall denied that could be so: "Had Thomas Nash been an impressed American, the homicide on board the Hermione would, most certainly, not have been a murder. The act of impressing an American is an act of lawless violence. The confinement on board a vessel is a continuation of the violence, and an additional outrage" (ibid. 617).

Interpretations of "Sole Organ"

Some scholars have interpreted Marshall's "sole organ" remark as the president merely being the organ of communication with another nation (Levy 1988, 52; Koh 1990, 81). In the debate of 1800, Marshall meant more than that. He meant communications with other nations plus the president's duty to carry treaties into effect. Marshall's formulation of the sole organ theory built on earlier observations about the authority of a chief executive to communicate national policy to other countries. Thomas Jefferson, serving as secretary of state in 1790, wrote: "The transaction of business with foreign nations is Executive altogether. It belongs then to the head of that department, *except* as to such portions of it as are specially submitted to the Senate. *Exceptions* are to be construed strictly" (Boyd 1961, xvi. 379).

This passage from Jefferson is sometimes read to define presidential power broadly and exclusively in foreign affairs. By making the transaction of business with foreign nations "Executive altogether," it has been argued that the Constitution makes foreign policy "an executive prerogative" (Powell 2002, 45–6; Yoo 2005, 19). However, Jefferson wrote about a very narrow dispute concerning the Senate's role in the appointment of ambassadors and consuls. President George Washington had asked Jefferson whether the Senate had a right to veto the appointee and decide what grade the president might want for a foreign mission (Boyd 1961, xvi. 379). Jefferson concluded that if the Constitution intended to give the Senate power to veto the grade, "it would have said so in direct terms, and not left it to be effected by a sidewind" (ibid. 380). In responding to this specific issue, Jefferson had no reason to address the larger role of Congress in foreign affairs or the particular prerogatives of the House, such as the power to grant or withhold legislation and appropriations.

Jefferson spoke of *transactions*, which means some kind of communication between two parties. In that sense, Jefferson's statement is consistent with Marshall's speech in 1800. Whenever Congress and the president act jointly to formulate foreign policy, it is the president who communicates, transmits, and explains that policy to other nations. Presidents may initiate foreign policies on their own, such as the Monroe Doctrine, but those executive statements of national policy survive only with congressional acquiescence. Congress has the authority to revoke or modify presidential announcements at any time.

During the controversy over President Washington's issuance of the Neutrality Proclamation in 1793, competing definitions of presidential power were offered. In one of his "Pacificus" essays, Alexander Hamilton wrote that the "legislative department is not the *organ* of intercourse between the United States and foreign nations" (Lodge 1904, iv. 436, emphasis in original). The executive department is "the *organ* of intercourse between the nation and foreign nations" (ibid. 437, emphasis in original). This language did not adopt the Blackstone view of exclusive executive power over foreign affairs. Hamilton understood that under the US Constitution "the Legislature can alone declare war, can alone actually transfer the nation from a state of peace to a state of hostility" (ibid. 443). Writing a few months later, Jefferson made the same observation about the "right to go to war." The US Constitution "gives that power to Congress alone" (Ford 1895, vi. 381).

Writing on 12 May 1798, Hamilton again expressed his understanding of the degree to which the US Constitution broke with Blackstone's model of external affairs under the executive. American ships at sea were always entitled to repel force by force and to repress hostilities within US waters, but "any thing beyond this must fall under the idea of reprisals & requires the sanction of that Department which is to declare or make war" (Syrett 1974, xxi. 462). Jefferson had earlier, in 1793, reached the same conclusion: "if the case were important enough to require reprisal, & ripe for that step, Congress must be called on to take it; the right of reprisal being expressly lodged with them by the constitution, & not with the executive" (Ford 1895, vi. 259).

As Chief Justice of the Supreme Court, Marshall held to his position that the making of foreign policy was a joint exercise by the executive and legislative branches (through treaties and statutes), not a unilateral or exclusive authority of the president. With the war power, Marshall looked solely to Congress—not the president—for the authority to take the country to war against another power. For the Quasi-War against France, Marshall looked for guidance to statutory policy: "To determine the real situation in regard to France, the acts of congress are to be inspected."[10] Marshall had no difficulty in identifying the branch that possessed the war power: "The whole powers of war being, by the constitution of the United States, vested in congress, the acts of that body can alone be resorted to as our guides in this enquiry."[11]

In an 1804 case, Marshall ruled that when a presidential proclamation issued in time of the Quasi-War with France conflicts with a statute enacted by Congress, the statute prevails. Presidential instructions "cannot change the nature of the transaction, or legalize an act which without those instructions would have been a plain trespass."[12] Having followed a presidential proclamation contrary to an act of Congress, the commander of a US vessel "must be answerable to damages to the owner of this neutral vessel."[13]

In his celebrated opinion in *Marbury* v. *Madison* (1803), Marshall recognized certain presidential actions as exclusive in nature and therefore not subject to checks from the judiciary. Those actions, however, did not create a privileged area for the president with regard to foreign affairs, external affairs, or national security. Marshall wrote: "By the constitution of the United States, the president is invested with certain important political powers, in the exercise of which he is to use his own discretion, and is accountable only to his country in his political character and to his own conscience."[14] Here Marshall described the president's control over executive officers and a range of executive discretionary actions that were exclusive. But when Congress

proceeds to impose on that officer other duties; when he is directed peremptorily to perform certain acts; when the rights of individuals are dependent on the performance of those acts; he is so far the officer of the law; is amenable to the laws for his conduct; and cannot at his discretion sport away the vested rights of others. . . . [W]here a specific duty is assigned by law, and individual rights depend upon the performance of that duty, it seems equally clear that the individual who considers himself injured, has a right to resort to the laws of his country for a remedy.[15]

The president's conclusive and wholly discretionary decisions applied to orders given to executive officials appointed to carry out his policies. Actions by those officers "can never be examinable by the courts" unless Congress intervened to impose statutory duties on the officers. At that point courts are available to interpret those duties and the individual rights attached to them. Marshall said that if the head of an executive department "commits any illegal act, under colour of his office, by which an individual sustains an injury, it cannot be pretended that his office alone exempts him from being sued in the ordinary mode of proceeding, and being compelled to obey the judgment of the law."[16] That principle applied to both domestic and external affairs, as can be seen in the case a year later of Captain Little's actions during the Quasi-War.

The *Curtiss-Wright* Decision

Although the Court's decision in *Curtiss-Wright* is the standard citation for the "sole organ" doctrine and the existence of inherent executive power in the field of foreign affairs, the case itself did not concern independent presidential power. The issue before the judiciary was whether Congress had delegated too broadly *legislative power* when it authorized the president to declare an arms embargo in South America. A joint resolution by Congress allowed the president to prohibit arms in the Chaco region whenever he found that it "may contribute to the reestablishment of peace" between belligerents (48 Stat. 811, ch. 365). In imposing the embargo, President Franklin D. Roosevelt relied solely on statutory—not inherent—authority. His proclamation prohibiting the sale of arms and munitions to countries engaged in armed conflict in the Chaco begins: "NOW, THEREFORE, I, FRANKLIN D. ROOSEVELT, President of the United States of America, acting under and by virtue of the authority conferred in me by the said joint resolution of Congress ... " (ibid. 1745). The proclamation does not assert any inherent, independent, extraconstitutional, or exclusive presidential power.

It has been argued that the joint resolution passed by Congress was not really law but something inferior to it: "In the strictest sense, Congress did not choose to legislate in this case. It did not pass a statute that would act generally and prospectively; a statute that would bar arms to any nations engaged in an armed conflict" (Arkes 1994, 198). Congress "acted, instead, through the device of a joint resolution" (ibid.). The embargo imposed by President Roosevelt "seemed to be supported, in this case, by an act of Congress, but that act of Congress did not have the solemnity and the properties of a statute" (ibid. 204). However, a joint resolution has the identical legal properties of a bill passed by Congress and enacted into law. Both must pass the two Houses. Both must be presented to the president and signed into law or have both Houses override a veto. Roosevelt's proclamation indicated that he was acting solely under legislative authority.

There was no talk of inherent presidential authority when the case was litigated in the lower courts. The issue, instead, was the extent to which Congress could transfer its legislative power to the president. In 1935, the Court had twice struck down the delegation by Congress of *domestic* power to the President.[17] The issue in *Curtiss-Wright* was whether Congress could delegate legislative power more broadly in international affairs than it could in domestic affairs. A district court, holding that the joint resolution represented an unconstitutional delegation of legislative authority, said nothing about any reservoir of inherent presidential power.[18] The district court decision was taken directly to the Supreme Court, where none of the briefs on either side discussed the availability of independent or inherent powers of the president. To the Justice Department, discussing the issue of jurisdiction, the question for the Court went to "the very power of Congress to delegate to the Executive authority to investigate and make findings in order to implement a legislative purpose" (Kurland and Casper 1975, xxxii. 898). The government argued that previous decisions by the Supreme Court, including those in the field of foreign relations, supported the delegation of this legislative power to the president (ibid. 910). Past delegations covering the domain of foreign relations represented "a valid exercise of legislative authority" (ibid. 912).

The brief for the private company, Curtiss-Wright, also focused on the issue of delegated legislative power and did not explore the existence of independent or inherent presidential power. The brief charged that the joint resolution (1) represented an unlawful delegation of legislative power, (2) did not go into operation because the president's proclamation failed to contain all the findings required by the joint resolution, (3) the president could not have consulted other governments as contemplated by the joint resolution, and (4) the effect of the president's second proclamation of 14 November 1935 extinguished the alleged liability of private companies involved in selling arms and munitions abroad (ibid. 937). A separate brief, prepared for other private parties, also concentrated on the delegation of legislative power (ibid. 979–81).

There was no need for the Supreme Court to explore the existence of independent, inherent, or exclusive powers. Nevertheless, in extensive dicta, Justice Sutherland went far beyond the specific issues before the Court and discussed extraconstitutional powers of the president. Many of the themes in *Curtiss-Wright* were drawn from Sutherland's writings as a US Senator from Utah. According to his biographer, Sutherland "had long been the advocate of a vigorous diplomacy which strongly, even belligerently, called always for an assertion of American rights. It was therefore to be expected that [Woodrow] Wilson's cautious, sometimes pacifistic, approach excited in him only contempt and disgust" (Paschal 1951, 93).

Sutherland's Orientation

The dicta in Sutherland's opinion reflected the product of many forces. One was James Valentine Campbell, Chief Justice of the Michigan Supreme Court and Sutherland's professor at the Michigan Law School. Campbell's lectures "clearly articulated the theory of the foreign relations powers which prevails today as a result of two of Sutherland's most celebrated opinions," one of them being *Curtiss-Wright* (ibid. 17). The other decision was *United States v. Belmont* (1937). Sutherland developed the view that every nation has a fundamental duty to survive, and the source of that power of the government "in the field of foreign relations does not depend for its existence on the Constitution. Rather, it is an inherent power arising by virtue of the United States' membership in the family of nations" (ibid. 221).

Sutherland served two terms as a US Senator from Utah, from 4 March 1905 to 3 March 1917, and was a member of the Senate Foreign Relations Committee. His opinion in *Curtiss-Wright* closely tracks his article, "The Internal and External Powers of the National Government," printed as a Senate Document in 1910 (S. Doc. No. 417, 61st Cong., 2d Sess.). The article began with this basic principle: "That this Government is one of *limited* powers, and that absolute power resides nowhere except in the people, no one whose judgment is of any value has ever seriously denied..." (ibid. 1, emphasis in original).

Yet the article later moved in the direction of independent presidential power that could not be checked or limited by other branches, even by the people's representatives in Congress. He first faulted other studies for failing "to distinguish between our *internal* and our *external* relations" (ibid., emphasis in original). As to the first category, the states possessed "every power not delegated to the General Government, or prohibited by the Constitution of the United States or the state constitution" (ibid. 3). With regard to external relations, Sutherland argued that with the Declaration of Independence the American colonies lost their character as free and independent states and that national sovereignty passed directly to the central government" (ibid.). In the article Sutherland connects external matters with the national government (ibid. 12), but in *Curtiss-Wright* he would associate national sovereignty and external affairs with the presidency, greatly expanding executive power. In addition to identifying express and implied constitutional powers in the article, Sutherland spoke of "inherent" and "extra-constitutional" powers (ibid. 8–9). This article was also published in the *North American Review* (US Congress 1910).

Sutherland's Book

The same themes appear in Sutherland's book, *Constitutional Power and World Affairs*, published in 1919. He again distinguishes between internal and external powers (Sutherland 1919, 26). When Great Britain entered into a peace treaty with America following the War of Independence, "it is impossible to escape the conclusion that all powers of external sovereignty finally passed from the Kingdom of Great Britain to the people of the thirteen colonies as one political unit, and not to the people separately as thirteen political units" (ibid. 38). In carrying out military operations, the president "must be given a free, as well as a strong hand. The contingencies of war are limitless—beyond the wit of man to foresee... To rely on the slow and deliberate processes of legislation, after the situation and dangers and problems have arisen, may be to court danger—perhaps overwhelming disaster" (ibid. 111). As will be explained later, scholars have generally rejected his treatment of the Declaration of Independence, national sovereignty, and the sources and scope of presidential authority.

Regarding popular sovereignty, Sutherland was inconsistent in his book as he was in his article. Early passages in the book speak of "sovereignty—the plenary power to determine all questions of government without accountability to any one—is in the people and nowhere else" (ibid. 2). The American Revolution "proceeded upon the principle that sovereignty belongs to the people, and it is by their consent, either express or implied, that the governing agency acts in any particular way, or acts at all. This is the animating principle of the Declaration of Independence. It is the very soul of the Constitution" (ibid. 10). In an apparent rejection of inherent or extraconstitutional powers, Sutherland wrote this about the Constitution: "One of its great virtues is that it *fixes* the rules by which we are to govern" (ibid. 13, emphasis in original). He warned against "the danger of centralizing irrevocable and absolute power in the hands of a single ruler" (ibid. 25). On "all matters of external sovereignty" and the general government, the "result does not flow from a claim of inherent power" (ibid. 47).

Further into the book, however, Sutherland begins to flesh out the concepts of inherent and extraconstitutional powers as applied to external affairs and presidential authority. He described the Louisiana Purchase "as an exercise of the *inherent right of the United States as a Nation*" (ibid. 52, emphasis in original). What he attributed here to *national power* (exercised by both elected branches) he later attributed to independent presidential power. He acknowledged that the framers broke with Blackstone by placing many powers of external affairs with Congress, in Article I (ibid. 71). Yet once war is declared or waged, he saw in the president as commander in chief a power that is supreme: "Whatever any Commander-in-Chief may do under the laws and practices of war as recognized and followed by civilized nations, may be done by the President as Commander-in-Chief. In carrying on hostilities he possesses sole authority, and is charged with sole responsibility, and Congress is excluded from any direct interference" (ibid. 75).

Martial law, when invoked, "finds no limitations in the Constitution, or in the general laws of the land" (ibid. 80). Legislative or judicial checks do not exist: "The length of time during which military government shall be allowed to continue over conquered and acquired territory after the conclusion of a treaty of peace, is a matter wholly for political determination, in no manner controlled or affected by the Constitution, or subject to judicial review or determination" (ibid. 82). Here Sutherland failed to take into account the judicial checks that have repeatedly placed limits on military occupation and martial law.[19]

In time of war, Sutherland argued that traditional rights and liberties had to be relinquished: "individual privilege and individual right, however dear or sacred, or however potent in normal times, must be surrendered by the citizen to strengthen the hand of the government lifted in the supreme gesture of war. Everything that he has, or is, or hopes to be—property, liberty, life—may be required" (ibid. 98). Freedom of speech "may be curtailed or denied," along with freedom of the press (ibid.). Congress "has no power to directly interfere with, or curtail the war powers of the Commander-in-Chief" (ibid. 109). Statutes enacted during World War I invested President Wilson "with virtual dictatorship over an exceedingly wide range of subjects and activities" (ibid. 115). Sutherland spoke of the need to define the powers of external sovereignty as "unimpaired" and "unquestioned" (ibid. 171).

Sutherland's Decision

Writing for the Court in *Curtiss-Wright*, Justice Sutherland reversed the district court and upheld the delegation of legislative power to the president to place an embargo on arms or munitions to the Chaco. He said whether the joint resolution "had related solely to internal affairs" it would be open to the challenge of unlawful delegation "we find it unnecessary to determine" because the "whole aim of the resolution is to affect a situation entirely external to the United States, and falling within the category of foreign affairs."[20] Sutherland argued that the two categories of external and internal affairs are different "both in respect of their origin and their nature."[21] The principle that the federal government is limited to either enumerated or implied powers "is categorically true only in respect of our internal powers."[22] The purpose, he said, was "to carve from the general mass of legislative powers *then possessed by the states* such portions as it was thought desirable to vest in the federal government, leaving those not included in the enumeration still in the states."[23] But that doctrine, Sutherland continued, "applies only to powers which the states had . . . since the states severally never possessed international powers. . . ."[24] The states may not have possessed "international" powers. They did, as will be explained, possess and exercise sovereign powers.

As a step in his analysis, Sutherland concluded that as a result of the Declaration of Independence "the powers of external sovereignty passed from the Crown not to the colonies severally, but to the colonies in their collective and corporate capacity as the United States of America."[25] By transferring external or foreign affairs directly to the national government, and then associating foreign policy with the executive, Sutherland was in a position to argue for a broad definition of inherent presidential power.

But Sutherland relied on a misconception. External sovereignty did not circumvent the colonies and the independent states and pass directly to the national government. When Great Britain entered into a peace treaty with America, the provisional articles of 30 November 1782 were not with a national government. Instead: "His Brittanic Majesty acknowledges the said United States, viz. New-Hampshire, Massachusetts-Bay, Rhode-Island and Providence Plantations, Connecticut, New-York, New-Jersey, Pennsylvania, Delaware, Maryland, Virginia, North-Carolina, South-Carolina, and Georgia," and referred to them as "free, sovereign and independent States" (8 Stat. 55). The colonies formed a Continental Congress in 1774 and it provided a form of national government until replaced by the US Constitution. Until that time, the states operated as sovereign entities in making treaties and exercising other powers that would pass to the new national government in 1789.

It would not be accurate to say that sovereignty and external affairs passed from Great Britain to the US president. In 1776, at the time of America's break with England, there was no president and no separate executive branch. Only one branch of government functioned at the national level: the Continental Congress. It carried out all governmental powers, including legislative, executive, and judicial (Fisher 1972). When the new national government was established in 1789, sovereign powers were not placed solely in the president. They were divided between Congress and the president, with ultimate sovereignty placed in the people.

Much of *Curtiss-Wright* is devoted to Sutherland's discussion about independent and inherent presidential powers in foreign affairs. Having made the distinction between external and internal affairs, he wrote: "In this vast external realm, with its important, complicated, delicate and manifold problems, the President alone has the power to speak or listen as a representative of the nation. He *makes* treaties with the advice and consent of the Senate; but he alone negotiates. Into the field of negotiation the Senate cannot intrude; and Congress itself is powerless to invade it."[26] In his book, Sutherland took a less rigid view. He recognized that senators did in fact participate in the negotiation phase and that presidents often acceded to this "practical construction" (Sutherland 1919, 122–4; see Fisher 1989). It was at this point of his decision that Sutherland quotes John Marshall out of context, implying a belief in presidential power that Marshall never embraced: "The President is the sole organ of the nation in its external relations, and its sole representative with foreign nations."[27] Justice Sutherland developed for the president a source of power in foreign affairs that did not depend on authority delegated by Congress:

It is important to bear in mind that we are here dealing not alone with an authority vested in the President by an exertion of legislative power, but with such an authority plus the very delicate, plenary and exclusive power of the President as the sole organ of the federal government in the field of international relations—a power which does not require as a basis for its exercise an act of Congress, but which, of course, like every other governmental power, must be exercised in subordination to the applicable provisions of the Constitution. It is quite apparent that if, in the maintenance of our international relations, embarrassment—perhaps serious embarrassment—is to be avoided and success for our aims achieved, congressional legislation which is to be made effective through negotiation and inquiry within the international field must often accord to the President a degree of discretion and freedom from statutory restriction which would not be admissible were domestic affairs alone involved.[28]

In freeing the president from statutory grants of power and legislative restrictions, Justice Sutherland did not explain how the exercise of presidential power would be constrained by requiring that it "be exercised in subordination to the applicable provisions of the Constitution." Which provisions in the Constitution could check or override presidential initiatives? On that he was silent. Justice McReynolds' dissent was brief, without any elaboration: "He is of opinion that the court below reached the right conclusion and its judgment ought to be affirmed."[29]

Justice Stone did not participate. He later wrote to Edwin M. Borchard, a prominent law professor: "I have always regarded it as something of a misfortune that I was foreclosed from expressing my views in...*Curtiss-Wright*...because I was ill and away from the Court when it was decided" (Stone 1942). In another letter to Borchard, Stone said he "should be glad to be disassociated" with Sutherland's opinion (Stone 1937). Borchard later advised Stone that the Court, in such cases as *Curtiss-Wright*, "has attributed to the Executive far more power than he had ever undertaken to claim" (Borchard 1942).

Scholarly Reaction to *Curtiss-Wright*

Most of the studies of *Curtiss-Wright* in professional journals and books have been highly critical. An article by Julius Goebel in 1938 attacked the principal tenets of Sutherland's opinion, concluding that his view of sovereignty "passing from the British crown to the union appears to be a perversion of the dictum of Jay, C. J. in Chisholm's Executors v. Georgia, 3 Dall. 419, 470 (US 1799) to the effect that sovereignty passed from the crown to the people" (Goebel 1938, 572 n. 46). As to Sutherland's comment that the president "alone negotiates" treaties and that into this field the Senate "cannot intrude," Goebel regarded that as "a somewhat misleading description of presidential authority in foreign affairs," citing earlier examples of presidents consulting the Senate before negotiation (ibid. n. 47). To Goebel, Sutherland chose "to frame an opinion in language closely parallel to the description of royal prerogative in foreign affairs in the *Ship Money Case*" of 1637 (ibid. 572–3).

Writing in 1944, C. Perry Patterson regarded Sutherland's position on the existence of inherent presidential powers to be "(1) contrary to American history, (2) violative of our political theory, (3) unconstitutional, and (4) unnecessary, undemocratic, and dangerous" (Patterson 1944, 297). He argued that the doctrine of *Curtiss-Wright* "that Congress acquired power over the entire field of foreign affairs as a result of the issue of the Declaration is contrary to the facts of American history" (ibid. 308). Also writing in 1944, James Quarles objected to Sutherland's reasoning that foreign affairs, as distinguished from domestic affairs, invest the federal government with "powers which do not stem from the Constitution, are not granted, but are inherent" (Quarles 1944, 376–7). He noted that the question of inherent presidential power was not "raised by counsel for either side, either in the District Court or in the Supreme Court; nor is there any allusion to any issue of that sort in the opinion of the District Judge. Indeed, the pages of Mr. Justice Sutherland's opinion devoted to a discussion of that question appear to the present writer as being little, if any, more than so much interesting yet discursive *obiter*" (ibid. 378).

A particularly incisive article by David M. Levitan in 1946 not only found fault with Justice Sutherland's distinction between internal and external affairs and the belief that sovereignty flowed from the British crown directly to the national government, but expressed alarm about the implications for democratic government. Sutherland's theory marked "the furthest departure from the theory that [the] United States is a constitutionally limited democracy. It introduces the notion that national government possesses a secret reservoir of unaccountable power" (Levitan 1946, 493). Levitan's review of the political and constitutional ideas at the time of the American Revolution and the Constitutional Convention left "little room for the acceptance of Mr. Justice Sutherland's 'inherent' powers, or, in fact, 'extra-constitutional' powers theory" (ibid. 496). The Sutherland doctrine "makes shambles out of the very idea of a constitutionally limited government. It destroys even the symbol" (ibid. 497).

Charles Lofgren and other scholars have pointed out that the states in 1776 operated as sovereign entities and not as part of a collective body, as Sutherland claimed. The creation of a Continental Congress did not disturb the sovereign power of the states to make treaties, borrow money, solicit arms, lay embargoes, collect tariff duties, and conduct separate military campaigns (Lofgren 1973, 1). The Supreme Court has recognized that the American colonies, upon their separation from England, acquired certain elements of sovereignty.[30] To Lofgren, the historical evidence does not support Sutherland's reliance on inherent or extraconstitutional sources: "Federal power in foreign affairs rests on explicit and implicit constitutional grants and derives from ordinary constitutive authority" (ibid. 29–30). Further, John Marshall in 1800 "evidently did not believe that because the president was the sole organ of communication and negotiation with other nations, he became the sole foreign policy-maker" (ibid. 30).

Even if the power of sovereignty had somehow passed intact from the crown to the national government, the US Constitution allocates that power both to Congress and the president. The president and the Senate share the treaty power and the House of Representatives has discretion in deciding whether to appropriate funds needed to enforce treaties. The president receives ambassadors from other countries, but the Senate must approve US ambassadors as part of the confirmation process. Congress has the power to declare war, issue letters of marque and reprisal, raise and support military forces, make rules for their regulation, provide for the calling up of the militia to suppress insurrections and repel invasions, and to provide for the organization and disciplining of the militia. The Constitution also explicitly grants to Congress the power to lay and collect duties on foreign trade, to regulate commerce with other nations, and to establish a uniform rule of naturalization.

Other studies have rejected the line of reasoning found in *Curtiss-Wright*. Michael Glennon described Sutherland's opinion as "a muddled law review article wedged with considerable difficulty between the pages of the United States Reports" (Glennon 1988, 13). Glennon asked how constitutional limits could possibly check presidents who invoke inherent and extraconstitutional powers: "There is no logical reason why a power flowing from a source that transcends the Constitution should be subject to the prohibitions and limitations prescribed by the Constitution" (ibid.). Michael Ramsey offered a similar critique. The issue to Ramsey was not the broad scope of presidential power in foreign affairs, which he was prepared to concede. It was Sutherland's "claim that the power arose outside the Constitution" (Ramsey 2000, 382).

Roy Brownell wrote a more favorable assessment of *Curtiss-Wright*, concluding that Justice Sutherland had legitimate grounds for recognizing inherent presidential power in the field of national security and for making the distinction he did between external and internal affairs (Brownell 2000, 21–39). However, he also wrote that the "net result of *Curtiss-Wright's* deficiencies is that it places a disproportionate amount of constitutional power in the hands of the Executive Branch vis-à-vis Congress. . . . The notion that Congress may be excluded from the conduct of national security affairs, as implied by *Curtiss-Wright's* 'plenary/sole organ' passage, clearly does violence to the text of the Constitution" (ibid. 40–1).

The dicta in Justice Sutherland's decision in *Curtiss-Wright* depend to a great degree on his ability to make a clear distinction between internal and external powers. Yet it is difficult and often arbitrary to draw a bright line between the two. In 1991, President George H. W. Bush remarked: "I guess my bottom line . . . is you can't separate foreign policy from domestic."[31] Two years later President Bill Clinton made a similar point: "There is no longer a clear division between what is foreign and what is domestic."[32] There never was.

Judicial Citations to "Sole Organ"

Anthony Simones, after reviewing the academic literature and judicial decisions following Sutherland's opinion, concluded that "for every scholar who hates *Curtiss-Wright*, there seems to exist a judge who loves it" (Simones 1996, 415). The litigation record supports that judgment. Courts have repeatedly cited *Curtiss-Wright* favorably, not only to sustain delegations of legislative power but to support the existence of inherent and independent presidential power in foreign affairs.

In a 1942 case involving an executive agreement with Russia, the Supreme Court cited *Curtiss-Wright* and the "sole organ" doctrine, but described the president as acting under "a modest implied power"—not an inherent power.[33] In the Nazi saboteur case the same year, the Court spoke of the need to treat statutory grants of authority to the president as being "entitled to the greatest respect."[34] For that proposition it referred to three cases, including *Curtiss-Wright*.[35] At issue here was authority granted by Congress, not inherent presidential power. In one of the Japanese-American cases, the Court looked to *Curtiss-Wright* to support the granting of broad powers to the president during wartime.[36] Again, the Court relied on Sutherland's opinion to sustain the delegation of legislative power, not the exercise of independent, exclusive, and inherent executive powers.

In 1948, the Court decided that presidential actions in authorizing applications by carriers to engage in overseas air transportation were beyond the competence of the courts to adjudicate.[37] The president was acting under a provision of the Civil Aeronautics Act. The Court's opinion, written by Justice Jackson, cited *Curtiss-Wright* and adopted much of its language, but the thrust of the decision was to remove the judiciary, not Congress, from these questions. Justice Jackson wrote:

It would be intolerable that courts, without the relevant information, should review and perhaps nullify actions of the Executive taken on information properly held secret. Nor can courts sit in camera in order to be taken into executive confidences. But even if courts could require full disclosure, the very nature of executive decisions as to foreign policy is political, not judicial. Such decisions are wholly confided by our Constitution to the political departments of the government, Executive and Legislative.[38]

When Justice Jackson wrote those words, courts had in fact been hearing executive confidences *in camera* as part of a judge's duty to determine what evidence could be admitted at trial.[39] Moreover, in recent years Congress has specifically authorized federal courts to receive confidential documents from the executive branch and examine them in camera.[40]

In a military tribunal case decided in 1948, Justice Douglas said in a concurrence: "The President is the sole organ of the United States in the field of foreign relations. See *United States* v. *Curtiss-Wright Corp.*, 299 US 304, 318–321. Agreements which he has made with our Allies in furtherance of our war efforts have been legion. Whether they are wise or unwise, necessary or improvident, are political questions, not justiciable ones."[41] As with Justice Jackson above, this passage appears to read the judiciary out of the picture, not Congress, and does not endorse unlimited, unchecked presidential actions taken pursuant to inherent powers.

In 1950, the Court used *Curtiss-Wright* to support inherent presidential power to exclude aliens. The case involved questions of statutory authority and agency regulations adopted to enforce the statute, but the Court also relied on inherent presidential power: "there is no question of inappropriate delegation of legislative power involved here. The exclusion of aliens is a fundamental act of sovereignty. The right to do so stems not alone from legislative power but is inherent in the executive power to control the foreign affairs of the nation. *United States* v. *Curtiss-Wright Corp.*, 299 US 304; *Fong Ye Ting* v. *United States*, 149 US 698, 713. When Congress prescribes a procedure concerning the admissibility of aliens, it is not dealing alone with a legislative power. It is implementing an inherent executive power."[42] This ruling would support the exercise of inherent executive power taken in the absence of congressional policy. It is less clear how a court would rule if presidential action violated statutory policy.

In another military tribunal case, decided in 1950, the Court discussed legal challenges being brought against the "conduct of diplomatic and foreign affairs, for which the president is exclusively responsible. *United States* v. *Curtiss-Wright Corp.*, 299 US 304; . . ."[43] A deportation case in 1952 cited *Curtiss-Wright* but nevertheless recognized the role of the legislative branch in deciding policy in this area. Aliens "remain subject to the plenary power of Congress to expel them under the sovereign right to determine what noncitizens shall be permitted to remain within our borders."[44]

In the Steel Seizure Case of 1952, Justice Jackson observed that the most that can be drawn from *Curtiss-Wright* is the intimation that the president "might act in external affairs without congressional authority, but not that he might act contrary to an act of Congress."[45] He noted that "much of [Justice Sutherland's] opinion is *dictum*."[46] In 1981, a federal appellate court cautioned against placing undue reliance on "certain dicta" in Justice Sutherland's opinion: "To the extent that denominating the President as the 'sole organ' of the United States in international affairs constitutes a blanket endorsement of plenary Presidential power over any matter extending beyond the borders of this country, we reject that characterization."[47]

A right to travel case in 1965 cited *Curtiss-Wright* in upholding the authority of the secretary of state to restrict travel to Cuba.[48] Inherent presidential power, however, was not at issue. The case turned on the Court's recognition that Congress, in delegating legislative power to the president, "must of necessity paint with a brush broader than that it customarily wields in domestic areas."[49] Several Justices in the Pentagon Papers Case in 1971 made reference to *Curtiss-Wright*. In a concurrence, joined by Justice White, Justice Stewart described the president's power in national defense and international affairs as "largely unchecked by the Legislative and Judicial branches."[50] He left unclear whether the lack of checks was constitutionally mandated or merely a reflection of Congress and the courts not doing their jobs. The reference to Justice Sutherland's decision is included in a footnote related to the judicial branch, suggesting that *Curtiss-Wright* stands as a limiting factor on the judiciary, not on Congress.

A concurrence by Justice Marshall recognized that *Curtiss-Wright* gives the president "broad powers by virtue of his primary responsibility for the conduct of our foreign affairs and his position as Commander in Chief."[51] A dissent by Justice Harlan quoted Marshall's speech in 1800 ("The President is the sole organ of the nation in its external relations, and its sole representative with foreign nations") and remarked: "From that time, shortly after the founding of the Nation, to this, there has been no substantial challenge to this description of the scope of executive power."[52] A citation to *Curtiss-Wright* is added at that point. But what is "this description of the scope of executive power"? Marshall's sentence, standing by itself, does not delineate any particular scope of presidential power, and the context of the House debates rejects any notion that Marshall believed in exclusive, inherent, or unchecked executive power.

A year after the Pentagon Papers Case, Justice Rehnquist announced the judgment of the Court in a case involving the expropriation of property in Cuba. He first cited a case from 1918 that recognized that the "conduct of the foreign relations of our Government is committed by the Constitution to the Executive and Legislative—'the political'—Departments... "[53] Having discussed *concurrent* power, he then proceeds down the opposite path by citing *Curtiss-Wright* and quoting from Marshall's sole organ speech to buttress the point that the executive branch has "exclusive competence" in the field of foreign affairs.[54] In other decisions, Rehnquist also used *Curtiss-Wright* to argue that the limits on the authority of Congress to delegate its legislative powers are "less stringent in cases where the entity exercising the delegated authority itself possesses independent authority over the subject matter,"[55] and that the president occupies a "pre-eminent position... with respect to our Republic," particularly "in the area of foreign affairs and international relations."[56]

In a treaty termination case decided in 1979, Justice Powell relied on *Curtiss-Wright* to argue that Congress may grant the president wider discretion in foreign policy than in domestic affairs.[57] In the same case, Rehnquist (joined by Burger, Stewart, and Stevens) cited *Curtiss-Wright* for the more sweeping proposition that the judiciary should decline to decide political questions involving "foreign relations—specifically a treaty commitment to use military force in the defense of a foreign government if attacked."[58] A year later, in a concurrence, Rehnquist cited *Curtiss-Wright* to observe that delegations of legislative authority are upheld "because of the delegatee's residual authority over particular subjects of regulation," and that in the area of foreign affairs Congress (quoting from Justice Sutherland) "must often accord to the President a degree of discretion and freedom from statutory restriction which would not be admissible were domestic affairs alone involved."[59] There is nothing here about unchecked, extraconstitutional presidential power.

In 1981, in a case involving the revocation of an American citizen's passport, Chief Justice Burger relied in part on language from *Curtiss-Wright* that the president "has his confidential sources of information. He has his agents in the form of diplomatic, consular and other officials. Secrecy in respect of information gathered by them may be highly necessary, and the premature disclosure of it productive of harmful results."[60] In the same year, Justice Rehnquist wrote for the Court in sustaining President Carter's decision to freeze Iranian assets. The decision turned in large part on statutory authority under the International Emergency Economic Powers Act (IEEPA), but Rehnquist referred to language in *Curtiss-Wright* about the existence of presidential power "which does not require as a basis for its exercise an act of Congress."[61] The Court noted that "Congress has not disapproved of the action taken here. . . . We are thus clearly not confronted with a situation in which Congress has in some way resisted the exercise of Presidential authority."[62] This seems to recognize a legislative check on presidential power.

In 1984, the Court upheld presidential authority under the Trading With the Enemy Act (TWEA) to limit travel-related transactions with Cuba, referring to language in *Curtiss-Wright* about the "traditional deference to executive judgment '[i]n this vast external realm.' "[63] A 1988 decision by the Supreme Court concerned the authority of the Central Intelligence Agency (CIA) to terminate an employee on grounds of homosexuality. The Court decided that a provision of the Administrative Procedure Act precluded judicial review of the agency's decision, and reversed the DC Circuit on that ground.[64] Concurring in part and dissenting in part, Justice O'Connor stated that the functions performed by the CIA "lie at the core of 'the very delicate, plenary and exclusive power of the President as the sole organ of the federal government in the field of international relations.' *United States* v. *Curtiss-Wright Export Corp.*, 299 US 304, 320 (1936)."[65] In a dissent, Justice Scalia repeated the same language, adding the rest of the sentence from *Curtiss-Wright*: "a power which does not require as a basis for its exercise an act of Congress."[66]

In 1993, the Supreme Court held that neither a statutory provision nor Article 33 of the United Nations Convention Relating to the Status of Refugees limited the president's power to order the Coast Guard to return undocumented aliens, intercepted on the high seas, to Haiti.[67] The Court interpreted congressional legislation as granting to the president "ample power to establish a naval blockade that would simply deny illegal Haitian migrants the ability to disembark on our shores."[68] Whether the president's method of returning Haitians posed a greater risk of harm to them was considered "irrelevant to the scope of his authority to take action that neither the Convention nor the statute clearly prohibits."[69] The presumption that a congressional statute does not have extraterritorial application unless the intent is clear "has special force when we are construing treaty and statutory provisions that may involve foreign and military affairs for which the president has unique responsibility. Cf. *United States* v. *Curtiss-Wright Export Corp.*, 299 US 304 (1936)."[70] Left unexplored in the 1993 decision was the constitutional authority of Congress to legislate and reshape national policy in this area.

Curtiss-Wright remains a frequent citation used by the judiciary to uphold broad definitions of presidential power in foreign relations. Scholarly criticism has been directed at several points: the reliance on dicta in Justice Sutherland's opinion, taking John Marshall's speech out of context, and arguing that sovereignty passed directly from England to the national government and particularly to the president. Also objected to is Sutherland's distinction between external and internal affairs for the purpose of vesting exclusive powers with the president. The case is frequently cited by the courts to support not only broad delegations of legislative power to the executive branch but also the existence of independent, implied, inherent, and extraconstitutional powers for the president. Although some Justices of the Supreme Court have described the president's foreign relations power as "exclusive," the Court itself has not denied to Congress its constitutional authority to enter the field and reverse or modify presidential decisions in the area of national security and foreign affairs.

Inherent Powers under Truman

Curtiss-Wright remains a convenient, if erroneous, citation for those who promote inherent powers for the president. Another major source is the action of President Harry Truman, the first chief executive to initiate a major war without coming to Congress for either a declaration of war or authorization by statute. Acting under two resolutions passed by the UN Security Council, he ordered armed force against North Korea in June 1950. Unlike Lincoln, he never came to Congress after the fact to seek legislative approval for his actions. His reliance on the Security Council resolutions violated the Constitution, the UN Charter, the UN Participation Act, and his own promises made to the Senate in 1945 when it debated the Charter, when he pledged to first come to Congress for authority before being engaged in any UN military operation (Fisher 2004*b*, 81–104; Fisher 1995).

After two years of a costly war against North Korea, Truman faced a nation-wide strike of steelworkers in 1952. He reacted by issuing an executive order that directed the secretary of commerce to take possession of and operate the plants and facilities of 87 major steel companies. As justification, he referred to his proclamation of 16 December declaring the existence of a nationwide emergency and the dispatch of American soldiers to Korea. The order called steel "indispensable" for producing weapons and war materials (*Federal Register*, 17: 3139).

Although Truman based the order on authority under "the Constitution and laws of the United States, and as President of the United States and Commander-in-Chief of the armed forces of the United States," the Justice Department later argued in court that Truman had acted solely on inherent executive power without any statutory support. The department told the district judge that courts were powerless to control the exercise of presidential power when directed toward emergency conditions.[71] At a news conference on 17 April 1952, Truman was asked by reporters whether, if he could seize the steel mills under his inherent powers, he could also seize newspapers and radio stations. Truman said he could do "whatever is for the best of the country."[72]

On 29 April 1952, District Judge David Pine wrote a blistering opinion repudiating this theory of inherent presidential power. In holding Truman's seizure of the steel mills to be unconstitutional, he acknowledged that a nationwide strike could do extensive damage to the country but believed that a strike "would be less injurious to the public than the injury which would flow from a timorous judicial recognition that there is some basis for this claim of unlimited and unrestrained Executive power, which would be implicit in a failure to grant the injunction."[73] The Supreme Court upheld the district court's ruling.[74] These judicial rulings reflected a broad resentment throughout the country that condemned Truman's theory of inherent and emergency power. Newspaper editorials ripped him for acting in a manner they regarded as arbitrary, dictatorial, dangerous, destructive, high-handed, and unauthorized by law (Fisher 2000, 48).

Inherent Powers under George W. Bush

In the immediate aftermath of the terrorist attacks on 11 September 2001, President George W. Bush came to Congress to seek statutory authority for military action against Afghanistan and against Iraq, and to broaden law enforcement powers through the USA Patriot Act. At the same time, he turned to inherent powers to authorize military tribunals, designated US citizens as "enemy combatants" and held them indefinitely without trial, sent suspects abroad to countries that practice torture (extraordinary rendition), and authorized eavesdropping by the National Security Agency (NSA).

On 13 November 2001, President Bush issued a military order authorizing the creation of military commissions to try noncitizens as part of the "war on terrorism." He relied on his authority as commander in chief, "the laws of the United States," and sections 821 and 836 of Title 10 of the US Code (*Federal Register*, 66: 57833). The principal statute cited by the administration was the Authorization for Use of Military Force (AUMF), enacted within a week of 9/11. That statute was enacted to authorize military action against the Taliban and al-Qaeda in Afghanistan. No one during congressional debate spoke about military commissions, much less authorized them. Sections 821 and 836 specifically mention military commissions, but nothing in those sections imply plenary and unchecked powers for the president. Essentially, the administration is relying on what it considers to be the president's inherent authority in time of war or emergency.

The Justice Department argues that Congress "has recognized and approved the president's historic use of military commissions as he deems necessary to prosecute offenders against the laws of war."[75] The historical record is quite to the contrary. Military commissions have been authorized by statute and are considered to flow not from presidential but from legislative authority (Fisher 2005a). It is quite true that Congress has not protected its authority in this area in recent decades, but the case for independent and unrestricted presidential power is not convincing. The judicial ruling principally cited by the administration, the Nazi saboteur case of *Ex parte Quirin* (1942), was so unappealing to the Roosevelt Administration that it decided not to use the Nazi tribunal as a precedent two and a half years later, and Justices of the Supreme Court subsequently regretted how the Court decided the case (Fisher 2003, 134, 138–44).

Bush's military order covered only noncitizens. However, the administration claimed the right to detain US citizens by calling them "enemy combatants," holding them indefinitely without being charged, and not providing them with counsel or trial. A plurality of the Supreme Court in 2004 accepted the administration's argument that the AUMF constituted "explicit congressional authorization for the detention of individuals," thus supposedly satisfying the Non-Detention Act of 1971 that prohibits the detention of US citizens without an "Act of Congress."[76] Similar to the lack of connection between the AUMF and military commissions, no one during debate on the AUMF discussed the president's authority to detain US citizens. Unless lawmakers consciously discussed the the Non-Detention Act when they passed the AUMF and announced their intention to authorize detention of US citizens, the limitations in the 1971 statute remain in place and are not satisfied. The plurality cited nothing in the text or legislative history of the AUMF that "explicitly" indicated a willingness of Congress to authorize the detention of US citizens. In fact, a few paragraphs later the plurality said "it is of no moment" that the AUMF "does not use specific language of detention."[77] If not explicit or specific, where does the authority come from? Quite likely it is inherent powers.

On 29 June 2006, the Supreme Court again addressed the issue of military tribunals. In *Hamdan* v. *Rumsfeld*, a 5:3 majority rejected a number of the arguments put forward by the Bush Administration. The Court denied that legislation enacted on 30 December 2005 (119 Stat. 2740–44) took from the Court its jurisdiction to hear the case. The Court also held that the tribunals had not been expressly authorized by any congressional statute, and that nothing in the AUMF would be read to expand or alter the authorization set forth by Congress in the Uniform Code of Military Justice (UCMJ). Finally, the Court ruled that the structure and the procedures of the tribunals created by the Bush Administration violate both the UCMJ and the four Geneva Conventions signed in 1949. Given the consistent arguments from the administration that President Bush had plenary and exclusive powers as commander in chief to discharge his Article II powers during time of war, the Court's decision put a sizable dent in the theory of inherent executive authority.

Another controversy over inherent presidential powers involved the decision by the Bush Administration shortly after 9/11 to authorize the NSA to eavesdrop on American citizens. In December 2005, the *New York Times* broke the story (Risen and Lichtblau 2005). Before passage of the Foreign Intelligence Surveillance Act (FISA) in 1978, the constitutionality of national security wiretaps was murky. President Franklin D. Roosevelt had asserted that authority in a secret 1940 memo to Attorney General Robert Jackson (Fisher 2005b, 730), the Supreme Court sidestepped the issue in a 1967 decision,[78] and Congress similarly ducked the controversy in a 1968 wiretapping statute (82 Stat. 214, § 2511(3)). A Court decision in 1972 put pressure on Congress to decide what procedures to adopt for national security wiretaps.[79]

Uncertainty about the law disappeared in 1978 when Congress passed FISA, requiring the Justice Department to seek warrants from a newly created FISA Court before engaging in national security eavesdropping. Statutory policy now became the "exclusive means by which electronic surveillance ... and the interception of domestic wire and oral communications may be conducted" (92 Stat. 1797, § 2511(2)(f)). FISA specifically addressed how it would work in time of war, authorizing the president to conduct electronic surveillance without a court order to acquire foreign intelligence information for a period "not to exceed fifteen calendar days following a declaration of war by the Congress" (ibid. 1796, § 111).

The administration chose two grounds for ignoring FISA. The first was the claim that Bush was operating under authority implied by the passage of the AUMF. The argument is unpersuasive because no member of Congress in debating that statute thought about, or talked about, NSA spying on US citizens. The second ground is what the administration considers to be the president's inherent powers under Article II of the Constitution. In a press briefing on 19 December 2005, Attorney General Alberto Gonzales said that FISA lacked "the speed and the agility" that the administration needed "to deal with this new kind of enemy" (Press Briefing 2005, 2). When asked why the administration had not asked Congress to amend FISA to grant broader powers, he replied: "We have had discussions with Congress in the past— certain members of Congress—as to whether or not FISA could be amended to allow us to adequately deal with this kind of threat, and we were advised that that would be difficult, if not impossible" (ibid. 4). His explanation appeared to concede that the administration knowingly chose to act contrary to law.

President Bush met with reporters on 1 January 2006 to discuss the NSA wiretaps. On three occasions he used the expression "within the law" to characterize what the administration had done.[80] The White House obviously wanted to tell the public that the president is not above the law. However, when one reads these statements in context, it seems clear that "within the law" did not mean that the president was acting pursuant to legislation passed by Congress. Instead, the phrase seemed to cover actions by the president pursuant to what lawyers within the administration could argue were within the inherent executive powers under Article II.

Similarly, on 11 January 2006, President Bush said that the NSA eavesdropping program had "been authorized, reauthorized many times."[81] Without question, the "authority" here was solely within the executive branch. Congress did not authorize it and reauthorize it many times. Bush also spoke these words on the same day: "We are a rule—a country of law. We have a Constitution, which guides the sharing of power. And I take that—I put that hand on the Bible, and I meant it when I said I'm going to uphold the Constitution."[82] The rule of law means that the legislative branch makes the law and the president sees that it is faithfully carried out. As Justice Jackson said in the Steel Seizure Case of 1952: "With all its defects, delays and inconveniences, men have discovered no technique for long preserving free government except that the Executive be under the law, and that the law be made by parliamentary deliberations."[83] That source of law is absent from NSA eavesdropping.

In a major legal analysis released on 19 January 2006, the Justice Department argued: "The NSA activities are supported by the president's well-recognized inherent constitutional authority as Commander in Chief and sole organ for the Nation in foreign affairs to conduct warrantless surveillance of enemy forces for intelligence purposes to detect and disrupt armed attacks on the United States" (US Department of Justice 2006, 1). This argument, linking inherent powers to the sole organ doctrine, is remarkably shallow and vapid. The department also argued that if FISA were interpreted to "impede the President's ability to use the traditional tool of electronic surveillance to detect and prevent future attacks by a declared enemy that has already struck at the homeland and is engaged in ongoing operations against the United States, the constitutionality of FISA, as applied to that situation, would be called into very serious doubt." More directly: "In fact, if this difficult constitutional question had to be addressed, FISA would be unconstitutional as applied to this narrow context" (ibid. 3). In other words, even if Congress adopted legislation explicitly restricting NSA eavesdropping, it could not limit what the president decided to do.

The public and congressional reaction to NSA surveillance has been muted to some degree by President Bush's claim that the interception of international communications is confined to "people with known links to Al Qaeda and related terrorist organizations" (Bush 2006, 30). However, the public and most members of Congress do not know the extent of the surveillance. The administration consistently refused to discuss "operations." Unlike President Truman's seizure of steel mills—a public act in broad daylight—the extent of NSA eavesdropping is not visible or known. No one outside a handful of people in the administration understand the degree to which these operations invade the privacy of communications unrelated to al-Qaeda and terrorist organizations. Uncertainty about what the administration has authorized was highlighted by newspaper reports in May 2006 that the NSA had collected records of millions of domestic phone calls (Lichtblau and Shane 2006, A1).

On 18 May 2006, General Michael Hayden appeared before the Senate Select Committee on Intelligence on his nomination to be CIA Director. His testimony sheds light on a number of legal and constitutional issues. During his tenure as NSA Director, the assurance he received from agency attorneys was purely oral, not written. At different times, three separate attorneys "told" him that the NSA eavesdropping program was legal. No formal legal analysis was ever prepared. Moreover, the hearing transcript seems to indicate that these were agency attorneys at various levels, not the NSA General Counsel (Senate Hearing 2006, 22–3, 35, 69). Second, Hayden repeatedly made it clear that the legal justification for the program was not statutory (the AUMF) but rather the president's inherent powers under Article II (ibid. 35, 69, 121, 143–4, 170).

Third, Hayden seemed to acknowledge that the administration understood that FISA did not authorize the NSA eavesdropping and consequently decided to go against statutory law and rely on Article II arguments. He was asked by CIA Director George Tenet "could you do more? I said not within current law. He says, well, what could you do more? And I put it together with, as I said, technologically possible, operationally relevant" programs (ibid. 68). Fourth, when Hayden (1) pledged "to follow the law," (2) testified that the CIA "will obey the laws of the United States," and (3) said he had no doubts about the legality of the NSA eavesdropping program (ibid. 39, 74, 116), he was relying on Article II, inherent authority, not statutory authority. He testified: "I did not believe—still don't believe—that I was acting unlawfully. I was acting under a lawful authorization" (ibid. 138). He meant an authorization from the executive branch, not from Congress. As he told Senator Orrin Hatch: "The way I describe it, Senator, is I had two lawful programs in front of me, one authorized by the president, the other one would have been conducted under FISA as currently crafted and implemented" (ibid. 88). Faced with two choices, executive law and statutory law, he selected the former.

The Bush Administration also invoked inherent authority by sending suspected terrorists to other countries for possible torture during interrogation ("extraordinary rendition"). It merits the special adjective because customary rendition allowed the president to render (send) someone to a foreign jurisdiction, moving the person from one judicial process to another. A series of opinions by attorneys general concluded that presidents may not act under some form of implied, inherent, or extraconstitutional authority. They needed authority granted either by treaty or a law passed by Congress.[84] As recently as 1979, the Office of Legal Counsel in the Justice Department decided that the president "cannot order any person extradited unless a treaty or statute authorizes him to do so."[85]

Extraordinary rendition thus leaves the legal and judicial system, subordinate to the rule of law, and enters into the field of presidential law and inherent authority. Under this system the president acts not only in the absence of statutory or treaty law but even in the face of restrictive statutes or treaties. Those who advocate extraordinary rendition argue that the president is at liberty to act in whatever manner he decides is necessary to accomplish his objectives as commander in chief during time of war.

Officials in the Bush Administration defended the practice of interrogating suspected terrorists outside the country. James L. Pavitt, after retiring from the CIA in August 2004, claimed that the practice of extraordinary rendition had been done in consultation with the National Security Council and disclosed to the appropriate congressional oversight committees (Priest 2004, A21). Instead of relying on law made by statutes or by treaty, the administration decided it could make law unilaterally and touch base with a few members of Congress.

To counter criticism directed at extraordinary rendition, Secretary of State Condoleezza Rice presented the administration's views in a detailed statement on 5 December 2005. She claimed that rendition "is not unique to the United States, or to the current administration," and offered two examples where suspected terrorists were transferred from one country to another.[86] One example, Ramzi Youssef, was brought to the United States after being charged with the 1993 bombing of the World Trade Center and plotting to blow up airlines over the Pacific Ocean. "Carlos the Jackal," captured in Sudan, was brought to France. Rice neglected to add that the purpose of rendition in those two cases was not to take them to a secret interrogation center outside the judicial process for possible torture, but to bring them to court to face public charges, trial, conviction, and sentencing.

Conclusions

Inherent powers are back in vogue, but on a scale far more vast than during the Truman Administration. The health of representative government and constitutional limits cannot depend on checks created within the administration by a few "in the know," nor by briefings conducted by executive officials with a handful of lawmakers. The administration has told the public that such initiatives as NSA eavesdropping have been carefully vetted and cleared. The program is "within the law" and regularly "authorized" and "reauthorized." All of this constant scrubbing might seem reassuring, but the scrutiny is being done within one branch and by a small group of people. What constitutes law in this area is what the administration has decided fits within the president's inherent powers. The statutory system available in FISA was sidestepped, as was the process of judicial warrants available through the FISA Court. The rule of law, the Constitution, and "the sharing of power" cannot coexist with one-branch government.

On 20 March 2006, President Bush told a gathering in Cleveland, Ohio, that General Hayden of the NSA believed that FISA "was designed for a previous period and is slow and cumbersome."[87] If that were true, FISA could have been amended, as it has been many times since 1978, including after 9/11. Bush said he was concerned about the legality of the NSA program, "and so I asked lawyers . . . to determine whether or not I could do this legally. And they came back and said yes."[88] Of course the lawyers were from the executive branch.

Courts need to be much more assertive in exercising their independence. Too often, in the past, they have been content to function as an arm of the executive branch on matters concerning foreign affairs and national security (Fisher 2006). Congressional committees will have to invoke powers of legislative oversight that have remained dormant in recent years. The media plays a key role in ferreting out information within agencies and encouraging executive officials to blow the whistle on agency corruption. For its part, the public needs to register whether it wants to be part of a democratic system and continue to enjoy the freedoms and liberties associated with checks and balances, or sit back passively and watch autocracy take root.

References

Arkes, Hadley. 1994. *The Return of George Sutherland: Restoring a Jurisprudence of Natural Rights*. Princeton: Princeton University Press.

Borchard, Edwin M. 1942. Letter to Harlan Fiske Stone, Papers of Harlan Fiske Stone, Container No. 6, Manuscript Room, Library of Congress.

Boyd, Julian P. (ed.) 1961. *The Papers of Thomas Jefferson*. 33 vols. Princeton: Princeton University Press.

Brownell, Roy E., II. 2000. "The Coexistence of *United States* v. *Curtiss-Wright* and *Youngstown Sheet & Tube* v. *Sawyer* in National Security Jurisprudence," *Journal of Law & Politics* 16: 1–111.

Bush, George W. 2006. "Bush on the Patriot Act and Eavesdropping," *The New York Times*, 18 January: 30.

Cullen, Charles T. (ed.) 1984. *The Papers of John Marshall*. 4 vols. Chapel Hill: University of North Carolina Press.

Fisher, Louis. 1972. *President and Congress*. New York: Free Press.

——— 1989. "Congressional Participation in the Treaty Process," *University of Pennsylvania Law Review* 137: 1511–22.

——— 1995. "The Korean War: On What Legal Basis did Truman Act?" *American Journal of International Law* 89: 21–39.

Fisher, Louis. 1997. *Constitutional Conflicts between Congress and the President*. 4th edn. Lawrence: University Press of Kansas.

____ 2000. *Congressional Abdication on War and Spending*. College Station: Texas A&M University Press.

____ 2003. *Nazi Saboteurs on Trial: A Military Tribunal & American Law*. Lawrence: University Press of Kansas.

____ 2004a. *The Politics of Executive Privilege*. Durham, NC: Carolina Academic Press.

____ 2004b. *Presidential War Power*. 2nd edn. Lawrence: University of Kansas Press.

____ 2005a. *Military Tribunals and Presidential Power: American Revolution to the War on Terrorism*. Lawrence: University Press of Kansas.

____ 2005b. *American Constitutional Law*. 6th edn. Durham: Carolina Academic Press.

____ 2005c. "Judicial Review of the War Power," *Presidential Studies Quarterly* 35 (September): 466–95.

____ 2006. *In the Name of National Security: Unchecked Presidential Power and the* Reynolds *Case*. Lawrence: University Press of Kansas.

Ford, Paul Leicester (ed.) 1895. *The Writings of Thomas Jefferson*. 10 vols. New York: G. P. Putnam's.

Glennon, Michael J. 1988. "Two Views of Presidential Foreign Affairs Power: *Little* v. *Barreme* or *Curtiss-Wright*?" *Yale Journal of International Law* 13: 5–20.

Goebel, Julius, Jr. 1938. "Constitutional History and Constitutional Law," *Columbia Law Review* 38: 555–77.

Koh, Harold Hongju. 1990. *The National Security Constitution*. New Haven: Yale University Press.

Kurland, Philip B., and Casper, Gerhard. 1975. *Landmark Briefs and Arguments of the Supreme Court of the United States: Constitutional Law*. 326 vols. Arlington, Va.: University Publications of America.

Levin, Ronald M. 1974. "In Camera Inspections Under the Freedom of Information Act," *University of Chicago Law Review* 41: 557–81.

Levitan, David M. 1946. "The Foreign Relations Power: An Analysis of Mr. Justice Sutherland's Theory," *Yale Law Journal* 55: 467–97.

Levy, Leonard W. 1988. *Original Intent and the Framers' Constitution*. New York: Macmillan.

Lichtblau, Eric, and Shane, Scott. 2006. "Bush is Pressed over New Report on Surveillance," *The New York Times*, 12 May, A1.

Lodge, Henry Cabot (ed.) 1904. *The Works of Alexander Hamilton*. New York: G. P. Putnam's.

Lofgren, Charles A. 1973. "*United States* v. *Curtiss-Wright Export Corporation*: An Historical Reassessment," *Yale Law Journal* 83: 1–32.

Paschal, Joel Francis. 1951. *Mr. Justice Sutherland: A Man Against the State*. Princeton: Princeton University Press.

Patterson, C. Perry. 1944. "In Re The United States *v.* The *Curtiss-Wright* Corporation," *Texas Law Review* 22: 286–308.

Powell, H. Jefferson. 2002. *The President's Authority over Foreign Affairs*. Durham, NC: Carolina Academic Press.

Press Briefing. 2005. Attorney General Alberto Gonzales and General Michael Hayden, Principal Deputy Director for National Intelligence, 19 December

⟨http://www.whitehouse.gov/news/releases/2005/12/print/20051219-1.html⟩, accessed 21 November 2006.

Priest, Dana. 2004. "Ex-CIA Official Defends Detention Policies," *Washington Post*, 27 October.

Quarles, James. 1944. "The Federal Government: As to Foreign Affairs, Are Its Powers Inherent as Distinguished from Delegated?" *Georgetown Law Journal* 32: 375–83.

Ramsey, Michael D. 2000. "The Myth of Extraconstitutional Foreign Affairs Power," *William and Mary Law Review* 42: 379–446.

Richardson, James D. 1897. *A Compilation of the Messages and Papers of the Presidents.* 20 vols. New York: Bureau of National Literature.

Risen, James, and Lichtblau, Eric. 2005. "Bush Lets U.S. Spy on Callers Without Courts," *The New York Times*, 16 December, A1.

Senate Hearing. 2006. Senate Select Committee on Intelligence on the Nomination of General Michael V. Hayden to be the Director of the Central Intelligence Agency, 19 May, hearing transcript.

Simones, Anthony. 1996. "The Reality of *Curtiss-Wright*," *Northern Illinois University Law Review* 16: 411–31.

Stone, Harlan Fiske. 1937. Letter to Edwin M. Borchard, 13 May 1937. Papers of Harlan Fiske Stone, Container No. 6, Manuscript Room, Library of Congress.

―――― 1942. Letter to Edwin M. Borchard, 11 February 1942. Papers of Harlan Fiske Stone, Container No. 6, Manuscript Room, Library of Congress.

Sutherland, George. 1919. *Constitutional Power and World Affairs.* New York: Columbia University Press.

Syrett, Harold C. 1974. *The Papers of Alexander Hamilton.* 27 vols. New York: Columbia University Press.

US Congress. 1910. "The Internal and External Powers of the National Government." S. Doc. 417, 61st Cong. 2nd Session.

US Department of Justice. 2006. "Legal Authorities Supporting the Activities of the National Security Agency Described by the President," 19 January.

Yoo, John. 2005. *The Powers of War and Peace.* Chicago: University of Chicago Press.

Notes

The views expressed here are personal, not those of the Law Library of the Library of Congress.

1. *United States* v. *Lopez*, 514 US 549, 552 (1995).
2. *Boerne* v. *Flores*, 521 US 507, 516 (1997).
3. *The Prize Cases*, 67 US 635, 660, 668 (1863).
4. Ibid. 668.
5. Ibid. 669.
6. Ibid. 668.
7. Ibid. 660 (emphasis in original).
8. 10 *Annals of Cong.* 613 (1800), cited in *United States* v. *Curtiss-Wright Corp.*, 299 US 304, 319 (1936).

9. 10 *Annals of Cong.* 515; See *United States* v. *Robins* [*sic*], 27 Fed. Cas. 825, 832 (1799) (Case No. 16, 175).

10. *Talbot* v. *Seeman*, 5 US 1, 29 (1801).

11. Ibid. 28.

12. *Little* v. *Barreme*, 2 Cr. (6 US) 170, 179 (1840).

13. Ibid.

14. *Marbury* v. *Madison*, 5 US (1 Cr.) 137, 165 (1803).

15. Ibid. 166.

16. Ibid. 170.

17. *Panama Refining Co.* v. *Ryan*, 293 US 388 (1935); *Schechter Corp.* v. *United States*, 295 US 495 (1935).

18. *United States* v. *Curtiss-Wright Export Corporation*, 14 F.Supp. 230 (SDNY 1936).

19. e.g. *United States* v. *Brown*, 12 US (8 Cr.) 110, 128–9 (1814); *Mitchell* v. *Harmony*, 54 US (13 How.) 115, 132–3, 135 (1851); *Jecker* v. *Montgomery*, 54 US (13 How.) 498, 515 (1852); *United States* v. *Anderson*, 76 US (9 Wall.) 56, 70–1 (1870); *Dooley* v. *United States*, 182 US 222, 234, 235 (1901); *Ex parte Orozco*, 201 F. 106, 112 (WD Tex. 1912) dismissed, 229 US 633 (1913). See Fisher (2005c.)

20. *United States* v. *Curtiss-Wright Corp.*, 299 US 304, 315 (1936).

21. Ibid.

22. Ibid. 316.

23. Ibid. (emphasis in original).

24. Ibid.

25. Ibid.

26. 299 US at 319 (emphasis in original).

27. 299 US at 319.

28. Ibid. 319–20.

29. Ibid. 333.

30. *United States* v. *California*, 332 US 19, 31 (1947); *Texas* v. *White*, 74 US 700, 725 (1869).

31. *Public Papers of the Presidents*. 1991. ii. 1629.

32. *Public Papers of the Presidents*. 1993. i. 2.

33. *United States* v. *Pink*, 315 US 203, 229 (1942). *Curtiss-Wright* was also cited in *United States* v. *Belmont*, 301 US 324, 331–2 (1937).

34. *Ex parte Quirin*, 317 US 1, 41–2 (1942).

35. Ibid. 42.

36. *Ex parte Endo*, 323 US 283, 298 n. 21 (1944).

37. *C. & S. Air Lines* v. *Waterman Corp.*, 333 US 103 (1948).

38. Ibid. 111.

39. *Haugen* v. *United States*, 253 F.2d 850, 851 (9th Cir. 1946).

40. e.g. 88 Stat. 1562 (1974) (a district court has jurisdiction to "enjoin the agency from withholding agency records and to order the production of any agency records improperly withheld from the complainant. In such a case the court . . . may examine the contents of such agency records in camera"). See Levin 1974.

41. *Hirota* v. *MacArthur*, 338 US 197, 208 (1948). The concurrence by Justice Douglas was announced 27 June 1949.

42. *Knauff* v. *Shaughnessy*, 338 US 537, 542 (1950).

43. *Johnson* v. *Eisentrager*, 339 US 763, 789 (1950).
44. *Carlson* v. *Landon*. 342 US 524, 534 (1952).
45. *Youngstown Co.* v. *Sawyer*, 343 US 579, 636 n. 2 (1952).
46. Ibid.
47. *American Intern. Group* v. *Islamic Republic of Iran*, 657 F. 2d 430, 438 n. 6 (DC Cir. 1981).
48. *Zemel* v. *Rusk*, 381 US 1, 17 (1965).
49. Ibid.
50. *New York Times Co.* v. *United States*, 403 US 713, 727 (1971).
51. Ibid. 741.
52. Ibid. 756.
53. *First Nat. Bk.* v. *Banco Nacional de Cuba*, 406 US 759, 766 (1972) (citing *Oetjen* v. *Central Leather Co.*, 246 US 297, 302 (1918)).
54. Ibid. (citing *United States* v. *Belmont*, 301 US 324 (1937)).
55. *United States* v. *Mazurie*, 419 US 544, 556–7 (1975).
56. *Nixon* v. *Administrator of General Services*, 433 US 425, 550–1 n. 6 (1977) (dissenting op.).
57. *Goldwater* v. *Carter*, 444 US 996, 1001 n. 1 (1980).
58. Ibid. 1003–4. See also 1004–5.
59. *Industrial Union Dept.* v. *American Petrol. Inst.*, 448 US 607, 684 (1980).
60. *Haig* v. *Agee*, 453 US 280, 307–8 (1981).
61. *Dames & Moore* v. *Regan*, 453 US 654, 661 (1981).
62. Ibid. 687–8.
63. *Regan* v. *Wald*, 468 US 222, 243 (1984).
64. *Webster* v. *Doe*, 486 US 592 (1988).
65. Ibid. 605–6.
66. *Ibid.* 614–15.
67. *Sale* v. *Haitian Centers Council, Inc.*, 509 US 155 (1993).
68. Ibid. 187.
69. Ibid. 188.
70. Ibid.
71. "US Argues President is Above Courts," *New York Times*, 25 April 1952, 1. For oral argument before the district court, see H. Doc. No. 534 (Part 1), 82d Cong., 2d Sess. (1952).
72. *Public Papers of the Presidents* (1952), 273.
73. *Youngstown Sheet & Tube Co.* v. *Sawyer*, 103 F.Supp. 569, 577 (DDC 1952).
74. *Youngstown Co.* v. *Sawyer*, 343 US 579, 637 (1952).
75. "Brief for the Respondents in Opposition," *Hamdan* v. *Rumsfeld*, No. 05-184, US Supreme Court 24, filed 7 Sept. 2005.
76. *Hamdi* v. *Rumsfeld*, 542 US 507, 517 (2004).
77. Ibid. 519.
78. *Katz* v. *United States*, 389 US 347, 358 n. 23 (1967).
79. *United States* v. *United States District Court*, 407 US 297, 322–3 (1972).
80. *Weekly Compilation of Presidential Documents* 42: 2–3.
81. Ibid. 46.
82. Ibid.

83. *Youngstown Co.* v. *Sawyer*, 343 US at 655.
84. e.g. 3 Op. Att'y Gen. 661 (1841) (the president depends on authority by a law or treaty to surrender someone to a foreign jurisdiction); 2 Op. Att'y Gen. 559 (1833) (requiring a law or treaty for extradition); 1 Op. Att'y Gen. 68, 69–70 (1797) ("[H]aving omitted to make a law directing the mode of proceeding, I know not how, according to the present system, a delivery of such offender could be effected. . . . This defect appears to me to require a particular law.")
85. 4A Op. OLC 149 (1979).
86. Condoleezza Rice, US Secretary of State, Remarks Upon Her Departure for Europe (5 Dec. 2005), available at ⟨http://www.state.gov/secretary/rm/2005/57602.htm⟩ accessed 21 November 2006.
87. *Weekly Compilation of Presidential Documents* 42: 511.
88. Ibid.

3

Torture of Detainees and Presidential Prerogative Power

Richard M. Pious

In conducting a "war" on terrorism any government faces legal and moral choices in its treatment of captives. One can argue that the government should accord due process of law to all prisoners it classifies as civilians or treat those it considers prisoners of war according to the laws of war. But two problems arise: unlike prisoners in a conventional war, who usually possess only tactical information about their units, those detained in a war on terror may have information about future operations, including those that involve the use of weapons of mass destruction. Should the magnitude of such a threat outweigh protections against inhuman treatment? The other problem is that some detainees do not neatly fit into the civilian or the prisoner of war classifications. What are terrorists, and what protections must the government grant to them after they are captured and when they are interrogated?

To gain the greatest flexibility in obtaining intelligence from detainees in conflicts in Afghanistan and Iraq, President Bush used the prerogatives (as he defined them) of his office: the powers of the commander in chief; the power to interpret and reinterpret treaty and convention language defining American obligations regarding the treatment of prisoners of war and other detainees; and the power to "take care that laws be faithfully executed," enabling him to interpret domestic statutory law dealing with torture and inhuman treatment of detainees.

When presidents rely on prerogatives, they claim that their constitutional powers are controlling. They often rely on a combination of statutory delegation and constitutional power in order to claim that they are acting according to a specific delegation of power, or according to the intent of Congress—what constitutional lawyers call "joint concord." Presidents defend the legitimacy of their exercise of prerogative power, while the opposition party calls into question not only the policy but also the prerogative power used to implement it. Were their own party in the White House, they would be defending the prerogative while the opposition party attacked it.

When presidents rely on prerogative power, there are three possible outcomes. If a president succeeds, there is a "frontlash" effect: the president's party unites while the opposition is divided and demoralized, Congress is supportive or at least acquiescent, and the "living presidency" of custom and precedent absorbs the presidential prerogative. Courts rule for the executive or decline to take jurisdiction. If the policy is not consonant with American values, or if it fails, the result may be a "backlash" effect: the opposition calls into question the president's competence; his own party is demoralized while most of the opposition unites against him; Congress is likely to modify his policies or even abandon them; and it increases oversight and may pass a statute requiring policy co-determination. Courts are likely to rule in ways that limit presidential power, and their decisions do not incorporate presidential claims into the powers of the office. In extreme cases there may be an "overshoot and collapse" effect leading Congress to censure or impeach the president.

In most cases of covert action or scandals (such as the U-2 flights, Watergate, CIA assassination attempts, and the Iran-Contra affair), events follow a progression: first, the White House claims that nothing happened (a weather plane is missing), or only an insignificant event occurred (a "third-rate" burglary). The White House attempts to shift blame downward (Cuban burglars) or outward (Israel sending arms to Iran, then private arms dealers). It claims that only minor players in the administration were involved (Watergate), acting on their own in a rogue operation (CIA attempted assassination investigations). Blame is placed on "the process" not working properly (the Tower Commission in the Iran-Contra affair). If the president is directly linked to illegal behavior, he and his lawyers employ constitutional and legal "damage control": they claim that intelligence operations need not comply with statutory laws prohibiting certain activities; or that the law was not violated, since the administration exploited loopholes or ambiguities; or that only "technical" provisions were violated but not the spirit of the law, and that the president acted in "joint concord" with congressional intent. In a last line of defense, the White House may claim that a legal prohibition was unconstitutional or an international commitment unenforceable because it infringed upon the president's constitutional prerogatives.

Usually these maneuvers work and the process flames out after lower-level officials are punished. But occasionally debate in Congress and in the media focuses on White House misdeeds, and the president drops precipitously in the polls, his party abandons him, and he loses influence in Congress. Congressional investigations and hearings and investigation by prosecutors commence. The president is forced to accept high-level resignations of aides or cabinet-level officials. A new chief of staff who has the confidence of Congress comes in to restore "adult supervision"; within the cabinet the secretary of state and other senior secretaries assume leadership roles. The president may be censured, and there may be moves to impeach—or even an impeachment trial. The imperial presidency collapses, to be followed by the "imperiled" presidency, of limited political resources, constrained by new framework legislation.

Since the allegations of abuse of detainees at Abu Ghraib prison were first disclosed by media sources late in 2003, there have been investigations of inhuman treatment and torture of prisoners which occurred in the following locations: at Abu Ghraib during the "night shift"; at Quaim the Third Armored Cavalry's "Blackstone Hotel"; at the Black Room at Camp NAMA (standing for "Nasty-Ass Military Area") at Baghdad International Airport (where the CIA conducted interrogations of detainees picked up by Iraq Force I-21, a unit hunting for high-ranking fugitives, along with Ft. Bragg's Task Force 6-26, a special operations command unit working a "Special Access Program" for high-value detainees); at Guantanamo's Camp Delta; and in Afghanistan at Gardez, Khost, Asadabad, and Jallalabad, at Bagram Control Point, at the CIA's "Salt Pit," and at the Special Forces "Camp Slap Happy" detention center in Kandahar. Investigations by the Pentagon, by members of Congress, and by international organizations such as the Red Cross, Human Rights Watch, and Amnesty International have substantiated inhuman treatment.[1] According to Mark Sappenfeld (2005), the Pentagon has confirmed over 600 credible cases of abuse, accounting for about 1 per cent of detainees. Army statistics indicate that 27 detainees died during 2002–4, in cases that might have involved murder, negligent homicide, or assault. At least 19 homicides may have occurred during extreme interrogations.

Some abuses occurred because "rogue" officers go beyond sanctioned interrogation techniques, but it is clear that the Bush Administration developed policies that led to inhuman treatment and torture in the "extreme interrogation" of "high value assets," either by the military or by the CIA and its contractors. Other interrogations took place after the CIA's Counterterrorism Center Rendition Group sent detainees to other countries for interrogation through a power known as "extraordinary rendition." According to Dana Priest (2005b), the highest value detainees are held in CIA "black sites" in host countries, and interrogated by CIA officers using CIA approved "Enhanced Interrogation Techniques." The CIA has sent lower priority detainees to Egypt, Jordan, Morocco, Syria, Saudi Arabia, Uzbekistan, and Thailand.

Why have allegations of torture and inhuman treatment resulting in the maiming or even the death of detainees not risen to the level of an Iran-Contra affair? Or a Watergate? What does this tell us about the politics of prerogative power?

Administration Decision Making

President Bush, Vice President Cheney, Secretary of Defense Rumsfeld, and Attorney General Gonzales made decisions about the treatment of prisoners that went against international law conventions and commitments, customary international law, American statutory law, and existing guidelines for interrogation that the military had developed over more than two centuries. The Bush Administration justified these decisions on its reading of the constitutional authority of the president (as administration lawyers defined it), and that in turn left open the probability that lower-level officials would subject detainees to inhuman treatment and torture as defined by international law. The CIA and Defense Department developed guidelines that turned inhuman treatment into government policy that resulted in torture, maiming, and even death of detainees during interrogation.

Interrogation Procedures

From the mid-1960s until February 2002, the military had confined its interrogations to techniques described in *Army Field Manual 34-52*, which followed methods permissible under the Geneva Conventions, and the Uniform Code of Military Justice. The manual specified that "The use of force, mental torture, threats, insults, or exposure to unpleasant and inhumane treatment of any kind is prohibited by law and is neither authorized nor condoned by the US government." It noted that humane treatment would render prisoners more susceptible to interrogation, and that "brutality by either capturing troops or friendly interrogators will reduce defections and serve as grist for the insurgents' propaganda mill."

The Geneva Conventions of 1949 on the Protection of War Victims, including the Third Convention dealing with prisoners of war and the Fourth Convention applying to civilians under enemy control, were ratified by the US in July 1955. It later ratified the Convention Against Torture and Other Cruel, Inhuman and Degrading Treatment applying to Prisoners of War in 1994. Article 75 of Additional Protocol I (1977), protects all detainees captured in international or internal armed conflict, regardless of their legal status. The United States is not a party to this Protocol (having rejected it during the Reagan Administration in 1987) and the government did not believe it was required to comply.[2] Additionally, in 1975 the United Nations General Assembly passed Resolution 3452, Declaration on the Protection of All Persons from Being Subjected to Torture and Other Cruel, Inhuman and Degrading Punishment. These Conventions and the Declaration apply in all cases of armed conflict between two or more states (whether recognized *de jure* or merely *de facto*), and apply whether or not an enemy state has bound itself to, or is party to, the Conventions.

Under the Conventions ratified by the United States, prisoners of war have the right to humane treatment, there are limits on what interrogators may do, and, while imprisoned, detainees have the right to communicate with protective agencies such as the Red Cross and Red Crescent. Article I of the Convention Against Torture prohibits torture and defines it as:

[A]ny act by which severe pain or suffering, whether physical or mental, is intentionally inflicted on a person for such purposes as obtaining from him or a third person information or a confession, punishing him for an act he or a third person has committed or is suspected of having committed, or intimidating or coercing him or a third person, or for any reason based on discrimination of any kind, when such pain or suffering is inflicted by or at the instigation of or with the consent or acquiescence of a public official or other person acting in an official capacity.

Article 2a states that "No exceptional circumstances whatsoever, whether a state or war or a threat of war, internal political instability or any other public emergency, may be invoked as a justification of torture." Article 17 states: "No physical or mental torture, nor any other form of coercion, may be inflicted on prisoners of war to secure from them information of any kind whatever. Prisoners of war who refuse to answer may not be threatened, insulted, or exposed to unpleasant or disadvantageous treatment of any kind."

Civilians detained also have certain rights. Under the Fourth Convention's Article 27, they "shall at all times be humanely treated, and shall be protected especially against all acts of violence or threats thereof." Unlawful combatants are protected under Common Article 3 (so named because it is common to each of the Geneva Conventions), which provides that detained persons "shall in all circumstances be treated humanely," and that "[t]o this end" certain specified acts "are and shall remain prohibited at any time and in any place whatsoever." What are termed "grave breaches" of the conventions by captors mistreating "protected persons" in their custody are considered to be war crimes. The acts which contracting parties are required to prosecute criminally include the following: (1) willful killing of protected persons such as injured combatants, POWs, and civilians under their control; (2) murder, mutilations, torture, inhuman treatment, outrages upon personal dignity, humiliating or degrading treatment, or causing great suffering or bodily injury to protected persons.

The War Crimes Act of 1996, in sect. 2441 (1996) makes it a criminal offense for an American citizen or a member of the US Armed Forces (citizen or non-citizen) to commit in the US or abroad a grave breach of the Geneva Conventions. A grave breach includes the deliberate "killing, torture or inhuman treatment" of detainees. Violations of the *War Crimes Act of 1996* that result in death carry the death penalty. But if the administration can substitute its own definition of torture or inhuman treatment under the conventions, the law becomes a nullity. Under the most restrictive interpretation (which the government favors), if causing harm is not the primary objective—if intelligence gathering is the goal instead—there is no torture, therefore no violation of a Geneva Convention, and therefore the law does not apply. Section 2340 of the law defines torture as "an act committed by a person acting under the color of law specifically intended to inflict severe physical or mental pain or suffering." So the plain meaning of the statute cannot be squared with the reinterpretation of the meaning of the Geneva language. In any event, even if the *Geneva Conventions* are deemed not to apply, and customary international law is considered not to be binding on the United States, the US criminal code prohibits torture (Elsea 2004, 11).[3]

Article 16 of the Convention Against Torture requires the signatories to "undertake to prevent in any territory under its jurisdiction other acts of cruel, inhuman or degrading treatment or punishment which do not amount to torture as defined in article 1, when such acts are committed by or at the instigation of or with the consent or acquiescence of a public official or other person acting in an official capacity". The administration claimed that the article simply incorporates protections of the Constitution's Due Process clause in the Fifth Amendment; it then claimed that Fifth Amendment due process protections do not apply to aliens detained overseas, and therefore Article 16 cannot apply to such aliens. Moreover, it claimed that the US is obligated under the article only in territory under US jurisdiction, which excludes facilities in any sovereign nation—a narrow definition that excludes bases abroad as well as at Guantanamo, Cuba. Federal courts have rejected this argument with regard to Guantanamo.[4]

There are restrictions on interrogation procedures in the Uniform Code of Military Justice that "prohibit US armed forces from engaging in cruelty, oppression, or maltreatment of prisoners (art. 93), murder (art. 118), manslaughter (art. 119), maiming (art. 124), assaulting prisoners (art. 128), a demonstration of violence that results in reasonable apprehension of immediate bodily harm), communicating a threat to wrongfully injure a detainee, and negligent homicide, (art. 134). There are also general offenses of attempt (art. 80), conspiracy (art. 81), accessory after the fact (art. 78), and solicitation (art. 82). Article 128 is the article most likely to be violated because an unlawful demonstration of violence may create in the mind of another detainee a reasonable apprehension of facing immediate bodily harm. United States Army Regulation 190–8 states: "All persons taken into custody by US forces will be provided with the protections of the GPW until some other legal status is determined by competent authority."

Changes in Existing Interrogation Policy

All these obligations and restrictions were in force by the end of the winter of 2001, at a time when thousands of Taliban prisoners had been captured on the battlefields of Afghanistan by warlords, and some had been turned over to American military units, who in turn handed over the most significant detainees to the CIA. The Bush Administration calculated that if it abided by the Geneva Conventions, international and domestic law, and military codes and manuals that required humane treatment, it would make it difficult for its military and CIA interrogators to gather intelligence.

Since the president had announced a "war on terror"—arguing that al-Qaeda had declared war on the US and carried out a warlike action—it might be assumed that detainees in Afghanistan were prisoners of war. But al-Qaeda terrorists were not organized as a military force, nor were they sponsored by a nation-state; nor did they wear uniforms, use conventional weapons, or fight conventional battles, all of which defined the military forces of a state. According to an aide to Secretary of State Colin Powell quoted in *CNN News* (21 November 2005), Vice President Dick Cheney (who talked about "the dark arts") and Secretary of Defense Donald Rumsfeld both recommended that the president deny the protections of the Geneva Convention to al-Qaeda and Taliban captives. Department of Justice Counsels John C. Yoo and Robert J. Delahunty advised their superiors that the Geneva Conventions did not apply to the war against al-Qaeda, and that the Taliban lost POW privileges by violating the "laws of war." They viewed members of these groups as "unlawful combatants." Their argument was that the terrorist acts committed by al-Qaeda signaled a new and unprecedented threat to American national security: war had changed, and the laws of war would have to change as well. Terrorists operating without regard to borders, not constrained by the need to protect their own forces or civilian populations, and making no distinction in their actions between combatants and civilians, should not be included in the protections of "treaty-based" warfare. Adhering to the Conventions would not protect either our own forces or civilians from terrorist atrocities. Following their reasoning, on 25 January 2002 White House Counsel Alberto Gonzales sent a memorandum to President Bush recommending that the detainees be denied the protection of the Geneva Conventions.

The Department of State objected strongly. Powell, who had already met twice with President Bush to argue against this approach, sent his own memorandum to the White House the following day, indicating that the advantages in adhering to the Geneva Conventions far outweighed the disadvantages. He argued that if we did not apply them "it will reverse over a century of US policy and practices...and undermine the protections of the law of war for our own troops." He also thought it would weaken world support for American actions in Afghanistan. General Richard Myers, chair of the joint chiefs of staff agreed, as did the top-ranking officers of the US Central Command, responsible for combat in Afghanistan. On 2 February 2002, a memorandum to Gonzales from William H. Taft IV, the legal adviser to the State Department, warned: "A decision that the conventions do not apply to the conflict in Afghanistan in which our armed forces are engaged deprives our troops there of any claim to the protection of the conventions in the event they are captured." An attachment to the memo noted that CIA counsel requested that the administration's public pledge to abide by the "spirit" of the conventions did not apply to its operatives.

The Decider Decides

The president sided with Gonzales against Powell. On 7 February 2002, he issued a directive establishing the procedures for handling the prisoners captured in Afghanistan. He decided that the US would not uniformly abide by Common Article 3 of the Geneva Conventions, holding that its terms did not apply to al-Qaeda and the Taliban. The US would treat detainees in a way consistent with the "principles" of Geneva "to the extent appropriate and consistent with military necessity." The Bush Administration decided that interrogations of certain high-value al-Qaeda and Taliban detainees would take place at Guantanamo on soil the administration claimed was not part of the United States. This location was designed to shield detainees from the jurisdiction of federal courts; moreover the federal anti-torture statute excluded military bases.

President Bush in his executive order of 7 February 2002, decided not only *as a matter of law* that the customary standards of Common Article 3 would not pertain to Taliban and al-Qaeda prisoners or other terrorists detained, but also that they would not be applied *as a matter of policy*: in past conflicts the US had adhered to these standards even when it claimed that it was not legally required to do so—as with the Viet Cong in the Vietnam War.[5] President Bush claimed the power, as other presidents had done before him, to interpret and reinterpret treaty obligations as he saw fit, rather than conform to pre-existing interpretations at the time of treaty negotiation, Senate consent, and ratification. Following his decision, Attorney General Alberto Gonzales rejected the definition of torture in the Convention Against Torture (although the US is a signatory), and rejected definitions used by other international bodies, including the European Human Rights Court.

Pentagon and DOJ Implementation

Civilian counsel within the Department of Defense prepared memoranda developing legal protections for the interrogators: since prisoners in the war on terror were not entitled to protection under the Geneva Convention the US could not violate the conventions; if the government were not violating Geneva, then it also was not violating the Uniform Code of Military Justice prohibitions against war crimes, because the UCMJ requires a violation of the Geneva Conventions to establish that a war crime has been committed.

Legal counsel in the Department of Justice defined torture to include only methods used by knowledgeable interrogators, designed to inflict severe pain and suffering, which would have lasting physical or mental effects akin to organ failure or permanent disability. They did not include in their definition tactics that inflicted temporary pain or suffering, or mental disorientation. None of these interpretations were consistent with black letter provisions of the Geneva Convention, which prohibited cruel, inhuman, or degrading treatment: the UN Committee Against Torture had already indicated in several reports that measures such as severe sleep deprivation or forcing someone to sleep on the floor of a cell, or handcuffing in unusual positions, were prohibited by the Convention.

Jay S. Bybee, then a lawyer in the Office of Legal Counsel in the Department of Justice (later a federal judge), prepared the most important memorandum defining "torture" at the behest of the CIA, the Pentagon, and the Office of the Vice President, all of which wanted guidance on how torture statutes should be read to apply to top al-Qaeda leaders, According to his memo torture "must be equivalent in intensity to the pain accompanying serious physical injury, such as organ failure, impairment of bodily function, or even death." He specified prohibited techniques, such as severe beatings with truncheons and clubs, threats of imminent death, burning with cigarettes, electric shocks to genitals, sexual assaults, and forcing a prisoner to watch the torture of a third party. (A companion memorandum, which remains classified, outlined specific methods that the Central Intelligence Agency could use.)

The Bybee memo went well beyond standard military interrogation practices: the Army's *Field Manual 34-52, Intelligence Interrogations* permitted seventeen interrogation techniques, but prohibited pain induced by chemicals or bondage; forcing an individual to stand, sit, or kneel in abnormal positions for prolonged periods of time; and food deprivation. It also prohibited sleep deprivation, mock executions, and chemically induced psychosis. Bybee argued in the memo that the president's power as commander in chief would insulate lower-level officials from prosecution: "Any effort to apply Sec. 2340A [the War Crimes Statute] in a manner that interferes with the president's direction of such core war matters as the detention and interrogation of enemy combatants thus would be unconstitutional."

On 25 October 2002 General James Hill forwarded to the Pentagon a set of proposed counter-resistance techniques and asked Pentagon lawyers to review them. Responding to the request from Guantanamo, Defense Department Counsel William J. Haynes II on 27 November 2002, proposed 14 interrogation techniques "involving standing in unusual stress positions" for up to four hours, and "mild, non-injurious physical contact such as grabbing, poking in the chest with the finger and light pushing." Secretary of Defense Donald Rumsfeld was unimpressed, and scribbled on Haynes' memo "I stand for 8–10 hours a day. Why is standing limited to 4 hours?" On 2 December 2002,

Rumsfeld approved 16 interrogation techniques, including grabbing, yelling, and stress positions, 20-hour interrogations, removal of clothing, and playing on phobias such as fear of dogs.

Rumsfeld put pressure on military commanders to use harsh methods. According to *Human Rights Watch* (2006), a military investigation conducted by Lt. General Randall M. Schmidt indicated that Rumsfeld had been "personally involved" in the interrogation of a key al-Qaeda operative, al-Qahtani, talking weekly with the senior commander at Guantanamo, General Geoffrey Miller, about it. According to Schmidt, Rumsfeld did not specifically authorize the tactics, but his vague instructions permitted interrogators to commit abuses, since "there were no limits." They deprived al-Qahtani of sleep (20 hours of daily interrogation for 48 days) and kept him standing, forced him into painful positions, and subjected him to forced exercises and sexual humiliation. They gave him an intravenous drip so that he would have to urinate on himself, and also gave him an enema. They put him in a cell with extreme air conditioning to slow his heartbeat. They led him on a leash and forced him to perform dog tricks.

In March 2003 a Defense Department legal task force determined that members of the military were immune from domestic and international law regarding torture if the interrogators believed that they were acting on lawful orders from superiors, "except where the conduct goes so far as to be patently unlawful." The Pentagon report claimed: "If a government defendant were to harm an enemy combatant during an interrogation in a manner that might arguably violate criminal prohibition, he would be doing so in order to prevent further attacks on the United States by the al Qaeda terrorist network...he could argue that the executive branch's constitutional authority to protect the nation from attack justified his actions." One of the task force's memos took the position that, given "the President's inherent constitutional authority to manage a military campaign," laws against torture were inapplicable to interrogations undertaken pursuant to his authority as commander in chief (*Working Group Report*, 6 March 2003, 21).

There was significant opposition within the military to these proposals. Members of the Pentagon Criminal Investigation Task Force (CITF) who were working with FBI agents at Guantanamo to develop evidence of crimes that could lead to criminal prosecution, reported allegations of abuse of prisoners. Their commanders were concerned that the tactics could lead to prosecutions of interrogators. Retired Col. Brittain P. Mallow, who commanded the task force in late 2002, wrote in an e-mail to his superiors dated 2 December 2002, the same day Rumsfeld approved harsher techniques: "Our folks should make it clear that our participation in dialogues related to the aggressive strategies does not amount to an endorsement of the technique or the interrogation plan." All deployed CITF personnel were instructed "to disengage, stand clear, and report any questionable interrogation techniques," a legal adviser to the task force wrote in a memo dated 15 January 2003: "CITF maintains that its personnel will not utilize non-law enforcement techniques or participate, support, advise, or observe aggressive interrogation techniques or strategies." The Navy outrage caused Rumsfeld to call for a review of procedures being used at GITMO. Dr Michael Gelles, the chief psychologist of the Navy Criminal Investigative Service (NCIS) reviewed Guantanamo interrogations in December 2002 that included extracts of interrogation logs. According to Charlie Savage (2005), Gelles reported to the service director, David Brant, that interrogators were using "abusive techniques and coercive psychological procedures."

Uniformed military lawyers in the services' Judge Advocate General offices believed that use of aggressive interrogation techniques would lessen the likelihood that they could obtain the surrender of enemy forces, or gain the cooperation of local communities, or the assistance of friendly nations. The information they obtained would be of questionable value, since those they subjected to torture might say anything if they were broken.

Faced with this opposition, on 15 January 2003 Rumsfeld rescinded his 2 December approval of Haynes' recommendations and ordered a new study. In February and March 2003 the uniformed lawyers in the Judge Advocate General offices in each of the services circulated memoranda that attempted to develop policies that would protect interrogators and military lawyers against legal liability. They believed that courts might reject Bush's definition of torture, and that the directives under which interrogators were operating might be held by courts to violate domestic criminal law, international law, and the Uniform Code of Military Justice. They also believed that the US would be weakened in the war on terror because it would lose the moral high ground. According to a memo written on 27 February 2003 by Brigadier General Kevin M. Sandkuhler, judge advocate general of the United States Marine Corps: "The authorization of aggressive counter-resistance techniques by service members will adversely impact . . . human intelligence exploitation and surrender of foreign enemy forces, and cooperation and support of friendly nations." As Air Force Major General Jack Reves, the deputy judge advocate general, wrote:

[T]he use of the more extreme interrogation techniques simply is not how the US armed forces have operated in recent history. We have taken the legal and moral "high-road" in the conduct of our military operations regardless of how others may operate. Our forces are trained in this legal and moral mindset beginning the day they enter active duty. It should be noted that law of armed conflict and code of conduct training have been mandated by Congress and emphasized since the Viet Nam conflict when our POWs were subjected to torture by their captors. We need to consider the overall impact of approving extreme interrogation techniques as giving official approval and legal sanction to the application of interrogation techniques that U.S. forces have consistently been trained are unlawful.[6]

75

Mary Walker, general counsel of the Air Force, was appointed by Secretary of Defense Rumsfeld to chair a task force to review the policies. Most of the legal analysis came from the Department of Justice. The task force reaffirmed the administration's claim that Bush was not bound by the Geneva Conventions. Its lawyers, consisting of civilian counsel from the service departments, the joint chiefs of staff, and the intelligence community, examined 36 techniques for what it called "exceptional interrogations." On 8 March 2003, these Pentagon civilian lawyers concluded "we need a presidential letter approving the use of the controversial interrogation to cover those who may be called upon to use them" (*ABC News*, 15 June 2005). John Yoo provided a memorandum, "Military Interrogation of Alien Unlawful Combatants," on 14 March 2003 to Pentagon General Counsel William Haynes. Yoo's reasoning later appeared in the Working Group's *Final Report*, dated 4 April 2003.

The Department of Justice's Office of Legal Counsel argued that interrogators were constitutionally permitted to use methods that on their face violated the international commitments of the United States, the anti-torture statutes, the federal assault statute, and the Uniform Code of Military Justice, and these conclusions were incorporated into the Pentagon's final report to Secretary of Defense Rumsfeld, which noted that the president would have the authority, as commander in chief, to override these laws and regulations. It stated that "[d]efenses relating to Commander-in-Chief authority, necessity and self-defense or defense of others may be available to individuals whose actions would otherwise constitute these crimes, and the extent of availability of those defenses will be fact-specific.... Where the Commander-in-Chief authority is being relied upon, a Presidential written directive would serve to memorialize this authority."

After a review on 16 April, Rumsfeld approved 24 of the proposed interrogation techniques, with four of the most extreme requiring his advance approval. He dropped several proposed techniques because of JAG opposition, including a "waterboarding" proposal (which makes prisoners feel as if they were drowning). According to investigative reporter Seymour Hersh (2004), he also approved the "special access" programs allowing extreme interrogation in the ghost facilities, with no reporting to Congress. Although many top officials in the Pentagon, such as Matthew Waxman, deputy assistant secretary of defense, tried to restore Common Article 3 protections, according to Tim Naftali (2005), David Addington of the vice president's office, along with DOD Undersecretary Stephen Cambone, and DOD General Counsel William J. Haynes, opposed Waxman's efforts. Uniformed lawyers of the JAG even tried to revise Directive 23.10 "DOD Program for Enemy Prisoners of War and Other Detainees" if necessary agreeing to discuss it as a revision of policy rather than as a requirement of adherence to international and domestic law, but they too were unsuccessful.

CIA Interrogation and Rendition Authority

Bush's executive order of 7 February 2002 did not apply to the CIA. Eric Schmitt and Douglas Jehl (2004) quoted Army General Paul Kern's congressional testimony before the Senate Armed Services Committee that "the CIA has held as many as 100 'ghost' detainees in Iraq without revealing their identities or locations" to the International Red Cross (IRC). For prisoners held by the CIA in American facilities, six "Enhanced Interrogation Techniques" were authorized as of mid-March 2002, including "waterboarding." By spring 2004, CIA Inspector General John L. Helgerson wrote a classified report reviewing interrogation procedures approved by the CIA after 9/11, and warned that they might have violated provisions of the Convention Against Terror. According to Douglas Jehl (2005b), the report did not characterize the techniques as torture, but concluded that they constituted cruel, inhuman, and degrading treatment under the convention.

President Bush did not bar inhuman treatment or torture by the CIA, which leaves open the question of whether that omission was a backhanded authorization. The suspicion that it was is fed by the testimony of former CIA director Porter Goss, who testified in March 2005 at his confirmation hearing that the CIA was not torturing detainees. Goss refused to testify about *past* practices unless it was at a closed hearing. Similarly Alberto Gonzales, in written responses to questions posed by members of the Senate Judiciary Committee considering his nomination to be attorney general, indicated that provisions of Bush's 2002 directive that had pledged humane treatment of prisoners did not cover CIA interrogators and other non-military personnel. He also wrote in response to a senator's written question that the statute banning cruel, unusual, and inhuman treatment had "a limited reach" and did not always apply to "aliens overseas." He wrote that if we "were to begin ruling out speculated interrogation practices, we would fairly rapidly provide Al Qaeda with a road map concerning the interrogation that captured terrorists can expect to face and would enable Al Qaeda to improve its counter-interrogation training to match it."

According to Douglas Jehl and David Johnston (2005), just after 9/11 President Bush signed a still-classified secret directive giving the CIA authority to conduct renditions (the practice of transferring prisoners from American custody to foreign prisons). Subsequently the CIA relied on a retroactively drafted memo written on 19 March 2004 by the Office of Legal Counsel of the Department of Justice as legal support for transfers of ghost detainees to other nations. It permitted the CIA to take Iraqis and non-Iraqis out of the country to be interrogated for a "brief but not indefinite period," and allowed permanent removal of persons deemed to be "illegal aliens" under "local immigration law." The memo was intended to immunize CIA officials who had participated in the transfers and interrogations from violations of Article 49 of the *Fourth Geneva Convention*, which protects civilians during wartime and occupation, and prohibits "individual or mass forcible transfers, as well as deportations of protected persons from occupied territory... regardless of their motive." Jack Goldsmith, then an assistant attorney general (now professor at Harvard Law School) concluded in the memo that the *Convention* allowed transfers out of Iraq "for a brief but not indefinite period, to facilitate interrogation." Yet a footnote to the memo recognized that a violation of this provision constitutes a "grave breach" of the accord and a "war crime" under US law: "For these reasons, we recommend that any contemplated relocations of 'protected persons' from Iraq to facilitate interrogation be carefully evaluated for compliance with Article 49 on a case by case basis."

In order to develop a rendition program, the president had to exercise his prerogative to interpret and reinterpret provisions of international law, through what is known as "dual meaning" doctrine. This allows the United States to interpret provisions according to its own domestic law rather than use customary international understandings. So when the US ratified the 1984 Convention Against Torture it specified its "understanding" on the definition of torture: it indicated that the term would be taken to be consistent with the US definition under American constitutional law, and violations would have to be constitutional violations of the Bill of Rights or statutory violations of US law.

Article 3 of the Convention Against Torture provides that "[n]o State Party shall expel, return ('refouler') or extradite a person to another State where there are substantial grounds for believing that he would be in danger of being subjected to torture." To determine such grounds, the government is to take into account whether or not a foreign government has demonstrated "a consistent pattern of gross, flagrant, or mass violations of human rights." The US Senate consented to this obligation on the understanding that "the phrase 'where there are substantial grounds for believing that he would be in danger of being subjected to torture,' as used in Article 3 of the Convention, [is] to mean 'if it is more likely than not that he would be tortured." But according to Attorney General Alberto Gonzales, responding with a written answer to the Senate Judiciary Committee's Question 11 at his confirmation hearing, the president uses his prerogative to interpret treaty language based on the claim that Article 3 applies only when a detainee is sent from the United States, and does not apply when a detainee in American custody is transferred from one location outside the United States to another—even if it was from the American base at Guantanamo. Such an interpretation is both restrictive and absurd.

The Bush Administration was willing to accept assurances that detainees would not be tortured from countries that the State Department has long cited for torture of prisoners. As President Bush put it in a statement to reporters (Priest 2005a), in "the post-9/11 world, the United States must make sure we protect our people and our friends from attack. And one way to do so is to arrest people and send them back to their country of origin with the promise that they won't be tortured. That's the promise we receive. This country does not believe in torture. We do believe in protecting ourselves."

Some FBI officials believed that such renditions were illegal. A 27 November 2002 memo from a supervisory special agent to a senior FBI lawyer (Isikoff 2005) contained a legal analysis of interrogation techniques that had been approved by Pentagon officials for use against a high-value al-Qaeda detainee. The agent discussed a plan to send the detainee to Jordan, Egypt, or an unspecified third country for interrogation. "Inasmuch as the intent of this category is to utilize, outside the US, interrogation techniques which would violate 18 U.S.C. sec. 2340 if committed in the US, it is a per se violation of the US Torture Statute," the agent wrote. "Discussing any plan which includes this category could be seen as a conspiracy to violate [the Torture Statute]" and "would inculpate everyone involved."

Outcomes of Prerogative Governance

President Bush asserted his prerogative power in interpreting and reinterpreting conventions and customary international law obligations, and in interpreting the obligations of government officials to execute faithfully statute law, the Uniform Code of Military Justice, and various directives. He made a decision to "take the gloves off" in the war on terror, believing that prior restrictions involving the treatment of prisoners and noncoercive interrogation techniques were, in the words of his lawyers in the Office of Legal Counsel, "quaint" and "obsolete." These were debatable propositions, which would lead to responses from Congress and the judiciary. Would Congress approve of these actions? If so, that would indicate "joint concord" (president and Congress acting toward the same goals), and it would be a strong signal to federal courts either to decline to adjudicate cases, or alternatively to uphold these exercises of executive power. Alternatively Congress and the courts could check and balance the president, Congress could even determine that such conduct was a "high crime and misdemeanor" worthy of impeachment, or at the very least censure.

Frontlash, Backlash, or Collapse Outcomes

A theory of prerogative power describes these alternative outcomes. In "frontlash," Congress responds favorably to the presidential initiative: passing perfecting legislation (congressional delegations of broad authority, and reorganizations of administrative responsibilities proposed by the executive); legislating for contingencies suggested by the executive; providing retroactive authorizations; immunizing or indemnifying officials who have carried out orders from judicial process; even at times limiting or eliminating the jurisdiction of the federal judiciary. When there is a backlash effect Congress passes obstructive or prohibitory provisions and funding cut-offs, places conditions on expenditures, narrows delegations of power, increases legislative oversight, provides consultation and "report and wait" requirements, institutes reporting mechanisms and requires that Committees be kept "fully and currently informed" and informal clearances and concurrences be obtained (the equivalent at times of a legislative veto), takes reprisals on unrelated legislation, holds up presidential nominations, refuses to pass reorganization proposals, and passes laws making it easier to bring suits in federal courts. In the rare cases of "overshoot and collapse," Congress holds comprehensive hearings, calls for the resignation of top White House officials or cabinet secretaries, proposes a complete change of policy, supports blue ribbon investigating panels, and even passes resolutions of censure or votes of impeachment.

Why, as of late summer 2006, had there been no strong backlash effect on the torture issue? Why had there been no "overshoot and collapse" effect? What follows are some hypotheses (none of which are mutually exclusive) which may help explain why checks and balances have not come strongly into play—at least not in the first five years of the war on terror.

Bottom-up Investigations

As of May 2006, Army statistics indicated that more than 600 investigations had been conducted into allegations of abuse involving more than 460 detainees, and at least 259 service personnel had been court-martialed or received other punishment. The military investigators have worked their way up the chain of command, but they have not usually given offers of immunity or leniency to low-level enlisted personnel (the overwhelming majority of those facing discipline) and officers that would induce these personnel to discuss the command policies of their superiors.

Army and Navy Criminal Investigation Division personnel conducted 68 death and homicide investigations and 308 investigations of assault, sexual assault, and theft or detainee abuse as of mid-April 2005. In a report submitted to the UN Committee Against Torture, the government claimed to have substantiated 190 instances of mistreatment and "the US government has acted swiftly to investigate and take action to address the abuses."[7] Penalties have included 30 courts martial, 15 reprimands or administrative actions, and in 46 cases there was no judicial punishment. In only 12 of the deaths of detainees did military courts impose punishment, and the longest term was five months in prison. In more than half prosecutors brought no charges. The highest-ranking officer convicted as of May 2006 was Army Captain Shawn Martin, sentenced to 45 days in jail. Given the light sentences courts martial meted out (as of April 2006 only 10 enlisted personnel had been sentenced to more than one year in prison, only 40 to any prison time) there would be no incentive for personnel to plea bargain in exchange for testimony implicating higher-ups, even if higher-ups had been targets of investigation.[8]

The highest official the military reprimanded was Brigadier General Janis Karpinski, who was in charge of the Abu Ghraib prison compound in Iraq— she was demoted in rank to colonel, even though intelligence officers discouraged her from inspecting the cellblocks where abuses were occurring. Pentagon investigators cleared three generals senior to her in the chain of command: "Every senior-officer allegation was formally investigated," the Army said in its 5 May 2005 summary. Lieutenant General Ricardo Sanchez was investigated, it said, for "dereliction in the performance of duties pertaining to detention and interrogation operations" and for "improperly communicating interrogation policies." The Army inspector general "found each of the allegations unsubstantiated." He cleared Sanchez in late April 2005, even though Sanchez had been disingenuous when he had denied authorizing techniques at Abu Ghraib when he testified before the Senate Armed Services Committee, in May 2004, and said "I never approved any of those measures to be used . . . at any time in the last year." In fact he had authorized 29 of these techniques in a 14 September 2003 memo, "CJTF-CG-7, Interrogation and Counter-Resistance Policy." The military did not mete out punishment to Sanchez's deputy, Major General Walter Wojdakowski, or the top legal officer, Colonel Marc Warren (who had not reported abuses). Major General Barbara Fast, former chief intelligence officer at Abu Ghraib, not only was not punished or reprimanded, but she was named by the Army chief of staff to be commander of Fort Huachuca's US Army Intelligence Center and School, the facility for training interrogators to deal with Muslim prisoners.

Other general officers have avoided (through 2006) significant penalty. In 2004 the Criminal Investigation Division named General Miller in an inquiry of FBI claims that detainees held at Guantanamo were being mistreated. The CID report recommended that Miller be reprimanded for not monitoring the interrogation tactics used on Mohamed al-Qahtani, who allegedly intended to be the twentieth hijacker in the 9/11 plot. Miller's superior officer General Bantz Craddock overruled the reprimand, arguing that there was no evidence that laws had been broken. Generals Randall Schmidt and John Furlow, in their report on Guantanamo interrogations, concluded that there was "no evidence of torture or inhumane treatment." "[E]very technique employed against [Qahtani] was legally permissible under the existing guidance" they concluded. Later Lieutenant General Stanley Green, the Army inspector general, exonerated Miller of allegations that he lied to Congress when he said he had "no direct discussion" with Undersecretary of Defense for Intelligence Stephen Cambone. Green distinguished between "discussion" and a "briefing" that Miller had given to Cambone.

There have been no high-level investigations outside of the Pentagon or CIA. Twenty civilians, including CIA agents, have been referred by CID investigators to the Department of Justice for abusing detainees, but there have been no indictments of CIA personnel and as of spring 2006 only one civilian contractor had been charged (Human Rights Watch, and Human Rights First, New York: 26 April 2006). The inspector general of the CIA has conducted investigations of at least ten "erroneous" renditions to countries where their interrogators might have committed human rights abuses. The Department of Justice has the responsibility to investigate and prosecute CIA officials if a crime is committed, but the memoranda setting forth new standards for interrogation were prepared by the DOJ itself, and would be used by the defense in any trial. If it were serious about investigating CIA abuses the DOJ would have to provide for a special prosecutor, which is something the current administration has no intention of doing.

The Bush Administration gives the impression that it investigates abuses. Secretary of Defense Rumsfeld proclaimed at a congressional hearing on May 7, 2004: "Mr. Chairman, I know you join me today in saying to the world: Judge us by our actions. Watch how Americans, watch how a democracy deals with wrongdoing and scandal and the pain of acknowledging and correcting our own mistakes and weaknesses." Pentagon spokesperson Lawrence Di Rita claims: "The US military has successfully detained and interrogated nearly 70,000 individuals since 9/11. The vast majority of these interrogations have been conducted professionally and with impressive results. Where policies were violated, people are being held accountable and, where necessary, procedures revised and improved" (2005).

Sleight of Hand

How did the Pentagon revise these procedures? Consider the promulgation of the 3 November 2005 Defense Directive No. 3115.09, "DoD Intelligence Interrogations, Detainee Debriefings, and Tactical Questioning." Purporting to clear up questions of muddled lines of command and accountability, it assigns responsibilities for interrogations to senior Pentagon civilians and commanders. It requires the CIA to follow Pentagon guidelines when questioning military prisoners. The Pentagon must approve all non-standard interrogation techniques.[9] But the directive disavows the Geneva Conventions. The old *Army Field Manual 34-52* stated that the convention "shall apply," but in the new directive, governing standards "may include the law of war, relevant international law, US law and applicable directives." Not only is "may" substituted for "shall," but also it is so "unless otherwise authorized" by the secretary of defense, who according to this language may change the requirements to obey international conventions, the laws of war, and statutory war. The secretary may exempt operations or personnel from the directive, just as he has authorized rules of engagement for special units that are irreconcilable with the *Army Field Manual*.[10] The directive is limited in its reach to detainees under the control of the military, yet in many circumstances foreign nations provide our military interrogators with access to their detainees.

Artful Dodging

When necessary to deflect congressional and media criticism, members of the administration make statements that seem to reflect core American values, but if read closely it is clear that they are dodging key issues. Consider the rendition procedures that have sent detainees to other countries: President Bush claimed at a news conference on 30 April 2005: "We seek assurances that nobody will be tortured when we render a person back to their home country." The statement is meaningless because (1) assurances from many of these countries are worthless and (2) the US sends many detainees not back to their home countries but on to other nations. When Secretary of State Condoleezza Rice visited Germany and Ukraine, she wanted to reassure Europeans that American treatment of detainees follows the Convention Against Torture. But she carefully sidestepped the question of renditions: she did not claim that as a matter of law the CIA had to follow convention, but in a statement on 7 December 2005 at a news conference reported by Reuters, said "[A]s a matter of US policy, the United States' obligations under the CAT which prohibits cruel, inhumane and degrading treatment—those obligations extend to US personnel wherever they are, whether they are in the United States or outside of the United States." Personnel of other nations, not US officials, however, engage in the inhuman treatment or torture of prisoners in CIA programs. According to Douglas Jehl (2005a), when Porter Goss, the nominee for CIA director, was asked at his confirmation hearings about interrogation abuses, he carefully answered only in the present tense: "Torture is not productive. It is not professional interrogation; we don't do torture." When Alberto Gonzales, the nominee for attorney general, gave his testimony at his confirmation hearings before the Senate Judiciary Committee on 6 January 2005, he too gave an artful response, claiming that he was "deeply committed to ensuring that the United States government complies with all of its legal obligations as it fights the war on terror, whether those obligations arise from domestic or international law. These obligations include, of course, honoring the Geneva Conventions whenever they apply . . . ".

Gonzales has left it unclear exactly to what extent the various memoranda prepared to justify presidential decision making have determined administration policy or currently reflect it. In a press briefing on 22 June 2004, he characterized the memoranda as efforts "to explore the limits of the legal landscape as to what the Executive Branch can do within the law and the Constitution as an abstract matter." In contrast, he described Bush's military order and other directives as the "documents that reflect the actual decisions issued by the President and senior administration officials directing the policies that our military would actually be obliged to follow." He called the memoranda "legal theory" and the directives "the actual policy guidance that the President and his team directed." He claimed that "the policies ultimately adopted by the President are more narrowly tailored than advised by his lawyers, and are consistent with our treaty obligations, our Constitution and our laws." He referred to some of the theoretical conclusions as "irrelevant and unnecessary to support any action taken by the President," and "Unnecessary, over-broad discussions in some of these memos that address abstract legal theories, or discussions subject to misinterpretation, but not relied upon by decision-makers." He announced that these documents are "under review, and may be replaced, if appropriate." He said the memoranda circulated only among government lawyers, and that they never "made it into the hands" of soldiers neither in the field "nor to the President." Earlier that month the adminis-tration had decided to repudiate its August 2002 torture memorandum, a fact Justice Department lawyers leaked to a reporter, indicating that CIA counsel were angry that the agency was being left by the administration to take the responsibility for interrogation excesses. Later Acting Assistant Attorney General Daniel Levin prepared a new memorandum that repudiated the Bybee memo.[11]

The Illusion of Candor

Often in presidential scandals the cover-up leaves officials more vulnerable than the underlying acts. Borrowing a leaf from the Reagan Administration in the Iran-Contra affair, the Bush Administration seemed to eschew a cover-up. It announced that the Pentagon was investigating abuses. It condemned mis-treatment at Abu Ghraib after photographs were distributed over the Internet. The president and other top-level officials artfully offered a "half-defense": on the one hand condemning torture and mistreatment, but on the other hand insinuating that tough tactics were necessary, as in this interchange at a presidential news conference of 28 April 2005:

Question: Mr President, under the law, how would you justify the practice of rendition-ing, where US agents . . . [send] terror suspects abroad, taking them to a third country for interrogation? . . .

Answer: . . . We operate within the law and we send people to countries where they say they're not going to torture the people. But let me say something: The United States government has an obligation to protect the American people. It's in our country's interests to find those who would do harm to us. . . . We still [are] at war.

Similarly John Bellinger, the legal adviser at the State Department, told a committee of the United Nations (as reported by Reuters, 5 May 2006), that the US was "absolutely committed to uphold its national and international obligations to eradicate torture." He suggested that allegations of US abuse were so exaggerated they had become "absurd," and claimed that "relatively few actual cases of abuse and wrongdoing have occurred in the context of US armed conflict with al Qaeda." Nevertheless, he also claimed that "As a purely legal matter, we think [the Torture Convention] does not apply to transfers that take place outside of the United States."

When officials state that the president is commander in chief, and is using his powers to protect the American people in a time of war, they put the focus on constitutional disagreements over the scope of the president's powers as commander in chief, rather than on violations of international and statutory law prohibitions against torture. Because it appears that the administration is defending its position in the open, the acts of inhuman treatment and torture do not take the trajectory of a scandal involving a cover-up.

Passing the Buck

It is not uncommon for the United States to pass the blame to other nations for our own fiascos. In the case of CIA renditions, the Bush Administration has simultaneously tried to shift the blame while reminding foreign governments to keep a lid on their own criticisms of US actions. As reported by Reuters (7 March 2005), Attorney General Gonzales claims that when the CIA sends prisoners abroad, "We can't fully control what that country might do," but we expect them to comply with their representations to us. Secretary of State Rice in a major speech in Germany claimed that "The United States does not transport, and has not transported, detainees from one country to another for the purpose of interrogation using torture. The United States does not use the airspace or the airports of any country for the purpose of transporting a detainee to a country where he or she will be tortured." But according to Sidney Blumenthal (2005), Rice reminded her European hosts in a veiled hint not to make the CIA rendition flights to European airports an issue, since their own intelligence services were involved and the CIA had received logistical assistance from hub countries and host countries: "What I would hope that our allies would acknowledge is that we are all in this together."

The Illusion of Congressional Oversight

Congressional oversight of CIA and Pentagon interrogation activities was pro forma until newspapers published accounts of prisoner abuse at Abu Ghraib. But with the Senate and House controlled by Republicans, committees did not direct their investigations at Attorneys General Ashcroft or Gonzales, Secretary of Defense Rumsfeld, Vice President Cheney, or President Bush. Democrats did not have the kind of institutional resources they would have enjoyed if they had controlled either house of Congress, as they had during both the Watergate and Iran-Contra affairs—and if one wishes to go back further in history, as the Democrats had in investigating the CIA in the 1970s, or the U-2 incidents in the 1950s. The International Relations Committee rejected three resolutions introduced by Representative Edward Markey (D-MA) that would have required the administration to provide the committee with documents relating to renditions.

Congress did pass Senator McCain's (R-ARIZ) anti-torture amendment, by a margin of 90 to 9, even though existing laws already prohibited torture, and even though a similar amendment sponsored by Senator Richard Durbin (D-ILL) in an $82 billion military operations financing measure for Iraq and Afghanistan had just been passed by 100 to none and signed into law by the president, barring the government from using funds to subject anyone in American custody to torture or "cruel, inhuman or degrading treatment" forbidden by the Constitution. McCain, along with Senator Lindsey Graham (R-SC), a reserve officer in the Air Force JAG, sponsored his amendment to a $440 billion Department of Defense Appropriation Act of 2006 (the amendment is referred to as the Detainee Treatment Act or DTA), requiring that detainees in the custody of the military could be subjected only to interrogation techniques of the *Army Field Manual*, and that "no individual in the custody or under the physical control of the United States Government, regardless of nationality or physical location, shall be subject to cruel, inhuman, or degrading treatment or punishment."[12] It covered ghost detainees and CIA interrogations. McCain initially seemed open to allow a presidential waiver, "if the president determines that such operations are vital to the protection of the United States or its citizens from terrorist attack," but after Vice President Cheney attempted to pressure him to withdraw the amendment, McCain stiffened his terms, and got more than three dozen retired high-ranking military officers to sign letters of support. A White House effort in December to get the House not to recede in the conference committee failed, as did President Bush's threat to veto any bill containing the provision.

The White House used a strategy of seeming accommodation. According to Associated Press (14 December 2005), McCain met with national security adviser Steven Hadley, after which Karen Hughes, Undersecretary of State for Public Diplomacy and Public Affairs expressed her belief that they would reach "consensus," since "the goal is to make it very clear that the United States is a nation of laws and that we operate our detainee policy within our laws, within our international obligations, and without torture." Then McCain met Bush in the Oval Office, after which Bush agreed not to exercise his veto. There was no reason for him to do so: the Pentagon was already in the process of revising the *Army Field Manual* to increase authority for extreme interrogations; the language of the amendment did not provided specific definitions of cruel, inhuman, and degrading treatment; and McCain had compromised on two key points—CIA officers and other civilians accused of abusive interrogation techniques could raise as a defense that they believed they were obeying a legal order, and they would have the right to government counsel.

A separate provision of the DTA sponsored by senators Graham and Jon Kyl (R-ARIZ) was more to the Bush Administration's liking: Graham changed a prior draft that had forbidden the use of evidence from coercive interrogations, into the following provision: "to the extent practicable" courts would assess whether testimony was obtained as a "result of coercion." It allowed the courts to consider the "probative value" of illegally obtained evidence in military tribunals. In effect Congress had decided through the McCain amendment to ban torture, but then through the Graham-Kyl provisions to allow courts to admit evidence that it had just ruled was illegal. This was the first time Congress had legitimated using the fruit of torture in the courts.[13] The DTA also stripped the federal courts of the right to review detentions through habeas corpus petitions from detainees.[14] It provided in sect. 1005(e)(2) that "no court justice or judge shall have jurisdiction to hear or consider (1) an application for a writ of habeas corpus filed by or on behalf of an alien detained by the Department of Defense at Guantanamo Bay, Cuba; or (2) any other action against the United States or its agents relating to any aspect of the detention by the Department of Defense." The amendment provides that Guantanamo detainees could have access to the courts only to appeal their enemy combatant status determinations and convictions by military commissions.

As the bill moved through the Senate, Senators Carl Levin (D-MI) and Graham reached an agreement (the Graham-Levin-Kyl Amendment), modifying the "effective date" clause, whereby cases *already* before the courts would not be subject to the court-stripping aspects of the amendment. The revised amendment passed the Senate by 84 to 14. But when President Bush signed the measure on 30 December 2005, he issued a signing statement that construed the amendment to bar federal jurisdiction in *all* existing cases. The solicitor general then informed the Supreme Court in mid-January that it no longer had jurisdiction over detainee cases, and asked the court to drop jurisdiction over the *Hamdan* case. Graham and Kyl backed him up by referring to the "legislative history" of the bill: they noted their colloquy on the Senate floor on 21 December 2005 discussing the habeas corpus provisions to claim that "Congress was aware" that the bill would strip the Supreme Court of "pending cases." But as Emily Bazelon notes in *Slate* (2006), the discussion *had never taken place on the floor of the Senate*; instead, the language of the colloquy had been inserted into the record by the two senators just before passage of the law under the "revise and extend" courtesy. The only discussion of the provision on the Senate floor before the vote had come from Levin, based on his understanding that pending cases would not be stripped. Because the insertion means that other senators had not heard any of the so-called legislative history of the amendment before casting their votes, the Court of Appeals for the District of Columbia Circuit subsequently refused to allow a brief filed in March 2006 by Graham and Kyl in a detainee case that relied on this bogus legislative history. Later the Supreme Court, in *Hamdan* v. *US*, concluded that Congress in passing the DTA had not stripped the court of jurisdiction over detainee cases.

Bush's signing statement dealt directly with the McCain amendment. "The executive branch shall construe [the law] in a manner consistent with the constitutional authority of the President . . . as Commander in Chief," Bush wrote, adding that this approach "will assist in achieving the shared objective of the Congress and the President . . . of protecting the American people from further terrorist attacks." And so the president immediately reopened the loophole that the McCain amendment was supposed to have closed. "We believe the president understands Congress' intent in passing by very large majorities legislation governing the treatment of detainees," McCain responded, according to Rosa Brooks (2006): "The Congress declined when asked by administration officials to include a presidential waiver of the restrictions included in our legislation. Our committee intends through strict oversight to monitor the administration's implementation of the new law." For all McCain's tough posturing, his amendment was more symbolic than substantive: its focus on a new statutory prohibition diverted attention from other congressional mechanisms of check and balance, such as the possibility of authorizing a full-scale investigation of White House involvement in developing the policies through congressional legislation to authorize a commission. Congress has not passed any of a dozen or so measures introduced by members that would limit renditions to countries where detainees might face torture (Garcia 2006).

Judicial Evasions and Evading the Judiciary

In a few cases federal courts have checked executive power: courts have reaffirmed their jurisdiction to hear cases, as well as their power to issue writs of habeas corpus, and the Supreme Court in *Hamdi* v. *Rumsfeld* has imposed minimal standards of due process in preliminary military proceedings at Guantanamo.[15] Hardly any cases have reached issues involving inhuman treatment or torture of prisoners. The administration has not brought prosecutions against wrongdoers: without the administration's appointment of a special prosecutor, there is no coordinated strategy for granting immunity in grand jury investigations, plea-bargaining in exchange for testimony incriminating superiors, or indeterminate sentencing to induce cooperation in the investigations. Without a special prosecutor the media has no "story arc," and the public does not focus on the White House involvement.

Private lawsuits brought by those suffering maltreatment or torture have been dismissed by the courts. In the case that most directly deals with the issue, a rendition case involving a lawsuit for damages brought by Maher Arer against former attorney general John Ashcroft, Judge David Trager dismissed the lawsuit on the grounds that entertaining the suit could embarrass a friendly government by exposing its involvement—in this case Canada. In a footnote to the decision, Trager recognized the *Filátarga* precedent (the right of foreign torture victims to sue their torturers in American courts under the Alien Tort Statute), but held that nothing in the case addressed "the constitutionality of torture to prevent a terrorist attack."[16] Arer's claim for damages was thrown out on the grounds that the questions presented were exclusively the province of the president and Congress, and that it would be embarrassing to our government and its Canadian ally if the case went forward.[17]

In theory, officials who authorized inhuman treatment or torture could be held liable in civil lawsuits holding them to account for pain and suffering and mental anguish, but in practice it is likely that courts would find reasons not to take jurisdiction, as in the Maher case; and if they did, Congress would pass legislation stripping the courts of jurisdiction, or immunizing officials, or indemnifying them. As of early 2006, Defense Secretary Donald Rumsfeld, Lieutenant General Ricardo Sanchez, Colonel Thomas Pappas, and Brigadier General Janis Karpinski were involved in the preliminary stages of lawsuits in federal courts in Illinois, South Carolina, Texas, and Connecticut. They could also (though this is highly unlikely) face criminal prosecutions under the War Crimes Act of 1996 and the Anti-Torture Act of 1996 for approving torture memoranda.[18] But the attorney general would have to appoint a special prosecutor because otherwise it would not be possible for the Justice Department to indict, since the actions of these officials were based on memos justifying the treatment that had been written in the Department of Justice.

According to law professor Naomi Roht-Arriaza, writing in *The Daily Journal*, 9 May 2005, high-ranking officials could also be held liable in courts of other nations for crimes against humanity and violations of international law. Some nations have universal jurisdiction laws, which allow them to prosecute offenses that have taken place in other nations. There is usually no statute of limitations on such offenses. But most countries with such statutes use an extreme version of prosecutorial discretion: the idea that NATO allies will use universal jurisdiction laws to arrest current or former Bush Administration officials is highly unlikely. Not only would such a prosecution severely fray trans-Atlantic relations, but it would also open up to judicial scrutiny the activities of allied nations in cooperating with interrogations, detention facilities, and renditions. The first such indictment would mean the end of NATO—or at least its location in Brussels.

Although most federal courts have evaded the issue of maltreatment of prisoners, the Supreme Court in *Hamdan* v. *US* (2006), a case holding that military tribunals in Guantanamo were unconstitutional, also held that

Common Article Three does apply to detainees.[19] Even so, the case would have a limited impact. It was a close decision: had Chief Justice Roberts not recused himself, it would have been decided by only a narrow 5 to 4 margin, so one more Bush appointment to the high court would likely overturn key holdings in the case. The decision involved military tribunals and detainees in military custody and not the CIA. As the administration acted to implement the decision, its guidelines only covered DOD employees, and did not reach the CIA or its ghost detainees.[20] The White House and Pentagon both claimed that the decision would not change practices at Guantanamo, because prisoners were being treated in accordance with the McCain Amendment, and therefore were not being mistreated.

Public Opinion

A partial explanation for the failure of courts and Congress to put an end to inhuman treatment and torture may be offered through analysis of public opinion. An illegitimate policy or a scandal does not reach the "overshoot and collapse" stage unless there is a precipitous drop in public support for the president that is directly linked to the issue. As of spring 2006 the steep decline in President Bush's popularity and job approval ratings did not correlate closely with the torture and maltreatment revelations. The drop was linked to Iraq, Katrina, the Dubai Ports deal, and the price of gasoline, and the key dimension was incompetence and not malevolence. Media disclosures and military and congressional investigations of inhuman acts or torture committed against those believed to be sworn enemies of the United States, against the plotters and accomplices of those who planned 9/11 and other atrocities against civilians around the world, has not created the same kind of outrage that Watergate or Iran-Contra did.

Allegations of inhuman treatment and torture have never had a single dramatic storyline that dominated the news, except perhaps for the synecdochic imagery of the prisoner with electrodes, and the image of the Koran being flushed down the toilet, which in any event had more impact in the Islamic world than in the United States. The recurring charges by critics of patterns of abuses of power, unconstitutional practices, illegalities, and deception seem to have led, not to outrage and insistence on accountability, but rather to a lowering of expectations, a numbing of the public to revelations of lawbreaking, and a renormalization downward about the expectation of governmental adherence to the rule of law.

Individual Americans held ambivalent attitudes that polling questions could not capture, since they involved a tension between the values the nation professes and the interrogation techniques it practices. Although majorities supported some extreme interrogation techniques, they strongly opposed others. A May 2004 *ABC News/Washington Post* poll indicated that

63 percent of Americans thought torture was never acceptable, while 35 percent found it acceptable in some cases. However 46 percent said it was acceptable to use physical abuse falling short of torture, while 52 percent said it was not acceptable: in partisan terms 40 percent of Republicans and Independents said torture may be acceptable in some cases, but only 27 percent of Democrats agreed. In a *USA Today* poll in early January 2005, 59 percent of respondents said that they would *not* be willing to have the US government torture known terrorists even if they knew details about future terrorist attacks in the US. Although a bare majority supported depriving prisoners of sleep for several days, 49 to 48 percent, most other techniques were strongly opposed: forcing prisoners to remain naked and chained in uncomfortable positions in cold rooms for several hours by 79 to 18 percent; threatening to transfer prisoners to a country known for using torture by 62 to 35 percent; threatening prisoners with dogs by 69 to 29 percent; waterboarding by 82 to 18 percent. In a *New York Times/CBS News Poll* of 21–5 July 2006, asking if in treating prisoners of war the US should follow international agreements it has agreed to or do "what it thinks is right," a large majority (72 percent) agreed that the US should follow international agreements. Other than that indirect question, pollsters for national news organizations were not asking Americans their opinion about torture and inhuman treatment of detainees as of 2006. With the administration denying that it used torture and claiming adherence to the rule of law, yet at the same time hinting that the president would use his powers as commander-in-chief to order interrogations that would safeguard Americans, it seemed as if the issue had been contained with the symbolic passage of the McCain amendment, and whatever rules the federal courts might impose.

Conclusion: Prerogative Power in the War on Terror

As of the winter of 2007, it would seem that whatever issue might result in checking the president, up to and including censure or impeachment, it was *not* going to be inhuman treatment or torture of detainees, nor the power of the president as commander in chief to detain indefinitely citizens or non-citizens linked to terrorism. In measuring the reaction to the assertion of presidential prerogative, the relevant comparison is not to Watergate (impeachment) or Iran-Contra (administrative paralysis), and not even to the U-2 Crisis (embarrassment). At best, it might have been compared with the Steel Seizure, Nixon's impoundments, or disclosures about CIA assassination attempts on foreign leaders: an assertion of prerogative that led to limited judicial checks and congressional oversight.

But it seems that the resolution of the issue has not even reached that outcome. Instead, the torture scandals have resulted in the *illusion* of a backlash effect. Congress investigated and held hearings, but as with Iran-Contra, they were deflected from the top ranks of the Pentagon and Department of Justice. The military investigated and prosecuted low-level officers and enlisted personnel but offered them no incentives to move the inquiry upwards. Congress passed an anti-torture amendment, but it was watered down, and the president emasculated it with a signing statement. Congress passed a law requiring a report to congressional committees before any "special access" interrogation program can be implemented, but this too was subverted by a presidential signing statement. The Supreme Court held that prisoners were entitled to Common Article Three protections against mistreatment, but its decision was based on construction of a statute, and the limited reach of its holdings invited Congress to override these protections by passing new laws if it wished. As in past scandals, legislators characterized CIA agents or special operations units as "rogue elephants" while the president was portrayed as duped by subordinates (Eisenhower), inexperienced and manipulated by advisers (Ford), asleep at the switch and prone to excessive delegation (Reagan), or as the Boy in the Bubble, incapable of understanding the complexities of the issues (W. Bush).

The ineffectiveness of congressional checks and balances is best explained as a consequence of a public distracted by multiple crises and conflicted in its attitude toward treatment of those detained in the war on terror, combined with the inability of Democrats to control either chamber of Congress: in the U-2, Watergate, Iran-Contra, and Clinton scandals, the opposition party controlled Congress, and the assertion of executive prerogative could be checked by legislative prerogative. But when party government exists, the congressional party in power provides only the illusion of checks; the most some members of the opposition party can do is to propose measures the opposition doesn't have the votes to pass, such as censure or impeachment.[21]

The torture case seems to be a variant in the theory of prerogative power that involves the substitution of illusory checks and balances for the real thing. It is likely to remain that way until public opinion can be mobilized against violations of international and domestic law, and until the opposition party gains control of at least one house of Congress.

References

Bazelon, Emily. 2006. "Invisible Men." *Slate*. 31 March.

Blumenthal, Sidney. 2005. "Condi's Trail of Lies." *Salon*. 8 December.

Brooks, Rosa. 2006. "McCain to Bush: Don't Try it Pal." *Los Angeles Times*. 6 January.

Detainee Abuse and Accountability Project. 2006. *By the Numbers*. New York: New York University's Center for Human Rights and Global Justice, Human Rights Watch, and Human Rights First. 26 April.

Di Rita, Lawrence. 2005. "Don't Tie Our Hands." *USA Today*. 5 August.

Elsea, Jennifer. 2004. "U.S. Treatment of Prisoners in Iraq: Selected Legal Issues." *Congressional Research Service Report for Congress* (RL32395). 2 December.

Garcia, Michael John. 2006. "Renditions: Constraints Imposed by Laws on Torture." *Congressional Research Service Report for Congress* (RL32890). 5 April.

Hersh, Seymour. 2004. "Torture at Abu Ghraib." *New Yorker*. 20 May. On-line at ⟨www.newyorker.com/fact/content/?040510fa_fact⟩, accessed 21 November 2006.

Human Rights Watch. 2006. "Rumsfeld Potentially Liable for Torture." 15 April.

Isikoff, Michael. 2005. "Exclusive: Secret Memo—Send to be Tortured." *Newsweek*. 8 August.

Jehl, Douglas. 2005a. "C.I.A. Chief Defends Interrogation Policy and Disavows Torture." *New York Times*. 17 March.

——— 2005b. "Report Warned on C.I.A.'s Tactics in Interrogation." *New York Times*. 9 November.

——— and Johnston, David. 2005. "Rule Change Lets C.I.A. Freely Send Suspects Abroad to Jails." *New York Times*. 6 March.

Naftali, Tim. 2005. "Superiority Complex." *Slate* website, 2 November.

Priest, Dana. 2005a. "CIA's Assurances on Transferred Suspects Doubted." *Washington Post*. 17 March.

——— 2005b. "CIA Holds Terror Suspects in Secret Prisons." *Washington Post*. 2 November.

Sappenfeld, Mark. 2005. "How Common is US Abuse of Detainees?" *Christian Science Monitor*. 8 December.

Savage, Charlie. 2005. "Abuse Led Navy to Consider Pulling Cuba Interrogators." *Boston Globe*. 16 March.

Schmitt, Eric, and Jehl, Douglas. 2004. "Army Says C.I.A. Hid More Iraqis Than It Claimed." *New York Times*. 10 September.

Working Group Report on Detainee Interrogations in the Global War Against Terrorism: Assessment of Legal, Historical, Policy, and Operational Considerations. 2003. 6 March.

Notes

1. The Afghanistan Independent Human Rights Commission, Human Rights Watch, and the Crimes of War Project as of 2005 had logged 800 complaints against US forces for brutality, torture, and other human rights abuses. Government documentation about abuses in Iraq and at Guantanamo include the following: Vice Admiral Church's *Report to Congress* (classified, 11 March 2005); *Final Report of the Independent Panel to Review Department of Defense Detention Operations*, reprinted in *The Abu Ghraib Investigations*, ed. Steven Strasser (New York: Public Affairs, 2004; the Fay/Jones Report on Abu Ghraib, *Investigation of the Abu Ghraib Detention Facility and 205th Military Intelligence Brigade* by Major General George R. Fay, Investigating Officer, reprinted in *The Abu Ghraib Investigations*; *AR 15-6 Investigation of the Abu Ghraib Detention Facility and 205th MI Brigade*, by LTG Anthony R. Jones, reprinted in *The Torture Papers: The Road to Abu Ghraib*, ed. Karen J. Greenberg and Joshua L. Dratel (New York: Cambridge University Press, 2005); the report by Generals Randall Schmidt and John Furlow on interrogations at Guantanamo, summarized at ⟨www. defenselink.mil/news/detainee_investigations.html⟩, accessed 21 November

2006; Antonio M. Taguba, *Article 15-6 Investigation of the 800th Military Policy Brigade* (26 February 2003), reprinted in Greenberg and Dratel, *The Torture Papers*; the 1,200 pages of documents obtained by the American Civil Liberties Union on treatment of detainees in Iraq; the 36,000 pages of documents and reports of 130 investigations by the Army and FBI obtained by the ACLU; the 1,000 photos from Abu Ghraib obtained and posted on the internet by Salon and analyzed at Mark Benjamin, "Salon Exclusive: The Abu Ghraib Files," 16 February 2006; the *Report of the International Committee of the Red Cross (ICRC) on the Treatment by the Coalition Forces of Prisoners of War and other Protected Persons by the Geneva Conventions in Iraq During Arrest, Internment and Interrogation*, reprinted in Greenberg and Dratel, *The Torture Papers*, 383–404; Human Rights First, *Command Responsibility* (New York: Human Rights First Report, 2006); data from the declassified Combatant Status Review Tribunals proceedings of 314 Guantanamo prisoners; details from 132 habeas corpus petitions filed by Guantanamo prisoners; reports of the UN Commission on Human Rights on conditions at Guantanamo; the reports from the European Union on Extraordinary Renditions.

2. Some commentators believe that this provision has become part of customary international law, and therefore as *The U.S. Army Field Manual of the Law of Land Warfare* observes: "unwritten or customary law of war is binding upon all nations." The US then would be bound to treat detainees humanely.

3. The War Crimes Act of 1996 defines war crimes as "grave breaches" of the Geneva Conventions and violations of Common Article 3. Source: P.L. 104-192, 110 Stat. 2104 (1996), 18 USC par. 2441.

4. *Rasul v. Bush*, 542 US 466 (2004).

5. The *Final Report of the National Commission on Terrorist Attacks Upon the United States* recommended (at 380) that the United States "engage its friends to develop a common coalition approach toward the detention and humane treatment of captured terrorists," and expressly urged the US to "draw upon Article 3 of the Geneva Conventions on the law of armed conflict," which was "specifically designed for those cases in which the usual laws of war did not apply." Common Article 3's minimum standards, according to the Commission, "are generally accepted throughout the world as customary international law."

6. Marty Lederman, "The Heroes of the Pentagon's Interrogation Scandal—Finally, the JAG Memos" ⟨www.balkin.blogspot.com⟩, 27 July 2005, accessed 21 November 2006.

7. Human Rights First alleges that since August 2002, nearly 100 detainees have died while in US custody. It counts 34 suspected or confirmed homicides, and another 11 deaths in which physical abuse or harsh treatment in detention may have played a role, claiming "Overall eight people in U.S. custody were tortured to death." *Command Responsibility* (New York: Human Rights First Report, 2006), 1.

8. In its first investigation of conditions at Guantanamo, the US Southern Command assigned a one-star officer, Brigadier General John Furlow, to conduct an investigation. The commanding officer of Camp Delta at the time, Army Major General Geoffrey Miller, was a two-star general and thus Furlow could not investigate him. The failure of the Bush Administration to investigate whether senior civilian officials in the Pentagon, Department of Justice, or other agencies ordered mistreatment or torture of prisoners may violate the Convention Against Torture,

which requires that each signatory state conduct an investigation whenever there is reasonable ground to believe that an act of torture has been committed in any territory under its jurisdiction. While specific acts involving detainees have been investigated, the "act" of ordering inhuman treatment through policy directives has not.

9. Accompanying the directive was a revision of the *US Army Field Manual*, FM 2-22.3, "Human Intelligence Collector Operations," which now prohibited stripping prisoners, keeping them in stressful positions, imposing dietary restrictions, using police dogs, and depriving prisoners of sleep. It also would not allow the CIA to keep ghost prisoners at army facilities. It would require soldiers to report violations of treaties or standards of humane treatment.

10. The directive states: "Intelligence interrogations will be conducted in accordance with applicable law, this directive and implementing plans, policies, orders, directives, and doctrine developed by DoD components and approved by USD (I), unless otherwise authorized, in writing, by the secretary of defense or deputy secretary of defense." USD (I) refers to the undersecretary of defense for intelligence.

11. "Memorandum for James B. Comey, Deputy Attorney General from Acting Assistant Attorney General Daniel Levin Re: Legal Standards Applicable Under 18 U.S.C. par. 2340-2340A."

12. Title X, Defense Appropriation Act, 2006 (H.R.2863); Sections 1402–5, Defense Authorization Act, 2006.

13. This amendment contradicts the flat prohibition on the use of testimony secured through torture or extreme coercion, contained in the Uniform Code of Military Justice, 10 USC sect. 863.

14. The Graham amendment was designed to render the Supreme Court decision in *Rasul* v. *Bush* 542 US 466 (2004) a nullity. The court held that detainees at Guantanamo could file habeas petitions to contest their detentions. The amendment limits such review to the validity of decisions of the Combatant Status Review Tribunals, a preliminary proceeding. It would mean that federal courts could not determine if the McCain anti-torture amendment had been violated. Sect. 1005 of the Detainee Treatment Act of 2005, "Procedures for Status Review of Detainees Outside the United States."

15. *Hamdi* v. *Rumsfeld*, 542 US 507 (2004).

16. *Filátarga* v. *Peña-Irala*, 630 F.2d 876 (2d Cir. 1980); *also Kadic* v. *Karadzic*, 70 F.3d 232 (1995); *Arar* v. *Ashcroft*, 414 F. Supp. 2d 250 (2006).

17. *Arar* v. *Ashcroft*, ibid. at 284.

18. They argue that those involved with the memoranda may be accessories to crimes committed by interrogators and involved in a criminal conspiracy, if the deaths were held to be foreseeable consequences of the legal advice given or the approvals granted. *United States* v. *Alstotter* et al. ("The Justice Case") 3 TWC 1 (1948).

19. *Hamdan* v. *Rumsfeld*.

20. Gordon England, "Memorandum for Secretaries of the Military Departments," Office of the Secretary of Defense, 7 July 2006. OSDA 10735-06.

21. The Conyers Resolutions, HR 635, HR 636, HR 637 calling for a House select committee and the censuring of Bush and Cheney had 30 co-sponsors as of May 2006.

4

Bending so as Not to Break: What the Bush Presidency Reveals about the Politics of Unilateral Action

William G. Howell and Douglas L. Kriner

Whatever future historians may say about the George W. Bush presidency, one thing is clear: their verdict will hinge upon evaluations of the president's "war on terror" and his military campaigns in the Middle East. Though social security reform and ballooning deficits may constitute prominent policy failures, and tax cuts and educational accountability systems may rank among his victories, the security of this president's legacy ultimately depends upon democracy taking hold in the Middle East and the successful dismantling of terrorist networks both at home and abroad.

Because Bush has consciously crafted his as a wartime administration, the recent and rapid escalation of presidential power should come as little surprise, for when the nation stands on a war footing, presidential power almost always expands. Locked in a struggle of will and might against a foreign foe, with reports of advances and retreats printed daily, the president exerts influence at home like at no other time. " 'When the blast of war blows in our ears,' " Clinton Rossiter (1956, 24) reminds us, "the President's power to command the forces swells out of all proportion to his other powers." And when a perceived enemy does not so much line up in formation as lurk within shadows, when the casualties of war are as likely to be carried from a marketplace as from a battlefield, when the threat of future attacks appears imminent at home as well as abroad, the president can push the limits of his powers to the fullest by merely gesturing towards the nation's security interests.

The expansion of executive power during times of war grants presidents a full arsenal of administrative tools to forge and execute their policy objectives. Using national security directives, executive orders, proclamations, and a wide assortment of other measures, this president has exercised extraordinary control over military actions waged against foreign regimes and the terrorists that they purportedly harbor. Bush has not hesitated to use any and all means at his disposal. In the aftermath of September 11, Bush unilaterally created a series of agencies—the Office of Homeland Security, the Office of Global Communications, and the Commission on the Intelligence Capabilities of the United States Regarding Weapons of Mass Destruction—to collect and disseminate new intelligence while coordinating the activities of existing bureaus. He issued a national security directive lifting a ban (which Ford originally instituted via executive order 11905) on the CIA's ability to "engage in, or conspire to engage in, political assassination"—in this instance, the target being Osama bin Laden and his lieutenants within al-Qaeda. He signed executive orders that froze all financial assets in US banks that could be linked to bin Laden and his terrorist networks. Bush unilaterally established special military tribunals to try noncitizens suspected of plotting terrorist acts, committing terrorism, or harboring known terrorists.[1] And through national security directives, the president has developed a massive international infrastructure to detain and interrogate (and, some charge, torture) foreign combatants.

The most visible of Bush's unilateral actions consisted of military strikes in Afghanistan and Iraq. Having secured congressional authorizations to respond to the mounting crises as he saw fit, in the fall of 2001 Bush directed the Air Force to begin a bombing campaign against Taliban strongholds, while Special Forces conducted stealth missions on the ground. In the spring of 2003, he launched a massive air and ground war against Iraq, plunging the United States into the most protracted military conflict since the Vietnam War. During the subsequent occupation, most policies related to intelligence gathering, the rebuilding of infrastructure, the training of Iraqi troops, and the governing transition came not through laws, but through unilateral actions of one sort or another. Though not packaged as traditional policy directives, these commands nonetheless instigated some of the most potent expressions of executive power. Within a year Bush's orders resulted in the collapse of the Taliban and Baathist regimes, the flight of tens of thousands of refugees into Pakistan, Iran, and Turkey, the destruction of Afghanistan's and Iraq's social and economic infrastructures, and the introduction of new democratically elected governments.

How should we evaluate these extraordinary displays of presidential power? There is, at present, a burgeoning literature on unilateral powers that lends guidance on the matter (see e.g. Cooper 2002; Deering and Maltzman 1999; Howell 2003, 2005a, b; Howell and Lewis 2002; Krause and Cohen 1997, 2000; Marshall and Pacelle 2005; Mayer 1999, 2001; Mayer and Price 2002; Moe and Howell 1999a, b; Pious 1991). The more formal and empirically minded contributors to this research have offered two core lessons about unilateral powers. First, and perhaps foremost, presidents are able to accomplish things unilaterally that would not survive the legislative process. If their policy agenda ultimately depends upon Congress's goodwill, shared convictions, or induced preferences, presidents invite regular disappointment. But by issuing any number of unilateral directives, presidents manage to eke out a measure of discretion that they otherwise would sorely miss. The second lesson concerns how the boundaries of presidential power are defined. Unilateral power is not absolute; rather, it expands and contracts according to the variable capacity and willingness of other political actors to amend or overturn an order already given. The politics of unilateral action do not halt instantaneously the moment the president signs off on an executive order or proclamation. Should a president overextend his (someday her) unilateral authority, Congress and the courts stand poised, albeit with variable levels of determination, to reverse his actions.

During the course of the Bush presidency, even casual observers appear awestruck by the sheer amount of evidence in support of the first lesson. Indeed, this president's willingness to bypass Congress in pursuit of a sweeping set of foreign policy objectives reveals considerable aplomb, audacity even. *The Economist* (2006a) recognizes that "most presidents like to try and expand their powers. But in repeatedly invoking his constitutional authority as commander-in-chief in the 'war on terror' to bypass both domestic laws and international treaties, George Bush has taken the art to new heights." David Moberg (2006, 4) laments "the threat of an imperial presidency, which has reached its highest level under Bush." Stephen Graubard (2004, 32) notes that, "the perils of exaggerated executive power were never more conspicuous than in the first years of the twenty-first century when the king, courtiers, and warriors domiciled in Washington, D.C." And other scholars within this volume speak more eloquently still about the various constitutional, legal, and moral implications of the current administration's brash exercise of presidential power. Unequivocally, this president has gleaned considerable influence from his unilateral powers.

Evidence of the second lesson, however, appears in shorter supply—at least, as of this writing in the summer of 2006. During the past five years, Congress has done precious little legislatively to rein in the president. For the most part, Bush's policy agenda, or at least the part that has been unilaterally instituted, has not suffered grand defeats at the hand of congressionally enacted statutes or judicial rulings. Though an epic inter-branch showdown may yet erupt, thus far, conflicts have proven rather muted—even though the president, quite explicitly, has sought to exalt his own power and to denigrate Congress's, insisting on more than a few occasions that members should not, and constitutionally cannot, meddle in his campaigns against terrorism at home and abroad. Among critics, the president's defiant stance has generated a growing consensus, articulated in a recent *New York Times*

(2006*a*) editorial, that "the system of checks and balances is a safety net that doesn't feel particularly sturdy at present."

Two factors, in our judgment, help explain why friction between Congress and the presidency has not yielded the kinds of spark that might allay scholars' growing worries about the health of our system of separated powers. First, the Bush Administration has proven remarkably adept at measuring the level of opposition it faces within Congress and adjusting accordingly. Facing or anticipating unified and vocal objections from Capitol Hill against a unilaterally instituted policy—an admittedly rare occurrence, given the Republican majorities that reside there—Bush has not been shy about dropping its most controversial provisions. And when Congress has stood poised to enact sweeping laws that Bush himself opposes, the president has often taken the initiative himself to pre-empt Congress and unilaterally institute more moderate policy changes, thereby derailing the more extreme versions circulating in the legislature. Though resolute and ideologically committed, this administration, like so many of its predecessors, is not foolhardy.

Second, there is much that members of Congress can do short of enacting laws that formally amend or overturn especially objectionable unilateral actions taken by the president. Indeed, to focus exclusively on the dearth of legislative challenges to presidential actions is to overlook the more subtle, yet tangible, ways through which members of Congress can affect the president's strategic calculus. By holding hearings, advancing criticisms, and issuing public appeals for a change in course, members can, and have, materially raised the political costs of unilaterally creating public policy. And here again we find evidence of Bush's sensitivity to these costs. Repeatedly, Bush has taken firm stances in support of his favored foreign policy position only to backtrack later when critics assemble and object in unison. The current administration is certainly bold, but it also is highly strategic, wary of overextending its reach in a contested policy domain and suffering the political fallout. When the costs of either advancing or merely defending an especially controversial unilateral action become prohibitive, Bush often bends so as not to break.

This chapter focuses on congressional efforts to curtail the president's foreign policy over terrorism and the Middle East, almost all of which has been unilaterally instituted. With a series of case studies and new experimental survey data, we show that congressional opposition to the president systematically influences the willingness of average citizens to support the president's military campaigns abroad and, moreover, that such opposition has occasionally induced the president to back off from his preferred policies. So doing, we demonstrate that congressional checks on presidential war powers, though certainly diminished, remain a core feature of unilateral politics.

Studies in Strategic Action

When presidents unilaterally change public policy, they can accomplish things that would not survive the legislative process—and in such instances, the mark of presidential influence is plain for all to see. The fact, though, that presidents can create policy outside the legislative process does not ensure that they will secure every aspect of their policy agenda. For when Congress and the courts stand poised to amend or overturn him, or when the adjoining branches of government can raise the expected political costs of defending an especially controversial policy initiative, the president will usually back off from his preferred policy. This section presents four brief case studies that illustrate these dynamics.[2] In the first three, Bush conceded on key dimensions (some small, others large) of a policy initiative in order to protect gains on other dimensions; in the fourth, Bush conceded nothing at all and watched his entire policy initiative run aground.

Warrantless Wiretaps

Questions regarding the legality of and proper procedures for wiretapping and electronic surveillance have a long history in the United States. The Court first addressed the legality of wiretapping in *Olmstead* v. *United States* (1928) when chief justice and former president William Howard Taft ruled that wiretapping a public phone did not violate the Fourth Amendment's search and seizure provision. Forty years later the Court reversed *Olmstead* and required warrants for domestic wiretaps in *Katz* v. *United States* (1967). The following year, Congress addressed wiretapping directly by passing the Omnibus [Crime] Controls and Safe Streets Act, which placed general restrictions on the impositions of wiretaps.[3] Even though it permitted electronic surveillance only when authorized by a "court of competent jurisdiction," the act still recognized the president's constitutional power to "protect the United States against the overthrow of the Government by force or other unlawful means, or against any other clear and present danger to the structure or existence of the Government" (Markels 2005).

Following the Church Committee's investigation into past executive branch abuses of electronic surveillance, particularly the Nixon Administration's eavesdropping on Vietnam War protesters and Civil Rights activists, Congress in 1978 enacted the Foreign Intelligence Surveillance Act (FISA) to redress ambiguities in previous legislation.[4] Attempting to balance national security interests and civil liberties, the legislation authorized wiretaps against a "foreign power" or "agents of a foreign power," but created a special FISA Court from which the Attorney General must first seek a warrant before initializing wiretaps.[5] In cases of extreme exigency, the law gave the attorney general 72 hours after the initial surveillance to seek a retroactive warrant from the FISA Court.

And thus the law stood until the immediate aftermath of September 11, when the Bush Administration began re-evaluating the nation's intelligence gathering capabilities in light of new challenges posed by the war on terror. John Yoo, a former official in the Justice Department's Office of Legal Counsel, wrote an internal memorandum shortly after the September 11 attacks arguing that "the government might use 'electronic surveillance techniques and equipment that are more powerful and sophisticated than those available to law enforcement agencies in order to intercept telephonic communications and observe the movement of persons but without obtaining warrants for such uses' " (Risen and Lichtblau 2005). In the fall of 2001, the administration quickly moved to implement these ideas. Although details about the program remain shrouded in secrecy, officials familiar with the program say that the National Security Agency (NSA) conducts wiretapping without warrants on up to 500 people in the United States at any given time.

The administration informed several members of Congress of the NSA program prior to its inception. In separate meetings on 25 October 2001 and 14 November 2001, Vice President Richard Cheney, Director of Central Intelligence George Tenet, and Michael Hayden, a lieutenant general and director of the NSA, briefed four members of Congress about the agency's new domestic surveillance, including Senator Bob Graham (D-FL) and Representative Nancy Pelosi (D-CA). Though Graham later claimed to recall "no discussion about expanding [NSA eavesdropping] to include conversations of US citizens or conversations that originated or ended in the United States," officials associated with the administration insisted that the meetings provided a comprehensive announcement of the new program (Gellman and Linzer 2005).

After sitting on the story for over a year, the *New York Times* exposed the warrantless wiretapping policy on 16 December 2005. Congressional Democrats immediately attacked the program (Arena 2005; Johnston 2006). The Senate's leading defender of its institutional prerogatives, Robert Byrd (D-WV), denounced the program as an assumption of executive power previously "reserved only for kings and potentates," and Barbara Boxer (D-CA) said there was "no excuse" for the president's actions (*Economist* 2006b). Former vice president Al Gore made perhaps the most cogent denunciation of the president, arguing that Bush had broken "the law repeatedly and persistently" (CNN 2006). Even the few Democrats who had previously been briefed on the program quickly expressed their disapproval publicly. Senate Intelligence Committee ranking member John D. Rockefeller IV (D-WV) released a letter he had sent to Vice President Cheney on 17 July 2003 complaining that "given the security restrictions associated with this information and my inability to consult staff or counsel on my own, I feel unable to fully evaluate much less endorse these activities" (Lichtblau and Sanger 2005). In the House, ranking Intelligence Committee member Jane Harman (D-CA) distributed a 14-page legal analysis she had requested from former CIA counsel Jeffrey H. Smith, which called the administration's defense of the program "'weak' in light of the language and documented purpose of the Foreign Intelligence Surveillance Act of 1978" (Sanger and Shane 2006).

Perhaps more surprising was the cool reception the program's disclosure received from a number of key Republicans. Judiciary Committee chair Arlen Specter (R-PA) warned "I am skeptical of the attorney general's citation of authority," and "I think it does not constitute a check and balance." South Carolina's Lindsay Graham similarly conceded that the justifications for Bush's power grab were "a stretch" (Kuhnhenn and Henderson 2006). Many conservatives outside Congress were even more scathing in their denunciations. Former Georgia congressman and civil libertarian Bob Barr declared the program "an egregious violation of the electronic surveillance laws" (King 2005). Bruce Fein, former deputy attorney general in the Reagan Administration, suggested that the program might constitute grounds for impeachment:

On its face, if President Bush is totally unapologetic and says I continue to maintain that as a war-time President I can do anything I want—I don't need to consult any other branches—that is an impeachable offense. It's more dangerous than Clinton's lying under oath because it jeopardizes our democratic dispensation and civil liberties for the ages. It would set a precedent that ... would lie around like a loaded gun, able to be used indefinitely for any future occupant.

Norm Ornstein, from the Conservative-leaning American Enterprise Institute, seconded this view: "I think if we're going to be intellectually honest here, this really is the kind of thing that Alexander Hamilton was referring to when impeachment was discussed" (Rehm 2005).

In a 42-page Justice Department "white paper," the administration defended the program on the basis of the Authorization to Use Military Force (AUMF) against international terror and on the grounds of inherent presidential authority as commander in chief. And the administration's claims received support from a small cadre of legal scholars, most notably from John Yoo and the attorney general, Alberto Gonzales. The majority of constitutional scholars, however, sharply criticized the administration's legal arguments (see *Fox News* 2006; Lichtblau and Liptak 2006; Lichtblau and Sanger 2006). A group of fourteen constitutional law scholars including Kathleen Sullivan, Ronald Dworkin, and Laurence Tribe rejected the administration's contention that Congress implicitly authorized the NSA program by passing the AUMF (Bazan and Elsea 2006; Nolan et al. 2006). Even Robert Levy, constitutional scholar and Federalist Society Board Member, said of the program, "The text of FISA §1809 is unambiguous: 'A person is guilty of an offense if he intentionally engages in electronic surveillance...except as authorized by statute.' ... I know of no court case that has denied there is a reasonable expectation of privacy by US citizens and permanent resident aliens in the types of wire communications that are reportedly monitored by the NSA's electronic surveillance program" (Federalist Society 2006).

When details of the secret program first became public, Bush vehemently opposed any congressional hearings into the matter. Publicly airing the government's tactics, the president warned, would play into the hands of al-Qaeda: "any public hearings on programs will say to the enemy, 'Here's what they do—adjust' " (Sanger and Shane 2006). With 58 percent of Americans supporting an investigation into the program's legality, however, Bush quickly backed off and claimed to welcome hearings; so doing, though, he made a conscious effort to reframe the debate in terms of national security objectives rather than civil liberties (Brookes 2006). In a Louisville conference center "decorated with signs that said 'Winning the War on Terror,' " Bush professed support for congressional hearings but again raised the specter of al-Qaeda: "there will be a lot of hearings to talk...that's good for democracy...just so long as the hearings, as they explore whether or not I had the prerogative to make the decision I made, doesn't [sic] tell the enemy what we're doing. See that's the danger" (Sanger and Shane 2006).

The White House then began an all-out media blitz in support of the program and the president's authority to order it. Attorney General Gonzales spoke at the Georgetown University Law Center and then made seven television appearances between 23 and 24 January, in which he invoked the policies of previous presidents (including George Washington, Woodrow Wilson, and Franklin Roosevelt) as precedents for the administration's actions. The president himself emphasized that the NSA program was an essential tool in a different type of war in a "different era." Claiming that FISA was inadequate to meet the nation's security needs in the post-September 11 world, the president explained: "We use FISA still...But FISA is for long-term monitoring. What is needed in order to protect the American people is the ability to move quickly to detect...Do I have the legal authority to do this?... The answer is, absolutely" (Bush 2005). The administration's belief that the terrorism angle would resonate with public concerns was so strong that Karl Rove, the president's chief political advisor, even signaled to the National Republican Committee that the NSA wiretapping program would be at the heart of the GOP strategy in the 2006 Midterm elections. By the eve of the impending congressional hearings, a 27 January 2006 *New York Times*/CBS News poll revealed the fruits of the administration's efforts. A majority of Americans now approved of eavesdropping without prior court approval "in order to reduce the threat of terrorism."[6]

Congressional hearings into the NSA program began when Attorney General Alberto Gonzales appeared before the Senate Judiciary Committee on

6 February 2006. During the hearings, most Democrats criticized the program, and most Republicans defended it. Party lines, however, were not impervious to passage. Chair Specter, for instance, warned Gonzales that that the Supreme Court in *Hamdi* v. *Rumsfeld* (2005) ruled that the AUMF was not a "blank check;" and in response to Gonzales' continued assertion that the president had sufficient statutory and constitutional authority to initiate the program, Specter quipped "you think you're right, but there are a lot of people who think you're wrong" (*New York Times* 2006*b*).[7] Though less blunt, a number of other Republicans echoed Specter's concerns including Lindsey Graham (R-SC), Sam Brownback (R-KS), Mike DeWine (R-OH), John McCain (R-AZ), Chuck Hagel (R-NE), Susan Collins (R-ME), and Larry Craig (R-ID).

The congressional inquiry accelerated on 16 February when the House Intelligence Committee, prompted by New Mexico Republican Heather Wilson, opened its own investigation into the NSA program, and a federal judge ordered the administration to begin turning over "internal documents on the surveillance program" to Congress (Babington and Leonnig 2006). Democrats on the Senate Intelligence Committee then pushed to open the committee's own investigation into the matter. To diffuse such calls, however, chair Pat Roberts (R-KS) announced the White House's agreement to "negotiate on legislation that would give Congress authority to oversee the eavesdropping" (Lichtblau and Stolberg 2006).

Though the administration had previously refused to admit any need for new statutory authorization for the NSA surveillance program, legislative reform quickly became the best way to quell unrest among party moderates. Alluding to past experience in the Civil War, the White House expressed its hope that these "talks will lead to legislation to approve the program, much as Congress eventually approved Abraham Lincoln's suspension of *habeas corpus* during the Civil War." Toward that goal, the president dispatched Chief of Staff Andrew Card, White House Counsel Harriet Miers, and others to the Hill to forge a compromise with congressional Republicans (Stolberg and Sanger 2006).

On 17 March 2006, Senators DeWine, Graham, Hagel, and Snowe introduced the Terrorist Surveillance Act of 2006 (S. 2455). The bill placed modest limits on the duration of warrantless wiretapping and created augmented congressional reporting requirements, but also recognized the president's legal right to authorize surveillance of American citizens' international communications without a FISA court order. Under the compromise, the NSA would retain the right to wiretap international communication without a warrant for the first 45 days, after which the administration would have to choose between discontinuing the surveillance, securing a court order, or certifying in writing to Congress the need for the wiretap's continuation. The administration also agreed to expanded briefings and reports on the program to new subcommittees drawn from the ranks of both chambers' Intelligence

Committees.[8] Finally, the compromise required that the president establish and maintain a Terrorist Surveillance List "of groups and organizations that are subject to electronic surveillance authorized under the Terrorist Surveillance Program."

Many Democrats cried foul, noting that the alleged "compromise" gave the White House virtually everything it wanted, including the absence of any judicial review—a qualification that some Republicans, including South Carolina's Lindsey Graham who co-sponsored S. 2455, just a few weeks earlier had declared essential (Stollberg and Sanger 2006). The deal's authors, however, rejected such claims. Pat Roberts lauded the compromise as an assertion of congressional power to curb the president's actions: "There was a lot of pushback...So we kept saying, I am sorry, that is not acceptable, and the reality is such that you will either do this or you will face bigger obstacles and we will get into confrontation." Similarly, Chuck Hagel also sought to dispel the Democratic claims, calling them "laughable" and saying that he had "never been accused of buckling to White House pressure" (Shane and Kirkpatrick 2006). The compromise measure currently is referred to the Judiciary Committee awaiting further action.

Although the Senate compromise appeared to resolve the inter-branch tensions, the confluence of two additional developments in May of 2006 compelled the White House to give further ground. On 5 May, CIA Director Porter Goss abruptly resigned, prompting the White House to tap former NSA director and architect of the agency's surveillance program Michael Hayden for the vacant post. The battle for Hayden's confirmation became more complicated, however, when *USA Today* then reopened the winter's wounds and revealed the existence of another secret NSA program compiling a massive database of nearly all domestic calls logged within the United States. Although the database comprised only the records of numbers dialed and did not involve any electronic surveillance of the content of communications, the sheer scope of the program raised hackles both on Capitol Hill and alarmed the general public. Senators from both parties openly speculated that the new revelation would seriously jeopardize Hayden's confirmation and, at the very least, set the stage for a renewed battle over the controversial program (Babington 2006).

Sensing the deteriorating environment on the Hill, the White House on 16 May finally agreed to brief all members, rather than just a select few, of both the House and Senate Intelligence Committees on the operational details of the NSA surveillance program. Pat Roberts acknowledged the critical importance of the impending Hayden confirmation as the catalyst that prompted the administration's about-face: "This issue will be central to the committee's deliberations on General Hayden's nomination and there was no way we could fulfill our collective constitutional responsibilities without that knowledge" (Wilson 2006).

Despite initially denouncing any public hearings or added congressional oversight of his secret NSA surveillance program, President Bush, confronted with open discord from moderate Republicans and near unanimous opposition from Democrats, ultimately softened his stance on warrantless wiretapping. The legislative compromise currently working its way through the Judiciary Committee inherently recognizes Congress's constitutional power to limit warrantless surveillance longer than 45 days—a power the administration previously claimed was inherent in the Constitution's commander-in-chief clause. Moreover, the administration's most recent decision to brief the full membership of the House and Senate Intelligence Committees on the operational details of the NSA program directly contradicts the White House's previous position that greater disclosure of the program's details would only aid the terrorists. But provided that the intelligence committees do not demand further reforms after learning the full scope of the NSA program, the Terrorist Surveillance Act will protect the basic framework of the president's initiative. Having succeeded in casting the debate in terms of terrorism rather than civil liberties, the Bush Administration has shored up public support for the NSA program even as the president's own job approval ratings have slid into the low 30s. This steady popular support for the program has thus far helped the administration bring renegade Republicans in Congress back to the party fold and turn back their and congressional Democrats' demands for judicial review and even greater congressional oversight.

A Department of Homeland Security

In the immediate aftermath of the September 11 attacks, members of Congress, particularly those in the then Democratic-controlled Senate, began publicly calling for a dramatic overhaul of the nation's intelligence infrastructure. These members sought to create a new bureaucracy charged with coordinating the efforts of a vast array of federal, state, and local agencies involved in intelligence gathering and law enforcement. By leading the charge for administrative reorganization, they hoped to cast themselves as proponents of bold, forceful actions to shore up the nation's defense against another attack—while also preserving some measure of congressional influence over the expansion of presidential power needed to oversee the nascent war on terror.

The first salvo in the struggle over bureaucratic reorganization came on 21 September 2001, when Senate Intelligence Committee Chair Bob Graham (D-FL) and a number of other prominent Democrats introduced S. 1449, a bill to establish the National Office for Combating Terrorism. Agreeing with Michigan Democrat Carl Levin that "the President has got to have the flexibility as to how he organizes the executive branch," the bill proposed creating an office charged with coordinating different intelligence agencies and developing a comprehensive budget for the nation's counter-terrorism strategy within the Executive Office of the President (Kane and Pershing 2001). The Office's Director, however, would require Senate confirmation before taking his post, and the legislation specifically provided for congressional oversight of the Office's activities, noting that "the location of the Office in the Executive Office of the President shall not be construed as affecting access by Congress, or any committee of Congress, to any information, document, record, or paper in the possession of the Office or any study conducted by or at the direction of the Director; or any personnel of the Office."

As the Governmental Affairs Committee prepared to hold hearings on the proposal, President Bush pre-empted congressional action on 8 October 2001 by issuing Executive Order 13228, which established his own Office of Homeland Security (OHS). The goal of the new agency "to coordinate the executive branch's efforts to detect, prepare for, prevent, protect against, respond to, and recover from terrorist attacks within the United States" overlapped with S. 1449's mandate for a new coordinating intelligence bureau. But to maximize his personal control of the new agency, President Bush not only lodged OHS within the Executive Office of the President, but he created a new special assistant to the president for homeland security to head the new agency. As such, OHS's newly appointed director, former Pennsylvania governor Tom Ridge, would not require Senate confirmation, nor would he be subject to the oversight requirements of a departmental head.[9]

Many in Congress reacted to Bush's gambit negatively, proclaiming the OHS woefully inadequate. To insulate themselves from charges of being soft on national security, most Democratic attacks on the president's action emphasized the need to go further by strengthening the agency and augmenting the resources at the director's disposal. In the House, California Democrat and ranking member of the Homeland Security subcommittee Jane Harman supported efforts to authorize OHS legislatively and increase its budget, warning: "Mr. Ridge has the critical job in the US government now, aside from the president's. In the long term, he needs the power to do more" (Becker and Sciolino 2001). Senators on both sides of the aisle concurred.

On 11 October 2001, Arlen Specter (R-PA) and Joe Lieberman (D-CT) introduced a counterproposal, S. 1534, which insisted that Ridge and his office be specifically sanctioned by and held accountable to Congress. Asserting the need for legislative oversight, Lieberman argued: "the office [Ridge's] isn't authorized by law, and he isn't confirmed by the Senate. We need to create a robust, cabinet-level agency, led by a strong director, that has the clout and resources to make the homeland security mission work" (Labaton and Pear 2001). Senator Bob Graham echoed Lieberman's views when he declared that a legislative act of Congress was needed to create an agency equipped with the full powers and tools needed to accomplish the vital goal of coordinating the nation's response to the terrorist threat: "My own feeling is that for Governor Ridge or any other human being to be able to effectively direct [the agencies]... [it] will require more authority than the president can give him in an executive order" (Mitchell 2001*a*). Finally, in his testimony before the Governmental Affairs Committee on 12 October former congressman and future 9/11 Commission member Lee Hamilton (D-IN) explicitly raised the importance of congressional oversight of homeland security initiatives. Hamilton seconded Lieberman's call for the creation of a new cabinet department with its own budget and staff, and he encouraged Congress to reorganize its internal institutional operations to provide better support for and oversight of the department (Hamilton 2001).

The White House, however, refused to bend to congressional demands and stood by its unilaterally created agency. When asked whether the OHS should be restructured and Ridge face Senate confirmation, Press Secretary Ari Fleischer replied:

President just doesn't see the need for it. It's just not necessary. The office can get up and running... without needing to take that step... Similar to the National Security Council. Dr. Rice has done a very good job, of course, for this country. She's not Senate-confirmed. It is not a necessary prerequisite for a government official to do a good job on behalf of the President and on behalf of the war against terrorism. There is no need for it. (Fleischer 2001)

Other allies also came to the administration's defense, including Robert M. Gates, former director of Central Intelligence under President George H. W. Bush, who asserted in a *New York Times* editorial that "granting the office [of Homeland Security adviser] statutory authority could hurt more than help. It would reduce the flexibility President Bush and Mr. Ridge need to experiment—to work out, for example, which agency does what best" (Gates 2001).

Inter-branch tensions simmered throughout the rest of 2001, only to boil when the administration finally sought congressional funding for its bureaucratic creation. On 24 January 2002, Bush announced his request for an additional $38 billion in funding for Homeland Security operations in the forthcoming year. Congress appeared prepared to grant the president the funds he requested; in the words of one Senator, "In the end, he'll get what he wants, maybe more" (Sanger 2002). Before signing the check, however, a growing number of members demanded that Ridge testify on behalf of the administration's request.

The White House immediately refused, citing Ridge's status as an adviser to the president, not a cabinet officer subject to standard congressional reporting and oversight requirements.[10] Many Republicans supported Bush's stance—Senator Phil Gramm (R-TX) jokingly asked "should we subpoena [Bush's] mother? It is well-known that the president gets advice, and often good advice, from the former first lady. Maybe she ought to testify" (Jones and

Stevens 2002). A growing number of the president's co-partisans, however, began breaking ranks and joining Democrats in demanding Ridge's testimony. Senators Robert Byrd (D-WV) and Ted Stevens (R-AK) sent a letter to Ridge on 2 March 2005, reminding him that his "views and insights on the policies necessary to meet these objectives are critical to the committee and the nation." Maverick Republican Senator Chuck Hagel of Nebraska chastised the administration's approach: "I don't think that is a wise way to do these things. The fact is we are a co-equal branch of government...[and secrecy] does not facilitate cooperation and the spirit of working together" (Mitchell 2002a). Even apart from the issue of Ridge's testimony, many in Congress viewed the whole affair as an affront to their institutional and constitutional prerogatives, a rare feat in an atomized deliberative body with a penchant for the parochial.[11] According to Ernest Istook (R-OK), "the point is not whether a presidential adviser testifies, it's whether somebody can be given express major responsibilities under an executive order and then be exempted from accountability. I see it as respecting the Constitution" (Milbank 2002a).

Bush refused to yield, insisting that Ridge would not testify. In late March, the president declared, "He's part of my staff and that's part of the prerogative of the executive branch of government, and we hold that very dear" (Mitchell 2002b). But congressional critics also appeared unwavering. Rhode Island Republican Lincoln Chafee urged the White House to back down and even raised the possibility that Congress might withhold funds if the administration did not comply with its request. "In the balance, it's always a good idea to defend your budget and make a pitch. He's going to need money for his budget and it comes from that committee" (Jones and Stevens 2002). Buoyed by public opinion polls showing a clear majority of Americans supporting efforts to recast the Office of Homeland Security as a cabinet level agency (Penn, Schoen & Berland Associates 2002), Jane Harman seized the opportunity created by the uproar over Ridge's refusal to testify to advocate again for even greater congressional control over the new homeland security apparatus: "Tom Ridge needs to be a cabinet secretary subject to Senate confirmation, with budgetary authority and accountability to Congress for a homeland security strategy" (Becker 2002a).

Slowly, and reluctantly, the administration gave ground. Though Ridge informally discussed homeland security with the House Appropriations Committee on 10 April, House Democrats were not appeased. Representative Steny Hoyer (D-MD) insisted "this is a serious issue of significant importance to the country—Mr. Ridge has been given one of the most important jobs in government—and we made it very clear that this was no substitute for a formal hearing" (Becker 2002b). Eight Democrats wrote a letter to Dan Burton (R-IN), chair of the House Committee on Government Reform, requesting that discussions of homeland security be held on the record. Dennis Kucinich (D-OH) even walked out of a committee meeting in protest.

Signs that the White House would reconsider its insistence on maintaining the Office of Homeland Security as an agency within the EOP pleased Democrats further still. When speaking with a Senate panel, Mitchell Daniels, Jr., the director of the Office of Management and Budget, explained "the president has said from the outset that the structure for organizing and overseeing homeland security may evolve over time as we all learn more and as circumstances change." Said Ridge, "I embrace it [making OHS a cabinet department] enthusiastically but the only way to do it is here—in Congress" (Becker 2002c).

Two months later, Bush refashioned congressional calls for the creation of a Department of Homeland Security as his own and publicly announced his proposal in a radio address. According to the president, the initiative was "the most extensive reorganization of the Federal Government since the 1940s;" and the president then brazenly asked the public for "your help in encouraging your Representative to support my plan" (Bush 2002a). Days later, the president again claimed credit for the idea and shared his reasons for the legislative request. "In order to get good results," he said, "it's important to hold people accountable and align authority and responsibility. And that's part of my thinking, is to take the functions and put them under one—in one Cabinet agency" (Bush 2002b). Though Ari Fleischer acknowledged that discussions about creating a cabinet level agency began in earnest after the Ridge testimony row with Congress (Bumiller and Sanger 2002), at a meeting with congressional leaders Bush insisted that he had been considering the idea all along: "Ever since we first got going, I've been exploring this idea [creating a Cabinet-level department of homeland security]. My mind was never made up one way or the other . . . I've been listening to members of Congress, who have been quite articulate on the subject" (Bush 2002c).

Bush's switch in time quickly paid political dividends. Polls immediately after the president's announcement showed more than 70 percent of Americans supporting the creation of a new cabinet Department of Homeland Security (see Gallup/CNN/*USA Today* Poll, 7 June 2002; CBS News Poll, 18 June 2002; *Time*/CNN/Harris Interactive Poll, 19 June 2002). Even congressional Republicans who had previously championed the administration's efforts for exclusive White House control over the Office of Homeland Security now rallied behind the new cabinet department initiative. Democrats, robbed of their political thunder, were left to lament with House Leader Richard Gephardt (D-MO) that "it would have been better to do this five months ago, but, you know, we are where we are" (Mitchell 2002c).

On 24 June 2002, House majority leader Dick Armey (R-TX) introduced H.R. 5005, the administration's legislative proposal creating the Department of Homeland Security. The bill bore a remarkable resemblance to earlier proposals opposed by the White House, including both S. 1534 and S. 2452. The administration successfully defeated Democratic proposals further to integrate the CIA and FBI and to include stronger protections for employees of the new Department of Homeland Security. On most issues, though, the White House capitulated to congressional demands. The new Secretary of Homeland Security would be subject to Senate confirmation and the Department bound by reporting requirements and mechanisms for congressional oversight.

Why, in the end, did the administration capitulate to congressional demands? Proposals for legislatively mandated reorganization of homeland security, after all, had floundered for months. Instead, a confluence of factors likely pressured the administration to give ground. First, the prospects for continued congressional intransigence were politically unappealing. Ultimately, Congress would almost certainly have approved the requested funds for the administration's agency, but the growing unease within even Republican ranks threatened to spill over into other policy areas if allowed to fester. Second, the growing impetus for congressional investigations into specific intelligence failings leading up to September 11 threatened to embarrass the president precisely on the grounds where his appeal was strongest, his handling of national security. Indeed, several leading Democrats including John Conyers (D-MI) would accuse the administration of hastily introducing the Department of Homeland Security bill to distract attention from investigations into its past failings (Pear 2002). Finally, it became increasingly difficult to ignore the nascent public support for a Department of Homeland Security. In this unique political climate, through its concerted opposition to the president's actions, Congress managed to rein in presidential unilateral powers, replacing an independent office responsible only to the president with a cabinet level department subject to Senate confirmation and congressional oversight.

The 9/11 Commission

In the immediate aftermath of September 11, 2001, both the White House and leaders of the House and Senate Select Intelligence Committees resisted calls for an investigation into the governmental failures that contributed to the attacks. Though proposals for a comprehensive investigation gained little traction in the initial weeks and months, on 18 December 2001, Robert Torricelli (D-NJ) and Chuck Grassley (R-IA) introduced a bipartisan bill (S. 1837) calling for an independent commission to investigate the events surrounding September 11. Two days later, Connecticut Democrat Joseph Lieberman and Arizona Republican John McCain introduced similar legislation (S. 1867) calling for the establishment of an independent commission with full subpoena powers to investigate failures leading up and in response to the terrorist attacks on the World Trade Center and Pentagon. Rejecting the White House's argument that such an inquiry would undermine the fledgling war on terror, Torricelli insisted on the need for a thorough independent review: "An event of this magnitude historically cannot occur without people demanding some

111

accountability and some review of how it happened and what failed." McCain emphasized that the sheer scope of the issues involved and the intricacies of the requisite solutions demanded an independent investigation: "Neither the administration nor Congress is alone capable of conducting a thorough nonpartisan independent inquiry into what happened on September 11, or to propose far-reaching measures to protect our people or our institutions" (Mitchell 2001*b*).

Initially, the White House did not appear especially amenable to launching a major investigation into the intelligence failures surrounding September 11. As late as mid-January, media reports indicated that Vice President Dick Cheney had called upon the Senate majority leader to withhold any investigation whatsoever because it would "take resources and personnel away from the effort in the war on terrorism." By month's end, though, the administration had reconciled itself to some sort of investigation, but the president called on leaders in both chambers to limit its scope to the narrow inquiries proposed by the Select Intelligence Committees, whose proceedings could be kept confidential (Allen 2002; Morris 2002). By supporting the Intelligence Committee investigation, the White House hoped it could undercut support for a more wide-ranging independent investigation. The White House then opened negotiations with Intelligence Committee chairs Porter Goss (R-FL) and Bob Graham (D-FL). On 14 February 2002, the two chairs publicly announced they had reached an agreement for a joint investigation limited to examining pre-September 11 intelligence failures.

Even as the Intelligence Committees began to launch their own inquiry, advocates of an independent commission continued to press the initiative. The Committee on Governmental Affairs opened hearings on the Lieberman-McCain bill the first week of February, and by 21 March the committee voted unanimously to report it favorably to the full chamber. The White House promptly denounced the committee action. White House spokesperson Claire Buchan toed the administration line, telling the press that while the president endorsed the limited inquiry of the Intelligence Committees, he feared that a broader investigation would risk "pulling people off the front lines who are fighting the war on terrorism" (Stout 2002). When a few weeks later the committee submitted its written report on the Lieberman-McCain bill and had it placed on the Senate calendar, the president himself publicly rejected the legislation's premise that a further independent investigation was needed. At a news conference in Germany, Bush warned: "I, of course, want this Congress to take a look at what took place prior to September 11. But since it deals with such sensitive information, in my judgment, it's best for the ongoing war against terror that the investigation be done in the intelligence committees." Warren Rudman of the Hart/Rudman US Commission on National Security in the 21st Century summed up the White House's reasons for opposing the independent commission in one word: control. "The White House feels it can control a Congressional committee better than it can an investigative commission and the senators [McCain, Lieberman, and their allies] are afraid that may be the case" (Rosenbaum 2002).

A number of Republican allies in Congress swiftly came to the president's defense. Dismissing the need for an independent commission, they accused Democrats of jeopardizing national security and undermining the war on terror for their own political gain. The majority whip Tom DeLay (R-TX) claimed that a public report on the deficiencies of the nation's homeland security would endanger the country, insisting that "our work should prevent another terrorist attack and not make Osama bin Laden's job easier." DeLay vehemently opposed the commission's creation, suggesting the Democrats' course of action "during a time of war is ill conceived and frankly irresponsible... We will not allow our president to be undermined by those who want his job" (Mitchell 2002*d*). Representative Jennifer Dunn (R-WA) also chastised Democrats for "politicizing [the attacks]... a very, very low-level, underhanded use of a terrible incident" (Sanger and Bumiller 2002).

While the debate raged across both sides of the aisle, on 21 May, majority leader Tom Daschle announced his intention to sponsor new legislation creating an independent commission. Amid reports that the ongoing Intelligence Committees investigation was encountering difficulties obtaining information from key intelligence agencies and personnel, Daschle promptly shifted his support to the Lieberman–McCain cause. "At the very least," he said, "we ought to have a good debate about whether or not it's important to do this. Let those who oppose this idea come forth and explain themselves" (Mitchell 2002*d*).

Supporters of the commission sought to build momentum for their proposals over the course of the summer and enlisted a powerful ally in their cause to mobilize public opinion: families of September 11 victims. In early June, these families held a rally with a few lawmakers on the steps of the Capitol to support the creation of an independent commission. At the rally, Senator Joe Lieberman chided, "the reasons that they [administration officials] give [for opposing the creation] are without consequence and, in some cases, they're foolish." Senator Torricelli exhorted supporters, "there will be a national commission. It may be this week, it may be next month, it may be next year, it may be 10 years—but history is a demanding master. History will demand an answer, and we want that answer now" (Vasquez 2002).

Ironically, perhaps, it was the Intelligence Committee hearings' obvious defects that would generate the political pressure needed to force the administration to give ground. Just as soon as the inquiry began, lawmakers on both sides of the aisle began to decry the administration's stonewalling. "Are we getting the cooperation we need? Absolutely not," said Senator Richard Shelby (R-AL), the ranking Republican on the Senate Intelligence Committee. Senate Intelligence Committee chair Graham echoed Shelby's lament: "What we're trying to do is get people who had hands on these issues.... And what we're being told is, no, they don't want to make those kind of witnesses available." Frustrated by the administration's refusal to cooperate, both lawmakers endorsed an independent commission to expand upon the joint investigation. Shelby sent a clear warning to the White House that "there may come a day very soon when it will become apparent that ours must be only a prelude to further inquiries" (Milbank 2002b).

In the committee room, after the joint inquiry heard from a number of government officials, Kristen Breitweiser, whose husband perished in the World Trade Center and who was now co-chair of the September 11th Advocates group, took the stand and delivered a politically fatal blow to the president's efforts to ward off an independent investigation. Noting the widespread failure at all levels of government to anticipate and respond to the attacks, Breitweiser emotionally and cogently appealed for an independent and more wide-ranging investigation. "It goes without saying," Breitweiser argued, "that the examination of the intelligence agencies by this Committee does not detract, discount or dismantle the need for a more thorough examination of all of these other culpable parties." To supplement the Intelligence Committees' inquiry, Breitweiser urged Congress to create an independent commission as provided for in the Lieberman–McCain and Daschle initiatives: "An independent blue-ribbon panel would be the most appropriate means to achieve such a thorough and expansive examination, in large part, because it would not be limited in scope or hindered by time limits. An independent blue-ribbon panel would provide a comprehensive, unbiased and definitive report that the devastation of September 11th demands." Finally, Breitweiser curtly rejected the administration's contentions that such an inquiry was inappropriate and even counterproductive in the current political and strategic climate:

Soon after the attacks, President Bush stated that there would come a time to look back and examine our nation's failures, but that such an undertaking was inappropriate while the nation was still in shock. I would respectfully suggest to President Bush and to our Congress that now, a full year later, it is time to look back and investigate our failures as a nation. A hallmark of democratic government is a willingness to admit to, analyze and learn from mistakes. And, it is now time for our nation to triumph as the great democracy that it is. The families of the victims of September 11th have waited long enough. We need to have answers. We need to have accountability. We need to feel safe living and working in this great nation. (Breitweiser 2002)[12]

Two days later, the administration orchestrated a complete about-face and called for the establishment of an independent commission to investigate the attacks, a commission it had consistently opposed throughout the previous year. In a letter to Speaker Hastert, the president's legislative liaison Nicholas Calio audaciously expressed concern that the Intelligence Committee investigations "did not address the panoply of other important and related issues as they may relate to September 11," and announced that the White House now strongly supported "a focused inquiry into these matters [that] will help strengthen our ability to prevent and defend against terrorism and protect the security of the American public" (CNN 2002).

In the aftermath of the president's reversal, key congressional Democrats jumped on the opportunity to score political points. Minority leader Richard Gephardt (D-MO) emphasized the administration's stubborn refusal to endorse the commission for the past year. "I am encouraged that the White House today ended its opposition to an independent commission to investigate all aspects of the September 11th terror attacks. As I have been saying for months, we need a commission that can build on the good work of the congressional intelligence committees' joint inquiry, and help us all understand what happened, why it happened, so we can dramatically strengthen all aspects of our nation's homeland defenses." Similarly, an aide to Senator Joseph Lieberman, who introduced legislation calling for the commission in December of 2001, noted "we appreciate the White House switching its position," adding that it had taken ten months of prodding by members of Congress (Firestone and Risen 2002).

The White House, however, argued that any new commission should not re-examine intelligence failings before September 11, as this was the focus of the joint Intelligence Committee inquiry. Ignoring the administration's concerns, the Senate by a 90 : 8 vote inserted an amendment into the Homeland Security Bill establishing an independent commission charged with investigating the lead-up and response to September 11 at all levels, including intelligence. The administration made its last stand by lobbying House Republicans to oppose similar language in the House version, and many privately withdrew their support for the commission. Indiana Democrat Tim Roemer feared that "the White House may try to run the clock out as we near the end of the session and might not be as supportive of this concept as they have indicated" (Dewar 2002a). Minority whip Nancy Pelosi (D-CA) charged that while "the White House is professing openly to support an independent commission . . . privately they're moving to thwart the commission." Yet, both Lieberman and McCain vowed to fight on, even if they had to continue the battle in the next legislative session. "It's going to happen," declared a resolute John McCain (Dewar 2002b).

Again, despite continued White House objections, the administration gradually abandoned its opposition to, and even openly supported, the commission's creation and its authority to investigate all aspects, including intelligence failures, of the September 11 attacks. On 27 November 2002, more than 11 months after calls for an independent investigation into the terrorist attacks of September 11, 2001, President Bush signed H.R. 4628, the Intelligence Authorization Act. This bill created the National Commission on

Terrorist Attacks upon the United States, an organization comprised of ten members, five Democrats and five Republicans. The commission's chair was to be appointed by the president, and the assent of six members would be required to issue a subpoena.[13] The resulting legislation was a political victory for McCain and Lieberman, and for the 9/11 families who so forcefully advocated its passage. Stephen Push, the treasurer of the lobbying group Families of September 11, explained that the new commission met their most important criteria: "We're not crazy about the president appointing the chairman," Push said, "but our greatest concern was the subpoena power" (Firestone 2002). In almost every aspect, the president had caved in to congressional and public pressure.

On the day Bush signed H.R. 4628, White House spokesperson Scott McClellan (2002) praised the creation of the 9/11 Commission and the Department of Homeland Security as "two of our highest priorities." The administration's rhetorical tactics to co-opt the popular initiatives for political gain, however, should not obscure the fact that these new-found "priorities" came about through congressional pressure. Moreover, the administration's acquiescence would ultimately come at a political cost, as the 9/11 Commission provided political ammunition to the administration's enemies in the 2004 election cycle. From the revelation that the administration had not acted on an August Presidential Daily Briefing titled "Bin Laden determined to Attack Inside the United States," to the Commission's disavowal of the administration's implied linkages between the events of September 11 and Iraq, the Commission provided plenty of fodder to presidential critics. Though the Commission's final report placed much of the blame at the feet of the FBI and CIA, with chairman Kean saying neither Presidents Clinton nor Bush had been "served properly by the intelligence agencies of this country," none of the embarrassing details about both administrations' failings would have ever been unearthed had the president possessed sole power to determine the composition and scope of the inquiry into terrorist attacks.

The Dubai Ports Deal

In the three preceding cases, the president asserted his ability to remake politics unilaterally with varying effect. Even when the president most visibly gave ground, as in the debate over the creation of the Department of Homeland Security or the independent 9/11 Commission, Bush succeeded in muting some of the most objectionable aspects of congressional proposals and even attempted to turn his acquiescence to congressional demands to his own political advantage. Though these successes reflect the president's inherent institutional advantages *vis-à-vis* the legislature, the administration's failed efforts to authorize DP World's acquisition of operations at several major US seaports—a defeat shocking both for its rapidity and totality—reminds us that during times of war presidents are not always guaranteed even partial victories.

With little fanfare outside the nation's business pages, on 10 February 2006, Dubai-owned DP World successfully outbid other competitors in a battle to control Peninsular & Oriental Steam Navigation, a British company that had operated terminals at several American ports (Timmons 2006). Prior to the sale, the Treasury Department's Committee on Foreign Investments in the United States (CFIUS), comprised of representatives from 11 executive departments and agencies, held a routine 23-day inquiry into the deal's implications for American national security. In the body's only official meeting on the merger, the committee routinely approved of DP World's acquisition.

On the very day the deal was announced, New York Senator Charles Schumer warily discussed the national security implications of the deal and urged the administration to reconsider its support. Emphasizing the critical economic importance of the nation's maritime infrastructure, Schumer warned "just as we would not outsource military operations or law enforcement duties, we should be very careful before we outsource such sensitive homeland security duties" (Bridis 2006). But Schumer's admonition was only the calm before the storm. A week later a political maelstrom erupted within Congress when Schumer, joined by fellow Democrats Hillary Clinton (NY) and Robert Menendez (NJ) announced their intention to introduce legislation preventing the sale of US port operations to companies owned by foreign governments. As Menendez explained, "I just don't believe that our ports should be handed over to foreign governments," especially to the United Arab Emirates, with its "serious and dubious history" of terrorist activity (McGeehan 2006). Raising the specter of Dubai's connection with September 11, Menendez cited reports that two of the hijackers were from the United Arab Emirates, and that money used in the attacks had flowed through banks there.

Vocal objections to the deal raised by a number of key Republicans, particularly those representing constituencies directly affected by the pending merger, troubled the administration even more. New York Representative Peter T. King, chair of the House Homeland Security Committee, and Vito Fossella were early critics of the deal (McGeehan 2006), as was Florida Congressman Mark Foley who insisted that "the potential threat to our country is not imagined, it is real" (Magnet 2006). Stalwart Bush supporter Tom Coburn (R-OK) echoed Foley's sentiment: "Handing the keys to US strategic ports to a regime that recognized the Taliban is not a sound next step in our war against terror" (Blustein 2006a).

A few Republicans publicly supported the president and the administration's decision to allow the deal to proceed. Senator John Warner of Virginia, for example, worried that opposition to the deal would jeopardize America's relationship with Dubai; citing America's interests in the Middle East, he urged his fellow legislators to "move carefully in considering the implications of what we do." Republican leaders in both chambers of Congress, however, quickly abandoned the president. Both House Speaker Dennis Hastert (R-IL) and Senate majority leader Bill Frist (R-TN) publicly criticized the deal and called for an extended 45-day period to assess the threat that the deal posed to national security. Frist even warned the White House that if it failed to order the review on its own initiative, he would "plan on introducing legislation to ensure that the deal is placed on hold until this decision gets a more thorough review" (Sanger and Lipton 2006).

DP World's acquisition of operations at American ports hardly ranked among the most important elements of the administration's programmatic priorities. In the days following the announcement, White House Press Secretary Scott McClellan revealed that Bush himself was unaware of the merger until after CFIUS had approved it. Treasury Secretary John Snow was similarly out of the loop, telling reporters "I learned of this transaction probably the same way as members of the Senate did, by reading it in the newspapers" (VandeHei and Weisman 2006). Precisely because the White House was not heavily invested in the decision, Bush could have easily reversed course, mollified critics on both sides of the aisle within Congress, and avoided a potentially damaging political battle.

The administration, however, refused to abide congressional objections. Treasury Secretary John Snow publicly emphasized Dubai's role as a strong ally in the Middle East and war on terror, and Secretary of State Condoleezza Rice declared Dubai "a very good friend" of the United States that should not be alienated (McGeehan 2006). Bush then escalated the stakes of a showdown with Congress by publicly threatening to veto any legislation that would interfere with the port deal. If carried out, it would be the first veto of his presidency. With a flair for the dramatic, Bush summoned reporters to the front of Air Force One for a press conference at which he proclaimed his continued support for the deal. Reasserting his toughness on issues of national security, the president dismissed the congressional concerns as unfounded: "And so, look, I can understand why some in Congress have raised questions about whether or not our country will be less secure as a result of this transaction. But they need to know that our government has looked at this issue and looked at it carefully. Again, I repeat, if there was any question as to whether or not this country would be less safe as a result of the transaction, it wouldn't go forward." Echoing concerns previously voiced by Warner, Snow, and Rice, Bush closed by emphasizing that "this is a company that has played by the rules, that has been cooperative with the United States, a country that's an ally in the war on terror, and it would send a terrible signal to friends and allies not to let this transaction go through" (Office of the Press Secretary 2006).

At the administration's request, on 24 February DP World reaffirmed its commitment to close the deal, but also announced that it would delay any "exercise of control" over the port terminals it sought to acquire. The administration hoped that the move would give it enough time to win over skeptics in Congress. Senior presidential political adviser Karl Rove summarized the administration's strategy: "Our interest is in making certain the members of Congress have full information about it, and that, we're convinced, will give them a level of comfort with this" (Hulse and Shane 2006).

Despite the administration's efforts to reassure the nation, Congress and the public remained unconvinced. Two polls conducted in the waning days of February showed that between 59 and 69 percent of Americans opposed the deal (see *Los Angeles Times Poll*, 25 February–1 March 2006; *Fox News Poll*, 28 February–1 March 2006). Feeling the heat from their constituents, even more members of Congress, particularly on the Republican side of the aisle, ceased straddling the fence and openly broke with the White House. As his job approval numbers slid even further, from 42 percent in January to just 34 percent by 26 February, the president's calls for party loyalty yielded few dividends. Florida's Mark Foley lamented: "We've defended [the administration] on wiretaps, we've defended them on Iraq, we've defended them on so many things [Bush has] tried to accomplish, that to be left out here supporting this thing in a vacuum is kind of offensive" (Stolberg 2006). Even in conservative southern states, the political pressures to abandon the president were steep. According to Republican Governor Mike Huckabee of Arkansas, the deal "put a lot of elected officials in an impossible position . . . The visceral reaction they got from their constituents left them no choice in opposing it" (Sanger 2006a). Perhaps the most blunt attack on the administration's decision came from staunch North Carolina conservative Sue Myrick whose one-line letter to Bush ran: "Dear Mr. President: In regards to selling American ports to the United Arab Emirates, not just NO but HELL NO!" (VandeHei and Weisman 2006).

Seeking still more time to convince Congress on the merits of the deal and to allow passions to subside, the administration on 27 February persuaded DP World to request a formal 45-day review of the sale as authorized by US law. The review would include background checks on port employees, inspections at the ports, and an examination of the UAE's efforts to fight terrorism (Hulse and Shane 2006). DP World also made further concessions by announcing that the company would attempt to "segregate" its US operations from its other global interests (Sanger 2006b). Despite the virulent domestic political criticism, on 28 February Bush reaffirmed his decision to approve the acquisition, urging "lawmakers and the public to withhold judgment" until the new review was completed (Hulse 2006a).

The extended review did help the administration, as a few former critics, most importantly majority leader Frist, now announced that they were "satisfied" that the deal did not pose serious security risks (Sanger 2006b). But other Republicans such as King, Foley, Hastert, and Coburn remained opposed, and Democrats refused to give any ground. Indeed, critics of the deal began articulating altogether new concerns, citing DP World's agreement to an Arab boycott of Israel and the US Coast Guard's apprehensions about farming out port operations to a foreign government-owned company (Hulse 2006a). The continued congressional opposition took more concrete form in two measures introduced on 27 and 28 February. With Joint Resolutions in both the House and Senate (SJ Res 32 and HJ Res 79), Susan Collins (R-ME) and Jane Harman (D-CA) directed CFIUS to provide more information to Congress before the sale could become final. Senator Byron Dorgan (D-ND) went further by introducing S. 2341, which would explicitly prohibit DP World from acquiring control of port operations within the United States.

Even as the administration escalated its lobbying effort—a front on which it was so active that Congressman Peter King chided that Bush "was viewing the 45 days more as a chance to lobby Congress than to investigate security concerns"—the ranks of vocal opponents in Congress, even among Republicans, steadily grew (Hulse 2006a). Senators John Kyl (R-AZ) and Jeff Sessions (R-AL) publicly criticized the administration over the deal. Again, pressure from constituents fueled the objections. Sessions acknowledged, "I traveled my state last week, and I got it at every stop from people...The average citizen believes that maintaining American control of our ports is important" (Hulse and Shane 2006). The barrage of criticism of the DP World acquisition both within Congress and over the air waves only further eroded support for the deal. A new poll conducted from 2 to 5 March revealed that only 15 percent of Americans supported the deal (see ABC News/Washington Post poll, 2–5 March 2006). Though sources within Congress acknowledged that many legislators "concede[d] that the White House and its Congressional allies [could] make a persuasive argument for the arrangement," the adamant refusal of a number of core critics, coupled with intensifying public opposition to the proposal, made a showdown with the White House all but inevitable (Hulse and Shane 2006).

On 7 March, less than a month after DP World's acquisition of American port operations became public, the Republican leadership in Congress announced that they would immediately move ahead with efforts to scuttle the deal, without even waiting for the results of the 45-day investigation. House Appropriations Committee chair Jerry Lewis (R-CA) unveiled his intention during the committee's next session to add a provision to a critical defense appropriations bill that would prevent the deal from going forward. Speaker Hastert endorsed the move, as did other prominent members of the Republican House leadership.

The president continued to insist "my position hasn't changed" and maintained his threat to veto any legislation that would block the deal (Lipton and Sanger 2006). The congressional leadership, however, moved to counter that threat by adding its amendment to kill the acquisition to H.R. 4939, a

supplemental appropriations bill providing needed funds for military operations in Afghanistan and Iraq, as well as for victims of Hurricane Katrina.
Chair Lewis's measure passed the committee by an overwhelming 62:2 vote
on 8 March. Despite explicit warnings from congressional leaders that they
had the votes needed to override any presidential veto, the administration, at least publicly, continued to stand behind its decision to approve
the sale. Administration spokesmen insisted that the White House "would
continue to work with Congress to try to resolve the matter, giving the
company, DP World, the right to operate some shipping terminals" (Hulse
2006b).

Ultimately, the administration was spared the embarrassment of a direct
defeat in Congress as DP World abandoned its efforts to assume control of
the port terminals and agreed to sell its US operations to an American-owned
firm. Senator John Warner broke the news on the chamber floor two hours
before a scheduled vote on a motion to move forward with a Democratic bill
to block the sale (Kirkpatrick 2006). Though there is no direct evidence that
DP World did so at the White House's behest, officials involved in negotiations
suggested that the administration had "prodded" DP World to give up on the
planned deal. A senior official in Dubai acknowledged: "A political decision
was taken to ask DP World to try and defuse the situation. We have to help
our friends" (Sanger 2006c).

On 15 March, DP World issued a written statement that it would sell its US
holdings to an "unrelated American buyer" within six months. A spokesman
for P&O Steam Navigation, the British company that had been acquired by DP
World, said, "I cannot emphasize enough that this will be an American buyer"
(Blustein 2006b). As of this writing, a deal has not been completed, but the
company's statement confirmed that until US terminal operations were sold to
an American buyer, they would be operated separately from DP World's other
operations, under an agreement that the Dubai company had reached with
the Bush Administration. While some legislators had reacted with suspicion
to the vague language of DP World's original 9 March announcement, the new
statement placated even the most vociferous critics.

Ultimately, both the breadth of bipartisan and public opposition to the
administration's position and the president's tactical refusal to give sufficient
ground led to the demise of the DP World Ports deal. In the wiretapping
case, the administration had managed to overcome virtually unanimous
opposition among congressional Democrats and considerable concern within
Republican ranks by reframing the debate over Americans' constitutional
rights and civil liberties in terms of effectively fighting the war on terror.
In the Dubai context, however, congressional opponents overwhelmed the
president's vigorous assurances that he had looked into the matter and would
never have approved the acquisition if it would jeopardize national security.
Indeed, public support for the Dubai deal actually declined over time with

disapproval of the sale, peaking at over 80 percent in some polls. Refusing to make even modest concessions to members of his own party standing for re-election in the fall, the president completely alienated those who had stood by his side in previous crises. New York Republican Peter King spoke for many when he said that lawmakers were no longer willing to "take a lot of tough votes and...not get much in return." South Carolina Republican Lindsay Graham, who had previously objected to the administration's assertions of unbridled executive power in the wiretapping debate, suggested that the Dubai deal struck a deeper chord resonating with many members' concern with the aggrandizement of presidential power. "What you see here," Graham explained, are "people within the president's party pushing back against the administration's view of executive power" (Hulse 2006c). The constellation of public and political interests allied against the president's policies, combined with the administration's intransigence in the face of opposition, defeated the White House's policy.

Assessing Congressional Influence

When gauging the robustness of congressional constraints on presidential unilateral action, we cannot simply tally the number of times that Congress formally overturns an executive action and legislatively restores the status quo. As the preceding four cases make clear, when formulating their policies presidents often anticipate the likely reaction of Congress and adjust their chosen course, making formal congressional votes no longer necessary to induce a policy change. In stark contrast to its previous claims about executive independence, the administration gradually acknowledged the need for congressional oversight of the NSA wiretapping program in order to placate congressional opposition. Moreover, when lingering questions about the program threatened the confirmation of the president's choice for CIA director, the administration abruptly announced its intention to expand congressional briefings, a move it had heretofore flatly rejected, and promised further concessions. Similarly, in the immediate wake of September 11 Bush vehemently opposed the creation of both a Department of Homeland Security and an independent commission to investigate the government's preparation for and response to the attacks. But facing sustained congressional insistence, the administration ultimately executed an about-face and embraced both initiatives. Finally, in the only case in which Bush did not bend, his policy broke completely as congressional and public outcry forced the administration to abandon its approval of Dubai World's acquisition of operations at several major US ports.

These short case studies illustrate Congress's capacity to influence presidential behavior even absent enacting legislation compelling a change in course. Moreover, they suggest an alternative mechanism through which members of

Congress affect the president's strategic calculus: by priming and informing public opinion and raising the political costs to the president of defending his preferred policy. The next section takes this suggestion seriously and moves beyond case studies in order to test more systematically its central implications. More specifically, we employ an experimental research design to probe the capacity of Congress and other political elites to influence the public's foreign policy preferences, in this instance regarding the withdrawal of American troops from Iraq.

Rallying Public Opinion

When checking the president's unilateral powers, members of Congress are most effective when they unite around a common cause and stand ready to reverse his actions. Nothing signals defeat quite like a newly enacted law that guts a presidential initiative. The trouble, of course, is that Congress rarely has the votes required to override a presidential veto; and hence Congress's institutional capacity to constrain the president's unilateral powers would appear substantially diminished.

Fortunately, as the preceding case studies make plain, members of Congress sometimes can influence presidential decision making even when they lack the votes either to amend or overturn his orders. Through hearings, speeches, and media appearances, members of Congress, even those within the minority party, can sway public opinion and thereby raise the political costs of either advancing a new presidential action or defending an old one. By engaging the public, members of Congress can occasionally realize a measure of influence over the White House that they otherwise could only achieve through the more cumbersome legislative process. This section more systematically examines how this happens. With new experimental data, we assess the various ways in which congressional position-taking shapes the public's willingness to support the Iraq War. So doing, we pay special attention not only to the overall effectiveness of Congress as an institution in checking presidential power, but also to the ways in which appeals made by different kinds of political elite (defined by their institutional affiliation and/or partisanship) resonate with different kinds of citizens.

A Very Brief Literature Review on Political Elites and Public Opinion on War

It is a well-established truism in political science that most Americans lack even rudimentary political information (Campbell et al. 1960; Converse 1964), particularly in foreign affairs (Almond 1950; Light and Lake 1985; but see Aldrich, Sullivan, and Borgida 1989). Because experience alone cannot serve as a guide, average citizens appear especially reliant upon political elites to formulate their foreign policy opinions (Jordan and Page 1992; Zaller 1994a).[14] In the absence of criticism by other political elites, the public typically rallies behind the president. Conversely, when political actors come out and criticize the president, the public expresses less support for a presidential initiative (Brody 1991; Zaller 1992, 1994a, b). And on matters involving war, most especially, the public goes wherever political elites take them.

This literature, to be sure, aptly describes the general relationship between the public and political elites on foreign policy issues. From our vantage point, however, the literature does not adequately differentiate the various publics and political elites who contribute to contemporary debates about the presidential use of force. If only implicitly, this literature assumes that all arguments have equal weight in shaping public opinion, and that the overall balance of elite discourse best predicts popular reactions to a proposed military venture. It is not at all clear, though, that average citizens give equal credence to all political elites who participate in public debates concerning war. At least since Hovland and Weiss (1951) and Asch (1987 (1952)), scholars have understood the basic principle that the identity of the actor making a specific argument has great importance for its interpretation (Lupia and McCubbins 1998; Sniderman, Brody, and Tetlock 1991).[15]

Two kinds of signal from political elites are likely to be especially informative. The first we label "trusted" signals. Because citizens are especially responsive to cues offered by political elites with whom they most closely align (Druckman 2001a, b), and because they tend to view their co-partisans as more trusted sources of political information than their partisan opponents (Groeling 2001), Republican citizens may find little need to update their opinion of Bush when Democratic members of Congress criticize him; similarly, Democratic citizens may not change their opinion of Bush in light of Republican speeches supporting the president. Signals are also likely to prove influential if deemed "costly." Scholars have long argued that citizens can distinguish costly and cheap talk, and that they naturally place more weight on the former than the latter (Spence 1973). If true, then both Democratic and Republican citizens ought to change their views about the president's foreign policies when either prominent Republicans come out and oppose them or Democrats come out and support them.

For the most part, though, the existing literature on war and public opinion pays scant attention to the persuasive appeal of trusted and costly signals. Though a number of scholars have examined the president's efforts to drum up public support for war (Holsti 1996; Mueller 1973; Sobel 2001), none have systematically tracked the capacity of different individuals and organizations to check the president's claims; none, that is, have shown whether opposition to or support for the president that is articulated by different kinds of political elites factor into the public's evaluation of an ongoing war.

For a variety of reasons, the oversight is readily understandable. It is extraordinarily difficult to tease out from survey data and even the most careful documentations of political speeches and hearings whether the public is following elected officials, or whether elected officials are following the public. Moreover, from survey evidence alone, it is virtually impossible to determine from whom, if anyone, the public is taking its cues—be they members of Congress, interest groups, international organizations, or whomever else. Given the empirical challenges of characterizing the relationship between political elites and the public writ large, it is little wonder that scholars have not managed to use observational data to identify the various relations between different public constituencies and political elites. Indeed, without employing an experimental framework, one wherein subjects are selectively exposed to different kinds of arguments advanced by different types of political elites, trying to distinguish the causal effect of Republican or Democratic members of Congress on Republican or Democratic citizens' foreign policy views is virtually impossible.

Two teams of scholars, however, have recently accepted the challenge. Using a series of Gallup surveys from World War II, Adam Berinsky (2005) demonstrates that during periods of partisan conflict in foreign policy, opponents and supporters of the president split on the war as their levels of political information increased, with each group taking its cues from the political elites of their affiliated party. Conversely, when elites of both parties spoke with one voice, mass opinion on US policy also converged. Matthew Baum and Timothy Groeling (2004) test a more nuanced theory of how a congressperson's party identification moderates the influence that her support for (or opposition to) the president has on his public approval ratings. From content analyses of ABC news broadcasts and Gallup polls, Baum and Groeling confirm Berinsky's finding that partisan identifiers take their cues primarily from elites of their own party. They also show that more credible evaluations of a president's actions—criticisms from members of his own party and support from the opposition—have a greater impact on popular judgments of the president than do other elite arguments appearing in the national media.

In three respects, we build on the foundations that Baum, Berinsky, and Groeling have erected. First, we expand the scope of inquiry by examining how the same argument's influence on public opinion varies when it is made by different political actors who frequently appear in the media. Second, by shifting the level of analysis from the aggregate to the individual level, we explore how source identity effects are moderated by the partisan attachments of each respondent.[16] Finally, and perhaps more importantly, we introduce an experimental design that alleviates concerns about identification and endogeneity, which regularly plague observational studies that correlate the actions of political elites with the opinions of average citizens.

A Simple Experiment

In coordination with Time-Sharing Experiments for the Social Sciences and Knowledge Networks, an online polling firm, in the spring of 2006 we conducted a simple experiment designed to gauge the relative influence of political elites on the public's willingness to back the president's preferred policy on the Iraq War. With a nationally representative sample of 1,617 adults,[17] we randomly assigned individuals to one of nine (one baseline, eight treatment) conditions that presented various vignettes about the positions of different members of Congress, the United Nations, and international aid organizations on the Iraq War. We then asked the respondents whether they supported the president's preferred policy. Given random assignment, differences in the levels of support for the president's position that are observed across the various conditions can reliably be attributed to the treatments applied.

Subjects assigned to the baseline condition were told the following: "According to President Bush, considerable progress is being made toward building a stable, democratic government in Iraq. President Bush opposes setting a fixed timetable for withdrawal of American troops from Iraq." Subjects then were asked whether they "strongly agreed," "agreed," "somewhat agreed," "neither agreed nor disagreed," "somewhat disagreed," "disagreed," or "strongly disagreed" with the following statement: "The US government should not set a fixed timetable for the withdrawal of troops from Iraq." Agreement, as such, connotes support for Bush's policy, and disagreement connotes opposition.

For each of the treatment conditions, subjects read exactly the same text on Bush and were asked exactly the same question. After learning Bush's position, however, subjects were told that either "many Democrats within Congress," "many Republicans within Congress," "many members of the United Nations," or "many international aid organizations" either agreed or disagreed with the president's claims, and that these individuals or groups either supported or opposed setting a fixed timetable for the withdrawal of troops. The four groups and two positions generate the eight treatment conditions ($4 \times 2 = 8$) that complete the experiment.

Several features about this experiment deserve notice, each of which suggests that whatever differences we observe across the various experimental conditions are likely to represent a lower-bound on the actual influence that different political elites wield on public support for a presidential use of force. First, in order to recognize the president's privileged stature in public debates about war, Bush's position is always listed first. Second, the experiment focuses on an issue that has already received extensive public attention, and about which respondents are already likely to have formulated an opinion. Unlike prospective military ventures (e.g. Iran) or smaller past ones (e.g. Liberia), the Iraq War had dominated public debate for fully three years by the time this experiment was conducted. Third, the "treatment" itself is quite modest. Respondents only receive the president's view of the situation in Iraq—namely, that considerable progress is being made. When the treatment conditions introduce the positions of other political elites, they offer no new information or competing characterizations of conditions on the ground. Hence, rather than being given a long list of reasons either to support or oppose a fixed timetable for the withdrawal of troops, respondents are merely informed that certain individuals in certain organizations support or oppose the president. As a result, we do not present any competition among elites over the framing of the situation in the field or the nature of the policy choices available; in this experimental context, the only way other elites can influence public opinion is by simply expressing their support for or opposition to the president's position.

Findings

Table 4.1 presents the main results. Each of the figures represents respondents' average levels of support for the president's position.[18] Possible responses ranged from 1 to 7, with higher values representing greater support for the president's position, lower values representing less support. As one might expect, Republicans (column 1) and Democrats (column 2) differ markedly from one another. In the baseline condition (row 1), the mean Republican

Table 4.1. Support for president across experimental conditions

	Republicans	Democrats	All respondents
Control condition	5.01	2.92	3.73
Treatment conditions that present *opposition to* the president from:			
Republican members of Congress	4.91#	2.71	3.74
Democratic members of Congress	5.79*	2.97	4.18*
United Nations	4.81#	2.94#	3.82
International aid organizations	4.86#	2.76#	3.64#
Treatment conditions that present *support for* the president from:			
Republican members of Congress	5.59#*	2.99	3.69
Democratic members of Congress	5.77*	2.98	4.16*
United Nations	5.91#*	3.45#*	4.03*
International aid organizations	5.38#	3.16#	4.16#*
(N)	41–62	47–64	166–90

Notes: Table presents weighted, mean results on 7-point scale, where 1 represents strong disagreement with the president's position on Iraq and 7 represents strong agreement.

* denotes differences with the control condition that are statistically significant at p < .10 on a one-tailed test.

# denotes differences with the corresponding opposite condition that are statistically significant at p < .10 on a one-tailed test.

response was "somewhat agree" (5.01 on the 1–7 scale), as compared to "somewhat disagree" (2.92) for Democrats. This difference is both substantively and statistically significant.

The most important findings concern the differences observed across experimental conditions. Here, we highlight two sorts of comparisons. First, we contrast respondents' support for the president when they are exposed to only his position (row 1) with their support when also exposed to other views (rows 2–9). Such comparisons that are statistically significant are denoted with an asterisk (∗). Second, we compare respondents' support for the president when they are told that different political elites *oppose* him (rows 2, 3, 4, and 5) with their support when told that the same political elites *support* him (rows 6, 7, 8, and 9, respectively). In this instance, statistically significant differences are denoted with a no. sign (#). We summarize the main findings associated with each comparison in turn.

COMPARISON 1: TREATMENT VERSUS BASELINE CONDITIONS

When told that members of Congress, the United Nations, or international aid organizations supported the president, Republican and Democratic respondents consistently offered higher levels of support for Bush than when they were told only the president's position. In every instance, the values in rows 5–9 are higher than those in row 1. In three of four instances for Republicans, and one in four instances for Democrats, the differences are statistically significant.

For the most part, meanwhile, opposition to the president also had the expected effect on respondents' views about withdrawing from Iraq. Momentarily putting aside those cues coming from Democratic members of Congress (row 3), we find that almost every value in rows 2, 4, and 5 is smaller than those observed in the baseline condition. Though none of these differences as presented are statistically significant, when using unweighted data, the responses of Democrats exposed to opposition from Republican members of Congress (row 2, column 2) is statistically significantly different from the baseline condition. Moreover, the sheer consistency of these findings suggests that opposition from political elites may depress, if only moderately, the support of both Republican and Democratic respondents.

The clear exception to this pattern of results is row 3. It is not altogether surprising that opposition from Democratic members of Congress did not affect the views of Democratic respondents. Given the widespread disaffection with the Iraq War among Democrats, combined with the fact that at the time of the experiment most Democratic members of Congress were openly criticizing the president, the mere exposure to Democratic opposition offered little additional information above and beyond the baseline condition. The significant and positive effect for Republican responses, however, hardly comports with our theoretical expectations. Among Republican respondents, support for the president actually *increased* when they were told that Democratic members of Congress opposed the president. It is possible that when told that Democrats oppose the president, and thus given two cues rather than one, Republicans were better able to discern their preferred position. Additionally, the perceived stridency of Democratic dissent that received such prominent media coverage at the time of this experiment also may have contributed to Republicans' reticence to support any policy endorsed by the opposition party. Whatever the explanation, though, these findings suggest that opposition voiced by some political elites occasionally can be counterproductive, at least when directed at partisan opponents within the public.

COMPARISON 2: DIFFERENCES ACROSS TREATMENT CONDITIONS

Given that most political speech is contested, that no single actor monopolizes public debate about any policy agenda, the second comparison—between respondents receiving the same group's cues supporting and opposing the president's policies—is especially instructive. Members of Congress, the United Nations, and international aid organizations regularly participate in public discussion regarding war. Does it matter, then, what they say? The findings presented here overwhelmingly suggest that it does. Again and again, Democrats and Republicans alike expressed higher levels of support for the president when told that other political actors supported the president (rows 6, 7, 8, and 9) than when told that these same actors opposed the president (rows 2, 3, 4, and 5, respectively); and in three of four instances for Republicans, and two of four for Democrats, the differences are statistically significant.

Republicans appeared especially susceptible to appeals made by members of their own party within Congress and by the United Nations. Told that these two groups supported the president, Republicans were 0.68 and 0.90 points (or 0.36 and 0.48 standard deviations) more likely to support him than when they were told that these respective groups opposed him. Democrats, meanwhile, took special notice of the positions assumed by international aid organizations and the United Nations. For these two respective groups, differences of 0.40 and 0.51 points (or 0.21 and 0.27 standard deviations) were observed across the experimental conditions.

KEY LESSONS

Two aspects of these findings deserve special notice. First, the views of Republicans tended to be more pliable than those of Democrats.[19] Three years into the war, most Democrats may have made up their minds about the efficacy of staying the course, such that the mere presentation of supporting or opposing positions by other political elites only marginally affected their propensity to support the president. Still, Democrats were not entirely impervious to

129

influence. Differences between Democrats receiving supporting and opposing group cues are statistically significant for both the United Nations and international aid treatments; and in the former instance, differences between the supporting treatment and baseline conditions were also statistically significant. And consistent with theoretical expectations, Democrats receiving the "credible" signal of elite Republican opposition to the White House expressed lower, albeit not statistically significantly different, mean levels of support for the president than did either Democrats assigned to the baseline condition or those assigned to the mirror treatment condition in which subjects received supporting Republican cues.[20]

Second, both Democratic and Republican respondents tended to update their views on Iraq to a greater extent when told about the positions of the United Nations or international aid organizations than when told about those of either political party within Congress. This result may be due to the fact that the public already possessed considerable information on both parties' positions on Iraq, but comparatively little information about the positions of the United Nations or aid organizations.[21] In similar experiments we report elsewhere (see Howell and Kriner forthcoming), we asked respondents whether they would support or oppose military action against nations accused by the administration of harboring terrorists and of committing human rights abuses. In these hypothetical scenarios, the effects associated with Republican and Democratic congressional cues appeared larger than those associated with the United Nations or international aid organizations.

No single experiment, of course, can establish once and for all how public appeals made by members of Congress affect the content of public opinion. Much depends upon the wording of the questions asked, the amount of information that subjects are afforded, their prior views of the president, and the specific features of the military deployment itself. And in any experiment, particularly one with relatively modest sample sizes, responses observed across treatment conditions may vary at least in part for idiosyncratic reasons. Hence, before rushing to Capitol Hill to inform Democratic members that all their efforts to persuade Republican citizens are in vain, we strongly recommend the replication and extension of this research.

Nonetheless, the brief experiment examined here suggests a valuable lesson about the politics of unilateral action: should its members wish to challenge a president intent on either advancing or defending a controversial public policy, even one that strictly involves the use of military force, Congress is not completely at a loss if it cannot build the coalitions required to enact new laws that amend or overturn the president—something remarkably difficult to accomplish in a process laden with collective action problems, transaction costs, and multiple veto points. Members, instead, can stake out positions that may profoundly affect the public's support for war. As we have seen, who exactly makes these appeals matters greatly for different segments of the American public; on the whole, the findings observed here lend modest empirical support to prior literatures that emphasize the importance of credible and costly signals. But coming from the right political elites, and directed at the right constituencies, public appeals can either augment or deplete the pool of public support for military ventures conducted abroad.

Conclusion

One of the most remarkable facts about inter-branch politics during the past five years, we believe, is just how rarely open conflicts have arisen. This is a president, after all, who as of this writing still has not seen fit to issue a single veto, and a Congress which has done precious little outwardly to check even the most egregious (perhaps even unconstitutional) displays of executive power. Though some of his most ambitious domestic policy initiatives have either been laid asunder (Social Security) or vitiated (the choice provisions of No Child Left Behind), this president's ability to wage war—whether against Afghanistan, Iraq, or a nebulous band of terrorists—would appear unassailable.

It certainly is the case that this president has unilaterally issued some of the most significant and controversial foreign policies witnessed in the modern era and that Congress has abdicated some of its constitutional responsibilities to oversee matters involving war. Republican majorities in Congress, September 11, the looming threat of new terrorist attacks, and a history of transferring war-making authority from the legislative to the executive branches have contributed mightily to the current president's freedom to write and implement foreign policy. The absence of visible congressional checks on Bush's unilateral powers, however, should not be confused with a total derogation of the nation's system of checks and balances. Although this president has sought aggressively to expand and protect his power, as modern presidents are wont to do, he also has proceeded strategically, selectively, and at times even cautiously, careful not to issue policies that he knows full well Congress or the courts will promptly reverse.

The case studies presented above reveal a consistent pattern: the president comes out strongly on behalf of his preferred policy, members of Congress object vocally, and the president then promptly, though sometimes assuming airs of triumph, retreats to less controversial ground. This president, like all presidents, has not exercised his unilateral powers with reckless abandon. Instead, he has used them to push outward on the boundaries of his own authority just as far as he can, but then he has consistently stopped; and when it has become clear that he actually has gone further than most members of Congress would prefer, he then has backtracked. When Congress has moved to amend or overturn his actions, and even when sufficient numbers have vocally expressed their disapproval, something our experiment shows can have a tangible impact on public opinion, the president has quickly sought compromise, and for good reason. In the one instance when the president refused to budge at all, the Dubai ports deal, Bush's loss was near complete.

Trying to predict when, and whether, a president will exercise his unilateral powers, it will not do to simply divine the president's true preferences and juxtapose them against the existing corpus of law. One must assess the probability that Congress and/or the courts will object to a unilaterally instituted executive order, executive agreement, proclamation, or directive, and then forecast the likely outcome of the ensuing struggle—be it deleterious judicial ruling, the loss of appropriations, an amended order, or a hostile public. Though the influence gleaned from unilateral powers is considerable, it is not absolute. In the wake of congressional opposition, Bush often has settled for policies that do not map perfectly onto his true preferences, as best they can be discerned. And so doing, the Bush presidency reminds us that politics persist, even in a policy domain where all concede that presidential power reaches its zenith.

References

Aldrich, John, Sullivan, John, and Borgida, Eugene. 1989. "Foreign Affairs and Issue Voting: Do Presidential Candidates 'Waltz' before a Blind Audience?" *American Political Science Review* 83:123–41.

Allen, Mike. 2002. "Bush Seeks To Restrict Hill Probes Of Sept. 11: Intelligence Panels' Secrecy Is Favored." *Washington Post.* 30 January, A4.

Almond, Gabriel. 1950. *The American People and Foreign Policy.* New York: Praeger.

Ansolabehere, Stephen, and Iyengar, Shanto. 1995. *Going Negative: How Political Advertisements Shrink and Polarize the Electorate.* New York: Free Press.

Arena, Kelli. 2005. "Bush Says He Signed Wiretap Order." CNN/website, 17 December ⟨http://www.cnn.com/2005/POLITICS/12/17/bush.nsa/⟩, accessed 21 November 2006.

Asch, Solomon. 1987(1952). *Social Psychology.* Oxford: Oxford University Press.

Babington, Charles. 2006. "Lawmakers Call for Hearings: Report May Complicate Hayden CIA Confirmation." *Washington Post.* 12 May, A4.

——and Leonnig, Carol D. 2006. "Senate Rejects Wiretapping Probe; But Judge Orders Justice Department to Turn Over Documents." *Washington Post.* 17 February, A6.

Baum, Matthew. 2002. "The Constituent Foundations of the Rally-Round-the-Flag Phenomenon." *International Studies Quarterly* 46: 263–98.

——2005. "What Gets Covered?: How Media Coverage of Elite Debate Drives the Rally-Round-the-Flag Phenomenon, 1979–1998," in L. Cox Han and D. Heith (eds.) *In the Public Domain: Presidents and the Challenges of Public Leadership.* New York: SUNY.

_____ and Groeling, Timothy. 2004. "Crossing the Water's Edge: Elite Rhetoric, Media Coverage, and the Rally-Round-the-Flag Phenomenon, 1979–2003." Paper read at Annual Meetings of the American Political Science Association.

Bazan, Elizabeth, and Elsea, Jennifer. 2006. "Presidential Authority to Conduct Warrantless Electronic Surveillance to Gather Foreign Intelligence Information." Congressional Research Service. 5 January.

Becker, Elizabeth. 2002a. "Ridge to Brief 2 House Panels, but Rift Remains." _New York Times_. 4 April, A19.

_____ 2002b. "Ridge Briefs House Panel, but Discord Is not Resolved." _New York Times_. 11 April, A23.

_____ 2002c. "Bush is Said to Consider a New Security Department." _New York Times_. 12 April, A16.

_____ and Sciolino, Elaine. 2001. "A Nation Challenged: A New Federal Office Opens Amid Concerns That its Head Won't Have Enough Power." _New York Times_. 9 October, B11.

Berinsky, Adam. 2005. "Assuming the Costs of War: Events, Elites, and American Public Support for Military Conflict." Paper read at Annual Meetings of the Midwest Political Science Association, at Chicago.

Blustein, Paul. 2006a. "Some in Congress Object to Arab Port Operator." _Washington Post_. 17 February, A11.

_____ 2006b. "Ports Deal Expected within 6 Months." _Washington Post_. 16 March, D6.

Breitweiser, Kristen. 2002. "Joint Inquiry into Intelligence Community Activities Before and After the Terrorist Attacks of Sept. 11, 2001." Senate Intelligence Committee, S. Hrg. 107-1086, 18 September, 21–57.

Bridis, Ted. 2006. "UAE company poised to oversee six U.S. ports" _Associated Press_. 11 February.

Brody, Richard. 1991. _Assessing the President: The Media, Elite Opinion, and Public Support_. Stanford: Stanford University Press.

Brookes, Adam. 2006. "White House Defends Spying Policy." _BBC News_. 24 January ⟨http://news.bbc.co.uk/2/hi/americas/4645412.stm⟩, accessed 21 November 2006.

Bumiller, Elizabeth, and Sanger, David. 2002. "Bush, as Terror Inquiry Swirls, Seeks Cabinet Post on Security." _New York Times_. 7 June, A1.

Bush, George W. 2002a. "The President's Radio Address: June 8, 2002." _The Public Papers of the Presidents: George W. Bush_, i. 947–8.

_____ 2002b. "Remarks at Oak Park High School in Kansas City, Missouri." _The Public Papers of the President: George W. Bush_. i. 962.

_____ 2002c. "President Meets with Congressional Leaders on Homeland Security." 7 June ⟨http://www.whitehouse.gov/news/releases/2002/06/20020607-1.html⟩, accessed 21 November 2006.

_____ 2005. "The President's News Conference." _Weekly Compilation of Presidential Documents_. 26 December, 41: 1885–96.

Campbell, Angus, Converse, Phillip, Miller, Warren, and Stokes, Donald. 1960. _The American Voter_. New York: John Wiley.

CNN. 2002. "Bush Accepts Independent but Focused 9/11 Probe." 1 December ⟨http://archives.cnn.com/2002/ALLPOLITICS/09/20/independent.probe/index.html⟩, accessed 21 November 2006.

CNN. 2006. "Two Groups Sue over NSA Wiretap program." 17 January ⟨http://www.cnn.com/2006/LAW/01/17/aclu.nsa/⟩, accessed 21 November 2006.

Converse, Phillip. 1964. "The Nature of Belief Systems in Mass Publics," in D. Apter (ed.), *Ideology and Discontent*. New York: Free Press.

Cooper, Phillip. 2002. *By Order of the President: The Use and Abuse of Executive Direct Action*. Lawrence, Kan.: University Press of Kansas.

Deering, Christopher, and Maltzman, Forrest. 1999. "The Politics of Executive Orders: Legislative Constraints on Presidential Power." *Political Research Quarterly* 52 (4): 767–83.

Dewar, Helen. 2002a. "House GOP Stops 9/11 Probe Plan; Proponents of Proposal Point to White House Opposition." *Washington Post*. 11 October, A14.

____2002b. "House GOP Stops 9/11 Probe Plan; Proponents of Proposal Point to White House Opposition." *Washington Post*. 11 October, A6.

Druckman, James. 2001a. "The Implications of Framing Effects for Citizen Competence." *Political Behavior* 23: 225–56.

____2001b. "On the Limits of Framing Effects: Who Can Frame?" *Journal of Politics* 63: 1041–66.

Economist, The. 2006a. "The President's Wartime Powers under Challenge." 14 January, 38.

____2006b. "The Paranoid Style in American Politics." 7 January, 32.

Feaver, Peter, and Gelpi, Christopher. 2005. *Choosing Your Battles: American Civil–Military Relations and the Use of Force*. Princeton: Princeton University Press.

Federalist Society. 2006. ⟨http://www.fed-soc.org/pdf/domesticsurveillance.pdf⟩, accessed 21 November 2006.

Federal News Service. 2006. "Wartime Executive Power and the National Security Agency's Surveillance Authority." Senate Judiciary Committee Hearings. 6 February.

Firestone, David. 2002. "Threat and Response: The Inquiry; White House Gives Way on a September 11 Commission; Congress Is Set to Create It." *New York Times*. 15 November, A19.

____and James Risen. 2002. "White House, in Shift, Backs Inquiry on 9/11." *New York Times*. 21 September, A1.

Fleischer, Ari. 2001. "White House Press Briefing." 5 October ⟨http://www.whitehouse.gov/news/releases/2001/10/20011005-3.html#GovernorRidge⟩, accessed 21 November 2006.

Fox News. 2006. "John Yoo Defends Warrant-less Wiretapping." 30 January ⟨http://www.foxnews.com/story/0,2933,183179,00.html⟩, accessed 21 November 2006.

Gartner, Scott, Segura, Gary, and Wilkening, Michael. 2000. "Race, Casualties, and Opinion in the Vietnam War." *Journal of Politics* 62: 115–46.

Gates, Robert. 2001. "The Job Nobody Trained For." *New York Times*. 19 November, A19.

Gellman, Barton, and Linzer, Dafna. 2005. "Pushing the Limits of Wartime Powers." *Washington Post*. 18 December, A1.

Graubard, Stephen. 2004. *Command of Office: How War, Secrecy, and Deception Transformed the Presidency, from Theodore Roosevelt to George W. Bush*. New York: Basic Books.

Groeling, Timothy. 2001. "When Politicians Attack: The Causes, Contours, and Consequences of Partisan Political Communication." Diss., University of California, San Diego.

Hamilton, Lee. 2001. "Legislative Options To Strengthen Homeland Defense." Senate Committee on Governmental Affairs, S. Hrg. 12 October, 107–212.

Holsti, Ole. 1996. *Public Opinion and American Foreign Policy*. Ann Arbor: University of Michigan Press.

Hovland, Carl, and Weiss, Walter. 1951. "The Influence of Source Credibility on Communication Effectiveness." *Public Opinion Quarterly* 15: 625–50.

Howell, William G. 2003. *Power without Persuasion: The Politics of Direct Presidential Action*. Princeton, NJ: Princeton University Press.

——2005a. "Power without Persuasion: Rethinking Foundations of Executive Influence," in G. Edwards (ed.), *Readings in Presidential Politics*. Belmont, Calif.: Wadsworth.

——2005b. "Unilateral Powers: A Brief Overview." *Presidential Studies Quarterly* 35 (3): 417–39.

——and Kriner, Douglas. Forthcoming. "Political Elites and Public Support for War."

——and Lewis, David. 2002. "Agencies by Presidential Design." *Journal of Politics* 64 (4): 1095–1114.

Hulse, Carl. 2006a. "New Concerns Are Raised in Congress on Port Deal." *New York Times*. 1 March, A13.

——2006b. "In Break with White House, House Panel Rejects Ports Deal." *New York Times*. 9 March, A20.

——2006c. "Setback to Bush on Ports Deal Casts a Shadow over his Agenda." *New York Times*. 11 March, A10.

——and Shane, Scott. 2006. "Doubts Back Home Fuel GOP Worries over Ports Deal." *New York Times*. 2 March, A22.

Jentleson, Bruce. 1992. "The Pretty Prudent Public: Post Post-Vietnam American Opinion on the Use of Military Force." *International Studies Quarterly* 36: 49–74.

Johnston, David. 2006. "Inquiry Into Wiretapping Article Widens." *New York Times*. 12 February. 26.

Jones, Mary Lynn, and Stevens, Allison. 2002. "Senate GOP Divided over Ridge Testimony." *The Hill*. 20 March, 1.

Jordan, Donald, and Page, Benjamin. 1992. "Shaping Foreign Policy Opinions: The Role of TV News." *Journal of Conflict Resolution* 36: 227–41.

Kane, Paul, and Pershing, Ben. 2001. "Hill Weighs Oversight of Anti-Terror Chief." *Roll Call*. 21 September.

King, Neil, Jr. 2005. "Wiretap Furor Widens Republican Divide; While Security Camp Claims Justification, Civil Libertarians See an Intrusion on Rights." *Wall Street Journal*. 22 December, A4.

Kirkpatrick, David. 2006. "How the Clock Ran Out on the Dubai Ports Deal." *New York Times*. 10 March, A18.

Krause, George, and Cohen, David. 1997. "Presidential Use of Executive Orders, 1953–1994." *American Politics Quarterly* 25 (October): 458–81.

——and Cohen, Jeffrey. 2000. "Opportunity, Constraints, and the Development of the Institutional Presidency: The Case of Executive Order Issuance, 1939–1996." *Journal of Politics* 62: 88–114.

Kuhnhenn, James, and Henderson, Stephen. 2006. "Alito Faces Grilling on Executive Power." *Chattanooga Times Free Press*. 8 January, A1.

Kuklinski, James, and Hurley, Norman. 1994. "On Hearing and Interpreting Political Messages: A Cautionary Tale of Citizen Cue-Taking." *Journal of Politics* 56: 729–51.

Kull, Steven, and Clay, Ramsey. 2001. "The Myth of the Reactive Public: American Public Attitudes on Military Fatalities in the Post-Cold War Period," in P. Everets and P. Isneria (eds.), *Public Opinion and the International Use of Force*. London: Routledge.

Labaton, Stephen, and Pear, Robert. 2001. "Anthrax Menace Exposes Badly Coordinated Defense." *New York Times*. 17 October, B7.

Larson, Eric. 1996. *Casualties and Consensus: The Historical Role of Casualties in Domestic Support for U.S. Military Operations*. Santa Monica, Calif.: Rand.

―― 2000. "Putting Theory to Work: Diagnosing Public Opinion on the U.S. Intervention in Bosnia," in M. Nincic and J. Leogold (eds.), *Being Useful: Policy Relevance and International Relations Theory*. Ann Arbor: University of Michigan Press.

Lichtblau, Eric, and Liptak, Adam, with Barclay Walsh. 2006. "Bush and his Senior Aides Press on in Legal Defense for Wiretapping Program." *New York Times*. 28 January, A13.

―― and Sanger, David, with Eric Schmitt and Sheryl Gay Stolberg. 2005. "Administration Cites War Vote in Spying Case." *New York Times*. 20 December, A1.

―― and Stolberg, Sheryl Gay. 2006. "Accord in House to Hold Inquiry on Surveillance." *New York Times*. 17 February, A1.

Light, Paul, and Lake, Celinda. 1985. "The Election: Candidates, Strategies and Decision," in M. Nelson (ed.), *The Elections of 1984*. Washington, DC: Congressional Quarterly Press.

Lipton, Eric, and Sanger, David. 2006. "Officials Say Ports Company Faces More Intensive Review." *New York Times*. 4 March, A10.

Lupia, Arthur, and McCubbins, Matthew. 1998. *The Democratic Dilemma: Can Citizens Learn What They Need to Know?* New York: Cambridge University Press.

McClellan, Scott. 2002. "Press Gaggle." Office of the Press Secretary. 27 November ⟨http://www.whitehouse.gov/news/releases/2002/11/20021127-8.html⟩, accessed 21 November 2006.

McGeehan, Patrick. 2006. "2 Senators Seek to Stop Ports Deal, Citing Security." *New York Times*. 18 February, B2.

Magnet, Alec. 2006. "Tide of Opposition to Port Deal Swells Despite Assurances that it is Safe." *New York Sun*. 17 February, 3.

Markels, Alex. 2005. "Timeline: Wiretaps' Use and Abuse." *National Public Radio*. 20 December ⟨http://www.npr.org/templates/story/story.php?storyId=5061834⟩, accessed 21 November 2006.

Marshall, Bryan, and Pacelle, Richard. 2005. "Revisiting the Two Presidencies: The Strategic Use of Executive Orders." *American Politics Research* 33 (1): 81–105.

Mayer, Kenneth. 1999. Executive Orders and Presidential Power. *Journal of Politics* 61 (2): 445–66.

―― 2001. *With the Stroke of a Pen: Executive Orders and Presidential Power*. Princeton, NJ: Princeton University Press.

―― and Price, Kevin. 2002. "Unilateral Presidential Powers: Significant Executive Orders, 1949–99." *Presidential Studies Quarterly* 32 (2): 367–86.

Mayhew, David. 1974. *Congress: The Electoral Connection*. New Haven: Yale University Press.

Milbank, Diana. 2002*a*. "Congress, White House Fight Over Ridge Status." *Washington Post*. 21 March, A33.

_____ 2002*b*. "Barriers to 9/11 Inquiry Decried; Congress May Push Commission." *Washington Post*. 19 September, A14.

Mitchell, Alison. 2001*a*. "Disputes Erupt on Ridge's Needs for His Job." *New York Times*. 3 November, B7.

_____ 2001*b*. "Senators Press for an Inquiry on U.S. Intelligence Lapses." *New York Times*. 21 December, B5.

_____ 2002*a*. "Letter to Ridge Is Latest Jab in Fight over Balance of Powers." *New York Times*. 5 March, A8.

_____ 2002*b*. "Ridge Offers Compromise on Testimony before Congress." *New York Times*. 26 March, A3.

_____ 2002*c*. "Plan for Security Agency Draws Bipartisan, but not Unconditional, Support." *New York Times*. 7 June, A21.

_____ 2002*d*. "Daschle is Seeking a Special Inquiry on Sept. 11 Attack." *New York Times* 22 May, A1.

Moberg, David. 2006. "An Imperial President." *In These Times*. January 21. ⟨http://www.inthesetimes.com/site/main/article/2470⟩, accessed 21 November 2006.

Moe, Terry, and William Howell. 1999*a*. Unilateral Action and Presidential Power: A Theory. *Presidential Studies Quarterly* 29 (4): 850–72.

_____ _____ 1999*b*. "The Presidential Power of Unilateral Action." *Journal of Law, Economics, and Organization* 15 (1): 132–79.

_____ and Wilson, Scott. 1994. "Presidents and the Politics of Structure." *Law and Contemporary Problems* 57: 1–44.

Morris, Vincent. 2002. "VEEP Tries to Stop 9/11 Spy Probe." *New York Post*. 30 January, 8.

Mueller, John. 1973. *War, Presidents and Public Opinion*. New York: Wiley.

New York Times. 2006*a*. "A Stumble a Day." 15 March, 26.

_____ 2006*b*. "Excerpts From Senate Hearing on Eavesdropping Program." 7 February, A17.

Nolan, Beth; Bradley, Curtis; Cole, David; Stone, Geoffrey; Hongju Koh, Harold; M. Sullivan, Kathleen; Tribe, Laurence H.; Lederman, Martin; Heymann, Philip B.; Epsten, Richard; Dworkin, Ronald; Dellinger, Walter; Sessions, William S.; and Alstyne, William Van. 2006. "On NSA Spying: A Letter to Congress." *New York Review of Books*. 9 February, 53: 2.

Office of the Press Secretary. 2006. White House Press Release. 21 February.

Page, Benjamin, Shapiro, Richard, and Dempsey, Glenn. 1987. "What Moves Public Opinion." *American Political Science Review* 81: 23–44.

Pear, Robert. 2002. "Lawmakers Asking if Plan on Terror Goes Far Enough." *New York Times*. 8 June, A1.

Penn, Schoen & Berland Associates 2002. "Democratic Leadership Council Poll." 19–21 November 2001, released January 2002.

Pious, Richard. 1991. "Prerogative Power and the Reagan Presidency." *Political Science Quarterly* 106 (Fall): 499–510.

Rasmussen Reports. 2005. "National Security Agency." 28 December ⟨http://www. rasmussenreports.com/2005/NSA.htm⟩, accessed 21 November 2006.

Rasmussen Reports. 2006. "Americans Okay with Current Balance between National Security and Individual Liberty." 4 January ⟨http://www.rasmussenreports.com/2006/January%20Dailies/Security%20v%20Liberty.htm⟩, accessed 21 November 2006.

Rehm, Diane. 2005. "Conservatives Condemn Bush's Domestic Spying Scandal." *The DianeRehm Show*. 19 December ⟨http://www.democrats.org/a/p/conservatives_condemn_bushs_domestic_spying_scandal.html⟩, accessed 21 November 2006.

Risen, James, and Lichtblau, Eric. 2005. "Bush Lets U.S. Spy on Callers without Courts." *New York Times*. 16 December, A1.

Rosenbaum, David. 2002. "Bush Bucks Tradition on Investigation." *New York Times*. 26 May, 18.

Rossiter, Clinton. 1956. *The American Presidency*. 2nd edn. New York: Harcourt, Brace & World.

Sanger, David. 2002. "Domestic Security Spending to Double under Bush Plan." *New York Times*. 25 January, A11.

——2006a. "Dubai Expected to Ask for Review of Port Deal." *New York Times*. 26 February, A1.

——2006b. "Dubai Deal Will Undergo Deeper Inquiry into Security." *New York Times*. 27 February, A1.

——2006c. "Under Pressure, Dubai Company Drops Deal." *New York Times*. 10 March, A1.

——and Bumiller, Elisabeth. 2002. "No Hint of Sept. 11 Report in August, White House Says, but Congress Seeks Inquiry." *New York Times*. 17 May, A1.

——and Lipton, Eric. 2006. "Bush Would Veto Any Bill Halting Dubai Port Deal." *New York Times*. 22 February, A1.

——with Shane, Scott. 2006. "In Shift, Bush Says He Welcomes Inquiry on Secret Wiretaps." *New York Times*. 12 January, A24.

Shane, Scott, and Kirkpatrick, David D. 2006. "G.O.P. Plan Would Allow Spying without Warrants." *New York Times*. 9 March, A20.

Sniderman, Paul, Brody, Richard, and Tetlock, Phillip. 1991. *Reasoning and Choice: Exploration in Political Psychology*. Cambridge: Cambridge University Press.

Sobel, Richard. 2001. *The Impact of Public Opinion on U.S. Foreign Policy Since Vietnam*. New York: Oxford University Press.

Spence, A. M. 1973. *Market Signaling*. Cambridge, Mass.: Harvard University Press.

Stollberg, Sheryl Gay. 2006. "How a Business Deal Became a Big Liability for Republicans in Congress." *New York Times*. 27 February, A14.

——and Sanger, David E. 2006. "Facing Pressure, White House Seeks Approval for Spying." *New York Times*. 20 February, A9.

Stout, David. 2002. "A Nation Challenged: Congressional Action; Panel Votes for Wide Scrutiny into Attacks." *New York Times*. 22 March, A13.

Timmons, Heather. 2006. "Dubai Wins Bidding Battle for P&O." *New York Times*. 11 February, C4.

VandeHei, Jim, and Weisman, Jonathan. 2006. "Republicans Split with Bush on Ports: White House Vows to Brief Lawmakers on Deal with Firm Run by Arab State." *Washington Post*. 23 February, A1.

Vasquez, Michael. 2002. "Sept. 11 Families Rally for Probe; Some Congressmen Also Urge Forming Independent Panel." *Washington Post.* 12 June, B8.

Wawro, Gregory. 2000. *Legislative Entrepreneurship in the U.S. House of Representatives.* Ann Arbor: University of Michigan Press.

Wilson, Brian. 2006. "Administration Officials to Brief Lawmakers on NSA Terrorist Surveillance Program." *FOX News.* 16 May ⟨http://www.foxnews.com/story/0,2933,195752,00.html⟩, accessed 21 November 2006.

Zaller, John. 1992. *The Nature and Origins of Mass Opinion.* Cambridge: Cambridge University Press.

—— 1994a. "Elite Leadership of Mass Opinion: New Evidence from the Gulf War," in W. L. Bennett and D. Paletz (eds.), *Taken by Storm: Media, Public Opinion, and U.S. Foreign Policy in the Gulf War.* Chicago: University of Chicago Press.

—— 1994b. "Strategic Politicians, Public Opinion, and the Gulf Crisis," in W. L. Bennett and D. Paletz (eds.), *Taken by Storm: Media, Public Opinion, and U.S. Foreign Policy in the Gulf War.* Chicago: University of Chicago Press.

Notes

1. However, in a vivid example of the limits on presidential unilateral power, the Supreme Court on 29 June 2006 struck down Bush's unilateral creation of military tribunals to try terror suspects as in violation of both the congressionally enacted Uniform Code of Military Justice and the Geneva Conventions (*Hamdan* v. *Rumsfeld*). Invoking Jackson's concurring opinion in *Youngstown* v. *Sawyer* (1952), Justice Kennedy in his concurring opinion argues that because the president's action directly contradicts congressional statute, the tribunal case falls within Jackson's third category in which presidential "power is at its lowest ebb."

2. We thank Ben Sedrish, Brad Feldman, and Charles Griffin for their assistance in compiling these case studies.

3. The legislation was in part inspired by Hal Lipset's unsettling demonstrations detailing the advantages of concealed recording technology in front of a Senate Subcommittee.

4. The formal name of the committee, which Idaho Democratic Senator Frank Church chaired, was "The United States Select Committee to Study Governmental Operations with Respect to Intelligence Activities."

5. The attorney general was permitted to bypass the FISA Court if surveillance was solely directed at communications used exclusively "between or among foreign powers or on property or premises under the open and exclusive control of a foreign power" (Bazan and Elsea 2006, 25).

6. Other polls showed similar results. See *Rassmussen Reports* 2005, 2006.

7. For complete testimony, see Federal News Service 2006.

8. The deal would also provide classified briefings to seven members, four Republicans and three Democrats, of the Senate Intelligence Committee: Democratic Senators Carl Levin (MI), Dianne Feinstein (CA), and John D. Rockefeller IV (WV) as well as Republican Senators Pat Robert (KS), Orrin G. Hatch (UT), Mike DeWine (OH), and Christopher S. Bond (MO).

9. A parallel situation arose when the 9/11 Commission sought the testimony of Bush's national security adviser, Condoleezza Rice. The White House initially refused requests for her public sworn testimony, which the administration claimed infringed upon the president's need for private counsel. Only later, after political clamoring from Democrats and Republicans, did the administration acquiesce.

10. Alison Mitchell (2002a) describes the situation as follows: "The dispute over whether Mr. Ridge will appear formally before Congress stems in part from Mr. Bush's decision to create a homeland security office inside the White House and not as a separate cabinet agency run by an official confirmed by Congress. The president and Mr. Ridge have repeatedly said that because Mr. Ridge, former governor of Pennsylvania, is close to Mr. Bush, he will have enough power to be effective and does not need a separate agency or his own budget powers. That he is a White House adviser and not a cabinet official also means that he is subject to less congressional oversight—a fact that is becoming an irritant between Congress and the administration."

11. For the difficulties Congress has in protecting its institutional prerogatives, see Mayhew 1974; Wawro 2000; Moe and Wilson 1994.

12. See also ⟨http://intelligence.senate.gov/0209hrg/020918/breifweises.pdf⟩, accessed 21 November 2006.

13. Bush initially tapped former Secretary of State Henry Kissinger for the post, but Kissinger later stepped down due to business conflicts of interest. Instead, the administration turned to former New Jersey Governor Tom Keane, while congressional Democrats (who had first asked former Senate majority leader George Mitchell) selected former Indiana congressman Lee Hamilton for the vice chairmanship.

14. A number of scholars have examined how features of a proposed deployment—the character of a mission (Jentleson 1992); the success of a mission (Kull and Clay 2001; Feaver and Gelpi 2005); and casualties (Larson 1996, 2000; Gartner, Segura, and Wilkening 2000)—affect public opinion. We do not intend to test their claims here. Instead, we focus on the capacity of different political elites, in a competitive political environment, to sway public opinion for or against the use of military force.

15. The literature on source effects, however, focuses primarily on issues that do not concern foreign policy and tends to vary aspects of source identities apart from their place in government. For general differences in the persuasive power of appeals made by various government and non-governmental sources, see Page, Shapiro, and Dempsey 1987; for the reinforcing effects of partisanship, see Ansolabehere and Iyengar 1995; and for the effects of the race and perceived credibility of the source, see Kuklinski and Hurley 1994 and Druckman 2001a, b respectively.

16. At the aggregate level, work by Baum (2002) has shown that popular responses even to "rally events" are moderated by individuals' party attachments.

17. We had a completion rate of 70.3 percent, and a response rate of 30.6 percent.

18. Because respondents were randomly assigned to control and treatment conditions, the differences in means reported in Table 4.1 are unbiased. (To make sure that the randomization worked, we compared the background characteristics of subjects assigned to the nine conditions. On no dimension except age do we find any

evidence that individuals across conditions differ systematically from one another.) There are modest efficiency gains to be had from pooling the observations and estimating regressions that include background controls. We have estimated a series of multivariate models, which yield results virtually identical to those observed in Table 4.1.

19. When using unweighted data, however, the observed differences between Democrats and Republicans attenuate.

20. When using unweighted data, the difference between the supporting and opposing Republican congressional treatment conditions for Democratic respondents also is statistically significant.

21. Moreover, even a casual observer of the news is more likely to react skeptically to the cues that many Republicans in Congress oppose the president or many congressional Democrats support the administration's policies than they would to similar cues made by the United Nations or outside interest groups. While there are a handful of Republicans and Democrats who do hold these views, most news coverage emphasizes the partisan divide in Congress on Iraq policy. If these treatment conditions conflict with respondents' prior understanding of the state of the congressional debate, it could significantly muddle the experimental effects. The hypothetical experimental scenarios discussed briefly below and more fully in Howell and Kriner (forthcoming) address such concerns.

Part II

Decision Making

5

"The Decider's" Path to War in Iraq and the Importance of Personality

Thomas S. Langston

At some point following 9/11, President George W. Bush decided upon war in Iraq. In the years since the invasion commenced, on 20 March 2003, the president's decision has become immensely controversial. Critics allege that the operation to topple Saddam Hussein was begun under false pretenses: that the White House fabricated or at the least exaggerated evidence of the threat that Iraq posed to the West in order to justify the invasion. Presumably, the president's "real" reasons for deciding upon war were too nefarious, too personal, or perhaps merely too nuanced for public consumption. The president insists that he decided upon war in national self-defense, and as a last resort. Clearly, this is a decision that deserves scrutiny on several levels.

The purpose of this chapter is not to second-guess the president's decision, but to inquire into the possibility that it represents an outstanding example of the influence of personality upon decision making of the highest importance. The decision for war against Iraq may or may not have served the nation's interest; it most certainly satisfied the president's character-rooted needs and conformed to his beliefs and world-view. I demonstrate this relationship by breaking the decision for war into a series of smaller decisions that led to invasion. Reconstructing those smaller decisions reveals, to begin, that the president on occasion made policy by proclamation. Acting impulsively, without the benefit of advice, he narrowed the range of options for dealing with Iraq, making military conflict more likely. The president reached other decisions after consulting with only a very few aides and advisers. The rhetoric the president used in expressing his decisions revealed a highly personal perception of the conflict with Iraq, as well as the president's own peculiar understanding of his, and the nation's, religiously grounded destiny. Along the path to war, President Bush shunned doubt and doubters, and otherwise demonstrated his famous resolve. In the process, he also showed that—in a rather important instance of executive decision making—it is not possible to understand a presidency without trying to understand the president.

This chapter proceeds first by presenting a composite view of the personality of the president, taking into account both his major personality traits and his world-view. Next, it breaks down the decision for war in Iraq into seven discrete decisions. The first six progressively made war increasingly likely. The last was the final decision to launch the invasion. I characterize each decision as to the major actors who influenced the president's choice, the manner in which the decision was made, and the practical consequences of each choice for the likelihood of war. In the final substantive section of the chapter, I examine this seven-step path to war by referencing back to the president's personality traits and world-view. In the conclusion, I observe that there is compelling evidence that personal factors drove "the" decision to wage war in Iraq. A different person would have *chosen differently*, in both senses of the term. The analysis also suggests, ironically, that the president's emotionally charged, factually shaky rhetoric in the final months before the invasion was not evidence of the influence of personality on decision making; the decision for war had already been made.

The Personality of George W. Bush

Alexander L. George has demonstrated the utility of a catholic perspective for studying decision making. George's preferred method incorporates the analysis of traits, their psychoanalytic foundations, and an individual's "cognition," or, to use the term more commonly employed to describe a person's knowledge, beliefs, and conceptual framework, his or her "world-view." George even considers the skills that a decision maker possesses as components of personality, or a "personality system." All must be observed, according to George, in relation to a decision maker's situation and role (1980, 1–8).

Steve Yetiv (2004), in a recent book seeking to combine multiple perspectives upon executive decision making, presents a complementary analysis. Personality traits are significant, but not by themselves. A decision maker's knowledge, experience, personal motivations, and skills combine with an element of historical chance to provide, on occasion, an opportunity for individual influence to flourish. A decision maker's beliefs and values mediate his or her knowledge and experience.

Yetiv suggests a counterfactual as an illustration of the sort of conditions that make personal factors salient: consider a different president in 1990, facing Saddam Hussein's invasion of Kuwait. A different president from the one in office might have had: no particular knowledge or experience with dictators or appeasement, no personal motivation to prove his mettle, no impulsive or combative personality traits, and no exceptional skill at diplomacy.

George Herbert Walker Bush had those characteristics, and they propelled him towards a military response. A different president—one less likely to see Hussein as another Hitler (the influence of experience and knowledge), less in need of proving himself (a personal motive), less impulsive and combative (prominent personality traits of the president), less competent at diplomacy (a skill enabling the formation of a coalition that made military intervention less costly in a number of ways)—would likely have reached a decision that reflected less his personality and more the influence of other factors, such as domestic politics, bureaucratic dynamics, "Groupthink," or—even—a thorough, rational, calculation of state interests. With the right combination of personality and chance, the individual decision maker can make all the difference.

What of the intersection of George W. Bush and the threat from Iraq, as seen in the wake of 9/11? The presence of personal knowledge, experience, motives, and traits relevant to the situation and the role that the president saw himself playing suggests that this situation was indeed ripe for personal influence. About personal knowledge and experience, Saddam Hussein was not just any tyrant in the Middle East, but the "guy who tried to kill my dad." This understanding of the situation speaks also to the president's possible personal motives: either to avenge or best his father. From the latter perspective, the war to remove Hussein from office can be seen as the culmination of a lifelong effort on the part of "Jr." to live up to and, finally, surpass the first President Bush. Even if we leave this level of psychoanalytic speculation at a safe distance, many observers of George W. Bush through the years have seen him as at least as determined as his father to demonstrate toughness. W. is, moreover, commonly characterized as impulsive and aggressive—personality traits that predispose an actor to take control of just the sort of situation that the president found himself in after 9/11. With regard to skill, the son lacked his father's talent for diplomacy, but because his administration had already, before 9/11, made clear its willingness to act "unilaterally," this was not as great a barrier to individual influence as it might have been.

What, then, can we say about the personality of George W. Bush, simplifying our analysis by searching only for well-defined personality traits and examining limited aspects of the president's world-view, namely his knowledge and beliefs about God, Iraq, and the presidency?

Personality Traits of "The Guy Making History"

George Bush's major personality traits are rooted in his psychology. A brief review of some of the psychological literature on the president will allow us to situate his personality traits in his biography, and to suggest how deepseated they are. Deep-seated traits are the ones most likely to come to the fore in a crisis and to influence decision making over time.

George W. Bush has been described as struggling in "his father's shadow" (Renshon 2004). Throughout his youth and into adulthood, Bush sought to emulate his loving but absent father. Indeed, in the words of two psychologists who have made a systematic study of the personal attributes of American presidents, "many of (Bush's) life decisions seem like dutiful emulations of him" (Rubenzer and Faschingbauer 2004, 299). Like his father, he "prepped" at Andover before attending Yale, where, like his father, he played baseball and was tapped for Skull and Bones. When he left college, he told a friend that he intended to join the Texas Air National Guard to be a fighter pilot "because my father was" (ibid. 300). He even became engaged, temporarily, at 25, the age at which his father became engaged to his mother. Later, like his father, he moved to Midland, started an oil exploration company, and ran for a seat in the United States House of Representatives.

Unfortunately for the younger Bush, he was not as successful as his father in any of these undertakings, and suffered a series of setbacks, including the collapse of "Arbusto," his ill-named oil company, and a decisive defeat in his first political campaign. The future president, a binge drinker in college, developed an abusive relationship with alcohol that threatened his marriage. This was not a confidence-building path to independence. Bush was, in his own words, "the black sheep of the family" well into his thirties (Frum 2003, 41; Schweizer and Schweizer 2004, 136, 426, 517, 524). What happened?

George W. Bush tells the story of his transformation as one of Christian redemption, emphasizing the power of prayer and the tutelage of the Reverend Billy Graham. Other observers, both secular and religious, underline the president's power of will. Doug Wead, an evangelical minister and friend of the president, explains Bush's decision to turn his life around as a matter of priorities. "George W. Bush can be defined," Wead says, "in two words—Dad and daughters." He had almost ruined his life trying to live up to his image of his father, and when he reached his fortieth birthday, he was about to lose his family as a result. "(H)e woke up one morning … and he said," Wead relates, "Eureka, that's it. I'll take God. I'll beat drinking. I keep Laura [Mrs. Bush] and the girls. That simple. I will never take a drink again the rest of my life. Done" (Wead 2004).

Political psychologists and biographers generally concur with the analysis of Bush's evangelist friend. Stanley Renshon, a political psychologist, finds the key to Bush's presidency in his successful mid-life transformation, and the key to his transformation in discipline and self-control. When Bush stopped drinking, he notes, he did so "cold turkey." When, about the same time, he took up exercise, he did not "jog;" he "ran." (In Bush's first term, before a knee injury forced a switch to bicycling, Secret Service agents ran relay-style with the president in order to sustain the frenetic pace. Runners read with envy, following one of his well-publicized annual check-ups, that the president's resting heart rate was a superbly conditioned 44 (LaGay 2002).) From mid-life on, self-control has been a pivotal element of Bush's psychology, upon which other traits, principally focus and resolve, have been constructed (Renshon 2004, 76).

The authors of a composite biography of the Bush family, Peter and Rochelle Schweizer (2004, 433), similarly note W's intense focus, post-transformation. Bush has, they believe, an "addictive personality," which "requires him to fix on something and maintain a hold on it." The Schweizers (ibid. 413) believe that Bush fixed on a new image of himself in 1994. That was the year in which Bush, with sobriety and business success at last to his credit, defeated incumbent Governor Ann Richards to become Governor of Texas. His parents had urged him not to run, thinking he would surely lose. In the campaign, his opponent attacked Bush mercilessly, hoping to provoke an immature outburst. Bush kept his cool and stuck with his script, focusing keenly on a few agenda items throughout the campaign. After watching him debate his sharp-tongued opponent with an unfamiliar measure of self-control, a stunned cousin of the president sent a cable to her aunt Barbara, inquiring: "WHAT DID HE DO?" (Minutaglio 1999, 286).

Whatever he did, Bush has had numerous opportunities to test his self-mastery since then. Bush creates these opportunities for himself, by virtue of his lifelong extraversion and action orientation. In 1999, Aubrey Immelman (1999) conducted "an indirect assessment of the political personality" of Bush as governor of Texas. Bush's "primary personality patterns," he found, were "outgoing" and "adventurous." This combination of traits makes for independent-minded leaders who "seek to do things their own way," sometimes behaving "impulsively and irresponsibly." The basic strength of Bush's personality, according to Immelman, is his enthusiasm and engaging personal style. The president's gravest personality-based handicap is his lack of deliberativeness. "A less-than-deliberative President Bush," Aubrey wrote *before* Bush took office, "will run the risk of failing at times to fully appreciate the implications of his decisions, displaying sufficient depth of comprehension, or effectively weighing alternatives and long-term consequences of policy initiatives." A similarly grounded study by a team of psychological researchers reached similar conclusions. George W. Bush, concluded Steven Rubenzer and Thomas Faschingbauer (2004, 303), exhibits considerable "angry hostility" and "assertiveness," while scoring low on openness to ideas, values, and deliberation.

George W. Bush's personality has not changed in the crucible of the presidency; if anything, its major features have become more starkly defined. Indeed, during his presidency, a number of persons, from harsh critics to warm admirers, have offered descriptions of the man that highlight the very traits identified by biographers and analysts of his earlier years.

Panelists at a conference on the president assembled by Princeton political scientist, Fred Greenstein, reportedly "marveled repeatedly at [the] decisiveness" of the president (Allen 2003). A number of disaffected former White House officials have written and spoken of the president's focus, certainty, and decisiveness in more critical terms. Former Environmental Protection Agency administrator Christine Todd Whitman complained that she was branded as "disloyal" for asking whether the administration had any facts to support its policies (Suskind 2004b). What she realized, too late for her own career ambitions within the administration, was that meetings with the president to review policy "choices" were not in fact policy-making forums. Paul O'Neill had the same experience. The president's first secretary of the treasury found that decisions he believed should have been made through a deliberative process were made in an often ad hoc, mysterious manner. The president would then "explain" his decisions with reference to his "instinct" (Suskind 2004a, 165).

Ironically, President Bush has himself attested repeatedly to a self-image in conformity to the profile drawn by people he dismisses as "psychobabblers."[1] In an interview with *Time* magazine, September 2004 (Dickerson and Gibbs, 2004), Bush responded to a question about how history might judge him by observing, "I'm not the historian. I'm the guy making history." In the same interview, the president offered his analysis of the essence of the presidency. "If you say, Write your job description, I'd say, 'Decision maker.'" The president echoed this remark two years later at a press conference, when he said, with reference to the continuation in office of his embattled secretary of defense: "I'm the decider, and I decide what's best" (Hunt 2006). In talking at length to Bob Woodward (2002, 341) about the decisions he faced in his war on terror, the president returned time and again to the value he placed on being resolute, having no doubt, and taking confident action. It is not necessary to persuade others to follow you, the president suggested at one point. "Confident action," not talk or bargains, will lead "reluctant nations and leaders" to follow the United States, by creating a "slipstream" redirecting the metaphorical winds of change.[2]

In the president's vocabulary, "doubt" is a pejorative. "I know it is hard for you to believe," he insisted at one point during his administration's first war, the one in Afghanistan, "but I have not doubted what we're doing. I have not doubted.... There is no doubt in my mind we're doing the right thing. Not one doubt" (ibid. 256). When National Security Adviser Rice reported to the president, 25 October 2001, that the principals were having doubts about the Afghan operation, his response was instructive. The president first conducted a "gut check" on Rice herself. After asserting, "We have a good plan," the president "asked," "You're confident in it?" Rice ducked the question and told the president he needed to "take the pulse" of the principals the next day, and "if he was committed to the strategy," to "let people know it." Otherwise, people might start to fall off. Paraphrasing Bush's response, Woodward has the president reply: "Starting to fall off? Who was nervous?

Who was concerned?" "The president," Woodward writes, "wanted to take names." The president later commented on this conversation: "If I weaken, the whole team weakens . . . it's essential that we be confident and determined and united. I don't need people around me who are not steady." The next day, the president "took the pulse" of his team, telling them, "I just want to make sure that all of us did agree on this plan, right?" "He was almost demanding," Woodward comments, "they take an oath."

Bush's admirers as well as his critics comment also upon one final trait that flows from his decisiveness: his fatalism. "There is a fatalistic element," says his former speechwriter, David Frum. "You do your best and accept that everything is in God's hands" (Fineman 2003, 29). To his critics, such as the libertarian conservative Bruce Bartlett, Bush's faith gives him a "weird, Messianic idea of what he thinks God has told him to do" (Suskind 2004*b*, 1).

To summarize, George W. Bush is impulsive, extroverted, strong-willed, and confident. Before his mid-life retooling, these traits were not "working for him" well, to adopt the language of the popular television psychological counselor, "Dr. Phil," with whom the president and first lady sat down for a friendly interview during his re-election campaign ("Exclusive" 2004). When Bush added to this constellation of traits self-discipline, his became a formidable personality.

Even in his early adulthood, Bush exhibited considerable self-confidence, continuously placing himself in situations in which a purely objective analysis of strengths and weaknesses should have inspired anxiety. From Andover to the White House, Bush has exhibited the confidence of a man better prepared for his life's challenges than he himself has been. The source of this confidence seems to be Bush's extraordinary comfort in his identity. A Bush, presumably, or at least this particular Bush, his father's son in even his looks, can do anything, and is entitled to the opportunity. When the ultimate son came to occupy his father's former position in the cockpit of the nation's government, it was "Top Gun" time, all the more so when one considers Bush's world-view, in addition to his personality.

World-View: George Bush's Ideas about God, Iraq, and the Presidency

Knowledge, beliefs, and conceptual frameworks are critical elements of a personality system. A generally combative, impulsive, and fatalistic individual might nonetheless hesitate to react to a threat that reminds him or her of some particularly salient event from their past, or their understanding of history, in which quick action led to disaster. In the case before us, George W. Bush's beliefs and ideas on a number of topics inclined him, rather, to give free rein to his instincts. In particular, the president's ideas about God, Iraq, and the presidency reinforced his inclination towards military action against Saddam Hussein.

Although it is unexceptional for an American president to speak, as Bush often does, of the nation's goodness and destiny, President Bush expresses a peculiarly intense and personal rendering of the American civil religion. His is truly a "presidency of good and evil" (Singer 2004).

All presidents are symbolic leaders of the civil religion; this president is in addition a born-again Christian with strong beliefs about the relationship of the earthly and spiritual realms (Kegnor 2004, 325). The substance of his beliefs, not just the intensity with which they are expressed, stand out. First, the president's beliefs are those of an "evangelical." Indeed, after 9/11, the president continued what some say is a practice of lacing his speeches with "code" words easily recognizable by his fellow evangelicals, as in the promise to hunt down "evildoers" in their caves, and in his praise of the "wonder-working power" of America's spiritual values ("George Bush and God" 2004, Lincoln 2004). Perhaps the president, and his chief speechwriter, Michael Gerson, also an evangelical Christian, are simply drawn to a language that they know well. Either way, evangelicals believe that God works his will upon the world through grace, which they see as direct, unmediated, action by God upon the individual, that Satan is real, Hell is a place, and that with God's help, and only with God's help, evil can be overcome.[3]

But does Bush believe he was specifically chosen by God for the presidency? Although Kegnor holds that Bush has a "humble grasp" of the ambiguity at the heart of a Christian belief in the working of providence, Richard Land (2004), the director of the Southern Baptist Convention claims that Bush told him and others on the day he was re-elected governor of Texas that "God wants me to be president." The liberal Christian commentator, Jim Wallis (2004), says that after 9/11, the "self-help Methodist became now almost a messianic American Calvinist, speaking of . . . his perhaps divine appointment to be president at a time such as this." According to Michael Duffy (2002) of *Time* magazine, Bush spoke privately on or after 9/11 of having been "chosen by the grace of God to lead at that moment." The president has certainly not taken issue with the many evangelical Christians who have proclaimed that this is so. On the issue of whether President Bush ever said God told him to invade Iraq (as the late Yasser Arafat once claimed the president told him), his spiritual defender, Kegnor (2004, 246) sensibly concludes that he never made the statement. Besides, "(e)ven if he thought so, he knew better than to say so."

George W. Bush adds to these ideas about evil and providence a belief about freedom as a gift from God. The idea that human freedom is a universal, God-given right, is itself hardly original with the president. Thomas Jefferson, and presumably Al Gore and John Kerry as well, would likely agree at some level. It is the president's combination of this idea with his preference for action and his unwillingness to acknowledge ambiguity (plus his command of the nation's armed forces) that gives this idea its power in the Bush presidency.

The president has repeated his belief in freedom as "the Almighty God's gift to each and every individual" numerous times in the war on terror (ibid. 116, 246). He was, moreover, adamant in his conversations with Woodward for the author's first two books on Bush that Woodward "get" the importance of the idea of freedom to his presidency. "Let me make sure you understand," the president said at one point, "what I just said about the role of the United States. I believe that the United States is *the* beacon for freedom in the world. And I believe we have a responsibility to promote freedom that is as solemn as the responsibility is to protecting the American people, because the two go hand-in-hand. No, it's very important that you understand that about my presidency" (Woodward 2004, 88).[4] Because the United States is called to do God's work on earth, this country, the president stated plainly to Woodward on one occasion, has a "duty to free people" (ibid.).

Among the other important ideas that Bush brought to bear upon his decision making about Iraq, two stand out: his belief that Saddam Hussein had been coddled by the Clinton Administration, and his belief that the presidency is, in essence, an office from which to lead the nation in war. That Iraq was a very bad place, a "rogue" nation, was a truism of the 1990s. The Iraq Liberation Act of 1998, passed unanimously by the senate, even expressed the sense of Congress that US policy should promote "efforts to remove the regime" of Saddam Hussein (HR 4655). Only Iraq had the distinction of being targeted in this manner by the US government for "regime change." President Clinton, however, did little to promote this outcome. As a consequence, when the Bush team came to office, they had, if not a policy, a definite "attitude" about Iraq. *Something* should be done about it, they believed, and something more forceful than what Clinton had dared to attempt (Gordon and Trainor 2006, 10). Taking action of some sort on Iraq was sufficiently important to the administration that Iraq was the focus of the president's first meeting of his NSC, ten days into his first term (Suskind 2004a, 70–5). The president memorably described what he thought of the Clinton precedent in a meeting with several senators, including the former president's wife, two days after 9/11. "When I take action," Bush said, "I'm not going to fire a $2 million missile at a $10 empty tent and hit a camel up the butt. It's going to be decisive" (Fineman 2003).

Finally, President Bush came to the presidency with a uniquely intimate perception of the office. As has often been noted, the present President Bush and his father are, with the Adamses, the only father–son duo in the history of the presidency. Unlike John Quincy Adams, however, only eight years separated this son's assumption of the office from his father's departure, lending the transition from Clinton to Bush an air of familial, if not imperial, restoration. (Fully 24 years separated the two Adamses.)

The younger President Bush, who learned the job of being president by watching his father, became heavily involved in his father's re-election campaign of 1992. What he, and the world, saw that year was a man proud of his accomplishments in foreign affairs, especially his victory in war. In his acceptance speech that year, the president boasted of his foreign policy success, of having "locked a tyrant [Hussein] in the prison of his own country." Of his sought-after second term, he promised to "do what is right for the national security of America, and that is a pledge from my heart" (quoted by Parmet 1997, 504). He sought to distinguish himself from his opponent by questioning his suitability to handle foreign affairs. The world, he warned, was still a dangerous place, and he would sooner let his dog, Millie, be responsible for America's foreign relations than he would Bill Clinton, the "leader of the Arkansas National Guard" (ibid.; Schweizer and Schweizer 2004, 403). Although the majority of voters that year saw a relatively placid world and a domestic environment in need of strong leadership, George Bush saw the obverse.[5]

And what does "43" think of the office now that he is in it? First, he thinks it is an enjoyable job, representing the pinnacle of personal accomplishment. In an interview with *Time*, quoted from above, the following exchange took place:

TIME: What's the most important thing you've learned from the past four years? [This was the magazine's first question to the president.]
BUSH: I've learned I really enjoy the job. It's a fantastic moment in my life, obviously.

Perhaps the president was merely channeling the late Ronald Reagan or the late James David Barber, both of whom taught that it was good for a president to enjoy his work, but it is hard to imagine any other modern president answering *Time*'s question in this way.[6]

The president's enjoyment, if not his pride, might have roots in his distinctly non-Neustadtian perspective on presidential power (see Neustadt 1960). Talking to Woodward (2002, 144) about his frustration at the slow pace of movement towards military action against the Taliban in Afghanistan, the president said "One of my jobs is to be provocative . . . to provoke people into—to force decisions, and to make sure it's clear in everybody's head where we're headed . . . I was beginning to get a little frustrated." The president was not about to leave the actual decision to intervene to his war cabinet, however. What he wanted, he went on to say, was "to make sure that the people [his advisers and cabinet members] understood that we were getting ready to attack." Worried that the members of his own administration were losing their sense of "purpose and forward movement," he decided he would push them, provoke them even, by asking "Does anybody doubt?" Did he explain to his national security adviser or anyone else what he was doing? Woodward asked. "Of course not. I'm the commander—see, I don't need to explain—I do not need to explain why I say things. That's the interesting thing about being the president. Maybe somebody needs to explain to me why they say something, but I don't feel like I owe anybody an explanation" (ibid. 145–6).

The personality system of the president did not *compel* him to war. It did make war more likely, though, when events came together on 9/11 that brought urgency to the responsibilities of the president. Because of the president's impulsive personality, he was prone to act on instinct; because of his assertiveness and fondness for decisive action, he was apt to choose, when following his instincts, more over less belligerent alternatives. And because of his tremendous confidence, and his fatalism, he was not inclined to ask a lot of questions about consequences. The crisis of 9/11, finally, brought into play the president's beliefs about God, Iraq, and the presidency. To see how these propensities influenced the course of events, we next look at the decision for war.

Decisions Leading to War

The decision for war against Iraq was not actually one decision, but many. There were in truth any number of smaller decisions made along the path to war. Six stand out prior to the ultimate decision for invasion. Below, I reconstruct each of these decisions to show how it was reached and how, progressively, options were narrowed, making the final choice for war all but inevitable. From, then, 11 September 2001 to 6 April 2002, the president decided that:

1. The nation was "going to war" (11 September 2001).
2. The United States would not distinguish between terrorists and states which support them (11 September 2001).
3. Action against Iraq would be deferred until al-Qaeda and the Taliban were hit (15 September 2001).
4. The military would plan and prepare for an Iraq war (12 November 2001).
5. Iraq, because of its presumed weapons of mass destruction (WMD) and unreliable history, would be publicly identified as a possible target for the implementation of a doctrine of pre-emptive war (29 January 2002).
6. Disarmament equaled regime change (6 April 2002).

Then there was the final decision to launch the war. This decision, unlike those that led up to it, can be observed only by the shadows that it cast.

Decision 1: "We Were Going to War"

When his chief of staff, Andrew Card, leaned over to whisper in the president's ear that a second plane had hit the World Trade Center in New York, "I made up my mind at that moment that we were going to war" (Woodward 2002, 15). In truth, the president's public statements that day reflected more hesitancy than he was willing later to acknowledge. In his very first remarks, made at a Sarasota, Florida school, the president began by expressing regret at having to cut short his trip—"I, unfortunately, will be going back to Washington after my remarks"—and thanked his hosts—"I do want to thank the folks here at Booker Elementary for their hospitality." Then he moved to the task at hand. "Today," he said, "we've had a national tragedy... an apparent terrorist attack on our country." Terrorism, the president said, echoing his father's famous remark about Saddam Hussein's occupation of Kuwait, "will not stand" (Bush 2001a). It was not war, though, but a criminal investigation that the president described when he next said that he had spoken "to the Vice President, to the Governor of New York, to the Director of the FBI and have ordered that the full resources of the Federal Government go to help the victims and their families and to conduct a full-scale investigation to hunt down and to find those folks who committed this act."

At Barksdale Air Force Base in Louisiana that afternoon, the president once again expressed resolve, but not a decision for war. "(F)reedom will be defended," he said (Bush 2001b). "The resolve of our great Nation is being tested... we will pass this test." The president's rhetoric still left doubt, though, about the relevance of military force. "The United States will," he said, "hunt down and punish those responsible," possibly, but not clearly, a military mission. If the president had truly already decided that "we were going to war," he had not yet found the words to express that decision.

That evening, the president spoke to the nation from the Oval Office, having insisted—against the advice of the Secret Service—upon returning to the White House that day. Before his speech, there was debate among unidentified West Wing staff members over whether the president should be more firm than he had been already that this was war. The president decided to strike from the speech the sentences, "This is not just an act of terrorism. This is an act of war" (Woodward 2002, 30).

But the president did make his first reference in that speech to a "war against terrorism" (Bush 2001c). The president also seemed to promise action incommensurate with a criminal justice campaign in his declaration that "we go forward to defend freedom and all that is good and just in our world." The next day, after meeting with his national security advisers in the morning, the president for the first time stated bluntly that the attacks "were acts of war" (Bush 2001d).

The president was more decisive, however, about the nature of the struggle. In his remarks at Barksdale, he had declared "Freedom, itself, was attacked this morning." In his speech that evening, the president elaborated on this theme. "America was targeted for attack," the president declared, not because of its policies or its actions, but "because we're the brightest beacon for freedom and opportunity in the world." The struggle to come, the president stated the following morning, would be "monumental," pitting "good versus evil." His first reference to the enemy as "evildoers" was made on 13 September, in a statement proclaiming a "National Day of Prayer and Remembrance" (Bush 2001g). His first spoken use of the term came on Sunday, 16 September, in remarks to reporters upon his return to the White House from a war council at Camp David the day before. The president referenced "evildoers" five times in answer to seven questions (Bush 2001j).

There was, over the course of the same few days, a change in the president's visible emotions.[7] On the day of the attacks, the president had expressed shock, sadness, and resolve. In the following days, shock receded, and "angry hostility," along with a desire for action, came into focus. In the first of several such references, the president said in brief remarks at the Pentagon that seeing the destruction made him sad, but also angry (Bush 2001e). The following day, in a public phone conference with the mayor of New York city and the governor of New York state, Bush declared an overtly bellicose "intention to rout out and whip terrorism" now that "an act of war" had been "declared" on the United States (Bush 2001f). "Whipping terrorism," the president repeated, was "now the focus of my administration." At the National Day of Prayer and Remembrance Service, the president returned again to these themes, and offered a clear sign of his decision to employ force. The nation's "responsibility" was clear: "To answer these attacks and rid the world of evil" (Bush 2001h). An angry nation, President Bush averred, would answer these acts of war, "in a way, and at an hour, of our choosing." On 14 September, the president ordered the call-up of Army reservists. "The message," he said speaking to reporters briefly the next morning at Camp David, "is for everybody who wears the uniform: Get ready" (Bush 2001i).

Decision 2: "We Will Make No Distinction . . ."

"We will make no distinction," the president declared in his evening televised address on 9/11, "between the terrorists who committed these acts and those who harbor them." It was the president's idea. An initial draft of his remarks for that evening, prepared by Gerson, had included a more vague statement about not distinguishing between those who carry out attacks and those who encourage or tolerate them. Gerson had found the idea in a speech Bush had given during the campaign. The president changed the language to "harbor." He then asked his national security adviser what she thought of this part of the speech.

In asking Rice her opinion, the president was inviting her to comment on its substance, not simply the timing or style of its articulation. Rice's understanding of her role, though, was as strict and focused as the president's personality. She did not present her own views to the president unless pressed.

"You can say it now or you'll have other opportunities to say it," Rice replied (Woodward 2002, 30). The president decided he would say it now.

After the speech, the president met first with the full National Security Council, along with invited guests, and afterwards with his war cabinet. To the latter group, he made a pronouncement. "We have made the decision," he said, using the royal plural, "to punish whoever harbors terrorists, not just the perpetrators" (ibid. 31).

These first two decisions had important consequences. Among them was raising the costs of inaction against state sponsors of terror. Now that the president had identified such states as threats to the nation's security, on a par with those emanating from "evildoers" who had murdered thousands of American civilians, should the president *not* act aggressively against such states, the outcome might well be to embolden, and thereby increase the threat from, precisely those states.

Decision 3: "We'll Get This Guy... at a Time and Place of Our Choosing"

Using military force against Iraq to implement the nation's long-standing preference for regime change had been considered, in at least an abstract fashion, by Bush's national security advisers before 9/11. On 1 July 2001, a Principal's Committee meeting reviewed four options regarding Iraq, ranging from a continuation of the present containment policy—through "no-fly zones" and sanctions—to a full-scale invasion. The two intermediate options also involved the use of additional force, either by arming opposition forces (option 2), or by taking and holding a piece of Iraq (option 3) (Gordon and Trainor 2006, 10). Bush's advisers reached no consensus at this meeting on a policy to recommend to the president. There was, however, considerable interest within parts of the administration in pursuing military options against Iraq, and had been since the transition.

The presence within the Bush Administration, principally in the office of the vice president and the secretary of defense, of committed "neoconservatives" has been well documented (Halper and Clarke 2004; see also Mann 2004). The neoconservatives had lobbied throughout the 1990s to focus the government's attention on what they perceived to be a considerable, growing threat to the West from Iraq, insufficiently mitigated by the actions of the United Nations or the Clinton Administration. In the second Bush Administration, a rather remarkable migration occurred from neoconservative niches outside the government into the Bush Administration (Sanders and Langston 2004). In part as a result of the work of this group from within the government, two senior members of the war cabinet, the vice president, Dick Cheney, and the secretary of defense, Donald Rumsfeld, had come to see Iraq's containment as a failed policy. Rumsfeld was also concerned that target-poor Afghanistan might be a difficult environment for the exercise of

US military power, relative in particular to Iraq. Although Cheney, at this early date, had perhaps not yet come down with the Iraq war "fever" that Secretary of State Colin Powell diagnosed him as exhibiting a year later, he had been pushing since the transition for prioritizing Iraq on any listing of threats facing the United States (see Woodward 2004, 175). At the sub-cabinet level, the interest in toppling Hussein was intense at the Department of Defense (see Dolan and Cohen 2006). There, Undersecretary for Policy Douglas Feith, in fact told the "J-3," the general officer in charge of operations for the Joint Staff, on the day of September 11, that he should not be "working on Afghanistan. You ought to be working on Iraq" (Gordon and Trainor 2006, 15).

It was not Rumsfeld's style to be so forthright, but at Camp David on the 15th, he brought briefing materials for three sets of targets, Afghanistan, Iraq, and al-Qaeda, along with a written argument that only the last two were strategic threats to the nation (ibid.). Rumsfeld also brought his deputy, Paul Wolfowitz, who presented to the group his own favored war plan, option three from the discussion of July. (Powell, believing this was to be a principals-only meeting, had left his deputy behind.) Among the reasons for pursuing this plan now, Wolfowitz said, was that there was up to a "fifty percent chance" that Saddam was involved in the 9/11 attacks. Although in the morning, Bush encouraged Wolfowitz to say more about his ideas, he "sent a message," in Bob Woodward's (2002, 85) reporting, to the group before lunch, presumably through either Card or Rice, that "he had heard enough debate over Iraq."[8]

In the afternoon session, the president asked the principals—the secretaries of state and defense, the director of central intelligence, the chief of staff and the director of the FBI—for their recommendations. Powell led off, arguing for the primacy of Afghanistan and al-Qaeda, declaring that going with the "Iraq option" now would "lose the coalition" for the war against terror (ibid. 87). Although Rumsfeld, in particular, took issue with Powell's reasoning, none of the principals advocated taking action on Iraq at this point. At the end of the meeting, the president informed the group, "I'll let you know what I've decided." Before the session broke up, he exchanged a few words with chair of the joint chiefs of staff General Hugh Shelton. "We'll get this guy," the president said, "but at a time and place of our choosing" (Gordon and Trainor 2006). When the national security team next convened Monday morning, the president told the group what he had told Shelton: although "I believe Iraq was involved," he said, "I'm not going to strike them now" (Woodward 2002, 97).

Decision 4: "Let's Get Started on This"

After an NSC meeting on 12 November 2001, Bush reportedly pulled Rumsfeld aside. "How do you feel about the war plan for Iraq," the president asked. "Let's get started on this. And get Tommy Franks [combatant commander for the Middle East, presently conducting the war in Afghanistan] looking at what it would take" to remove Hussein (Woodward 2004, 2). His final instruction to Rumsfeld was to keep this secret, even within the government. (He authorized an exception be made so that Rumsfeld could speak to George Tenet at the CIA.)

The making and revision of war plans is a routine exercise in the Pentagon. Rumsfeld, as part of his effort at military "transformation," had in fact already begun a systematic review and redrafting of all major war plans for the department. There is, however, a fine line between drafting war plans and preparing for war. Given the tension between the United States and Iraq, and the intense interest in an Iraq war among civilian elites at the Pentagon, it is not surprising that the order to plan led quickly to practical preparations. The armed forces could go at any time, the general insisted when queried by the president, but to go with confidence, and without unnecessary cost in American lives, required a great deal of advance work: people and things had to be put into new configurations, not just on paper but on the ground. This would take money and time, probably a year, the general told the president in February 2002. Throughout the planning and preparation, the president approved a number of steps, each small and incremental in itself, which established a momentum for military action, including the reprogramming of funds for a command and control headquarters in Qatar, and an incremental build-up of American forces (ibid. 59; Franks 2004, 343, 376). General Franks, under continuous pressure from the secretary of defense, decreased to a minimum the time that would elapse between an execute order and the commencement of military operations.

Decision 5: "I Will Not Wait on Events, While Dangers Gather"

With victory in Afghanistan already behind him, the president reported on the state of the union on 29 January 2002 (Bush 2002a). This was the memorable "axis of evil" speech. Iraq, along with North Korea and Iran—included in the drafting process, so as to soften the message regarding Iraq—was identified as a particularly bad state, one whose regime "leav[es] the bodies of mothers huddled over their dead children."[9] Because these states, along with their terrorist "allies," seek WMD, said the president, they "pose a grave and growing danger." They could blackmail other states, or give weapons of catastrophic power to terrorists. To defend against this threat, the president said, the United States would not "wait on events."

The president elaborated on this theme in several other speeches during 2002, in particular at a West Point commencement address on 1 June (Bush 2002b). On that occasion, the president set forth many of his administration's developing ideas about national security in the aftermath of 9/11. In particular, he identified the nexus of WMD and terrorist groups—especially radical Islamic terrorist groups—as the "gravest danger to freedom" (Halper and Clarke 2004, 140). The United States, he said, must be alert not only to new threats, though, but to new opportunities, because the "war on terror will not be won on the defensive." Americans must be prepared, he said, for "preemptive action when necessary." On 17 September, the president's declarations received the imprimatur of a doctrine, with the publication of the Bush Administration's first formal *National Security Strategy* (2002).

Under this new doctrine, the United States might be justified to engage Saddam Hussein's Iraq if he did not comply with even existing United Nations demands to abandon WMD and WMD programs in chemical, biological, and nuclear weapons. UN weapons inspectors had not been permitted into Iraq since 1998; in the meantime, Hussein had presumably continued to seek the means to threaten his neighbors and perhaps even his distant adversaries. In response to Hussein's 1998 decision no longer to cooperate with weapons inspectors, the UN had expressed "alarm" (Resolution 1205, 5 November 1998) and President Clinton had ordered retaliatory missile strikes to "degrade" Iraq's capacity "to develop and deliver weapons of mass destruction" (Clinton 1998).

By 2001, to "demand" Iraqi disarmament was routine. It was the sort of demand that, for "reasons that have a lot to do with the US government bureaucracy . . . everyone could agree on."[10] To mean it with the literal force of an imperative: "prove beyond a shadow of a doubt that you no longer possess weapons of mass destruction or we will invade you and take over your country," was a radical innovation embodied in the Bush Doctrine. This decision established an incentive for action sufficiently great so as to demonstrate the credibility of the president's threatening words.

Decision 6: "He Goes"

Because President Bush saw Hussein as irrevocably untrustworthy, he would not be prone to give him the benefit of any doubts when it came time for the Iraqi government to demonstrate its disarmament. To Bush, disarmament in Iraq came quickly to mean regime change. The president said as much himself in an interview with a UK television network after hosting Tony Blair and his family at the Crawford ranch, 6–7 April 2002. "I made up my mind that Saddam needs to go," the president told the reporter. "The policy of my government is that he goes" (Woodward 2004, 119). Later in 2002, Powell became concerned that "the discussions of Iraq were increasingly focused on military planning" and sought a private meeting with the president to urge him to consider other options. In a two-hour session with the president, 5 August, to which Bush invited Rice, Powell urged diplomacy, but acknowledged that diplomacy, rather than force, might mean "no war," and a result "less clean" than "going in and taking the guy out." Powell recalled later that he felt constrained in his advice to stay within the parameters of what he saw as the president's settled belief that disarmament meant Hussein's removal, one way or another (ibid. 148–51).

The Final Decision: The Choice for War

So at what point did the president at last decide to take the final, irreversible step? As late as early January 2003, the president questioned several people about when they thought he would have crossed a point of no return. General Franks told him, when you commit Special Forces on the ground inside Iraq for offensive operations, which was planned for 48 hours before the official start of war (ibid. 258). Rumsfeld, involved in negotiations for the formation of a military coalition, said it was "When your people, Mr. President, look people in the eye and tell them you're going" (ibid. 261). These conversations took place when the president was engaged in a very public effort at disarmament through diplomatic action at the United Nations. Was Bush serious, though, about diplomacy? Was he truly keeping an open mind?

The head of the British intelligence service, MI6, was doubtful. "There was a perceptible shift in attitude," he reported to his colleagues about what he had learned in a visit with Rice and Tenet in July 2002 (Manning 2005). "Military action was now seen as inevitable. Bush wanted to remove Saddam through military action, justified by the conjunction of terrorism and WMD." The "intelligence and facts were being fixed around the policy." "The NSC," the memo continues, "has no patience with the UN route..."[11] We will likely never know if the British intelligence chief's understanding was correct, or even if it was, whether his impressions, formed from conversation with Bush's advisers, accurately reflected Bush's thinking. It is, however, one among a number of indications that the president had indeed decided upon war before it was possible for him to reveal his decision.

Shortly before making his choice known to the world, the president did take into his confidence a small number of associates. Karl Rove may have gotten the message first (though Cheney has not spoken of when *he* knew). "We've got a war coming" the president confided to Rove at the Crawford ranch over Christmas, 2002 (Woodward 2004, 256). On 2 January, Bush told Rice, "Probably going to have to; we're going to have to go to war" (ibid. 254). Shortly thereafter, the president made similar remarks to a handful of people, including, in chronological order, Rumsfeld, Prince Bandar bin Sultan, the ambassador to the United States from Saudi Arabia, and Powell, who was informed—after Rice told Bush it was the thing to do—14 January. Along the way, he asked for advice on his final decision from only Rice and Karen Hughes, his Texas friend and communications adviser (ibid. 251).

Well before the president felt comfortable revealing the imminence of war, however, a number of people with a close working relationship with him had moments of clarity of their own, similar to that of the British intelligence chief. In chronological order, the following epiphanies have been recorded:

1. First, reflecting a good sense of prudence, was Tommy Franks, who in briefing component commanders in Germany about the evolving war plans for Iraq warned them, "if you guys think this is not going to happen, you're wrong" (ibid. 113).[12] Either Hussein is going to leave, or Bush is going to war, he told them, before observing dryly that Saddam Hussein was not about to leave. (21 March 2002.)

2. Condoleezza Rice reportedly informed an associate in the State Department that, in his words, "that decision's been made, don't waste your breath" (Lemann 2003).[13] (July 2002.)

3. The president's legislative affairs director, Nick Calio, judged on the basis of "side comments and body language" that the "question was not if but when there would be a war" (Woodward 2004, 168–9). (3 September 2002.)

4. Finally, there is the testimony of the champions of an Iraq war from even before 9/11. In hindsight, both Dick Cheney and Paul Wolfowitz perceived Bush as someone who understood what "had to be done." At a celebratory dinner at the vice president's residence after the launch of war, Cheney got together with Wolfowitz, Scooter Libby, Cheney's top aide and another True Believer in the Iraq option, and Kenneth Adelman, a foreign policy veteran who had advocated war from outside the administration. Reconstructing the conversation from his usual highly placed but unnamed sources, Woodward (ibid. 210) has Cheney saying that from the time of 9/11, Bush "understood what had to be done," that "he had to do Afghanistan first" but "knew he had to do Iraq." (13 April 2003.)

Personality on Display

The president's major personality attributes include impulsiveness, fatalism, and disdain for deliberation. All were at work in the decisions leading to war. "What you saw was my gut instinct," the president said in recounting his solo decision making on the day of September 11 (Woodward 2002, 15, 342). In reaching his first two important decisions on the path to war in Iraq— that the nation was "going to war" and that this war would target states, not just terrorists—he acted literally on impulse. In making these decisions, the president did not discuss with others the consequences of his decisions, and given the speed with which the decisions were made, could hardly have given much thought to the topic himself.

Bush's rashness makes sense in light of, and only in light of, his fatalism, both a personality trait and an aspect of his religious world-view. Consequences are important to the president, but they are not under his control. This is all the more true for Bush as president, for he believes that the president leads the nation in, quite literally, doing God's work. That the president saw himself and his actions in this way is suggested strongly by the language he adopted when articulating his initial decisions. He placed them rhetorically not only in the familiar context of American civil religion, but framed them by reference to his more idiosyncratic belief of a national obligation assertively to defend a God-granted right to human freedom.

Decision making by pronouncement was followed chronologically by an anomalous example of deliberation. At Camp David on the Saturday after September 11, the president and his national security advisers, along with several of their deputies, considered a range of options for the government's response. Although the president believed Iraq was complicit in the attacks on the United States, he was not yet willing to declare it a target for war. In several sessions that day, Bush allowed both advocates and opponents of an Iraq attack to present their views. Although this has the appearance of a "rational" decision-making session, the events of that day, as we have them indirectly from Woodward and others, suggest that the president maintained control over the conversation, perhaps even setting boundaries in order to ensure a predetermined outcome.[14] By allowing his Iraq hawks to make their case in detail, only to be rebutted, predictably, by the secretary of state, the president demonstrated to the former that he would have to overcome internal opposition before he might embrace their goal, while maintaining credibility with the latter. By polling his advisers after signaling to them that he had heard enough, he suggested to them the desired response.

After taking the Iraq option off the table by consensus, the president placed it back on by fiat. He did so, first, by issuing a stealthy order for secretive war preparations. Before making this decision, the president, typically, asked for no advice, though he recalled informing Rice (Woodward 2004, 4). As to whether he consulted Vice President Cheney, the president told Woodward he could not recall. There was no deliberation; in fact, the meeting of 15 September may have been the first and last time when a full range of options with regard to Iraq were open for conversation in the president's presence.

The president followed this covert move by an overt declaration of a rationale for offensive war against an imperfectly realized threat. From a realist perspective on international relations, it was only a matter of time after the end of the Cold War before the United States began to assert itself more forcefully. If "the new assertiveness of U.S. hegemony is accidental, the product of a reaction of personalities and events," Robert Jervis (2003, 83–7) has written, it was "an accident waiting to happen." How that would happen, though, was anyone's guess until President Bush's State of the Union address of 2002. Again, and typically, the president made the decision to identify Iraq as part of an "axis of evil" without deliberation, and without excessive consideration of consequences.

The president's preparation for war against Iraq gave expression not only to his religious beliefs, but to his disdain for his predecessor's alleged failures in Iraq policy as well. Clinton's (and Bush Sr.'s) containment of Saddam betrayed intolerable weakness. The president's belief that his predecessor had exhibited a damning weakness against Hussein also led him to shift responsibility for the avoidance of war to the target of war itself, which was the result of decision six, that disarmament equaled regime change. Even had Hussein cooperated more fully with the UN weapons inspectors, it is likely that Bush would have continued on the path to war. So long as Hussein was in office, Iraq posed an unacceptable threat to the United States, as that threat was perceived by the president.

Throughout the course of events, the president's belief in the nature of presidential command leadership was also, finally, in evidence. The president thought he was under no obligation to inform his secretary of state, for instance, before deciding that states as well as terrorist groups would be targeted in the nation's new war. The secretary, like the rest of us, could learn the government's policy by watching TV. President Bush's understanding of his role as "the decider" made it difficult at times for advisers to impinge upon his mindset. Thus, when Powell attempted to dissuade the president from war in their after-hours conversation of 5 August, the president seemed not to hear. "Basically what he was saying," Bush recalled, "was that if in fact Saddam is toppled by military [action], we better have a strong understanding about what it's going to take to rebuild Iraq" (Woodward 2004, 152). Powell, Bush said, was talking tactics; Bush's job was strategy. In fact, Powell had been trying to tell the president that too much could go wrong to justify war.

As for the president's questioning late in the process of when he would have reached a "point of no return," that too manifested the president's perception of the president as the man (always) in charge—"the decider." From the start of the planning process, the secretary of defense had stressed to the combatant commander that he must not go so far in his preparations as to "commit the nation to war" inadvertently (Franks 2004, 342, 359, 389, 425). Continuing the conversation on this topic deep into the process, as the president did, likely eased the president's anxiety, which he otherwise did not permit himself to express. It is difficult, after all, for a president to acknowledge that he has in fact relinquished control of events. President John Kennedy similarly maintained with his top aides what can be seen in hindsight as a polite fiction that, at almost any moment up to the final order to initiate operations, the president might simply choose to say "no" to the Bay of Pigs operation.[15]

A president without Bush's combination of personal qualities would likely have chosen differently in the wake of 9/11. Consider a president, for instance, who was deliberative and habitually anxious about the consequences of decisions. Such a president might well have considered regime change by force in Iraq—it was a policy strongly desired by a sufficient number of people to guarantee that any president would at least have been lobbied to "do Iraq"—but in the context of a more careful consideration of a range of options. If war had been chosen even so, it would likely have been chosen after greater consideration for its consequences, leading perhaps to a different sort of war. A president with a less imperturbable self-confidence would presumably have been more interested in examining alternative scenarios for the unfolding of the war and its aftermath. Consider, further, a president with more conventional views about the American civil religion and the role of the president in relation to his advisers. Such a president would have judged the costs and benefits of war differently, and would probably not have been so blithe about opposition from within the administration.

Conclusion: When Personality Matters

When President Bush chose war in Iraq, he gave expression to personal motivations, personality attributes, and highly personal views on his enemy, his religion, and his office. It seems unlikely, on the evidence of his public statements, that the president truly formed quite as instant a determination to begin on the path that led to war as he recounts. Bush is apparently so enamored of the image of himself as "the decider" that he would rather appear to have erred on the side of rashness than of indecision. In truth, his words in the first twelve hours of the 9/11 crisis revealed the same sort of natural uncertainty that some say his father experienced much later on the way to *his* Iraq war. In the father's case, it possibly took a visit with British Prime Minister Margaret Thatcher to stiffen the president's resolve. This was no time, Thatcher had lectured the president, to "go wobbly."[16] Perhaps the son, too, had his Thatcher moment—an encounter with a trusted associate that struck in him a "challenge chord."[17] No such conversation has been reported. In any event, by the time the president spoke that evening from the Oval Office, he had made some important decisions, decisions that constrained future choices and created momentum for war.

How and why did Bush move from the decision that "we were going to war" in principle, to the actual—if inaccessible—decision to invade Iraq? He did so through a series of small decisions, often rashly made. More specifically, Bush ended up at war because:

- He continuously went with his gut, making one decision after another with no or minimal deliberation beforehand. Each decision moved him closer to war.

- Once George W. Bush fixed upon a policy, or began down a path to which he had publicly committed himself, he did not tolerate doubt.

- He followed his beliefs—his "vision thing"—which instructed him that, in invading Iraq, he was leading the United States in the fulfillment of its providential mission to restore freedom to the oppressed, and also fulfilling the potentialities of his office.

- He had a passionate contempt for Saddam Hussein and for the allegedly soft way in which he had been treated in the recent past.

The president's personality and world-view were critical to the decision for war. Personality determined the procedural framework of decisions. Important choices would be made by instinct, without deliberation or consultation. This is not a process for decision making that we can diagram in a flow chart, but it is a process nonetheless. Because his personality led the president to choose impulsively, his world-view did not merely shape the decisions he actually made, it determined them, in the sense that several of the president's critical decisions were reflexive manifestations of pre-existing beliefs and orientations. To think that the president might at some point have been reasoned off the path that led to war would be to miss the point. George W. Bush could not be reasoned out of his choices that led to war, because he did not reason his way into those choices in the first place.

This analysis also suggests that in studying a decision for war, it is worthwhile to open up the time frame for analysis and look at early path-setting decisions. To do otherwise might lead to an *overstatement* of the extent to which a president was motivated by either emotion or a radically incomplete or biased examination of facts.

To "take a nation to war" implies that the nation would rather be someplace else. In this case, certainly, the president acted in the final months before the war as if it were his duty to inflame the passions of the entire world against Saddam Hussein. The president was so determined by January 2003 to "make his case" against Saddam that he and, particularly, his vice president, dismissed, denied, and even ridiculed doubts and deficiencies in the intelligence upon which the administration built its political and legal case for war.[18] He encouraged Colin Powell to lay out not a judicious, but a lawyerly indictment against Hussein before the United Nations (Woodward 2004, 250, 288). He also made some of his harshest comments about Hussein and his regime during this time. The enemy was no abstract evildoer, but a regime under whose misrule innocent civilians' "tongues are cut off; their eyes are gouged out; and female relatives are raped in their presence" (Bush 2003).

By looking at the decision to go to war as one made up of several smaller decisions over a long time, it is possible to see all this for what it was, not part of the record of decision making at all—the decision had already been reached—but the first phase of war, that of "information operations."

The confluence of George W. Bush as president and 9/11 created a "perfect storm" for the influence of personality upon foreign policy decision making. The consequent damage, to the process as well as the substance of decisions, was done months before the president at last ordered the first military personnel into harm's way. It may, or may not, turn out for the good. Either way, it is a remarkable demonstration of the simple fact that the American people often get more than they could imagine from their selection of a chief executive.[19]

References

Allen, Mike. 2003. "Close Look at a Focused President." *Washington Post*. 27 April, A4.

Barber, James David. 1992. *Presidential Character: Predicting Performance in the White House*, 4th ed. Englewood Cliffs, NJ: Prentice-Hall.

Bush, George. 1991. "State of the Union Address." *Public Papers of the President*. January 29.

_____ and Scowcroft, Brent. 1998. *A World Transformed*. New York: Knopf.

Bush, George W. 2001a. "Remarks in Sarasota, Florida, on the Terrorist Attack on New York City's World Trade Center." *Public Papers of the President*. 11 September.

_____ 2001b. "Remarks at Barksdale Air Force Base, Louisiana, on the Terrorist Attacks." *Public Papers of the President*. 11 September.

_____ 2001c. "Address to the Nation on the Terrorist Attacks." *Public Papers of the President*. 11 September.

_____ 2001d. "Remarks Following a Meeting with the National Security Team." *Public Papers of the President*. 12 September.

_____ 2001e. "Remarks While Touring Damage at the Pentagon in Arlington, Virginia." *Public Papers of the President*. 12 September.

_____ 2001f. "Remarks in a Telephone Conversation with New York City Mayor Rudolph W. Giuliani and New York Governor George E. Pataki and an Exchange with Reporters." *Public Papers of the President*. 13 September.

_____ 2001g. "Proclamation 7462: National Day of Prayer and Remembrance for the Victims of Terrorist Attacks on September 11, 2001." *Public Papers of the President*. 13 September .

_____ 2001h. "Remarks at the National Day of Prayer and Remembrance Service." *Public Papers of the President*. 14 September.

_____ 2001i. "Remarks in a Meeting with the National Security Team and an Exchange with Reporters at Camp David, Maryland." *Public Papers of the President*. 14 September.

_____ 2001j. "Remarks on Arrival at the White House and an Exchange with Reporters." *Public Papers of the President*. 16 September.

_____ 2002a. "Address Before a Joint Session of Congress on the State of the Union." *Public Papers of the President*. 29 January.

———2002*b*. "Commencement Address at the United States Military Academy at West Point, New York." *Public Papers of the President.* 1 June.

———2003. "President Bush Discusses Iraq in Radio Address." *Public Papers of the President.* 15 March.

Clinton, Bill. 1998. "Address to the Nation Announcing Military Strikes on Iraq." *Public Papers of the President.* 16 December.

Dickerson, John F., and Gibbs, Nancy. 2004. "'I've Gained Strength': The President Who Reads History Books Like a User's Manual Talks about Where he Fits in Himself." *Time.* 6 September.

Dolan, Chris, and Cohen, David B. 2006. "The War about the War: Iraq and the Politics of National Security Advising in the George W. Bush Administration's First Term." *Politics and Policy* 34 (March): 30–64.

Duffy, Michael. 2002. "9/11, One Year Later: The President." *Time,* 1 September. Online at ⟨http://www.time.com/time/covers/1101020909/abattle.html⟩, accessed 21 November 2006.

"Exclusive: The Bush Family." *D. Phil.* September 29. Online at ⟨http://drphil.com/shows/show/529/⟩, accessed 21 November 2006.

Fineman, Howard. 2003. "Bush and God, How Faith Changed His Life and Shapes His Presidency." *Newsweek,* 10 March.

Franks, Tommy. 2004. *American Soldier.* New York: Regan.

Frum, David. 2003. *The Right Man: The Surprise Presidency of George W. Bush.* New York: Random House.

George, Alexander L. 1980. *Presidential Decisionmaking in Foreign Policy: The Effective Use of Information and Advice.* Boulder, CO: Westview.

"George Bush and God: A Hot Line to Heaven." 2004. *The Economist.* 16 December. Online at ⟨http://www.economist.com/printedition/displayStory.cfm?Story_ID=3502861#top⟩, accessed 21 November 2006.

Gordon, Michael R., and Trainor, General Bernard E. 2006. *Cobra II: The Inside Story of the Invasion and Occupation of Iraq.* New York: Pantheon.

Halper, Stefan, and Clarke, Jonathan. 2004. *America Alone: The Neo-Conservatives and the Global Order.* Cambridge: Cambridge University Press.

Hunt, Terence. 2006. "Bush, 'The Decider', Vows More Changes." *ABC News: Nightline.* 18 April. Online at ⟨http://www.abcnews.go.com/Politics/wireStory?id=1856539⟩, accessed 21 November 2006.

Immelman, Aubrey. 1999. "The Political Personality of George W. Bush: Brief Research Report." *Clio's Psych: The Journal of the Psychohistory Forum* 6 (September): 74–75. Online at ⟨http://www.csbsju.edu/uspp/Bush/Political-Personality.html⟩, accessed 21 November 2006.

Jervis, Robert. 2003. "The Compulsive Empire." *Foreign Policy* (July/August): 83–7.

Kegnor, Paul. 2004. *God and George W. Bush: A Spiritual Life.* New York: Regan.

LaGay, Faith. 2002. "Running in First Place." *AMA Virtual Mentor, Ethx Bytes.* October. Online at ⟨http://www.ama-assn.org/ama/pub/category/8868.html⟩, accessed 21 November 2006.

Land, Richard. 2004. "The Jesus Factor: Interview with Richard Land." *PBS Frontline.* 29 April. Online at ⟨www.pbs.org/wgbh/pages/frontline/shows/jesus/interviews/land.html⟩, accessed 21 November 2006.

Lane, Robert Edwards. 1962. *Political Ideology: Why the American Common Man Believes What He Does*. New York: Free Press.

Langston, Thomas S. 1997. *With Reverence and Contempt: How Americans Think About Their President*. Baltimore, Md.: Johns Hopkins University Press.

―――2006. *Cold War Presidency*. Washington DC: CQ Press.

Lemann, Nicholas. 2003. "How it Came to War." *The New Yorker*. 31 March. Online at ⟨http://www.newyorker.com/fact/content/articles/030331fa_fact⟩, accessed 21 November 2006.

Lincoln, Bruce. 2004. *Holy Terrors: Thinking about Religion after September 11*. Chicago: The University of Chicago Press.

Mann, James. 2004. *The Rise of the Vulcans: The History of Bush's War Cabinet*. New York: Viking.

Manning, David. 2005. "The Secret Downing Street Memo." *Times Online*. 1 May. Online at ⟨http://www.timesonline.co.uk/article/0,,2087-1593607,00.html⟩, accessed 21 November 2006.

Minutaglio, Bill. 1999. *First Son: George W. Bush and the Bush Family Dynasty*. New York: Times Books.

National Security Strategy of the United States of America. 2002. September. Online at ⟨http://www.whitehouse.gov/nsc/nss.pdf⟩, accessed 21 November 2006.

Neustadt, Richard E. 1960. *Presidential Power: The Politics of Leadership*. New York: John Wiley and Sons.

Parmet, Herbert S. 1997. *George Bush: The Life of a Lone Star Yankee*. New York: Scribner.

Renshon, Stanley A. 2004. *In His Father's Shadow: The Transformations of George W. Bush*. New York: Palgrave Macmillan.

Rubenzer, Steven J., and Faschingbauer, Thomas R. 2004. *Personality, Character, and Leadership in the White House: Psychologists Assess the Presidents*. Washington, DC: Brassey's.

Sanders, Elizabeth, and Langston, Thomas S. 2004. "Taking Ideologues Seriously, Neo-conservative Influence and Theories of the Presidency." Paper presented at the Annual Meeting of the American Political Science Association, Washington, DC.

Schweizer, Peter, and Schweizer, Rochelle. 2004. *The Bushes: Portrait of a Dynasty*. New York: Doubleday.

Sidey, Hugh. 2003. " 'He Had No Respect for Our Military Then', The President's Father on Saddam, the First Gulf War and What His Son Faces Now." *Time*. 17 March.

Singer, Peter. 2004. *The President of Good and Evil: The Ethics of George W. Bush*. New York: Dutton.

Suskind, Ron. 2004*a*. *The Price of Loyalty: George W. Bush, the White House, and the Education of Paul O'Neill*. New York: Simon & Schuster.

―――2004*b*. "Without a Doubt." *New York Times Magazine*. 17 October.

Wallis, Jim. 2004. "The Jesus Factor: Interview with Richard Land." *PBS Frontline*. 29 April. Online at ⟨www.pbs.org/wgbh/pages/frontline/shows/jesus/interviews/wallis.html⟩, accessed 21 November 2006.

Wayne, Stephen J. 1993. "President Bush Goes to War: A Psychological Interpretation from a Distance," in Stanley Renshon (ed.), *The Political Psychology of the Gulf War: Leaders, Public, and the Process of Conflict*. Pittsburgh: University of Pittsburgh Press.

Wead, Doug. 2004. "The Jesus Factor: Interview with Doug Wead." *PBS Frontline.* 29 April. Online at ⟨www.pbs.org/wgbh/pages/frontline/shows/jesus/interviews/wead.html⟩, accessed 21 November 2006.

Wolfowitz, Paul. 2003. "Deputy Secretary Wolfowitz Interview with Sam Tanenhaus, *Vanity Fair.*" News Transcript, United States Department of Defense. 9 May. Online at ⟨www.defenselink.mil/Transcripts/archive.aspx⟩, accessed 21 November 2006.

Woodward, Bob. 2002. *Bush at War.* New York: Simon & Schuster.

——2004. *Plan of Attack.* New York: Simon & Schuster.

Yetiv, Steven A. 2004. *Explaining Foreign Policy: U.S. Decision Making and the Persian Gulf War.* Baltimore, Md.: Johns Hopkins University Press.

Notes

1. Bush, naturally, discounts as "psychobabble" accounts that seek the roots of his behavior in his past (see Minutaglio 1999, 311).
2. In the index to *Bush at War* (Woodward 2002, 359) there are twenty entries for "Bush, George W.: action desired by." There are three entries for "Bush, George W.: advice sought by."
3. As Peter Singer has noted, the president uses the term "evil" a great deal, and did so even before 9/11. According to Singer, the president spoke of evil in fully 30 per cent of the speeches he delivered between his inaugural and 16 June 2003. Moreover, evil, in Bush's rhetoric, is usually a noun, a "thing, or a force, something that has a real existence apart from the . . . acts of which human beings are capable" (Singer 2004, 2).
4. The president was defending to Woodward his choice to name Iran as within the "axis of evil." Bush said he "made a calculation" that the reformers would be pleased by his statement. In fact, the president's remarks created a backlash against the reformers which contributed to the success of harshly anti-American parties and leaders in the struggle for power within Iran.
5. The Bushes' perspective on the presidency conforms to the perspective, in this regard, of the "American common man" of the High Cold War era. See Lane 1962. That this confirms to the Bush family's perspective on the presidency is suggested by the emphasis at the Bush Presidential Library and Museum upon the Gulf War. On a stone wall of the museum are inscribed, in enormous letters designed to be visible by visitors making their way by car to the site, a quotation from the president's 1991 State of the Union Address, delivered 12 days after the air war had begun: "Let future generations understand the burden and the blessings of freedom. Let them say, we stood where duty required us to stand" (Bush 1991). It also bears noting that the president, the only modern president not to publish traditional memoirs, instead co-authored a book on his foreign affairs leadership with his national security adviser (Bush and Scowcroft 1998).
6. James David Barber (1992) popularized this idea in a series of op-ed essays on presidential candidates from 1972 into the 1990s. The president's father says he hears no complaints from his son about the job. See Sidey 2003.

7. I take the idea of chronicling the president's observable emotions from Stephen J. Wayne (1993, 20–48), who found more interesting variation over time in the emotions of the elder Bush in the Gulf War.

8. Gordon and Trainor (2006, 16) suggest that at the morning sessions, Wolfowitz and Rumsfeld were acting out a preconceived plan to advance the Iraq option together, in such a way as partially to hide Rumsfeld's hand.

9. Speechwriter David Frum had initially named only Iraq part of an "axis of hatred." Rice and her deputy, Stephen Hadley, suggested the addition of Iran and North Korea. Talking it over with the president, though, they expressed doubt about the wisdom of listing Iran. The president, characteristically, lunged: "No, I want it. . . . No question about it." Scooter Libby, in the vice president's office, had wanted Syria named too, but Rice had demurred (Woodward 2004, 88–90).

10. The words are from a perhaps over-interpreted statement by Paul Wolfowitz, at the end of a lengthy interview with a journalist. Wolfowitz was replying, incautiously, to a question about the "motive" for war. See Wolfowitz 2003.

11. This statement from the memo is curious, in that the NSC included Secretary Powell, who seems to have had quite a lot of enthusiasm for the "UN route." Perhaps the speaker and/or writer meant, rather, the NSA, the national security adviser, Rice herself.

12. Compare, though, with Franks's (2004, 382–4) somewhat less dramatic account. In Franks's own account, he tells his component commanders that the "NSC believes . . . diplomacy might work," before then shaking his head. "There's a burglar in the house," he told them—a situation requiring their urgent and complete attention.

13. Rice herself told Woodward that she thought the president had truly reached his decision point on 2 January 2002 (Woodward 2002, 254).

14. Wolfowitz (2003) speaks briefly of the conversations at Camp David in his interview for *Vanity Fair*.

15. The relevant literature is large. For an overview, see Langston 2006, ch. 4.

16. The president thought the comment gratuitous. His major biographer concurs (see Parmet 1997, 454).

17. The term is from Wayne 1993.

18. See James Pfiffner's chapter in this volume on this point.

19. On this last point, see Langston 1997, ch. 5.

6

From Success to Failure? Iraq and the Organization of George W. Bush's Decision Making

John P. Burke

How does one account for the evolution in performance of the Bush presidency? Bush and his associates began with what is generally regarded as a successful transition to office and a generally able response to the events of September 11. However, by the administration's third and fourth year in office its performance appeared flawed. Much of its case for war against the Saddam Hussein regime in Iraq proved to be based on faulty evidence and the postwar reconstruction of Iraq was poorly planned and executed. Although a free, democratic, and politically stable Iraq may yet emerge, few major decisions made by a modern president were so defective in terms of *process*. Indeed, decisions on Iraq will provide the bulk of my more detailed examination of this administration's difficulties in decision-making organization and outcomes.

As well, the start of Bush's second term was inauspicious: few major policy initiatives reached fruition. Social security reform especially garnered limited support, congressional opposition increased (even within the president's own party), the administration's response to Hurricane Katrina was poorly executed, the White House was put on the defensive by revelations of a secret eavesdropping program, the ill-advised nomination of Harriet Miers to the Supreme Court had to be withdrawn, media reports were increasingly critical in tone, and the president's approval ratings with the public dropped below 40 per cent by November 2005. Bush may well recover over the remaining years of his presidency. But despite his successful re-election effort, the period from 2003 through 2005 was one of questionable performance.

Although a number of factors were undoubtedly at work that can account for change in presidential performance over time, my aim is to examine it through the lens of presidential decision making, particularly its organization and operations. I take this approach not to suggest that decision making explains all, only that it may be especially illuminating: if decision outcomes are problematic, decision-making processes are likely a strong explanatory variable. Furthermore, the Bush presidency may be particularly instructive in this regard. Bush was the chief executive of a large state and the first president to hold an MBA degree. During his transition to office, he was sensitive to his needs as a decision maker and frequently exhibited an awareness of the merit of presidential management of personnel and processes. His key principals— Vice President Richard Cheney, Defense Secretary Donald Rumsfeld, Secretary of State Colin Powell, Chief of Staff Andrew Card, Director of the Central Intelligence Agency George Tenet, and National Security Council Adviser Condoleezza Rice—had all served in past presidencies. More notably, both Bush and a number of his chief advisers had observed first-hand the strengths and weaknesses of his father's presidency. The awareness of the inner workings of a presidency was thus high and in marked contrast to the learning curve that Jimmy Carter, Bill Clinton, or even Ronald Reagan faced upon taking office.

Yet awareness of the internal workings of the presidency and the attempt to mold a staff structure and decision-making processes around presidential preferences, although potentially contributing to successful deliberations, are not necessarily guarantors of them. The conventional wisdom that such processes must fit a president "like a suit of clothes," can fail to account for the need (as indeed holds in fashion design) appropriately to "tailor" them; simple "fit" is not enough. Presidential predilections are not always effective, appropriate, or success-encouraging. Further alterations may be required: What presidential weaknesses need to be compensated for? What strengths need to be accentuated? These questions, moreover, are particularly important when directed at this presidency. As Donald Kettl has noted, Bush is a master at making "the organization fit your personality. Bush imposed his ways on the Oval Office, not the other way around" (Kettl 2003, 36).

But organizational "mastering" to fit the president's personality, even if well executed, is only part of the equation. Other flaws in organizational structure and routines can affect presidential performance. Also, as I have argued elsewhere, the broader institutional context of the presidency may have negative effects and, in turn, necessitate managerial attention (Burke 2000). So too with personnel choices, especially among the principal actors. Roles get defined, not just by the president but by the actors themselves. How players interact, in turn, can be consequential for decision making.

A Successful Transition in Difficult Circumstances

The signs of successful decision-making organization looked auspicious as Bush took office. Although he faced a unique challenge—the uncertainty until mid-December 2000 of an Electoral College majority—his transition to office proceeded smoothly (see Burke 2004, 11–62). Pre-election planning had been undertaken early (starting in the spring of 1999, the earliest to date). Tensions and conflict with the campaign war room, which had plagued the Carter and Clinton efforts and negatively affected their early presidencies, were avoided. Selection of a chief of staff was made before election day. After election day, Cheney brought his considerable experience to bear in directing the transition. Even as the controversy over the Florida vote wore on, chief of staff designate Card used the interlude, with little publicity, to organize the White House and start making personnel decisions. Following Al Gore's concession on 13 December 2000, key staff appointments were announced, well ahead of Clinton's timetable in 1992. By 2 January 2001, cabinet selection was finished, only a week behind Clinton's schedule in 1992.[1]

The White House staff that emerged also bore signs of concern for effective organization. For example, drawing on his father's experience with John Sununu as an overly powerful chief of staff, Bush wanted the role defined differently: a "facilitator," and "honest broker." As Clay Johnson, Bush's gubernatorial chief of staff and the head of his pre-election transition effort, notes,

[Bush] did not want someone to be chief of staff who was over territorial, or was a control freak, or felt like they had to control the content or the recommendations that flowed to the president. He wanted somebody who was more a facilitator, an orchestrator, and a tie breaker; as they say an honest broker. . . . The president's knowledge about the way he likes to work led him to choose Andy Card.   (Burke 2004, 19)

Similar concerns also factored in with the selection of Rice as NSC adviser. As Bush himself noted in an interview during the transition, Rice was "both a good manager and an honest broker of ideas" (Sciolino 2000).

The senior-level appointments of Karl Rove as senior adviser to the president and Karen Hughes as counselor to the president also reflected an organizational arrangement that was designed to meet Bush's policy needs. It brought two long-time associates into the very top of the White House. Their broad organizational responsibilities and standing with Bush lessened the possibilities of a Sununu-like chief of staff. Their duties also reflected a heightened awareness of the need for strategic planning and effective public communication, thereby reflecting some lessons learned from the George H. W. Bush presidency. Both participants and observers of the elder Bush's White House have noted that too much was delegated to the chief of staff alone and that its communications and political affairs units were poorly organized and utilized. Those errors were not repeated.

Other organizational changes were made. Like the successful legislative strategy group that James Baker developed as chief of staff under Reagan, Rove and Card also created a number of White House staff groups in order to further the Bush policy agenda. One was an Office of Strategic Initiatives, under Rove's direction, designed to emphasize long-range planning and provide input to meetings of senior White House aides. Other groups were established to deal with long-range scheduling and communications, and some were created to deal with policy efforts, such as faith-based initiatives (see Burke 2004, 69–86; Milbank 2001). After September 11, other units were created such as the White House Office of Homeland Security (followed by the cabinet-level Department of Homeland Security), the Office of Global Communications,[2] a short-lived Domestic Consequences Group, and the USA Freedom Corps (Burke 2004, 175–85).

The need for staff management was also recognized early on. The transition was a time to instill a particular "organizational culture" that Bush valued. According to one account, transition advisers "said Bush insists that loyalty can flower in an institution known for distractions and back-stabbing" (Allen 2001a). James Barnes of the *National Journal* later observed that although "the Clinton White House was more of a coalition—with aides from all parts of the Democratic Party," the Bush White House was more cohesive: "Because so many people on the Bush White House staff worked together either on the campaign or, even before that, in Austin, they've not only demonstrated their fidelity to Bush, they've operated as a team and formed bonds with each other, which may diminish prospects for internecine warfare" (Barnes 2001, 1869).

The final days of the transition even saw what Clay Johnson termed "practicing to be in the White House," which Andrew Card had instigated: "The senior staff of the White House had begun to meet for the last ten days to two weeks of the transitions, twice a day, to get in the habit of meeting with each other, communicating with each other, and to begin to talk about the president's schedule as if we were in the White House." In sum, in Johnson's view, "a lot of planning, a lot of focus, a lot of rigor and discipline" (Burke 2004, 52–3, 62).

Organizational Blend

Although Bush favored an organized structure whether within the White House staff or in his dealings with cabinet members, it has not been a rigid structure. In many ways, the Bush staff and advisory system has been a blend of two models—the more tightly organized, "hierarchical" model of the Eisenhower and Nixon presidencies, as well as the more collegial, "spokes-and-wheel" arrangement of recent Democratic presidencies. Although most recent presidencies have some facets of each—the models are "ideal types" defining a continuum—Bush is unique in having captured and incorporated key elements of each to such a significant degree.

But that noted, the issue remains whether Bush was able to reap the benefits of hierarchy and formal structure—closer to the Eisenhower experience—or whether he fell victim to its weaknesses, more akin to the isolation and its consequences that beset Richard Nixon. Likewise, were his collegial deliberations closer to those of John F. Kennedy during the Cuban missile crisis, or were they more analogous to the decision-making fiasco of the Bay of Pigs invasion?

During the campaign, Bush summarized for reporters his decision-making and management style: "I'm the kind of person who trusts people. And I empower people. I am firm with people. On the other hand, I'm a decider. I do not agonize. I think, I listen, and I trust my instincts and I trust the advice I get. And I'm an accessible person" (Balz and Neel 2000). This self-characterization offers a useful starting point for examining the strengths and weaknesses of both the formal and collegial elements of his decision making.

The Strengths and Weaknesses of the Formal Structure

One difficulty with more formal, organized advisory arrangements is that, although orderly, their hierarchy can isolate a president, with a key aide such as the chief of staff or the NSC adviser serving as a powerful "gatekeeper," if not "choke point," controlling access and limiting the information and advice that flows to the president. Bush's own organizational instincts indicate, however, that he was potentially on guard for this phenomenon; as he told reporters, *"I'm an accessible person."* Clay Johnson also reflects this in his comments, quoted above, concerning what led Bush to select Card as chief of staff. Indeed Bush himself observes in his campaign memoir, *A Charge to Keep*, that he didn't want a strong gatekeeper as chief of staff: "I had seen that problem in my dad's administration. Key members of his staff felt stifled because they had to go through a filter to get information to the president." Not only was his father's experience an important example of what to avoid, Bush's own gubernatorial practices provided lessons in how problems might be countered. As governor, Bush also notes in *A Charge to Keep*, "I wanted a flat organizational chart rather than the traditional chief-of-staff approach; I wanted the senior managers of different divisions in my office to report directly to me. . . . I like to get information from a lot of different people, plus I knew that high-powered people would be frustrated unless they had direct access to the boss" (Bush 1999, 97).

Organizational Structure and Access: War with Iraq

But although access may have been more open in the Bush White House (and Card and Rice were not gatekeepers in the mold of a Henry Kissinger, Donald

Regan, or John Sununu), was the formal structure permeable enough so that dissenting views and dissonant information percolated upward? Early in this presidency, the absence of discordant analysis and advice may have been less problematic; the policy agenda was driven by key campaign proposals, as it had been during his governorship. But as new challenges and issues arose, did the decision process function effectively and yield wise policy choices?

Although a full analysis of Bush's later economic and domestic policy decisions cannot be rendered here, the administration's case for war against Iraq indicates that the organizational structure for decision making was ineffective in vetting information, exploring a full range of analysis, and considering competing views. Errors, faulty inferences, exaggerations, and misplaced assumptions ranged across the administration's case for war: links between Iraq and al-Qaeda; claims about Iraq's nuclear capabilities; its attempts to acquire "yellowcake" uranium ore; its efforts to purchase aluminum tubes for centrifuges used in uranium enrichment; its use of mobile weapons labs; its continued possession of chemical and biological weapons; and its presumed fleet of manned and unmanned aerial vehicles to deliver them (see Ackerman and Judis 2003a; Barstow, Broad, and Gerth 2004; Pfiffner 2004; Pollack 2004; Stone 2003; for a defense of the administration, see R. Kessler 2004, 196–205).[3]

Defenders of the administration have noted that the White House was not alone in these claims and assessments. The intelligence services of other nations believed many of them too. And claims about Iraq's possession of chemical and biological weapons were clearly and widely held in the US intelligence community during the Clinton years (see Gordon and Trainor 2006a, 125–6).

Yet what is also notable is that within the administration agreement was not universal. Some dissent existed in the US intelligence community, yet those doubts largely failed to resonate at the highest levels. A March 2002 State Department intelligence analysis, for example, questioned assertions about the sale of yellowcake uranium by Niger to Iraq. Such sales were "unlikely" because it would have required "25 hard-to-conceal 10-ton tractor-trailers," traveling across 1,000 miles and crossing at least one international border (Lichtblau 2006).[4] Lower-level officials in the Department of Energy and in the State Department's Bureau of Intelligence and Research (INR) raised questions whether the aluminum tubes Iraq had purchased were suitable for the centrifuges used in uranium production or were really just for use in conventional weapons (see Barstow, Broad, and Gerth 2004).[5] In a late 2005 interview with the BBC, Colin Powell noted that, in preparation for his key February 2003 speech before the UN laying out the case for war with Iraq, although "Nothing was spun to me. What really upset me more than anything else was that there were people in the intelligence community that had doubts about some of this sourcing, *but those doubts never surfaced up to us*" (Leiby 2006, emphasis added). Some dissent did find its way into the National Intelligence Estimate (NIE) of

October 2002.[6] The NIE was the most important, comprehensive prewar assessment of the case for war against Iraq.[7] However, as the Senate Select Committee on Intelligence later concluded, the "key findings" of the NIE were "overstated, or were not supported by the underlying intelligence reporting" (Risen 2006, 121–2). Moreover, by the time the NIE was pulled together in October 2002, the White House was well down the path to war.

Problems in the "surfacing up" of doubts were especially problematic for those at the CIA who were concerned about the reliability of the evidence underlying the case against Iraq. In the view of one CIA official in the agency's Directorate of Operations, "Who can they speak up to? There's no forum for someone who's involved in operations to talk to anyone and say, 'We don't have Iraqi assets, we don't have information on WMD [weapons of mass destruction], we don't have anything there'" (Bamford 2004, 337). In the account that James Risen provides in his book *State of War*, CIA intelligence presented to the president concealed both its limitations (outdated evidence, questionable sources) and reservations about it held by analysts at lower levels in the agency. "If someone had spoken up clearly and forcefully, the entire house of cards might have collapsed. A little bit of digging might have revealed the truth" (Risen 2006, 121–2).

The problem may also have been compounded by the distrust of the CIA's analysis on the part of some of the principals, notably Cheney and Rumsfeld, and their eagerness to make their own intelligence judgments. As Gordon and Trainor note, "Cheney had never forgotten how U.S. intelligence had underestimated the Iraqis before the Gulf War," especially their hidden nuclear program (Gordon and Trainor 2006a, 126). A number of accounts have noted a breakdown in the intelligence vetting process as a source of the faulty assumptions about Iraq's capabilities. In particular, raw intelligence—sometimes from dubious sources—was "stovepiped" directly to Cheney's office and Rumsfeld's Special Plans unit, without proper vetting by the CIA (see Ackerman and Judis 2003a; Hersh 2003; Hosenball, Isikoff, and Thomas 2003; Pollack 2004, 88).[8]

Questions and doubts, moreover, were not confined to lower-level functionaries. According to Bob Woodward, "Well-placed officials in the administration were skeptical about the WMD intelligence on Iraq—among them [Richard] Armitage [Powell's chief deputy at State], some senior military officials and even the CIA spokesman Bill Harlow.... This skepticism apparently did not make it in any convincing form to the president. The unambiguous pronouncements of the heavyweights Tenet, Cheney and Rumsfeld prevailed" (Woodward 2004, 295). During work on one article in which administration sources were interviewed, Woodward concluded the case against Iraq was "pretty thin": "Several of these sources, I know, did voice their reservations within their various organizations but they also did not have enough to robustly challenge the conclusions that had been already reached. I have no evidence that the reservations of these particular sources reached the president" (ibid. 356).[9]

Organizational Structure and Access: Iraq's Postwar Reconstruction

Similar difficulties also beset the surfacing of dissent from those who had a less sanguine view of what Iraq's postwar reconstruction would entail. As Fallows observes, "The problems the United States has encountered are precisely the ones its own expert agencies warned against" (Fallows 2004a, 54). Prewar studies undertaken by the Army War College and the CIA's National Intelligence Council warned of the dangers likely to arise during reconstruction (see Gordon and Trainor 2006a, b; O'Hanlon 2004). Rice's own NSC military aides had prepared a report for her in early 2003 titled "Force Security in Seven Recent Stability Operations." Although each situation was unique they noted, if Iraq was like Kosovo, 480,000 peacekeepers would be needed; if like Bosnia, 364,000; but if like Afghanistan, only 13,900 (Gordon 2004a).

These troop level projections (as well as problems in the organization of the postwar effort) were confirmed in a December 2004 post-mortem study by the Defense Science Board, an independent advisory body to the secretary of defense. The report on the general topic of post-conflict stabilization and reconstruction concluded that stabilization of disordered nations might require 20 troops per 1,000 population [the ratio was 6:1000 for Iraq], that reconstruction and stabilization should be a "core competency" of *both* State and Defense, that the *State Department* (not Defense) should be "the locus for this reconstruction integration," and that "certain critical capabilities *require preparation years in advance*" (Defense Science Board 2004, pp. viii, ix, xvii, emphasis added). As Gordon and Trainor point out with respect to these troop projections and parallels for Iraq, "The implicit question was whether Iraq would be more like the Balkans or Afghanistan. The NSC briefing made clear that in one key respect Iraq had more in common with the Balkans than Afghanistan": dense urban areas requiring more troops. Yet no alarm bells sounded: "Hadley seemed to take comfort in the Afghan parallel. At the White House, the briefing never prompted any second-guessing of Rumsfeld's position" (Gordon and Trainor 2006a, 104).

But Hadley did have other concerns. Since November 2002, the NSC deputies committee, which he chaired, had been examining the administration's postwar planning. In Hadley's view, General Tommy Franks's "stability operations" needed further definition (Franks, head of US Central Command, was the chief architect of Iraq war planning). "They needed," in Woodward's words, "a comprehensive postwar plan. It was a long distance between stability and democracy" (Woodward 2004, 282).

Just as with the case for war, dissenting views on postwar planning existed. Powell had concerns and even had "back channel" contacts with General

Franks (ibid. 413–14; Gordon and Trainor 2006a, 70–1). Most importantly, the State Department's Future of Iraq project had undertaken extensive analysis since October 2001 and had produced some thirteen volumes of reports. Rumsfeld, however, distrusted State's efforts, and sought to block participation in the reconstruction effort of some of the project's members.[10] According to several reports, General Jay Garner, the initial head of the postwar Office of Reconstruction and Humanitarian Assistance (OHRA) in Iraq, was told simply to ignore the Future of Iraq project (Fallows 2004a, 72; Rieff 2003, 32).

Paul Bremer, Garner's successor, was also successful in the exclusion game, in this case preventing Zalmay Khalilzad from participation in what was now the Coalition Provisional Authority. Khalilzad, then an NSC official, had extensive experience in dealing with Iraqi exiles and had been a "presidential envoy" to civilian leaders in Baghdad right after the war (he would eventually become US ambassador to Iraq after serving in the same capacity in Afghanistan). According to one report, Powell was kept in the dark about that decision, and Rice "had nothing to do" with it. For Powell and his aides, the decision "demonstrated the administration's tendency to make important decisions without consulting key officials." The report also noted that Powell and Rice were not told in advance of the decision to disband the Iraqi army, and that "as he was preparing to leave office, Mr. Powell told Mr. Bush that the national security process was broken" (Gordon and Trainor 2006c; also see Bremer 2006, 11, 44, 83). Gordon and Trainor also note that the joint chiefs of staff were out of the loop on disbanding the Iraqi army and that General John Abizaid, Franks's deputy at US Central Command, and General David McKiernan, Franks's chief theater commander and military planner, also had strong reservations (Gordon and Trainor 2006a, 476, 482–85).

Not only may Powell and Rice have been out of the loop regarding the Iraqi army, so too may have been the president. According to another report, the decision to disband "may have been made without President Bush's advance knowledge, according to a senior White House source. The well-placed source said he is virtually certain that the president did not know of the decision before it was taken." Disbanding the army, moreover, "contradicted the recommendations of the [NSC's] interagency planning group" (Risen 2006, 3). Interestingly, Bush *had* been briefed on the latter (see ibid. 133).

Both in its case for war and in planning for its aftermath, the administration was not monolithic in its views. Dissent was present both at lower and higher levels. But the structure operated poorly. Dissent was either blocked (State's Future of Iraq Project), misrepresented (Tenet's "slam dunk" case, discussed below), or lacked an adequate vehicle for expression (the CIA's reservations). There is of course no guarantee that a fuller expression of dissent might have changed the decision to go to war—the principals may still have weighed the evidence and come to the same conclusion. But imperfect knowledge and information reduces the probabilities that they might have decided differently.

Coordination and Management

Other aspects of the decision structure were problematic. Problems in the coordination and management of the national security process by NSC Adviser Rice also may have played a part (see Burke 2005*b*). Part of the NSC adviser's role is to serve as an honest broker (as Bush himself recognized in appointing Rice): to make sure that dissenting opinion is adequately explored, assumptions and options fully probed, and necessary information is at hand. Effective brokerage can act as a check on imperfections in the organization and workings of the decision process (see Burke 2005*a*).

Yet almost the opposite of effective coordination and brokerage emerged, especially once Iraq was on the front burner. According to several accounts, a number of administration officials complained that the NSC process had become "dysfunctional": "Decisions go unmade at the deadlocked 'deputies' meetings or get kicked back or ignored by the president's 'principals,' his top advisers" (Thomas 2002).[11] At interagency meetings at lower levels in the process, according to one report, "the Defense Department sometimes doesn't even bother to show up" (Thomas 2003). According to one former senior NSC staff member, in Rice "you've never really had a national security adviser who's ready to discipline the process, to drive decisions to conclusions and, once decisions are made, to enforce them" (G. Kessler and Slevin 2003).

The controversy over the claim that Iraq had tried to purchase uranium for nuclear weapons production especially raises questions about Rice's knowledge of a crucial part of the case for war, her management of the NSC staff, and her hands-on effectiveness as coordinator and broker of the decision process. One of the CIA's October 2002 warnings (cautioning against mentioning it in a major address that month by the president) listed her as a recipient. CIA concerns were also raised in the October 2002 NIE, albeit in an annex to the report. In July 2003, a senior administration official asked if Rice had read the report, said that she may not have fully read it: "We have experts who work for the national security adviser who would know this information." As for the annex, she "did not read footnotes in a ninety-page document.... The national security adviser has people who do that." Nor had her deputy, Stephen Hadley, discussed with her the removal of the reference to uranium purchases in the October speech: "there was no need," he told reporters. As for the CIA memo listing her as a recipient, "I can't tell you she read it. I can't tell you she received it," Hadley noted (Milbank and Allen 2003; also see Milbank and Priest 2003; Sanger and Miller 2003).

By early July 2003, the White House publicly acknowledged that it should not have included the claim about uranium purchases in Bush's 2003 State of the Union address (Pincus 2003*a*). In the view of Senator Pat Roberts (R-KA), chair of the Senate Intelligence Committee, the error indicated that "the process was broken" and was a sign of "sloppy coordination between State and CIA and the NSC and the White House" (Pincus 2003*b*). The president's Foreign Intelligence Advisory Board, following a study requested by President Bush, was also reportedly critical of how the claims and evidence about uranium purchases were evaluated. The board, chaired by former NSC adviser Brent Scowcroft, raised concerns that "there was no organized system at the White House to vet intelligence, and the informal system that was followed did not work" (Pincus 2003*c*).[12]

Rice would also encounter difficulties over postwar reconstruction. An NSC Executive Steering Group had been created in August 2002 by Rice and Hadley to oversee and coordinate reconstruction efforts, and it was headed by Frank Miller. Yet Miller's experience signaled trouble: "Miller formally reported to the deputies committee and moved the paper and the policy decisions up to the principals and then to the president if necessary. But he found such chaos that he had to have an off-line meeting each week with Card, Rice, Hadley and [I. Lewis] Libby [Cheney's chief of staff] to outline problems and blow the whistle so that they could nudge Rumsfeld or others. Communications between the civilian and military sides of the Defense Department are catastrophically broken, Miller reported" (Woodward 2004, 322; on Miller's difficulties with Defense, especially see Gordon and Trainor 2006*a*, 148–9).

According to a *Time* magazine account, Rice also established four working groups, but they too experienced difficulty: "Rice's working groups failed on two counts. First, they never succeeded in getting State and the Pentagon on the same page." Second, "the Rice group responsible for postwar planning led by Elliott Abrams [from the NSC] and Robin Cleveland [from OMB] woefully underestimated the cost of reconstructing Iraq" (Gibbs and Ware 2003). According to another *Time* account, "The process never got much traction. Both Defense and State had their planning operations on Iraq (looking at very different things in very different ways), and according to one participant, Pentagon officials regularly skipped meetings of Rice's group that was planning for postwar Iraq" (Elliott and Calabresi 2004; on Rumsfeld's successful effort to control post-war Iraq and Rice's difficulties with Defense and more passive role in postwar planning, see Gordon and Trainor 2006*a*, 141, 147–9).

Rice's situation is especially in contrast to the role of her mentor, Brent Scowcroft, during the first Persian Gulf War. As one account notes, Scowcroft's effective coordination of "both military and diplomatic policy has prevented either [Secretary of State] Baker or Secretary of Defense Dick Cheney from dominating the stage alone." The White House rather than State or Defense coordinated and held center stage (Lauter 1990). But during Rice's tenure as NSC adviser, the formal NSC processes below the level of the principals appears problematic. Interagency coordination—a traditional NSC adviser's function—was weak, while Rumsfeld's Pentagon and Cheney's staff were dominant. Intelligence coordination by the NSC adviser and staff was also problematic. More generally, as Rothkopf notes, Rice's closeness to Bush drew her "inexorably to his side and away from process and the institution she might otherwise have managed quite like Scowcroft had" (Rothkopf 2005, 436).

Limits of Delegation and Trust

More formal staff and advisory systems also depend upon a high degree of delegation. As Bush himself observed, *"I'm the kind of person who trusts people. And I empower people."* The organization of the Bush White House, the responsibilities given Vice President Cheney, and the presence of able and experienced persons in the major cabinet departments, as well as in the White House, signaled that delegation would be a hallmark of this presidency.

According to Thompson and Ware's study of Bush's leadership style, "Bush's staff do understand when its time to pull their boss in." As one staff member observes, "You set the table and insert him at key points in the process" (Thompson and Ware 2003, 115; also see Dickerson, Cooper, and Waller 2001). The downside, of course, is that it is the *staff's* job to "set the table" and decide when to "insert him"—the success of delegation turns on the skills and knowledge of those to whom much is delegated. And that proved to be no minor matter later in his presidency. As Bruce Buchanan has observed, Bush is "not a policy wonk, so he has to rely on people who are." But that reliance can create vulnerability to error: "Bush's biggest weakness is that he may not be in a position to discern the credibility of the options his advisers lay out for him" (Carney 1999). Similarly, in the view of Donald Kettl, the success of the Bush decision-making process "depends critically on his staffers' skill in boiling complex issues down to their essence. If they miss important facts, they risk blinding Bush to things he ought to know.... The process, then, risks making the president especially vulnerable to what he and his staff don't know—or don't know to ask" (Kettl 2003, 150).

Delegation especially carried risks given Bush's deliberative style. As Fred I. Greenstein has noted, Bush "shows little intellectual curiosity, and appears not to have been drawn into the play of ideas" (Greenstein 2004, 281). Likewise, as Hugh Heclo notes, "Bush learns quickly and becomes deeply informed about what he is interested in. But this sort of learning capacity turns into a liability when it comes to things that should interest him but do not" (Heclo 2003, 46).

The issue of whether delegation served Bush well especially arises concerning the administration's Iraq deliberations. One telling occasion occurred on 21 December 2002 (when the UN inspection process was well underway). That day CIA Director Tenet and his deputy, John McLaughlin, presented a briefing on the positive case for Saddam's possession of WMD. In addition to the president, Cheney, Rice, and Card attended but not the other principals. At the end of the presentation, Bush was underwhelmed: "Nice try. I don't think it is quite—it's not something that Joe Public would understand or would gain confidence from." Turning to Tenet, Bush asked, "I've been told all this intelligence about having WMD and this is the best you have got?" Tenet replied that "It's a slam dunk case!" Bush again pressed: "George, how confident are you?" Again, Tenet told him, "Don't worry, it's a slam dunk case." Bush cautioned Tenet (several times according to Woodward), "Make sure no one stretches to make our case" (Woodward 2004, 249–50).[13]

Although, as noted above, significant reservations existed within the CIA concerning the case against Iraq, for Tenet—in front of the president—it was a "slam dunk." As Risen observes, "In public, Tenet struck a pose as an honest broker of intelligence; in private, he was sometimes seen as someone who would tell people what they wanted to hear but would later say the opposite to others" (Risen 2006, 12). Other accounts also blame Tenet for being overconfident, too eager to be a team player, and not sufficiently proactive in protecting established vetting procedures (see Ackerman and Judis 2003a, b). According to Seymour Hersh (2003, 80), "In the view of many CIA analysts and operatives, [Tenet] was too eager to endear himself to the administration's hawks and improve his standing with the President and the Vice President."

Delegation also proved problematic because it did not check those who were more eager advocates for war with Iraq, especially the Office of Special Plans (OSP) in the Pentagon. Created by Douglas Feith, undersecretary of defense for policy, the OSP would play crucial roles both in advancing the case for war and then in planning for postwar reconstruction. In both instances, its work product would be criticized. According to one account of its efforts to build a case for war, "Feith's intelligence unit had cherry-picked the most damning items...they were then sent to the OSP to be turned into 'analysis' and 'talking points.' Then the OSP would brief senior administration officials." In 2002, one of these briefings concerned links between al-Qaeda and Iraq. However, criticism raised at a 15 August session at the CIA, "was largely ignored."[14] Later, without notifying the CIA or taking into account its reservations, "Feith's road show turned around and gave the same briefing at the White House for senior officials [on the NSC staff] and the Vice President's office." They had added, however, a "slide harshly critical of the CIA for disagreeing with them." Moreover, "Despite the inaccuracy of the information contained in the high-level briefings, the top down pressure worked and the CIA quickly reversed itself" (Bamford 2004, 317–18; also see Gordon and Trainor 2006a, 127).

Starting in January 2003, Feith's OSP also became the Pentagon's centerpoint for postwar planning. It was another organizational choice that mattered. Whereas the State Department had handled postwar Afghanistan, Defense would handle Iraq. Yet Feith's work and his operating style generated criticism. According to one report, he operated "in an atmosphere of near-total secrecy." Feith's team even "pointedly excluded *Pentagon* officials with experience in postwar reconstructions." In the view of Thomas White, secretary of the army until April 2003 when he was fired, "You got the impression in this exercise that we didn't harness the best and brightest minds in a concerted effort." The issue for the Defense Department was "'We've got to control this thing'—so everyone else was suspect." Feith's group "had the mind-set that this would be a relatively straightforward, manageable task, because this would be a war of liberation and therefore reconstruction would be short-lived" (Packer 2003, 62, emphasis added).

On 21 and 22 February 2003 (less than a month before the onset of the war), some 200 officials gathered for a "rock drill" of the plans made so far. "Plans for running the country's ministries were rudimentary; [General Garner's] ORHA had done little research," according to one account, "The drill struck some participants as ominous." In the view of one ORHA member, "I got the sense that the humanitarian stuff [Garner's specialty] was pretty well in place, but the rest of it was flying blind" (ibid.).

But Feith's efforts made their way upwards largely without challenge. He made a Power Point briefing on reconstruction at a 4 March meeting of the NSC, just weeks before the war began. According to Woodward, "Feith displayed his organizational charts. It was a lot of abstract political science." "The president didn't have much to say other than to remark that he wanted to see information on how they would deal with the military and intelligence services" (Woodward 2004, 329). Feith returned for another briefing on 12 March. Plans were presented for dismantling the Iraq intelligence service, the Special Republican Guards, and the Fedayeen Saddam special militia. The regular Iraqi army might remain intact and be used "as a reconstruction force." Yet, according to Woodward (ibid. 343), "What they didn't plan for was the possibility that hundreds of thousands of soldiers would just go home, that the workforce to rebuild the country would just melt away." According to O'Hanlon, they "assumed that much of the regular Iraqi army would survive and be available to play a large role in keeping postwar order." Basic tasks, moreover, such as "policing the streets, guarding huge weapons depots, protecting key infrastructure, maintaining public order were simply not planned for." "Such planning as there was," conducted out of Feith's office, "was reportedly unfocused, shallow, and too dependent on optimistic scenarios" (O'Hanlon 2004, 3).[15]

O'Hanlon also faults General Franks's Phase IV [postwar period] planning. "One need only consult the Third Infantry Division's after action report, which reads: 'higher headquarters did not provide [us] with a plan for Phase IV. As a result, Third Infantry Division transitioned into Phase IV in the absence of guidance'" (ibid. 2, 3). According to another account, "There was no plan for oversight and reconstruction, even after the division arrived in

Baghdad" (Brinkley and Schmitt 2003; also see Rieff 2003, 44). Moreover, according to O'Hanlon, "A broader Department of Defense report on the war similarly observed that 'late formation of Department of Defense [Phase IV] organizations limited time available for the deployment of detailed plans and pre-deployment coordination.'" "Although Franks himself always cautioned that this stage of the operation could take years, it was ultimately assumed that much of the regular Iraqi army would survive and be available to play a large role in keeping postwar order." Rumsfeld's efforts to pare down the size of US forces won an ally in Franks. As O'Hanlon notes, Bremer later viewed this as a mistake and argued that "the single most important change . . . would have been having more troops in Iraq at the beginning and throughout." Bremer later claimed to have "raised this issue a number of times with our government" (O'Hanlon 2004, 2, 3, 4.) As for Gen. Franks, he had warned Rumsfeld of the need to focus on postwar period more, but, in Woodward's words, "Rumsfeld and the others had been focused on the war." As for Powell, as war planning occurred over sixteen months, he "felt that the easier the war looked, the less Rumsfeld, the Pentagon and Franks had worried about the aftermath" (Woodward 2004, 413, 414). In General Franks's view, "I wish some things had been done differently. I wish Don Rumsfeld and Colin Powell had forced the Defense and State Departments to work more closely together" (Franks 2004, 544; for an extended analysis of Franks's and the Pentagon's postwar planning, see Gordon and Trainor 2006a, 139–63; Gordon and Trainor also offer a compelling narrative about problems in combat planning and operations, especially lack of preparation for dealing with the Fedayeen Saddam militia in the early stages of the war).

Loyalty and Discipline: Pressure from Above?

Bush's emphasis on ensuring loyalty and discipline, particularly of the staff but also the cabinet, was another hallmark of this presidency. His pre-election day comments to reporters—"*I am the kind of person who trusts people*" but "*I am firm with people*"—provide early testimony. Few of his recent predecessors were so attentive to the need for teamwork and for staying on message, while avoiding the infighting and backbiting that often plagued his predecessors. Yet as time wore on did discipline go too far?

One issue is whether a too pervasive sense of loyalty may have compromised the candor, openness, and honesty needed in the deliberative process. Even during the first term Treasury Secretary Paul O'Neill saw problems: "Loyalty to a person and whatever they say or do, that's the opposite of real loyalty, which is based on inquiry, and telling someone what you really think and feel—your best estimation of the truth instead of what they want to hear" (Dickerson 2004). According to another account, "In the Bush White House, disagreement is often equated with disloyalty" (Thomas and Wolffe 2005).

With respect to the war in Iraq, journalist James Risen's extensive analysis of the CIA's intelligence failures indicates that the loyalty of some may have stifled dissent by others: "Many CIA officials—from rank-and-file analysts to senior managers—knew before the war that they lacked sufficient evidence to make the case for the existence of Iraq's weapons programs. Those doubts were stifled because of the enormous pressure that officials at the CIA and other agencies felt to support the administration." CIA Director Tenet and his chief lieutenants were "fearful of creating a rift with the White House," and created a climate in which warnings about the weakness of intelligence "were either ignored or censored" (Risen 2006, 109). Similar concerns are echoed in James Bamford's *Pretext for War*: within the CIA "there was a great deal of pressure to find a reason to go to war with Iraq. And the pressure was not just subtle, it was blatant" (Bamford 2004, 333; also see 334–7).

That pressure came from sources besides Tenet, moreover. According to David Rothkopf, "Cheney's active consumption of Iraq intelligence and his trips to the CIA in the run-up to the invasion of Iraq were cited by some in the CIA as White House political pressure to produce evidence justifying an invasion of Iraq" (Rothkopf 2005, 424–5). According to Hersh, "Some CIA analysts were constantly being urged by the Vice-President's office to provide worst-case assessments on Iraqi weapons issues. 'They got pounded on, day after day,' one senior Bush Administration official told me, and received no consistent backup from Tenet and his senior staff. 'Pretty soon you say, F**k it.' And they began to provide the intelligence that was wanted" (Hersh 2003, 80).[16]

Loyalty and Discipline: Ignored at the Top?

Although discipline may have translated into pressure for some lower down the policy food chain, sufficient discipline may not have extended to the top levels of the Bush inner circle. Larry Wilkinson, Powell's chief of staff, felt that Cheney and Rumsfeld operated as a secretive "cabal." When asked about Wilkinson's characterization, Powell wouldn't share the "cabal" label, but he did note that "very often maybe Mr. Rumsfeld and Vice President Cheney would take decisions to the president that the rest of us weren't aware of. That did happen, on a number of occasions" (Leiby 2006).

A number of accounts especially note that Rumsfeld operated freely with little restraint but great effect on the deliberative process. According to one account,

Time and again in the Bush administration, Rumsfeld simply ignored decisions made by the president in front of his war cabinet, according to several senior administration officials. . . . Rumsfeld succeeded by using a passive-aggressive style in which he would raise an unending series of questions and concerns about a proposal without flatly stating his opposition to it. If a decision went against him in one meeting, he and his aides would simply arrange another meeting with a different group of administration officials and would repeat the process until the Pentagon view prevailed. Rumsfeld succeeded by wearing out his bureaucratic foes, and by refusing to take no for an answer, even from the president.

Powell, by contrast, was at a disadvantage since he "made the mistake of playing by the rules" (Risen 2006, 161–2).

Other principals, notably Rice, who might have been in the position to curb Rumsfeld didn't do so: "Rice, who was supposed to be managing the interagency policy process, seemed either unwilling or unable to rein in Rumsfeld, so the defense secretary simply got away with pursuing his own foreign policy." "Early on," Rumsfeld made it clear that "he worked for George W. Bush, not Condoleezza Rice." Within the NSC staff a strong belief developed that "Rumsfeld had told his aides at the Pentagon that they too could ignore directions from the NSC" (ibid. 63, 161).

Yet, Rumsfeld's tactics—shared by others at Defense—affected Rice's own operations and coordinating role: the numerous "dysfunctional" critiques noted above. Also, as Rothkopf learned, Pentagon pressure would be exerted after the fact: "one senior official told of 'fairly regular' instances in which, after deputies meetings, notes would be adjusted on the basis of comments that appeared to come from the Department of Defense." On one occasion, a Defense official tried to amend conclusions "that had been collectively reached by the group. Hadley obliged" (Rothkopf 2005, 414). Another of Rothkopf's sources notes that Defense officials "would come to meetings in one of two postures. Either they would say that they couldn't decide because they didn't know what the secretary wanted or they would decide and then come back later and say they had changed their minds. So in either case it was worthless" (ibid. 419).

Not only was Hadley compliant, so too was Rice. According to one former senior NSC staff member, Rice "will never discipline Don Rumsfeld." "Never any sanctions. Never any discipline. He never paid a price" (G. Kessler and Slevin 2003). According to another account, Rice "could not rein in the Pentagon in order to get its leadership to adhere to the normal interagency processes" (Risen 2006, 63–4).

At the same time, it must be borne in mind that Bush's senior advisers were political heavyweights and skilled at bureaucratic maneuver. As one account notes, "Bush's war cabinet has included some very strong and independent-minded figures. Because they were at the end of their careers, with no office left to seek, Dick Cheney and Donald Rumsfeld were seen as liberated to call things the way they saw them." Moreover, "the headstrong Cheney and Rumsfeld seemed to almost relish scoffing at dissent. Cheney in particular has acted as Bush's unofficial prime minister, playing a heavy hand in the war on terror and handling (or often mishandling) Hill relations" (Thomas and Wolffe 2005).

Loyalty and Ideology

Bush was able to bring into the highest levels of his administration a number of individuals who had close personal connection to him and others who had considerable experience in past Republican presidencies. But there appears to have been little interest in political and ideological diversity. The latter is not without its costs, it should be noted. The early Clinton presidency was a coalition building exercise among disparate elements of the Democratic party that often led to policy confusion and political muddle. Yet, did Bush end up with an equally problematic outcome: ideological rigidity?

On the domestic side, one might argue that Rove's political calculus rather than ideology was the prime mover. Others offer different assessments. For John DiIulio, an early adviser on faith-based initiatives and a professor of political science at the University of Pennsylvania, the problem was the "*policy-lite* inter-personal and organizational dynamics of the place" (DiIulio 2002, emphasis added). Still others have argued that ideology was dominant, especially in the sway of the neoconservatives over the positive merits of war with Iraq and their optimism over its swift transition to democracy (Dolan and Cohen 2006).

According to Colin Campbell (2004, 97), there has been a high degree of "unrestrained ideological entrepreneurship." The administration has a "surfeit of doctrinaire players," and one consequence is that it "invests very little structure or effort in ensuring that policy initiatives receive intense collegial scrutiny." For Gary Mucciaroni and Paul Quirk (2004, 162, 182), "Much as the Clinton White House was dominated by liberal ideologues in 1993 and 1994," there was the hazard for Bush "that his agenda, or parts of it, would be hijacked by the right." In their view, moreover, the result was that "Bush and his advisers did not deliberate carefully about the actual consequences of their policies." Perhaps the problem is summed up best in Bush's own words: "I... want to make sure that the people are there for a cause as opposed to themselves" (Balz and Neal 2000). Wariness of self-interest may be laudable, but perhaps the emphasis on "there for a cause" proved too overbearing.

Access Outside the Official Family?

One check on a formal decision-making system that may be fraught with some problems—whether stifled access, poor coordination, problems in delegation, and too heavy a dose of loyalty and ideology—is the ability of a president to move beyond formal channels in search of information and advice: Eisenhower's wide circle of business friends and former military associates as sources of counsel, Kennedy's penchant for contacting lower-level officials and also expanding the membership of ExCom to include the "Wise Men" of the foreign policy establishment at the time of Cuban missile crisis. Moreover, even if an advisory system is relatively open and functioning well, a president may still benefit from reaching out beyond his *formal* set of advisers in search of further information and advice or to test that which his staff provides him—Alexander George's theory of multiple advocacy (George 1972). Here Bush's decision-making instincts and practices are less positive despite his personal belief in "access." Access connotes a kind of passive willingness to let others come forward. But was Bush more proactive in reaching out, not just to lower echelons of his official family but outside that family circle?

A number of accounts have noted that Bush operates within a "bubble" or an "echo chamber." In the view of his biographer, Treasury Secretary O'Neill felt that Bush "was caught in an echo chamber of his own making, cut off from everyone other than a circle around him that's tiny and getting smaller and in concert on everything." Bush lacked "disinterested perspective about what's real and what the hell he might do about it" (Suskind 2004, 126, 293). According to *Newsweek's* Evan Thomas and Richard Wolffe (in an article titled "Bush in the Bubble"), "Bush may be the most isolated president in modern history, at least since the late-stage Richard Nixon." Bush's outside contacts are largely social: "Bush's real friends are his old Texas and school buddies from Andover, Yale and Harvard Business School. He calls them all the time—but the talk is usually comforting and jocular, of sports and old days. They rarely dispense pointed political advice or brace him with bad news" (Thomas and Wolffe 2005). Whether George H. W. Bush was a powerful source of outside advice remains a mystery. Yet given that this son of a former president had unprecedented access to a range of former officials in past Republican administrations (Reagan's as well as his father's), the lack of reported extramural contact is noteworthy.

Absence of informal congressional contact is also notable. According to Senator Richard Lugar (R-IN), chair of the Senate Foreign Relations Committee, Bush needs to "have much more of a cadre of people in both houses, from both parties" visiting the White House "very frequently" (ibid.). According to one report in December 2005, "When Senate Judiciary Committee chairman Arlen Specter wanted to have a private word with the President . . . about the extension of the Patriot Act, he put on a tuxedo and waited in line at one of the White House Christmas parties." But that same report also noted that, at social gatherings, Bush had begun "to circulate with an intensity his friends haven't seen before." In the view of one adviser, "He's listening a little more because he's looking for something new. He's looking for ideas. He wants to hear what people are saying because something might strike him as worth following up on" (Tumulty and Allen 2005).

In January 2006, Bush convened a meeting of 13 former secretaries of state and defense from both Democratic and Republican administrations in order to solicit their advice about Iraq policy. Participants did not hesitate to express their views, some in conflict with administration policy. According to one account, "The meeting marked the first time that Bush convened such a gathering," and that it was "an outreach effort recommended to him by senior Republican members of Congress, among others." It was a response, moreover, "to criticism that his administration has become too insular and resistant to contrary views" (Branigin 2006). Although reports indicated the meeting was candid and at times "feisty," and "chastening," one noted that "Colin L. Powell said nothing—a silence that speaks volumes to many in the White House" (Sanger 2006).

Not only were few outside "Wise Men" brought in as a reality check—as has occurred from time to time in previous presidencies—but discordant voices from even within the Bush political family were sidelined. Brent Scowcroft, George H. W. Bush's trusted NSC adviser, raised concerns about the administration's Iraq policy and his fears that Bush had been "mesmerized" by Israeli prime minister Ariel Sharon. Yet, as one account (of a number) has noted, "Scowcroft was ostracized by the White House and fired from the one small assignment he had been given, the chairmanship of the President's Foreign Intelligence Advisory Board" (Risen 2006, 222).

At best, outside voices were registered not through the president's contacts but those of his key aides, especially Karl Rove. As Kessler notes, "Longtime Washington Republicans—not to mention Democrats—complain that the Bush White House did not consult them." But Rove "maintained an intricate system for obtaining feedback from political leaders throughout the country" (R. Kessler 2004, 250). Rove also was the link to the concerns of the Republican Party base, especially the religious right. But where was the Rove-like figure when it came to foreign policy and extramural advice on Iraq?

The Strengths and Weaknesses of Collegial Deliberations

The other side of Bush's decision-making processes is his collegial deliberation, especially with his principal advisers. At one level, it is fair to characterize Bush as an active participant. According to one press report at the end of Bush's first 100 days, "In meetings briefers never get through presentations; Bush interrupts without hesitation when he feels he has heard enough.... There is little doubt that it is Bush—his personality, his likes and dislikes, his political values—who is the animating force of this White House" (Harris and Balz 2001). Assistant Attorney General Eric Holder, a Clinton holdover who represented the Justice Department at cabinet meetings until John Ashcroft was sworn in as attorney general, found Bush "formidable." Holder recalled that Bush conducted the cabinet meeting off an index card with just four or five items listed: "There is no question who was in charge. He has a light touch, but he takes up the space" (Allen 2001b). Moreover, in Kettl's view, Bush's engagement had positive benefit. It allows him "to keep focused on the task at hand. Bush watches the small things to sharpen his focus" (Kettl 2003, 36). For Bush, it also brought other benefits: "One of my jobs is to be provocative, seriously to provoke people into—to force decisions, and to make sure in everybody's mind where we are headed" (Woodward 2002, 144).

Bush and the Collegial Deliberative Process

Yet there were also personal nuances to Bush's involvement, some of which may signal problems. According to one account, "Bush generally prefers short conversations—long on conclusion, short on reason" (Thomas and Wolffe 2005). According to another report, "Bush is not disengaged, but there are clear signatures to the way he engages. His questions at meetings, say participants, usually focus on practicalities: What coalitions back a particular bill? Has someone or other been consulted? Bush's curiosity has an almost tactile quality to it." According to Senator Bill Frist (R-TN), "You can watch him click and register with individuals as they speak, and if he's not clicking he will quickly move on." At one meeting on health care, one person began "talking in very esoteric terms," according to Frist. Bush interrupted, asking "What can we do in six months?" In Frist's view, "He'll turn a person off unless you make it practical" (Harris and Balz 2001).

For Colin Powell, Bush's practical perspective was also of import. Unlike his father who was attuned to "a more deliberate process," George W. Bush "is guided more by a powerful inertial navigation system than by intellect. He knows what he wants to do, and what he wants to hear is how to get it done" (Rothkopf 2005, 401). For former White House aide John DiIulio, Bush's more practical bent may have led him to tune out more intellectually sophisticated analysis: "compared to other presidencies since that of Franklin D. Roosevelt, the Bush Administration is largely bereft of policy intellectuals" (DiIulio 2003, 248). Still other accounts point not just to the absence of policy reasoning but the reliance on ideological faith: "Occasional outsiders brought into the Bush Bubble have observed that faith, not evidence, is the basis for decision making" (Thomas and Wolffe 2005).

That said, others have found Bush's pattern of interpersonal engagement of positive benefit. According to Clay Johnson, Bush "encourages people to push. He is interested in good ideas and to give people confidence to have a dialogue with him, to have that exchange of ideas and difference of opinion" (Kumar 2002, 37). And even in Powell's view, Bush "allows his principal advisors freedom to present all sides of an argument...he encourages us to discuss with one another, debate with one another, and disagree with one another. And he then works hard to draw out the best ideas from everyone" (R. Kessler 2004, 177).

Yet was Bush fully engaged when his advisers wanted to raise issues outside his immediate agenda or perhaps even in challenge of it? Early in Bush's presidency, Treasury Secretary Paul O'Neill, who had reservations about the Bush tax cut plan, found his meetings with the president unproductive. At one early meeting, according to his biographer, Ron Suskind, "There were a dozen questions that O'Neill had expected Bush to ask. He was ready with answers." O'Neill raised some issues, "Bush didn't ask anything." O'Neill continued with other issues. "The president said nothing. No change in expression. Next subject." One important cabinet meeting in March 2001, "was like many of the meetings I would go to over the course of two years," according to O'Neill, "The only way I can describe it is that, well, the president is like a blind man in a roomful of deaf people. There is no discernible connection" (Suskind 2004, 57–8, 149).[17]

After September 11, the picture changed: a continual cycle of NSC and other meetings of the principals was held, and most accounts of them portray a process of vigorous give-and-take among the president's advisers. As well, most depict a more engaged president (Moens 2004, 133–40). According to one aide, "From the very beginning the president decided he wanted to chair the NSC meetings ... because I think he didn't want a process where options were coming up to him, where we had to say 'A thinks this, B thinks this, the consensus should be this'.... In the earliest phases, he chaired and we had our intellectual discussions about strategy—everybody, with the president there. It was great" (McManus and Gerstenzang 2001).[18] According to Bob Woodward (2002, 38), "This was a commander in chief function—it could not be delegated. He also wanted to send the signal that it was he who was calling the shots, that he had the team in harness."

Yet problems in collegial deliberations mounted once Iraq was on the front burner. The problem was *not* that Bush was a passive participant. As planning progressed, according to one account, "Aides said he questioned whether the plan was too conventional, what the Iraqis might have learned from the 1991 Persian Gulf War, and he constantly asks what can go wrong with the plans and how ready the generals are if something does go wrong." Once the war was underway, Bush continued to press questions about Iraqi troop strengths, coalition troop morale, and the effectiveness of US media communications with the Iraqi people (Balz and Allen 2003). According to Rumsfeld, Bush would often interrupt briefings, asking "What about this? What about that? If this occurs, what would the approach be?" Bush "pushes people to think about things he does not know whether or not they have thought through" (R. Kessler 2004, 184).

But, that said, two notable areas of possible omission would emerge after the war was over: Had the president pressed his inner circle with sufficient vigor concerning the reliability of some of the evidence on which the case for war was based? Had the political, economic, and military situation in a postwar Iraq been sufficiently anticipated and had Iraq's pacification and reconstruction been adequately planned for?

Perhaps the most glaring decision-making error was that the case for war against Iraq was apparently not directly engaged by the principals. Broad planning had begun even before September 11 and contingency plans were ordered shortly after (see Gordon and Trainor 2006a, 3–5, 24–54, 62–70). Yet at no point is there evidence of a thorough and sustained debate among the principals about the merits of the case against Iraq and the evidence and assumptions underlying it. According to one administration official, "There was absolutely no debate in the normal sense."[19] According to another account, when administration officials were asked "to recall how and when the president decided to invade Iraq, they had a hard time picking out one turning point." In the view of one State Department official, "We never had a decisive moment. It was like water dripping" (Thomas 2003).

According to Woodward, Bush never even directly asked Rumsfeld whether he recommended going to war against Iraq.[20] Nor had Bush asked Powell or Cheney: "I could tell what they thought. I didn't need to ask..." For Powell especially, Woodward (2004, 272, 416) notes, "in all the discussions, meetings, chats and back-and-forth, the president never once asked Powell, Would you do this? What's your overall advice? The bottom line?"

Omissions here are particularly striking for a president with so little pre-presidential national security experience. As Kettl notes, "No matter how intense Bush's attention to a subject might be, his instincts for the jugular of some issues might not be as sharp as for others" (Kettl 2003, 150). Although Bush could question his war cabinet and other advisers on some matters, he may have lacked the ability to press for more detailed explanations of assumptions or have a sense when options were too narrow and needed to be expanded.

Bush's dependence on his principals was thus problematic with respect to Iraq; indeed he may have been in greater jeopardy given the strong advocacy by some for war. In the view of Gregory Theileman, a senior State Department intelligence official, not only were there strong advocacy efforts from Feith and the OSP, but they were matched by eagerness from the very top to find evidence confirming the case for war, especially in the preparation of the October 2002 National Intelligence Estimate: "Instead of our leadership forming conclusions based on a careful reading of the intelligence we provided them, they already had their conclusions to start out with, and they were cherry-picking the information that we provided them to use whatever pieces of it fit their overall interpretation. Worse than that, they were dropping qualifiers and distorting some of the information...to make it seem more alarmist and more dangerous" (Bamford 2004, 328).

The public presentation of the case for war—especially when France, Russia, and Germany began to balk at intervention in early 2003—was also skewed in ways that would later come back to haunt the administration when no WMD were found.[21] As Alexander Moens points out, "The Bush team did what many decision makers have done in similar cases; they started to bolster their arguments. The UN would no longer authorize war so they had to make the strongest indictment of Iraq and proceed to war with few allies. Bush and his advisers... began to make the case more compelling than the information at hand could support. As political scientist Alexander George has pointed out, such bolstering typically leads to distortions in information" (Moens 2004, 188).

Bush may also have had difficulties grasping the complexity and challenge of a postwar Iraq. Powell had clearly warned him in August 2002 (discussed further below). In 2003, as war loomed, according to Gordon and Trainor, "Bush and his team had begun to focus on the postwar phase but with little of the attention and energy devoted for sixteen months to the invasion plan." On 5 March 2003, General Franks made his final presentation before Bush and the NSC. Bush asked about Franks's plans for Phase IV, the postwar period. Franks replied the "military would have 'lord mayors' in every Iraqi city and town.... Franks's response seemed to satisfy Bush and there was little follow-up" (Gordon and Trainor 2006a, 160).

An Unbalanced Playing Field?

There was also a significant imbalance of power and influence among the principals that likely affected the quality of the Iraq deliberative process. In the view of Richard Haass, director of policy planning in the State Department, "the process didn't work well." Compared to George H. W. Bush, there was "a bias much more toward one side of the field" (Rothkopf 2005, 407). Imbalances existed among the principals and they also had effect below, at the interagency level.

Cheney's powerful role was especially notable. According to Rothkopf (ibid. 391), "what happened during the first term of the presidency of George W. Bush was hardly anticipated by anyone—that the dominant role in that inner circle would be played by a vice president who would himself occasionally assume the role envisioned for the national security adviser and have unprecedented influence over the president." According to Haass, "the vice president's office has become the equivalent of a separate institution or bureaucracy. When I was in the White House [under George H. W. Bush], the vice president's office had one or at most two people doing foreign policy... In this administration, the vice president has his own mini-NSC staff. And at every meeting they had a voice and a vote" (ibid. 407). According to another account, "On the road to war, Cheney in effect created a parallel government that became a real power center" (Hosenball, Isikoff, and Thomas 2003).

For his part, Cheney had "three bites at the apple" according to Haass: his staff at lower-level meetings, his own role among the principals, and his private meetings with Bush. As a result "at just about every meeting, the State Department began behind two and one half [the half being the NSC] to one...You had the vice-president's office [OVP], Defense, and the NSC tilting in the direction of what OVP and Defense favored. I thought there was not enough quality control in terms of countering that leaning. Too many assumptions got accepted or built in" (Rothkopf 2005, 408). According to Rothkopf (ibid. 421), Cheney was not "just a wise old principal without portfolio" as Rice characterized him. For others "He is seen as an 800-pound gorilla whose views carry much more weight than the others', and which skews discussion and quashes open dissent—inadvertently or otherwise."

Rumsfeld was perceived by some as a stumbling block. According to one administration source, "Rumsfeld would never come to meetings prepared. He'd come not having read any of his briefing papers and so would extemporize, which was frustrating for everyone else". Yet Rumsfeld's bureaucratic skill and maneuvering allowed Defense to keep "a thumb on the scale" throughout the process, according to Rothkopf. And his "willful unpredictability affected every meeting in which Defense participated, whether he...was there or not" (ibid. 414, 419).

The imbalance among the principals especially attenuated Powell's influence. Such was the skew in the process that Powell had to resort to "back channel" efforts to reach Bush, never a sign of an effective process. As Fred I. Greenstein (2004, 208) notes, such efforts carry risk: "policy making by end run...places a premium on an adviser's bureaucratic skill and not just the merits of his or her recommendations."

By the summer of 2002, Powell was frustrated both by his lack of a good personal relationship with the president[22] and by a deliberative process that seemed to focus only on war plans with Iraq not the case for war itself. He approached Rice who arranged private meetings with Bush (with Rice sitting in). Powell's concerns are particularly telling about problems in the deliberative process: "I really need to have some private time with him to go over issues that I don't think he's gone over with anyone yet." And it was at a meeting on 5 August, that Powell pressed his case for asking for a UN resolution resuming inspections and warned the president of postwar consequences: the so-called Pottery Barn rule of "You break it, you've bought it" (Woodward 2004, 149, 150).[23]

Powell prevailed over Cheney on the need for a UN resolution. Yet Powell missed a fork that had already been passed by: one that might have challenged the premises of the case for war and taken a different route. Nor could he anticipate that the UN path would prove a political and diplomatic dead end, and that the language of the resolution that the administration ultimately negotiated for and agreed to would force the US to seek a second resolution, an effort that would lead to failure. The UN path was taken, but it would lead back to war, with little ability to backtrack further. As Woodward (2004, 227) observes, "For his larger, ultimate purposes of avoiding war... [Powell] may have done too well with the resolution."

The way the debate unfolded in September 2002—unilateral intervention versus a UN resolution and an inspections process—may also have been constrained by the way Powell's concerns initially entered: Rice's arrangement of *private* meetings with the president. Had Powell *initially* pressed his case not privately but with the other principals present, would the case for war and other issues (such as postwar reconstruction) have been more directly joined and debated?

The ability of Bush's top military advisers and field commanders to raise concerns may also have been stifled by perceptions of what Bush, Cheney, and Rumsfeld wanted, especially concerning troop levels needed for Iraq's reconstruction.[24] According to Risen, "The docility of the American officer corps is particularly striking. One senior administration source notes that during his visits to Iraq, he invariably heard American commanders complain about such problems as the lack of sufficient troops. But during meetings and videoconferences with Bush and Rumsfeld in which this source participated, those same military commanders would not voice their complaints" (Risen 2006, 4).

Bush cannot be faulted for asking his commanders what they needed (which he did), but did he ask the right questions in ways that would elicit a genuine response? According to one former senior member of the Coalition Provisional Authority in Baghdad, "The president would ask the generals, 'Do you have what you need to complete the mission?' as opposed to saying, 'Tell me, General, what do you need to win?'—which would have opened up a whole new set of conversations." Bush's phrasing of questions and his lack of interest in long, detailed discussions might have had a "chilling effect": "It just prevented the discussion from heading in a direction that would open up the possibility that we need more troops" (Thomas and Wolffe 2005).

Rice as Honest Broker?

The NSC adviser's role as a coordinator and honest broker not only covers the workings of the organizational bureaucracy (discussed earlier), it also applies to deliberations at the highest levels. In the aftermath of September 11 and as planning for the war in Afghanistan unfolded, Rice's role as an honest broker appeared to counter some of these imbalances among the principals. As Pfiffner observes, "Rice's role as NSC adviser had expanded during the months after 9/11. Beginning the administration as junior to the other principals in age and experience, she demonstrated her skill in her role as neutral broker as well as enforcer of the president's wishes" (Pfiffner 2005, 86). As the war in Afghanistan was underway, Rice also acted as a brake on Bush's penchant for quick action and results. And Rice's braking was welcomed by the president:

"Sometimes that's the way I am—fiery. On the other hand, [Rice's] job is to bear the brunt of some of the fire, so that it—takes the edge off a little bit. And she's good at that." "I was growing a little impatient. I can be an impatient person." Asked by Woodward why he backed off a bit on a more hurried timetable, Bush replied, "That's the Rice influence there, you know. Who says she isn't powerful. I'm a realistic person . . . " More generally, according to Woodward, "Rice's job was to tell him things. Sometimes he liked to hear them, sometimes he didn't." "Rice felt it was her job to raise caution flags, even red lights if necessary, to urge the president to rethink" (Woodward 2002, 158, 167–8, 256, 258).

Rice's role as broker in the process, however, lessened as Iraq replaced Afghanistan in the principals' deliberations. As one former White House official observed, "Maybe the Secretary of Defense and his people are short-circuiting the process, and creating a separate channel to the Vice President. Still, at the end of the day, all the policies have to be hashed out in the interagency process, led by the national security adviser." Instead, there was "a real abdication of responsibility by Condi" (Hersh 2003, 87). According to a number of the administration sources Rothkopf interviewed, her role as counselor to Bush, "body man," and "alter ego" "let the NSC become weak, and worse, the NSC processes become weak." According to one source, "She is earnest and dedicated and very smart. But she can't be in two place at once, and [her then-deputy] Steve Hadley hasn't stepped in to fill the void. The guys in this administration are old hands, experienced players, and you can't leave them to their own devices, or they will eat your lunch" (Rothkopf 2005, 406).

In fact, there is some evidence that the case for war against Iraq may have been a closed issue for Rice. Richard Haass recalled a meeting with Rice in the first week of July 2002 when he raised the issue of whether Iraq should be the focus of concern in the war on terrorism: "she said, essentially, that the decision's been made, don't waste your breath" (Lemann 2003, 39; also see Bumiller 2004; Frum 2003, 197–201).

Conclusions

Four caveats about the organization of decisions and its relation to decision outcomes should be noted at the outset. First, well-organized and functioning decision-making processes do not guarantee correct policy choices or success-ful policy outcomes. At most, they can increase their probability. It might have been entirely possible, for example, that had the administration's formal processes worked better and dissenting views on WMD been more effectively expressed at the highest levels, that the principals would still have evaluated intelligence in the net direction that they actually did, however much in error. Dissent can weaken but it does not necessarily trump.

Second, correct choices and successful outcomes can issue from flawed decision-making processes. Probability of success is surely lessened here. But it may be case, for example, that history will prove that regime change in Iraq was a wise course of action despite the fact that other parts of this administration's case for war proved largely unfounded. It may also prove true that a democratic and politically stable Iraq may emerge, despite errors in planning for and executing its postwar reconstruction. Time will tell.

Third, my intent here is to offer an analysis that is instrumental in nature. That is, it is not based on an assessment of the administration's *decisions* made from a normative perspective, but on the internal quality of the process that led to a decision outcome. As Greenstein and I note in our work *How Presidents Test Reality*, which comparatively examined Eisenhower's and Johnson's Vietnam decision making, "Our comparative advantage as students of decision making is not in judging what policies were warranted. It is in establishing whether policy alternatives were systematically and rigorously addressed" (Burke and Greenstein 1989, 3).

Finally, the decision process outlined here relies on an evidentiary base drawn from Iraq decision making. Thus it remains open whether problems in the formal structure and collegial deliberations described herein prevailed in other areas, whether other foreign and national security challenges or in economic and domestic policy-making settings.

That said, however, what can we learn from this analysis of the Bush Administration's decision making? Perhaps the most important lesson is that although the formal and collegial parts of its processes must "fit" the president's predilections as a decision maker, simple fit is not enough as noted at the outset. The fit with George W. Bush seems largely present, but an effective process seems to have required more than that.

One deficiency, as we have seen, is that dissent over the case for war with Iraq as well as differing views on the course of reconstruction were not adequately expressed to and enjoined by the principals. Few internal channels or organizational routines existed to ensure that dissent had its day in higher court. The written record appears flawed. The October 2002 NIE did have some expression of dissent on some parts of the case for war. But even the NSC staff acknowledged that Rice, whose role should have been attentive to such matters, may not have paid it sufficient attention. More generally, Rice's role as an effective coordinator and broker of the process was deficient. As I have argued elsewhere, she *was* effective after September 11 and in the planning for and execution of the war in Afghanistan, but much less so with Iraq (Burke 2005*b*).

The NSC deputies committee also appears dysfunctional at times. Since the introduction of the "Scowcroft model" of NSC organization under George H. W. Bush, it should have been the venue for interagency surfacing of disagreement. But it was a far cry from the Planning Board of the Eisenhower era, where consensus was sought but dissent clearly reported to the NSC principals. Nor did it operate under the organizational norms of the Eisenhower era, where allegiance to the quality of the decision process rather than bureaucratic norms and position-taking or preset ideological commitment was the order of the day.

Organizational process was also compromised by the direct "stovepiping" of intelligence by Cheney and Rumsfeld. Their mistrust of the CIA analysts may have been well placed, but, operating outside normal channels, there was no organizational check on what had been "cherry picked" and adequate vetting appears lacking.

This was a presidency with a high degree of delegation, but at least during its Iraq deliberations, dependence on those to whom much had been delegated was sometimes misplaced and, here too, lacking corrective check. CIA Director Tenet not only failed to express the dissent of some in his agency on the case for war, he was the overly reassuring voice to the (somewhat skeptical) president that case for war was a "slam dunk." Postwar reconstruction plans drawn up in the Pentagon's Office of Special Plans were woefully inadequate, as were General Franks's efforts. Coordination between Defense and State over postwar stabilization and reconstruction not only were ineffective, but bureaucratic rivalry, if not antagonism, were the order of the day. A common organizational culture dedicated to the mission at hand was sorely lacking.

Loyalty and discipline were other hallmarks of Bush's managerial expectations. In some of its operations over the last six years, this has served the administration well: there have been far fewer unauthorized leaks and reports of factional infighting than had occurred in the Carter, Reagan, Clinton, or even his own father's presidencies. Yet with Iraq, an emphasis on loyalty may have led to the conflation of disagreement with disloyalty, a detriment to the candor and honesty needed for effective decision making. For some of the principals, the opposite problem prevailed: discipline was sometimes lacking, especially so in Rumsfeld's lack of commitment to the NSC's interagency process.

The collegial deliberations among the principals were also problematic. The issue was not that Bush was a passive a participant; he often engaged actively in deliberations. The problem was how Bush engaged: what triggered his interest (practical issues), how long he would engage (a preference for short conversations). Who Bush chose to engage was also problematic: reliance on the closed circle of his principals and little in the way of competing, informal channels of information and advice, much less the ideals of multiple advocacy.

More generally, a number of reports indicate that there was no full debate over the case for war; some participants could not even pinpoint when the decision to go to war had been made. The playing field was also imbalanced among the principals. Cheney and Rumsfeld were advantaged, Powell was outmaneuvered (and sometimes forced to resort to back channel contacts to get his views heard). Military advisers were restrained by protocol. Most importantly, Rice largely failed to act as an honest broker. She failed not just in making the broader system work, but also in righting any imbalances among the principals and making sure their deliberations worked effectively— a concern at the highest levels that some of her predecessors, such as Robert Cutler under Eisenhower and Brent Scowcroft under George H. W. Bush, had embraced and with positive effect. Nor was there anyone else (save Powell in a limited way) who would act as a devil's advocate, perhaps providing an entrée to challenge assumptions or otherwise explore or expand the range of policy options, whether about the case for war with Iraq or plans for its stabilization and reconstruction.

Finally, President Bush was remiss in his responsibilities to take the necessary steps to ensure that the decision-making process effectively enhanced the most important choice any president must make: a commitment to war. For a president who was normally so insistent on staff discipline and internal order, it was Bush who ultimately allowed Cheney and Rumsfeld to operate as free agents, outside the control of the NSC process and ultimately to its detriment. As Rothkopf notes, Bush never "put his foot down [and said] 'This has to stop'" (G. Kessler and Ricks 2004). More generally, as Pfiffner observes, "It is the *president's responsibility* to create an atmosphere in which the White House staff and cabinet officers give the president all of the relevant evidence to help him make an informed decision. If they bend their advice to suit his preconceptions, they are not serving his best interests, nor the country's" (Pfiffner 2004, 45, emphasis added). The causal tissue of failed responsibility is complex here, but its anatomy also points to the head.

References

Ackerman, Spencer, and Judis, John B. 2003a. "The Selling of the Iraq War: The First Casualty." *New Republic*. 30 June, 14–25.
___2003b. "The Operator." *New Republic*. 22 September, 18–29.
Allen, Mike. 2001a. "A Team Built on Conservative Discipline," *Washington Post*. 3 January.
___2001b. "Bush on Stage: Deft or Just Lacking Depth". *Washington Post*. 19 February.
Balz, Dan, and Allen, Mike. 2003. "CEO Bush Takes Over Management of Message." *Washington Post*. 28 March.
___and Neal, Terry. 2000. "For Bush, Questions, Clues and Contradiction." *Washington Post*. 22 October.
Bamford, James. 2004. *A Pretext for War: 9/11, Iraq, and the Abuse of America's Intelligence Agencies*. New York: Doubleday.
Barnes, James A. 2001. "Bush's Insiders." *National Journal*. 23 June, 1866–72.

Barstow, David, Broad, William, and Gerth, Jeff. 2004. "How the White House Embraced Disputed Arms Intelligence." *New York Times*. 3 October.

Branigin, William. 2006. "Bush Takes Suggestions on Iraq." *Washington Post*. 5 January.

Bremer, Paul. 2006. *My Year in Iraq*. New York: Simon & Schuster.

Brinkley, Joel, and Schmitt, Eric. 2003. "Iraqi Leaders Say U.S. Was Warned of Disorder After Hussein, but Little Was Done." *New York Times*. 30 November.

Bruni, Frank. 2002. *Ambling into History: The Unlikely Odyssey of George W. Bush*. New York: HarperCollins.

Bumiller, Elisabeth. 2004. "A Partner in Shaping an Assertive Foreign Policy." *New York Times*. 7 January.

Burke, John P. 2000. *The Institutional Presidency: Organizing and Managing the White House from FDR to Bill Clinton*. Baltimore: Johns Hopkins University Press.

——2004. *Becoming President: The Bush Transition, 2000–2003*. Boulder: Lynne Rienner.

——2005a. "The Neutral/Honest Broker Role in Foreign Policy Decision Making: A Reassessment." *Presidential Studies Quarterly* 35 (June): 229–58.

——2005b. "Condoleezza Rice as NSC Adviser: A Case Study of the Honest Broker Role." *Presidential Studies Quarterly* 35 (September): 554–75.

Burke, John P., and Greenstein, Fred I. 1989. *How Presidents Test Reality: Decisions on Vietnam 1954 and 1965*. New York: Russell Sage.

Bush, George W. 1999. *A Charge to Keep*. New York: William Morrow.

Butler Committee. 2004. "Review of Intelligence on Weapons of Mass Destruction," 14 July 2004 〈www.butlerreview.org.uk〉, accessed 21 November 2006.

Campbell, Colin. 2004. "Unrestrained Ideological Entrepreneurship in the Bush II Advisory System," in Colin Campbell and Bert Rockman (eds.), *The George W. Bush Presidency: Appraisals and Prospects*. Washington DC: CQ Press, 73–104.

Carney, James. 1999. "Why Bush Doesn't Like Homework." *Time*. 15 November.

Central Intelligence Agency. 2002. "Iraq's Weapons of Mass Destruction Programs. October. 〈www.odci.gov/cia/reports/iraq_wmd/Iraq_Oct_2002.htm〉, accessed 21 November 2006.

Cloud, David S., and Schmitt, Eric. 2006. "More Retired Generals Call for Rumsfeld's Resignation," *New York Times*. 14 April.

Commission on the Intelligence Capabilities of the United States Regarding Weapons of Mass Destruction. 2005. "Report to the President of the United States," 31 March 〈www.wmd.gov/report〉, accessed 21 November 2006.

Defense Science Board. 2004. *Transition to and from Hostilities*, Washington, DC: US Department of Defense, Office of the Undersecretary of Defense for Acquisition, Technology, and Logistics. December 〈www.acq.osd.mil/dsb/reports/2004-12-DSB_SS_Report_Final.pdf〉, accessed 21 November 2006.

Dickerson, John. 2004. "Confessions of a White House Insider," *Time*. 19 January.

Dickerson, John, Cooper, Matthew, and Waller, Douglas. 2001. "Bush's Two Sides." *Time*. 6 August.

DiIulio, John. 2002. "To Ron Suskind: Your Next Essay on the Bush Administration, October 24, 2002." 2 December 〈www.drudgereport.com〉, accessed 21 November 2006.

——2003. "A View from Within," in Fred I. Greenstein (ed.), *The George W. Bush Presidency: An Early Assessment*. Baltimore: Johns Hopkins University Press, 245–59.

Dolan, Chris J., and Cohen, David B. 2006. "The War About the War: Iraq and the Politics of National Security Advising in the G. W. Bush Administration's First Term." *Politics & Policy*, 34 (1): 30–64.

Elliott, Michael, and Calabresi, Massimo. 2004. "Is Condi the Problem?" *Time*. 5 April.

Fallows, James. 2004a. "Blind into Baghdad." *Atlantic Monthly*. January/February, 52–74.

___ 2004b. "Bush's Lost Year." *Atlantic Monthly*. October, 68–84.

Federal Documents Clearing House. 2003. "U.S. Senate Armed Services Committee Holds a Hearing on Nominations." Washington, DC. 27 February.

Franks, Tommy. 2004. *American Soldier*. New York: Regan.

Frum, David. 2003. *The Right Man: The Surprise Presidency of George W. Bush*. New York: Random House.

George, Alexander L. 1972. "The Case for Multiple Advocacy in Making Foreign Policy." *American Political Science Review* 66 (3): 751–85.

Gibbs, Nancy, and Ware, Michael. 2003. "Chasing a Mirage." *Time*. 6 October.

Goldberg, Jeffrey. 2005. "Anticipating Problems." *New Yorker*. 9 May, 36–41.

Gordon, Michael R. 2004a. "The Strategy to Secure Iraq Did Not Foresee a 2nd War." *New York Times*. 19 October.

___ 2004b. "Faulty Intelligence Misled Troops at War's Start." *New York Times*. 20 October.

Gordon, Michael, and Trainor, Bernard. 2006a. *Cobra II: The Inside Story of the Invasion and Occupation of Iraq*. New York: Pantheon.

___ 2006b. "Even as U.S. Invaded, Hussein Saw Iraqi Unrest as Top Threat." *New York Times*. 12 March.

___ 2006c. "After Invasion, Point Man for Iraq was Shunted Aside." *New York Times*. 13 March.

Greenstein, Fred I. 2004. *The Presidential Difference: Leadership Style from FDR to George W. Bush*. Princeton: Princeton University Press.

Harris, John F., and Balz, Dan. 2001. "First 100 Days Go By in a Blur." *Washington Post*. 29 April.

Heclo, Hugh. 2003. "The Political Ethos of George W. Bush," in Fred I. Greenstein (ed.), *The George W. Bush Presidency: An Early Assessment*. Baltimore: Johns Hopkins University Press, 17–50.

Hersh, Seymour M. 2003. "The Stovepipe." *New Yorker*. 27 October, 77–87.

Hosenball, Mark, Isikoff, Michael, and Thomas, Evan. 2003. "Cheney's Long Path to War." *Newsweek*. 17 November.

Ignatius, David. 2003. "A Foreign Policy Out of Focus." *Washington Post*. 2 September.

Jehl, Douglas. 2004. "U.S. Report Finds Iraqis Eliminated Illicit Arms in 90s." *New York Times*. 7 October.

___ and Sanger, David. 2004. "Prewar Assessment on Iraq Saw Chance of Strong Divisions." *New York Times*. 28 September.

Kagan, Robert, and Kristol, William. 2004. "The Right War for the Wrong Reasons." *Weekly Standard*. 23 February, 20–8.

Kessler, Glenn, and Ricks, Thomas E. 2004. "Rice's NSC Tenure Complicates New Post." *Washington Post*. 16 November.

___ and Slevin, Peter. 2003. "Rice Fails to Repair Rifts, Officials Say." *Washington Post*. 12 October.

Kessler, Ronald. 2004. *A Matter of Character: Inside the White House of George W. Bush*. New York: Sentinel.

Kettl, Donald F. 2003. *Team Bush: Leadership Lessons from the Bush White House*. New York: McGraw-Hill.

Kumar, Martha. 2002. "Recruiting and Organizing the White House Staff." *PS: Political Science and Politics*, 35 (March): 35–40.

Lauter, David. 1990. "The Man Behind the President." *Los Angeles Times*. 14 October.

Leiby, Richard. 2006. "Breaking Ranks." *Washington Post*. 19 January.

Lemann, Nicholas. 2003. "How It Came to War. *New Yorker*. 31 March, 36–40.

Lichtblau, Eric. 2006. "2002 Memo Doubted Uranium Sale Claim." *New York Times*. 17 January.

McManus, Doyle, and Gerstenzang, James. 2001. "Bush Takes CEO Role in Waging War." *Los Angeles Times*. 23 September.

Mazzetti, Mark, and Ruttenberg, Jim. 2006. "Pentagon Memo Aims to Counter Rumsfeld Critics." *New York Times*. 16 April.

Milbank, Dana. 2001. "Serious Strategery." *Washington Post*. 22 April.

—— and Allen, Mike. 2003. "Iraq Flap Shakes Rice's Image." *Washington Post*. 27 July.

—— and Priest, Dana. 2003. "Warning in Iraq Report Unread." *Washington Post*. 20 July.

Moens, Alexander. 2004. *The Foreign Policy of George W. Bush: Values, Strategy and Vision*. Burlington, Vt.: Ashgate.

Mucciaroni, Gary, and Quirk, Paul. 2004. "Deliberations of a 'Compassionate Conservative': George W. Bush's Domestic Presidency," in Colin Campbell and Bert Rockman (eds.), *The George W. Bush Presidency: Appraisals and Prospects*. Washington, DC: CQ Press, 158–90.

National Intelligence Estimate. 2002. "Key Judgments, Iraq's Continuing Programs for Weapons of Mass Destruction." October ⟨www.gwu.edu/~nsarchive/NSAEBB/NSAEBB80/wmd15.pdf⟩, accessed 21 November 2006.

O'Hanlon, Michael. 2004. "Iraq Without a Plan," *Policy Review* 128 (December): 1–9 ⟨www.policyreview.org/dec04/⟩, accessed 21 November 2006.

Packer, George. 2003. "War after the War." *New Yorker*. 24 November, 58–85.

Pfiffner, James P. 2004. "Did President Bush Mislead the Country in His Arguments for War with Iraq? *Presidential Studies Quarterly* 34 (March): 25–46.

—— 2005. "National Security Policymaking and the Bush War Cabinet," in Richard S. Conley (ed.), *Transforming the American Polity: The Presidency of George W. Bush and the War on Terrorism*. Upper Saddle River, NJ: Pearson Prentice Hall, 84–100.

Pillar, Paul R. 2006. "Intelligence, Policy, and the War in Iraq." *Foreign Affairs* 85 (March/April): 15–27.

Pincus, Walter. 2003a. "White House Backs Off Claim on Iraqi Buy." *Washington Post*. 8 July.

—— 2003b. "Tenet Says He Didn't Know About Claim." *Washington Post*. 17 July.

—— 2003c. "White House Faulted on Uranium Claim." *Washington Post*. 24 December.

Pollack, Kenneth M. 2004. "Spies, Lies, and Weapons: What Went Wrong?" *Atlantic Monthly*. January/February, 78–92.

Priest, Dana, and Pincus, Walter. 2004. "U.S. 'Almost All Wrong' on Weapons," *Washington Post*. 7 October.

Rieff, David. 2003. "Who Botched the Occupation?" *New York Times Magazine*. 2 November.

Risen, James. 2006. *State of War: The Secret History of the CIA and the Bush Administration*. New York: Free Press.

Risen, James, and Miller, Judith. 2003. "No Illicit Arms Found in Iraq, U.S. Inspector Tells Congress." *New York Times*. 3 October.

Rothkopf, David. 2005. *Running the World: The Inside Story of the National Security Council and the Architects of American Power*. New York: Public Affairs.

Sanger, David. 2006. "Visited by a Host of Administrations Past, Bush Hears Some Chastening Words." *New York Times*. 6 January.

Sanger, David, and Miller, Judith. 2003. "National Security Aide Says He's to Blame for Speech Error." *New York Times*. 23 July.

Schmitt, Eric, and Brinkley, Joel. 2003. "State Department Foresaw Trouble Now Plaguing Iraq." *New York Times*. 19 October.

Sciolino, Elaine. 2000. "Compulsion to Achieve: Condoleezza Rice." *New York Times*. 18 December.

Senate Intelligence Committee. 2004. *Report of the Select Committee on Intelligence on the U.S. Intelligence Community's Prewar Intelligence Assessments on Iraq*. Washington, DC: Government Printing Office, 7 July.

Stone, Peter H. 2003. "Were Al Qaeda–Iraq Links Exaggerated?" *National Journal*. 9 August, 2569–70.

Suskind, Ron. 2004. *The Price of Loyalty: George W. Bush, the White House, and the Education of Paul O'Neill*. New York: Simon & Schuster.

Thomas, Evan. 2002. "The Quiet Power of Condi Rice" *Newsweek*. 16 December.

——— 2003. "The 12 Year Itch." *Newsweek*. 31 March.

Thomas, Evan, and Wolffe, Richard. 2005. "Bush in the Bubble." *Newsweek*. 19 December.

Thompson, Carolyn B., and Ware, James W. 2003. *The Leadership Genius of George W. Bush*. Hoboken, NJ: Wiley.

Tumulty, Karen, and Allen, Mike 2005. "His Search for a New Groove." *Time*. 19 December.

Waas, Murray. 2006a. "What Bush Was Told About Iraq." *National Journal*. 4 March, 40–1.

——— 2006b. "Insulating Bush." *National Journal*. 1 April, 36–40.

Woodward, Bob. 2002. *Bush at War*. New York: Simon & Schuster.

——— 2004. *Plan of Attack*. New York: Simon & Schuster.

Notes

1. Linda Chavez's nomination as secretary of labor was withdrawn on 9 January, 2001 and she was replaced by Elaine Chao on 11 January.
2. The Office of Global Communication was disestablished when Karen Hughes returned to the administration in 2005 as undersecretary of state for public diplomacy and public affairs.

3. The best analysis of intelligence failures on Iraq can be found in the report of the Robb-Silverman Commission, appointed under President Bush's executive order (Commission on the Intelligence Capabilities of the United States Regarding Weapons of Mass Destruction 2005, 3–11, 45–249). It is also important to note that the reports of the postwar Iraq Survey Group, although not finding the actual presence of WMD, a nuclear capability, and other evidence that the Bush Administration had alleged in its case for war, still concluded that Iraq had been in violation of UN Resolutions 1441 and 687. In inspector David Kay's preliminary report, delivered to congressional intelligence committees on 2 October 2003, he indicated that his team had found equipment and activities never declared to the UN inspectors, covert research on biological warfare agents, signs that Iraq was exploring chemical weapons programs, design work on prohibited missiles, and an ongoing interest in developing a future nuclear capability (see Kagan and Kristol 2004; Pollack 2004, 81; Risen and Miller 2003). Similar points were made in inspector Charles Duelfer's (Kay's successor) report to Congress a year later. Duelfer noted that Saddam sought to preserve "the capability to reconstitute weapons of mass destruction when the [UN] sanctions were lifted" but he had made no "concerted effort to restart programs." The report also indicated that Saddam had used the UN's oil-for-food program's vouchers to buy influence in a number of different countries with the aim of getting the sanctions lifted (Jehl 2004; also see Priest and Pincus 2004). Saddam's top military commanders also believed that Iraq possessed WMD and that they would use them in case of attack, according to a classified 2005 US military report. According to one account, Saddam "was so secretive and kept information so compartmentalized that his top military leaders were stunned when he told them three months before the war that he had no weapons of mass destruction" (Gordon and Trainor 2006b; also see Gordon and Trainor 2006a, 118–20)

4. It should be noted that in his 2003 State of the Union address, President Bush claimed, based on British intelligence, only that Iraq *had sought* to purchase the uranium.

5. In contrast, the CIA, the Defense Intelligence Agency, and the National Ground Intelligence Center viewed the tubes as linked to nuclear purposes (see Gordon and Trainor 2006a, 128–9).

6. It should be noted that the NIE was hastily put together in one month, following a request by Senator Bob Graham (D-FL), vice chair of the Senate Intelligence Committee. Moreover, as Gordon and Trainor note, "for those who read the NIE carefully the document had already poked a gaping hole in the White House's case for war" (ibid.). Ironically, Powell and his staff had based his UN speech on the NIE, believing it more reliable than information they had been provided for the speech from Douglas Feith's Special Plans Pentagon operation and the vice president's staff. Material from both of the latter, according to one Powell aide, "was unsourced, a lot of it was just out of newspapers... it was nuts" (Bamford 2004, 368–69).

7. A partially (8 of 90-plus pages) declassified version of the NIE was made public on 18 July 2003, and it notes, on p. 2, that "DOE agrees that reconstitution of the nuclear program is underway but assesses that the tubes probably are not part

of the program." In a box on pp. 4–5, the report notes the dissent of State's INR on the extensiveness of Iraq's pursuit of a comprehensive effort to acquire nuclear weapons as well as its view that the aluminum tubes are "poorly suited" for uranium enrichment. Page 6 of the declassified version is labeled "Annex A" and has a boxed paragraph on INR's dissent on the aluminum tubes. Page 3 of the report notes an Air Force dissent on whether unmanned aerial vehicles are primarily intended for delivering chemical and biological weapons. Page 7 notes that Iraq "began vigorously trying to procure uranium ore and yellowcake" and then discusses the report from a "foreign government" that as of 2001 Niger planned to send yellowcake uranium to Iraq and the two countries "reportedly were still working out arrangements for this deal," as well as other reports where Iraq "sought" uranium ore from Somalia and "possibly" the Congo. With respect to Niger, the report is somewhat equivocal ("We do not know the status of this arrangement") and, generally with respect to all three nations, "We cannot confirm whether Iraq succeeded" in its acquisition attempts. It is not clear from the declassified version where all of these items appeared in the longer, classified report (National Intelligence Estimate 2002). Also see the CIA's unclassified report on WMD also issued in October 2002, "Iraq's Weapons of Mass Destruction Programs," often referred to as the unclassified NIE (Central Intelligence Agency 2002). It should also be noted that two instances of dissenting views made their way *directly* to the president. The first, a one-page presidential summary of the October 2002 NIE (read by Bush in Tenet's presence) noted the dissent by the State and Energy Departments on the use of aluminium tubes. The second, delivered in January 2003, noted State's INR dissent over whether Saddam would attack the US if Iraq itself was under attack; State felt that he was unlikely to conduct clandestine attacks against the U.S. homeland even if [his] regime's demise is imminent (Waas 2006*a*, 40–1; also see Waas 2006*b*).

8. One might also defend Cheney's and Rumsfeld's efforts as Stephen Cambone did at his confirmation hearings as undersecretary of defense for intelligence on 27 February 2003 when he noted that the "consumers" of intelligence should question how the analysts "arrived at those conclusions and what the sources of information were" (Federal Document Clearing House 2003, 10). According to Kessler, "By questioning analysts, Cheney was doing his job, making sure he and Bush understood the intelligence before going to war" (R. Kessler 2004, 198). Similarly, as Kenneth Pollack notes, "no policymaker should accept intelligence estimates unquestioningly. While I was at the NSC, I regularly challenged analysts as to why they believed what they did.... Any official who does less is derelict in his or her duty" (Pollack 2004, 88). But by the same token, this approach places more burden on top policy makers to make sure that they, the "consumers," have got it right. For a critique of the principals' assessment of intelligence information, as well as Cheney's and Rumsfeld's stovepiping, see Pillar 2006. According to Pillar, then the CIA national intelligence officer for the Near East and South Asia, the administration turned the standard intelligence model "upside down. The administration used intelligence not to inform decision-making but to justify a decision already made" (ibid. 17).

9. The article appeared in the *Washington Post* on 16 March 2003 under Walter Pincus's byline titled "U.S. Lacks Specifics on Banned Arms."

10. According to Woodward's account, Thomas Warrick, who supervised the study, and Meghan O'Sullivan, a sanctions expert, were sent over to Defense to coordinate and work with the Office of Reconstruction and Humanitarian Assistance, the unit that Jay Garner and then Paul Bremer would eventually head (and which would later become the Coalition Provisional Authority). Although Garner wanted Warrick, Rumsfeld reportedly kicked them out of the Pentagon, "ordering them to leave by sundown." The White House was forced to intervene, allowing O'Sullivan back in but not Warrick. It took another week to resolve the status of another seven; five were eventually allowed to participate in ORHA. "Powell couldn't believe the silliness" (Woodward 2004, 283–4; also see Fallows 2004a, 72; Jehl and Sanger 2004; Packer 2003, 62; Schmitt and Brinkley 2003). Gordon and Trainor note, however, limitations in State's study. It was "of uneven quality," and "proposed some good ideas but was far short of a viable plan" (Gordon and Trainor 2006a, 159).

11. Similar criticisms appeared in a *Washington Post* piece on Rice published in October, 2003 and based on four dozen interviews. One senior State Department official, "voicing an opinion that few in the government disputed," stated that "if you want a one-word description of the NSC since January 21, 2001: dysfunctional" (G. Kessler and Slevin 2003). Woodward also discusses the issue, especially Armitage's criticisms of Rice's performance in precisely those terms (Woodward 2004, 414–15). Yet Armitage was not the only high-level critic; according to one former Republican *cabinet secretary*, "The interagency process is completely dysfunctional. In my experience, I've never seen it played out this way" (Ignatius 2003).

12. Some positive developments did come out of the controversy: a CIA officer was assigned to participate in the speech-writing process. It should also be noted that the uranium purchase issue may still be an open question. As Kessler notes, "the British House of Commons Intelligence and Security Committee [the Butler Committee] reviewed the MI6 intelligence about the Niger claim and concluded in September 2003 that, based on the information MI6 gathered [which was not based on the forged documents], the finding was 'reasonable'." MI6 was also "justified in continuing to claim that the intelligence was credible" (R. Kessler 2004, 199). The Butler Committee also found that Bush's statement in the 2003 State of the Union Address "was well-founded" (Butler Committee 2004, 123).

13. But the "case" itself was not apparently put under scrutiny, only its public relations deficiencies. Bush told the group: "Needs a lot more work. Let's get some people who've actually put together a case for a jury" (Woodward 2004, 250). Stephen Hadley and I. Lewis Libby, Cheney's chief of staff and key foreign policy adviser, were assigned the task. Both were lawyers by training, and, as part of their work, they visited the CIA. Libby then presented the case on 25 January 2003 to Rice, Hadley, Richard Armitage (Powell's deputy), Paul Wolfowitz (Rumsfeld's deputy), White House communications director Dan Bartlett, speechwriter Michael Gerson, Rove, and Karen Hughes (who had left the White House but was still serving as an informal adviser). Although some were impressed, according to Woodward (ibid. 290), Armitage thought the case "overreaching and hyperbole," and Hughes "said it didn't work" as a public relations effort.

14. As one participant's CIA notes states, "Much of [OSP's case] we had discounted already" (Bamford 2004, 317).

15. A May 2005 profile of Feith in the *New Yorker* indicates that Feith did consider the "possibility that the invasion and its aftermath could be disastrous," and that concerns were forwarded to the president, the latter notably in Rumsfeld's October 2002 "parade of horribles" memo. According to Feith, "Instead of saying, 'How can we conceal from the President those things that would make him reluctant?,' we decided we had to go to him before he makes such an important decision with a list of all those things that could go wrong." Likewise, Feith sent a memo to General Franks, who was in charge of postwar planning, arguing that "'we're going to have major law-and-order problems after the war . . . I wrote a memo anticipating problems'" (Goldberg 2005, 40–1).

16. However, it should be noted that the July 2004 report of the Senate Intelligence Committee contains testimony from a number of CIA analysts disputing charges that they had been "pressured" (Senate Intelligence Committee, 357–63, 445–6, but also see 455–9). According to Kessler, "Even though Hill staffers interviewed more than a hundred [CIA] analysts after the war, none ever came forward to say he or she had felt any pressure" (R. Kessler 2004, 198). Alternatively, Paul Pillar (2006) argues that the efforts of Cheney and others did have a chilling effect within the CIA.

17. It should be noted that O'Neill later publicly disavowed this and other of his characterizations of the Bush Administration (see R. Kessler 2004, 236–7).

18. Similarly, in the view of journalist Frank Bruni, "Aides said he was asking more questions in . . . meetings, grilling his advisers with more requests for explanations and often demanding to talk not only to the deputy from an administration agency who was giving him a briefing but to the head of the agency" (Bruni 2002, 248). Once decisions were made, strategy determined, and plans set, Bush did not micromanage the effort, as Lyndon Johnson had done during Vietnam. According to Chief of Staff Card, "He gets consulted, but consistent with how does that tactic help us achieve the overall mission. He isn't saying 'I want eight more tanks here,' [or] 'Why are you taking this division up this road.'" In the view of another aide, "He does not and will not micro-manage the plan. Instead, what he does is pepper people with questions to ascertain how the plan is going and to get the latest details and the latest information" (Balz and Allen 2003).

19. According to James Fallows, "The three known exceptions to this pattern actually underscore the limits on top-level talks. One was the discussions at Camp David just after 9/11: they led to 'Afghanistan first,' which delayed rather than forestalled the concentration on Iraq. The second was Colin Powell's 'You break it, you've bought it' warning to the president in the summer of 2002 [in a private meeting with none of the other principals present except Rice]; far from leading to serious questions about the war, it did not even persuade the administration to use the postwar plans devised by the State Department, the Army, and the CIA. The third was a long memo from Rumsfeld to Bush a few months before the war began, when a campaign against Iraq was a foregone conclusion . . . its only apparent effect was that Bush called in his military commanders to look at the war plans" (Fallows 2004*b*, 79).

20. When Woodward asked Rumsfeld about it, Rumsfeld replied that he agreed with the president's decision, but added "Whether there ever was a formal moment where he asked me...I can't recall it." According to Woodward, Bush later told him that "he had not asked Rumsfeld" (Woodward 2004, 416).

21. How the administration presented the public case for war also raises issues about organization and its operations discussed in the first part of this chapter. In August 2002, the White House Iraq Group was created by Chief of Staff Card to engage in "public education" about Iraq's "grave and gathering danger." Its members included, among others, Card, Rove, Hughes, Rice, Hadley, Libby, and Mary Matalin from Cheney's staff, James Wilkinson from the Office of Communications, and Nicholas Calio, the then head of the White House congressional liaison unit. Unfortunately, there is little in the public record about the group's activities and much seems inferential, yet its activities may have played a major role in "ginning up" public evidence—and public comments by members of the administration—of the various components of the case for war, including selective leaks to the media (see Bamford 2004, 317–31, 369–70; Woodward 2004, 168–9, 172, 286). That the group drew so heavily from non-national security officials may have been a further organizational factor causing them perhaps to miss some of the nuances in the evidence against Iraq and publicly overstate the case.

22. As Woodward observes, "In his first months as secretary of state, Powell had never really closed the personal loop with Bush, never established a comfort level—the natural, at-ease state of closeness both had with others. There existed a distance between these two affable men—a wariness—as if they were stalking each other from afar, never sitting down and having it out, whatever the 'it' was" (Woodward 2002, 13).

23. In Woodward's account, Powell laid out his concerns, including the instability war might cause in the Middle East and the problems to be confronted in Iraq following the war; "You need to understand not just a military timeline but the other things that are going to be facing you." According to Woodward, Powell "did not feel the downsides had been brought out in sufficient, gory detail." "The president listened, asked some questions but did not push back that much. Finally, he looked at Powell. 'What should I do? What else can I do?'" At that point, Powell laid out his own plan for taking the issue to the United Nations (Woodward 2004, 150–2). It is also important to note that Powell may not have been dead set against regime change in Iraq. As Moens observes, "there is no evidence that Powell ever opposed regime change in Iraq, as the question for him was not 'whether' but 'how' and 'when.' Clearly, this leaves considerable daylight between Cheney and Powell, but it is not about continuing the existing policy versus regime change" (Moens 2004, 169; also see Gordon and Trainor 2006a, 71–2).

24. In 2006, a number of retired generals who held command positions during the Iraq war publicly criticized Rumsfeld and called for his resignation. They included Major General John Batiste, commander of the Army First Infantry Division, Major General Paul Eaton, commander of Iraqi security forces training, Lieutenant General Gregory Newbold, director of operations of the Joint Chiefs of Staff, Lieutenant General John Riggs, director of the Objective Force Task Force, and Major General

Charles H. Swannack, Jr., commander of the Army 82nd Airborne Division. General Anthony Zinni, former head of the US Central Command before the war was also an outspoken critic (see Cloud and Schmitt 2006). On 14 April 2006, the Pentagon issued an e-mail memo to former commanders and military analysts noting the military's "unprecedented degree" of involvement in the Pentagon's decision making, citing 139 meetings of Rumsfeld and the JCS and 208 meetings with senior commanders since 2005; as well, President Bush strongly defended Rumsfeld as did General Tommy Franks, the former Central Command head, and General Richard Myers, the recently retired chair of the JCS (Mazzetti and Ruttenberg 2006).

7

Intelligence and Decision Making before the War with Iraq

James P. Pfiffner

President Bush made the fateful decision to go to war in Iraq sometime in 2002 or 2003, but he never addressed explicitly the question of whether to go to war in a formal NSC or cabinet meeting. The evidence adduced as the justification for war was ambiguous and incomplete, yet the administration claimed unwarranted certainty about it. The administration attempted to influence the intelligence process to support its case for war, and even though the effort did not fully succeed, it gave insufficient attention to alternative explanations for the intelligence.

The use of intelligence before the Iraq war underscores the insights of Richard Betts (1978, 61) in his analysis of intelligence failures:

In the best-known cases of intelligence failure, the most crucial mistakes have seldom been made by collectors of raw information, occasionally by professionals who produce finished analysis, but most often by the decision makers who consume the products of intelligence services. Policy premises constrict perception, and administrative workloads constrain reflection. Intelligence failure is political and psychological more often than organizational.

As Robert Jervis (2006a, 1) succinctly puts it, "Policy-makers say they need and want very good intelligence. They do indeed need it, but often do not want it."

In the case of Iraq, high officials in the Bush Administration accepted without critical examination the conclusions of the intelligence community that fit their policy preferences. However, they challenged, pressured, and bypassed the intelligence community when intelligence products did not fit their expectations. As a result, the flawed decision-making process, combined with misinterpretation of intelligence, led to a war based on mistaken premises.

Although the bureaucratic pathologies highlighted in Graham Allison's model II (Allison 1971) may have been at work, this chapter argues that in the case of Iraq, a rigid mindset on the part of administration policymakers led to disaster. The commitment to regime change in Iraq blinded the administration to evidence that did not support their arguments for war in Iraq. Thus, they came to conclusions with much more confidence than the intelligence evidence warranted.

The administration had understandable and plausible reasons for seeing Saddam Hussein as a threat to his neighbors in the Middle East. He had used chemical weapons in the past and had made some progress toward a nuclear capacity in the late 1980s. The administration also had reasons to want to thwart Saddam's military ambitions. Saddam was a brutal tyrant who threatened his neighbors and oppressed his own people.

The United States had used military power to oppose Saddam's ambitions since the 1991 Gulf War and had sought to hinder him with economic sanctions and the enforcement of no-fly zones. Saddam, however, seemed determined to continue his internal domination and pursue his external ambitions. Iraq controlled a good portion of the world's oil reserves and Saddam would not hesitate to use this leverage in support of his ambitions. In addition, President Bush believed that Saddam had sponsored an attempt on his father's life. Thus, the conclusion that the Middle East in particular and the world in general would be better off without Saddam was compelling.

Other attempts to remove Saddam from power had been unavailing, and a military confrontation seemed to be the only way to remove Saddam as a threat. Therefore, President Bush resolved to remove Saddam from power through military means. However, in its eagerness to go to war with Saddam, the administration followed a flawed decision-making process, selectively used intelligence, and tried to politicize the intelligence process. Administration officials argued that Saddam had reconstituted his nuclear weapons programs and that he had chemical and biological weapons that were a threat to the United States homeland. They also maintained that Saddam had a cooperative relationship with al-Qaeda.

This chapter examines the use of intelligence by George W. Bush and his administration in decision making before the war in Iraq. I first argue that as the administration moved toward war, decision making was neither deliberate nor deliberative but consisted of a series of decisions that cumulatively led to war. Second, I analyze the arguments of the administration that Iraq was closely linked to al-Qaeda and that it possessed weapons of mass destruction (WMD) that were a threat to the United States. The intelligence produced by the intelligence community was sketchy and ambiguous; political officials in the administration, however, presented it with unwarranted certainty to bolster their case for war. Third, I argue that the administration sought to shape the conclusions of intelligence agencies and downplayed or ignored contrary evidence and the reservations of intelligence professionals. As a result of flawed decision making, the administration went to war in Iraq under misperceptions that resulted in the undermining of US credibility throughout the world.

Deciding to go to War in Iraq

It is not clear when President Bush finally decided to go to war in Iraq, but from the beginning of his administration he had a predisposition for deposing Saddam Hussein. His first two NSC meetings focused on Iraq (Suskind 2004a, 74–6). Immediately after the terrorist attacks of 9/11 he told his top terrorism expert, Richard Clarke, three times to find a link between Saddam and the 9/11 attacks, even though Clarke told him that the intelligence community had concluded that al-Qaeda was behind the attacks (Clarke 2004, 32).[1] Officials in the war cabinet meetings at Camp David discussed attacking Iraq rather than Afghanistan, but the president thought this option was premature. Nevertheless, the president ordered the Defense Department to examine the possibility of a military confrontation with Iraq (National Commission 2004, 334–6; Kessler 2003).

Plans for war became much more concrete when the president told Donald Rumsfeld on 21 November 2001, to develop an operational war plan. General Tommy Franks pulled together a group of DOD planners and presented his results to Rumsfeld and Bush in a series of meetings between December 2001 and 7 February 2002 (Woodward 2004, 96–115). At that time, the Pentagon began shifting intelligence, personnel, and planning resources from the war in Afghanistan to focus on Iraq (Bob Graham 2004, 126; Ricks 2006, 38).

The president began his public campaign for war with Iraq in his State of the Union address on 29 January 2002, in which he warned of the growing menace from the "Axis of Evil" states: Iraq, Iran, and North Korea. During the spring of 2002, the administration started talking about "regime change" in Iraq, and President Bush began to signal publicly that he was committed to removing Saddam from power. In his meeting with British prime minister Tony Blair in April 2002, he asked for Blair's support in a war against Saddam. Blair agreed, but emphasized that there had to be a political plan in place to convince public and world opinion that war was necessary.

In the summer of 2002, military planning became more intense, and leaks from the Pentagon voiced the concerns of the professional officer corps, particularly the Army, about war with Iraq (Ricks 2006, 40–2). By mid-summer, President Bush had seemingly made up his mind. When State Department official Richard Haass broached the issue with National Security Adviser Condoleezza Rice, she told him that the decision had already been made (Lemann 2003, 36). The British foreign secretary characterized US intentions in July of 2002: "It seemed clear that Bush had made up his mind to take military action, even if the timing was not yet decided. But the case was thin" (Downing Street Memo 2002).

With opposition to war growing in elite circles, the administration decided to make the case for war publicly and explicitly. On 26 August Vice President Cheney, in a speech to the Veterans of Foreign Wars, declared, "Many of us are convinced that Saddam will acquire nuclear weapons fairly soon. . . . There is no doubt he is amassing [WMD] to use against our friends, against our allies, and against us" (Cheney 2002). Colin Powell met with the president on 5 August 2002 to try to warn him of the dangers of invading Iraq. Although Powell's reasoning about war with Iraq did not convince the president, Bush did agree to go to the United Nations Security council for a resolution. Tony Blair had also insisted that this was necessary for international support for war.

In September the administration began to gear up its campaign to sway public opinion about the need for war with Iraq. Chief of Staff Andrew Card explained the timing by pointing out, "From a marketing point of view, you don't introduce new products in August" (Woodward 2004, 172). On 3 September the White House Iraq Group (WHIG) was created to coordinate the administration's message on Iraq. Its members included Card, Condoleezza Rice, Stephen Hadley, Lewis Libby, Dan Bartlett, and Nicholas Callio (ibid. 168).

During September 2002 the administration in its public statements began to focus heavily on the direct threat to the United States from Iraq's WMD, chemical, biological, and nuclear. In early September the administration leaked information to the *New York Times* that Saddam was purchasing aluminum tubes in order to refine uranium for nuclear fuel. Vice President Cheney and National Security Adviser Rice quickly confirmed the authenticity of the leak in press interviews. The next disclosure came in a dossier released by the Blair government on 24 September 2002 in which it claimed that Saddam had sought uranium oxide (yellowcake) from Niger and that Saddam could attack with chemical weapons within 45 minutes of warning.

The classified National Intelligence Estimate prepared for Congress on 2 October 2002, followed the British dossier. The NIE asserted that Saddam had chemical and biological weapons and that if he acquired fissile material, he could manufacture a nuclear bomb within one year (CIA 2002*a*). The NIE also contained dissents by the Departments of State and Energy and the Air Force that undercut the broad assertions in some of the major findings of the document. Shortly after the NIE was given to members of Congress, a White Paper was made public that contained the most disturbing assertions of Iraq's WMD but few of the reservations expressed in the original document (Ricks 2006, 52).[2]

The president used the intelligence reported in the NIE, most importantly in his 7 October speech in Cincinnati, to convince members of Congress to vote for a resolution allowing the president to initiate war with Iraq. The timing was important, because congressional elections were coming up in November, and the president wanted to use the votes as campaign issues for those who did not support his request for authority to take the nation to war. With the positive votes from Congress and the Republicans regaining control of the Senate in the November elections, the administration succeeded in winning a unanimous vote from the UN Security Council to force Saddam to give UN weapons inspectors free access to any suspected weapons sites in Iraq.

On 21 December 2002 CIA Director George Tenet and Deputy Director John McLaughlin briefed President Bush in the Oval Office about WMD in Iraq. After McLaughlin had gone over the highly classified evidence for the existence of Saddam's WMD, President Bush was not impressed. He told them, "Nice try. I don't think this is quite—it's not something that Joe Public would understand or would gain a lot of confidence from." Bush said to Tenet, "I've been told all this intelligence about having WMD and this is the best we've got?" Tenet replied, "Don't worry, it's a slam dunk!" The president had concluded that the evidence was less than compelling, but aside from asking his aides to prepare a more effective presentation, there is no indication that he insisted on a fundamental reanalysis of the evidence to ensure that there was a more compelling case (Woodward 2004, 247–250). After the incident, however, neither Tenet nor McLaughlin could recall Tenet having used those words (Suskind 2006, 188).[3]

The president appears to have made the final decision to go to war in January 2003, but not after any formal meeting. Bob Woodward reported that President Bush had asked Rice and Karen Hughes their judgment about going to war and had informed Rumsfeld (Woodward 2004, 251–265). The president said that he knew how the different members of his administration felt and informed them at different times of his decision. The fact that Rice had to prompt the president to inform Powell that he had made up his mind to go to war highlights the lack of a formal process of decision making. So on 13 January the president brought Powell in for a 12-minute meeting to inform him of his decision. Notably, he did not ask his advice. Even Prince Bandar of Saudi Arabia had known of Bush's final decision before Powell (Pfiffner 2004, 25–46; Woodward 2004, 269–74). On 31 January 2003 the president met with Prime Minister Blair and informed him that he intended to invade Iraq, even if there were no new UN resolution and no WMD were found. At this meeting both Bush and Blair expressed doubts that WMD would be found quickly in Iraq, despite Colin Powell's upcoming speech to the UN (Van Natta 2006).[4]

Although UN weapons inspectors had carte blanche to inspect whatever sites they chose, President Bush became impatient with their inability to locate WMD in Iraq. In his 2003 State of the Union Address, he declared, "If Saddam Hussein does not fully disarm for the safety of our people, and for the peace of the world, we will lead a coalition to disarm him." Hans

Blix, head of the UN inspectors, said that more time was needed to complete the inspections, but President Bush remained skeptical of the UN's ability to locate the weapons. President Bush then insisted that the UN inspectors be withdrawn as US and British troops massed on the borders of Iraq in preparation for the invasion. On 19 March the war began.

The striking thing about the decision to go to war was that there seemed to be no overall meeting of the principals in which the issue of whether to go to war with Iraq was debated. According to Richard Haass, director of policy planning for the State Department, "It was an accretion, a tipping point.... A decision was not made—a decision happened, and you can't say when or how" (Packer 2005, 45). Thomas Ricks characterized the decision to go to war as being made "more through drift than through any one meeting" (Ricks 2006, 58).

The traditional interdepartmental policy development process of the NSC did not guide the decision-making process. Vice President Cheney and Secretary Rumsfeld dominated the planning for war; Condoleezza Rice did not play the traditional brokering role of the national security adviser (Burke 2005a, b); and Colin Powell was often marginalized. As Colin Powell said, "very often maybe Mr. Rumsfeld and Vice President Cheney would take decisions in to the president that the rest of us weren't aware of. That did happen, on a number of occasions" (Leiby 2006). According to Deputy Secretary of State Richard Armitage, "There was never any policy process to break, by Condi or anyone else. There was never one from the start" (Suskind 2006, 225). President Bush's tendency to consult only a few of his closest aides and the vice president exacerbated the lack of process. According to Christopher DeMuth, president of the American Enterprise Institute, the circle of Bush advisers was "both exclusive and exclusionary." "It's a too tightly managed decision-making process. When they made decisions, a very small number of people are in the room, and it has a certain effect of constricting the range of alternatives being offered" (Suskind 2004b, 8).

Although an orderly decision-making process cannot guarantee that wise decisions will be made, the lack of a deliberative process in which major decisions are formally debated is more likely to lead to mistakes. The mistake in this case was going to war based on faulty premises (Pfiffner 2005b). As President Eisenhower said, "Organization cannot make a genius out of an incompetent.... On the other hand, disorganization can scarcely fail to result in inefficiency and can easily lead to disaster" (Eisenhower 1963, 114).

The *Casus Belli*: Saddam's Link to al-Qaeda and WMD

Both the Senate Select Committee on Intelligence in 2004 and the Robb-Silberman Commission in 2005 concluded that US intelligence agencies were at fault for the incorrect and misleading information used by policy makers in the run-up to the war with Iraq. According the SSCI, "Most of the major key judgments in the Intelligence Community's October 2002 National Intelligence Estimate . . . either overstated, or were not supported by, the underlying intelligence reporting." The report stated that the committee had found "no evidence that the IC's mischaracterization or exaggeration of the intelligence on Iraq's weapons of mass destruction (WMD) capabilities was the result of political pressure" (Senate Select Committee, 203–4). The Robb-Silberman report said, "We conclude that the Intelligence Community was dead wrong in almost all of its pre-war judgments about Iraq's weapons of mass destruction." They also found that the IC did not change any judgments in response to political pressure (Commission on Intelligence Capabilities 2005, 335–46). The implication of these findings was that Bush Administration policy makers were innocent victims of faulty intelligence reporting and analysis. However, this chapter argues that, even though the IC was sometimes mistaken, administration officials consistently ignored contrary evidence and selectively focused on those bits of intelligence that seemed to support their policy preference for war with Iraq.

This section examines the way the administration used intelligence in its decision making about war. The analysis reinforces Betts's insight that, "The use of intelligence depends less on the bureaucracy than on the intellects and inclinations of the authorities above it" (Betts 1978, 61). The administration's commitment to depose Saddam Hussein led it to dismiss or ignore any arguments by the intelligence community that seemed to undermine its case for war. As Betts argued, "a leader mortgaged to his policy tends to resent or dismiss the critical [analyses], even when they represent the majority view of the intelligence community" (ibid. 64).

Strong psychological tendencies push policy makers toward interpreting intelligence in ways that are consistent with their expectations and not counter to their preferences. Robert Jervis (2006b, 4) observes, "people are prone to avoid painful value trade-offs if they possibly can. Decision makers talk about how they make hard decisions all the time. But, like the rest of us, they prefer easy ones and will use their great abilities of self-deception in order to turn the former into the latter."

The administration made several primary arguments to convince Congress, the American people, and even themselves that war with Iraq was necessary. The administration claimed that there was a link between Saddam and al-Qaeda, and it strongly implied that this was an operational link and that Saddam was connected to the 9/11 terrorist attacks. It also asserted that Saddam possessed chemical and biological weapons and was working on the ability to deliver these weapons to the US homeland (the unpiloted aerial vehicles, UAVs). Administration officials also asserted that Saddam's regime was well on the way to reconstituting its nuclear weapons capacity. (Although it never had such a capacity, it was making serious progress before 1991.) It was only after war was virtually inevitable that the administration began to argue that the United States needed to relieve the suffering of the Iraqi people by removing Saddam and that a democratic Iraq would be a beacon of hope for repressed peoples in the Middle East.

The Asserted Link Between Saddam and al-Qaeda

Immediately after the attacks of 9/11, much of the US public believed that Saddam Hussein was connected to the attacks, and statements by the president and other administration officials reinforced this impression over the next several years. Within 24 hours of the attacks, President Bush told Richard Clarke several times to look into "any shred" of evidence of a link, despite Clarke's report that the intelligence community had concluded that al-Qaeda was behind the attacks (Clarke 2004, 30–3). In September 2002 Secretary Rumsfeld said evidence for the link was "bulletproof" "factual," and "exactly accurate" (Schmitt 2002). In his 7 October 2002 speech, President Bush asserted, "we've learned that Iraq has trained al-Qaeda members in bomb-making and poisons and deadly gasses" (Associated Press 2004). The main evidence adduced to prove the relationship was (1) an asserted meeting of hijacker Mohamed Atta with an Iraqi intelligence official in Prague in April 2001; (2) the presence of the terrorist al-Zarqawi in Iraq; (3) several inconclusive meetings in the 1990s; and (4) the confession under aggressive interrogation of Ibn al-Shaykh al-Libi.

ATTA MEETING IN PRAGUE

The administration claimed that there had been a meeting between hijacker Mohamed Atta and an Iraqi diplomat in Prague on 9 April 2001. However, the CIA and FBI found no evidence of such a meeting. They had firm evidence that Atta was in Virginia Beach on 4 April and in Coral Springs, Florida on 11 April and that his phone had been used in the United States on 6, 9, 10, and 11 April (National Commission 2004, 228–9). In the President's Daily Brief (PDB) of 21 September 2001, the CIA reported the conclusion that there was no evidence that demonstrated a link between Saddam and al-Qaeda (Waas 2005). Nevertheless, Secretary Rumsfeld and Vice President Cheney continued to claim the existence of a link, and on 25 September 2002 President Bush said, "You can't distinguish between al Qaeda and Saddam when you talk about the war on terror" (ibid.).

Contrary to the administration's claims, the Senate Select Intelligence Committee concluded that "Despite four decades of intelligence reporting on Iraq, there was little useful intelligence collected that helped analysts determine the Iraqi regime's possible links to al Qaeda" (ibid.). The administration, however, did not allow the Senate Select Intelligence Committee to examine the PDB.[5]

The 9/11 Commission judged that "The available evidence does not support the original Czech report of an Atta–Ani meeting" (National Commission 2004, 228–9).

ZARQAWI IN IRAQ

In June 2004, President Bush said that the terrorist, Musab al-Zarqawi, was "the best evidence of connection to Al Qaeda affiliates and Al Qaeda" (CNN 2004). Although al-Zarqawi was a terrorist, the CIA doubted that he was closely connected with al-Qaeda. A CIA report of August 2004 said that they did not think that Saddam harbored the Jordanian terrorist or members of his group (Bergen 2004; Jehl 2004*b*). Aside from possible medical treatment in Baghdad, Zarqawi operated from Kurdish territory in Iraq that was not fully under Saddam's control.

AL-QAEDA IN IRAQ

In the 1990s, some meetings between al-Qaeda and Iraq representatives probably did take place, but there is no evidence that they led to any cooperation. According to the 9/11 Commission, meetings between bin Laden or aides "may have occurred in 1999." "But to date we have seen no evidence that these or the earlier contacts ever developed into a collaborative operational relationship. Nor have we seen evidence indicating that Iraq cooperated with al Qaeda in developing or carrying out any attacks against the United States" (National Commission 2004, 66).

CONFESSION OF SHAYKH AL-LIBI

In his major speech about the need for war with Iraq on 7 October 2002 President Bush said, "We've learned that Iraq has trained al-Qaeda members in bomb-making and poisons and deadly gasses." The main source of this claim was the interrogation of Ibn al-Shaykh al-Libi, a Libyan captured in Pakistan, who had been a senior member of al-Qaeda. However, in February 2002 the DIA had judged that al-Libi's statements were suspect because he could not provide credible details about the types of weapons involved, the Iraqis he dealt with, or the location of the meetings. In addition, he was probably subjected to torture to obtain his confession. In November 2005, Senator Carl Levin released portions of the 2002 Defense Intelligence Agency report (DITSUM 044-02) that undermined al-Libi's credibility (Levin 2004).

The DIA concluded in 2002, "it is more likely this individual is intentionally misleading the debriefers. Ibn al-Shaykh has been undergoing debriefs for several weeks and may be describing scenarios to the debriefers that he knows will retain their interest." The report added that, "Saddam's regime is intensely secular and wary of Islamic revolutionary movements. Moreover, Baghdad is unlikely to provide assistance to a group it cannot control."[6] Libi recanted his claims in February 2004, after he was returned to US custody and was held at Guantanamo Bay. It was reported that he had been subject to "aggressive interrogation techniques" in order to get him to talk (Isikoff 2004; Jehl 2004b; Priest 2004). Al-Libi confessed to aiding Iraq only after he had been questioned by Egyptian interrogators to whom the US had transferred him. Despite the DIA's judgment in February 2002 that Ibn al-Shaykh was probably "intentionally misleading" his interrogators, President Bush included the claim about al-Qaeda training Iraqis in "poisons and deadly gasses" in his speech on 7 October 2002 (Jehl 2005b).

Paul Pillar, who was in charge of coordinating the intelligence community's assessment of Iraq from 2000 to 2005, wrote: "the greatest discrepancy between the administration's public statements and the intelligence community's judgments concerned...the relationship between Saddam and al Qaeda. The enormous attention devoted to this subject did not reflect any judgment by intelligence officials that there was or was likely to be anything like the 'alliance' the administration said existed" (Pillar 2006).

The Intelligence Community (IC) reported its conclusions on the link in five separate reports from September 2001 to January 2003, according to the Senate Select Committee on Intelligence (Levin 2004). In its January 2003 report, "Iraqi Support for Terrorism," it said that the evidence for such a relationship was "contradictory" and that it "appears to more closely resemble that of two independent actors trying to exploit each other" and that there was "no credible information" that Iraq had any foreknowledge of the 9/11 attacks (ibid. 9).

Despite the lack of support from the Intelligence Community, on 1 May 2003, President Bush still called Iraq an "ally" of al-Qaeda. On 9 January 2004 Vice President Cheney said that a leaked document from Douglas Feith's office in the Pentagon was the "best source of information" on the alleged link (ibid. 32). The report, which was published in the conservative *Weekly Standard*, included many unverifiable assertions purporting to demonstrate the link (Hayes 2003).[7] However, the Department of Defense disavowed the accuracy of the leaked report.[8]

Thus the administration's decision to go to war in Iraq was based in part on its conclusion that Saddam was allied with al-Qaeda—a conclusion that was explicitly challenged by the intelligence community, especially the CIA and the Office of Intelligence and Research of the State Department.

Chemical and Biological Weapons

Suspicions that Saddam had significant quantities of chemical weapons in 2002 were based on the facts that he had large quantities of chemical munitions in the 1980s and that he had used them internally against the Kurds and in his war with Iran. When Saddam could not account for the weapons having been destroyed and the UN inspectors could not locate them, intelligence agencies made the reasonable inference that he still possessed them (Hersh 2003c, 87).[9] Nevertheless, the Defense Intelligence Agency had doubts as the NIE was being prepared in September 2002, though their reservations were not reported in the NIE. DIA concluded, "there is no reliable information on whether Iraq is producing or stockpiling chemical weapons" (Auster, Mazzetti, and Pound 2003; Whitelaw 2004).

The primary, contemporary evidence for the biological weapons and mobile labs claim that Colin Powell asserted in his 5 February UN speech originated with Curveball, who was an Iraqi defector held by the Germans (Kerr 2004).[10] Despite doubts about his reliability, the CIA assured Colin Powell before his UN speech that the sources were multiple and credible. Yet senior German officials of the Federal Intelligence Service (BND) said that they had warned US intelligence officials in the fall of 2002 that Curveball was unreliable. According to them, Curveball was "not a stable, psychologically stable guy." "This was not substantial evidence. We made clear we could not verify the things he said." After hearing the US claims about chemical and biological weapons, the Germans said "We were shocked. Mein Gott! We had always told them it was not proven.... It was not hard intelligence" (Drogin and Geotz 2005a, b).[11]

The German judgment that Curveball was not reliable was passed on to the CIA through Tyler Drumheller, chief of the Directorate of Operations European Division. After he had read a draft of Colin Powell's upcoming speech to the United Nations, Drumheller tried to warn CIA Deputy Director John McLaughlin that the Germans doubted Curveball's mental stability and reliability. McLaughlin reportedly said that Curveball was at "the heart of the case" for Iraq's biological weapons programs. Drumheller also warned Tenet on the night before Powell's speech that Curveball's information was not reliable. Later, Tenet and McLaughlin told the Robb-Silberman Commission that they did not remember Drumheller's warnings about Curveball (Drogin and Goetz 2005a; Drogin and Miller 2005; Risen 2006, 116–20).[12]

In May 2003, after the initial military phase of the war, the US sent nine bioweapons experts, each with ten years' professional experience, to Iraq to examine two trailers that were thought to be mobile biological weapons labs. After a careful examination, the technical team reported back to the CIA on 27 May 2003 that the trailers were not designed for bioweapons production but rather for producing hydrogen for weather balloons. Nevertheless the next day, 28 May 2003, the CIA issued a report stating that the trailers "were the strongest evidence to date that Iraq was hiding a biological warfare program" (Warrick 2006b). The next day, citing the trailers, President Bush declared, "We have found the weapons of mass destruction" (ibid. 2006). Despite the 122-page final report of the technical team, over the next several months administration officials continued to cite the trailers as evidence of

Saddam's WMD.[13] And on 5 February 2004, George Tenet said in a speech at Georgetown University that the trailers were plausibly bioweapons labs (Warrick 2006a, b). Over the summer and early fall of 2003, the Iraq survey group could not discover any mobile labs or biological weapons. Interestingly, David Kay said that he was not told of the report of the technical team until late in 2003 (Warrick 2006a).[14]

The NIE also reported that Saddam had unpiloted aerial vehicles. President Bush claimed in his 7 October 2002 speech, "Iraq has a growing fleet" of UAVs that "could be used to disperse chemical or biological weapons across broad areas. . . . We are concerned that Iraq is exploring ways of using these UAVs *for missions targeting the United States*" (emphasis added). The Air Force, however, registered a dissent in the NIE: "The Director, Intelligence, Surveillance, and Reconnaissance, US Air Force, does not agree that Iraq is developing UAVs primarily intended to be delivery platforms for chemical and biological warfare (CBW) agents. The small size of Iraq's new UAV strongly suggests a primary role of reconnaissance, although CBW delivery is an inherent capability" (CIA 2002a, 7). After the initial war, the Air Force was proven correct in its judgment of Saddam's UAVs (Bradley Graham 2003; Pfiffner 2004, 40–1).

Thus, although the premise that Saddam possessed chemical and biological weapons was plausible, policy makers ignored several warnings that did not support their assumptions.

Nuclear Weapons

Although Saddam's supposed participation in 9/11 constituted a strong political argument for revenge against Iraq, the argument that Saddam was close to obtaining nuclear weapons made the most compelling argument for war. Even those most skeptical about the need for war and its consequences had to be shaken by the possibility of Saddam with nuclear weapons. Therefore, the administration played the nuclear card with significant effects in its public campaign for war. The main evidence upon which it relied, however, was shaky. This section first examines the claim that Saddam sought uranium oxide from Niger; it then focuses on the question of the aluminum tubes.

The suspicion that Saddam was in the process of reconstituting his nuclear capacity was not unreasonable. After the 1991 Gulf War, it was discovered that Saddam had made much more progress toward a nuclear capacity than either the UN or the CIA had suspected. That capacity was destroyed by US forces in the war and by UN inspectors after the war. Given Saddam's record, it seemed reasonable that he would again seek nuclear weapons. The problem was that there was no convincing evidence that he was doing so— except for his supposed attempt to acquire yellowcake from Niger and his purchase of thousands of aluminum tubes that the administration asserted were intended to be used as centrifuges to produce fissile material for making nuclear bombs. Therefore, the administration fastened on these two claims of evidence to make its case that Saddam was on the verge of having nuclear weapons.

URANIUM OXIDE—YELLOWCAKE, FROM NIGER

In January 2002 a report that Iraq might be seeking nuclear materials provoked Vice President Cheney's concern, and an inquiry by his office led the CIA to send former ambassador Joseph Wilson to Niger to investigate. Wilson's report, along with reports from the US ambassador to Niger, concluded that the rumors were false. The conclusions from this report were circulated in the Intelligence Community.

The public disclosure on the reported yellowcake from Niger came in the British dossier that was released on 24 September 2002. The claim was also included in the CIA's NIE of early October (though not in the public White Paper). The State Department's Bureau of Intelligence and Research, however, concluded in the NIE: "Finally, the claims of Iraqi pursuit of natural uranium in Africa are, in INR's assessment, highly dubious" (CIA 2002a, 84). George Tenet had warned the British that the Niger story was probably not true, but it was included in the dossier nonetheless, and the claim was asserted in a draft of the president's 7 October speech in Cincinnati. However, after two memoranda from the CIA and a personal call from Tenet to Rice's deputy, Steven Hadley, the claim was taken out of Bush's speech (Associated Press 2003; Pfiffner 2004, 31).[15]

The report about Niger and yellowcake may have originated in several letters obtained by Italian intelligence sources. On 11 October 2002 Italian journalist Elisabetta Burba gave copies of the Niger letters to the US Embassy in Rome. A summary of the letters was distributed to US intelligence agencies with the caveat that they were of "dubious authenticity." The letters themselves, however, were not given to the CIA until after the president's State of the Union speech on 28 January 2003 (Hersh 2003a; Pincus and Priest 2003b; Priest 2003; Priest and DeYoung 2003; Priest and Milbank 2003). When Mohamed ElBaraedei, Director of the International Atomic Energy Commission was given the documents on 7 February 2003, he quickly concluded that they were clumsy forgeries. It is an open question why the CIA did not get the documents until after the president's speech and why, once they did, they did not expose the forgeries but let the IAEA make them public (Isikoff and Thomas 2003; Priest 2003).[16]

Given that the basis for the claim for the Niger yellowcake was known by the CIA to be dubious and was disavowed by the State Department, how did the claim make it into the president's State of the Union address? When the State of the Union speech was being prepared, NSC official Robert Joseph faxed a paragraph on uranium from Niger to CIA official Alan Foley.

Foley told Joseph that the reference to Niger should be taken out. Joseph insisted that a reference remain in the speech, so they compromised: Niger was changed to Africa; they did not include any specific quantity; and the source was attributed to the British rather than to US intelligence (Cooper 2003; Pincus and Priest 2003b). Thus there was high-level doubt about the wisdom of including the dubious claim about Niger in the president's State of the Union message, particularly since the same claim had been deleted from the president's 7 October 2002 speech in Cincinnati.

THE ALUMINUM TUBES

In early 2001 a CIA analyst ("Joe") discovered that Iraq wanted to buy thousands of highly specialized aluminum tubes. On 10 April 2001 a CIA report asserted that the tubes "have little use other than for a uranium enrichment program" (Barstow, Broad, and Gerth 2004; Linzer and Gellman 2004; Pfiffner 2004, 34–37). However, the next day the Energy Department said that the tubes were the wrong size for centrifuges and that the openness of the solicitation by Iraq indicated that the tubes were intended for conventional weapons. In June 2001 a shipment of the tubes was seized in Jordan, and the United States assigned its best nuclear centrifuge engineers to examine the case. The Energy Departments (and British) experts concluded that the tubes were meant for conventional purposes, but Joe at the CIA still maintained that they were intended for nuclear centrifuges.

Over the next year and a half the disagreement over the purpose of the tubes was debated within the intelligence community, and the CIA sent fifteen reports on the nature of the tubes to top administration officials. The CIA and Energy experts maintained that they told the top officials about the debate within the intelligence community. On 8 September 2002 the story of the tubes was leaked to the *New York Times*, but without any of the reservations expressed by the nuclear experts. Cheney and Rice, who expressed certainty that the tubes were intended for nuclear purposes, quickly confirmed the validity of the leak. Rice confirmed that the tubes "are only really suited for nuclear weapons programs" (Barstow, Broad, and Gerth 2004, 11). However, on 13 September the Energy Department forbade its scientists from talking with the press, so no reservations about the claim were made public (ibid. 1).

The claim was included in the NIE, but the Energy and State Departments dissented and said the tubes were not likely meant for nuclear purposes. The declassified version of the NIE (the White Paper) stated, "All intelligence experts agree that Iraq is seeking nuclear weapons and that these tubes could be used in a centrifuge enrichment program." Though in the next sentence it stated that "some" believe the tubes were for conventional weapons purposes (CIA White Paper 2002b, 71–6).

Despite the doubts of the best experts, the tubes were mentioned as evidence of Saddam's nuclear intentions in both the president's 7 October 2002 speech and the State of the Union address as well as in many statements by administration officials before the war. In preparing the secretary of state for his speech to the UN on Saddam's WMD, the Bureau of Intelligence and Research warned him that the tubes were not likely meant for nuclear purposes. Nevertheless, Powell in his speech to the UN said that there was "no doubt in my mind" that they were for nuclear purposes (Barstow, Broad, and Gerth 2004).[17]

The Senate Select Committee on Intelligence and the Robb-Silberman reports both decided that the administration's conclusions that the tubes were meant for nuclear purposes were wrong. The administration claimed that this was the conclusion of the intelligence community and included in the supposedly authoritative NIE of October 2002. National Security Adviser Condoleezza Rice said, "All that I can tell you is that if there were doubts about the underlying intelligence in the NIE, those doubts were not communicated to the president. The only thing that was there in the NIE was a kind of a standard INR footnote, which is kind of 59 pages away from the bulk of the NIE. That's the only thing that's there.... So if there was a concern about the underlying intelligence there, the president was unaware of that concern and as was I" (White House 2003). Even though the State Department's INR dissent was placed toward the end of the document, the "Key Judgments" section near the front called attention to the "INR alternative view at the end of these Key Judgments" (Milbank and Allen 2003; Mufson 2003; Priest and Milbank 2003; Waas 2006b).[18]

In fact, top officials of the Bush Administration, including the president, knew of the doubts within the intelligence community about the nature of the aluminum tubes. Murray Waas of the *National Journal* reported that George Tenet presented a "President's Summary" of the October 2002 NIE to President Bush and that the president read it in his presence (Waas 2006a, b). The classified summary stated that the Departments of State and Energy doubted that the aluminum tubes were intended to be centrifuge rotors. It said that "most agencies judge" that the tubes were intended for nuclear purposes, but that "INR and DOE believe that the tubes more likely are intended for conventional weapons uses."[19]

In its selective use of intelligence, the Bush Administration also ignored what might be viewed as an impressive intelligence coup. Although the CIA was criticized after the Iraq War for its lack of "humint," that is, human intelligence sources who had penetrated the government of Saddam Hussein, Naji Sabri, the foreign minister of Iraq, had been recruited to divulge information. Tyler Drumheller, who had been with the CIA for 26 years and who was the head of covert operations for the CIA in Europe, ran the operation. Drumheller reported that the president was enthusiastic about the recruitment when told of it by George Tenet. However, when Sabri reported that Saddam had no active WMD programs ongoing, the White House lost its enthusiasm. According to Drumheller, when he told the White House group that was preparing for the Iraq War of Sabri's denial of WMD, they dropped their interest in Sabri. "And we said, 'Well, what about the intel?' And they said, 'Well, this isn't about intel anymore. This is about regime change.'" Drumheller concluded: "The policy was set. The war in Iraq was coming. And they were looking for intelligence to fit into the policy, to justify the policy" (*Sixty Minutes* 2006).

As Betts observed, "Policy perspectives tend to constrain objectivity, and authorities often fail to use intelligence properly" (Betts 1978, 67). In the case of the purported link between Saddam and al-Qaeda, policy workers ignored CIA doubts and continued to imply that there was such a link. Although the premisses of chemical and biological weapons in Iraq were plausible, policy makers suppressed or ignored Tyler Drumheller's warnings about Curveball's credibility and the warning of the team of experts who examined the purported mobile bioweapons labs. In the case of nuclear weapons, policy makers resisted the CIA warnings about Niger yellowcake. They also accepted the CIA's judgment that the aluminum tubes were intended to be nuclear centrifuges, despite the judgment of US centrifuge experts in the Department of Energy that the tubes were not well suited for such purposes. Finally, policy makers discounted the high-level human intelligence obtained from Iraq's foreign minister.

Politicizing Intelligence

The traditional role of the career services in the US government is to provide to political superiors their best judgment about whatever policies are being considered; it is the rightful prerogative of the president and political appointees to make policy decisions within the executive branch. In the case of intelligence, this means that intelligence professionals should present their best judgment as to the evidence in question whether or not it seems to support the policy preferences of the political administration in office.

There is some evidence that the Bush administration may have tried to politicize the intelligence process in several ways in order to bolster its case for war with Iraq. It arguably did this in three ways:

1. it created a separate bureaucratic unit to provide alternative analyses of evidence;
2. it "stovepiped" the separate analyses directly to policy makers; and
3. it brought political pressure to bear on intelligence analysts to affect their conclusions.

British officials articulated a more pithy description of the politicization in the Iraq case. According to the "Downing Street Memo" of July 2002, the head of Britain's Secret Intelligence Service (MI6), after his meeting in Washington with US officials, reported, "Military action was now seen as inevitable. Bush wanted to remove Saddam, through military action, justified by the conjunction of terrorism and WMD. *But the intelligence and facts were being fixed around the policy"* (Downing Street Memo 2002, emphasis added). The normal intelligence process is that analysts carefully vet all "raw" reports from the field to ensure that the sources are credible and that the information fits with what else is known about the particular issue. This might include examining the history of the issue or checking with other US or allied intelligence agencies.

In Betts's (1978, 67) analysis, "The ultimate causes of error in most cases [of intelligence failure] have been wishful thinking, cavalier disregard of professional analysts, and, above all, the premises and preconceptions of policy makers." As was argued in the previous section, the Bush Administration's policy preference for regime change in Iraq influenced how it interpreted intelligence. In addition, its mindset influenced what intelligence was provided (and not provided) to policy makers. As Robert Jervis (2006*b*) observed about the Bush Administration and Iraq, "Here as in many cases, policy decisions precede and drive intelligence rather than the other way around."

New Bureaucratic Units

In 2002 the political leadership in the Department of Defense and in the White House had become convinced that the US intelligence community, and the CIA in particular, were discounting the link between Saddam and Osama bin Laden and ignoring the information coming from Ahmed Chalabi and his associates. This fit with the general low regard in which many administration officials held the CIA. As articulated by Richard Perle, chair of DOD's Defense Policy Board: "I think the people working on the Persian Gulf at the C.I.A. are pathetic." "They have just made too many mistakes. They have a record of over 30 years of being wrong." He said they "became wedded to a theory" that al-Qaeda was not working with Iraq (Risen 2004, 1; Pillar 2006).

This led Douglas Feith to use the Policy Counterterrorism Evaluation Group, created shortly after 9/11, to provide alternative analytic perspectives to those being produced by the CIA (Goldberg 2005; Hersh 2003*c*; Jehl 2003; Phillips 2003).[20] Feith's units had close working relationships with the Iraqi National Congress, which the United States had funded, and was headed by Ahmad Chalabi. The CIA, DIA, and the INR at State, however, had become skeptical of the reliability of Chalabi and the defectors from Iraq that he supported. They concluded that Chalabi was unreliable and that the defectors had a stake in overthrowing Saddam and thus were exaggerating or fabricating reports of Saddam's WMD. Feith, however, thought the defectors were reporting accurately and that the CIA was ignoring a valuable intelligence source (Ricks 2006, 104–6).

The leaders of the Counter Terrorism Evaluation Group briefed Undersecretary of Defense for Intelligence Stephen Cambone weekly, and according to one official left "no dot unconnected" (Risen 2004, 4–5). Former analyst for Middle East intelligence for DIA, Patrick Lang, summed up the problem from the perspective of career intelligence professionals: "But the problem is that they brought in people who were not intelligence professionals, people brought in because they thought like them. They knew what answers they were going to get" (ibid. 2). The administration seemed to want to convince itself that its preconceptions were correct and block any alternative analysis.

"Stovepiping" Intelligence

So instead of allowing the CIA to vet the intelligence from Chalabi and the defectors, Feith "stovepiped" the reports of the Iraqi defectors straight to the White House (the vice president's staff and NSC staff) without any opportunity for comments by career intelligence professionals. According to Kenneth Pollack, who wrote a book supporting the war with Iraq, the Bush Administration: "dismantled the existing filtering process that for fifty years had been preventing the policy makers from getting bad information. They created stovepipes to get the information they wanted directly to the top leadership. Their position is that the professional bureaucracy is deliberately and maliciously keeping information from them" (Hersh 2003c).

On the issue of a link between Saddam and al-Qaeda, Feith's office presented different versions of the link evidence to the CIA and to the White House. In the White House version, among other differences, Feith presented as a "known" fact the claimed meeting of Atta with the Iraqi Ani in Prague in 2001, despite the IC skepticism that any meeting had taken place. George Tenet testified that he did not know about these prewar White House meetings until February 2004 (Levin 2004, 17–20).

The point here is not that White House officials should not get raw intelligence or direct reports from the field, but rather that to be fully informed, they ought also to get the best judgment of career intelligence professionals about the credibility of the sources and interpretation of the information. However, the administration's political leadership was convinced that the CIA was biased, and so Feith purposely bypassed the intelligence community in order to present his own analysis directly to White House officials without any vetting by career intelligence professionals. Thus the White House officials, who were predisposed to believe Feith and Chalabi, were misled about the evidence for WMD and Saddam's link with bin Laden. The result was the use of faulty evidence and non-credible intelligence in decision making about going to war with Iraq and obtaining public support for it.

Cheney's Visits to Langley

Policy makers may also have tried to politicize the intelligence process by putting pressure on intelligence analysts to arrive at the conclusions favored by the Bush Administration. During the summer and fall of 2002 Vice President Cheney made multiple visits to CIA headquarters in Langley in order to ask sharp questions about CIA analysis of intelligence relating to Iraq. Although it is appropriate for the vice president or other high-level officials to question intelligence conclusions, there is a fine line between skeptical questioning and pressure for a given outcome. Vice President Cheney, having been chief of staff to President Ford and secretary of defense for President George H. W. Bush, was a sophisticated political and bureaucratic operator. He clearly understood the impact that a personal visit and sharp questioning from the vice president would have on CIA analysts. According to one retired career CIA analyst, "During my 27-year career at the Central Intelligence Agency, no vice president ever came to us for a working visit" (McGovern 2003).

Senator Rockefeller, ranking minority member of the Senate Select Intelligence Committee, concluded that there was an atmosphere of "intense pressure in which the intelligence community officials were asked to render judgments on matters relating to Iraq when the most senior officials in the Bush Administration had already forcefully and repeatedly stated their conclusions publicly" (*New York Times* 2004).

Some intelligence officials said they felt pressure from these visits to write reports that would help the administration make the case for war (Risen 2003). One "senior Bush Administration official told Seymour Hersh: "They got pounded on, day after day.... Pretty soon... they began to provide the intelligence that was wanted" (Hersh 2003*b*). Some intelligence professionals felt that "intense questioning" and "repetitive tasking" created pressure to conform to administration expectations. One intelligence veteran said that the pressure on analysts was greater than he had ever seen at the CIA in his 32-year career (Miller and Reynolds 2004). "They were the browbeaters," according to a former DIA official who was at some of the meetings. "In interagency meetings Wolfowitz treated the analysts' work with contempt" (Pincus and Priest 2003*a*).

In one meeting in August 2002 representatives from Feith's office attended an Intelligence Community meeting to finalize a report about the suspected links between Saddam and al-Qaeda. It was highly unusual for representatives of the Office of the Secretary of Defense to attend such intelligence meetings. Feith's people pressed for a more positive statement about the link and asked for 32 changes to the draft, about half of which were made (Bamford 2004, 333–4, 337; Levin 2004; Miller and Reynolds 2004).[21]

Another effect of administration pressure on the CIA amounted to self-censorship in one case in which the Agency failed to report what turned out to be accurate information obtained from human intelligence. In the summer of 2002 the CIA located relatives of Iraqi scientists and convinced them to contact their relatives in Iraq to get information on Iraq's WMD programs. One of them was Dr Sawsan Alhaddad whose brother had worked in Saddam's nuclear program in the 1980s. She traveled to Baghdad to talk with her brother and reported back to the CIA that her brother said that Iraq's nuclear program had been abandoned in the 1990s. In total, thirty relatives of Iraqi scientists reported back to the CIA that Saddam had no nuclear programs of which the scientists were aware. The CIA, however, was convinced that Saddam was pursuing a nuclear program, and they did not forward the reports to senior policy makers in the administration (Risen 2006, 106, 185–208).

In the summer of 2003 Robert L. Hutchings, former chair of National Intelligence Council, told his staff not to inflate the intelligence on Syrian weapons programs at the insistence of State Department political appointee John Bolton. Even though the Syrian incidents with Bolton took place after the Iraq invasion, the attitude of administration officials toward the professional intelligence officials is relevant. According to Hutchings, "This is not just about the behavior of a few individuals but about a culture that permitted them to continue trying to skew the intelligence to suit their policy agenda. . . . When policy officials come back day after day with the same complaint and the same instructions to dig deeper for evidence to support their preformed conclusions, that is politicization." "When those officials seek to remove from office analysts whose views they do not like, that is politicization. The mere effort, even when it is successfully resisted, creates a climate of intimidation and a culture of conformity" (Jehl 2005a).

In one case an important message that Curveball was unreliable did not make it through to Colin Powell. When one DOD biological weapons analyst (the only US intelligence official who had met Curveball) went over Colin Powell's draft speech the day before it was to be delivered to the UN, he felt he had to warn Powell that Curveball, the main source of the reports of the mobile biological weapons labs, was not reliable. But the deputy chief of the Iraqi Task Force wrote him an e-mail saying: "Let's keep in mind the fact that this war's going to happen regardless of what Curve Ball said or didn't say, and that the Powers That Be probably aren't terribly interested in whether Curve Ball knows what he's talking about" (Senate Select Committee 2004, 249; Johnston 2004).[22]

Confirmation that pressure was applied to the Intelligence Community with respect to the claimed link between Saddam and al-Qaeda came in a special report by a team headed by Richard J. Kerr, former deputy director of central intelligence. The Report, "Intelligence and Analysis on Iraq: Issues for the Intelligence Community," was issued in July 2004 and declassified in August 2005 (Kerr 2004). With respect to the claimed link between Saddam and al-Qaeda, the Report concluded:

In the case of al-Qa'ida, the constant stream of questions aimed at finding links between Saddam and the terrorist network caused analysts to take what they termed a "purposely aggressive approach" in conducting *exhaustive and repetitive searches* for such links. *Despite the pressure*, however, the Intelligence Community remained firm in its assessment that no operational or collaborative relationship existed.

(ibid. 11; emphasis added)

At one point, the deputy director for intelligence, Jami Miscik, threatened to quit if she was forced to rewrite a report about the purported link between Saddam and al-Qaeda again. She had responded to inquiries from the vice president's office a number of times, but they continued to come back to her to insist on further rewrites to meet their expectations. Tenet convinced her to stay and rebuffed the demand (Suskind 2006, 190).

The Report pointed out that when the Intelligence Community conclusions supported the administration's policy goals—that is, reported that Saddam had WMD—that there was little discernible pressure applied. The irony was that the administration applied pressure when the Intelligence Community had it right (i.e. no link) and applied no pressure when the IC was wrong (i.e. the IC conclusion that there were WMD). The Report also noted that personal briefings "at the highest levels" probably influenced policy makers to have more confidence in their conclusions than written reports, which most often contain caveats about the limitations of the evidence, would have conveyed. In the case of WMD the oral briefings "probably imparted a greater sense of certainty to analytic conclusions than the facts would bear" (Kerr 2004, 11).

Perhaps the most authoritative evidence that policy makers tried to politicize intelligence prior to the Iraq War is the testimony of Paul R. Pillar. Pillar was the national intelligence officer who had responsibility for Middle East intelligence from 2002 to 2005 and directed the coordination of the intelligence community's assessments of Iraq. In an article in *Foreign Affairs*, Pillar (2006, 1) charged that (1) "official intelligence analysis was not relied on in making even the most significant national security decisions"; (2) "intelligence was misused publicly to justify decisions already made"; and (3) "the intelligence community's own work was politicized." According to Pillar, "intelligence on Iraqi weapons programs did not drive [the administration's] decision to go to war," because sanctions were working; rather the Bush Administration wanted to "shake up the sclerotic power structures of the Middle East and hasten the spread of more liberal politics and economics in the region" (ibid.).

According to Pillar, the proper role of policy makers is to influence what areas the intelligence community should focus on, but not insist on specific conclusions. Intelligence professionals, on the other hand, should avoid policy judgments. Among intelligence professionals the term "policy prescriptive" is a pejorative because it implies that the analyst stepped beyond his or her appropriate role (ibid. 2). In Pillar's judgment, "the administration used intelligence not to inform decision-making, but to justify a decision already made" (ibid.). In addition, the administration "aggressively [used] intelligence to win public support for its decision to go to war. This meant selectively adducing data—'cherry-picking'—rather than using the intelligence community's own analytic judgments" (ibid. 3).

According to Pillar, the "principal way" that intelligence was politicized was the continued repetitive questioning of reports that did not match the administration's version of events. The Bush Administration "repeatedly called on the intelligence community to uncover more material that would contribute to the case for war. The Bush team approached the community repeatedly and pushed it to look harder at the supposed Saddam-al Qaeda relationship.... The result was an intelligence output that... obscured rather than enhanced understanding of al Qaeda's actual sources of strength and support."

The consequences of politicization may have led to "policymaker self-deception," that is, members of the Bush national security team may have actually believed the conclusions that they had preordained with their pressure on the intelligence community. According to Pillar (2006, 5): "The process did not involve intelligence work designed to find dangers not yet discovered or to inform decisions not yet made. Instead, it involved research to find evidence in support of a specific line of argument—that Saddam was cooperating with al Qaeda—which in turn was being used to justify a specific policy decision." President Bush typified the administration's attitude toward the intelligence community in July 2004 when the CIA station chief in Baghdad wrote a pessimistic analysis of US progress in Iraq. The president's reaction was, "What is he, some kind of defeatist?" (Robinson and Whitelaw 2006).

Although Robert Jervis doubts that the Bush Administration successfully politicized the intelligence process, he pointed out that, "At the very least, it created (and probably was designed to create) an atmosphere that was not conducive to critical analysis and that encouraged judgments of excessive certainty and eroded subtleties and nuances" (Jervis 2006a, 33, 36).

Thus, although officials may intend their attempts to politicize intelligence as ensuring that the strongest case is made for a policy decision that has already been made, the consequences can be disastrous, because administration officials will not have an accurate perception of reality. Or at least they will not have the benefit of the best, honest judgment of intelligence professionals. The longer-term consequences are the undermining of the capacity of the intelligence community to provide professional intelligence analysis to future administrations. The attitude on the part of the Bush Administration that "Langley is enemy territory" (Pillar 2006, 6) may have seriously hurt the institution and professionalism of the CIA. The purge of top CIA officers by Director Porter Goss in 2004 and 2005 and the loss of traditional CIA functions to the newly created Director of National Intelligence undermined the CIA even further. The CIA director no longer reports directly to the president, and it is now merely one of 15 agencies in the intelligence community.

Conclusion

In this chapter I have argued that the Bush Administration's decision making regarding the war in Iraq was flawed, that it misinterpreted some of the intelligence it received, and that it attempted to influence the nature of that intelligence. As a consequence, decisions about war were made based on faulty conclusions about the nature of WMD in Iraq, and American credibility was undermined throughout the world.

The decision to go to war was fragmented, serial, and neither deliberative nor comprehensive. President Bush may have made up his own mind about going to war, and his actions led in the direction of war, but there is no public evidence that he formally deliberated with his cabinet and White House advisers about the question of whether or not war was necessary. In this respect, he did not follow the approach of President Eisenhower in his decision not to intervene in Vietnam in 1964 or John Kennedy's approach to deliberation over the Cuban Missile Crisis of 1962. The closest President Bush came to fostering "multiple advocacy" (George 1972; Pfiffner 2005b) was his dinner with Colin Powell in August 2002 when Powell laid out the potential dangers of invading Iraq. Otherwise, the White House staff, the vice president, and the secretary of defense marginalized Powell and ignored warnings from the professional Army officer corps (Ricks 2006, 40–3). The failure to treat these reservations seriously blinded the administration to flaws in its logic about the consequences of war with Iraq.

The administration's use of intelligence before the war was also flawed in that it systematically ignored or refused to consider evidence that challenged its preconceptions about Iraq's connection with al-Qaeda and its WMD. Again, Bush Administration officials reflected Betts's prediction that, "receptivity of decision makers to information that contradicts preconceptions varies inversely with their personal commitments, and commitments grow as crisis progresses" (Betts 1978, 81). In this case, the administration's commitment to regime change in Iraq grew over the course of 2002 up to the beginning of the war in 2003. The administration ignored or dismissed the analyses and some of the conclusions of the State Department, the Air Force, the Department of Energy, and the CIA in the run-up to the war.

Finally, in its search for evidence and analysis to corroborate its preconceptions about Iraq, the administration used several devices of politicization to affect the intelligence process in order to support its conclusions. In doing so, it led itself to incorrect conclusions that had lasting negative effects on the United States. The intelligence community was caught in the dilemma of balancing its objectivity with its influence. According to Betts (1978, 81), "analytic integrity is often submerged by the policy makers' demands for intelligence that suits them." However "In order to avert intelligence failures, an analyst is needed who tells decision makers what they don't want to hear, dampening the penchant for wishful thinking" (ibid. 80). Some parts of the intelligence community tried to "speak truth to power," but other parts decided that insisting on interpreting intelligence in ways inconsistent with the administration's preference for regime change was either hopeless or dangerous to their bureaucratic self-interest.

Although there is no guarantee that a sound decision-making process or accurately interpreting intelligence will ensure wise policy decisions, we have learned from this experience that the analytic objectivity of the intelligence community must be protected if policy makers are to base their decisions on realistic evaluations of our adversaries' behavior. The lack of a deliberative decision-making process and the compromising of the objectivity of the intelligence community can easily lead to disaster.

References

Allison, Graham. 1971. *Essence of Decision*. Boston: Little Brown.

Associated Press. 2003. "White House Official Apologizes for Role in Uranium Claim." *New York Times*. 22 July, website.

———2004. White House Statements on Iraq, al-Qaeda. 16 June, website.

Auster, Bruce B., Mazzetti, Mark, and Pound, Edward T. 2003. "Truth and Consequences." *U.S. News & World Report*, 9 June, 17.

Bamford, James. 2004. *A Pretext for War*. New York: Doubleday.

———2005."The Man Who Sold the War." *Rolling Stone*. December 1, 53–62.

Barstow, David, Broad, William J., and Gerth, Jeff. 2004. "How the White House Embraced Disputed Arms Intelligence." *New York Times*. 3 October, 1.

Bergen, Peter. 2004. "This Terrorist is Bad Enough on His Own." *New York Times*. 26 June, A27.

Betts, Richard K. 1978. "Analysis, War, and Decision: Why Intelligence Failures Are Inevitable." *World Politics* (October) 31 (1): 61–89.

Burke, John P. 2005a. "The Neutral/Honest Broker Role in Foreign-Policy Decision Making: A Reassessment." *Presidential Studies Quarterly* 35 (2): 229–58.

———2005b. "Condoleezza Rice as NSC Advisor: A Case Study of the Honest Broker Role." *Presidential Studies Quarterly* 35 (3): 554.

Central Intelligence Agency. 2002a. "Key Judgments [from the October 2002 NIE]: Iraq's continuing Programs for Weapons of Mass Destruction." Declassified excerpts published on the CIA website, p. 7 ⟨www.odci.gove/nic/pubs/research⟩, accessed 10 October 2003.

____ 2002*b*. "White Paper: Iraq's Weapons of Mass Destruction Program," repr. in John Prados. 2004. *Hoodwinked: The Documents that Reveal How Bush Sold Us a War*. New York: The New Press, 51–76.

Cheney, Richard. 2002. "Remarks by the Vice President to the Veterans of Foreign Wars 103rd National Convention." 26 August, White House website.

Clarke, Richard A. 2004. *Against All Enemies*. New York: Free Press.

CNN. 2004. Bush Stands by al Qaeda, Saddam Link. 15 June, website.

Commission on the Intelligence Capabilities of the United States Regarding Weapons of Mass Destruction. 2005. Printed in Craig R. Whitney (ed.) 2005. *The WMD Mirage*. New York: Public Affairs, 335. Also available at ⟨www. wmd.gov⟩, accessed 21 November 2006.

Cooper, Matthew. 2003. Pinning the Line on the Man. *Time*. 28 July, 31.

Downing Street Memo. 2002. "Secret and Strictly Personal—UK Eyes Only. To: David Manning, From Matthew Rycroft S 195/021 Re: Iraq: Prime Minister's Meeting, 23 July." Published by the *The Times*, ⟨www.timesonline.co.uk⟩, accessed 21 June 2005.

Drogin, Bob, and Goetz, John. 2005*a*. "How U.S. Fell Under the Spell of 'Curveball'." *Los Angeles Times*. 20 November. Los Angeles Times website.

____ ____ 2005*b*. "CIA Was Warned On Iraq Informer." *Washington Post*. 21 November. A10.

____ and Miller, Greg. 2005. "Curveball Debacle Reignites CIA Feud." *Los Angeles Times*. 2 April.

Eisenhower, Dwight D. 1963. *Mandate for Change*. Garden City, NY: Doubleday.

George, Alexander L. 1972. "The Case for Multiple Advocacy in Making Foreign Policy." *American Political Science Review* 66 (3): 751–85.

Goldberg, Jeffrey. 2005. "A Little Learning." *New Yorker*. 9 May, 36–41.

Graham, Bob. 2004. *Intelligence Matters*. New York: Random House.

Graham, Bradley. 2003. "Air Force Analysts Feel Vindicated on Iraq Drones." *Washington Post*. 26 September, A23.

Hayes, Stephen. 2003. "Case Closed: The U.S. Government's Secret Memo Detailing Cooperation Between Saddam Hussein and Osama bin Laden." *Weekly Standard*. 24 November.

Hersh, Seymour M. 2003*a*. "Who Lied to Whom?" *New Yorker*. 31 March, 41–3.

____ 2003*b*. "Selective Intelligence." *New Yorker*. 12 May.

____ 2003*c*. "The Stovepipe." *New Yorker*. 27 October, 87.

Isikoff, Michael. 2004. "Forget the 'Poisons and Deadly Gasses'." *Newsweek*. 5 July, 6.

____ and Thomas, Evan. 2003. "Follow the Yellowcake Road." *Newsweek*. 28 July, 23–5.

Jehl, Douglas. 2003. "Agency Belittles Information Given by Iraq Defectors." *New York Times*. 29 September, A8.

____ 2004*a*. "High Qaeda Aide Retracted Claim of Link with Iraq." *New York Times*. 31 July.

____ 2004*b*. "A New C.I.A. Report Casts Doubt on a Key Terrorist's Tie to Iraq." *New York Times*. 6 November, A12.

____ 2005*a*. "Tug of War: Intelligence vs. Politics." *New York Times*. 8 May, 10.

____ 2005*b*. "Report Warned Bush Team About Intelligence Doubts." *New York Times*. 6 November, 6.

Jehl, Douglas. 2005c. "The Reach of War's Intelligence; Qaeda-Iraq Link U.S. Cited Is Tied to Coercion Claim." *New York Times.* 9 December.

Jervis, Robert. 2006a. "Reports, Politics, and Intelligence Failures: The Case of Iraq." *Journal of Strategic Studies,* 29 (1): 3–52.

——2006b. "The Politics and Psychology of Intelligence and Intelligence Reform." *The Forum* 4 (1): 1.

Johnston, David. 2004. "Powell's 'Solid' C.I.A. Tips Were Soft, Committee Says." *New York Times.* 11 July, 11.

Kerr, Richard J. 2004. "Intelligence and Analysis on Iraq: Issues for the Intelligence Community." *Studies in Intelligence* 49. Issued in July 2004 and declassified in August 2005. MORI DocID: 1245667, 29 July.

Kessler, Glenn. 2003. "U.S. Decision On Iraq Has Puzzling Past." *Washington Post,* 12 January, 1, A20.

Leiby, Richard. 2006. "Breaking Ranks." *Washington Post.* 19 January, C1.

Lemann, Nicholas. 2003. "How It Came to War." *New Yorker.* 31 March, 36.

Levin, Senator Carl. 2004. *Report of an Inquiry into the Alternative Analysis of the Issue of an Iraq-al Qaeda Relationship.* Senate Armed Services Committee, 21 October, 4, posted on Senator Levin's website.

Linzer, Dafna, and Gellman, Barton. 2004. "CIA Skewed Iraq Reporting, Senate Says." *Washington Post.* 11 July, A19.

McGovern, Ray. 2003. "Cheney and the CIA: Not Business as Usual." 27 June (Truthout.org), accessed 21 November 2006.

Milbank, Dana and Allen, Mike. 2003. "Iraq Flap Shakes Rice's Image." *Washington Post.* 27 July, 1, A18.

Miller, Christian T., and Reynolds, Maura. 2004. "Senate Intelligence Report: Question of Pressure Splits Panel." *Los Angeles Times.* 10 July.

Mufson, Steven. 2003. "Forget WMD. What's an NIE?" *Washington Post.* 20 July, B3.

National Commission on Terrorist Attacks upon the United States. 2004. *The 9/11 Commission Report,* authorized edition. New York: W. W. Norton.

New York Times. 2004. "Excerpts From Two Senators' Views About Prewar Assessments of Iraq." 10 July, website.

Packer, George. 2005. *The Assassins' Gate.* New York: Farrar, Straus & Giroux.

Pfiffner, James P. 2004. "Did President Bush Mislead the Country in his Arguments for War with Iraq?" *Presidential Studies Quarterly* 34 (1): 25–46.

——2005a. "Presidential Decision Making: Rationality, Advisory Systems, and Personality. *Presidential Studies Quarterly* 35 (2): 217–28.

——2005b. "Presidential Leadership and Advice about Going to War." Paper prepared for presentation at the Conference on Presidential Leadership. University of Richmond, 9–10 September.

Phillips, David L. 2003. "Listening to the Wrong Iraqi." *New York Times.* 20 September.

Pillar, Paul R. 2006. "Intelligence, Policy, and the War in Iraq." *Foreign Affairs* 85 (2): 15–28.

Pincus, Walter. 2003. "CIA Seeks Probe of Iraq-Al Qaeda Memo Leak." *Washington Post.* 18 November.

——2005. "Newly Released Data Undercut Prewar Claims." *Washington Post.* 6 November, A22.

____and Priest, Dana. 2003a. "Some Iraq Analysts Felt Pressure from Cheney Visits." *Washington Post.* 5 June, 1.

____ ____2003b. "U.S. Had Uranium Papers Earlier." *Washington Post,* 18 July, 1.

Prados, John. 2004. *Hoodwinked: The Documents that Reveal How Bush Sold Us a War.* New York: The New Press.

Priest, Dana. 2003. "Uranium Claim was Known for Months to be Weak." *Washington Post.* 20 July, A22.

____2004. "Al Qaeda-Iraq Link Recanted." *Washington Post.* 1 August, A20.

____and DeYoung, Karen. 2003. "CIA Questioned Documents Linking Iraq, Uranium Ore." *Washington Post.* 22 March, A30.

____and Milbank, Dana. 2003. "President Defends Allegation On Iraq." *Washington Post.* 15 July, 1.

Ricks, Thomas E. 2006. *Fiasco.* New York: Penguin.

Risen, James. 2003. "C.I.A. Aides Feel Pressure in Preparing Iraqi Reports." *New York Times.* 23 March, B10.

____2004. "How Pair's Finding on Terror Led to Clash on Shaping Intelligence." *New York Times.* 28 April, 1.

____2006. *State of War.* New York: Free Press.

Robinson, Linda, and Whitelaw, Kevin. 2006. "Seeking Spies." *U.S. News and World Report.* 13 February, website.

Scheer, Robert. 2006. "Now Powell Tells Us." 11 April ⟨www.truthdig.com⟩, accessed 21 November 2006.

Schmitt, Eric. 2002. "Rumsfeld Says U.S. Has 'Bulletproof' Evidence of Iraq's Links to Al Qaeda." *New York Times.* 28 September.

Select Committee on Intelligence, United States Senate. *Report on the U.S. Intelligence Community's Prewar Intelligence Assessments on Iraq.* 2004. 7 July. Repr. in Craig R. Whitney (ed.) 2005. *The WMD Mirage.* New York: Public Affairs.

Sixty Minutes. 2006. "A Spy Speaks Out." *CBS News* website, 23 April ⟨www.cbsnews.com/stories/20006/04/21/60minutes/main1527749.shtml⟩, accessed 21 November 2006.

Suskind, Ron. 2004a. *The Price of Loyalty.* New York: Simon & Schuster.

____2004b. "Faith, Certainty and the Presidency of George W. Bush." *New York Times Magazine.* 17 October, 1–16, website.

____2006. *The One Percent Doctrine.* New York: Simon & Schuster.

Van Natta, Don, Jr. 2006. "Bush Was Set on Path to War, Memo by British Adviser Says." *New York Times.* 27 March.

Waas, Murray. 2005. "Key Bush Intelligence Briefing Kept from Hill Panel." *The National Journal.* 22 November.

____2006a. "Insulating Bush." *National Journal.* 30 March.

____2006b. "What Bush Was Told About Iraq." *National Journal.* 2 March.

Warrick, Joby. 2006a. "Lacking Biolabs, Trailers Carried Case for War." *Washington Post.* 12 April, 1.

____2006b. "White House Decries Report on Iraqi Trailers." *Washington Post.* 13 April, A18.

White House. 2003. "Press Gaggle with Ari Fleischer and Dr. Condoleeza [sic] Rice." 11 July, website.

_____ 2006. "A Decade of Deception and Defiance." ⟨www.whitehouse.gov/infocus/iraq/decade/book.html⟩, accessed 21 November 2006.

Whitelaw, Kevin. 2004. "We Were All Wrong." *U.S. News & World Report.* 24 February.

Woodward, Bob. 2004. *Plan of Attack.* New York: Simon & Schuster.

Notes

The author would like to thank particularly George Edwards and Mark Phythian for comments and help on an earlier version of this chapter. Help and comments also came from other friends and colleagues: Tom Coghlan, Philip Davies, Jason Dechant, Jack Goldstone, Jim Lucas, David Kay, Bob Kline, Bill Pope, John Ritzert, and Pete Zimmerman.

1. Secretary of Defense Rumsfeld also moved within hours of the 9/11 attacks to link Iraq with them. He told his aide Stephen Cambone, according to Cambone's hand-written notes, to get "best info fast. Judge whether good enough hit S.H. [Saddam Hussein] @ same time—Not only UBL [Osama bin Laden]. . . . So massive—sweep it all up. Things related + not. Need to do so to get anything useful" (underscoring in original). A facsimile of Cambone's handwritten notes was released under a Freedom of Information Act request and posted on ⟨www.outragedmoderates.org⟩, accessed 24 February 2006. See also CBS News, "Plans for Iraq Attack Began On 9/11 (4 September 2005) posted on ⟨www.cbsnews.com⟩, accessed 24 February 2006. These notes show an initial impulse to go after Saddam Hussein. This could indicate merely a suspicion that Saddam might have had a hand in the 9/11 attacks or it could be read as asking whether there was enough evidence to justify attacking Saddam, aside from whether he had been involved with 9/11 or not.

2. For a detailed analysis of how the White Paper differed from the NIE, see Prados 2004: 51–93.

3. Suskind (2006, 188) reported that the president was carefully prepared for the session in which Bob Woodward was told about the meeting.

4. This report was based on a secret British memorandum cited in the book *Lawless World*, by Philippe Sands, according to Van Natta (2006).

5. Despite President Bush's later claim that Congress had access to the same intelligence that the executive branch had prior to the Iraq War, the President's Daily Brief is one important example of intelligence not available to Congress. See the statement by Senator Feinstein on 15 December 2005 on her website (accessed 16 December 2005) and Memorandum to Senator Feinstein from Alfred Cumming, an analyst at the Congressional Research Service, "Congress as a Consumer of Intelligence Information," also posted on her website on 16 December 2005.

6. Letter from Kathleen P. Turner, chief of the Office of Congressional Affairs, Defense Intelligence Agency (26 October 2005); Press Release: "Levin Says Newly Declassified Information Indicates Bush Administration's Use of Pre-War Intelligence Was Misleading" (Senator Levin's website, 6 November 2005; see also Pincus 2005 and Jehl 2005*b*).

7. The report's title was, "Summary of Body of Intelligence on Iraq–al Qaeda Contacts (1990–2003)" (see Levin 2004, 25).

8. The Defense Department stated: "News Reports that the Defense Department recently confirmed new information with respect to contacts between al Qaeda and Iraq . . . are inaccurate." The memo published by the *Weekly Standard* "was not an analysis of the substantive issue of the relationship between Iraq and al Qaeda and drew no conclusions"(Pincus 2003).

9. Since they did not turn up after the US invasion, one theory was that Saddam actually used many more of them in the Iran war than he wanted to admit and that he wanted his adversaries to believe that he still had them.

10. The Kerr Report said that "different descriptions of the same source" often led "analysts to believe they had more confirmatory information from more sources than was actually the case."

11. David Kay raised the interesting question that "if the BND [German intelligence service] thought he was a fabricator why did not they just throw him to the US instead of trying to protect him as if he was a valuable source??" Personal e-mail to the author, 13 December 2005.

12. In the fall of 2003, the CIA discovered that Curveball had been fired in 1995, at the time that he claimed to have been working on biological weapons in Iraq. In May 2004 the CIA sent out a notice admitting the Curveball was not a solid source: "Discrepancies surfaced regarding the information provided by . . . Curveball in this stream of reporting, which indicate that he lost his claimed access in 1995. Our assessment, therefore, is that Curveball appears to be fabricating in this stream of reporting" (Drogin and Goetz 2005a, 14; see Drogin and Miller 2005).

13. White House spokesmen said that the president's assertions were based on faulty intelligence rather than an intent to deceive (Warrick 2006b).

14. It is difficult to understand, since so much was at stake, why Kay was not informed of such important evidence compiled by the US technical team (Warrick 2006a, 1).

15. Paul Pillar who coordinated the intelligence community's analysis of Iraq said, "U.S. intelligence analysts had questioned the credibility of the report making [the Niger] claim, had kept it out of their own unclassified products, and had advised the White House not to use it publicly. But the administration put the claim into the speech anyway" (Pillar 2006, 6).

16. The letterhead of one letter was from the military government that had been replaced before the 1999 date on the letter, and the signature on the letter indicated the name of a foreign ministry official who had left the position in 1989 (Isikoff and Thomas 2003: Priest 2003).

17. Later, Powell told Robert Scheer: "The CIA was pushing the aluminum tube argument heavily and Cheney went with that instead of what our guys wrote." He also said of the yellowcake claim in the President's State of the Union speech: "That was a big mistake. It should never have been in the speech. I didn't need Wilson to tell me that there wasn't a Niger connection. He didn't tell us anything we didn't already know. I never believed it." Powell also said of the claim of a nuclear threat from Saddam "That was all Cheney" (Scheer 2006).

18. Also, on 11 July 2003, Rice said on Air Force One: "Now, if there were any doubts about the underlying intelligence to that NIE, those doubts were not communicated to the president, to the vice president or me" (Waas 2006a).

19. Waas 2006 (p. 5 of the 10-page article on the website below). According to Waas, Bush was also informed in his intelligence briefings that Saddam was not likely an imminent threat to the US (pp. 2, 6). Another of the sources that the administration used to make its case that Saddam had chemical, biological, and nuclear weapons was Iraqi exile Adnan Ihsan Saeed al-Haideri. He had lived in Kurdistan and was dedicated to undermining Saddam Hussein's control of Iraq. He claimed to be a civil engineer who had helped hide many weapons of mass destruction for Saddam. The problem was that the CIA determined in a polygraph examination that Saeed was not telling the truth. Nevertheless, his claims were used in a campaign directed by the Rendon Group to influence public opinion about going to war with Iraq (Bamford 2005; 53–62). See the White House website, "A Decade of Deception and Defiance" (www.whitehouse.gov/infocus/iraq/decade/book.html), accessed 21 November 2006. David Kay said that Saeed was "a fabricator" and that when he was brought to Iraq that he was "totally useless" and "every one of his leads turned up nothing." Personal e-mail to the author 11 December 2005.

20. Paul Pillar explained it this way: "The administration's rejection of the intelligence community's judgments became especially clear with the formation of a special Pentagon unit, the Policy Counterterrorism Evaluation Group. The unit, which reported to Undersecretary of Defense Douglas Feith, was dedicated to finding every possible link between Saddam and al Qaeda, and its briefings accused the intelligence community of faulty analysis for failing to see the supposed alliance" (Pillar 2006: 19).

21. According to James Bamford, in January 2003 a CIA official told members of his unit, "if Bush wants to go to war, it's your job to give him a reason to do so" (Bamford 2004: 333–4, 337).

22. The deputy chief later told the Senate Select Committee staff that the DOD analyst had made similar points before and that in his judgment war was inevitable in any case (Senate Select Committee 2004, 246–50, quote on 249; see also Johnston 2004).

Part III

Governing by Campaigning

8

The Public, the President, and the War in Iraq

Gary C. Jacobson

George W. Bush began his second term as president in 2005 with Americans more widely divided by party in their evaluations of his performance than they have been about any president in the more than fifty years the approval question has been polled. They were also more widely divided by party about the wisdom and necessity of his Iraq War than they have been about any major US military action undertaken during the same time span. It is inconceivable that these two phenomena are not tightly linked, yet the structure of their relationship is far from obvious. Insofar as a president's performance ratings are based on reactions to his policies, then judgments about Bush's most consequential and costly undertaking, the invasion of Iraq, should powerfully affect overall evaluations of his presidency. But research on the psychology of political opinion formation also teaches that prior attitudes toward a president should strongly influence reactions to his policies; people favorably disposed toward Bush should be more willing to accept his justifications for decisions and thus to support his policies than people who are not. In short, the direction of causality is ambiguous. Moreover, whichever we take to be the independent variable, the question remains as to why party identification predicts its value so accurately.

In this chapter I review a selection of the inordinately abundant polling data on the president and the war to document the unprecedented partisan polarization in public attitudes that they have jointly provoked and to begin to explore some of the questions the data can be used to address concerning the formation, evolution, and consequences of mass opinion on the war.

A Divider, Not a Uniter

Ironically, the candidate who had pledged in his 2000 acceptance speech to be "a uniter, not a divider" had, by the end of his first term in office, become the most divisive president on record. The evolution of public reactions to Bush's presidency is displayed in Figs. 8.1 and 8.2. Bush's overall approval ratings languished in the mid-50s until the September 11, 2001, terrorist attacks on New York and Washington, DC, and the president's resolute response to them, provoked the greatest "rally" (Mueller 1973) in presidential approval ever observed, giving Bush the highest ratings ever accorded a president. Over the following fifteen months, his ratings returned gradually to where they had been before 9/11. The effects of another, more modest rally coinciding with the initial successful military phase of the Iraq War in April 2003 eroded more quickly, as did an even smaller spike in approval inspired by the capture of Saddam Hussein in December. Ratings dipped following the Abu Ghraib prison scandal in the spring of 2004 but revived to about 50 per cent at the time of his re-election. The decline resumed as administration problems mounted in late 2005 but revived modestly with the killing of al-Qaeda operative al-Zarqawa and the organization of a new government in Iraq in the spring of 2006.[1]

This overall trend, while intelligible, masks the more intriguing pattern that emerges when the data are disaggregated by the party of the respondent (Fig. 8.2). Democrats and, to a lesser extent, independents account for nearly all the temporal variation in evaluations of Bush. Largely though not entirely because of his controversial route to the White House through Florida and the Supreme Court, Bush took office with the widest partisan difference in approval of any newly elected president (Jacobson 2000). After 9/11, he received the highest ratings from the opposing party (and from independents) of any president ever. The subsequent downward trends in approval among Democrats and independents were reversed temporarily by the rally events already noted, but the overall pattern is one of increasing disaffection to the point where, by 2006, Bush was receiving the lowest ratings from the opposing party's identifiers yet recorded for any president.

Meanwhile, Republicans continued to approve of his performance by over-whelming margins. Indeed, Bush has so far received the highest approval ratings among his own partisans of any president since the question has been polled. Even after its decline in 2006, Bush's average level of approval among Republicans in the Gallup Polls taken through June 2006 of 90.2 per cent exceeds the next highest, that of Dwight D. Eisenhower (87.6 per cent) by a statistically significant margin ($p < .001$). Among the other party's supporters, however, his ratings had by the end of his first term fallen to their lowest point for any president to that date, only to fall even lower after his re-election; in May 2006, only 4 per cent of Democrats said they approved of his performance. To put this figure in perspective, it is seven points lower than Richard Nixon's nadir just before he resigned in disgrace. Before Bush and going back to Eisenhower, the partisan difference in approval ratings had never exceeded 70 percentage points in any Gallup Poll and never averaged

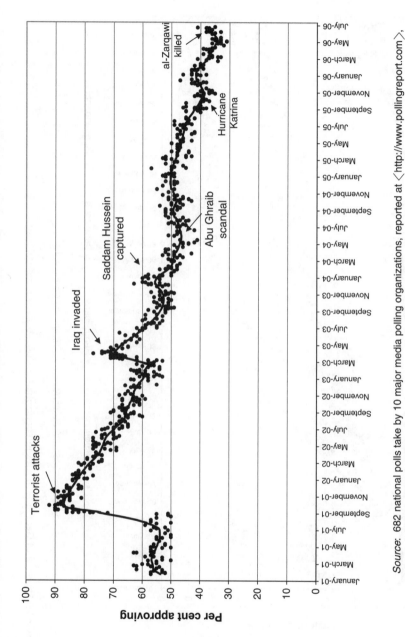

Figure 8.1. Approval of George W. Bush's job performance, January 2001–June 2006

Source: 682 national polls take by 10 major media polling organizations, reported at ⟨http://www.pollingreport.com⟩, accessed 21 November 2006.

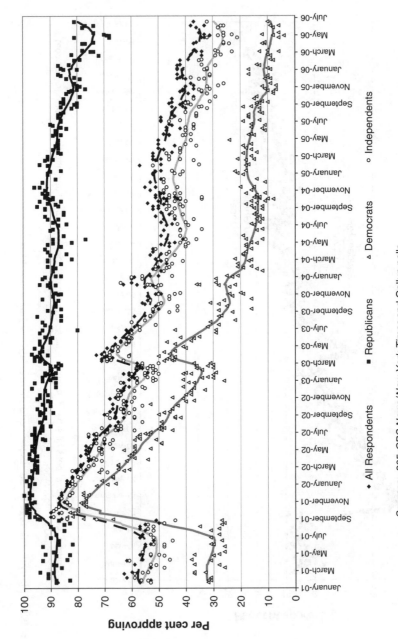

Figure 8.2. Approval of George W. Bush's job performance, 2001–6, by party identification

Sources: 305 *CBS News/New York Times* and Gallup polls.

◆ All Respondents   ■ Republicans   △ Democrats   ○ Independents

more than 66 points for any quarter. In 74 of the 94 Gallup Polls taken between January 2004 and June 2006, the gap exceeded 70 points; it averaged 73 points and reached an all-time high of 83 points in a couple of polls taken near the election.[2] The average partisan difference in approval of Bush during the fourth quarter of 2004, 79 points, was 13 points greater than greatest quarterly difference recorded for the second most polarizing president, Bill Clinton (Jacobson 2007, 6–7).

A Republican War?

Partisan differences in attitudes toward the Iraq War are, by historical comparison, even more striking than divisions over Bush's performance as president. Assessing support for the war is complicated by the diversity of questions used by pollsters to measure it, because different questions elicit different levels of support, and the frequency with which each has been asked has changed with evolving circumstances. Figure 8.3 displays the most general picture by including data from variants of eleven different questions and using Lowess smoothing to summarize the trend.[3] Support for invading Iraq was high right after 9/11, as most Americans suspected Saddam Hussein was at least partly responsible. It declined as the focus turned to Osama bin Laden and Afghanistan, revived with the administration's campaign accusing Saddam of hiding weapons of mass destruction (WMD) in defiance of United Nations sanctions and of aiding al-Qaeda, and peaked in the "mission accomplished" phase of the war in April 2003. It fell thereafter until Saddam's capture provoked a brief spike, fell again to a low point in May 2004 in the wake of the Abu Ghraib revelations, rebounded a few points later in the summer, then continued its very gradual decline for the next two years, averaging about 40 per cent by the spring of 2006. A small uptick in support followed the death of al-Zarqawi and the formation of an Iraqi government at that time.

The same trends appear when we examine separately those questions asked frequently enough for temporal comparisons (Fig. 8.4). Notice that support is highest when respondents are asked if the US had done the "right thing" in taking military action in Iraq or if the US had made a mistake going to war.[4] Support is as much as 20 points lower when people are asked if the results of the war were worth the cost in American lives. Although the levels differ, the trends are generally parallel.

Partisan assessments of the war, in contrast, have diverged sharply no matter how the question is posed. Figure 8.5 displays the data and Lowess-smoothed trends in support of the war, disaggregated by party. The gap between Republicans and Democrats grows steadily wider, with only a brief pause during the first month or so of the war. Figure 8.6 shows the widening partisan gap in responses to specific questions, which levels out to an average

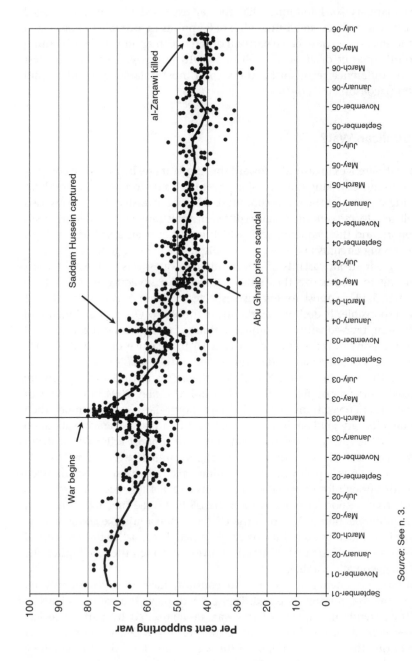

Figure 8.3. Popular support for the Iraq War (all question wordings)

Source: See n. 3.

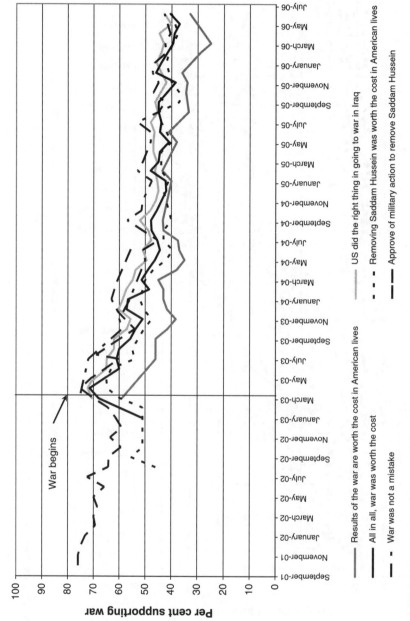

Figure 8.4. Popular support for the Iraq War (various question wordings) (monthly averages)

Legend:

—— Results of the war are worth the cost in American lives

—— All in all, war was worth the cost

– – War was not a mistake

—— US did the right thing in going to war in Iraq

- - - Removing Saddam Hussein was worth the cost in American lives

—— Approve of military action to remove Saddam Hussein

Y-axis: Per cent supporting war (0 to 100)

X-axis: September-01, November-01, January-02, March-02, May-02, July-02, September-02, November-02, January-03, March-03, May-03, July-03, September-03, November-03, January-04, March-04, May-04, July-04, September-04, November-04, January-05, March-05, May-05, July-05, September-05, November-05, January-06, March-06, May-06, July-06

War begins

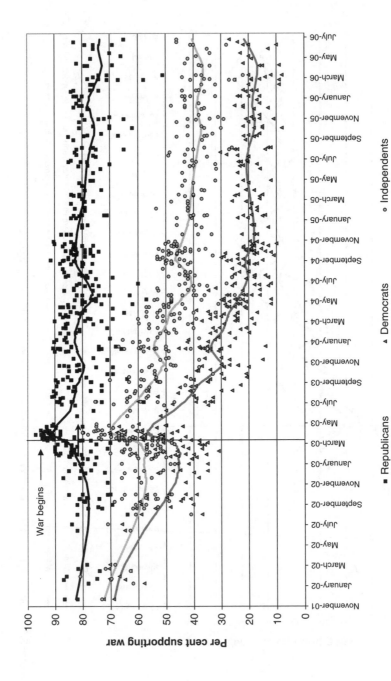

Figure 8.5. Party identification and support for the Iraq War

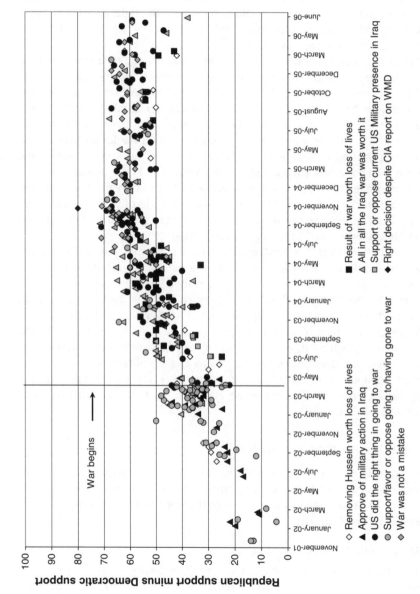

Figure 8.6. Partisan differences in support for the Iraq War

of about 62 percentage points from July 2004 through the end of 2005 before falling modestly in the first half of 2006. A *Los Angeles Times* poll question asking whether, in light of the CIA's report that Saddam had no WMD and no active program to produce them, Bush had made the right decision to go to war produced the biggest difference, with 90 per cent of Republicans but only 10 per cent of Democrats saying "yes."[5]

These data stand in striking contrast with comparable data from previous wars. In none is the gap anywhere near as large as it is for the Iraq War. Ironically, it is lowest in the most controversial of these engagements, Vietnam, averaging only 5 percentage points. The Vietnam War certainly divided Americans, but the division was much greater within than between the parties, and support for the war declined at about the same pace for partisans in all categories (Jacobson 2006, Fig. 14). Party differences on Korea, Kosovo, and Afghanistan were of a similar magnitude, averaging 11–12 points, although the absolute levels of public support differed widely between these conflicts; for example, the action in Afghanistan was supported by an average of 96 per cent of Republicans and 84 per cent of Democrats, much higher numbers than for any other conflict (Jacobson 2007, 83–4).

Bush's father's Gulf War produced the widest partisan gap in this set, and it is also the only one for which the data suggest increasing divergence over time. Still, the party difference averaged only 21 points and peaked at 29 points, months after the fighting had concluded. Ole Holsti (2004, 174), comparing these to earlier war support data, notes "rather substantial partisan differences", but they seem in retrospect quite modest by comparison to the more than 60-point partisan differences on Iraq. As we would expect, the party of the president determines whether support for military action is higher among Republicans or Democrats; it is true for every survey regarding the Iraq War and in 97 per cent of the surveys taken regarding the other five wars (Jacobson 2007, 135–6).

What is Different about the Iraq War?

The uniquely partisan responses to the Iraq War beg explanation. The most obvious place to look is in the distinctive features of the war itself, and they are, as we shall see, clearly a major part of the story. But they are by no means the whole story. Consider:

INITIAL CONDITIONS

George W. Bush took the White House after three decades of growing partisan polarization among both political activists and voters, a trend reaching what appeared to be crescendo with Clinton's impeachment and acquittal, only to be topped by the battle over Florida's electoral votes after the 2000 election (Jacobson 2001). The wide initial partisan differences over the legitimacy of

Bush's election killed any chance of a presidential honeymoon and lasted his entire first term (Jacobson 2005). Americans were more polarized over Bush than his predecessors from the start and so predisposed to sharp partisan differences in evaluating his decisions.

THE BUSH ADMINISTRATION'S OTHER POLICIES

Initial partisan differences in evaluations of Bush nearly disappeared after 9/11, when Americans of all persuasions rallied to his support, and Bush's job approval among Democrats remained above 50 per cent for nearly a year. But Democrats' approval of his response to terrorism did not change their opinions on his domestic agenda. With the exceptions of the education and prescription drug benefit bills, Bush spent his first term catering to his party's base among social conservatives and the corporate and small business sectors. His approach naturally pleased Republican regulars but alienated ordinary Democrats, majorities of whom opposed the administration's policies on taxes, energy, the environment, regulation, and stem cell research. A conservative program that reinforced partisan differences on issues other than the Iraq War may have strengthened the effect of partisan predispositions on reaction to the war.

THE BUSH ADMINISTRATION'S TACTICS

Bush has sought to achieve major changes in public policy despite narrow Republican margins in Congress, widespread political resistance, and general public indifference or opposition to what he wanted to do (Jacobson 2007). His administration's strategy for winning in this political context has followed a typical pattern. Policy proposals are designed in-house in great secrecy so that any internal disagreements are thrashed out and resolved before presenting a unified front to the outside world. The president then announces his proposal as "the right thing for the American people," and he and his team go to work turning it into policy. The public campaign takes the form of a multifaceted sales exercise; the aim is not to explain the product, but to sell it. Everyone on the team is expected to "stay on message," reiterating with little variation arguments and rhetoric carefully vetted in advance. Contrary messages and messengers are denounced (a favorite ploy is to portray opposition as motivated solely by partisanship). Probing questions from reporters are ducked or ignored if straightforward answers might undermine the message. The idea is to control not only the agenda, but also the framing, language, and definition of what count as relevant facts regarding the issue at hand.

This mindset and consequent emphasis on marketing has bred a cavalier approach to truth: dishonesty not by lying, but by a deceptive selection of truthful but misleading statements.[6] Republicans, positively disposed toward the president, have tended to accept his "facts" and arguments uncritically because of both their source and their fit with prior attitudes. Democrats and others not inclined to follow the president's lead or accept his word have been more receptive to analyses by critics busy parsing the rhetoric and pointing out the deceptions. Insofar as their initial reflexive doubts about the policy and its promoter appear to be confirmed, these attitudes are only strengthened. The administration's approach to selling its policies has thus been inherently polarizing.

IDEOLOGY

Democrats have been generally less hawkish than Republicans for a long time, and partisan differences on the use of force were clear before the Iraq War, with Democrats considerably more reluctant than Republicans to invade (Fig. 8.5). This is not a particularly compelling general explanation, however, because Democrats supported the military action in Kosovo under Clinton at higher rates than Republicans and backed the action in Afghanistan by huge majorities. Moreover, at least some evidence suggests that party differences on whether force or diplomacy was the better way to conduct foreign policy grew substantially wider only *after* the Iraq War (Pew Research Center for the People and the Press 2003, 2005). And ideological divisions cannot by themselves explain why partisan differences in war support grew dramatically with time only for the Iraq War.

OPINION LEADERSHIP

The public's (arguably rational) ignorance of foreign affairs enhances the importance of opinion leadership in matters of war and peace. For Republicans the chief opinion leader would of course be George W. Bush, but he was backed by Secretary of State Colin Powell (more broadly esteemed than the president) as well as virtually all Republicans of stature in or out of government. Ordinary Republicans thus had little inducement to break ranks, so they did not. However, this raises the question of why solidarity among Republican elites was so high and why it generally survived the collapse of the original case for war. It is at least conceivable that the president's continued rock-solid support among ordinary Republicans had something to do with it: Republican opinion leaders who dissented might well have lost that status.

Among Democrats as well, it is not obvious that opinion leaders led rather than followed. In light of the dire threat depicted by the administration and uncertainty about Saddam's WMD and connections to al-Qaeda, prudence lay in not opposing the war. If it turned out to be unjustified, unnecessary, or disastrous in some way, Bush would get the primary blame. But if Democrats opposed the war and Saddam's complicity in 9/11 and WMD were confirmed, or if the Iraqi people welcomed their liberators and democracy emerged from the ashes of Saddam's sadistic regime, Democrats could face a political reckoning. Worse, if they succeeded in hindering the president's plans and another terrorist attack occurred on American soil, no matter what its provenance, they could wind up scapegoats. The chaos and continuing violence that persisted long after Bush's "mission accomplished" moment in April 2003, combined with the failure to find WMD or evidence of Saddam's involvement in 9/11, greatly reduced this risk, but it was not until outsider Howard Dean, pursuing his party's presidential nomination, found a receptive audience among ordinary Democrats for criticism of the war that it became common among Democratic leaders. Just as in the case of Clinton's impeachment (Jacobson 2000), Democratic politicians appeared to be taking cues from their followers, not vice versa.

ALTERNATIVE REALITIES

As we shall see, Democrats and Republicans expressed very different beliefs in responses to factual questions about the Iraq War and its consequences. There is no question that these beliefs were strongly influenced by prior attitudes and responses to opinion leadership. But they are also strongly related to the sources respondents said they relied on for news (Kull, Ramsay, and Lewis 2003–4, 581–5). The fragmentation and ideological diversification of news media in recent years may thus have contributed to partisan polarization on the war by reducing the quantity of discordant news to which partisans were exposed (Jacobson 2007).

CASUS BELLI

As explanations of partisan differences in response to the Iraq War, these considerations are in the end, however, only important through their interactions with the particulars of the Iraq War itself. First, more than any of the other comparable military actions, the Iraq War was discretionary and preventive. The war's proximate provocation was the terrorist attacks of 9/11, but its public justification was not so much retaliation as pre-emption. Although Saddam Hussein was widely thought to have had his hand in 9/11, the evidence for his complicity was exceedingly tenuous (and of course postwar investigations found none). The administration's primary public case for using force to impose a "regime change" was thus that Saddam was defying the United Nations by producing and hiding WMD, posing an intolerable threat to the US and its allies that would only grow with time. The evidence for this claim was also, at best, ambiguous, and widespread doubt among many of its traditional allies about the need for immediate action deprived the US of broad international support.

Ambiguity gives priors full sway. Positively disposed toward the president, especially after 9/11, an overwhelming majority of Republicans resolved any doubts they might have had in his favor and accepted his word that action was imperative. Democrats were of no mind to resolve ambiguity in Bush's favor—rather the opposite—so their support depended crucially on the belief in Saddam's complicity in 9/11 and the threat his WMDs posed to American lives and interests. Lacking a partisan anchor, independents' support for the war was even more sensitive to these beliefs. Many Democrats and independents were apparently convinced by Colin Powell and other leaders more trusted than Bush that they were warranted.

The second exceptional feature of the Iraq War was that its central premises proved rather quickly to be faulty and were publicly, if reluctantly and with considerable hedging and backsliding, acknowledged to be so by those who initiated it, including the president himself. The partisan split on the war then widened, as most Republicans either refused to recognize that neither WMD or a 9/11 connection could be found or accepted the substitute justifications offered by the administration after the fact, while Democrats, with no inclination to miss the message or adopt new reasons for support, grew increasingly opposed to the war. Herein, I think, lies the proximal source of the extraordinarily wide partisan differences in responses to questions about the war.

The Evidence

The partisan gap in support of the Iraq War reflects differences in beliefs about its necessity, its consequences, and the president's honesty in statements about both. Among Democrats (and independents), these beliefs have shifted over time in response to events and information, while Republicans' views have been much less sensitive to changing circumstances. Moreover, the level of support for the war varies more strongly with those beliefs among Democrats and independents than among Republicans.

The Necessity for War

The Bush Administration's principal justifications for invading Iraq were that Saddam possessed or was about to possess WMDs, including possibly nuclear weapons, and was in cahoots with al-Qaeda and probably complicit in 9/11 (Pfiffner 2004). Although Republicans were more likely than Democrats to believe these allegations from the beginning (Figs. 8.7 and 8.8), differences prior to the war were small by later standards, on the order of 10–15 percentage points. Before the war, a large majority of Americans regardless of party believed Saddam was hiding WMD, and about half thought he was personally involved in 9/11. After the war, as time passed and the search for WMD and an al-Qaeda connection continued to turn up nothing of substance, Democrats abandoned these beliefs to a much greater extent than did

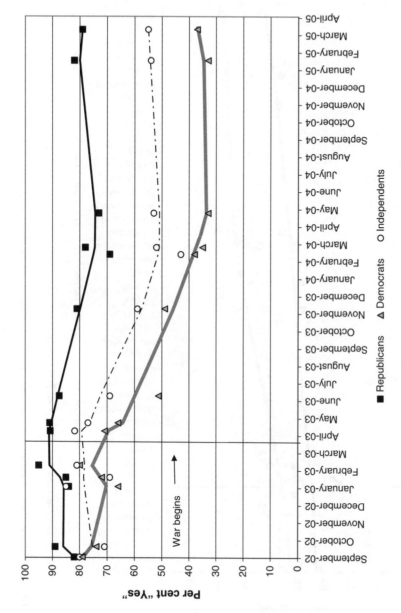

Figure 8.7. Does (did) Iraq possess weapons of mass destruction?

Source: CBS News/New York Times and ABC News/Washington Post polls.

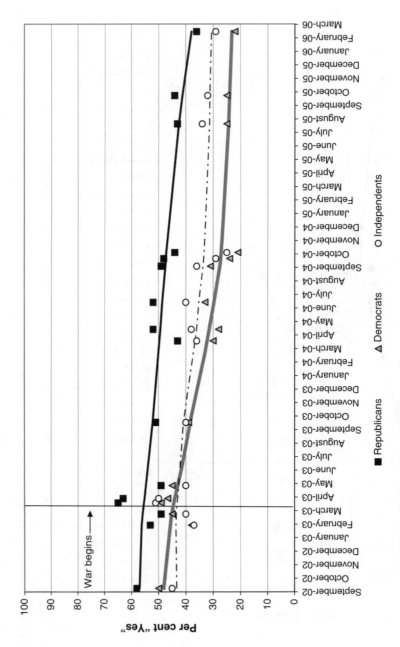

Figure 8.8. Was Saddam Hussein personally involved in 9/11?

Source: CBS News/New York Times polls.

Republicans. In February of 2003, 79 per cent of Democrats thought Saddam possessed WMD; within about 15 months, that figure had fallen to 33 per cent and has subsequently remained at that level. Among Republicans, belief in Saddam's WMD peaked at 95 per cent just before the war and has not fallen below 69 per cent since; it actually increased a bit to around 80 per cent in early 2005, when the partisan gap on this question reached about 45 points. Belief in Saddam's involvement in 9/11 also declined less steeply among Republicans than among Democrats or independents. From a peak right after the fall of Baghdad in April 2003 through March 2006, it dropped from 65 to 36 per cent among Republicans, from 51 to 29 per cent among independents, and from 49 per cent to 22 per cent among Democrats in these surveys.

Perhaps more surprising than these partisan differences is the extent to which even Democrats continued to believe the allegations long after well-publicized official reports had found no evidence to support them and the president and his administration had ostensibly disavowed them. Evidently, Saddam's evil reputation has continued to predispose Americans to think the worst and to ignore or forget exculpatory information. A March 2005 *ABC News/Washington Post* poll documented its staying power (Fig. 8.9). A majority of Americans continued to believe that solid evidence has been found proving that Iraq had directly supported al-Qaeda or at least to suspect such a connection. Partisan differences are apparent but not especially large. One important source of these continuing misperceptions is no doubt the Bush

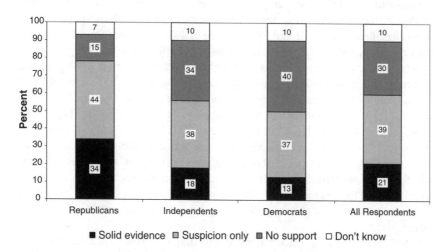

Source: *ABC News/Washington Post* poll, 10–13 March 2005.

Figure 8.9. Before the war, do you think Iraq did or did not provide direct support to the al-Qaeda terrorist group?

Administration's artfully insinuating rhetoric (Pfiffner 2004). On 20 March 2005, the second anniversary of the US invasion, the president put it this way: "We knew of Saddam Hussein's record of aggression and support for terror. We knew of his long history of pursuing, even using, weapons of mass destruction, and we know that September 11 requires our country to think differently" (Boudreaux 2005). With rhetoric like this—lumping together in two sentences Saddam Hussein, September 11, terror, and WMD—no wonder most Americans thought the administration had continued to advance claims unsubstantiated by its own investigations despite having officially abandoned them.[7]

The simplest interpretation of the patterns of belief in the two major justifications for the war is that Americans of all persuasions tended to have strong prior beliefs about Saddam Hussein that led them to assume his complicity in 9/11 and possession of illicit WMD, while Republicans also had a strong prior faith in the president and thus in his administration's version of Iraqi realities. Both sets of priors have kept subsequent revelations from fully undermining these beliefs, with their compound effect among Republicans explaining why the president's partisans have been especially slow to acknowledge new, discordant information. The classical theory of cognitive dissonance (Festinger 1957) effectively accounts for these patterns.

Republicans also were more likely to believe that the Iraq War was justified even if WMD were never found, and this view become more predominant after the war. In a survey taken on the day the war started, 31 per cent of Republicans thought the war "was justified only if the US finds conclusive evidence that Iraq has weapons of mass destruction," while 63 per cent said it was justified even if conclusive evidence of WMD was not found. Ten days later the proportion of Republicans expressing the first view had dropped to 11 per cent while the proportion expressing the second had risen to 83 per cent, a pattern that was repeated in surveys taken in December 2003 and February 2004. Among Democrats, the proportion saying the war was justified even without conclusive evidence of WMD stood at 46 per cent on 20 March, rose to 56 per cent ten days later, but by February 2004 had dropped to 35 per cent; the proportion of Democrats saying the war was unjustified with or without WMD rose from 9 to 25 per cent over the same period.[8] Asked in January 2005 whether the war "will have been worth the loss of American lives and other costs" if WMD are never found, 69 per cent of Republicans said it still would be worth it, compared to 42 per cent of independents and only 16 per cent of Democrats.[9]

Belief in the primary rationales for the Iraq War had a potent effect on support for the venture both before the invasion and afterwards (Figs. 8.10 and 8.11). More than 80 per cent of respondents interviewed in February 2003 (just before the invasion) who believed Saddam's regime was guilty on both counts supported the war. A substantial majority of those who

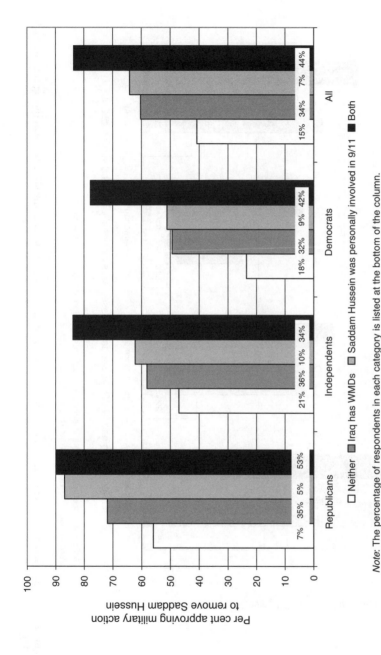

Per cent approving military action to remove Saddam Hussein

☐ Neither ▨ Iraq has WMDs ☐ Saddam Hussein was personally involved in 9/11 ■ Both

Note: The percentage of respondents in each category is listed at the bottom of the column.

Source: ABC News/Washington Post poll, 23–6, September 2002.

Figure 8.10. Beliefs about WMD and Saddam Hussein's involvement in 9/11 and approval of military action to remove Hussein from power (September 2002)

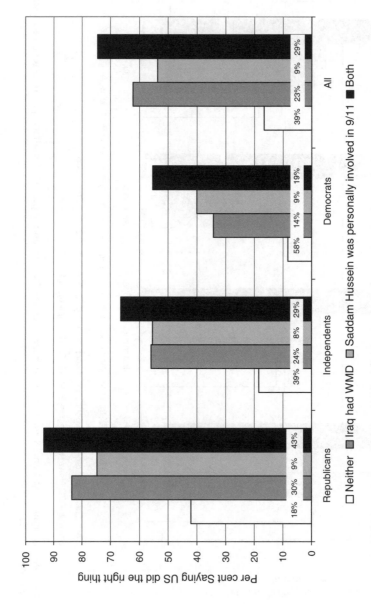

Figure 8.11. Beliefs about WMD and Saddam Hussein's involvement in 9/11 and belief that invading Iraq was the right thing to do (April 2004)

Note: Percent of respondents in each belief category is listed at the foot of the column.
Source: CBS News/New York Times poll, 23–7 April 2004.

thought him guilty on only one count (mostly of hiding WMD—only a small per centage who believed Saddam was involved in 9/11 did not also believe he had WMD) also supported military action to take him out. Only the small minority who believed neither accusation displayed a strong tendency to oppose the venture. By this time, Republicans had come to support military action by huge majorities regardless of which charges they believed; moreover, 97 per cent accepted at least one of the grounds for going to war, and more than half accepted both. Substantial majorities of independents who accepted either one or both (about 85 per cent of independents in this poll) also supported military action. Among Democrats, only the third who believed both charges favored going to war (slightly more than 70 per cent did so); support for war among those who believed only one of the charges was around 40 per cent, and among the minority who believed neither, it was below 20 per cent.

A year after Bush had announced the end of major military action, retrospective support for the war remained strongly linked to beliefs about WMD and Saddam's complicity in 9/11, although partisan differences were larger than before the war regardless of beliefs. The proportion of Republicans who still accepted as factual at least one of the war's primary justifications declined between February 2003 and April 2004, but by only 15 percentage points, from 97 to 82 per cent. The decline was much larger among Democrats (43 points, from 85 to 42 per cent), with independents falling in between (24 points, from 85 to 61 per cent), and this change accounts for much of the decline in support for the war among these two groups.

A naive reading of these results would be that popular support for the war depended largely on misinformation and would have collapsed had the public absorbed the reports of US investigators who had conceded that, despite their best efforts, they had found no convincing evidence of WMD or complicity of Saddam Hussein in 9/11. But by itself, the widespread resistance to this information suggests that, for many Americans, particularly Republicans, support for the war came first and the specifics of the factual case for it were of decidedly secondary importance. If forced to recognize that the war's original premises were faulty, they would be willing, as loyal followers of President Bush, to accept the others he proffered. Thus, for example, most Republicans continued to accept the Bush Administration's contention that Iraq posed a threat that could not be contained but required immediate action (Fig. 8.12); the proportion taking this view exceeded 80 per cent just after the war began and has not fallen below 60 per cent since. Forty-six per cent of Democrats shared this opinion at the onset of the war but by October 2004, just 12 per cent continued to do so; belief in the need for immediate action also lost ground among independents, falling from over 50 per cent to below 30 per cent.

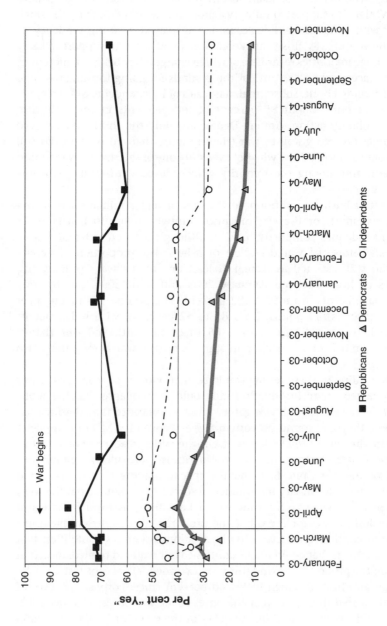

Figure 8.12. Was Iraq a threat that required immediate action?

Source: CBS News/New York Times polls.

Opinions on the necessity of the war were of course very strongly related to believing it was the right thing to do (Fig. 8.13), but the questions do not elicit parallel responses across partisan categories; observe the large partisan difference in support for the war among those respondents who believe Iraq was a threat that could have been contained (without immediate military action). Republicans who took this position backed the war at much higher levels than Democrats (60 to 24 per cent). Only the tiny fraction of Republicans who said Iraq was not a threat (3.2 per cent) opposed the war.

The Effects of the War on National Security

Assessments of the consequences of the Iraq War are also strongly influenced by partisanship, with party differences growing over time. And again, these assessments have a smaller effect on support for the war among Republicans than among independents or Democrats. The proportion of Republicans believing that the war contributed to the long-term security of the United States has stayed at about 80 per cent since the end of 2003 (when the *ABC News/Washington Post* poll first asked the question); the proportion of Democrats with this view has fallen about 20 per centage points, so the gap between partisans has widened by about the same count (Fig. 8.14). Estimates of the net effect of the war on the threat of terrorism in the US have been less stable but display the same growing partisan divergence (Fig. 8.15). Up through the onset of the war, the consensus was that going to war in Iraq would increase the threat of domestic terrorism. After Baghdad fell, that expectation declined, but more so among Republicans than among Democrats and independents. Republicans have become more likely to think that the war decreased than increased the threat, while Democrats and independents are more likely to believe the opposite. Again, these beliefs are strongly related to support for the war (Jacobson 2005).

The President's Credibility

Public reactions to the war and its aftermath amplified partisan differences in assessments of George W. Bush. The administration's campaign justifying the war, before and after Iraq was invaded, put Bush's credibility on the line. Republicans' faith was barely shaken, while Democrats became increasingly skeptical. A large majority of Republicans continued to believe that Bush made the case for war in good faith, while the proportion of Democrats who thought the president had intentionally misled the public grew from 50 to 80 per cent over the three years following the onset of hostilities; partisans are now 64 points apart on this question (Fig. 8.16). Bush has enjoyed the trust of an overwhelming majority of Republicans from the beginning of his

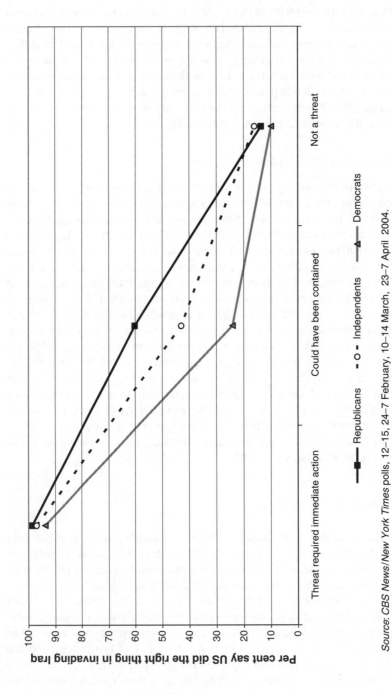

Figure 8.13. Opinions on the amount of threat posed by Iraq to the United States

Source: CBS News/*New York Times* polls, 12–15, 24–7 February, 10–14 March, 23–7 April 2004.

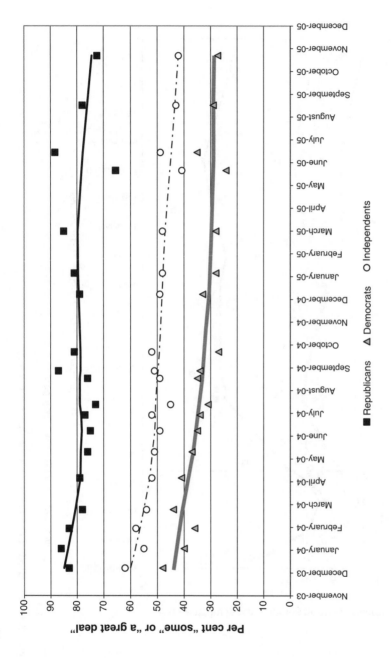

Figure 8.14. Has the Iraq War contributed to the long-term security of the US?

Source: *ABC News/Washington Post* polls.

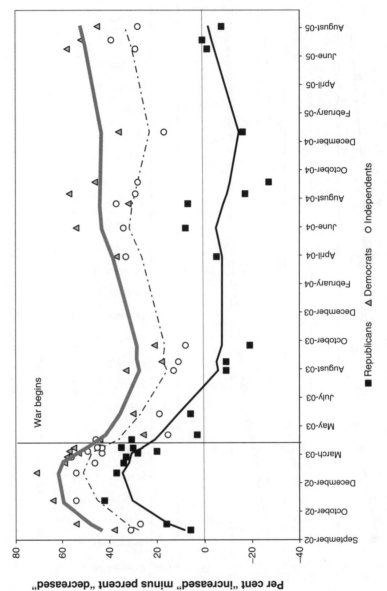

Source: CBS News/New York Times polls.

Figure 8.15. Net effect of the Iraq War on the threat of terrorism in the US

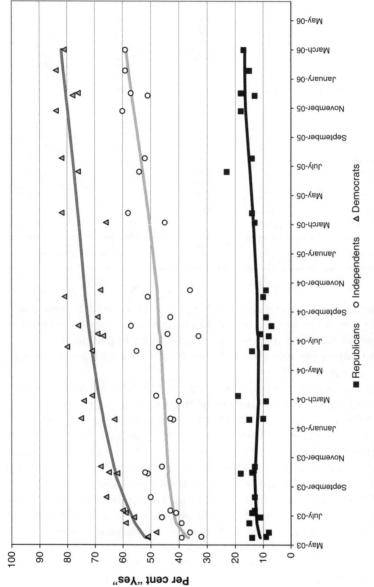

Source: *ABC News/Washington Post, CBS News/New York Times, NBC News/Wall Street Journal, Los Angeles Times, Time, Newsweek, Gallup, and PIPA Knowledge Networks polls.*

Figure 8.16. Belief that the Bush Administration deliberately misled the public in making the case for the Iraq War

Table 8.1. Sources of beliefs about George Bush's candor and the case for war in Iraq

	Bush's candor	Iraq had WMD	Saddam involved in 9/11	Saddam worked with al-Qaeda
Party identification	.266***	.310***	.198***	.271***
	(.018)	(.040)	(.028)	(.038)
Ideology	.125***	.197***	.115***	.208*
	(.019)	(.044)	(.031)	(.041)
Religious attendance	.106***	.127**	.093**	.038
	(.019)	(.044)	(.031)	(.042)
White, born-again Christian	.114**	.106	.104†	.233**
	(.035)	(.077)	(.055)	(.077)
Education	−.012	−.123***	−.174***	−.098***
	(.013)	(.029)	(.020)	(.028)
Male	.022	−.180**	−.277***	−.094
	(.026)	(.058)	(.041)	(.056)
African American	−.212***	−.126	.125†	.181†
	(.044)	(.098)	(.068)	(.093)
Constant	−.009	.388***	.298***	.206**
	(.034)	(.074)	(.053)	(.074)
Adjusted R^2	.27	.18	.12	.14
Number of cases	1808	926	1864	938

Note: Standard errors are in parentheses; †p < .10, *p < .05, **p < .01, ***p < .001, one-tailed test.

Source: CBS news/New York Times polls, 23–7 April 2004 (all cols.) and 23–7 June 2004 (cols. 1 and 3).

administration, and nothing that has happened since then has done much to shake it (Fig. 8.17). Initially, about 40 per cent of Democrats thought the phrase, "he is honest and trustworthy," applied to Bush; that figure exceeded 50 per cent during the year after 9/11 but by the fall of 2002 had fallen to about 22 per cent.

Multivariate models offer further insights into faith in Bush's candor. Table 8.1 reports regression estimates of the effects of party identification, ideology, religious attendance, identity as a born-again Christian, education, sex, and race on belief in Bush's candor about the case for war and in Saddam Hussein's alleged WMD, complicity in 9/11, and connections with al-Qaeda.[10] The data are from *CBS News/New York Times* polls.[11] Partisanship and ideology strongly influenced acceptance of claims that were central to the case for war and about Bush's candor in making that case, no surprise here. But the equations indicate that the respondent's religious beliefs and behavior also affected these beliefs. Reflecting the president's avowed born-again faith and strong rapport with religious conservatives, more frequent religious service attendees and white born-again Christians were significantly more likely to think him candid about the war and to accept his justifications for it. African Americans were significantly more skeptical about Bush but not necessarily about circumstances used to justify the war. Education and gender were unrelated to faith in Bush's candor, but skepticism about the case for

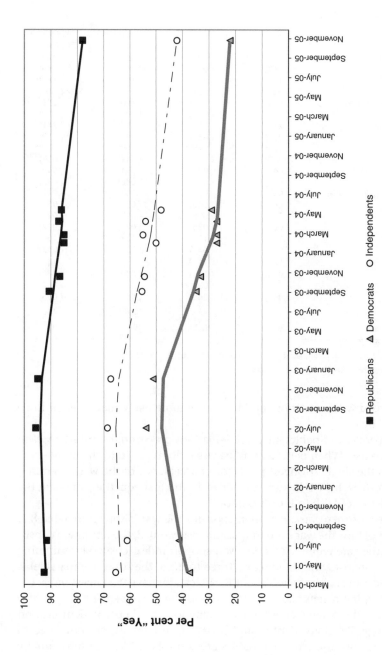

Source: ABC News/Washington Post polls.

Figure 8.17. Is George W. Bush honest and trustworthy?

Table 8.2. Effects of beliefs about George Bush's candor and his case for support for the war in Iraq

	Worth the cost	Right thing	Not a mistake	Support index
Bush's candor	.314***	.306***	.353***	.325***
	(.048)	(.046)	(.049)	(.040)
Iraq had WMD	.199***	.243***	.125***	.189***
	(.032)	(.031)	(.033)	(.026)
Saddam involved in 9/11	.074*	.208***	.170***	.151***
	(.031)	(.030)	(.032)	(.025)
Party identification	.232***	.211***	.279***	.241***
	(.038)	(.037)	(.039)	(.032)
Ideology	.114**	.145***	.107**	.122***
	(.040)	(.039)	(.041)	(.033)
Religious attendance	.047	.036	.034	.040
	(.039)	(.037)	(.040)	(.032)
White, born-again Christian	.033	−.059	−.007	−.011
	(.068)	(.066)	(.070)	(.056)
Education	.068**	.006	−.012	.020
	(.026)	(.025)	(.027)	(.022)
Male	.148**	.140**	.173**	.154***
	(.052)	(.051)	(.054)	(.043)
African American	−.109	−.153†	−.157†	−.140†
	(.088)	(.085)	(.090)	(.073)
Constant	−.457***	−.034	−.055	−.182***
	(.067)	(.065)	(.069)	(.056)
Adjusted R^2	.34	.42	.36	.46
Number of cases	902	902	902	902

Note: Standard errors are in parentheses; †p < .10, *p < .05, **p < .01, ***p < .001, one-tailed test.
Source: CBS News/New York Times poll, 23–7 April 2004.

war increased with education, and men were more likely than women to be persuaded by it.

The dependent variables in these equations are strongly linked to each other, of course. When belief about Bush's candor is added to the other equations, it is the single strongest predictor of acceptance of the war's premises, and when these beliefs in turn are added to the first equation, they are the best predictors of faith in Bush's candor.

The effect of these variables on support for the war is shown in Table 8.2. Regardless of how the war support question was worded, the results are consistent, and they are reiterated when a war support index (created by summing the three responses and dividing by three to make the scales comparable) is the dependent variable. Beliefs about Bush's candor have the largest impact of any variable, but beliefs about WMD and Saddam's involvement in 9/11 also have large and separable effects on war support.[12] So do party identification and ideology. Religious identity and behavior, in contrast, are unrelated to war support once these other variables are controlled. Men are substantially more likely than women to back the war; African Americans are less likely to support it, although none of the coefficients reaches the $p < .05$ level of significance (three come close). Education affected only responses to the question of whether the war was worth the cost.[13]

These results underline the contribution of religious conservatives to the president's success in maintaining support for his war policies among Republicans. Whites who identify themselves as born again are twice as likely as other respondents to identify themselves as Republicans. Those who do so approve of the president's performance both generally and in handling Iraq at significantly higher levels than other Republicans (94 to 87 per cent on general performance, 92 to 83 per cent on Iraq in the set of *CBS News/New York Times* polls under scrutiny here), and they are also the most likely to say that invading Iraq was the right thing to do (91 compared to 84 per cent for other Republicans; among Republicans identifying themselves as both born again and conservative, support for the war rises to 93 per cent).

Consequences

The War and the 2004 Election

The Iraq War was naturally a central issue in the 2004 presidential campaigns, which reinforced as well as reflected partisan differences over whether it was wise or necessary, and partisan differences on war-related questions tended to peak around election day. The pivotal disagreement between Bush and John Kerry, his Democratic opponent, about the Iraq War, highlighted in their first debate, concerned its relation to the fight against terrorism. Bush insisted that, regardless of mistaken assumptions about Saddam's WMD or complicity in 9/11, the war in Iraq was central to the war on terrorism, whereas Kerry argued that the Iraq invasion had unwisely taken resources from the pursuit of Osama bin Laden and other al-Qaeda terrorists who, unlike Iraq, had actually attacked the US. Not surprisingly, partisan differences on the question of whether the Iraq was or was not part of the war on terrorism widened during the election year (Fig. 8.18). From the war's beginning onward, large majorities of Republicans steadfastly continued to accept Bush's argument that the Iraq War was a major part of the war on terrorism, and only a small and shrinking minority thought it was separate from the war on terrorism. Democrats increasingly took the latter position, so the gap between partisans continually widened, reaching about 60 points just before the election.

Respondents' views of the connection between the war in Iraq and the war on terrorism were strongly related to support for the war, which in turn profoundly affected the decision to vote for Bush or Kerry on election day (Fig. 8.19).[14] Partisan divisions on the war thus contributed to the highest

a. Republicans

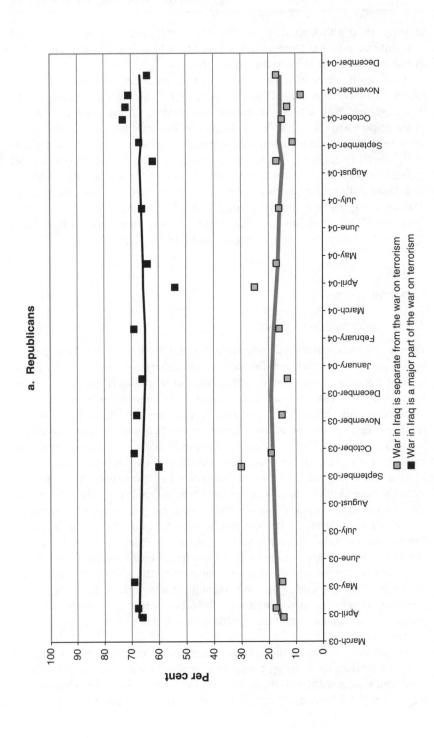

□ War in Iraq is separate from the war on terrorism
■ War in Iraq is a major part of the war on terrorism

b. Democrats

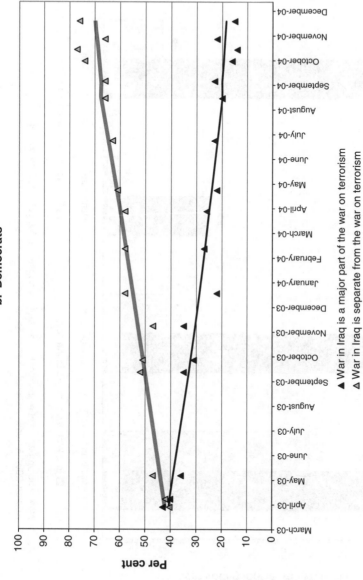

▲ War in Iraq is a major part of the war on terrorism
△ War in Iraq is separate from the war on terrorism

Source: CBS News/New York Times polls.

Figure 8.18. Is the Iraq War a major part of, a minor part of, or separate from the war on terrorism?

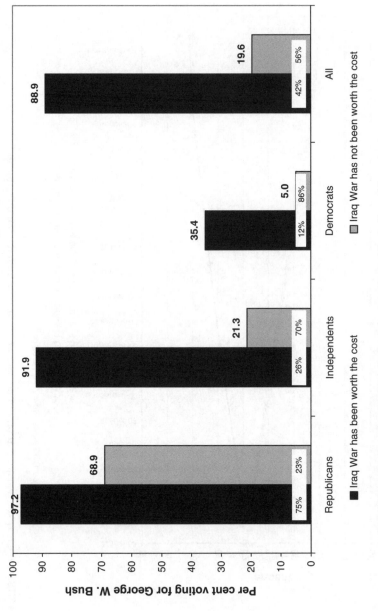

Note: The proportion of respondents in a category appears at the bottom of the column.
Source: 2004 America National Election Study.

Figure 8.19. Support for the Iraq War and the presidential vote choice

level of party loyalty—90 per cent—ever recorded in any of the fourteen NES presidential election surveys conducted since 1952.

Support for the Iraq Occupation

The steady and overwhelming support for US involvement in Iraq provided by Bush's core Republican constituents has given the administration considerable leeway in coping with the insurgents while trying to help Iraqi allies impose order and establish a viable representative government. As long as ordinary Republicans remain steadfast, any pressure to bring the troops home will be resistible. So far, Republicans remain largely optimistic about progress in Iraq—again, in striking contrast to Democrats—and are likely to remain so as long as there are signs of progress, such as the December 2005 parliamentary elections and the killing of al-Zarqawi in the spring of 2006, to counter any sense that Iraq has become another quagmire (Fig. 8.20). Here is another instance where an ambiguous reality permits prior attitudes and opinion leadership to exercise unhindered influence on perceptions of it. Any unmistakable progress should also attract increased support for administration policies from Democrats and independents, who have been responsive to changing circumstances in the past and whose support for staying the course has eroded only very slowly since 2004 (Fig. 8.21).[15] Notice that among ordinary Democrats, support for seeing the war through is nearly twice as high as support for having gone to war in the first place, a sign that the conundrum that has bedeviled Bush's Democratic opponents persists: even if the invasion was a serious mistake, could the United States now precipitously abandon Iraq without risking a worse disaster? Unless conditions in Iraq deteriorate badly or the palpable costs of the war touch a wider segment of the American electorate than they have so far, the administration should enjoy sufficient public patience—particularly among ordinary Republicans and therefore among Republicans in Congress—to continue its effort to redeem what has threatened to become a political debacle of the first magnitude.

The administration cannot, on the other hand, count on broad political support for other pre-emptive military actions. One (at least temporary) legacy of the Iraq War has been to make Democrats more dovish and Republicans more hawkish. A Pew Center study found that the proportion of Democrats agreeing with the statement, "good diplomacy is the best way to ensure peace," had risen from 62 per cent in 1999 to 76 per cent in 2004; among Republicans, the proportion agreeing had fallen from 46 per cent to 32 per cent. The share of Republicans agreeing that "we should all be willing to fight for our country whether it is right or wrong" had risen from 59 to 66 per cent, while the proportion of Democrats agreeing with this sentiment had fallen from 45 per cent to 33 per cent (Pew Research Center for the People and the Press 2005). Barring a direct attack on the US or its close allies,

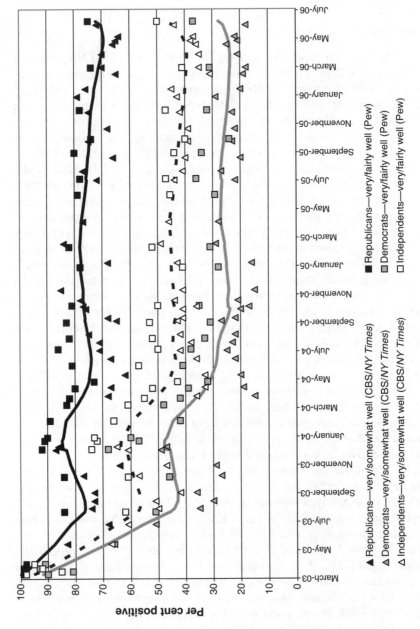

Figure 8.20. Evaluation of how well the Iraq War is going, by party

- ▲ Republicans—very/somewhat well (CBS/NY Times)
- ▲ Democrats—very/somewhat well (CBS/NY Times)
- △ Independents—very/somewhat well (CBS/NY Times)
- ■ Republicans—very/fairly well (Pew)
- ■ Democrats—very/fairly well (Pew)
- □ Independents—very/fairly well (Pew)

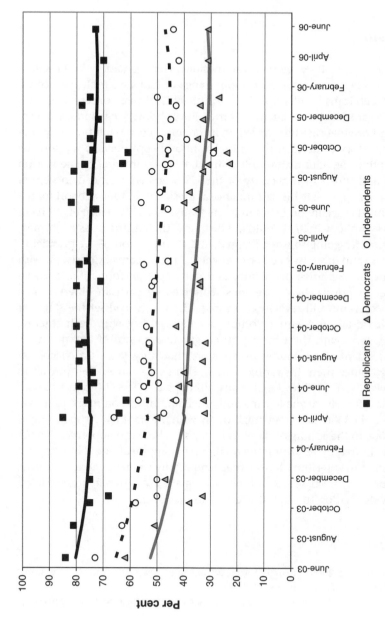

Sources: ABC News/Washington Post, CBS News/New York Times, and Pew Research Center for the People and the Press polls.

Figure 8.21. Support for keeping US troops in Iraq, by party

mobilizing bipartisan support for invading anyone will not be easy when distrust of the administration among Democrats is so high.

Conclusion

The public's unusually wide partisan divisions over evaluations of President Bush and his decision to force a regime change in Iraq are closely connected. Among Republicans of all stripes, but especially Christian conservatives, initial high regard for the president and trust in his honesty encouraged acceptance of his original case for war. When its premises proved faulty, they either missed that story or decided it was irrelevant and continued to support the war, accepting the administration's claim that it was integral to the war on terrorism and thus to the security of the US. Democrats tended to neither trust Bush nor appreciate his performance as president, so their support for the war depended crucially on belief in its necessity. When evidence of WMD or Saddam's complicity in 9/11 could not be found, their distrust was confirmed, their support for going to war collapsed, and their opinion of the president's performance and integrity became overwhelmingly negative. Consistent with the theories of cognitive dissonance and mass opinion formation, partisan differences in prior beliefs were thus reinforced by partisan differences in reactions to events and revelations in Iraq. The war helped set the stage for the most partisan presidential election in a half century, with Bush entering his second term with the widest partisan gap in approval of any newly re-elected president since polling began more than fifty years ago (Jacobson 2007, 202). Since then, his ratings among Democrats have fallen further to record lows (Fig. 8.2), while Republicans, although a bit less enthusiastic about their leader after Hurricane Katrina and other administration missteps in late 2005 and early 2006, have remained solidly with the president, responding in June of 2006 to the administration's campaign to shore up support for staying the course in Iraq by returning to an 80 per cent approval rate. Thus, at least barring some new terrorist horror that temporarily unifies Americans in the manner of 9/11, Bush seems destined to remain a divisive figure presiding over a divided nation through the rest of his presidency.

References

Boudreaux, Richard. 2005. "Insurgent Attacks Continue 2 Years After the U.S. Invasion." *Los Angeles Times*. 20 March, A4.

Festinger, Leon. 1957. *Theory of Cognitive Dissonance*. Stanford: Stanford University Press.

Fritz, Ben, Keefer, Bryan, and Nyhan, Brendan. 2003. *All the President's Spin: George W. Bush, the Media, and the Truth*. New York: Simon & Schuster.

Holsti, Ole. 2004. *Public Opinion and American Foreign Policy*. Ann Arbor: University of Michigan Press.

Jacobson, Gary C. 2000. "Public Opinion and the Impeachment of Bill Clinton," in *British Elections and Parties Review*, x, ed. Philip Cowley, David Denver, Andrew Russell, and Lisa Harrison. London: Frank Cass.

——— 2001. "A House and Senate Divided: The Clinton Legacy and the Congressional Elections of 2000." *Political Science Quarterly* 116 (Spring): 5–27.

——— 2005. "Partisan Polarization and the 2004 Congressional Elections." *Political Science Quarterly* 120 (Summer): 199–218.

——— 2006. "The President, the Public, and the War in Iraq." Presented at the Annual Meeting of the Midwest Political Science Association, Chicago, 7–10 April 2005.

——— 2007. *A Divider, Not a Uniter: George W. Bush and the American People*. New York: Pearson Longman.

Kull, Steven, Ramsay, Clay, and Lewis, Evan. 2003–4. "Misperception, the Mass Media, and the Iraq War." *Political Science Quarterly* 118 (Winter): 581–5.

——— with Clay Ramsay, Stefan Subias, Stephen Weber, and Evan Lewis. 2004. *The Separate Realities of Bush and Kerry Supporters*. PIPA/ Knowledge Networks Poll: The American Public on International Issues (21 October), at ⟨http://zz.tripod.com/cvb/pipa.html⟩.

Mueller, John E. 1973. *War, Presidents, and Public Opinion*. New York: John Wiley.

Pew Research Center for the People and the Press. 2003. *The 2004 Political Landscape: Evenly Divided and Increasingly Polarized*. Survey Report. Washington, DC (5 November).

——— 2005. *Politics and Values in a 51%–48% Nation*. Survey Report. Washington, DC (24 January).

Pfiffner, James P. 2004. "Did President Bush Mislead the Country in his Arguments for War with Iraq?" *Presidential Studies Quarterly* 34 (March): 25–46.

Notes

1. These data are from a set of national polls sampling all adults (not just registered or likely voters) conducted by the *CBS News/New York Times*, *ABC News/Washington Post*, *NBC News/Wall Street Journal*, *Los Angeles Times*, *Gallup*, Pew Center for the People and Press, Associated Press/IPSOS, *Newsweek*, *CNN/Time*, Marist, and Bloomberg polls reported at ⟨http://www.pollingreport.com⟩, accessed 21 November 2006. This and later charts also display Lowess-smoothed trends.

2. Evaluations of Bush's performance in different policy domains were also highly polarized along party lines during this period (Jacobson 2007, 10–13).

3. These data are from national polls sampling all adults or registered or likely voters conducted by the *CBS News/New York Times*, *ABC News/Washington Post*, *NBC News/Wall Street Journal*, *Los Angeles Times*, *Gallup*, Pew Center for the People and Press, *Newsweek*, *CNN/Time*, Fox News, Quinnipiac College, National Annenberg Election Study, Knowledge Networks, and Democracy Corps polls reported at ⟨http://www.pollingreport.com⟩ or at the polling outfit's website. The various question wordings are shown in Jacobson (2007, appendix).

4. These questions typically read, "Do you think the United States did the right thing in taking military action against Iraq, or should the US have stayed out?" and "In view of the developments since we first sent our troops to Iraq, do you think the United States made a mistake in sending troops to Iraq, or not?"

5. *Los Angeles Times Poll Alert*, Study 510, 25 October 2004.

6. Numerous well-documented examples may be found in Fritz, Keefer, and Nyhan (2003).

7. For example, a survey taken 12–18 October 2004 found that more than half of both Bush and Kerry supporters thought the Bush Administration had been saying that it had found clear evidence that Saddam Hussein worked closely with al-Qaeda. See Kull et al. (2004).

8. *ABC News/Washington Post* polls, 20 March, 3 April and 18–21 December 2003 and 10–11 February 2004, analyzed by the author. Among independents, the proportion saying WMD were not necessary to justify the war went from 50 per cent on March 20 to 63 per cent in April before declining to 58 per cent in February 2004; the proportion saying the war was not justified regardless went from 6 to 19 per cent.

9. *CBS News/New York Times* Poll, 14–18 January 2005, at ⟨http://www.cbsnews.com/htdocs/CBSNews_polls/bush_back.pdf⟩, accessed 10 February 2005.

10. Beliefs about Bush's candor are measured by responses to the question of whether, in making its case for the war, the Bush Administration was mostly telling the truth (1), hiding something (0), mostly lying (−1). The other three dependent variables are scored 1 if respondent believed Saddam had WMD, was complicit in 9/11, or had ties to al-Qaeda, 0 if uncertain, −1 if the respondent did not believe these things. Party identification is 1 if Republican, 0 if independent, −1 if Democrat; ideology is 1 if conservative, 0 if moderate, −1 if liberal. Education is 1 if high school or less, 2 if some college, 3 if college graduate, 4 if postgraduate degree. Religious attendance is 1 if weekly or nearly weekly, 0 if occasionally, −1 if never. White born-again Christian, African American, and male are all 1 if respondent is in the category, 0 otherwise.

11. The first and third equations combine data from the 23–7 April 2004 and the 23–7 June 2004 polls; the second includes only the April data, the fourth only the June data.

12. Responses to the al-Qaeda question have a similar effect under these controls, but they are not included here because the question was never asked in a survey that also included both the WMD and 9/11 questions.

13. I also tested for the effects of marital status and age in all of these equations and, finding none, have omitted these demographic variables.

14. Estimates of a multivariate logit model (not shown) indicated that support for the war continued to have a large, statistically significant effect on the presidential vote in 2004 under controls for ideology, party identification, overall approval of Bush's job performance, and all manner of demographic variables; see Jacobson (2007, 194–5).

15. Data are from responses to questions giving as alternatives staying until the situation in Iraq has stabilized or withdrawing troops "as soon as possible" or "immediately."

9

The Promotional Presidency and the New Institutional Toryism: Public Mobilization, Legislative Dominance, and Squandered Opportunities

Lawrence R. Jacobs

Contemporary textbooks, pundits, and students of American politics tell us that the critical power of the presidency is its public persona. Presidents use their unrivalled access to the airwaves and extensive travel publicly to promote themselves and their policies in order to attempt to move members of Congress and other elites to create support (Canes-Wrone 2001; Kernell 1997).

This power-enhancing interpretation of presidential promotion rests on the logic of electoral pressure. According to a common explanation of political motivation (Downs 1957), the competition of politicians for voters in a two-party system drives them to appeal to centrist public opinion. By extension, presidential success in mobilizing majorities of Americans for particular policy proposals is expected to create an irresistible electoral magnet for members of Congress and their allies. In effect, presidents practice a kind of "bank shot" off the public into Congress.

This power-enhancing view of presidential promotion has not gone without criticism. Some have shown that even enormous efforts by presidents to generate elite support by mobilizing the public have generally been inef-fectual in improving their success in Congress. Legislators' party loyalty, fidelity to philosophical principles of "good" policy, and attentiveness to constituents back home all combine, it is reported, to offset or, at a mini-mum, condition the president's influence (Bond and Fleisher 1990; Edwards 1989). Presidents generally react to onrushing events and media portray-als of them rather than shaping them (Edwards 2006; Edwards and Wood 1999).

This chapter makes a somewhat different argument. Changes in governing norms and the development of institutional capacity and routines that foster public presidential promotion generate incentives and expectations for the presidents to overestimate their personal power and underestimate durable institutional and political constraints. The result is a tendency—especially on major programmatic initiatives—to squander leadership opportunities and to leave themselves in weakened political positions. Presidential promotions may augment the White House's leverage at discrete moments, but it may also reflect inflated calculations of political feasibility, which prompt presidents to propose initiatives that politically overshoot what the public, interest groups, and congressional majorities will support.

This chapter examines the rise of presidential promotions and its impact on White House calculations by tracing changes in the White House's institutional capacity for reaching the public, a content analysis of presidential appeals, and comparative case studies of institutionally strong presidents—those who enjoyed the rare and advantaged position of unified party government. In an era before the promotional presidency, Franklin Roosevelt's Social Security proposal and Lyndon Johnson's Medicare proposal were both based on what were conservative institutional decisions to accommodate the legislative branch (omitting health insurance and coverage of medical costs, respectively). On the other hand, Bill Clinton and George W. Bush were buoyed by their confidence in the presidency's institutional capacity to mobilize public opinion in order to move the policy makers: Clinton's health reform proposal and Bush's partial privatization proposal pursued radical changes to remake large and complicated programs that were politically implausible given resistance by members of their own parties in Congress as well as opposition among stakeholders and doubts among Americans. Neither president even received a vote in Congress on his initiative despite its status as his top domestic priority. The promotional presidency offers enormous capabilities to educate and focus the public, but it can also seduce the most astute president into neglecting the enduring institutional constraints on any chief executive.

Although the development of the promotional presidency and the inflated expectations of presidential dominance seduced Bush and Clinton into squandering striking opportunities, they may reflect new norms of American governance that feature energetic and domineering executive power. This chapter's conclusion weighs the implications of what may be an emerging form of institutional Toryism—one that recalibrates the constitutional balance of authority under certain conditions and legitimizes a politically astute future Democratic president to use the new norms of governance for liberal ends.

Routinization of the Promotional Presidency: "Getting Away with Anything"

It is easy to forget that presidents once worked in the shadows of Washington, ceding the public spotlight to powerful members of Congress and party leaders. Theodore Roosevelt and Woodrow Wilson introduced a more publicly visible presidency, but presidents did not become a routine figure in the public eye until Franklin Roosevelt's radio appeals during the New Deal and World War II and John Kennedy's use of television (Tulis 1987; Jacobs 2005). Today, the press corps mans an around-the-clock watch on the president to capture his every statement, ensuring that he will be a featured part of every news cycle.

The transformation of the president into the premier political newsmaker reflects and has encouraged a series of linked developments in the institution of the presidency and in the expectations of White House officials over the past four decades or so. Routinization of White House procedures and capacities publicly to promote the president has fueled (and been fueled by) an expectation of presidential political dominance. The result is a kind of Caesarist mindset captured by one Clinton Administration official who explained that the White House can "get away with anything provided you believe in something, you say it over and over again, and you never change" (quoted in Jacobs and Shapiro 2000, 106).

Building the Institutional Capacity for Public Promotions

The modern presidency's capacity for public promotion is built on two institutional pillars—the tools to attempt to shape public thinking and the capabilities of tracking it with private polling. The emergence of the president as a routinely visible public force starts in earnest with William McKinley's efforts during the second half of the 1890s to control and centralize information in the White House and how it was released to the media.[1] Guided by Republican strategist Mark Hanna (Karl Rove's nineteenth-century counterpart), McKinley pinned the success of his top policy priority (his aggressive expansion of American power abroad) on marshaling public support. Mobilizing the public, he reasoned, required control over the information reaching Americans through the press, which led him to develop what became the precursor for the White House Press Office and press secretary. This new White House capacity was geared toward both generating a steady supply of information that would set the media's agenda to focus on the issues selected by the administration and shaping the content of press reporting in ways favorable to the administration. Today's staple of White House briefings, press releases, and advance copies of speeches began as part of McKinley's drive to manage the media.

Presidents following McKinley expanded on these new tools to strengthen their ability to appeal to the public. Teddy Roosevelt and William Taft continued the new relations with the press, but it was Woodrow Wilson who vigorously expanded relations with the press and centralized control in the White House. Wilson resurrected the tradition of the president orally delivering his State of the Union address to Congress (a tradition that had stalled after George Washington) and developed the White House's capacity to communicate directly with Americans by launching nationwide campaigns, such as his efforts to rally the country during World War I. The White House staff's relations with the press were solidified with Herbert Hoover's appointment of the first press secretary.

Franklin D. Roosevelt further expanded the White House's ties to the media and its administrative tools for publicly promoting himself and his policies. The press secretary was given greater authority systematically to structure the routines of the press and its contacts in the administration, and to discipline executive branch departments to project the public message that the White House designed. In addition, the Roosevelt White House encouraged ties with a new medium (radio) and strengthened existing ties with others (newspapers and film) (Steele 1985).

After World War II, a series of presidents cemented the press secretary and his base of operations, the Press Office, as the nerve center for the administration's press relations, focusing the attention of the press on the president. Presidents continued to introduce innovations aimed at more successfully managing media coverage and influencing public thinking. John Kennedy introduced television to presidential press conferences and his White House initiated a sustained effort to integrate executive branch agencies in a coordinated plan for feeding and managing the press in order publicly to champion the president and to distance him from unfavorable news. As part of the White House's drive to draft the executive branch into helping to promote the president, it routinely used the cabinet secretaries as public relations tools to travel the country singing the praises of the president and his administration's policies.

By Ronald Reagan, the White House combined its close press relations with professional public relations staff (often with experience in advertising and television) to develop sophisticated strategies for orchestrating how and where the President was presented in public. The White House's approach evolved from building press and public demand for information on the president to dictating the precise supply of images and messages that reached the press and public. Michael Deaver's famous efforts to determine which camera angles would be available to the press covering President Reagan illustrate the White House's orientations, abilities, and skill in crafting the president's public presentation. Bill Clinton's principal political strategy focused on developing a series of game plans to centralize control over the administration's public statement within the White House and to saturate the press with its message in the expectation that this would crowd out the opposing messages of reform opponents.

President George W. Bush has embraced and built upon the institutional capacity of the White House to promote himself and his policies. Bush has insisted that the administration "tal[k] about what we want to talk about, not what the press want to talk about."[2] The result has been a "funnel of information" from the president and his senior aides to the communications staff to the administration more widely. To achieve this domination over the flow of information to journalists and the public, the Bush Administration has increased the staffing of its communications. Martha Kumar estimates in her chapter in this volume that the number of people working in communications and supporting operations had ballooned to approximately 350 by the start of Bush's second term. The effect has been to strengthen the presidency's institutional routines for directly appealing to Americans and managing the press.

One of the Bush White House's major innovations in strengthening the president's sway over Americans has been to build up the institutional tools for directly delivering his messages. In particular, Bush and his aides expanded the White House's ability to communicate directly with Americans by building on its ties to political parties and interest groups and strengthening its tactical weaponry for writing speeches and arranging travel routinely to take the president's message to towns and cities across the country. Like other modern presidents, Bush used this capability to barnstorm the country for his legislative proposals and for his re-election campaign, targeting specific areas and segments of the country. In Florida, for instance, he traveled not only to the most widely known destinations, such as Miami and Tampa, but also to new suburbs that were relatively unknown outside the state, such as Niceville and New Port Richey.

Bush was particularly innovative in developing the capacity to organize grassroots support for his re-election and for his policy initiatives (from tax cuts to socially conservative legislation and judicial nominees). Previous administrations solicited the support of interest groups and voluntary associations, but the Bush White House was especially aggressive in building ties to community organizations from churches and synagogues to small businesses. In his 2004 campaign, these community ties helped Bush far exceed the number of volunteers he had in 2000 to make phone calls, leaflet neighborhoods, write personalized letters, and drive voters on Election Day. In Florida, for instance, the number of volunteers for Bush rose more than tenfold, from less than 10,000 to 109,000.

In addition to direct grassroots organizing, the Bush Administration ratcheted up White House control over the supply of information reaching the press. The White House has taken a strikingly disciplined and systematic approach to "get everyone on the same song sheet," as one senior official explained.

The press secretary and senior officials control who talks to the press, what is said in the White House and departments, and when and how the president appears in public. The president's communications staff meets with officials throughout the administration to distribute "talking points" to ensure they stay on the "message" defined by the White House and to make it possible for "everyone [to] say exactly the same thing."

The most uncommon events are the press conferences when Bush alone takes questions from reporters in front of television cameras. Bush has held fewer solo press conferences than any of his postwar predecessors because of his personal unease and the White House's determination to "control your message," as one aide responsible for communications put it (quoted in Auletta 2004).

In addition to tending to the national mass media, the White House caters to media outside the large mainstream press because they tend to be more accepting and less aggressive and suspicious. It also reaches out to religious publications and to the in-house networks operated by private gyms.

Modern presidents enjoy an extraordinary position for exerting unparalleled control over both the demand and supply of information on themselves and government policy. The century-long effort to stoke and sustain strong demand for information from the White House has now been combined with astonishing control over what images and news of the president and his administration are supplied.

Presidential Polling: The Guidance System for Public Promotions

The White House's development of institutions and procedures for shaping the public's perceptions of the president and his policies have paralleled and in some respects have been fueled by the rise of sophisticated and extensive private polling. By equipping presidents carefully to select popular topics and alluring wording for their presentations, polling has bolstered the confidence of presidents in their capacity to move public opinion much as lasers improved the military's faith that they could pinpoint aerial bombing to produce the impact it desired.

Although previous presidents had assembled private polls, the Kennedy White House initiated a significant expansion of the scope and sophistication of White House polling (Eisinger 2003; Heith 1998; Jacobs 1992, 1993, 2005). Private presidential polling started modestly under Kennedy, with Louis Harris providing 15 private reports to the White House. Oliver Quayle, whom Harris had recommended to replace him when he became a pollster for major media organizations, provided most of the 110 surveys that Lyndon Johnson received. Nixon escalated the number of private surveys to 173, relying on a stable of Republican pollsters to conduct his research, including established firms such as Opinion Research Corporation and new upstarts such as Robert Teeter (who later co-directed a polling firm that worked for the *Wall Street Journal* and directed George H. W. Bush's 1992 campaign) and Richard Wirthlin. Wirthlin conducted at least 204 private surveys for Reagan, though more may exist.

Along with the growing number of polls, the White House since Kennedy also increased the scope and sophistication of its polling. This development is partly reflected in the sheer growth of polling results that were collected by the White House's private polls. Archival research demonstrates that the number of poll questions and responses rose dramatically after Kennedy's term (Jacobs 2005). The two most recent presidents—Bill Clinton and George W. Bush—continued to expand on the polling apparatus constructed by their predecessors, pushing the White House's capabilities to new levels.

The increased number and sophistication of presidential polls since Kennedy coincided with their applications to a widening set of political challenges, from a tool for elections to the governing phase. In particular, they were used to fashion the president's travel schedule as well as to select which topics he would address and how he would discuss them. When the president went before Americans, his promotional message had been scientifically designed to appeal to the public and win its support.

Institutions that Fuel Expectations

The White House's capacities for publicly promoting the president have appeared to successive modern presidents as a remedy for their yearning to exert concerted and sustained leadership in a constitutional system designed to frustrate it. Political motivations have interacted with growing institutional capacity to feed the White House's confidence in its political capability to use its unmatched promotional power to overcome inherent constitutional weaknesses. Presidents committed to conservative policy goals (Reagan and Bush 43) and to liberal ones (Clinton) have turned to the White House's phalanx of tools to blanket the country with its crafted message as a means for rallying the public to its side and overcoming resistance in Congress and Washington.

For much of the nineteenth century, presidents rarely promoted themselves and their policies in public (Tulis 1987). The norms of governance generally looked down upon gestures that might appear demagogic; these norms discouraged presidents from verbally delivering the State of the Union address or routinely delivering demonstrable addresses to large public audiences.

In our time, ordinary Americans and presidents accept as "normal" not only ubiquitous public promotions of presidents but determined efforts by the White House to deploy its considerable public relations capacities toward *changing* public opinion. Bill Clinton's conduct in office was skewered for inappropriately opening up the White House for fund-raising and for unbecoming licentious behaviour; the White House's game plans to manufacture support for himself and his policies were accepted, indeed they were openly discussed as if they were theatre pieces to be reviewed. A similar *normalizing of presidential promotions* has been evident during President Bush's terms.

One of the most striking features of the various investigations and revelations of the Bush White House's efforts to rally public support for American military intervention in Iraq and for discrediting opponents such as Ambassador Joseph Wilson has been the acceptance of extensive and sustained administration efforts to shape news coverage and public thinking. The public criticism has largely focused on White House falsehoods (such as charges that Saddam Hussein was seeking uranium from Niger) and leaks (the revelation of Valerie Plame's undercover CIA status), not on whether determined efforts to mold press coverage and public thinking are appropriate. *What had once been extraordinary is now accepted as commonplace.*

In important respects, contemporary presidential power is equated not only with "going public" but with a far more pernicious activity that deeply troubled the framers of the US Constitution—determined efforts to shape public thinking to advance the personal and short-term interests of the president. It is now legitimate for presidents to dedicate the White House's administrative might to achieving what John Kennedy's senior advisers had seen as their innovation—"public communications—educating, persuading, and mobilizing [public opinion]" (quoted in Sorensen 1965, 310).

Presidents as the Public's Oracle

Presidential leadership is changing in ways that surpass the now common observation about going public (Kernell 1997). It is true that presidents are talking and traveling more. But Samuel Kernell's observation that presidents tend to talk to specialized audiences (such as business and labor leaders) when they travel and go public is much less true.[3] Presidents are not only out more but they are addressing the mass public more. The purpose of presidential promotion is predominantly directed at moving public opinion rather than engaging in debate with the "attentive public."

We conducted an extensive study of whether presidents since Richard Nixon addressed specialized elites or the mass public in order to examine patterns and trends in presidential leadership efforts. In particular, we conducted a rigorous content analysis of Nixon's and Reagan's oral statements (such as press conferences and addresses to the nation) and their written statements (such as messages to Congress or professional associations) as recorded in the *Public Papers of the Presidents of the United States* and the *Weekly Compilation of*

Presidential Documents (for more detail, see Jacobs et al. 2003). We analyzed an extensive number of Nixon's and Reagan's statements: all their news conferences and addresses to the nation as well as a random selection of other oral and written statements, which amounted to about 50 per cent of Nixon's statements and 25 per cent of Reagan's. For Bill Clinton and George W. Bush, we analyzed a random sample of 100 documents. This amounted to approximately 1 out of every 115 statements by Clinton and 1 out of every 100 documents for Bush, as chronically recorded in the *Public Papers of the President.*[4]

A particular focus of our analysis was whether the president's statements were directed at the mass public or specialized audiences. For instance, the State of the Union addresses and nationally televised speeches and press conferences were directed to the mass public. On the other hand, statements to more specialized audiences of political party leaders, government officials, interest groups, and narrow congressional topics or committees were aimed at segments of elites or the "attentive public."

The findings from the Nixon and Reagan analyses are quite reliable; the content analyses of Clinton's and Bush's statements are based on a far more limited number of documents. We consider them suggestive. On the other hand, the use of a random sample provides some sense of the relative proportion of statements aimed at the public and elite audiences. In addition, the findings we present below of the president's rising public orientation fit into a trend that includes Nixon and Reagan, the two most rigorously analyzed presidents.

The central trend in presidential appeals is a shift from addressing elite audiences toward addressing the mass public. Figure 9.1 shows that presidential appeals to the mass public sharply rose from Nixon to Reagan, Clinton, and Bush 43. Fifty-eight per cent of Nixon's statements were directed at the public compared to about 75 per cent under his successors. Presidential attention to elite audience declined by nearly half after the Nixon years.

The growing presidential preoccupation with the mass public is a steady development across administrations. Figure 9.2 indicates an overall increase in presidential appeals to the mass public over time. Presidential outreach to the general public hovered at about 60 per cent of Nixon's comments and then rose to about 80 per cent for most of the Reagan, Clinton, and Bush years (it was above 75 per cent for 13 of their 23 years in office).

A standard political model of governing expects presidents to focus their comments on the mass public during election years and then shift to elites when it comes time to govern. Indeed, the three highest peaks of Reagan's attention to the mass public were election years—1982, 1984, and 1986.

What is striking is that the spikes in Clinton's and Bush's appeals to the mass public are no longer tied to elections. Figure 9.2 shows that Clinton hammered Americans during 1993 when he was campaigning for his policy goals (health reform in particular) and 1999 as he fought off efforts to convict

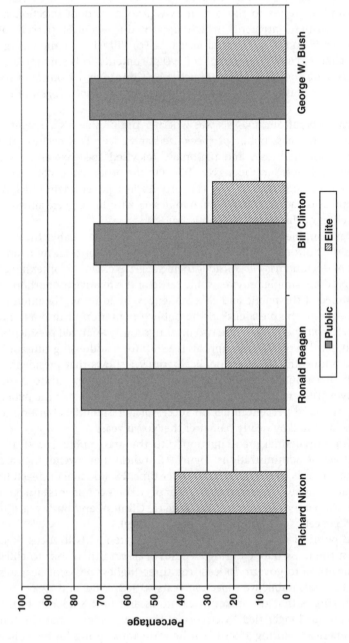

Denotes the percentage of presidential statements directed to elite and public audiences, aggregated yearly.
Source: content analysis of Public Papers of the President and Weekly Compilation of Presidential Documents.

Figure 9.1. Presidential addresses to public and elite audiences

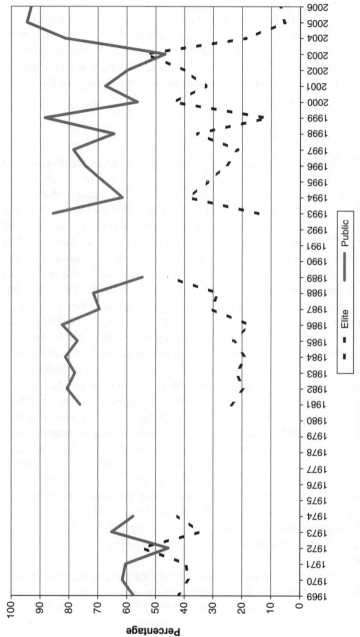

Denotes the percentage of presidential statements directed to elite and public audiences, aggregated yearly.
Source: Content analysis of Public Papers of the President and Weekly Compilation of Presidential Documents.

Figure 9.2. Presidential addresses to public and elite audiences over time

him of the charges of impeachment. In 2005, Bush targeted 95 per cent of his comments to the mass public.

Presidents are not only traveling more but are also targeting the mass public more. Modern presidents appear to equate their political power with their connection to the mass public; even during the period of governing, presidents only devote 20–30 per cent of their time to addressing elites. Presidential promotions and not elite collaboration are apparently the keys to the White House's political strategy.

The Caesarist Mindset: The Bush Presidency

The Bush White House has expanded on the innovations of the Reagan and Clinton White Houses in promoting the president's policy proposals. Bush's impact is not simply, though, on the extension of campaign strategy to the advocacy of policy proposals, though he has added to his predecessors' handiwork. Rather, the distinctiveness of Bush's impact was to broaden and intensify the White House's political expectation of policy dominance. The Bush White House embraced more fully what had been a more selective assumption under Reagan and Bush 41—namely, that the White House can move public opinion and that this (rather than basic institutional and political configurations) provides the foundation of presidential power.

Many, if not all, of the White House's major domestic and international policy initiatives relied on a political strategy of building public support through extensive travel and campaigning—what administration officials referred to as "Flood the Zone" (Allen 2003). The White House turned to a "mobile version of the bully pulpit" after failing to influence the direction of lawmaking through standard behind-the-scenes maneuvering (Allen 2002). The President's traveling promotions were expected to "press wavering lawmakers" (Stevenson 2003). When faced with congressional resistance, Bush engaged in "hardball politics" of rallying public opinion to "pressure reluctant lawmakers"—even those in the President's party (Allen 2003; Stevenson 2003). The point of Bush's extensive travel and appeals to the mass public was to generate—as one ally put it—"grass-roots pressure on the elected members" (Allen 2003). For instance, the White House attributed—according to the *Washington Post*—Bush's success in passing his first round of tax cuts to the impact of his "heavy travel schedule ... [in] building support" (Allen 2002).

As a general matter, the White House carefully crafted the president's messages on his policy proposals to resonate with his base of supporters as well as with Americans who were ambivalent or opposed to his plans. In 2003, for instance, the White House's response to the general public's unease with further tax cuts in a time of war and rising deficits was not to change policy but to activate its promotional capabilities. The White House settled on a "refined sales pitch" that publicly presented his proposal as the "President's jobs and growth package" instead of a "tax cut" (Allen 2003). Another approach to marshaling Americans was to capitalize—as the *New York Times* reported— on the "symbols of the nation's military might" by "speak[ing] from the commander in chief's platform about his tax-cut plan" (Stevenson 2003).

The White House attempted to change opinion in order to produce specific political effects in Washington. In particular, it concentrated the president's barnstorming on specific states and members of Congress where his "clout will make a difference" in "cranking up the political pressure" (Allen 2003; Stevenson 2003). In addition to attempting to turn constituents against moderate Democrats in Republican-friendly states (such as Arkansas, Nebraska, and Indiana), the White House also brought the heat on resistant moderate Republicans George Voinovich and Olympia Snowe. In addition to its own efforts, the White House mobilized an army of supporters that included—as the *Washington Post* reported—"barnstorming by Cabinet members [and] television advertisements by groups friendly to the White House" (Allen 2003).

The expectation in the Bush White House was that congressional opposition was a momentary stance; it would be altered with pinpointed presidential work on members' constituents.

Presidential efforts to rally public opinion are, of course, not new. Woodrow Wilson vigorously campaigned to rally the country behind entering World War I and adopting the League of Nations. There are two new elements, however. First, the technology for bringing the president and his message to the mass public has advanced as have the tools for calibrating his message to resonate with the public's preferences and emotions. These breakthroughs elevate the president as the single most influential force in shaping public opinion and have strengthened the potency of the White House's honed messages.

Second, the White House's promotional machinery has had a profound impact on the political calculations and expectations of the president and his aides and supporters. Ironically, the White House's growing efforts to impact how Americans think about public policy has also affected its own thinking. In particular, the rise of the promotional presidency has generated a near certainty among the president and his senior aides that public opinion and therefore opposition in Congress and other parts of Washington are malleable in the face of determined White House campaigning. In this mindset, opposition is always temporary and the president's capacity to work his will and dominate Washington faces few limits.

Presidential Overreaching

Despite the American hagiography that envelops the framing of the US Constitution and James Madison's much-cited wisdom, the Newtonian structure of government institutions that was designed to induce "delay and deadlock" has long been criticized (Burns 1963). In one of the earliest cogent critiques after the Constitution's ratification, Woodrow Wilson warned in *Congressional Government* (originally published in 1885) that the Constitution had dispersed authority to the point that responsibility and accountability were easily evaded. The result is that coherent government policy is sacrificed to the particularistic interests of decentralized wielders of power (Wilson 1973).

The election of one party into positions of control in both congressional chambers and the White House (i.e. "unified" government) has historically offered one of the few opportunities to navigate the Madisonian bulwarks against governing and passing significant legislation (Edwards, Barrett, and Peake 1997). Although "unified government" does not remove significant institutional friction, it creates the political circumstances for "conditional party government" within Congress (Aldrich 1995; Rohde 1991) and between the two lawmaking branches (Bond and Fleisher 1990; Edwards 1989). Presidential success in Congress is substantially higher under unified government than situations where partisan control over the legislative and executive is divided. This persistent pattern of stronger presidential success under unified government holds across presidents with varying political skills and professional reputations: Jimmy Carter, who was not politically gifted but enjoyed unified party control during his term, achieved more legislative success than the more politically deft Ronald Reagan who was opposed by the Democratically controlled House throughout his two terms and by Democratic majorities in the Senate during his last two years in office (Bond and Fleisher 1990).

George Bush has enjoyed extraordinary legislative success. Figure 9.3 shows *Congressional Quarterly's* scores for presidential success since Dwight Eisenhower. Although this measure has limitations (cf. Bond and Fleisher 1990, ch. 2), it does provide a rough comparative gauge of the proportion of roll-call votes on which the president took a clear position. Compared to his predecessors, Bush has consistently won on about three-quarters of legislation on which he has an announced position. His 78 per cent success in 2005 was the highest of any fifth-year president that has been studied—Lyndon Johnson was second at 74.5 per cent while Reagan considerably trailed at 59.9 per cent (Poole 2006). In part because of his success, Bush has yet to veto a single piece of legislation.

The primary source of Bush's legislative success is his partisan and ideological compatibility with members of Congress.[5] Bush benefited from disciplined Republican control in both chambers: his party wielded majorities in the House during his first six years in office and majorities in the Senate for four. In addition to the partisan dominance, the GOP has been able to exert remarkable unity due to ideological similarity (McCarty, Poole, and Rosenthal 2006). Figures 9.4 and 9.5 offer evidence of two important related over time

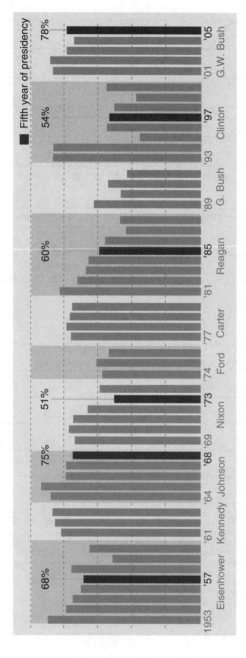

Source: Isaiah Poole, "Presidential Support: Two Steps Up, One Step Down." *Congressional Quarterly Weekly.* 9 January: 80–6.

Figure 9.3. Presidential success scores

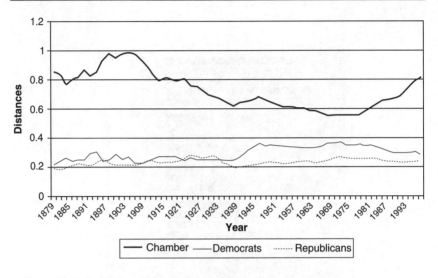

Source: McCarty, Poole, and Rosenthal 2006.

Figure 9.4. Average inter- and intra-party ideological distance in the House

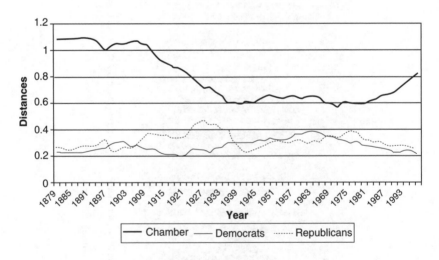

Source: McCarty, Poole, and Rosenthal 2006.

Figure 9.5. Average inter- and intra-party ideological distance in the Senate

developments. First, there has been a decline in the average ideological distance between House and Senate members of the same party; the dotted lines plot this increase in intra-party ideological similarity. Second, the ideological difference separating the average member of Congress in each party has widened during the same period; the bold lines plot this greater ideological polarization due to inter-party differences. Under the Clinton and Bush presidencies, each party has become more ideologically homogenous and drifted further from the other. President Bush has benefited from his partisan and ideological compatibility with the GOP's legislative caucuses. Deborah Pryce, chair of the House Republican Conference, attributed Bush's success to common policy goals—congressional Republicans "appreciate what's at stake."

An important analytic question arises: what political strategies do presidents adopt toward Congress when they are pursuing unusually significant legislative proposals and enjoy extraordinary institutional leverage through unified government? Do presidents defer to the preferences of members of Congress and adopt a cautious approach toward pursuing their policy goals or do they attempt to override congressional preferences by mobilizing Americans against members through their promotional capacities?

We investigate these questions by examining the political strategies of four presidents in the rare and advantageous position of unified party government; two operated both before the White House gained the institutional capacity for massive and sophisticated public promotions and after it had been established. In the era before the promotional presidency, we examine Franklin Roosevelt's formulation of his Social Security proposal in 1935 and Lyndon Johnson's design of Medicare in 1965. On the other hand, Bill Clinton's drive comprehensively to reform the health care system in 1993 and 1994 and George W. Bush's crusade partially to privatize Social Security in 2005 occurred after the promotional presidency had been established.

These presidential campaigns share two significant similarities. First, all four cases involve presidents who enjoyed an unusual institutional advantage—their political party controlled both legislative chambers. Nearly two-thirds of the Congresses elected since World War II were either split between the parties or faced a president of the opposing party. Figure 9.6 shows that Roosevelt and Johnson profited from exceptional majorities. Although Clinton and Bush had far smaller majorities, they did benefit from greater unity among their partisans—a factor that had eluded their predecessors.

A second similarity is that all four presidents treated their proposed reform as among their most important political and policy initiatives. Each saw their proposal as holding exceptional potential to shift the balance of party control, reconstitute the scope of government in the lives of individuals, and create a new philosophical orientation that would endure for generations.

Year	President	Size of Party House	Majority Senate
1935	Franklin Roosevelt (Democrat)	Dem +219	Dem +44
1965	Lyndon Johnson (Democrat)	Dem +155	Dem +36
1994	Bill Clinton (Democrat)	Dem +82	Dem +14
2005	George W. Bush (Republican)	Rep +30	Rep +11

Figure 9.6. Unified party government and presidential leadership

We suggest below that presidential strategy varied based on the development of the institutional capacity for policy promotions and the associated impact on the White House's political calculations. During the period before the promotional presidency was robustly institutionalized, Roosevelt and Johnson pursued conservative political strategies that explicitly acknowledged congressional resistance by omitting health insurance and coverage of medical costs, respectively. By contrast, Clinton and Bush were buoyed by their confidence in the presidency's institutional capacity to mobilize public opinion and thereby move policy makers; their signature proposals to remake large and complicated programs were politically implausible given the resistance of stakeholders, the general public, and members of their own parties in Congress.

The Conservative Institutionalists: Roosevelt and Johnson

Roosevelt and Johnson stand as the apostles of expanded government activism and are held up by supporters and opponents alike as cementing the Democratic Party's reputation for starting America's liberal welfare state. They are also counted among the most skilled and tenacious presidents in promoting change and exerting influence. It is striking, then, to think of them as institutionally conservative (at least compared to their successors), but their approaches to enacting priority domestic policy not only accepted the legislative branch's constitutional authority but compromised with the partisan and ideological distributions in Congress. The accommodation not only occurred during negotiations but also showed up in self-imposed restrictions that anticipated and accepted Congress and the preferences of legislators.

Roosevelt's and Johnson's conservative institutionalism on priority domestic policy is particularly notable given their extraordinary political strength and what would seem like ideal conditions for presidential trampling of opponents. As we discussed above, both presidents enjoyed unusually large majorities; although they faced a bipartisan coalition of conservatives, the size of their majorities and the social movements propelling their cause gave them unusual political strength in Congress. In addition, their legislative agenda was fueled by large and well-organized movements—the Townsend movement for Roosevelt and the Civil Rights and poor people's movement for Johnson. Moreover, each president exhibited an infamous hunger for power and mastery of politics; they certainly showed no personal predilection toward conservative institutionalism.

FRANKLIN DELANO ROOSEVELT AND THE OMISSION OF NATIONAL HEALTH INSURANCE

FDR was inaugurated in March in 1933 at a time of exceptional economic and political breakdown and turmoil. The crisis created a rare opportunity for bold action that broke with America's previous tradition of delegating sustained social and economic provision to the private sector and ad hoc local and state government programs.

Economic contractions and financial breakdowns put millions of Americans out of work and in desperate conditions. Millions more lived in fear that they too would lose their jobs and suffer deep deprivations; even a handful of years after the stock market crash, Americans were "uneasy, still-frightened, and longing for certainty" (Tugwell 1957, 334). By the spring of 1933, the run on banks prompted 38 states to close them and others operated them on a restricted basis. From 1929 to 1933, the number of people receiving assistance from state government increased approximately a hundredfold, from 1,000 to over 100,000, and the expense rose twenty-fivefold (Chambers 1963, 267; Leuchtenberg 1963, 38–41; Schlesinger 1959).

Franklin D. Roosevelt enjoyed enormous popular support. His leadership was rewarded during the 1934 midterm elections with a ringing national endorsement; the Democratic Party won remarkable gains in the elections for Congress, governorships, and other races. The economic and political breakdown created a groundswell of support and expectation that the federal government under Roosevelt's leadership would take the lead in making bold changes to restore the economy and stabilize the political order. As one commentator noted at the time: "There is a country-wide dumping of responsibility on the Federal Government. . . . All the other powers—industry, commerce, finance, labor, farmer, householder, state and city—virtually abdicate in its favor. [For] once Washington is the center of activity and the states beyond are passive, waiting for direction" (quoted in Axinn and Levin 1975, 165).

By 1933, large sections of the middle and lower strata had become increasingly active, moving the discontent from the fringe into the mainstream of American politics. James Schlesinger (1960) chronicles the "rising hurricanes" of upheaval led by Huey Long's call to "share the wealth" and Francis Townsend's movement for pensions of $500 for Americans of 60 and older. (Roosevelt declared that Long was "one of the two most dangerous men in America; the other was General McArthur.) Of particular relevance to the later Social Security Act, Townsend mobilized millions behind his declaration that the "time had arrived when the citizenry must take charge of their government and repudiate the philosophy of want and hunger in a land of wealth and abundance."

Roosevelt's experience as governor of New York and life around politics equipped him with a supreme sense of how to draw power to him and then exercise it to its maximum effect. He also possessed an acute sensitivity to the demands of his time; the preeminent historian Richard Hoftstadter (1948, 410–11) declared that "[n]o personality has ever expressed the American popular temperament so accurately or with such exclusiveness."

Roosevelt's use of his enormous political power to respond to the nation's crises was tempered, however, by the realization that his power was constrained and competitively shared with Congress (even though his party enjoyed lopsided legislative majorities).

Roosevelt's initial set of proposed legislation (the "First New Deal") attempted to resolve the country's problems by fostering the cooperation of federal bureaucrats and influential businessmen (Leuchtenberg 1963, 67). Among the programs enacted in 1933 were the National Industrial Recovery Act and its administrative arm, the National Recovery Administration, as well as the more significant Agricultural Adjustment Act. The Federal Emergency Relief Act in May 1933 dumped $500 million into existing state and local distribution channels (Schlesinger 1959, 267–9). Caution was the defining characteristic of this first set of federal responses in 1933; these acts were often temporary interventions and administered through existing state and local entities.

The Social Security Act emerged during the "Second New Deal" and laid the foundation for the American welfare state. By 1935, the First New Deal's programs were, according to historian Arthur Schlesinger, "faltering" under the weight of the ongoing economic downturn and were revealed as having "gone about as far as they could" (Schlesinger 1960, 2–3). Organized labor along with social movements led by Long, Townsend, and others clamored for far-reaching change, as did the newly elected Democrats who rode to office on the wave of support for the New Deal and tackling the country's economic collapse. Roosevelt came under growing political pressure to take bolder action. His initial supporters were now pressing him to go beyond the cautious First New Deal; some of his aides worried in 1934 and early 1935 that failure to satisfy these expectations could—if not addressed—hurt his re-election in 1936 (Burns 1956, 214; Schlesinger 1960, 4–7).

The door was now open to far-reaching change. With the possible exception of Abraham Lincoln, no other president enjoyed as much political latitude as Franklin Roosevelt in 1935. In the context of economic and political crisis, old shibboleths against national government activism in protecting and assisting individuals faded as the administration looked for "new political instrumentalities." The president concluded that it was "difficult to solve [the country's problems] piecemeal" and promised the nation "the security of the home, security of livelihood, and the security of social insurance" (Witte 1962, 6). The demand for bold change created political opportunity for Roosevelt: a "more complete plan" brought "maximum political effect" in unifying members of Congress (Schlesinger 1959, 304).

Roosevelt's actions were bold but notably reserved in one respect that continues to astound scholars and Democratic activists—he established a system of government financial support for senior citizens, the unemployed, and the poor but refused even to propose a health insurance program. In June 1934, Roosevelt gave a special message to Congress that promised a proposal to provide social security to Americans and established by Executive Order the Committee on Economic Security (CES). He instructed the Committee to draft a "new type" of bill that had "never come before the Congress" (Witte 1962, p. viii).

Roosevelt instructed the CES to make social insurance "national in scope...leaving to the Federal Government the responsibility of investing, maintaining, and safeguarding the funds" (quoted in Witte 1962, 6; Leuchtenberg 1963, 333; Perkins 1946). In scaling the old barriers against national government activism, Roosevelt wanted to move away from the "business of relief" and toward the more popular work of serving the respectable "employables" (quoted in Leuchtenberg 1963, 124).

At its first meeting in August 1934, the CES Executive Committee set out to develop a program that provided "protection of the individual against dependency and distress...[that] includes all forms of social insurance" (Social Security Administration). One of the Committee's four working groups was assigned the job of formulating a program to establish health insurance (the other working groups designed programs for unemployment insurance, public employment and relief, and old age security). The CES identified the cost of medical care as a major drain on the incomes of Americans and on their well-being. They assured the president that it could be administered using the contributory framework developed for old age insurance (OAI). The same political benefits of relying on "contributions rather than by an increase in general taxation" that Roosevelt identified for pensions in June 1934 extended to health insurance (Altmeyer 1966, 3; Witte 1962). This contributory approach would—Roosevelt explained—"give contributors a legal, moral, and political right [to their benefits]. With those [contributory] taxes in there, no damn politician can ever scrap my social security program" (quoted in Leuchtenberg 1963, 133).

The combination of Roosevelt's political dominance and the Committee's health insurance program arguably put America as close as it has ever come to creating a comprehensive government mechanism for financing medical care. The executive director of CES (Edwin Witte) explained in 1934 that the program designed by the Committee created "for the first time...a real prospect for the development of a program which will meet the crying need for the better distribution of the economic costs of illness in a way which will be fair and just to the men and women who devote their lives to the care of the sick" (Witte 1934).

Based on the Committee's work, Roosevelt presented legislation to Congress in January 1935 that led to the establishment of the old age insurance system that forms the core of what is now known as "Social Security."[6] One of Roosevelt's most historically consequential domestic policy decisions was to exclude health insurance from his Social Security legislation. Although one of Roosevelt's closest advisers (Harry Hopkins) strongly argued for including health insurance in the administration's package of protections, the president took the cautious advice of other administration officials (Frances Perkins and Arthur Altmeyer) to minimize opposition from Congress and the medical profession (Social Security Administration; Witte 1934).

Roosevelt decided it was more important and appropriate to reduce the risk of opposition than to press forward in pursuit of his preferred policy goal of a comprehensive package of social insurance protections. The old age insurance program, which would have formed the tandem program to a national health insurance program, did face some congressional opposition. In particular, Senators proposed that businesses with their own pension plans be allowed to opt out of OAI, but Roosevelt and his allies defeated this and other amendments.

By modern standards, Roosevelt's calculations are conservative and modest. He imposed on himself a significant (perhaps historic) compromise instead of pressing his enormous political advantage to secure a fuller set of his policy goals. The president's remarkably strong political position delivered a rare accomplishment—his restrained proposal made it through Congress essentially without serious revision (Witte 1962). When he signed it into law on 15 August, he achieved another remarkable accomplishment—his proposal made it through the House and Senate in just over half a year. Roosevelt saw himself as a "bridge between an old and new America"; he exerted significant self-restraint on what he would bring across that bridge (Tugwell 1957, 9).

Roosevelt's restrained approach to his main social policy initiative did coincide with bold action on other fronts; the complexity of his presidency defies simplistic and uniform conclusions. One of his most striking initiatives was to "pack" the US Supreme Court with his supporters in order to overcome its opposition to New Deal legislation. The number of justices on the Court is set by statute; the US Constitution is silent on it. Roosevelt proposed legislation to allow the president to appoint one judge for each sitting justice over age 70 and six months with at least ten years of experience.

Although Roosevelt's plan was brash, it actually illustrates in certain respects his fidelity to established institutions: he pursued his plan through the normal legislative process rather than attempting to circumvent it and he accepted his proposal's rejection rather than launching a sustained public campaign to try to force a victory and attempting to challenge the independent authority of the legislative branch.

LYNDON B. JOHNSON DEFERS TO CONGRESS
IN DESIGNING MEDICARE

Lyndon Johnson was dealt the political equivalent of a royal flush in 1965.[7] Johnson's victory over Republican nominee Barry Goldwater was apparent to the White House well in advance of Election Day. "[A]bsolutely certain" of victory early in the campaign, the Johnson team concentrated on using the campaign to define the agenda *after* the election. By the early summer of 1964, senior White House officials agreed that the president had "an opportunity... to shape the mandate he wants and needs."[8]

Months before Election Day, policy specialists were assembled to design specific policies for after the election. The campaign ranked the enactment of Medicare at the top of Johnson's "must" list. During the campaign, Johnson heavily promoted Medicare to prime the public and Washington for its passage, and his aides prepared to introduce legislation soon after Johnson's anticipated inauguration.

Although Johnson's team expected him to win, the magnitude of his victory and the scope of Democratic gains in Congress exceeded expectations. The Democratic landslide delivered a clear and unambiguous mandate for strong presidential initiative. Johnson fully appreciated his extraordinary political opportunity; officials in the executive branch department responsible for formulating Medicare described it as a "singular moment in history."[9] The president was ready to seize the moment, according to aides, by "whipping his staff into... [a] frenzy" within hours of the polls closing.

Members of Congress in both parties accepted Johnson's mandate, conceding that the passage of Medicare was a foregone conclusion. Symbolic of its top ranking, Democratic leaders designated it HR.1 and S.1 as the first legislation introduced into the new Congress. Conservative Democrats, who had previously held back in supporting Medicare after John Kennedy had introduced it in 1961, openly accepted that its passage was imminent. Even Republican leaders ceded to plain reality; they abandoned their previous stubborn opposition to health reform for seniors and put forward their own health insurance proposal. As one liberal Senator observed, "innovation by Republicans and conservative Democrats... [became] a sensible strategy."[10]

Opposition from the American Medical Association (AMA) lost its potency in the wake of Johnson's 1964 landslide. For decades, the AMA had bottlenecked reform through expensive advertising campaigns; it had run the first million dollar advertising blitz to defeat a policy proposal. In 1965, however, the threats of doctors to boycott Medicare and the ramping-up of another massive advertising blitz were largely ignored. It was dismissed as a "nuisance" by Democratic and Republican leaders for its "blind refusal to accept reality." Indicative of its isolation, the AMA was excluded from unofficial committee discussions and its testimony was derided for "spout[ing] the usual nonsense" and failing to respond to Congress's narrow need for the medical profession's technical advice on specific questions (Harris 1966, 179–80, 184–5).

Although Johnson's political position was Olympian, he pursued a strikingly conservative institutional approach to his top domestic priority. The content of his Medicare legislation was remarkably constrained, falling far short of what Congress would accept and the public expected. Instead of expanding on the Medicare legislation that he had previously proposed, Johnson insisted that the administration "stick with what we've got and not change horses in the middle of the stream." His principal health policy specialist (Wilbur Cohen) followed his lead by working to "keep a lot of things out."[11]

The gap between Johnson's enormous political capital and the conservatism of his Medicare proposal in 1965 was readily apparent in several ways. First, the administration's plan closely followed the one designed by John Kennedy, largely focusing on covering a limited number of days of hospitalization. In other words, the president with the electoral landslide sought no added political advantage over his predecessor who came into office with a weak and contested mandate after his razor-close win over Richard Nixon in 1960. Second, the conservatism of Johnson's proposal quickly became a political liability. Republicans actually criticized it as inadequate; congressional witnesses chastised it for only paying for a hospital bed but not the care that would be received in it. Third, his plan fell far short of what Americans expected. Shortly after his re-election, only 40 per cent of Americans correctly knew that the president's proposal did not cover physician fees (Schiltz 1970, 142).

Much like F.D.R., Johnson deferred to Congress. Johnson's deference could be considered a clever strategy for inviting Congress to take political ownership of his plan; but even this strategy rests on presidential acknowledgement of collaborative lawmaking—an acknowledgement that is anathema to later presidents Clinton and Bush. Instead, Johnson's approach appears to reflect a form (perhaps a norm) of institutional self-restraint—one that stands in stark contrast to his personal bluster. Officials in his administration insisted that their devotion was to "moderation" and "stand[ing] for all that is...calm and steady." Johnson and administration officials saw themselves as the "true moderates" that were committed to avoiding "excessive, drastic...and radical" measures. Johnson's outsized personality was channeled by a governing norm that favored building a "broad consensus...[behind] cooperative efforts."[12]

Johnson's legislation fell so far short of public expectations that the conservative Democratic chair of the House Ways and Means Committee (Wilbur Mills) felt compelled to step in. He found the president's proposal "too conservative...and too limited."[13] Although Mills was leery of government intervention, he also feared that failure to respond to strong public pressure would invite a steady march for expanded benefits. He sought to build "fences" around the program to contain future public demands (Marmor 1973).

Instead of the president pushing his clear political advantage, it was a conservative congressional Democrat who designed what became the foundation of government health insurance. Mills added Part B to Medicare, which covers physicians and outpatient services, and Medicaid for the indigent. Johnson's proposal omitted both of these essential components of the American health financial system.

Congress enacted Mills's expanded Medicare bill with no significant revisions. It won in the House by a 315 : 115 margin and in the Senate 68 : 12. The report of the Conference Committee, which largely followed Mills's handiwork, was also passed by lopsided margins—307 : 116 and 70 : 24.

Promotional Presidents and the Presumption of Institutional Dominance

The capacity of recent presidents to promote themselves and their policies has fostered a presumption of power within the White House and a shift from the governing norm in the Roosevelt and Johnson administrations—namely, that institutional and political parameters define and delimit presidential power. This presumed institutional dominance flows from the White House's elaborate apparatus for presidential promotion, which has both equipped the president with new capacities and inflated the White House's political self-assurance. Of course, presidential promotion and the erosion of institutional self-restraint and induced collaboration has also been fueled by other factors including political polarization, which motivate contemporary politicians to place greater strategic importance on single-mindedly pursuing policy goals.

BILL CLINTON'S OVERREACHING HEALTH PLAN AND POLITICAL COLLAPSE

The successive victories of Ronald Reagan and George H. W. Bush fueled a boutique cottage industry of books and articles that foretold an enduring Republican advantage and perhaps lock on the White House. Political prognosticators speculated that American voters were guided by a Madisonian temperament in strategically splitting political control of the lawmaking branches; others pointed to the differential skills of congressional Democrats to distribute pork and Republican presidents to respond to the broad philosophical conservatism of post-Great Society America.

Bill Clinton appeared to turn the world upside down in 1992 not only by surviving his first round of publicized salacious encounters but by defying the supposed Republican lock on the White House and voters' tilt toward divided government.[14] The Democratic sweep of the White House and both chambers of Congress created substantial institutional opportunities.

Despite this breakthrough, Clinton's institutional position was constrained. The president defeated George H. W. Bush with only 43 per cent of the vote (Bush received 37 per cent and Ross Perot picked up 19 per cent). Unlike Johnson, Clinton lacked a clear mandate. In addition, Democrats enjoyed an 82-seat margin in the House (258 to 176) but were three seats short of the 60 votes to defeat a filibuster. Indeed, the Party's historically modest majorities were somewhat mitigated by internal fissures.

After his package of proposals to stimulate the economy, Clinton's top domestic priority was comprehensive health care reform. The set of general institutional constraints that faced him were compounded in the area of health policy by three additional complications that White House officials incompletely appreciated as imposing severe restraints on them. First, unlike Kennedy and Johnson who inherited a reform approach that unified Democratic policy circles and was respected by independent health experts, Clinton faced a civil war over how to proceed. Democratic policy circles were split among advocates of a Canadian-style single payer approach, efforts to expand competition among health plans and providers through private markets, and incremental expansions of Medicare to "near retirees" and uninsured children. Clinton's aides as well as congressional leaders were convinced that no approach had a "majority behind it."[15] Clinton's top health policy aide Ira Magaziner described these competing clusters as "theologians who are prepared to wage holy war on behalf of their own ideologies."[16] The negative consensus on the failings of the health care system did not translate into an affirmative consensus on how to proceed forward.

Second, members of Congress and, especially, senior Democrats jealously guarded their institutional prerogatives and suspiciously eyed the White House as pretentious "outsiders" uninformed about the "ways of Washington" and the workings of national health policy. Congressional leaders and their staff fumed that White House invitations to discussions mocked their pecking order by treating "all staff as co-equal when Dan Rostenkowski's representative is not equal to Joe Blow congressman's junior assistant who happens to handle health."[17] In addition, the congressional process set fairly fixed restrictions on how it handled the President's proposal. Although the White House sought to insert its proposal into the budget reconciliation process in Congress in order to expedite its treatment and avoid a potential filibuster, congressional leaders refused because of existing rules and the limits on the capacity of committees to handle health care legislation at the same time as the budget.

Third, Clinton's health plan faced determined and sophisticated opposition from the outset. Most congressional Republicans were fierce opponents. Shortly after Clinton's electrifying national address introducing his proposal in September 1993, Republican strategist Bill Kristol openly called for the "defeat of the President's plan outright" instead of holding out for compromise legislation; he recommended an "aggressive and uncompromising counter-strategy."[18] The coming battle for the Party's 1996 nomination pressured the pragmatic Senate minority leader Bob Dole into working with hard-edged partisans to deny a major victory for the Democrats. In addition, Clinton's plan was intensely resisted by a diverse set of health care interest groups—especially representatives of small, medium, and large businesses, which had politically effective federated roots into congressional districts throughout the country.

Despite these significant barriers (obstacles that were collectively more imposing than those facing the politically better-positioned Roosevelt and Johnson), the Clinton team came to Washington convinced that their intelligence and the "merits of our case" as pioneering "New Democrats" gave them a dominating position in Washington. They often derided experienced health policy specialists and congressional Democrats as "Old Democrats." The Clinton team considered them out of touch with new ideas for incorporating the private sector and economic competition in government policy to offer "conservative means to liberal ends."[19] To members of Congress and other Washingtonians, the Clinton gang were "arrogant" and certain that the views of others could be "fit into their framework, interpret[ted] back in their own way and move[d] beyond."[20]

The Clinton White House worked to mold Congress to its will. The president viewed members of Congress as "independent operators" who could only be herded into coalitions by presidential success in mobilizing the public. Clinton's success in "shap[ing] public opinion" was expected to create "pressure that is reflected back to Congress." The critical assumption within the Clinton White House was that it could—with the correct strategy—"go out and sell a program to the public" and therefore as the president explained, "create new political capital all the time."[21] The key to success was to develop a message and "say it over and over again."

The White House's political strategy for passing its health plan rested, aides explained, on a carefully choreographed and "massive public communications campaign" that "deliberately and relentlessly communicated [its] health care message." The delivery mechanism for this promotional strategy was the White House's well-developed routines for honing the president's message and transmitting it directly and indirectly (through the media) to Americans.[22]

Even as the congressional process bogged down and Washingtonians could see the Clinton health plan heading for defeat, the White House stubbornly

311

clung to the conviction that public promotions would mobilize Americans and then compel members to sign on. Ira Magaziner warned against the costs of settling for less than comprehensive coverage and remained confident that Congress could be turned around. The president agreed and the White House refused to "imagine a scenario where we go to Plan B, which rolls our plan out in detachable pieces that goes into the next Congress." This unmoving insistence on the White House's basic approach flew in the face of the advice from seasoned congressional leaders; they recommended that the president shift to supporting incremental reforms that would extend Medicare's coverage to children and near seniors. Clinton would come to consider this intransigence a "blunder" as he came to embrace just these incremental reforms during his second term.[23]

The White House came to blame its defeat on tactical mistakes in crafting and delivering its message and on the failure of allies to amplify its message to Americans. But this account continues the myth that presidents can "shape public opinion," as Clinton and his aides confidently expected, and that this capacity allows them to preempt the Madisonian bulwarks against institutional domination. The Clinton White House's mistake was in presuming that presidents wield the capacity to "win" public opinion, which enables them to overcome institutional obstacles. The reality is that even laboriously drawn communications plans that are executed by a routinized and sophisticated promotional apparatus cannot consistently overcome resistance by interest groups, partisan divisions, and the interbranch tensions infused in a separation of powers system.

GEORGE W. BUSH OVERDRAWS POLITICAL CAPITAL ON SOCIAL SECURITY

For generations of political scientists who had championed the glories of responsible party government (American Political Science Association, 1950), the twenty-first century dawned with a startling realization: political parties were voting in Congress as durable unified blocks and Republicans were engaging in extensive interbranch cooperation. Many of the hoped-for benefits of responsible government emerged: ample, significant lawmaking instead of "deadlock and delay" and programmatic party platforms that offered voters clear and divergent policy choices for which elected officials could be held accountable. Characteristics of party government that had been overlooked by its American enthusiasts caught the notice of political observers and sparked renewed attention to the previously underappreciated benefits of the Madisonian system: moderates that had defied party discipline in the past were replaced by uncompromising partisans, and civil cooperation among lawmakers who regularly worked together in forming coalitions across party lines was replaced by tightly organized party caucuses that often ignored and locked out members of the minority party. With the filibuster teetering on the edge of abolition in a drive to sweep away obstacles to party government, the loudest voices call for Hamiltonian national energy, efficiency, and productivity; today's dissidents are regrouping around Madison's Newtonian system for stymied government.

As political observers searched to regain their bearings, the American political process gave birth after the 9/11 terrorist attacks to a supercharged presidency that wielded prerogative powers on national security matters and, of particular relevance for this chapter, wide institutional sway over the legislative process. Especially after the 2002 mid-term elections that gave Republicans a reliable two-seat majority in the Senate and expanded its majority in the House from 9 to 25 seats, Congress appeared to conform to President Bush's will.[24] The partisan and ideological unity among Republicans in Congress and the White House created a cohesive and potent juggernaut in which presidential positions routinely prevailed in law, seemingly reversing generations of research that catalogued the White House's legislative impotence (e.g. Wayne 1978). To enhance the effectiveness of his agenda setting, Bush substantially reduced his public position by taking to relatively few stances (Poole 2006).

Partially privatizing Social Security was to culminate the emergence of Republican Party government. The White House expected Social Security reform to be "one of the most significant conservative governing achievements ever," which would spearhead its effort to form an enduring Republican majority by attracting a new generation of younger and independent voters (quoted in Stevenson 2005; Chen 2003).

Hours after he won the 2004 election, President Bush emerged to claim a mandate to reform Social Security and launched—as his aides explained to reporters—a "public relations campaign to [establish] a system of private savings accounts." Conservative columnist Fred Barnes applauded Bush's promotion of Social Security privatization for demonstrating his uniqueness as a "conservative with the disposition of a radical" who "set[s] the bar very high...use[s] every bit of political capital and personal influence...to achieve [his] goals...and [was] ready to take chances." Rove similarly argued for "proactive, bold, [and] energetic" leadership for a "history-shaping moment" (Barnes 2005).

Well before Bush's crusade for Social Security privatization in 2005, the White House and congressional Republicans fully appreciated the resistance of voters, stakeholders, and many Republicans as well as unified Democratic opposition. Even before Bush's re-election campaign in 2004, the Republican-controlled House overwhelming passed a resolution against *full* privatization of Social Security politically to inoculate themselves from Democratic attacks; the resolution was clearly for show as all authoritative proposals focused on *partial* privatization. In the run-up to the 2002 congressional elections, some congressional Republicans pleaded with Bush to "stop talking about Social Security reform" and privately hoped he "doesn't utter one word about it." As Bush launched his campaign in 2005, the obstacles were clearly evident: a supportive Republican House leader confessed to feeling "a political queasiness and concern that this is a risky political venture" while another leader worried that Bush's proposal pushed the GOP "way out there beyond our defenses" given voters' enduring trust of Democrats on Social Security (Allen 2005; Andrews 2004a; Hook 2003; Morgan 2004; Ponnuru 2005; Stevenson 2005; Toner and Rosenbaum 2004; VandeHei and Eilperin 2002).

Despite these demonstrated signs of opposition and unease, the White House was convinced that these could be overcome through a "major public campaign to sell the nation" (Andrews 2004a). The game plan was straight-forward: presidential presentations that were poll-honed to resonate with existing public attitudes (both worry about government competence and support for greater choice and ownership) were expected to build strong public backing for the President's plan that would reassure uneasy or waffling legislators and even convert some naysayers.

Days after Bush was re-elected, the White House's public promotions wing moved into action—one administration ally explained—with all the weapons used in its "election campaign but [for] an issue rather than a candidate." The Social Security campaign deployed many of the White House's institutional capabilities that had built up since McKinley: a steady feeding and managing of the press corps to saturate the airwaves with the White House's agenda and particular presentation, presidential speeches calibrated to appeal to public opinion through extensive polling, television and radio advertisements by allied groups, and the mobilization of the cabinet to blanket the country with the same message (Morgan 2004; Stevenson 2004). The White House commit-ted these capabilities toward achieving precisely defined strategic objectives: establish a sense of urgency about the "problem" (or, as the White House put it, "crisis") that must be addressed to avert "bankruptcy" and flood the information system with precisely selected and alluring words that extolled the benefits of privatization (such as "choice" and "ownership") and obscured its costs (Allen and Eilperin 2002; Allen and Goldstein 2002; Andrews 2004b; Havemann 2004; Stevenson 2004; Weisman 2002).

Bush kicked off his "offensive" through his most powerful promotional platform—the State of the Union address. He then started a half year of intensive travel around the country, starting with visits to the home states of Democratic senators that had strongly supported the president in the 2004 elections (Allen 2005).

Even as the president's travel blitz failed to ignite public support by the spring of 2005 and became the subject of ridicule for late night comedy shows, the White House persisted in expecting Bush's promotions to rally the public and to congeal a supportive coalition in Congress. Faced with continuing legislative resistance, the President complained during his second trip to Kentucky in March that the problem was "too much politics," apparently considering his barnstorming to 27 states to be non-political. Indeed, according to the *Washington Post*, he "vowed to overcome [the continuing opposition] by continuing to take his case directly to the public" (Fletcher 2005).

By the fall of 2005, the White House's strategy had not only failed but had contributed to the general perception of Bush's falling political fortunes on several fronts including Iraq. As in the final stages of Clinton's efforts on health reform, the Bush Administration remained wedded to its approach and did not pursue incremental approaches recommended by seasoned Republican leaders such as Congressman Bill Thomas. Principled defeat appeared preferable to pragmatic compromise.

Despite Bush's extraordinary institutional position, he was unable to get even a single vote on his proposal. Congressional Republicans refused to bring his plan to a vote on the floor of either the House or Senate and no congressional committee voted on it. President Bush's expenditure of his much ballyhooed "political capital" produced no tangible benefit.

The startling congressional rebuff of Bush stemmed from a combination of familiar and new obstacles to presidential dominance—factors that were well-known before Bush's crusade in 2005 and that the White House calculated would be overcome by deploying the White House's promotional capacities.

Despite Bush's past success in Congress and assertion of constitutional prerogatives, party government remained conditional in several respects. Madison's system wired institutional and personal incentives for members of each branch—despite shared policy goals—to retain separate political identities and calculations. The two-year electoral cycle in Congress along with the limit on presidential terms intensified the focus of Republican legislators (especially after the 2004 elections) on immediate electoral conditions as opposed to the president's longer-term orientation to securing his historical legacy. While the White House dismissed polls, Congressional Republicans became increasingly concerned with each passing month of Bush's second term about the growing chorus of complaints from voters about the quagmire in Iraq, soaring gas prices, and other difficulties. As legislators focused on their own electoral mortality, the White House's unity with Congressional Republican majorities became whipsawed between the small but still indispensable group of Party moderates who defected (or threatened to defect) to the Democrats on critical floor votes and GOP stalwarts from conservative districts who increasingly insisted on returning to Party principles by cutting government spending and taxes and by protecting "law and order" through such measures as new restrictions on illegal immigration. Blocking coalitions of Republican legislators formed against either cutting benefits or raising the budget deficit to reform

Social Security. Although the filibuster remains on political life support, Senate Republicans continued to be compelled to compromise with Democrats in order to avoid filibusters—some of which have been supported by Republican moderates.

The enduring institutional impediments to Bush's Social Security campaign were reinforced by the immediate difficulties in navigating this policy area. Bush's closest Capitol Hill allies—Republican members of Congress—splintered and at times openly fought with each other. The differences arose in part from policy disputes. Some Republicans advocated large private accounts, allowing workers to redirect 4 percentage points of their 6.2 per cent payroll taxes, while others favored a more modest approach that would redirect 1 or 2 percentage points. Ferocious disputes erupted among Republicans over whether to consider increasing payroll taxes to pay for the costs of the new private accounts, with Republican Senator Lindsey Graham (SC) calling for raising the ceiling on payroll taxes for high-income workers. As most Republicans recoiled at raising taxes, the option of reducing benefits was the next logical place to make the program solvent—a central promise of Republican reforms. Even though the White House and many other Republicans preferred to cut benefits over increasing taxes, they tried to avoid public acknowledgment of these highly unpopular costs, which fueled criticism both from Democrats and other critics as well as from fiscal conservatives such as Senator Graham who called for an end to "Band-Aid solutions" and for an honest proposal that achieved solvency without "kick[ing] the can down the road" (quoted in Andrews 2004a). Republicans were fighting over not only taxes but also making the tough decisions about benefits, with former House Speaker Newt Gingrich deriding the White House's plan to reduce benefits as "political suicide" (Andrews 2004a; Hook 2003; Morgan 2004; Ponnuru 2005; Stevenson 2005; Toner and Rosenbaum 2004; VandeHei and Eilperin 2002).

Ready to lead, George Bush—not unlike Bill Clinton—found no clear approach to address an issue that his Party agreed was a fundamental problem: there was a negative consensus on the problem but no positive consensus that the president could promote. In addition to the disarray among Republicans, organized labor and powerful associations of seniors such as AARP were well coordinated and part of a broad coalition of one hundred groups dubbed the "New Century Alliance for Social Security." AARP's chief took to the airwaves to slam Bush's proposal as imposing "$2 trillion or more in benefit cuts, new taxes, or more debt" (Andrews 2004a and b). The opposition of stakeholders was amplified by the unified opposition of Democrats. Capitalizing on the public's growing doubts about the White House's credibility on Iraq and other policies, a Democratic spokesman warned that the "administration's blitz on Social Security is eerily reminiscent of the way they made their case for war" (Morgan 2004; Stevenson 2004).

The confluence of Republican infighting and furious attacks by Bush's opponents meant (as one reform advocate put it) that "both sides are priming the public to be against anything that is real reform" by "making the debate more partisan, more contentious and less beneficial to the public" (Weisman 2002). The demise of Bush's Social Security proposal is not surprising; many of the fatal political dynamics that led to defeat were predicted well before the president's campaign. What remain analytically noteworthy are the White House calculations—its unwavering confidence in its promotional capacities to overcome near certain opposition and refusal to fall back to a proposal that would accommodate known political blockages. Despite presidential presumptions, party government remains conditional not only on party control but also on institutionally induced electoral interests. Members of Congress—even those who share Bush's partisan and ideological orientations—remain largely autonomous and highly motivated to protect and promote their positions. The White House's intensive campaign to mobilize public support failed to win over Americans, and even Republican legislators remained convinced that the clear costs of the president's proposal would be traced back to them—to their electoral detriment.

Whigs for a New Age: Government Activism and Inter-Branch Collaboration

New forms of political mobilization echo and give shape to longstanding debates over the purpose and institutional contours of political authority in America. Recent developments in presidential promotions are layered on top of enduring debates crystallized by the framers of the US Constitution. The foundation of the US Constitution is, of course, the separation and counteracting of constitutional powers. There has also been, however, a powerful tug of war over the relative distribution of authority among the lawmaking branches. Although popular fears focused on the resurgence of a monarchy, the *Federalist Papers* repeatedly flagged the potential for legislative usurpation of executive powers. This tension in the American constitutional system, as with others, was left unresolved: as James Madison reasoned for a Newtonian counterbalancing structure in Federalist Papers 10 and 51, Alexander Hamilton forcefully outlined an energetic, proactive, and unitary executive in Federalist Papers 69, 70, and 71.

Contending interpretations of institutional authority burst into the open shortly after the Constitution's ratification, giving American voice to British eighteenth- and nineteenth-century debates between the Whigs who advocated legislative power and the Tories who promoted the power of the king. George Washington's declaration of American neutrality during the war between England and France (rebuffing the pro-French Jeffersonians) brought into full view the constitutional duel that had been simmering between Madison and Hamilton. Hamilton rushed forward to defend Washington's proclamation of a pro-British neutrality as justified by the executive's expansive enumerated and implied powers—authority that was limited only by expressed Constitutional grants in Article I—while Madison countered by defending legislative authority and institutionally hemming in the executive's.

The partisan tint of today's debate over a Republican president's actions on a range of issues from national security to social restrictions should not obscure the enduring and far-reaching implications of recent actions and arguments for constitutional authority in America. The current ascendance of Tory institutionalism is redrawing and legitimizing executive power and concerted and massive government action that may well be used later by a new president for quite different partisan and ideological purposes. *The ground is being prepared for new governing norms under conditions of unified party control.*

The new institutional Toryism in America has been cloaked in populism. The assertion of presidential power has been presented in the language of "the people" (a not unfamiliar formulation); it has been fueled by the expansion of institutional capacity for public presentations and by the growing White House expectations that Americans can be molded to fit its expectations.

Over time presidents have traveled more and increasingly talked directly (and indirectly) to Americans. President Bush has capitalized on the historic development of the White House's promotional capacities to attempt to rally the mass public for the purpose of forging supportive congressional coalitions: *the White House wields its institutional tools to tame Congress at the front of a populist pitchfork.* What is striking about the White House promotional activities is the interactions of institutions and presidential expectations: institutional development for routinized populism has reflected and fed White House expectations that public opinion can be shaped, that the White House has the capacity to shape public opinion, and that Congress can be bowed to presidential policy preferences by White House directed public pressure. The norm of accommodation that marked Roosevelt's and Johnson's monumental legislative programs has given way to an expectation of presidential domination.

Presidential efforts at legislative domination do not guarantee success in Congress; indeed, they might detract from it. Clinton's health reform initiative and Bush's Social Security crusade not only failed to produce new legislation but generated a political backlash—they set back efforts at incremental improvements and contributed to their party's political setbacks at the next midterm election.

In addition, both presidents squandered the remarkable institutional opportunities of unified government. Would Clinton and Bush have successfully enacted legislation if they followed the more accommodative approaches of Roosevelt and Johnson? Although no answer is clear, significant incremental proposals to extend Medicare to near retirees in 1993 and 1994 and to expand retirement plans to include a voluntary government program outside Social Security in the opening years of the twenty-first century would likely have won support from moderates in both parties and stood a higher probability of passing. These incremental approaches may have risked political defections among the extreme wings of each president's party, though the inflated expectations of these groups were themselves fanned by the president's maximalist promises. Tellingly, Clinton actually promoted Medicare extensions during his second term with the active support of Congressional Democrats.

The fundamental and perhaps paradoxical lesson is that enormous institutional capacities for presidential promotion appear to induce presidential presumptions of political mastery that are difficult to sustain and may lead to political backlash. Durable constraints continue to restrain presidential efforts at legislative dominance on domestic policy. Madison's system of competitive branches sharing power may be partly disabled by programmatically coherent unified government but the reality is that the president and legislators run in independent elections facing distinct constituents and possess their own reservoirs of authority. Moreover, even the White House's impressive institutional capacity to shape public opinion is restricted by the public's pre-existing attitudes, its reliance on alternative sources of information, and the avalanche of messages from political rivals and the media that contradict and challenge the president's presentations. In addition, the promotional presidency rests on the mistaken assumption that legislators routinely respond to public opinion as the Downsian model suggests. A growing body of research is demonstrating that party activists, contributors, lobbyists, wealthy Americans, and other vocal and well-organized groups have more influence on legislators and other policy makers than general public opinion (Bartels 2005; Jacobs and Page 2005; Jacobs and Skocpol 2005, ch. 3).

Institutional Toryism cannot be dismissed, though, as merely an idealistic or wrong-headed interpretation of the American political system. It is significant but its impact is conditional. Party control is a critical factor. Divided government activates Madisonian checks and poses a sturdy counter pressure to presidential self-aggrandizement. The Republican impeachment of Clinton in December 1998 may have misused constitutional means but it certainly displayed an energetic and active legislative branch. The White House's political and policy judgment of legislative preferences can also be decisive. Bush's public promotions of his first rounds of tax cuts succeeded in large part because they won broad support among his partisans as well as Democratic moderates.

Institutional Toryism has been building for some time and is unlikely to disappear quickly. It springs from Hamilton and courses through Woodrow Wilson's searing critique of "Congressional Government" for tawdry corruption and particularism and Morris Fiorina's (1989) autopsy of Congress as riven by collective action problems. This trajectory has been intensified by urgent national security threats during the Cold War and the aftermath of the 9/11 terrorist attacks.

America may well have crossed the Rubicon to a more assertive, if conditional, form of strong and secretive presidency. One of the ironies is that a Republican president carried out the boldest deployment of this institutional Toryism; he may have opened the door for a more politically astute liberal Democrat to capitalize on the new governing norms notably to expand the welfare state. Conservative beginnings may well produce liberal ends, a true perversion of traditional conservative concerns with means.

References

Aldrich, John. 1995. *Why Parties? The Origin and Transformation of Political Parties in America*. Chicago: University of Chicago Press.

Allen, Mike. 2002. "After His Bout With a Pretzel, President Turns to the Issues." *Washington Post*. 16 January, A4.

———2003. "Administration Launches Tax Cut Blitz." *Washington Post*. 19 April, A2.

———2005. "Congressional Republicans Agree To Launch Social Security Campaign." *Washington Post*. 31 January, A04.

——— and Juliet Eilperin. 2002. "Wary Words on Social Security, GOP Shunning Use of 'Privatization.'" *Washington Post*. 11 May.

——— and Goldstein, Amy. 2002. "Bush to Tout 'Retirement Security' Proposals." *Washington Post*. 28 February.

Altmeyer, Arthur. 1966. *The Formative Years of Social Security*. Madison: University of Wisconsin Press.

American Political Science Association. 1950. *Toward A More Responsible Two-Party System*. New York: Rinehart.

Andrews, Edmund. 2004*a*. "Bush Puts Social Security at Top of Economic Conference." *New York Times*. 16 December, A40.

———2004*b*. "Clamor Grows in the Privatization Debate." *New York Times*. 17 December.

Auletta, Ken. 2004. "Fortress Bush: How the White House Keeps the Press Under Control." *New Yorker*. 19 January, 53–65.

Axinn, June, and Levin, Herman. 1975. *Social Welfare: A History of the American Response to Need*. New York: Dodd, Mead.

Barnes, Fred. 2005. "Double or Nothing." *Weekly Standard*. 31 January.

Bartels, Larry. 2005. "Economic Inequality and Political Representation." Revised paper originally presented at the Annual Meeting of the American Political Science Association, Boston (August 2002).

Bond, Jon, and Fleisher, Richard. 1990. *The President in the Legislative Arena*. Chicago: University of Chicago Press.

Burns, James MacGregor. 1956. *Roosevelt: The Lion and the Fox*. New York: Harcourt, Brace.

_____ 1963. *The Deadlock of Democracy.* Englewood Cliffs, NJ: Prentice-Hall.

Canes-Wrone, Brandice. 2001. "The President's Legislative Influence from Public Appeals," *American Journal of Political Science* 45 (April 2001): 313–29.

Chambers, Clark. 1963. *Seedtime of Reform: American Social Services and Social Action, 1918–1933.* Minneapolis: University of Minnesota Press.

Chen, Edwin. 2003. "Now Directing Attention to Revamping Social Security." *Los Angeles Times.* 30 November.

Downs, Anthony. 1957. *An Economic Theory of Democracy.* New York: Harper & Row.

Edwards, George C. 1989. *At the Margins: Presidential Leadership of Congress.* New Haven: Yale University Press.

_____ 2006. *On Deaf Ears: The Limits of the Bully Pulpit.* New Haven: Yale University Press.

_____ and Wood, B. Dan. 1999. "Who Influences Whom? The President, Congress, and the Media." *American Political Science Review* 93 (June 1999): 327–344.

_____ Barrett, Andrew, and Peake, Jeffrey. 1997. "The Legislative Impact of Divided Government." *American Journal of Political Science* 41 (April): 545–63.

Eisinger, Robert. 2003. *The Evolution of Presidential Polling.* New York: Cambridge University Press.

Fiorina, Morris. 1989. *Congress: Keystone of the Washington Establishment.* 2nd edn. New Haven: Yale University Press.

Fletcher, Michael. 2005. "Bush Still Chief GOP Fundraiser Despite Flagging Polls." *Washington Post.* 3 June, A4.

Goodstein, Laurie, and Yardley, William. 2004. "President Benefits from Efforts to Build a Coalition of Religious Voters." *New York Times.* 5 November, A22.

Harris, Richard. 1966. *A Sacred Trust.* New York: New American Library.

Havemann, John. 2004. "Some Find Strong Pulse in Social Security." *Los Angeles Times.* 12 December.

Heith, Diane. 1998. "Staffing the White House Public Opinion Apparatus: 1969–1988." *Public Opinion Quarterly* 62: 165–89.

Hilderbrand, Robert. 1981. *People and Power: Executive Management of Public Opinion in Foreign Affairs, 1897–1921.* Chapel Hill: University of North Carolina Press.

Hofstadter, Richard. 1948. *The American Political Tradition.* New York: Alfred Knopf.

Hook, Janet. 2003. "GOP Divided Over Pushing Reform of Social Security," *Los Angeles Times.* 7 December.

Jacobs, Lawrence. 1992. "The Recoil Effect: Public Opinion and Policymaking in the U.S. and Britain." *Comparative Politics* 24 (January): 199–217.

_____ 1993. *The Health of Nations: Public Opinion and the Making of Health Policy in the U.S. and Britain.* Ithaca, NY: Cornell University Press.

_____ 2005. "Communicating from the White House: From Mass Communications to Specialized Constituencies," in Joel Aberbach and Mark Peterson (eds.), *Presidents and Bureaucrats: The Executive Branch and American Democracy.* New York: Oxford University Press.

_____ and Page, Benjamin I. 2005. "Who Influences U.S. Foreign Policy?" *American Political Science Review* 99 (February): 107–24.

_____ and Shapiro, Robert Y. 2000. *Politicians Don't Pander: Political Manipulation and the Loss of Democratic Responsiveness.* Chicago: Chicago University Press.

Jacobs, Lawrence, and Skocpol, Theda (eds.) 2005. *Inequality and American Democracy: What We Know and What We Need to Learn*. New York: Russell Sage Foundation.

——Page, Benjamin I.; McAvoy, Gregory; Burns, Melanie; and Ostermeier, Eric. "What Presidents Talk About: The Nixon Case." *Presidential Studies Quarterly* (December 2003): 751–71.

Kernell, Samuel. 1997. *Going Public: New Strategies of Presidential Leadership*. 3rd edn. Washington, DC: CQ Press.

Leuchtenberg, William. 1963. *Franklin D. Roosevelt and the New Deal, 1932–1940*. New York: Harper & Row.

McCarty, Nolan, Poole, Keith, and Rosenthal, Howard. 2006. *Polarized America: The Dance of Ideology and Unequal Riches*. Cambridge: MIT.

Marmor, Theodore. 1973. *The Politics of Medicare*. Chicago: Aldine.

Morgan, David. 2004. "Bush Plans a Media Blitz on Social Security." Reuters. 22 December.

Perkins, Frances. 1946. *The Roosevelt I Knew*. New York: Viking.

Poole, Isaiah. 2006. "Presidential Support: Two Steps Up, One Step Down." *Congressional Quarterly Weekly Report*, 9 January, 80–6.

Ponnuru, Ramesh. 2005. "The Case against Benefit Cuts." National Review Online. 7 January.

Rohde, David. 1991. *Parties and Leaders in the Postreform House*. Chicago: University of Chicago Press.

Schiltz, Michael. 1970. *Public Attitudes toward Social Security, 1935–65*. Washington, DC: Government Printing Office.

Schlesinger, Arthur, Jr. 1959. *The Age of Roosevelt: The Coming of the New Deal*. Boston: Houghton Mifflin.

——1960. *The Age of Roosevelt: The Politics of Upheaval*. Boston: Houghton Mifflin.

Social Security Administration. "Committee on Economic Security: Unpublished Study on Health Insurance" ⟨http://www.ssa.gov/history/reports/cesmedical.html⟩, accessed 21 November 2006.

Sorensen, Theodore. 1965. *Kennedy*. New York: Bantam.

Steele, Richard. 1985. *Propaganda in an Open Society: The Roosevelt Administration and the Media, 1933–41*. Westport, Conn.: Greenwood.

Stevenson, Richard. 2003. "To Save Tax Cut, Bush Banks on Political Capital." *New York Times*. 21 April, A21.

——2004. "Bush Says Social Security Plan Would Reassure Markets." *New York Times*. 17 December.

——2005. "GOP Divide as Bush Views Social Security." *New York Times*. 6 January.

Toner, Robin, and Rosenbaum, David. 2004. "Social Security Poses Hurdles for President." *New York Times*. 18 September.

Tugwell, Rexford. 1957. *The Democratic Roosevelt*. New York: Doubleday.

Tulis, Jeffrey. 1987. *The Rhetorical Presidency*. Princeton: Princeton University Press.

Van Natta, Don; Goodnough, Abby; Drew, Christopher; and Yardley, William. 2004. "Bush Secured Victory in Florida by Veering from Beaten Path." *New York Times*. 7 November, 1A.

VandeHei, Jim, and Eilperin, Juliet. 2002. "Bush's Plan for Social Security Loses Favor." *Washington Post*. 13 August.

Wayne, Stephen. 1978. *The Legislative Presidency*. New York : Harper & Row.

Weisman, Jonathan. 2002. " 'In Politics, Words Matter,' Social Security Memo Says." *Washington Post*. 13 September.

Wilson, Woodrow. 1973. *Congressional Government*, Gloucester, Mass.: P. Smith.

Witte, Edwin. 1962. *The Development of the Social Security Act*. Madison: University of Wisconsin Press.

——— 1934. "The Health Insurance Study of the Committee on Economic Security." (Presumably written December 1934). Social Security Administration. ⟨http://www.ssa.gov/history/reports/wittemedical.html⟩, accessed 21 November 2006.

Notes

The author acknowledges the helpful comments of George Edwards and conference participants as well as the research assistance of Eric Ostermeier. Presented at "Politics and Polarization: The George W. Bush Presidency," RAI and Nuffield College, University of Oxford, 25–7 May 2006. Ljacobs@polisci.umn.edu

1. Unless otherwise noted, the discussion of the history of presidential press relations is based on Hilderbrand (1981).
2. This section is based on Auletta (2004); Goodstein and Yardley (2004), and Van Natta et al. (2004).
3. Kernell distinguished between "major addresses" by the president to a national audience over the radio or television and "minor addresses" that are delivered to special audiences (cf. Kernell 1997, ch. 4 and table 4.1). As we discuss below, our measures overlap with Kernell's but more precisely distinguish between public audiences and elite or specialized audiences.
4. We have not yet analyzed the addresses of presidents Jimmy Carter and George H. W. Bush.
5. Strong congressional support for Bush also reflects the determined efforts of leaders to control the agenda to avoid areas of disagreement (Poole 2006). The terrorist attacks on 9/11 also boosted support (especially among Democrats) for a short period.
6. Roosevelt's legislation also proposed unemployment insurance and public assistance for the elderly, dependent mothers and children, and the crippled and blind that were state administered rather than administered by the federal government as was the case with the old age insurance program.
7. This section is based on Jacobs (1993, ch. 9).
8. LBJ Library, CF LE, Box 61, Memo to Jack Valenti from Bill Moyers, just before 5/30/64.
9. LBJ Library, interview with Jack Valenti by J. Frantz, 3 March 1971 (Tape 1); Administrative Histories, HEW, vol.1, pt.1, Office of the Assistant Secretary for Legislation, Recollections of Michael Parker.
10. LBJ Library, Ex IS, Box 1, Letter from Larry O'Brien to C. P. Anderson, 27 August 1965.
11. Interview with Wilbur Cohen by L. Jacobs, 1 April 1987.

12. LBJ Library, Ex FG1, Box 10, memo from H. A. Knowles to Secretary of Commerce, 6 November 1964, forwarded to Bill Moyers, 10 November 1964.
13. Interview with Wilbur Mills by L. Jacobs, 18 June 1987.
14. This section is based in part on Jacobs and Shapiro (2000).
15. Quoted ibid. 82.
16. White House records, Memo from Ira Magaziner to Hillary Rodham Clinton, 3 May 1993.
17. Quoted in Jacobs and Shapiro (2000, 91).
18. Quoted ibid. 132.
19. Quoted ibid. 79–83.
20. Ibid. 81–2.
21. Ibid. 103–6.
22. Memo to Hillary Rodham Clinton from Bob Boorstin and Lois Quam, 6 February 1993; Memo to H. R. Clinton from Senator Jay Rockefeller, 26 May 1993.
23. Quoted ibid. 115, 84.
24. The 2000 congressional elections split the Senate into 50 Democrats and 50 Republicans, which allowed Vice President Cheney to break ties in favor of the GOP. The Republicans lost their advantage with the defection of moderate Vermont Senator Jim Jeffords from the GOP and with his decision regularly to vote with Democrats. The 2002 midterm elections restored Republican control by giving them 51 seats as opposed to 48 for Democrats (Jeffords remained independent).

10

Going Public, Going to Baghdad: Presidential Agenda-Setting and the Electoral Connection in Congress

Scott B. Blinder

Describing the mood in the Bush Administration and its supporters in foreign policy circles in the summer of 2002, a senior British official said, "Everyone wants to go to Baghdad. Real men want to go to Tehran", but if the "real men" in the Bush Administration in 2002 wanted to take the country to war in Baghdad and even Tehran, they would not do so without first "going public" (Kernell 1997). Beginning in the late summer of 2002 and continuing through the invasion of Iraq in March 2003, President Bush and administration officials sought to persuade the domestic public, lawmakers in Washington, and the international community of the need to take military action against Saddam Hussein's regime, even after the decision to go to war had apparently been made (Pfiffner 2006). Using the power of the presidential bully pulpit and sending high-ranking officials to the airwaves and speech circuits, the administration spared no effort to make the case for "disarming" Saddam, by force if necessary.

But was "going public"—appealing to the American public to try to increase support for the president's preferred policy—a necessary or even useful step on the president's road to Baghdad? Despite the administration's efforts, public opinion polls show no sign that the president's public appeals actually increased support for invasion. The percentage of Americans in favor of military action changed little if at all during the fall of 2002 and winter of 2003 despite the public appeals during this period (Edwards 2006; Foyle 2004). Of course, this should not be surprising for scholars of the presidency, as prior research suggests that the president's capacity to lead public opinion is generally quite limited (Edwards 1989, 2003).

In this chapter, however, I will argue that "going public" was useful in at least one sense: improving the president's chances of success in the Congress (see Barrett 2004). The lack of impact on public preferences over war and peace, I will suggest, disguised subtler effects on public opinion that were nonetheless crucial to Bush's ultimate achievement of his policy goal in the legislative arena. In particular, my argument emphasizes the president's power of agenda-setting, and the effects of successful presidential agenda-setting on the behavior of members of Congress seeking re-election. At the beginning of the Bush Administration, Iraq rarely appeared on citizens' lists of important problems facing the nation. By raising the possibility of military action against Iraq, the Bush Administration mobilized pre-existing background animosity toward Saddam, converting it into a highly salient political issue at the very top of the public's agenda. This increased salience, in turn, activated the "electoral connection" (Mayhew 1974) for senators and representatives, creating electoral pressure on many lawmakers to accede to the president's agenda on Iraq (Foyle 2004).

First, I review the logic behind presidential appeals to public opinion in light of prior conditions, particularly pre-existing public opinion toward Iraq. Second, I show that the Bush Administration's public appeals increased the salience of Iraq as a political issue. Third, I analyze the roll-call votes in both houses of Congress on the joint resolution authorizing the use of force in Iraq. More specifically, I examine the hypothesis that issue salience in the context of an upcoming midterm election increased the pressure on Democratic legislators to side with the president and cast votes in favor of the use of force. Finally, I suggest that the case of Iraq shows that presidential leadership of public opinion can lead to tremendous change in policy, even if presidential persuasion works only "at the margins" (Edwards 1989). Without needing to persuade a single citizen or legislator that his preferred policy is a correct or wise one, the president can leverage public support into success in the legislative arena.

Preaching to the Choir: A Willing Public

Analyzing the effects of the Bush Administration's public appeals requires an understanding of the state of public opinion on Iraq before Bush began to make the case for confronting Saddam Hussein. In particular, it is crucial to note that the president faced a public that shared his initial hostility toward Iraq. Throughout the 1990s and into the current decade aggregate American public opinion remained hostile to Saddam and favorable to aggressive military action against him and his regime. Polls show that a majority of Americans came to regard the first Gulf War as successful but unfinished business. A solid 55 per cent of Gallup respondents supported sending American troops back to Iraq to remove Saddam from power when asked in April 1992, as did a startling 70 per cent when asked in June 1993.[1]

Nor was this support a matter of false bravado surfacing only when military action was off the agenda. In 1998, with Saddam denying access to weapons inspectors and President Clinton eventually retaliating with air strikes on Iraqi military targets that December, aggregate American public opinion again showed high levels of hostility toward Saddam. With Saddam balking at ongoing weapons inspections, and Clinton considering but delaying air strikes, 50 per cent thought Clinton's response "not tough enough" as compared to 39 per cent who thought it just about right and only 4 per cent who thought it "too tough."[2] After the air attack, public support remained strong, ranging from about 69 to 79 per cent in various news service polls in the days following the strikes.[3] Public support held across party lines, and in spite of the belief of a substantial minority that Clinton had chosen the timing of the attack to delay the pending vote in the House on his impeachment.

More recently, according to February 2001 national polling, almost two-thirds of Americans believed that the US "should have continued fighting Iraq until Saddam Hussein was removed from power" in Gulf War I.[4] Views on this question were remarkably non-partisan, as slightly more Democratic respondents than Republican respondents took the hawkish position.[5] Thus, even if President Bush had not uttered a word in public about weapons of mass destruction or Iraqi links to al-Qaeda, it should not have been surprising to find the majority of Americans in favor of using military force against Iraq in 2002 and 2003. Indeed, as the invasion drew near, public support for war was if anything weaker and more conditional than one might have expected given the pre-existing hostility toward Saddam. A plurality of Americans favored war only with some form of backing or approval for the president's plans, whether from Congress, from other allies, or from the United Nations; majorities did not back war without UN approval until it became a fait accompli, with the March 2003 invasion occurring under precisely those conditions (Foyle 2004).

Agenda-Setting and the Logic of Going Public

It was fortunate for the president that much of the American public was already hawkish toward Saddam Hussein, since the administration was not successful in convincing them of the need to depose Saddam Hussein through military force. Numerous public appearances by Bush and his surrogates did little to change aggregate public support for using military force in Iraq (Edwards 2006). Of course, the lack of presidential persuasion in the case of Iraq simply confirms the scholarly conventional wisdom. Despite the increasing use of public appeals in the age of television (Kernell 1997; Neustadt 1990), presidential efforts to persuade the public often fall "on deaf ears"

(Edwards 2003; also see Canes-Wrone 2006; Edwards 1989). Even Ronald Reagan, the "Great Communicator," had difficulty persuading the public on issues as important to him as aid to the Contras, the SDI ("Star Wars") missile defense program, and, later in his term, increases in defense spending (Edwards 2003). Bill Clinton had similar troubles in persuading citizens to support crucial initiatives, from health care reform and the 1993 budget to military interventions in Haiti and Kosovo (Edwards 2003). More recently, George W. Bush's numerous speeches on behalf of Social Security privatization seemed only to entrench public opposition to his plan (Edwards 2006).

These findings may buck the conventional wisdom on the power of the "bully pulpit," but they fit quite well with current scholarship on public opinion. Leading models of public opinion suggest at least two reasons why presidential persuasion is "marginal" at best (Edwards 1989, 2003; Zaller 1992). First, most citizens are not terribly attentive to news about politics, including presidential speeches. Second, even those who are paying enough attention to hear the president's appeals are often not open to persuasion, thanks to entrenched views about the topic at hand or about the credibility of the president himself. Indeed, highly attentive citizens are more likely to have strongly held attitudes on issues and toward the president, and thus are among the least likely to change their minds as a result of a presidential appeal.

But if the president cannot tell citizens what to think, perhaps he can tell them what to think about.[6] Presidential public appeals may have more success in shifting the public attention towards the president's priorities, even if appeals fail to persuade citizens to adopt the president's views on these high priority issues. Jeffrey Cohen (1995, 1997) finds that, through State of the Union addresses, the president can focus the public agenda on his priorities.[7] Moreover, although these effects seem to decay within a year for domestic issues, the agenda-setting effects of foreign policy priorities seem longer-lasting. Other work shows that agenda-setting may occur indirectly as well. The president, at least some of the time, can influence the mass media's priorities (Edwards and Wood 1999); media coverage, in turn, can influence the public's sense of the most important issues facing the nation (Behr and Iyengar 1985; Iyengar and Kinder 1987).

So if the president cannot persuade the public to adopt his views, then perhaps the best he can do is to shift the political terrain to his preferred turf.[8] If this is the case, several hypotheses about presidents' actions and political outcomes follow. First, a strategic president should be more likely to go public when he wishes to take an action that the public favors as well. Recent scholarship shows that presidents are more likely to go public with issue positions that are already popular with the public, and understandably so (Canes-Wrone and de Marchi 2002). Under these conditions, public appeals might help his own popularity through "priming" favorable issues (Iyengar and Kinder 1987), but more importantly for our purposes, public appeals might also help the president gain leverage in the legislative arena. More precisely, Canes-Wrone (2006) argues, and demonstrates formally, that the president stands to gain leverage over the Congress by going public when the public's view is closer to his than it is to that of Congress.[9] She also finds that presidents are, in fact, more likely to go public on issues on which their position is popular, at least in the domestic policy arena (ibid.; Canes-Wrone and de Marchi 2002).[10]

Second, this understanding of presidents' public appeals also suggests a mechanism through which public appeals help the president: increased issue salience. By raising the salience of an issue on which the majority of the public already agrees with his position, the president can pressure Congress to take the action he desires, in order to please their constituencies.[11] Members of Congress generally incline to act in accordance with constituency opinion, but this relationship is particularly strong for salient issues (Hutchings 1998; Kingdon 1989; Miller and Stokes 1963; see also Hill and Hurley 2003 for a more nuanced theory specifying conditions under which legislators follow constituency opinion). Increased issue salience, then, increases the likelihood that legislators' votes will reflect public opinion. Thus, when constituent preferences are aligned with the president's, increased issue salience works to the president's advantage. Thus, even if it fails to change a single citizen's preferences, "going public" on a popular issue position can help the president in the legislative arena. The president cannot usually shift public opinion in his direction, but, when it happens to coincide with his preferences, he can take advantage of this situation to put pressure on Congress to heed the public's wishes.

Conflict with Iraq was, therefore, an ideal issue for a presidential appeal to the public. As shown above, public hostility to Saddam Hussein remained high throughout the 1990s. On numerous polls throughout the decade, a majority of Americans favored military action to accomplish "regime change" in Iraq, which of course was Bush's preferred outcome as well. Aggregate public preferences, then, aligned well with the president's preferences. Distance between the public's preferences and Congress' preferences—the second condition that encourages "going public" in Canes-Wrone's model—was less clear, as we lack solid measures of the *ex ante* preferences of the House or Senate floor. With Bush facing a slim Democratic majority in the Senate and a polarized political climate (Jacobson 2003), however, it would have been at best risky for him to assume that the Senate's preferences aligned with his own. Foyle (2004: 290) suggests that the administration faced a "convinced public" but only a "persuadable Congress." Under these circumstances, the strategy of "going public" made sense as a way to increase pressure on reluctant members of Congress to follow the hawkish preferences of their constituencies.

Of course, regardless of the necessity or logic of the strategy,[12] the Bush Administration did in fact go public, and did so with gusto beginning in the late summer of 2002 (Foyle 2004; Pfiffner 2006). Vice President Dick Cheney asserted on national television that Iraq was close to reconstituting its nuclear weapons program, a claim that was backed by revelations, later falsified publicly, that Saddam was seeking yellowcake uranium and aluminum centrifuge tubes that were uniquely suited to the production of nuclear weapons (Pfiffner 2006). And President Bush himself, in a speech in Cincinnati just days before the Congressional vote to authorize military force, spoke of "a growing fleet" of unmanned aircraft which might be used for an attack with chemical or biological weapons on American soil, and claimed that Iraq was training al-Qaeda members in the use of unconventional weapons (Pfiffner 2006). Clearly, for the administration, going public preceded going to Baghdad, as it sought to build support in the domestic public, the Congress, and the international community (Foyle 2004). But, as noted above, public opinion remained essentially unchanged; a majority of the public had supported military action in Iraq throughout the 1990s; if anything, the public seemed more concerned about approval by the UN or European allies as the war came closer to becoming a reality. If the president was unable to persuade citizens to support military action, then what were the effects of this public strategy on the American public and, by extension, on congressional approval of military force?

The Effects of Going Public: Setting the Public Agenda

If going public works according to the logic outlined above, the president did not need to persuade the public of his views; he merely needed to shift Iraq to the top of the public agenda. This would increase the pressure on Congress to vote in his favor. I will show in this section that the impending conflict with Iraq indeed rose toward the top of the public's political agenda, with the increase in salience coinciding closely with Bush Administration rhetoric. Furthermore, although the data employed in studies of agenda-setting such as this one cannot establish cause-and-effect relationships, I will argue that the usual barriers to causal inference do not apply as strongly in this case, since the impetus for increased attention seemed to come so clearly from the White House rather than from external events.

Presidential appeals preceded sustained public and media attention to Iraq. Bush dropped the first major public hint at the coming war in his State of the Union address of 29 January 2002, and alluded to the need for "regime change" in Iraq throughout the spring of that year (Pfiffner 2006). In addition, as Pfiffner notes, leaks from the Pentagon escalated that summer as the military planned for an ever-approaching war. For the most part, however,

Bush and his proxies refrained from extensive public campaigning until late August or early September of 2002 because, in the words of White House Chief of Staff Andrew Card, "from a marketing point of view, you don't introduce a new product in August" (Bumiller 2002).

The president's public remarks on Iraq reflected this plan. Bush mentioned Iraq in speeches or public remarks just ten times between January and August 2002,[13] although this total does include one very high-profile mention: the inclusion of Iraq in the "axis of evil" in the aforementioned State of the Union address. Then, in September, Bush mentioned Iraq in public remarks or speeches 25 times, followed by 34 occurrences in October and 24 more in November. This sudden and dramatic increase is consistent with the notion of a strategy of public appeals beginning in September 2002, as reflected in Card's oft-quoted remark.

Of these dozens of public mentions of Iraq, many were reiterations of the president's campaign stump speech, as Bush did extensive campaigning on behalf of Republican congressional candidates leading up to the 2002 midterm elections. However, public appeals on the Iraqi threat were not limited to a throwaway line at campaign stops across the country. The president also focused on Iraq in high-profile venues, which he had not done earlier in the year aside from the State of the Union address. For example, his weekly radio address also showed newfound attention to Iraq in the fall of 2002; the address took Iraq as its subject only five times in 2002, none before 14 September. He also made major speeches on the Iraq issue beginning in the fall of 2002, including a 12 September speech at the UN outlining Saddam's violations of numerous UN resolutions, his 7 October speech in Cincinnati making a final pitch before the upcoming vote in Congress. Thus, although we might expect the salience of Iraq as a political issue to increase somewhat in early 2002 after the State of the Union speech, the evidence of presidential agenda-setting should be strongest in the fall of 2002.

To evaluate this prediction, I employ several commonly used indicators of salience (see Baum 2004), beginning with media coverage and letters to newspaper editors (see Lee 2002) before moving on to the self-reports of survey respondents. In all cases, it seems that public attention to Iraq increased rapidly as the Bush Administration began to talk about it publicly. First, media coverage, which scholars often use as an indicator of issue salience (Edwards, Mitchell, and Welch 1995; Hutchings 1998),[14] increased when the Bush Administration began its public campaign on the Iraq issue.

After a small spike in attention in the wake of the State of the Union message, coverage declined through the summer of 2002. Iraq did not completely disappear from the media's agenda; with the administration appearing non-committal, reporters and commentators speculated about when and if the "axis of evil" diagnosis would lead to military action. But when the

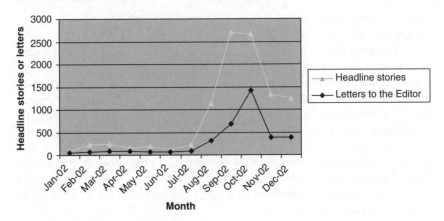

Figure 10.1. Newspaper coverage of Iraq

administration began its public campaign in late August and early September, media coverage quickly escalated to new peaks.

As an indicator of overall media coverage, I examine the number of news stories on Iraq appearing in newspapers nationwide, as well as coverage of Iraq on network television news, as recorded in the Vanderbilt Television News Archive.[15] As seen in Fig. 10.1, newspaper coverage of Iraq escalated dramatically in the fall of 2002. Indeed, over half of all headline stories on Iraq in 2002 appeared in September and October.

Television news followed a similar pattern. As Fig. 10.2 shows, there was little mention of Iraq on the nightly news. These results include all stories from the three major broadcast networks and CNN for which Iraq is mentioned in the Vanderbilt archive's abstracts. TV coverage of Iraq was concentrated in September and October almost as much as newspaper coverage was, with over 40 per cent of the year's stories appearing within that two-month period. Also, as with newspaper coverage, there was little attention to Iraq until August 2002, with only 128 stories about Iraq through July of 2002. By way

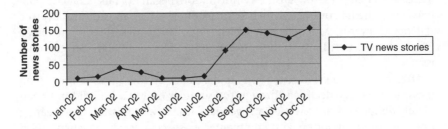

Figure 10.2. TV news coverage of Iraq

of comparison, there were 89 stories in August, 150 in September, and 140 in October.

The public agenda mirrored this heightened media attention. First, Fig. 10.1 also shows that along with increased coverage of Iraq, newspapers were publishing many more letters to the editor on the subject of Iraq. So, even among citizens interested and politically active enough to write letters to the editor, Iraq seemed largely off the radar until August 2002. Interest then increased in subsequent months with the increase in public appeals from the White House.

Among a more representative sample of the public, attention to Iraq also increased as the administrations' public appeals began in earnest. Gallup's monthly polls ask respondents to identify the "most important problem" facing the country, perhaps the survey item most often used as an indicator of issue salience (Baum 2004; Edwards, Mitchell, and Welch 1995; Soroka 2003). In early 2002, relatively few Americans surveyed named Iraq as one of the most important problems facing the nation; "fear of war" ranked relatively low among the public's stated priorities in January and February of 2002, and fell further to a low of about 3–4 per cent in two separate Gallup surveys in July.[16] By contrast, economic concerns seemed to loom larger than fears of war and even worries about terrorism, with the number of respondents citing economic issues even exceeding the sum of those citing fear of war and terrorism briefly in Gallup's July polls.

Then, as the Bush Administration escalated its hardline rhetoric toward Iraq beginning in early September, "fear of war" quickly rose from a relatively minor concern to a position close to the top of the public agenda. By October—the month of the congressional vote to authorize military force—fear of war was cited as the most important problem by almost 15 per cent of respondents; this remained steady at about 14 per cent by November—election month—and then proceeded to rise through the winter as war drew closer. Further, as Fig. 10.3 shows, the electorate's concerns shifted toward military and security issues at the expense of economic matters. Whereas in the July Gallup poll, slightly more respondents cited economic concerns as the most important problem than named terrorism and war combined, this also changed rapidly. By the fall, more Americans were focused on military or security issues as their most important problem, as Republican strategists desired and Democrats feared (Foyle 2004).

Given the state of political rhetoric at the time, Gallup poll results may well underestimate the public's concern with Iraq. With the Bush Administration rhetoric drawing illusory connections between Iraq and al-Qaeda (Kull, Ramsey, and Lewis 2003–4; Pfiffner 2006), those who believed administration claims and worried about a possible nexus between Iraq and terrorism might have reported terrorism as their most important concern, yet done so with Iraq on their minds. Unfortunately, we cannot determine from these data the

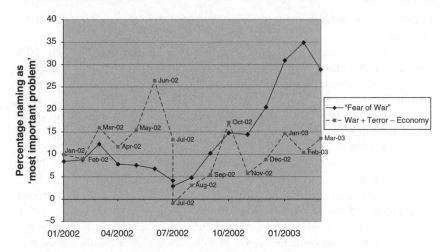

Figure 10.3. Salience of the Iraq War in US public opinion

number of respondents that fit this description, so claims for the existence and magnitude of this effect can only be speculative.

Additional supporting evidence comes from another poll question indicating a similar increase in Iraq's salience during the fall of 2002. A series of polls conducted by the Pew Research Center for the People and the Press asked respondents whether or not they are following a few prominent news stories.[17] Pew began to include "debate on war with Iraq" among its selected issues in September 2002, just when the salience of the issue was rising dramatically according to our other indicators. In September 2002, 48 per cent of Pew's respondents claimed to be following the debate on Iraq "very closely," a figure that rose to 60 per cent and 53 per cent in two different October polls. The 60 per cent figure from early October was Pew's second highest reading on any issue during 2002.[18]

Of course, concurrent trends over time do not establish a causal relationship between public attention to Iraq and Bush Administration rhetoric. The problem of establishing a causal relationship from corresponding trends over time plagues many studies examining agenda-setting; usually it is quite difficult to dispel the alternative explanation that both the public and the president (or, more commonly in studies of agenda-setting, the public and the mass media) are responding to the same real world events (but see Behr and Iyengar 1985). For example, a large increase in the unemployment rate may be followed by an increase in both presidential remarks about the economy and an increase in the number of citizens who cite the economy as the nation's most important problem. In such a scenario, citizens' increasing concern might reflect attention from the president and from the media, or it might have little to do with presidential speeches or media coverage of the president's activities.

Citizens' own experience with losing their jobs, or witnessing family, friends, and co-workers becoming unemployed, might drive increased public concern.

In this case, however, the claim that the Bush Administration, the media, and the public were simply responding concurrently to exogenous events is not compelling in retrospect. Events in Iraq—including Iraqi poverty and repression as well as development of weapons or military posturing—cannot explain the sudden increase in interest in and coverage of Iraq in September 2002. Events were not intrinsically more newsworthy than in July 2002 or July 2001. WMD claims and al-Qaeda ties turned out to be false, and increasingly appear to be the result of purposefully selective use of intelligence information; indeed, the lack of actual threatening events in Iraq seemed to frustrate the president's aims, as he reportedly suggested a ruse using UN planes flying under a US flag to bait Saddam into providing a *casus belli* (Pfiffner 2006).

Even contemporaneous views among American foreign policy experts saw little reason to make Iraq a priority. A poll of the public and of foreign policy elites by the Chicago Council of Foreign Relations conducted between May and July in 2002 found little concern with Saddam Hussein.[19] In fact, more experts named Saddam as among America's most important foreign policy problems in 1998 than in 2002. In 1998, 18 per cent of the poll's sample of opinion leaders named Iraq as one of the "two or three biggest foreign policy problems facing the United States today"; this fell to 4 per cent in 2002, even after the "axis of evil" mention in the 2002 State of the Union address.

It is notable that media coverage increased in August even though the president did not begin to make public remarks on Iraq until September. Prior studies (Baum 2004; Edwards and Wood 1999) have found evidence that the media can set the agenda as well, even leading the president to follow its lead at times. We might, then, be tempted to conclude that the media set the agenda on Iraq, with the president following. On the other hand, media attention seemed to follow earlier decisions by the president to make the ouster of Saddam Hussein a priority, and to plan accordingly. As Pfiffner (2006) notes, Bush's first national security meetings centered on Iraq; war planning began in late 2001 and escalated in the summer of 2002; Bush and Cheney held high-level meetings with foreign leaders on the issue of Iraq and "regime change," particularly with Tony Blair in April 2002; and, of course, Bush classified Iraq as part of an axis of evil in January 2002. Although these events were not the subject of presidential speeches or remarks, they nonetheless made news, whether through leaks from the Pentagon (Pfiffner 2006), reporters' questions at press conferences or brief public appearances, or through other channels. So, although increased coverage in August 2002 did not necessarily reflect a deliberate public relations campaign by the president, presidential attention to Iraq certainly preceded—and at least to some extent drove—media attention. And furthermore, as the administration escalated its rhetoric, media attention escalated as well.

Effects of Going Public: Tightening the Electoral Connection

We have seen that as President Bush and his surrogates spoke publicly about the need to confront Iraq, the salience of Iraq as a political issue increased dramatically. But did this help him in the legislative arena? Certainly, the Bush Administration was successful in achieving the outcome it sought in Congress—broad authorization to pursue a military campaign in Iraq, passed with bi-partisan support. Aside from unanimous support from Republicans in both chambers, the resolution authorizing military force gained support from 39 per cent of House Democrats (81 of 208 voting on the resolution) and 57 per cent of Senate Democrats (29 of 51 voting on the resolution).

Perhaps "going public" made little difference. Perhaps a combination of pre-existing hawkish public opinion, legislator preferences, and partisan influence would have been sufficient to produce similar results in Congress. The logic of going public suggests, however, that increasing the salience of a popular issue should have helped the president. More precisely, I suggest, it should tighten the "electoral connection" between legislative behavior and constituency preferences.

This argument has two clear implications; unfortunately, neither is directly testable with empirical data. The first is a counterfactual implication: absent the Bush Administration's public strategy, fewer Democratic legislators would have voted in favor of war. Obviously we cannot test directly the counterfactual claim (see Fearon 1991), but I will return to examine its plausibility below.

The second implication of the argument is that constituency opinion will have a stronger influence on the vote on use of force in Iraq than it has on other roll-call votes. If going public tightens mass-elite representative links, then we should see members of Congress doing their constituents' bidding on Iraq. This claim is more difficult to examine empirically than it might appear. The crucial barrier is the typical lack of publicly available constituency-level issue polling (Jackson and Kingdon 1992; see Aldrich and Kramer 2004 for review and rare counterexample), or adequate proxies for district-level opinion. Without good measures, we can neither capture constituent attitudes reliably nor disentangle the effects of constituency influence from legislator preferences as revealed in prior roll-call votes (Bond and Fleisher 1990; Jackson and Kingdon 1992). Furthermore, legislators seem to align their votes with their "re-election constituency" (Fenno 1978; Jacobson 2003) rather than median opinion in the district at large (Bishin 2000), and also are likely to try to anticipate future public opinion (Arnold 1990) rather than merely react to a static snapshot of public opinion that may well change, particularly for a vote with highly visible consequences such as a vote to authorize war.

Given these barriers, my empirical examination hinges on an additional implication of the theory of agenda-setting and the electoral connection. If the increased salience of Iraq intensified the pressure on legislators to heed constituent opinion or risk electoral defeat, then this pressure should have been the greatest for those facing the greatest electoral pressure. Moreover, additional pressure to heed constituency opinion would have been noticeable only for legislators for whom this factor clashes with other actors in the "field of forces" which they scan before making more complicated calculations on how to vote (Kingdon 1989). For Republicans representing moderate to conservative districts or states, any heightened electoral pressure from constituents from the president's public appeals would push them in the same direction as the other influences on their voting behavior, including their co-partisan president, their party leadership in the Congress, and their own ideological predilections (Bishin 2000).

For Democrats, however, the question is more complicated. For Democrats struggling to win re-election in 2002 (against Republicans campaigning on issues of national security), an antiwar vote might feel like giving a political gift to the opposition. For Democrats in safe seats, however, there might be less to fear from taking a position distinct from the president and his party on the impending war. Incumbents with a great deal of confidence in their electoral security might have felt sufficient "leeway" (Fenno 1978) to vote their conscience or personal preferences even in the face of potential constituent opposition. Also, Democrats' constituencies might range from somewhat conservative to quite liberal. Incumbents whose seats were safe because they represented relatively liberal districts might not even face a dilemma between preferences and constituency—while the nation as a whole seemed to support military action, the unusual degree of partisan polarization on the Iraq War (Jacobson 2006) suggests that aggregate public opinion in many safely Democratic congressional districts may well have run against war even in the fall of 2002. Thus, all else equal, we would expect Democratic incumbents in safe seats to be more likely to vote against the war, either because they were insulated from electoral pressure or because electoral incentives pushed them in an antiwar direction.

At first glance this prediction holds quite well. In the House, Democratic incumbents who were facing competitive races were 42 percentage points more likely to vote to authorize force in Iraq[20] than were Democrats representing safer seats (see Fig. 10.4). In the Senate, too, incumbent Democrats facing competitive races were more likely than other Democrats to vote with the president.[21]

However, is this relationship the result of increased electoral pressure of a salient issue, or simply the normal efforts to represent constituents' views? Perhaps the Democrats facing the prospect of electoral defeat were also representing relatively conservative districts; after all, incumbents whose partisanship, ideological preferences, or typical voting patterns are out of step with their constituents are more likely to be in electoral danger. Presumably, then,

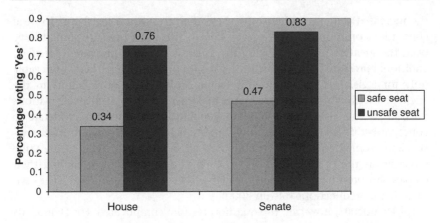

Figure 10.4. Effect of electoral threat on democratic votes to authorize force in Iraq

these incumbent Democrats would be more likely to vote with the Republicans on any given issue than would other Democrats representing more liberal constituencies. In other words, electoral threat might be correlated with conservative votes on Iraq simply because they both stem from the same underlying cause: Democratic attempts to represent conservative districts or states.

At first glance, this alternative explanation seems to have some merit. Whereas 85 per cent of the twenty Democratic senators from states that Bush carried in 2000 voted to authorize force, only 39 per cent of Democratic senators from Gore states did so. Moreover, endangered Democratic incumbents in both chambers were typically more conservative than the average Democrat in their voting patterns on foreign policy matters in 2001, according to *National Journal* rankings (described further below and in the Appendix).[22]

So, did electoral pressure increase the chances of these Democrats voting to authorize military force? Or were these Democrats simply more inclined than other Democrats to vote with the president on foreign policy matters, due to some combination of personal ideological preferences and constituency opinion? To test these explanations simultaneously, I analyzed legislators' roll-call votes in both chambers, using variables that represent each explanation to predict the probability that Democratic members would vote to authorize military force.

To represent the "electoral connection" hypothesis, I used a pair of dichotomous variables for House members. The first represented whether or not the incumbent faced a serious electoral challenge that fall; the second represented simply whether or not the incumbent was running for re-election at all, as opposed to those who were retiring, running for other offices, or had already lost in the party primary earlier in 2002. For the Senate, I created a simple additive index. Senators were scored one point higher on this scale for each of the following conditions they met: (1) running for re-election in 2002, as opposed to those either retiring or next running in 2004 or 2006; (2) facing a competitive election; (3) harboring ambitions for higher office;[23] and (4) being a first-term senator (Hill and Hurley 2002).

To represent the hypothesis that the Iraq vote was subject to the same blend of ideology and constituency that influences legislator behavior on all roll-call votes, I used the *National Journal* rankings of legislators' foreign policy ideology according to their voting records for 2001. The *National Journal* scores legislators' roll-call votes on selected foreign policy issues as liberal or conservative, and then ranks each legislator according to his or her likelihood of voting for the conservative position (see Appendix for details). When used as indicators of legislator ideology, such rankings can be justly criticized as conflating ideology with constituency pressures and other factors that might influence voting behavior (Jackson and Kingdon 1992). But for the purpose of capturing the way all of these forces, in combination, generally influence legislators' voting on foreign policy issues, the scores can be used without any need to parse out the relative contributions of constituents, legislator preference, and other forces. The theory here suggests that electoral pressure was unusually important for the vote on force in Iraq, over and above the normally operating "field of forces" (Kingdon 1989) that influence roll-call votes on foreign policy matters.

To test the relative influence of legislators' normal field of forces against the heightened electoral connection for the issue of force in Iraq, I estimated a model predicting the probability with which each senator or representative would cast a vote in favor of authorizing military force. The results from the probit models estimated for each chamber appear in Table 10.1.[24] As it turns out, both normal voting patterns and heightened electoral pressure are powerful predictors of voting to authorize force. Using just these variables, the probit models offer significantly improved prediction over the null model (in which, with no further differentiating information, the prediction is that each legislator would vote for the more popular outcome). The simple probit models correctly predict 78 per cent of votes in the House and 71 per cent in the Senate, compared with 61 per cent in the House and 57 per cent in the Senate for the null model.

Both normal voting patterns and heightened electoral pressure influenced legislators' votes. First, the same blend of legislator ideology, constituency opinion, and other factors that influenced votes on other foreign policy issues in 2001 influenced votes on military force in Iraq. Democrats with relatively conservative foreign policy records were significantly more likely to vote "yes" on force in Iraq (see Table 10.1). Using the estimates in Table 10.1 to generate predicted probabilities of a "yes" vote for differently situated members of Congress, we find that a typical Democratic incumbent running for re-election

Table 10.1. Effects of electoral pressure and foreign policy conservatism on House and Senate Democrats' votes to authorize military force in Iraq

Variable	House	Senate
Foreign policy voting record	**.06**	**.04**
(Conservatism)	(.01)	(.01)
Electoral pressure index	—	**.55**
		(.25)
Running in 2002? (1 = yes)	−.47	—
	(.31)	
Seat not safe? (1 = not safe)	**.89**	—
	(.33)	
Constant	**−1.52**	**−1.12**
	(.31)	(.41)
	n = 207	n = 51
	Log-likelihood = −95.88	Log-likelihood = −26.80
	Pr > chi2 = 0.0000	Pr > chi2 = 0.0003

Notes: Cell entries are coefficients estimated by probit, with standard errors below and in parentheses. Dependent variable is vote on authorization to use military force in Iraq (HJRes. 114), 1 = yes. **Bold** indicates p < .05.

in a safe seat had only about a 28 per cent chance of voting to authorize force, but a similar incumbent with a foreign policy conservatism score one standard deviation above the mean for House Democrats (a score of 41 as opposed to 24) would now have a predicted 65 per cent chance of voting "yes."[25]

But the evidence confirms the electoral connection hypothesis as well. Even taking into account the correlation between electoral challenges and foreign policy conservatism, Democrats facing electoral danger were significantly more likely to vote "yes" on the Iraq resolution than were those whose seats were safe. Indeed, by analyzing predicting probabilities from the probit equation in the first column of Table 10.1, we find that the effects of electoral pressure are about as strong as the effects of a substantial difference in foreign policy conservatism. In the House, we find that a Democrat whose foreign policy conservatism is at the mean for House Democrats in 2001 and who was running for re-election in a safe seat in 2002 had only a predicted 28 per cent chance of voting to authorize force. A similar member running in a competitive race had a predicted 61 per cent chance of voting "yes."

For House Democrats, then, an electoral challenge elevated probabilities of voting "yes" almost as much as having a foreign policy record a full standard deviation above the party's mean, as seen above.[26] In other words, the electoral pressure on the issue of Iraq was enough to make a Democratic incumbent whose typical voting pattern mirrors Henry Waxman or Eddie Bernice Johnson (*National Journal* foreign policy rankings of 24) look more like foreign policy centrists such as Dick Gephardt (ranking of 36) or Armed Forces Committee members John Spratt, Vic Snyder, and Susan Davis (all with rankings of 41).

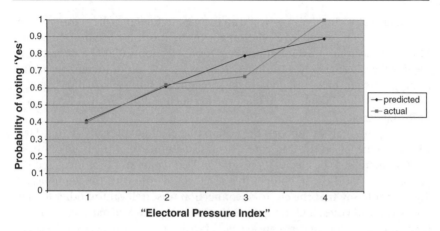

Figure 10.5. Senate Democrats' probability of voting to authorize military force

Meanwhile, in the Senate, predicted probabilities (from the probit equation in Table 10.1, col. 2) indicate similarly large effects for both foreign policy conservatism and electoral pressure. Again, electoral pressure changes our expectations of senators' votes on Iraq to the same extent as would substantial changes in ideology. At each point on the scale, an additional point on the electoral pressure index meant an increase of 10–20 percentage points in the probability of voting with the president for the typical Democratic senator.[27] Figure 10.5 shows the increases in predicted (and actual) probabilities of a vote to authorize force as electoral pressure increases, for a hypothetical senator whose foreign policy voting record is at the mean for his co-partisans in the chamber.

For a more concrete illustration, imagine a second-term incumbent senator not running for re-election until 2004 or 2006, and with no ambition for higher office. If this senator's voting pattern is at the mean level of foreign policy conservatism for Senate Democrats, her predicted probability of voting to authorize force in Iraq would stand at about 41 per cent. An otherwise similar senator positioned one standard deviation in the conservative direction on the *National Journal* rankings would have a 66 per cent likelihood of voting "yes" on force (again according to predicted probabilities from the Table 10.1 probit equation).

By manipulating electoral pressure instead, we can produce a similar effect. Let us return to our original senator with mean ideological tendencies for Senate Democrats, but this time instead of increasing her foreign policy conservatism, we add the electoral pressure of being a first-term Senator running for re-election in 2002. This change would increase her predicted probability of a "yes" vote rises from 41 to 67 per cent. In this case, then, two additional "points" on the electoral pressure scale has about the same effect on the probability of voting "yes" as would an increase in foreign policy conservatism to a position one standard deviation above the mean for Senate Democrats. Thus, the electoral pressure of running for re-election in 2002 as a first-term senator (or, alternatively, running in 2002 as a more senior incumbent facing a competitive race) is enough to make someone with the record of Harry Reid or Barbara Mikulski vote more like centrists such as John Breaux, Evan Bayh, or Joe Lieberman.[28]

In sum, the analysis supports the notion that electoral pressure changed legislators' behavior on the Iraq vote. The unusual salience of the issue of invading Iraq increased the electoral pressure on Democrats and thus increased the probability that those in competitive seats would vote with the Republicans. This is not to say that the electoral connection was irrelevant to other foreign policy roll-call votes, including those that made up the *National Journal* index. Clearly, re-election concerns are always a factor in legislator's voting decisions (Mayhew 1974). But the Iraq resolution presented itself as a particularly potent electoral issue, forcing members of Congress to choose sides a month before an election on a matter that had commanded the national news and the electorate's attention more than any other issue over the prior month or two. Under these circumstances, those facing electoral pressure did not simply vote according to their normal patterns (even allowing for random fluctuations around their mean tendencies). Rather, such legislators were systematically more likely to vote with the president. This finding in turn supports the argument that "going public," by increasing salience, helped the president in the legislative arena.

Admittedly, the overall argument for the effects of "going public" still rests on a counterfactual claim: that, absent Bush's appeals to the public, the political situation would have been substantially different. After all, one might wonder, how could a vote to authorize a major military offensive have been anything less than a gripping national concern, particularly in a post-9/11 environment of heightened sensitivity to foreign policy and threats to American security? Perhaps the Bush Administration had nothing to do with the salience of the Iraq issue; even without public appeals, a vote on the use of force in Iraq might have exerted similar pressures on legislators to heed their constituencies and vote with the president.

It is beyond the scope of this chapter to engage in the detailed case study required fully to refute these counterfactual claims, and argue for a counterfactual story that places more weight on the president's public relations strategy. I will simply point out briefly that these lines of argument rest on a narrow conception of "going public" and its effects. Critics might argue that a vote on war in Iraq would have been highly salient whether or not the president made any appeals to public opinion, simply because of the nature and magnitude of the decision at stake. But, imagining the president did not go public and holding all else equal, it may not be accurate to assume that there would have been a vote on the issue prior to the November 2002 elections. Admittedly, the president's priorities almost always find their way onto the congressional agenda (Edwards and Barrett 2000). But going public may have had an effect on the timing. If it had not been for the president's ability to set the agenda for the public as well, the Senate in particular might well have postponed consideration of the Iraq issue until after the midterm races.

In a more realistic counterfactual scenario, without public appeals and public pressure, majority leader Tom Daschle might well have held to his initial preference for postponing consideration of Bush's proposal.[29] Indeed, there is ample precedent to think that delay would have been a likely result— in considering the authorization for Gulf War I, the Democratic leadership in Congress consciously chose to wait until after the 1990 midterm elections to consider the resolution in an atmosphere less charged with immediate electoral pressure (Zaller 1994).[30] Zaller argues that a roll-call vote on the war was inherently a major political risk for all but the most electorally secure Democrats. Public appeals may have helped the White House by creating a new political risk: that inaction on such a salient, seemingly pressing issue would yield negative electoral consequences as well. This part of the argument is, of course, speculative (as is the counterfactual objection it addresses).

Conclusion: Putting the "Bully" Back in the "Bully Pulpit"?

Despite the enduring image of the presidential "bully pulpit," scholars of the presidency have long been skeptical of the president's influence on the public, and on the importance of the president's standing in the public for determining policy (Neustadt 1990). In the telling titles of Edwards's works on the subject, presidential leadership of the public seems to work only "At the Margins" (Edwards 1989) with attempts at persuasion often falling "On Deaf Ears" (Edwards 2003). Those who have studied the presidency and public opinion seem inclined to agree that the president lacks the power of persuasion, settling perhaps for the lesser ability to shape the public agenda (Canes-Wrone 2006; J. Cohen 1997; Hill 1998).

The case of the Bush Administration and the Iraq War suggests that it is a mistake to underestimate the power presidents can wield by setting the public agenda. This study gives no reason to dispute Edwards's conclusion that the president can only lead the public "where it already wants to go," but it does suggest that presidential leadership in agenda-setting can produce substantial shifts in policy outcomes. To be sure, a majority of Americans favored the use of military force to "go to Baghdad" in early 2002, but this was equally true throughout the 1990s. But as much as the public may have wanted to go to Baghdad, given the choice many citizens who favored an invasion of Iraq might have preferred going elsewhere first: perhaps to Tora Bora or Pakistan to pursue Osama bin Laden, or to the former Soviet Republics to secure "loose nukes," or even to places closer to home to act on domestic policy priorities.[31] Without extensive public appeals from the president and his administration, the invasion of Iraq would likely have remained a low-level priority, desirable in the eyes of the majority of American citizens, but by no means an imminent possibility.

By going public, I have argued, the president changed this situation dramatically, bringing Iraq to the top of the public's list of most important problems facing the nation. This newfound salience, combined with pre-existing hawkish public opinion, heightened the electoral pressure on members of Congress who might otherwise have been reluctant to support his planned course of action, thus helping the president attain passage of the resolution that authorized military force in Iraq. "Going public" can yield powerful consequences, even if the president fails to persuade a single citizen to change her mind to begin to support the president's preferred course of action.

Appendix: Key Variables in the Analysis

Foreign policy conservatism comes from 2001 *National Journal* rankings. The rankings are based on "key congressional roll-call votes" selected by *National Journal* editors and reporters. The *Journal* then uses a principal components analysis to determine a weighting scheme, with votes weighted 1, 2, or 3 according to how central each vote was to the underlying ideological dimension tapped by the principal component analysis. Each member of Congress is then given a score based on the percentage of conservative votes cast, with some votes weighted more heavily than others. Each member is then assigned a percentile based on this weighted average, so that a ranking of 60 on the foreign policy conservatism scale means that the member in question voted more conservatively than 60 per cent of the members of his chamber. For more details, see "National Journal Vote Ratings," *National Journal*, 1 February 2002.

Safe seat designations for the House (and for use in the creation of the "Electoral Pressure Index" for the Senate) come from contemporaneous observations at the time by *Congressional Quarterly Weekly* (Allen and Riehl 2002; Giroux 2002*a, b*) and the online version of the *National Journal*'s "Cook Political Report."

Electoral pressure is an additive index; each Senator received a point on the scale for (1) running for re-election in 2002, (2) facing a competitive race, (3) having ambitions for higher office, and (4) being a first-term Senator. No Senator scored a perfect 4 on the scale. (Incidentally, all four Senators who scored a 3 voted for the war: J. Carnahan (MO), M. Cleland (GA), T. Johnson (SD), and M. Landrieu (LA). Higher ambition was rated by the author, with the following Senators scored as having ambition: Bayh, Biden, Lieberman, Edwards, Kerry, Clinton, Feingold, and Graham. Bayh, Clinton, and Feingold were my subjective decisions and are admittedly speculative; the others ran for the presidential nomination in 2004.

References

Aldrich, John H., and Kramer, Claire V. 2004. "Tough Choices: The Influence of the Electoral Context and of Constituencies on Senators' Trade Votes." Paper delivered at Annual Meeting of the American Political Science Association, 1–5 September at Chicago Hilton Hotel, Chicago.

Allen, Jonathan, and Riehl, Jonathan. 2002. "Democrats Scramble to Recover From Sen. Torricelli's Downfall." *Congressional Quarterly Weekly* 60: 2580.

Arnold, R. Douglas. 1990. *The Logic of Congressional Action*. New Haven: Yale University Press.

Barrett, Andrew W. 2004. "Gone Public: The Impact of Going Public on Presidential Legislative Success." *American Politics Research* 32: 338–70.

Baum, Matthew A. 2004. "How Public Opinion Constrains the Use of Force: The Case of Operation Restore Hope." *Presidential Studies Quarterly* 34: 187–226.

Behr, Roy L., and Iyengar, Shanto. 1985. "Television News, Real-World Cues, and Changes in the Public Agenda." *Public Opinion Quarterly* 49: 38–57.

Bishin, Benjamin G. 2000. "Constituency Influence in Congress: Does Subconstituency Matter?" *Legislative Studies Quarterly* 25: 389–415.

Bond, Jon R., and Fleisher, Richard. 1990. *The President in the Legislative Arena*. Chicago: University of Chicago Press.

Bumiller, Elisabeth. 2002. "Bush Aides Set Strategy to Sell Policy on Iraq." *New York Times*. 6 September, A1.

Canes-Wrone, Brandice. 2006. *Who Leads Whom?: Presidents, Policy, and the Public, Studies in Communication, Media, and Public Opinion*. Chicago: University of Chicago Press.

—— and de Marchi, Scott. 2002. "Presidential Approval and Legislative Success." *Journal of Politics* 64: 491–509.

Cohen, Bernard Cecil. 1963. *The Press and Foreign Policy*. Princeton, NJ: Princeton University Press.

Cohen, Jeffrey E. 1995. "Presidential Rhetoric and the Public Agenda." *American Journal of Political Science* 39: 87–107.

—— 1997. *Presidential Responsiveness and Public Policy-Making: The Public and the Policies that Presidents Choose*. Ann Arbor: University of Michigan Press.

Edwards, George C., III. 1989. *At the Margins: Presidential Leadership of Congress*. New Haven: Yale University Press.

—— 2003. *On Deaf Ears: The Limits of the Bully Pulpit*. New Haven: Yale University Press.

—— 2006. *Governing by Campaigning: The Politics of the Bush Presidency*. New York: Longman.

—— and Wood, B. Dan. 1999. Who Influences Whom? The President, Congress, and the Media. *American Political Science Review* 93: 327–44.

—— and Barrett, Andrew. 2000. "Presidential Agenda Setting in Congress" in J. R. Bond and R. Fleisher (eds.), *Polarized Politics: Congress and the President in a Partisan Era*. Washington, DC: Congressional Quarterly.

—— Mitchell, William, and Welch, Reed. 1995. "Explaining Presidential Approval: The Significance of Issue Salience." *American Journal of Political Science* 39: 108–34.

Fearon, James D. 1991. "Counterfactuals and Hypothesis Testing in Political Science." *World Politics* 43: 169–95.

Fenno, Richard F. 1978. *Home Style: House Members in their Districts*. Boston: Little, Brown.

Foyle, Douglas C. 2004. "Leading the Public To War? The Influence of American Public Opinion on the Bush Administration's Decision to go to War in Iraq." *International Journal of Public Opinion Research* 16: 269–94.

Giroux, Gregory L., and CQ Politics Staff. 2002a. "Where the House Will Be Won." *Congressional Quarterly Weekly* 60: 449–54.

——— 2002b. "House Races: An Election Bucking Tradition." *Congressional Quarterly Weekly* 60: 2794–5.

Hansen, John Mark. 1998. "Individuals, Institutions, and Public Preferences over Public Finance." *American Political Science Review* 92: 513–31.

Hill, Kim Quaile. 1998. "The Policy Agendas of the President and the Mass Public: A Research Validation and Extension." *American Journal of Political Science* 42: 1328–34.

—— and Patricia A. Hurley 2002. "Symbolic Speeches in the U.S. Senate and their Representational Implications." *Journal of Politics* 64: 219–31.

——— 2003. "Beyond the Demand-Input Model: A Theory of Representational Linkages." *Journal of Politics* 65: 304–26.

Hutchings, Vincent L. 1998. "Issue Salience and Support for Civil Rights Legislation among Southern Democrats." *Legislative Studies Quarterly* 23: 521–44.

Iyengar, Shanto, and Kinder, Donald R. 1987. *News That Matters: Television and American Opinion, American Politics and Political Economy*. Chicago: University of Chicago Press.

Jackson, John E., and Kingdon, John W. 1992. "Ideology, Interest Group Scores, and Legislative Votes." *American Journal of Political Science* 36: 805–23.

Jacobson, Gary C. 2003. "Partisan Polarization in Presidential Support: The Electoral Connection." *Congress & the Presidency* 30: 1–36.

—— 2006. *A Divider, Not a Uniter: George W. Bush and the American People*. New York: Pearson Education.

Kernell, Samuel. 1997. *Going Public: New Strategies of Presidential Leadership*. 3rd edn. Washington, DC: CQ Press.

King, Gary, Tomz, Michael, and Wittenberg, Jason. 2000. "Making the Most of Statistical Analyses: Improving Interpretation and Presentation." *American Journal of Political Science* 44: 347–61.

Kingdon, John W. 1989. *Congressmen's Voting Decisions*. 3rd edn. Ann Arbor: University of Michigan Press.

—— 1995. *Agendas, Alternatives, and Public Policies*. 2nd edn. New York: Longman.

Kull, Steven, Ramsey, Clay, and Lewis, Evan. 2003–4. "Misperceptions, the Media, and the Iraq War." *Political Science Quarterly* 118: 570–99.

Lee, Taeku. 2002. *Mobilizing Public Opinion: Black Insurgency and Racial Attitudes in the Civil Rights Era*. Chicago: University of Chicago Press.

Mayhew, David R. 1974. *Congress: The Electoral Connection*. New Haven: Yale University Press.

Miller, Warren E., and Stokes, Donald E. 1963. "Constituency Influence in Congress." *American Political Science Review* 57: 45–56.

Neustadt, Richard E. 1990. *Presidential Power and the Modern Presidents: The Politics of Leadership from Roosevelt to Reagan*. New York: Free Press.

Pfiffner, James P. 2006. "The Use of U.S. Intelligence Before the War with Iraq." Paper delivered at "Politics and Polarization: The George W. Bush Presidency," 25–7 May 2006, at Rothermere American Institute and Nuffield College, University of Oxford.

Pomper, Miles A. 2002. "Bush Makes the Rounds to Build his Case Against Iraq." *Congressional Quarterly Weekly* 60: 2313–16.

Soroka, Stuart N. 2003. "Media, Public Opinion, and Foreign Policy." *Harvard International Journal of Press and Politics* 8: 27–48.

Taylor, Andrew. 2002. "Though Neither Party is Crying 'Politics,' Election Year Puts War Vote on Fast Track. *Congressional Quarterly Weekly* 60: 2317–18.

Tomz, Michael, Wittenberg, Jason, and King, Gary. 2003. CLARIFY: Software for Interpreting and Presenting Statistical Results. Version 2.1. Stanford University, University of Wisconsin, and Harvard University. 5 January. Available at ⟨http://gking.harvard.edu/⟩, accessed 21 November 2006.

Zaller, John. 1992. *The Nature and Origins of Mass Opinion*. New York: Cambridge University Press.

——— 1994. "Strategic Politicians, Public Opinion, and the Gulf Crisis," in W. L. Bennett and D. L. Paletz (eds.), *Taken by Storm: The Media, Public Opinion, and U.S. Foreign Policy in the Gulf War*. Chicago: University of Chicago Press.

Notes

I wish to thank George Edwards, Desmond King, and the participants at the conference "Politics and Polarization: The George W. Bush Presidency," Rothermere American Institute and Nuffield College, University of Oxford, 25–7 May 2006.

1. Aggregate data from this and subsequent polls cited are available at ⟨http://www.pollingreport.com⟩, accessed 21 November 2006.

2. *CBS News* poll. 16–17 November 1998.

3. *Gallup/CNN/USA Today* poll. 16 December 1998, *CBS News* poll. 16 December 1998, *CNN/Time* poll conducted by Yankelovich Partners. 17–18 December 1998, Newsweek Poll conducted by Princeton Survey Research Associates. 17–18 December 1998, *FOX News*/Opinion Dynamics poll. 17 December 1998. *ABC News* poll. 16 December 1998.

4. Conducted by *CBS News*, 10–12 February 2001.

5. Partisanship works against what we would think of as "normal" predispositions here. Republicans may usually be more hawkish in the aggregate, but it was a Republican president, George H. W. Bush, who made the decision to end Gulf War I with Saddam still in power.

6. This is a paraphrase of Bernard Cohen's (1963) frequently-cited statement about the mass media, which he viewed as similarly well suited for agenda-setting although lacking in powers of persuasion.

7. In a replication and extension, Hill (1998) finds that the relationship is reciprocal: issues that are salient to the public prior to the State of the Union address, the

president is more likely to mention in his speech. Hill also finds that the public is especially deferential to the president in the domain of foreign policy.

8. Edwards notes that, while presidents and their advisers often have an inflated notion of what they can accomplish by going public, occasionally practitioners' views converge with scholars'. For example, Edwards cites a memo written by Ronald Reagan's pollster Richard Wirthlin informing the president that his public appeals work in large part by raising the importance or salience of an issue where the president already has the upper hand with the public (Edwards 2003: 72).

9. Perhaps more precisely, the president should gain leverage over those legislators whose constituents' preferences are closer to those of the president than to those of their own representatives. Even this relationship may be more likely to hold when referring to a legislator's "electoral constituency" (Arnold 1990; Bishin 2000; Fenno 1978; Jacobson 2003) than to her district or state at large. Members of Congress are concerned not with national public opinion, but with the opinions of their own constituency or electoral subconstituency.

10. Canes-Wrone (2006) finds that in the area of foreign policy (more specifically, budget items related to foreign policy), prior issue popularity does not increase the likelihood that a president will go public on a given issue, but it does increase the chances that public appeals will be successful (in the sense of increasing the odds that Congress adopt the president's preferred policy direction). She suggests that prior issue popularity is less important to the president's decision to go public because the president is more likely actually to change public opinion on foreign policy matters; however, this claim is attenuated for an issue such as Iraq, for which citizens had more information thanks to Gulf War I and the ongoing American efforts to contain Saddam Hussein.

11. See Neustadt (1990) on public appeals as a form of "coercion" in the president's relationship with Congress, as opposed to the "bargaining" relationship Neustadt emphasized in the mid-twentieth-century presidency.

12. In Pfiffner's account, the public relations strategy may have been undertaken in large part to keep the British in the fold of the so-called "coalition of the willing." Unlike Bush, Tony Blair faced a more skeptical public and insisted that a strategy for convincing or at least preparing the public was needed (Pfiffner 2006).

13. This information was drawn from a search of the *Public Papers of the President* on-line archive at ⟨http://www.gpoaccess.gov/pubpapers/index.html⟩, accessed 21 November 2006. The counts here include speeches and remarks, while excluding interviews with journalists and news conferences in which the president's opening remarks did not mention or refer to Iraq.

14. Media attention might also be considered a precursor to public salience. Media coverage influences the importance citizens place on political issues, as shown by both statistical analysis (Behr and Iyengar 1985) and controlled experimentation (Iyengar and Kinder 1987).

15. Counts of stories were compiled by a Lexis-Nexis search for stories with Iraq in the headline. The search used the "US News" source within Lexis-Nexis, which indexes scores of newspapers across the US. The search excluded opinion stories, and included only stories which mentioned Iraq in the headline. This may not provide a perfect count, but it certainly offers a rough indicator of the extent of

coverage of Iraq, and furthermore screens out the occasional story that focuses on other Middle Eastern events but briefly mentions Iraq.

16. Gallup does not report using "Iraq" or "Saddam Hussein" as a category in coding responses to this item, making "fear of war" the closest matching category. In early 2002, responses coded under this category could reflect fears about Iraq especially after the debut of the phrase "axis of evil" in Bush's 2002 State of the Union address, but it might also reflect lingering feelings about the recently concluded military operation in Afghanistan. (The Taliban regime fell in November 2001.) Neither possibility changes the observed trend later in the year.

17. Pew selects six to eight issues for each month's poll and asks respondents if they are following the story "very closely, fairly closely, not too closely or not at all closely."

18. This figure was exceeded only by the 65 per cent that paid very close attention to a series of random sniper-like shootings in the Washington, DC area, also in October 2002.

19. Foreign policy elites as defined for the purposes of sampling and interviewing are: "those who are in positions of leadership in government, academia, business and labor, the media, religious institutions, special interest groups, and private foreign policy organizations." (See the Worldviews final report at ⟨http://www.worldviews. org/detailreports/usreport/index.htm⟩, accessed 21 November 2006).

20. The roll-call vote in question was on House Joint Resolution 114.

21. Unfortunately, with so few cases—only six Democrats faced competitive races in 2002—we cannot be confident that this difference is not due to chance ($p = .16$). Competitiveness in Senate races was initially assessed with the Cook Political Report's analysis (appearing in the *National Journal* in the months prior to the elections, and confirmed retrospectively by categorizing Senators who received 55 per cent of the vote or less as involved in a competitive race. The retrospective list was identical to the Cook Report's projections. Competitiveness in House races was drawn from Congressional Weekly's observations in the month before the election.

22. National Journal scores for foreign policy conservatism are percentiles, reflecting the percentage of the chamber that is less conservative than the legislator in question. So a score of 75 means that the legislator voted more conservatively more often than 75 per cent of her chamber. Among House Democrats, the mean *National Journal* conservatism score was 23 for incumbents with safe seats and 34 for those facing competitive races. This difference in means is statistically significant, $p < .01$ (two-tailed test).

23. Intuition as well as expert judgment (Pomper 2002) suggests that ambition for higher office was a form of electoral pressure in this case; certainly legislators contemplating a presidential run would have to consider the national constituency, more clearly pro-war than local or even state constituencies might be.

24. I present the results from the simplest specifications possible, omitting other variables that might be used as control or as additional attempts to pick up constituency influence. I do so for these reasons: first, typical proxies for constituent opinion (demographics; other aggregate statistics reflecting economic or other "interests" district- or state-wide) are quite weak as indicators of constituency opinion; second, the normal operation of constituent opinion should be reflected in the *National Journal* scores; third, numerous alternative specifications using controls for

demographic and economic variables at the district and state level (unemployment or poverty rates, racial make-up, number of veterans or active duty military personnel) were generally not significant predictors of legislator behavior in equations that included *National Journal* rankings and electoral pressure, and their inclusion did not alter the estimated influence of the variables of interest.

25. These predicted probabilities were calculated by CLARIFY (King, Tomz, and Wittenberg 2000; Tomz, Wittenberg, and King 2003).

26. As seen above, all else being equal, shifting a safe Democratic incumbent from the mean position on foreign policy ideology to a position one standard deviation more conservative than the mean resulted in increasing the probability of voting to authorize force from 28 to 65 per cent, very similar to the shift predicted here as a result of adding electoral pressure.

27. Predicted probabilities again used CLARIFY.

28. The former pair had foreign policy conservatism rankings of 27, slightly greater than the Senate Democrats' mean of 21; the latter trio each scored 43, slightly more than a standard deviation above the Senate Democrats' mean.

29. In September 2002 Daschle expressed a preference for doing things "right" rather than doing them "quickly", as had been done in 1990–1 when the vote on Gulf War I was not held until after the November 1990 elections in order to lessen the intensity of the electoral pressure on legislators. In 2002 Daschle faced strong resistance from the Bush Administration and ultimately was undermined when the Bush Adminstration struck a separate deal with House minority leader Dick Gephardt on a "compromise" resolution which Gephardt agreed to support. Clearly, then, backroom bargaining as well as public rhetoric was involved (Taylor 2002).

30. Both houses ultimately voted to authorize military force, but in a much closer vote, with a winning margin of only 52:47 in the Senate.

31. In the aggregate the public wants a great many things; in fact, the more questions one asks in an opinion poll, the more places one can find where a majority of the public wants to go. Most public opinion polls are poorly suited to capture agendas, priorities, or preferences over trade-offs; see Hansen (1998) for an illustration of the way in which offering explicit trade-offs in survey questions increases the interpretability and coherence of public opinion (in this case, on budgetary priorities).

11

Managing the News: The Bush Communications Operation

Martha Joynt Kumar

In his first term, President George W. Bush was viewed as having the most effective communications operation of any recent White House. Yet by the beginning of the president's sixth year, even the president's Republican allies criticized the White House communications operation and called on the president to make changes in his publicity staff. What was gold in his first term appeared to have turned into lead in his second. Did the communications operation work well in the first term and poorly in the second, and, if it did, why? The answer lies in the nature of the strengths and weaknesses of the Bush communications operation and in the limits of what such operations can accomplish for a president, including solving his policy problems.

The strength of the Bush communications operation was its ability in the president's first term to set priorities, plan ahead, coordinate among government units, and stick with the plan. The president and his staff focused on what they wanted to talk about and made news on the president's terms. In his first weeks in office, for example, he spent several days each on education, tax cuts, increased military spending, and faith-based initiatives. Their communications plan mixed presidential speeches with ones by surrogates. The goal was to focus public attention on the president's programs and on his appointees in those areas, which news organizations did.

Where the administration was less successful in its communications in its first term was handling unanticipated situations and criticisms of the president, and responding to what others wanted to talk about. All would require a staff capable of quick surveys of a situation, a fast communications response, and an ability to deal with the problem by assigning a communications team that responded to information enquiries. Those were qualities the communications team did not exhibit in the election year issue of the missing records of the president's National Guard service in the 1970s or the White House response to the charges that the president misstated the facts when he said in his 2003 State of the Union message that Saddam Hussein had sought yellowcake uranium from Niger. The unwillingness to deal publicly with those charges quickly led to an expanding problem that engulfed all the White House senior staff, including those of the vice president.

In the second term, the communications team experienced a great deal of political difficulty because of the ebbing public support for the president's Iraq policy and the lack of support of the president's signature issues, such as the personal retirement accounts as part of the Social Security program and a guest worker program as part of a proposed immigration bill. With criticism coming from members of the president's own party in Congress as well as the Democrats, the communications team was under fire, as was much of the White House staff.

In April 2006, as his job approval standings in public opinion polls reached the 30s in all of the major national polls, the president replaced his chief of staff and his press secretary. The president and his staff also made an effort to turn things around by doing something his administration was not known for: putting him and his surrogates in vulnerable situations where they responded to critics of their policies and reporters asking questions in areas of the president's weaknesses. Rather than provide less information, which they would have done in the first term, the president and his staff are currently providing more.

The current phase of openness dates to the period after the election campaign when the president increased the frequency and regularity of his solo press conferences as well as the number of speeches where he appeared before an audience untested for its support of the president and his programs. In addition to speaking to groups that often included a number of critics, he took questions from them on issues on the state of the war in Iraq and the lack of weapons of mass destruction there, the president's low approval ratings, issues related to the leaking of national security information, and the NSA wiretapping program.

To understand the Bush communications operation, one needs to look at the basic functions of communications operations and what kinds of staff demands each requires. White House communications operations call for offensive forces lined up to plan several months out and to coordinate among publicity units throughout government. There are also defensive operations, which call for staff and organizations capable of quick response. At the same time, there are natural limits to what communications operations can do that depend upon the president himself, the difficulties in most administrations of admitting communications problems, and the troubles that come with promoting unpopular policies.

White House Communications Units

The Bush Administration employs a vast communications system. When President Bush arrived at the White House in January 2001, there was a tradition in place of strong communications operations in Republican administrations and in the recent Clinton one as well. The Bush operation built upon these earlier efforts. In the fall of 2000, as soon as his election was certified, George W. Bush asked campaign spokesperson Karen Hughes to take charge of his incoming communications operations. When Hughes returned to Texas in the summer of 2002, she was replaced in her role as communications director by her deputy, Dan Bartlett, who now has her old title of counselor.

Contemporary White House communications operations involve several units and many people. The domain of Bush's first two communications directors extended from the Offices of Communications, Media Affairs, Speechwriting, and Global Communications to the Press Office and the Photography Office. In 2005, after the Office of Global Communications was eliminated, the remaining offices had 63 full-time employees. There were also another 21 aides working in communications and press in the Office of the Vice President, the Office of the First Lady, and the National Security Council. This communications staff of 84 was larger than all of the 67 people working in the White House economic and domestic policy operations, specifically in the Domestic Policy Council, Council of Economic Advisers, and the National Economic Council.[1]

There were other officials whose responsibilities included some aspect of communications, especially those in political offices. Most important of them all is Karl Rove, who has been responsible for integrating policy with politics and publicity. Another 42 staff members worked in the four offices he supervises. He serves as senior adviser to the president and his responsibilities include promoting administration messages via his contacts with government and Republican officials at the state and local levels, as well as with representatives of supportive interest groups.[2]

In addition to these 125 front-line employees, there were nearly 200 people working in communications-related White House support operations. That includes people at the top staff level, the chief of staff, for example, as well as those performing specific services, such as transcribing presidential speeches. Some of these aides staffed the offices responsible for scheduling public appearances, making travel arrangements, and analyzing all the public correspondence (paper and electronic) that arrives at the White House. Each office provides information important to the development of communications strategies.[3]

If one were to count into the communications orbit all those White House staff members working on the presentation of the president and the development of his communications, the number would indeed be large. By a conservative estimate at the beginning of his second term, approximately 325 people in the Bush White House worked in communications and supporting operations, including those from senior communications officials down to the military personnel who operate the recording equipment for presidential speeches, press conferences, and briefings, and transcribe the sessions.

White House Communications Operations: Advocating for the President

An effective White House communications operation is multifaceted, advocates for the president, and defends him as well. Presidents need communications operations that do offensive work for the administration, in particular advocating for the policies, laws, and programs that he wants. Increasingly, the president and his staff use their sophisticated communications apparatus to make the case for presidential programs. The publicity organization also promotes his brand of leadership and his political priorities. These are offensive operations where White House staff determine what communications actions they want to take in support of the president, such as scheduling and writing speeches and coordinating them with the introduction of legislative initiatives.

President Bush's advocacy operation is shaped by the larger White House staff structure organized around the president's management principles, the compartmentalized system set up by Chief of Staff Andrew Card, and the competing integrated system run by Karl Rove. All focused on establishing goals and planning ahead. The Bush management system had important implications for the president's communications because the staff structure made it easier to fashion presidential communications directives and to implement them. At the same time, the system did not prove sensitive to brewing trouble, which meant the president and his staff had substantial problems to deal with once disturbing issues became public ones, as was the case with the prison abuses in Abu Ghraib.

The Management System

The first part of the management system is the set of principles President Bush followed in his days as a business person and as governor of Texas. His core set of principles call for: setting goals; developing plans for getting to the desired goal; assigning operational responsibilities and then allowing staff to implement the plans.[4] Karl Rove described the system Bush followed: "set the goal, bring everybody together, focus them on the goal, let people find how to get from point A to point B; be clear about methods; be clear about philosophy; be clear about the goal. Define limits within which people can operate but make them wide and expansive" (interview: Rove 2002). Although they are Peter Drucker principles, Karl Rove indicated, Bush practiced them. "These are all things, whether it's because of his training or his nature, he does." The emphasis here is for the president to establish how the system is to work rather than managing the system himself. President Bush prefers to let others carry out the assignments he, the chief of staff, and others give them. He gets involved when he wants to.

Karen Hughes explained where the president's management system fit into the communications system (interview: Hughes 2002). "He'll want to know the plan. What's the plan? How are we rolling out?" Mary Matalin described it this way: "He throws out big projects, big goals, and then, you come back with pieces of it," she says (interview: Matalin 2002). "It's more meeting and talking, but tasks are given out, assignments are made."

The second element in the creation of the staff system was the structure chosen by Chief of Staff Andy Card. Card set up a system with two deputies and fairly independent positions for Senior Adviser Karl Rove and Counselor Karen Hughes. Except for Karl Rove, staff members had specific assignments and areas where their responsibilities lay. Rove was a floater who could move around in all three areas of policy, politics, and publicity. In the Card system, staff members other than Rove worked in one of the areas, not all three.

Chief of Staff Card described that system as a "compartmentalized" one (interview: Card 2001). "In my job, I am the Chief of Staff and so I am responsible for the staff. I am just a staffer responsible for the staff." Card described his system of communications with the staff, which was based on sharing only information he determined to be relevant for what individual staff members were doing.

I try to first of all have good communications with the people on the staff. But it is based on the "need to know" rather than the "want to know." And right after the war I had that discussion with the entire senior staff where I said we are going to now be very disciplined about "need to know" and "want to know." All of you will want to know everything. I am asking you to discipline yourself, to recognize that you will be told what you need to know. And if you come to me and you say you need to know something else, if it is a real need to know, you will know it. But focus on that which you have been assigned rather than try to get into that which you want to go.

The emphasis of the system on "need to know" restricted people to their assigned tasks, which in the communications area meant creating and carrying forward presidential messages.

Although this system was efficient in terms of avoiding overlap in staff duties, it turned out to be a system where the staff, and the president too, were caught by surprise on some major issues, including the status of legislation, resignations, nomination difficulties, and program problems. The system was effective at getting out messages related to presidential priorities; it ran into trouble picking up problems outside and inside the White House. Two major embarrassing issues for the White House where there were warnings that did not filter up the system were the prison conditions at Abu Ghraib prison in Baghdad and administration approval for Dubai Ports World to manage container operations at several US ports. Detailed International Red Cross reports came to the National Security Council at the White House but did not rise to the presidential level. Both situations were important issues that needed to be dealt with as early as possible.

The public learned of the extent of abuses by American guards at Abu Ghraib prison in Baghdad through photographs contained in a 28 April 2004 piece by Scott Pelley on the CBS program *60 Minutes II*. The White House was put in a position of catching up to a very bad story already shaped by photographs the public had seen. The communications staff was left to explain why the president had not known about the situation even though the National Security Council staff was aware of allegations contained in a 24-page report prepared by the International Committee of the Red Cross, which included graphic descriptions of types of alleged torture techniques. In talking to *Washington Post* reporter Mike Allen, presidential aides told him the "graphic images" of abuse "took the president by surprise" (Allen 2004). Although the story would have been bad whether or not the president had known about the extent of the prison abuses, coming on the problem so late left the president and his White House team with nothing left to do but respond to a story that was defined first by others. The system failed the president in a basic way. "The White House staff is there to insure there are no surprises," recently noted Reagan's senior communications adviser Tom Griscom (Griscom 2006).

The third element in the staff structure is the system George Bush used as governor of Texas. "Our starting point was really the President [George W. Bush]'s office in Texas, and then the campaign, where there had been this close integration between policy and politics and publicity" (interview: Rove 2002). In both the first and second terms, those three elements come together in Karl Rove's domain, which is a crucial one for planning out the publicity for the president's program.

A good example of how politics, policy, and publicity come together is the planning group that Rove created and managed. Rove chaired a monthly or bimonthly meeting of what he dubbed his "strategery" group. This name was borrowed from a television comedy program.[5]

Early in May of 2002, Rove illustrated what his "strategery" group did by describing what he expected for the year ahead. "Right now, for example, we had a strategy meeting last night, and we were talking about August. We have a model for between here and the end of the year, in terms of what we are attempting to achieve, what are our goals." For the shorter term, they had filled out their schedules three to four months out. "But in terms of, for example, planning the president's travels, and focusing on message, and focusing on thematic, and sort of helping make sense of our time here, we have a good handle on June. We've got the model for July; we've got the framework for August. Shortly we will have July filled out" (ibid.).

Although they plan way ahead, they are aware that their plans can easily go awry. "But last year, when we started, we were eight weeks ahead, and at other times we've been four weeks ahead, and at other times we've been twelve weeks ahead. We had September, October, November mapped out and guess what?" (ibid.). Even if they are blown off course by unpredictable events, as they were on September 11, 2001, their long-term strategizing gives them the stability of an overriding direction. In Rove's words, "It is better to walk into a day and say this is our model and we're going to discard it than it is to say, what is our model for today? What are we going to try to do?" (ibid.).

They work from a general planning document that identifies major scheduled events; "then the thematic for the day; then a specific POTUS [President of the United States] activity; and then the days that we're traveling are so indicated in green," Rove said while pondering a sample document. "This is just sort of the general, long-range planning calendar. There is a more detailed description of every one of those days."

Karen Hughes and then Dan Bartlett was involved in setting out the communications part of that general schedule. At the start of the administration, Karen Hughes held weekly communications planning meetings on Wednesdays and Fridays, so that the senior staff could map out high points of the president's schedule for the following three to four months. Based on the general goals that the president and his top associates had laid out, they would plan publicity events in which he could explain, promote, and illustrate his more specific aims. As soon as this schedule was set, perhaps two dozen staffers from various White House offices would work on implementing particular events with their counterparts in relevant Cabinet departments and with supportive officials in both governmental and non-governmental units at the state, regional, and local levels.

Once an event was scheduled, a senior person was assigned responsibility to work with the operations team, overseeing the deputies with the task to sketch it out in detail. It could be a communications, process, or policy person. This strategist would make certain that the purpose of the event was clear and that its proposed staging would effectively achieve that aim.

Communicating on the President's Terms

Jim Wilkinson, director for planning in the Office of Communications during the first term and Secretary of State Condoleezza Rice's communications deputy in the second, said that the president's goal as a communicator is "to make news on his own terms" (interview: Wilkinson 2002). A lot of the strategies the administration adopts derive from the effort of the administration to have the president covered when and how he and his staff want. Their information release strategies are based on the president as the focus of their efforts, including having him do the announcements without a lot of build-up in the press. As the staff set up events they do so in a way that works for them, including responding to press queries on their terms.

First, the president, not his staff or cabinet members, is the focus of presidential policy making. Ari Fleischer defined the president's desire in specific terms. "The president really believes, one, he's the newsmaker, not the staff" (interview: Fleischer 2001). That translates into White House news policy in two ways. First, the president does not want to see the staff in the news. An important result of the focus on presidential policy pronouncements is it is rare to have policy specialists come into the briefing room to provide background information on policy. That represents a substantial change from earlier administrations as most recent presidents have had a support operation for most of their initiatives where on-the-record sessions are held with policy specialists, including cabinet secretaries, explaining a presidential program.

In the Clinton Administration, for example, Cabinet Secretaries Donna Shalala (Health and Human Services), Richard Riley (Education), and Henry Cisneros (Housing and Urban Development) regularly briefed on the record in the White House Briefing Room as did economic adviser Gene Sperling, domestic policy adviser Bruce Reed, and budget chief Jack Lew.

In the Bush Administration, no cabinet secretary has come to the Briefing Room to explain a presidential initiative. During the first term, only National Security Adviser Condoleezza Rice regularly came out to brief reporters. But recent actions by the administration have involved several layers of White House officials going further than they previously have to explain the president's thinking and policy goals. When President Bush laid the groundwork for his address to the nation on immigration on Monday, 15 May 2006, the preceding Friday a senior administration official with a publicity rather than a policy specialty briefed two groups of reporters from first electronic and then print publications. The idea was to inform reporters about the basic provisions of the president's immigration initiative without focusing on the staff person providing the information. In the afternoon prior to the speech, two administration officials elaborated on the points of the speech. By so doing, White House reporters, who most often are generalists, could go through the particulars and implications of the programmatic angles of the speech with officials. The White House is interested in informing the stories reporters write, but to do so in a way so as not to draw attention to staff.

Second, as part of the focus of having the president announce policy in the first instance, there is little build-up to presidential announcements. Ari Fleischer explained, "You see a lot less of the pre-leaks before announcements.

When he has something to say, he says it and everyone hears it typically from him for the first time. It's our policy that . . . the American people should hear it from him first" (ibid.). Although in the second term the president is more willing than he was in his first term to have his staff advance policy initiatives with releases of information beforehand, the administration reserves such build-ups for major initiatives, such as the State of the Union address, rather than actions or smaller items he might be interested in.

In the second term, White House staff exhibited more of an interest than they did earlier in providing informed people to answer questions on the president's speech before he was to give it. Because reporters assigned to the White House do not specialize in domestic or foreign policy, the staff will prepare reporters on important speeches, such as the State of the Union address and addresses to the nation. For the 15 May immigration speech, senior White House staff members involved in the preparation of the address talked to reporters shortly before the president was to deliver it. Four aides, Communications Chief Dan Bartlett, Press Secretary Tony Snow, Homeland Security Adviser Frances Townsend, and Deputy Chief of Staff for Policy Joel Kaplan talked to and answered questions from reporters for an hour. Rather than discuss the policies in any depth, the four aides talked about the speech itself and what the president was aiming for.

Third, having the president covered in his terms has meant the administration decides what information they give to reporters and when they want to do so. White House communications senior adviser Dan Bartlett explained the administration's strategy of establishing a course of action and sticking to it. The communications team focuses on the risks involved in having open forums for discussion with reporters and policy people. Bartlett said there is a difference in how Republicans play the news cycle during campaigns and when they are governing, though he viewed Democrats as using the same strategies. "Sometimes they [Democrats] had to win every news cycle and you get that way in a campaign, for example. But in the governing stance we kind of, we'll pass up opportunities if something presents itself in the headlines that day or if television broadcast hits with some news" (Bartlett et al. 2003).

Republicans are reluctant to respond to reporters because often it does not fit in with the plans they have laid out. Bartlett continued, "We're not as eager to jump on something and ride that wave, so to speak, if it's not fulfilling or consistent with our strategic communications goal for that week, or that month, or that quarter or whatever it may be." They stick to the plan even though controlling the discussion meets with resistance from reporters, who want responses from the White House on their issues, not just the ones the president and his administration want to speak about. "So I think in that regard we kind of approach the news cycle a little bit differently which can be, frustrating for the press corps because they're in that news, that's them." From Bartlett's viewpoint, reporters want to get you to respond to their news priorities, which he regards as being dragged into the "deep end." "They're in the news cycle and they're wanting to play in that and they're trying to invite you into the deep end ... we tend to look at our long term goals or our mid term goals and say: 'Does it fit our communications priorities to do so?' " (ibid.).

For Bartlett, dealing with reporters reduces rather than enhances the president's flexibility. He provides the explanation of why the Bush Administration is reluctant to have policy people brief reporters on policy issues. If you were to bring in a reporter for in-depth discussion "about the complexities of Medicare" and "where we are in the Medicare debate and talk about how this is such an important issue but has complexities," you are taking a chance as the policy people do not have the training in how to deal with the press. The policy person might make news in an unintended way because, Bartlett argued, reporters are more experienced in such discussions than officials are. "That reporter is very smart [as to] how to ask questions to a policy person who doesn't deal with the press—and they say well, you know, Tommy [Thompson, Secretary of Health and Human Services], he really has this idea, but somebody over here has this [conflicting] idea."

What ends up in news articles can be harmful to the administration because it reduces the president's options. Bartlett observed, "The screaming headline the next morning, 'White House Divided Over Medicare' or you know 'White House Clashes.' " Neither the president nor the staff wants to see those kinds of stories on policy options in the public domain so they opt not to have the policy people speak, especially in preparation of an event or presidential speech.

And that's the challenge we have is that we want to do that, we want to enrich the reporting, we want to give context to reporting, at the same time it's difficult, particularly in policy making because the best thing that we can do for the president, when he's trying to make a policy decision, is to give him the most flexibility as possible; meaning he can entertain as many options as possible, but as soon as those options are in the public domain and given a certain characterization it then starts boxing him in, or her, but in his case it would say you're now putting a perception on a policy position or a certain way it's being communicated or reported makes it more difficult for him to have a free hand in deciding what he wants to do. (ibid.).

At the midpoint of the first term, communications staff were reluctant to risk the president's popularity by having him or someone else in his administration make a communications mistake. Above all, they wanted to avoid putting him or his surrogates in a position of vulnerability. In the second term, however, when they found themselves down in the polls, the president and his staff were more willing than they had been earlier to take communications risks. In the spring of 2006, they had little to lose by taking risks because they were facing criticism from so many political sources.

Instead of steering clear of risk, they courted it by allowing both staff and the president to answer questions from audiences likely to pose unwanted questions. Contrary to Bartlett's stated reluctance to let reporters query cabinet secretaries in an open setting, the day after the president's immigration speech policy specialists discussed the issue of border security. The officials included the secretary of the department of homeland security, the immigration chief, the head of border patrol, an assistant secretary of defense, and the chief of the National Guard. Rather than avoid letting reporters get an opportunity to talk to the policy specialists for fear they might get them to say something off the program, the communications staff created the event with the four policy specialists. With the president's job approval rating in the low 30s in the major public opinion polls, in order to get coverage on the specifics of the president's immigration proposals the staff needed to respond to reporters' requests for information. In both sessions, reporters questioned officials for at least a half hour following the initial remarks made by staff members.

While during the campaign and even earlier in the administration the president avoided audiences other than ones assured of being a friendly crowd, in 2006 he appeared before audiences that were not hand picked and faced questions dealing with issues the president and his staff would prefer not to focus on. White House staff found that news organizations were more likely to cover the president's remarks if he included questions from an audience with people the White House had not cleared. Instead of appearing solely before local Republican audiences or friendly business ones, the president mixed in venues such as the Johns Hopkins University's School for Advanced International Studies, where following his speech he faced a student audience with tough questions on Iran, the leak of information involving Ambassador Joseph Wilson's wife, Valerie Plame, and the president's democracy initiative (Bush 2006). That sort of event, which was covered by the cable television networks, is attractive because the press and the public are more likely to pay attention. Such sessions "definitely raise the interest level with the public and the press," said Scott Sforza, deputy communications director for television production, who arranges the stage settings for presidential events (interview: Sforza 2006). Reporters ask, "What is going to happen? And the president doesn't even know." Those are situations likely to be covered by television, exposure that the administration wants and has been willing to have at this point of low presidential approval numbers.

When the president went to Yuma, Arizona on 18 May 2006 to discuss his immigration initiative as it related to border control issues, the communications staff informed all five television networks beforehand that their correspondents would have an opportunity individually to conduct short interviews there with the president. As the staff were well aware, the reporters

361

went beyond the immigration subject to question the president on his low poll numbers as well as other issues they would have preferred not to discuss.

Presidential Speeches

The heart of the advocacy operation is the president himself and the speeches and remarks he regularly gives. Depending on the level of the events, the communications operation has to write the speeches, prepare the events, coordinate with governmental units at the federal, state, and local levels, and the Press Office arranges the briefings and back-up information. In the first term, the addresses and remarks of all kinds averaged 1.42 events for a six-day week, including Saturday. Each Saturday the president gives a radio address, though it is taped a day earlier. Table 11.1 demonstrates the large number of speaking occasions President Bush has had during his tenure.

President Bush's appearances are very much in line with the number of public presentations President Clinton had. Once cable television began carrying presidential speeches on a very regular basis, presidents could count on getting directly to their publics. President Bush has kept up the tradition set by Clinton of active speechmaking in the second term. It was during the latter half of the Clinton Administration that cable television broadened beyond CNN to include MSNBC and Fox. While the former began in 1981, the latter two established a White House presence in 1996. By 1997 and 1998, they were an important part of White House communications planning.

Coordinating Presidential Publicity

Communications staff coordinate White House publicity efforts with those of other governmental institutions and with recruited supporters in the private sector. They coordinate units within the White House with administrative departments and agencies, allies in Congress and at the state and local level. Interest groups back up administration efforts and work with the White House on promoting their policies to specific constituencies through news organizations.

We can view how coordination works in the Bush Administration by considering how the White House works together with executive branch units. Coordination within the executive branch involves several points. First, the president and his staff make use of the resources of the departments and agencies as he communicates his programs to the public. Communications coordination involves making use of the resources of the White House, departments, and agencies, including the cabinet secretaries and agency heads. In their coordination with others, White House officials use their wide range of resources to promote presidential priorities. Officials appear as surrogates for the president, as did, for example, Treasury Secretary John Snow in the 2005

Table 11.1. Addresses and appearances available for use by news organizations: George W. Bush

	2001	2002	2003	2004	To 20 Jan. 2005	Remainder 2005	To 16 June 2006	First Term	Second Term to 16 June 2006	TOTAL
Addresses to the nation	7	4	7	1	1	6	2	20	8	28
Oval Office	1	0	1	0	0	1	0	2	1	3
Other White House	1	1	4	0	0	2	0	6	2	8
Joint Session of Congress, incl. State of the Union and Inaugural	3	1	1	1	1	1	1	7	2	9
Other	2	2	1	0	0	2	0	5	2	7
Weekly radio addresses	48	51	52	52	3	49	24	206	73	279
Addresses and Remarks*	453	484	331	482	21	340	239	1,771	579	2,350
Total appearances available for media use	508	539	390	535	25	395	265	1,997	660	2,657

* This category represents those instances where the President gave an Address or Remarks. If the president had "Remarks" followed by an "Exchange with Reporters," the two were counted separately because they required work by separate staff operations, the Office of Communications and the Press Office. Only the "remarks" segment is counted in this chart while the "exchange" segment is counted in Table 11.3 Interchanges with Reporters. These are categories of remarks found in the *Weekly Compilation of Presidential Documents* and the *Public Papers of the President of the United States*.

Table 11.2. Addresses and appearances available for use by news organizations, by year, term, and tenure: President Clinton

	1993	1994	1995	1996	1997	1998	1999	2000–1
Addresses to the Nation*	7	5	3	2	2	5	3	3
Oval Office	4	4	2	0	0	1	2	1
Other White House	0	0	0	1	0	2	0	1
Congress	3	1	1	1	2	2	1	1
Weekly radio addresses	47	50	51	52	49	51	51	56
Addresses and Remarks†	410	475	426	531	438	545	567	645
Total appearances	602	530	480	585	489	601	621	704

* This section includes State of the Union messages as well as Inaugural addresses and other addresses found in the Document Category, "Addresses to the Nation" found in the *Public Papers of the President of the United States, William J. Clinton*. Weekly radio addresses and Addresses and Remarks also come from the *Public Papers*.

† In many instances in the events listed in Addresses and Remarks, there are sessions before or after the event where the president had an Exchange with Reporters where he took a small number of questions from reporters, usually a pool of reporters coming into the meeting at a specified time for a brief session. Counted here are the Addresses and Remarks where the president did have an exchange with reporters as well as one where he did not talk with reporters afterwards.

discussion of Social Security reform. When the administration came up with a program to promote its personal accounts for Social Security, White House and Treasury officials promoted it as "60 stops in 60 days" (Department of Treasury 2005). In the 60-day campaign, the following officials were some of those who spoke at the specified number of stops: President Bush spoke at 18, Vice President Cheney 5, Secretary Snow 13, Social Security administrators 29, Commerce Secretary Gutierrez 5, Treasury officials 7, Health and Human Services Secretary Leavitt 5, Secretary of Labor Chao 10, Housing and Urban Development Secretary Jackson 5, Small Business Administrator 13, and White House officials 5. Deputies to cabinet secretaries appeared as well. All these appearances by the president and his cabinet had little effect.

In the Social Security debate and in other discussions, the White House made use of their communications team in the executive branch. Having a communications team for all of the executive branch has entailed controlling appointments to the public affairs offices in the various departments, coordinating executive branch communications officials with White House senior officials, and then ensuring that certain statements coming out of the departments and agencies conform to perceived administration programs and presidential goals.

One of the early decisions of the Bush White House was to have the senior staff control several appointments at the department and agency level. Public affairs officer was one of the five positions at the administration level the White House would pay close attention to and sign off on. The other four are secretary, deputy secretary, legislative liaison, and counsel. When asked if controlling the appointment as public affairs officers means White House officials can be comfortable knowing the briefings are tied into the White

House, Chief of Staff Card said, "I believe that to be the case" (interview: Card 2001). In order to make certain the public affairs people are aware of White House themes and interests, Card said, "there is a call every morning with the communications teams from all of the Cabinet agencies. And I know [Deputy Chief of Staff for Policy] Josh [Bolten] keeps in touch with their policy wonk types and [White House Counsel] Al Gonzales with the lawyers and so White House liaison people are very important too." Thus, communication was one of several means used to tie the White House together with the departments in a way that created message consistency throughout the administration. In addition to their daily calls, the White House communications team has regular meetings in the Roosevelt Room at the White House to discuss administration programs and plans with departmental and agency public affairs officials.

The goal of this control over departmental publicity efforts is to make the most of administration resources and to ensure coordinated messages and initiatives. All recent administrations have tried to do the same. But the George W. Bush Administration has been willing to put in more resources than its predecessors and has faced front-page newspaper criticism as well as critical editorials. In the period between September 2000 and September 2004, public affairs officers have increased by 9 per cent, wrote *Newsday* reporter Tom Brune (2005). "The number of public affairs officials rose 9 per cent, from 4,327 to 4,703, in executive-branch agencies, according to US Office of Personnel Management statistics. Meanwhile, the federal work force grew 6 per cent." Moreover, despite talk of cost-consciousness and budget control, the funding for public affairs increased. "The cost of public affairs staffing has grown by more than $50 million, records show, from $279 million in 2000 to $332 million in 2003, the last year for which figures are available."

In the second term, the administration faced criticism for actions taken by public affairs officers viewed as trying too vigorously to enforce consistency in presidential messages. Scientists working for the National Oceanic and Atmospheric Administration (NOAA), the US Geological Survey, and the National Aeronautic and Space Administration publicly chafed at what the scientists regarded as administration efforts to interfere with their public descriptions of their own findings. One area of contention is the issue of global warming. The *Washington Post* reported the scientists "say they are required to clear all media requests with administration officials, something they did not have to do until the summer of 2004" (Eilperin 2006b). A NOAA official, Kent Laborde, said they were enforcing pre-existing policies on clearing interviews. "We've always had the policy, it just hasn't been enforced," Laborde told Juliet Eilperin of the *Washington Post*. "It's important that the leadership knows something is coming out in the media, because it has a huge impact. The leadership needs to know the tenor or the tone of what we expect to be printed or broadcast."

Other scientists publicly complained about the monitoring of their press contacts. In the case of NASA, scientist James Hansen complained that when he put up information on the agency's website that indicated 2005 might be the warmest year ever, he was told to take it down, "because he had not had it screened by the administration in advance" (Eilperin 2006a). It wasn't long before congressional Democrats got into the discussion and critical stories appeared.

Departments experienced other publicity problems, including the fallout from contracts designed to promote particular programs. Several of the contracts caused trouble for the administration. Long a source of friction with congressional committees responsible for overseeing the priorities and operations of various departments, departmental practices in this regard created so much resentment that the president himself felt compelled to put an end to certain routines.

President Bush spoke out against government contracts to media personalities who promoted administration policies without acknowledging that they had been paid to do so. The contract generating the most criticism was one granted to conservative talk show personality Armstrong Williams. Williams was paid $240,000 by the Department of Education to promote the administration's "No Child Left Behind" program. He often appeared on television and radio to discuss it. When he advanced the administration's programs, he failed to indicate he was being paid by the government to do so (Toppo 2005). After Williams's contract was first brought to light by a story in *USA Today*, contracts to media commentators Maggie Gallagher and Michael McManus were also reversed (Drinkard and Memmot 2005). It was not long before the president called for an end to the practice of paying media personalities.

In a report requested by Senators Edward Kennedy (D-Mass.) and Frank Lautenberg (D-NJ), the Government Accountability Office found the payments to Armstrong Williams to be illegal while the contract with Maggie Gallagher was permissible. The Department of Education responded through a spokesperson, Susan Asprey, that, "We've said for the past six months that this was stupid, wrong, and ill-advised" (Lee 2005b).

In addition to the contracts with media personalities, several departments sponsored the creation and distribution of videotapes for television that appeared as if they were news stories. Although the videos sent to local television stations identified the source, the stations often cut the videotape, including the government-funded identification. The result was the audience had no idea the film was paid for by the government. The comptroller general criticized such programs found in the Office of National Drug Control Policy and the Department of Health and Human Services. The Government Accountability Office in its report noted propaganda prohibitions found in law. "Television-viewing audiences did not know that stories they watched on television news programs *about the government* were, in fact, prepared *by the government"* (Lee 2005*a*). Video news releases, however, remained in place as the president and his staff felt they identified the source of information. If there was fault, administration officials reasoned, it was on the part of the local television stations, not the administration.

In addition to deploying departmental resources for presidential agendas, controlling departmental public affairs offices allows the president and his staff to avoid having such units serve cabinet secretaries and their goals rather than the president and his. The foundation of such control often lies in appointing to the departments people who have already demonstrated their loyalty to the president and his goals by working in his campaigns. Torrie Clark, the first public affairs officer at the Pentagon, worked in the presidential campaigns of George H. W. and George W. Bush. Mindy Tucker, who had worked the Florida shift in the wake of the contested 2000 election, was placed in the public affairs operation at the Justice Department. In the second term, several staff members went out from the White House to departments and agencies, including White House Deputy Press Secretary Clare Buchan to Commerce and Jennifer Millerwise Dyck from Vice President Cheney's office to the public affairs job at the CIA. By sending out people loyal to the president and vice president, the administration was ensuring the messages sent from the departments and agencies would be in sync with those of the White House.

White House Communications Operations: Defending the President against Critics

Defending a president often calls for a different tone and action timetable than advocating for the chief executive. Defensive operations call for a quick turnaround time and a flexible staff able to pull together a variety of people and resources as needed to support the president.

The Bush communications team has been weak in its defense operations. Defending a president calls for different strategies, timetables, and staff qualities than does advocating for a chief executive. Defensive communications operations are responsive ones with a short timetable. Defense is necessary when a president, his staff, or members of his administration are faced with criticism or unanticipated events, or make mistakes. It is also necessary when the president takes a newsworthy action and his critics view it as an opportune moment to try to get into his news story by making statements reporters will consider newsworthy. Defense also calls for press secretaries to challenge reporters when the president finds a news story unfair.

Critics act quickly where the president and his senior staff are involved. When President George W. Bush replaced Chief of Staff Andrew Card with Joshua Bolten, head of the Office of Management and Budget, his critics almost immediately provided reporters with information critical of the administration's budget policies and Bolten's role in them. President Bush made his announcement in the Oval Office at 8.31 a.m. on 28 March 2006. At 9.52 the Democratic National Committee sent out a statement attacking Bolten. "From stonewalling Congress about Katrina relief and the cost of the Medicare drug benefit to creating a 'shadow budget' with costs that will explode in 2009 to concealing the true reasons for the ballooning deficits this Administration has created, Josh Bolten is responsible for this Administration's long series of policy failures" (Shah 2006). Shortly after the DNC message, Senate Minority Leader Harry Reid criticized the appointment of Bolten as did House Minority Leader Nancy Pelosi.

At 11.11 a.m., approximately an hour after the Democratic National Committee and the congressional Democratic leaders, the Center for American Progress, a think tank operated by former Clinton White House Chief of Staff John Podesta, released its own attack on the newly named Bolten. "Replacing Andy Card with Josh Bolten is like rearranging chairs on the deck of the Titanic." Like the Democratic National Committee, the Center for American Progress released background briefing information on Bolten (Center 2006). The information they provided went into the early news stories on the appointment and into the questions asked at the press secretary's afternoon televised briefing with reporters.

Operating in a fast-moving news cycle has not been the strength of the Bush White House. Dan Bartlett described how much better Democrats were at responding to the needs of the news pace. "The best way that I can describe it is that in the daily news cycle they're kind of more day traders and we're more like long term investors. They play the cycle and much better than we do. They're very flexible, very agile" (Bartlett et al. 2003). The White House communications operation worked with its strength: planning and coordination. They laid out their agenda and stuck with it. Proportionately, they spent far less time in a mode where they defended the president outside the issues they were discussing.

One instance where the Bush communications team had trouble getting traction as they defended the president was on the issue of the accuracy of his statement in the 2003 State of the Union message that Saddam Hussein had sought to buy uranium in Africa. The president and his staff were reluctant to admit having given out incorrect information. Later, the administration was not able to support the allegation despite strong pressure to provide the information. The issue was important because it became part of the larger question of what types of weapon Saddam Hussein had and what he had sought to buy.

In the summer of 2003, memoranda began to surface casting doubt on the claim's accuracy. Initially, George Tenet, CIA director, accepted blame for the error. He said the "CIA should have ensured that it was removed." Yet, the CIA also got out the message that the White House shared in the fault. In the same article, the *Washington Post* reported, "The CIA director also made clear that it was members of the president's National Security Council staff who proposed including the questionable information in drafts of the Bush speech, although the CIA and the State Department had already begun questioning an alleged attempt by Iraq to buy uranium from Niger" (Pincus and Milbank 2003).

Day after day in the Briefing Room, reporters hammered Press Secretary Ari Fleischer with questions on who was at fault. Even his last briefing was dominated by questions related to the issue of what became known as the 16 words in the State of the Union (Milbank 2003). After weeks of the issue coming up, White House officials decided to take the topic out of the daily briefing by having a senior administration official take questions in one half-hour briefing devoted to the subject (18 July 2003). They provided selected pages from a National Intelligence Estimate discussion, but even that did not stop it.

Finally, four days later, Steve Hadley, deputy to the National Security Council adviser, took the blame in a briefing he jointly gave with communications director Dan Bartlett. In the briefing, they "revealed the existence of two previously unknown memos showing that Director of Central Intelligence George J. Tenet had repeatedly urged the administration last October to remove a similar claim that Iraq had tried to buy uranium in Africa" (Balz and Pincus 2003). After that, the issue moved to the background—but it had dominated White House information sessions for weeks.

Yet there was an aftertaste from the State of the Union incident that affected the relationship between the White House and reporters. Reporters were weary of what the White House had to sell. Two years later, in October, 2005, the issues came up in a daily briefing in which Press Secretary Scott McClellan received a large number of questions related to President Bush's Iraq speech earlier in the day. David Sanger, *New York Times* White House correspondent, asked McClellan for support for the president's description of ten attempted terrorist attacks halted by security forces. Sanger said, "after the '16 words incident' sometime ago, we are more interested than usual in having—seeing the footnotes that go with the speech. So just as a matter of maintaining credibility, it would be good if we could get at least outlines of the brief [on terrorism incidents]" (6 October 2005).

Closely related to the issue of the yellowcake uranium claims were the questions surrounding what White House aides Karl Rove and Lewis Libby, chief of staff to Vice President Cheney, had said to reporters Matthew Cooper, Judith Miller, and Robert Novak about CIA operative Valerie Plame. Day after day the press secretary was put on the spot to vouch for the credibility of what others in the White House had said and done on this issue but also on the president's National Guard records, and Vice President Cheney's hunting accident. Ultimately, the misstatements coming out of these briefings were a major factor in compromising Scott McClellan's credibility. It is unclear at this point whether the new press secretary, Tony Snow, will be able to move such issues away from the Briefing Room podium. In the Clinton Administration, the last three press secretaries successfully moved scandal from the daily sessions to a cadre of lawyers and communications people in the Office of White House Counsel.

In handling unanticipated agenda items, even victories, the Bush White House has had difficulty in taking advantage of opportunities. For example, when Libya renounced its weapons of mass destruction program, the Bush communications system failed to take advantage of a real victory when it meant responding to an unplanned event. On 19 December 2003 President Bush came out to the Briefing Room at 5.30 p.m. with ten minutes' notice to make the announcement that Libya's leader Col. Moammar Gaddafi agreed to renounce its nuclear, biological, and chemical weapons and to allow international inspection. The agreement, which was the result of British and American efforts, Bush declared, "will make our country more safe and the world more peaceful." Yet there was hardly any publicity of the victory because there was no advance notice given to reporters and no follow-up briefings from the White House to encourage reporting of the story. Just as with bad news, the White House had difficulty dealing with news for which they had no operational plan.

Coalition Information Centers

The one expressly defensive operation the White House created dealt with external issues. The White House experimented with a rapid response team in the days after 11 September when it created an operation to defend against charges coming from the Taliban from its base in Islamabad. The first effort was a short-term operation titled the Coalition Information Centers. Once that operation was viewed as no longer needed, the president and the communications staff developed a permanent White House operation designed to defend against erroneous claims of US conduct and to get ahead on issues of interest especially to the Arab world. The Office of Global Communications lasted barely two years before being allowed to expire.

After September 11, 2001, with the aim of responding to publicity critical of the US in Afghanistan and in other Muslim countries, the Bush Administration created the Coalition Information Centers to make its communications operation a global one. The aim was to respond within the same news cycle to information coming out of Afghanistan and surrounding countries.

Tucker Eskew, who headed the Office of Media Affairs at the time of the September attacks, moved to London to coordinate this new publicity initiative with Alastair Campbell, spokesperson for Prime Minister Tony Blair. The plan was to have both an offensive and a defensive operation where the American government and its allies could generate news and responses in the same news cycle as its opponents, most especially the Taliban.

Eskew explained the impetus for extending the existing communications operation: "We were being inflicted with disinformation, misinformation, outright lies, largely by a Taliban public information officer based in Islamabad in the days following the beginning of the bombing in Afghanistan," he said (interview: Eskew 2002). He related that officials in Tony Blair's government had told the White House that they were lagging behind in the news cycle. "I think we acknowledged that we needed to respond more aggressively, more rapidly, to defend ourselves in that global news cycle, and to do it more quickly so that we weren't letting the ten hours lapse from Islamabad's morning to DC's morning."

Once these discussions began, then "Alastair [Campbell] and Karen cooked up this idea of Coalition Information Centers designed to more effectively, rapidly, respond and coordinate information resources across agencies within the United States Government and between governments in the coalition.... So there's a briefing process at the White House. There is certainly one at Number 10 as well" (ibid.).

Because the challenge was to counter publicity resulting from Taliban briefings conducted in Islamabad, Campbell and Hughes decided they needed a briefer there on the spot. "We had to do it because the press was getting briefed by this Taliban information officer... The campaign became so successful that we didn't just rout the Taliban from most of Afghanistan; we routed that guy out of Islamabad. There was somewhat less need to respond to all of that but still a concentration of international media and regional media that was often very conspiracy-minded and in some ways anti-American. So throughout November and December particularly, we briefed, briefed frequently and regularly, daily in fact, and we knocked down some stories."

Four months after it was created, it was disbanded in favor of a longer-term operation designed to sell the administration viewpoint in a more coordinated way than the response operation represented by the Coalition Information Centers. Its successor was the Office of Global Communications.

Despite early hopes and grand expectations, by 2005, it ended up doing little beyond sending daily e-mails containing information favorable to the administration to a sizable mailing list. Generally, the e-mails contained two snippets of information: One, the "Fact of the Day," offered a fact or anecdote about progress in Afghanistan or Iraq, the second, "Global Messenger," reproduced quotations from presidential speeches as well as giving upbeat war reports. On 11 March 2005, for example, the Global Messenger gave information on the status of Iraq from the viewpoints of the Defense and State Departments. One bulleted item reported: "President Bush and his counterparts not only turned the page on Iraq, they wrote a new chapter. All 26 NATO allies are now contributing to the NATO Training Mission in Iraq" (White

House Global Messenger 2005). Unceremoniously on 18 March 2005, the messages stopped. The director and deputy directors of the office left for other assignments and the unit was quietly moved to the National Security Council. Executive Order 13283 creating the Office of Global Communications was signed on 21 January 2003 and was officially revoked on 30 September 2005.

The phasing out of the Office of Global Communications coincided with the return to the Bush Administration of Karen Hughes. Rather than working in the White House, Hughes is working on public diplomacy from a perch at the State Department holding ambassadorial rank. With no competition from the White House on the global communications stage, Hughes moved that portfolio with her to the State Department.

Presidential Interchanges with Reporters

One of the most important ways presidents defend themselves is by responding to reporters' questions. It is through questioning by reporters that we get a sense of what the president's thinking is, particularly on subjects where others have criticized him. Responses to press queries give the public an opportunity to hear from the president on topics he might not want to speak about, but on which others want to get his thinking.

Since the Eisenhower Administration, when presidents went on the record with their press conferences, presidential interchanges with reporters have been a dynamic area where presidents have developed a variety of ways of responding to reporters' queries. In the ten presidencies since Eisenhower, presidents have gradually reduced the number of solo press conferences they have held. At the same time, they have added three types of session where they respond to reporters' queries: short question-and-answer sessions; joint press conferences, mostly with foreign leaders; and single and group interviews with reporters. While each one of the three types of exchange existed prior to the Eisenhower Administration, all have become regular features of a president's contact with reporters, which was not the case prior to the on-the-record press conference.

President Bush followed patterns established by his recent predecessors in using all three types of reporter contacts in addition to press conferences. What is interesting is the mix of media contacts the president has had over his six years in office and how they have changed. He began with a large number of sessions where he answered a few questions from reporters, usually a pool of reporters ushered into the Oval Office, Roosevelt Room, or Cabinet Room. These encounters are much easier to control than is true of more open-ended sessions, such as press conferences where the president appears alone to respond to reporters' queries for a half hour or more. The reporters most frequently called on in short question-and-answer sessions are the wire service reporters for Associated Press and Reuters, who usually want a presidential response to a breaking news item or whatever the topic of the day is for reporters. Presidents typically are well prepared for such questions. One of the jobs of the press secretary and the communications operation is to anticipate questions and discuss possible responses with the president. In their contacts with reporters, the White House staff tries to meet reporters' demands for answers from the president himself while not putting the president in vulnerable situations, unless there is something to be gained by doing so.

The patterns of press interchanges found in Table 11.3 demonstrate the relatively high number of press contacts in the first year of the administration and then the different balances that are struck in different years among forums where President Bush entertains reporters' queries. In 2001, he had a weekly average of 4.2 press contacts in a five-day week while in 2004 it was down to 2.7. At the same time in 2004, though, the president gave a very high number of speeches. The president daily gave multiple speeches in the re-election campaign, but his team wanted to reduce his vulnerability to unwanted problems by reducing the occasions when he responded to press queries and stuck to his scripts.

In the early days of the administration, when the president was introducing his programs and his new appointees, there was little to fear in having the president answer a few questions on a regular basis. As critics emerge and the questions become tougher, the frequency of the sessions falls off. The election campaign is a time when short question-and-answer sessions are cut back as are solo press conferences because they are particularly high-risk.

The numbers that have their own rhythms are joint press conferences, which have come to have diplomatic as well as domestic political importance. These are sessions where the president and the visiting foreign dignitary give their descriptions of what happened in their meetings. It suits the purposes of any administration as it reduces the possibility of the visitor stepping outside the White House and giving his or her version of events without the president present to give his.

Presidential interviews have a rhythm with the heaviest number in the beginning of the administration when the president and his staff want specific groups of people to know what the administration is planning and then later leading up to and during the campaign season when they are appealing to particular states and regions. The president can do a round table with several reporters from targeted areas and get good play in the local media. Some of the round tables, though, are with foreign press prior to the president's trips abroad. Table 11.4 demonstrates the mix of interviews President Bush has had with reporters.

The interchanges that President George W. Bush has had with reporters are less frequent than those of President Clinton, but the former president had more interchanges with reporters than any recent president. Table 11.5 demonstrates the very high number of contacts he had with reporters,

Table 11.3. George W. Bush: public interchanges with reporters

	2001	2002	2003	2004	To 20 Jan. 2005	20 Jan. 2005 to 30 Dec. 2005	To 16 June 2006	First Term	Second Term to 16 June 2006	TOTALS
Public question-and-answer sessions other than press conferences, by location	143	96	66	47	3	40	20	355	60	415
White House, including Camp David, Air Force One, Blair House	92	48	36	26	2	21	13	204	34	238
In Washington, DC	9	8	3	1	1	6	0	22	6	28
Outside DC, inside US	32	31	18	17	0	8	3	98	11	109
Outside US	10	9	9	3	0	5	4	31	9	40
Press conferences	19	20	26	24	0	32	8	89	40	129
Solo	4	3	4	6	0	8	3	17	11	28
Joint	15	17	22	18	0	24	5	72	29	101
Interviews with news organizations as of 6 May*	49	34	45	69	12	33	14	209	47	256
Total interchanges with reporters	211	150	137	140	15	105	42	653	147	800

* The interview numbers were provided to me by the White House, and do not include off-the-record interviews. The numbers found in the *Weekly Compilation of Presidential Documents* and the *Public Papers of the Presidents of the United States* reflect only a portion of the interviews conducted. Those conducting the interview traditionally own the recording and control its release. The White House, however, does release interviews with foreign reporters where a translation is involved. It has an interest in making certain there is an accurate record in English of what was said by the president. The figures for round tables with reporters refer to sessions the president had with foreign journalists prior to visiting their countries, and with specialty reporters such as those focusing on economic issues, or where the White House organizes a group of reporters from a state or region for a presidential interview. The statistics in this table are tabulated from information found in the *Weekly Compilation of Presidential Documents*.

Table 11.4. George W. Bush: interviews with reporters

	2001	2002	2003	2004	To 20 Jan. 2005	20 Jan. 2005 to 30 Dec. 2005	To 6 May 2006	First Term	Second Term to 6 May 2006	TOTALS
Print interview	21	11	7	34	5	9	5	78	14	92
Television interviews	18	19	26	31	6	18	4	100	22	122
Round table interviews	10	4	12	4	1	6	5	31	11	42
TOTAL	49	34	45	69	12	33	14	209	47	256

Table 11.5. President Clinton: public interchanges with Reporters

	1993	1994	1995	1996	1997	1998	1999	2000–1	1993–6	1997–2001	1993–2001
Public question-and-answer sessions other than press conferences, by location	242	142	107	125	122	88	99	117	616	426	1,042
White House, including Camp David, Air Force One, Blair House	202	92	84	88	90	58	62	82	466	292	758
In Washington, DC	5	2	1	6	1	1	3	4	14	9	23
Outside DC, inside US	26	28	12	19	17	7	9	18	85	51	136
Outside US	9	20	10	12	14	22	25	13	51	74	125
Press Conferences	38	45	28	22	21	13	18	8	133	60	193
Solo	12	17	9	6	7	2	6	3	44	18	62
Joint	26	28	19	16	14	11	12	5	89	42	131
Interviews with news organizations*	52	79	34	24	16	32	36	95	189	179	368
TOTAL	332	266	169	171	159	133	153	220	938	665	1,603

Note: The Weekly Compilation of Presidential Documents and *The Public Papers of the Presidents of the United States* has two document categories, "Exchanges with Reporters" and "Remarks and Exchanges," which refer to sessions where either the whole event is one where the president takes questions from reporters or remarks where he takes questions, usually following his speech. These sessions differ from presidential press conferences in their shorter length, their restricted access, and sometimes their restriction to a particular subject or subjects. Press conferences include those sessions in the "news conferences" category in the *Weekly Compilation* and the *Public Papers*. The annual figures are calculated by calendar year rather than by elapsed time in office.

* The number of interviews found in the *Weekly Compilation of Presidential Documents* and the *Public Papers of the Presidents* does not reflect the total number of interviews conducted. In the Clinton Administration, there are transcripts that have not been made public, especially ones with print media. Additionally, there are interviews, especially radio interviews, in the Clinton Administration, where no permanent record was made of the President's remarks. On 6 and 7 November 2000, for example, President Clinton conducted 21 and 27 "get out the vote" radio interviews from his home in Chappaqua, New York. No transcripts were made. These figures come from an internal record kept by staff in the Clinton White House, "William Jefferson Clinton, Presidential Radio Interviews, As of January 15, 2001." A staff member who was present for the interviews said these were "individual interviews one after another after another. We started at about 2.00 p.m. on Monday the 6th and went until about 7.30 p.m. that night," she said. "And then on the 7th went from about 6.30 a.m. to 8.00 a.m. and 9.30 a.m. until 2.00 p.m." [Background information.] I have included television interviews not in the public record that are found on a list kept internally by White House staff: "President William Jefferson Clinton: Presidential Television Interviews 1993–2001."

particularly in his first two years in office. In looking at their figures in terms of how their administrations progressed, President Bush increased the number of solo press conferences in his second term while President Clinton had far fewer of them in his second. That is significant as the solo press conference is the forum where presidents are most vulnerable to questions about issues and events they don't want to talk about.

The Limits of Presidential Communications Operations

The Bush communications operation served the president well in his first term when he needed it to focus on what the president wanted to say and not get drawn off target by the president's critics who wanted him to respond to their issues. To accomplish his goal of making news on his terms, the president and his staff took few risks when it came to presenting administration officials other than the president to talk about their issues. They did not want to risk mistakes on their own part nor did they want others to get media attention. Even the president took few risks in his interchanges with reporters, except where being vulnerable suited his purposes. Although reporters were frustrated by not getting officials regularly to answer their questions, the White House staff stayed with their strategy of minimal contact with reporters and received the coverage they wanted. Yet their inability to defend the president with swift responses that disposed of issues left them with lingering unanswered questions that became important in the second term as well as the first.

In his second term, the previous communications strategies did not work. With his numbers falling, the president loosened up his communications operation by personally appearing in settings where he had to respond to the questions of others and began to go further in having his policies explained by people in his administration. The White House staff structure that focused on compartmentalizing gave way to what appears at this point to be a more open system where listening is given prominence. Whether these changes will be lasting ones will depend in part on whether they are viewed as making a difference in terms of the public's understanding of what he is doing and why.

White House communications operations provide the president with personnel, resources, and strategies as he seeks to develop, articulate, and reach his policy and political goals. Yet there are limits to what a communications operation can do for a president. Among the limits are those related to the president himself, his staff, his policies, and the public. Some presidents produce and perform with top-flight communications operations. Others allow their publicity efforts to drift. How a communications apparatus is structured depends on a president's choices, including how he organizes his staff. How it operates depends on the ability and desire of the president and his staff to explain his administration's policies and goals, and also on the interests of the public in hearing what the president has to say.

Policies Lacking Public Support

There are limits to the policies and the presidential explanations the public will accept. In the case of Hurricane Katrina, the federal government's disaster plans and organizational resources were inadequate for dealing with the problems spawned by the hurricane. President Bush's appearance of being slow to respond to Hurricane Katrina mirrored the demonstrably slow response by federal government agencies tasked with disaster planning, as broadcast far and wide by news media. Context also counts. Because billions have been spent on homeland security since September 11, 2001, both the Washington community and the public were surprised and dismayed that the federal government's capacity for handling a domestic disaster was so poor. There was no way to portray the federal government's handling of the hurricane as being successful. Thanks to extensive media coverage, too many people saw that it was not.

So too, the reforms in Social Security were a hard sell for the George W. Bush Administration. The president, his cabinet officers, and his agency heads went on the road in a high-profile campaign, "60 Cities in 60 Days," to sell his twin ideas: that the social security system was in a perilous state and that personal retirement accounts would benefit the public. The more the president spoke, the more the public disapproved of his handling of the issue. In early February, a CNN/*USA Today*/Gallup poll found 44 per cent approval, 50 per cent disapproval, and 6 per cent unsure in answering their question: "Based on what you have heard or read, in general, do you approve or disapprove of George W. Bush's approach to addressing the Social Security system?" In late July, the approval number went down to 29 per cent, the disapproval number rose to 62 per cent and unsure stood at 9 per cent (PollingReport.com).

After five months in Washington and on the road discussing the problems of Social Security and the importance of personal retirement accounts, the public was less likely to support the president's account plan. People responding to an ABC News/*Washington Post* poll question showed greater concern about personal retirement accounts after the president's tour than before he began it. When asked whether they would support or oppose a plan in which people could invest some of their Social Security contributions in the stock market, in mid-March 56 per cent supported the idea and 41 per cent opposed with 3 per cent unsure. In early June, support dropped to 48 per cent while those opposed increased to 49 per cent and unsure fell to 2 per cent (ibid.). The public simply was not buying personal retirement accounts.

A President's Personal Style

For the most part, the chief executive's personal style is a strength. It usually helps presidents get elected. Yet a president's personal style can also be a limitation in how an administration operates. Where the Bush communications operation might have made a difference on policy was in getting the president to listen to brewing trouble. Yet any such efforts ran counter to the president's personal style of sticking with a planned course of action. Although his ability to set out goals and plans and stick to them has been a personal and an administrative strength, it has also caused him problems. Once he makes plans, he and his team find it difficult to switch to another course of action. His response to Hurricane Katrina is a case in point.

President Bush was late in responding to Hurricane Katrina, in part because he was enjoying a long-planned vacation in Crawford, Texas. Two weeks before the hurricane, President Bush responded to a question to him posed by Cox Newspapers reporter Ken Herman about the importance of the vacation for him. When asked about antiwar protestor, Cindy Sheehan, who had camped out near his Crawford ranch during August, Bush replied, "I think it's important for me to be thoughtful and sensitive to those who have got something to say." Sheehan, whose son died in Iraq serving in the US military, wanted the president to talk to her about the Iraq war, which he did not do. He explained to Herman why he was not going to focus on her problems. "But I think it's also important for me to go on with my life, to keep a balanced life. I think the people want the President to be in a position to make good, crisp decisions and to stay healthy. And part of my being is to be outside exercising. So I'm mindful of what goes on around me. On the other hand, I'm also mindful that I've got a life to live, and will do so" (internal White House transcript, not publicly released, Bush 2005). He was sticking to his carefully planned schedule, including when Hurricane Katrina hit two weeks later.

As the hurricane gained strength, government officials issued warnings to residents in its potential path. On Saturday, 27 August, Bush declared a state of emergency in Louisiana from his Crawford ranch and authorized the Federal Emergency Management Administration to provide aid. On Sunday, 28 August, the day before the hurricane struck, he made comments on the emergency tucked into longer remarks about the Iraqi constitution. He had two Medicare speeches scheduled in Arizona and California on Monday and then a war on terrorism speech on Tuesday in San Diego. All three sets of planned scripts incorporated remarks at the beginning of the speeches dealing with the hurricane. But using add-ons to deal with the unfolding crisis made him seem strangely out of touch.

The situation on the ground in the hurricane zone was grave. Soon after the hurricane struck New Orleans, its levees were breached and serious flooding ensued. Gulf Coast towns in Mississippi and Alabama were also hard-hit. Still the president stuck with his schedule. Not until he was flying back to Washington on Wednesday did he get a glimpse of the impacted area. He got that view from his plane, which dipped down over New Orleans. By this time, New Orleans was flooded, people were stranded on roof tops, conditions at the Superdome and convention center where evacuees were sheltered were unsanitary and unsafe, and, except for the Coast Guard, the federal government agencies had little presence.

With the president out of Washington, Michael Chertoff, secretary of homeland security, the department in which FEMA is housed, was in charge of handling a federal response to the effects of this hurricane. In a news conference in Washington he declared that he was "extremely pleased with the response that every element of the federal government, all of our federal partners, have made to this terrible tragedy" (Chertoff 2006). But he had yet to visit the affected areas. So his comments made it seem like even administration officials left behind in Washington remained remote and out of touch. All of this was being shown on television, to an audience swelled with viewers free to watch television because, like the president, they, too, were on end-of-summer vacations.

Additional elements of President Bush's personal style made it difficult for him and his staff to alter the perception that he was out of touch and disengaged. One was his reputation for not following television news. The second was his well-known reluctance to fire, or even criticize, officials working for him.

President Bush often made a point of describing himself as someone who neither read newspapers nor watched television, although insiders, including his wife, have noted that he does do some of both and relies on others, including her, to fill him in. Because he was traveling during those first days of the hurricane, he saw little more than snippets of the television coverage. When an article in *Newsweek* reported that communications adviser Dan Bartlett made a DVD of news broadcasts to show the president as he traveled to the Gulf for the first time, the impression of an out-of-touch president was cemented (Thomas et al. 2005).

No matter whose administration it is, the White House staff structure reflects the president it serves. The flipside of a staff representing the strengths of a president is that they also reflect his weaknesses. They do not fill in for what he lacks. Those presidents who are good communicators spend their time and energy on publicity. So too do their staff. Those chief executives who are weak communicators choose to devote few staff resources to strengthen their own shortcomings. Instead, they focus resources on the areas they want to emphasize.

The George W. Bush Administration developed an exceptionally well-run communications operation capable of carrying forward a message the president wanted to deliver. By the same token, the system had difficulty getting those operations to change course when needed. One of the byproducts of a communications operation geared towards action is the difficulty in listening while selling the president's ideas. Operations focused on an agenda require the president and his staff to have a sense of their mission, to articulate it, to repeat it, and to hold to it. The administration took months to add corporate responsibility to its slate of pressing issues. Although President Bush discussed it repeatedly in his campaign speech in 2004, it was a long time before he and his staff viewed it as a salient issue when it surfaced in 2001. It took several months after the Enron collapse in December 2001, and the corporate fraud issues raised in the telecommunications field with the downfall of WorldCom Inc., Global Crossing Ltd., and QWest Communications International, before the president highlighted the issue. It was not until 9 July 2002 that the president gave a major speech on the issue. The following month he held a 13 August conference in Waco, Texas focusing on corporate responsibility as one of several key economic issues.

As successful as the administration appeared in its communications in its first term, it was clear even then that its operation was poor at listening, slow in responding to problems, and weak at taking advantage of unanticipated opportunities. All are critical elements in a communications operation's defensive responsibilities. Those weaknesses were important in the president's second term, but gradually the president and his staff experimented with a more flexible system open to risk. How long the president and his staff will be willing to take such risks will depend in great part on what they believe it produces. In the end, however, it will not be communications that moves public approval but what happens with the situation in Iraq.

References

Interviews conducted by Martha Joynt Kumar, Washington, DC:

Card, Andrew, 30 November 2001.
Eskew, Tucker, 13 June 2002.
Fleischer, Ari, 7 March 2001.
Griscom, Thomas, 3 May 2006.
Hughes, Karen, 13 June 2002.
Matalin, Mary, 3 October 2002.
Rove, Karl, 8 May 2002.
Sforza, Scott, 9 May 2006.
Wilkinson, James, 3 July 2002.

Other Sources

Allen, Mike, 2004. "Management Style Shows Weaknesses; Delegation of Responsibility, Trust in Subordinates May Have Hurt Bush." *Washington Post*. 2 June.

Balz, Dan, and Pincus, Walter. 2003. "Why Commander in Chief is Losing the War of the 16 Words." *Washington Post*. 24 July.

Bartlett, Dan; McCurry, Mike; Plante, Bill; Simendinger, Alexis; and Kumar, Martha Joynt. 2003. "The White House and the Press: Competitors in a Dependent Relationship," American Political Science Association and the White House Historical Association, Washington, DC, 9 October. Available from the White House Historical Association, ⟨http://whitehousehistory.org/03/subs_press/a.html⟩, accessed 21 November 2006.

Brune, Tom, 2005. "Cadre Grows to Rein in Message: Ranks of federal public affairs officials have swelled under Bush to help tighten control on communiqués to media, access to information," *Newsday*. 24 February.

Bush, George W. 2005. "Interview and Bike Riding with the President by Print Journalists," White House, Office of the Press Secretary, Internal Transcript, Bush Ranch, Crawford, Tex., 13 August.

____ 2006. "President Bush Discusses Global War on Terror," The Paul H. Nitze School of Advanced International Study, Johns Hopkins University, Washington, DC, 10 April.

Center for American Progress. 2006. "Talking Points: Not Playing with a New Deck of Cards," 28 March. A half hour later, a more extensive email provided biographical information and specifics about the administration's budget deficits. "Progress Report: Meet the New Chief."

Chertoff, Michael. 2006. "Press Conference with Officials from Homeland Security, the Environmental Protection Agency, and the Departments of Health and Human Services, Energy, Transportation, and Defense Press Room," Press Releases. Department of Homeland Security, 31 August 2006. Available from ⟨http://www.dhs.gov/xnews/releases/press_release_0724.shtm⟩, accessed 21 November 2006.

Department of Treasury. 2005. "March 3–May 1, 2005: 60 Stops in 60 days Accomplishments," available from ⟨http://www.strengtheningsocialsecurity.gov/60stops/accomplishments_042705.pdf⟩, accessed 21 November 2006.

Drinkard, Jim, and Memmott, Mark. 2005. "HHS Said It Paid Columnist for Help," *USA Today*. 27 January.

Eilperin, Juliet. 2006a. "Debate on Climate Shifts to Issue of Irreparable Change; Some Experts on Global Warming Foresee 'Tipping Point' When it is Too Late to Act," *Washington Post*. 29 January.

____ 2006b. "Climate Researchers Feeling Heat From White House," *Washington Post*. 6 April.

Lee, Christopher. 2005a. "Prepackaged News Gets GAO Rebuke," *Washington Post*. 21 February.

____ 2005b. "GAO Issues Mixed Ruling on Payments to Columnists," *Washington Post*. 1 October.

McClellan, Scott. 2005. Press Briefing, White House, Office of the Press Secretary, 6 October 2005.

Milbank, Dana. 2003. "Fleischer's Final Briefing is not Quite a Grand Slam," *Washington Post*. 15 July.

Pincus, Walter, and Milbank, Dana. 2003. "Bush, Rice Blame CIA for Iraq Error; Tenet Accepts Responsibility for Clearing Statement on Nuclear Aims in Jan. Speech," *Washington Post*. 12 July.

PollingReport.com. 2005. "Social Security," CNN/*USA Today*. 22–4 July 2005. Available at ⟨http://www.pollingreport.com/social⟩.

Shah, Shirpal. 2006. Email sent to White House correspondents from the Democratic National Committee by Communications Director Shripal Shah, ShahS@dnc.org. 28 March 2006.

Thomas, Evan, et al. 2005. "How Bush Blew It," *Newsweek*. 15 September.

Toppo, Greg. 2005. "Education Department Paid Commentator to Promote Law," *USA Today*. 7 January.

White House Global Messenger. 2005. "KEY POINTS." 11 March.

Notes

This chapter is part of a larger work on White House communications, *Managing the President's Message: the People, Policies and Politics Behind the Chief Executive's Message.* (forthcoming, Johns Hopkins University, 2007).

1. These numbers are based on compilations made from the May 2005 edition of the internal White House Phone Book as printed by the Bureau of National Affairs, "Daily Report for Executives: White House Phone Directory," no. 116, 17 June 2005.

2. The operations in Karl Rove's orbit in his role as senior adviser are: Office of Strategic Initiatives, Intergovernmental Affairs, Political Affairs, Public Liaison, and Policy and Strategic Planning.

3. The offices that are included in the secondary communications and press offices are: Chief of Staff, Oval Office Operations, Advance, Cabinet Liaison, Scheduling, Staff Secretary. In addition there are people in the Office of the Vice President and the Office of the First Lady who perform support operations for communications, including scheduling, advance, and correspondence. There are additional people who work in Presidential Correspondence, the Travel Office, and the White House Communications Agency, as well as speech transcribers, and military baggage handlers who move television equipment on presidential trips.

4. For a discussion of President Bush's management principles and an earlier description of how the communications operation worked in the first term, see Martha Joynt Kumar, "Communications Operations in the White House of President George W. Bush: Making News on His Terms," *Presidential Studies Quarterly* 33 (2): 366–93.

5. In titling the group the "strategery" group, Rove was playing on the spoof of candidate George W. Bush performed by Will Ferrell on *Saturday Night Live*. Ferrell portrayed the difficulties his character had in pronouncing words, such as "strategy," which always came out as "strategery."

Part IV

Building Congressional Coalitions

12

The US Congress and Chief Executive George W. Bush

Charles O. Jones

George W. Bush brought a chief-executive style of leadership to the White House in 2001. Explained originally by disposition and experience, this approach was then rationalized by circumstance, notably 9/11, followed by the war in Iraq and the attendant involvement in Middle Eastern governing and politics.

Republicans in 2000 retained majority status in the House by a slightly reduced margin and in the Senate by the vote of the vice president. These congressional Republicans were completing their sixth year as the majority party on Capitol Hill, their longest such segment of party control since the 1920s. Of special interest is the relationship between this "legislative" Republican Congress and the "chief executive" Republican president.

Scholars typically treat lawmaking between the branches as "presidential–congressional relations." The focus is on the president and his leadership of Congress. There are, however, good and sufficient reasons to do it the other way around, "congressional–presidential relations" and that is what I will attempt here.[1]

I will place more stress on continuity than on change. Congress, like the bureaucracy, mostly retains its structure and personnel following a national election. Much of the presidency, too, keeps its form and organization. But the White House, the president's cabinet, and other vital positions change markedly when new presidents are elected, especially given that those coming in are commonly of a different political party. As shown in Table 12.1, only three of the thirteen newly elected presidents, 1900–2004, were of the same party as their predecessors (less than a quarter of the changes by election). Coincidentally, each of the three (Taft, Hoover, and Bush 41) was a one-term presidency.[2] Just one of these occurred in the post-World War II era—Reagan

Table 12.1. Presidential succession, 1900–2004

Newly Elected Presidents

Party Change: R→D	1912 Taft to Wilson
	1932 Hoover to F. Roosevelt
	1960 Eisenhower to Kennedy
	1976 Ford to Carter
	1992 Bush to Clinton
Party Change: D→R	1920 Wilson to Harding
	1952 Truman to Eisenhower
	1968 Johnson to Nixon
	2000 Clinton to Bush 43
Same Party: R→R	1908 T. Roosevelt to Taft
	1928 Coolidge to Hoover
	1988 Reagan to Bush 41
Same Party: D→D	No cases
Takeover Presidents	
Republican	1901 McKinley to T. Roosevelt
	1923 Harding to Coolidge
	1974 Nixon to Ford*
Democrat	1945 F. Roosevelt to Truman
	1963 Kennedy to Johnson

* Due to resignation.
Source: Compiled by the author.

to Bush in 1988. Same-party control of the White House averaged 14 years, 1896–1952; it has shortened to 9 years, 1952–2008.

Also shown in Table 12.1 is that five other "new" presidents assumed the office upon the death or resignation of their predecessors, another variation affecting congressional–presidential relations. Predecessors' legacies varied, as did the pressures to retain or change White House staff and major appointments. Johnson had to move cautiously as the inheritor of the Kennedy heritage. Quite the opposite was the case for Ford, who would be evaluated by whether he cleaned house following Nixon's resignation in disgrace.

So the question is: How does an experienced Republican Congress interact with a chief-executive oriented president? I will make comparisons with other newly elected presidents so as to brighten the conclusions regarding the Bush 43 presidency and the theme of this conference: Politics and Polarization. Some broad historical and comparative perspective is the place to start.

Congress When a New President is Elected

How is it that Congresses come to new presidencies? Are leaders and members encouraged to pay extra heed to presidential leadership? To what extent is there congruence between how well the party did in the three national elections—House, Senate, and presidency? Is the natural tendency to start anew reinforced by election results?

Table 12.2. House and Senate incumbent return, 1952–2004*

President	Pres. election	First midterm	Pres. re-election	Second midterm
Eisenhower	H = 81.4	H = 87.1	H = 89.4	H = 81.8
	S = 84.4	S = 85.4	S = 89.6	S = 83.7
Kennedy-Johnson	H = 86.2	H = 84.6	H = 79.1[†]	H = 83.2
	S = 94.0	S = 90.0	S = 93.0[†]	S = 93.0
Nixon-Ford	H = 91.0	H = 87.1	H = 83.9	H = 79.9
	S = 86.0	S = 89.0	S = 87.0	S = 89.0
Carter	H = 84.6	H = 82.3		
	S = 83.0	S = 80.0		
Reagan	H = 83.0	H = 81.4	H = 90.1	H = 88.5
	S = 92.0	S = 95.0	S = 93.0	S = 87.0
Bush 41	H = 92.4	H = 89.7		
	S = 90.0	S = 96.0		
Clinton	H = 74.7	H = 80.0	H = 83.0	H = 90.1
	S = 88.0	S = 89.0	S = 85.0	S = 92.0
Bush 43	H = 90.1	H = 87.8	H = 90.1	H = 87.8
	S = 89.0	S = 91.0	S = 91.0	S = 90.0
Mean percentage	H = 85.4	H = 85.0	H = 85.9	H = 85.2
	S = 88.3	S = 89.4	S = 89.8	S = 89.1

* In every case, the percentage is of the total number of incumbents returning, not just those seeking re-election in the House and including the two-thirds not up for re-election in the Senate.

† Johnson was elected in 1964, not re-elected.

Source: Compiled by the author from data in Norman J. Ornstein, Thomas E. Mann, and Michael J. Malbin, *Vital Statistics on Congress, 2001–2002* (Cambridge, Mass.: AEI, 2002), tables 2-7, 2-8, and various internet sources for recent elections.

Table 12.2 shows the House and Senate incumbent return rates for presidential and mid-term elections, 1952–2004. Included in the turnover are those retiring plus those defeated for re-election in primary and general elections. The range of incumbent return for representatives is 74.7 per cent to 92.4 per cent; that for senators, 80 per cent to 96 per cent. The lowest rates are often associated with higher rates of retirement than normal. The overall mean return rates for this period are: House 85.3 per cent; Senate 89.1 per cent. As shown at the bottom of Table 12.2, there is no significant variation among the average return rates between the four types of election: presidential election and re-election, and the first and second mid-terms.

These data show both continuity and change. A return rate in a two-year period averaging between 85 and 90 per cent indicates steadiness for almost any organization. Yet the foundation for change is laid with a turnover of 15 per cent in the House (representing 65 members or 130 during a presidential term) and an 11 per cent turnover of senators (resulting in over one-fifth change during a presidential term). It is also the case that new members have been increasingly integrated into and socialized by both chambers in recent decades, thus facilitating adaptation to change.

It is noteworthy how replacement occurs in the two institutions. Newly elected members of Congress take their place at the bottom of the rosters, and when a congressional party leader or committee chair retires or is defeated, an experienced, senior member typically moves into his or her place, not a freshman.

By contrast, replacements in the executive branch come in at the top. Thus, for example, a new president may come from out of town, often bringing others who have not previously served in Washington. They assume the highest executive positions, then interact with party leaders and committee chairs who have long experience in lawmaking.

There are more data to consider in a quest to place the Bush 43 presidency in comparative perspective. Table 12.3 shows the political status of postwar presidents and congresses following national elections. Included are the results for individual presidents, along with how well they did in House districts,

Table 12.3. Status of elected presidents and Congress at inauguration, 1945–2000

President's win	House districts won (%)	Pres. party in Congress (%)	Pres. party gain/loss	Pres. party House vote (%)
DDE, 1952 PV = 55.1% EV = 82.6%	68.3	H = 50.8* S = 50.0*	H = +22 S = +1	49.3 (R)
JFK, 1960 PV = 49.7% EV = 56.3%	46.7	H = 60.0 S = 64.0	H = −21 S = 0	54.4 (D)
RMN, 1968 PV = 43.4% EV = 55.9%	n.a.	H = 44.1 S = 42.0	H = +5 S = +6	48.2 (R)
JEC, 1976 PV = 50.1% EV = 55.2%	50.6	H = 67.1 S = 61.0	H = +1 S = 0	56.2 (D)
RWR, 1980 PV = 50.7% EV = 90.9%	71.0	H = 44.1 S = 53.0*	H = +33 S = +12	48.0 (R)
GHWB, 1988 PV = 53.4% EV = 79.2%	68.7	H = 40.2 S = 45.0	H = −2 S = 0	45.5 (R)
WJC, 1992 PV = 43.0% EV = 68.8%	59.1	H = 59.3 S = 57.0	H = −9 S = +1	50.8 (D)
GWB, 2000 PV = 47.9% EV = 50.4%	52.4	H = 50.8 S = 50.0	H = −2 S = −5	50.4 (R)

Note: n.a = data not available.

* A switch in party control of the chamber.

Source: Compiled by the author from data in Ornstein, Mann, and Malbin (2002), ch. 2.

their party's showing in the House and Senate (percentages of membership and net gains or losses), and their party's share of the national House vote. The purpose of these data is to provide evidence of how members of Congress are likely to view the political advantages of a new president.

Presumably members will pay more heed to presidents with strongly positive numbers in all categories, less to those with weaker numbers. The five Republican presidents form two groups. Eisenhower and Reagan had strong wins and ran very well in House districts, the Republicans had net gains in the House and Senate and narrowly captured majority status in both houses in 1952 and the Senate in 1980. There were ample reasons for congressional Republicans to acknowledge the electoral standing of these presidents. Eisenhower and Reagan did differ in one important respect: the magnitude of their domestic agendas—limited in the case of Eisenhower, substantially grander in the case of Reagan.

Nixon, Bush 41, and Bush 43 fared substantially less well in electoral standing. Nixon had a marginal win in a three-person race. Republicans had net gains in the House and Senate but were still far from majority status in either chamber. Bush 41 had a comfortable win and ran well in House districts. But his win had no obvious effect on congressional races, with a net Republican loss of House seats, no gain in the Senate, and a huge disparity between how well he ran in House districts (68.7 per cent) and the share of vote won by Republican candidates in those districts (45.5 per cent).

Bush 43 fared no better. He lost the popular vote, won the lowest percentage of Electoral Vote as a winner since 1876, and won a slight majority of House districts. Republicans retained majority control in both houses of Congress but had a net loss of seats in both. Their losses in the Senate left them in a tie with Democrats that then had to be broken by the vice president so as to permit Republicans to organize that body.

There were notable agenda differences among these three Republicans. Nixon faced the daunting challenge of ending the Vietnam War but had a relatively light domestic program, as did Bush 41. By contrast, Bush 43 came to the White House with an ambitious domestic program in spite of his narrowest of wins.

The three Democrats—Kennedy, Carter, and Clinton—had little more claim than Nixon and the two Bushes to congressional following as a result of their elections. No one of the three had an impressive popular vote and though Democrats retained their House and Senate majorities in each case, they had either net losses or little or no gains. For all three, the party carried forward their relatively strong majorities gained in the mid-term elections preceding their own election—1958, 1974, and 1990. These three Democrats had robust agendas, possibly related to the strength of the Democratic majorities in Congress and less policy active Republican administrations—Eisenhower, Ford, and Bush 41.

One other feature of relevance is not shown in Table 12.3. There are three cases similar to the circumstances facing Bush 43. Kennedy, Carter, and Clinton each followed a Republican president working with a Democratic Congress: six years with Eisenhower for Kennedy (1954–60); eight years with Nixon-Ford for Carter (1968–76), and six years for Reagan and Bush 41 for Clinton (1986–92). Bush 43 inherited a Republican Congress having worked with a Democratic president (Clinton) for six years (1994–2000). I will refer to these analogues in the following analysis.

One final point of comparison. To what extent did leadership change follow the election of a new president? It is the case, as noted above, that experienced, typically senior, members replace party and committee leaders. But the replacements are taking on new jobs, thus giving the president an edge. He can make them look good through consultation and cooperation. Again, Eisenhower and Reagan had the most advantages because of party changeover. For Eisenhower, Republicans gained majorities in both chambers, accompanied by change in House and Senate majority leadership, to include all new committee chairs. One moderating factor was that most of these new leaders had served in their same positions during the 80th Congress—just four years prior. For Reagan, Republicans unexpectedly won majority status in the Senate, thus producing a change in floor and committee leadership. That shift influenced White House strategy in working with Congress, encouraging greater use of the Senate as the chamber of first action.[3]

Kennedy and Carter had similar experiences. Committee chairs remained stable for both but Speaker Rayburn's death in the fall of 1961 caused a shake-up of House party leadership, and Johnson's exit to become vice president meant a new majority leadership team in the Senate. Having Johnson in the White House also provided an advantage in working with the Senate, though several Senate Democrats expressed displeasure when it was proposed that Johnson preside over their caucus.[4] Carter too had a new Speaker and a House and Senate majority party team. As it happened, circumstances prevented his taking advantage of this change.

Majority party leadership changed for Bush 41 as well. The Speaker and whip resigned early in his administration and there was a new majority leadership team in the Senate. However, Republicans were in the minority, holding just 40 per cent of House seats and 45 per cent of Senate seats. The president was not in a strong position to take advantage of these shifts.

Party leadership and committee chair changes were not an advantage for either Nixon, Clinton, or Bush 43. House and Senate Republicans were in the minority during the entirety of the Nixon and Ford presidencies. There was but one change in House and Senate party leadership when Nixon took office (a new majority Senate whip). Clinton and Bush 43 gained no special advantage as the leadership teams for both parties remained the same. If anything, these two presidents from out of town relied on party and committee leaders to aid in orienting them to the lawmaking aspects of their new jobs. House and Senate party leadership changes had occurred for Republicans—a new Speaker and House leadership team in 1998 and a new Senate majority leader when Dole ran for president in 1996.

These cases for each party justify an effort to explore congressional–presidential relations. In more instances than not, the Congress greets the new president in a position sufficiently independent and advantageous as to encourage the advancement of a prudent and practical lawmaking strategy by the president and his aides. There is little to suggest that Congress need automatically accept presidential leadership. Quite the opposite. It is a fact, of course, that Congress cannot lead itself, being bicameral and having organized itself to serve its representative and deliberative functions. But it can and does often generate legislation with little or no presidential leadership or involvement. And whereas the president normally designates the agenda and its sequence, Congress contributes major refinements in shaping and maintaining the items on that agenda.

How, in summary, did Congress come to George W. Bush? A seasoned Republican majority awaited the president's inauguration. Incumbent Republicans returned at an above-average rate in 2000, fresh from battling President Clinton on ethical and domestic issues. Impeachment proceedings interrupted a legislative record that had been positive to that point. President Bush's political status in relationship to that of Congress was among the least impressive of any postwar president. His principal advantage was that of Republican majorities on Capitol Hill but there was limited evidence that he had much to do with their successful return. Had Gore won in Florida, Republicans would still have maintained their majorities.

There was one important point of congruity between Bush 43 and the Republican Congress. The president campaigned on a set of issues on which the 106th Congress had worked. In fact, as discussed below, the 2000 campaign focused on an agenda mostly laid out by Clinton in his 1998 State of the Union Address. The 106th Congress was, however, unlikely to make much progress on the Clinton agenda during the embittered impeachment struggle. Thus there was an issue basis for positive congressional–presidential relations in the 107th Congress, albeit set in the context of partisan ill will.

What Type of President?

The major theme of congressional–presidential relations is continuity (high incumbent return) integrating change (a new president). The type of president is vital to this accommodation. For who the president is, what he wants, and how he plans to get it are the elements of change to which Congress must adjust and respond. I noted the president's party affiliation above, along with the change that it may represent (see Table 12.1) and his political status upon being inaugurated, notably as contrasted with that of Congress (see Tables 12.2 and 12.3). Another distinction of relevance is that of presidential style being more *legislative* or more *executive*, a difference typically associated with experience and temperament.

The purely legislative manner is representative, reactive, responsive, collaborative, open and sharing, compromising, and narrowly accountable to constituencies. Presidents employing this style view issues from the perspective of constituents, reacting and responding accordingly. If a law is to be enacted, members of Congress must develop means for collaborating and compromising in a process that inevitably diffuses accountability. Ownership of an idea or proposal can get lost in the lawmaking process. Therefore a legislatively oriented president is accustomed to sharing responsibility and fault with others, that is, those who are implicated in lawmaking.

The purely executive manner is proactive, hierarchical, contained, programmatic, resolute, and broadly accountable. It stresses leadership. Hierarchy is established both symbolically and practically to promote initiative and accountability. It also provides the structural containers or organizational units for defining problems, planning, and making choices. Presidents as executives tend to be more programmatic, seeking to relate one policy to the next. That tendency, along with hierarchy, fosters more resoluteness than flexibility in supporting a plan or decision. Executive behavior invites command and its attendant risks and liabilities. After all, reliance on hierarchy leads right back to the top, whereas, as noted above, a more incorporative and horizontal process (for example, one more consultative with Congress) diffuses accountability.[5]

One measure of whether an incoming president's manner is likely to be more legislative or executive is background in government and politics. What has been his experience—more legislative or more executive? What was his position just prior to becoming president? Table 12.4 provides this information for all presidents, as well as whether they were elected to office or took over for someone else and whether they held an elective position upon winning the presidency. As shown, I rate presidents on a five-point scale: whether their background was "all executive," "all legislative," "more executive," "more legislative," and "balanced."

Table 12.5 provides a summary of prior experience and service at the time of election for the periods before and after the formation of the present two-party system. Note that a higher percentage of presidents in the earlier period had legislative experience. Even Washington served in the House of Burgesses for 15 years. The record since 1856 shows slightly less than half the presidents with mostly executive experience; the other half with mostly legislative or balanced backgrounds. There is little difference between the two periods in regard to jobs held at the point of being elected president. Two-thirds of

Table 12.4. Political experience prior to serving as president, 1789–2005

President	Accession	Background*	Just prior	Elected?
Washington[†]	Elected	5 (12/16)	Private	n.a.
J. Adams[‡]	Elected	3 (18/7)	Executive	Elected (VP)
Jefferson[†]	Elected	3 (13/6)	Executive	Elected (VP)
Madison[†]	Elected	4 (8/16)	Executive	Appointed
Monroe[†]	Elected	3 (15/8)	Executive	Appointed
J. Q. Adams[‡]	Elected	3 (22/6)	Executive	Appointed
Jackson[†]	Elected	2 (4)	Private	n.a.
Van Buren[‡]	Elected	4 (6/15)	Executive	Elected (VP)
W. Harrison	Elected	3 (14/9)	Private	n.a.
Tyler	Takeover	4 (2/23)	Executive	Elected (VP)
Polk	Elected	4 (2/16)	Private	n.a.
Taylor	Elected	1 (military)	Executive (military)	Appointed
Fillmore	Takeover	4 (3/10)	Executive	Elected (VP)
Pierce	Elected	2 (14)	Private	n.a.
Modern two-party system developed				
Buchanan	Elected	4 (8/22)	Executive	Appointed
Lincoln[†]	Elected	2 (10)	Private	n.a.
A. Johnson	Takeover	4 (6/24)	Executive	Elected (VP)
Grant[†]	Elected	1 (military)	Executive (military)	Appointed
Hayes	Elected	3 (8/2)	Executive	Elected
Garfield	Elected	2 (19)	Legislative	Elected
Arthur	Takeover	1 (7)	Executive	Elected (VP)
Cleveland[‡]	Elected	1 (3)	Executive	Elected
B. Harrison[‡]	Elected	2 (6)	Private	n.a.
Cleveland	Elected	1 (7)	Private	n.a.
McKinley[†]	Elected	4 (4/12)	Executive	Elected
T. Roosevelt§	Takeover	3 (11/2)	Executive	Elected (VP)
Taft[‡]	Elected	1 (8)	Executive	Appointed
Wilson[†]	Elected	1 (2)	Executive	Elected
Harding	Elected	4 (2/10)	Legislative	Elected
Coolidge§	Takeover	5 (5/5)	Executive	Elected (VP)
Hoover[‡]	Elected	1 (13)	Executive	Appointed
F. Roosevelt[†]	Elected	3 (11/2)	Executive	Elected
Truman§	Takeover	4 (2/10)	Executive	Elected (VP)
Eisenhower[†]	Elected	1 (military)	Executive (military)	Appointed
Kennedy	Elected	2 (12)	Legislative	Elected
L. Johnson§	Takeover	4 (3/24)	Executive	Elected (VP)
Nixon	Elected	5 (8/6)	Private	n.a.
Ford§§	Takeover	2 (24)	Executive	Appointed (VP)
Carter[‡]	Elected	5 (4/4)	Private	n.a.
Reagan[†]	Elected	1 (8)	Private	n.a.
GHW Bush[‡]	Elected	3 (13/4)	Executive	Elected (VP)
Clinton[†]	Elected	1 (14)	Executive	Elected
GW Bush[†]	Elected	1(6)	Executive	Elected

* Code: 1, all executive; 2, all legislative; 3, mostly executive; 4, mostly legislative; 5, balance. Numbers in parentheses represent years of executive and legislative experience.

[†] Successfully ran for re-election; Roosevelt three times.

[‡] Unsuccessful re-election bid.

§ Takeover president successfully ran for election.

§§ Takeover president unsuccessfully ran for election.

Source: Compiled by the author from biographical summaries in William A. DeGregorio, *The Complete Book of U.S. Presidents*, 6th edn. (New York: Gramercy Books, 2005).

Table 12.5. Prior executive and legislative experience of presidents in two time periods

Prior experience	1789–1857	1857–2005	Combined
Mostly executive	6 (43%)	15 (52%)	21 (49%)
Mostly legislative	7 (50%)	11 (38%)	18 (42%)
Balance	1 (7%)	3 (10%)	4 (9%)
TOTAL	14	29	43
Just prior			
Executive	9 (64%)	20 (69%)	29 (67%)
Legislative	0 (0%)	3 (10%)	3 (7%)
Private	5 (36%)	6 (21%)	11 (26%)
TOTAL	14	29	43

Source: Compiled by the author from biographical data in DeGregorio (2005).

the presidents held executive positions at the point of their moving to the White House—nineteen in elective positions (twelve as vice presidents), ten in appointive positions.[6] Just three (Garfield, Harding, and Kennedy) were serving as legislators; the rest were in private life when elected president.

Where does George W. Bush fit into this historical record? With whom might we compare him? These criteria, drawn from Bush's experience, are relevant: elected, not a takeover president; re-elected; all executive experience in previous posts; civilian elected executive position at the time of election. Remarkably, there are but two other presidents who meet these criteria: Woodrow Wilson and Bill Clinton. Others among presidents in the twentieth century come close in that their backgrounds are more purely executive: Franklin Roosevelt, Eisenhower, and Reagan.

Table 12.6 provides comparative data on these five presidents and Bush 43: the two purest cases (Wilson and Clinton) plus Roosevelt, Eisenhower, and

Table 12.6. Presidents with similar executive backgrounds: twentieth to twenty-first centuries

President	Elected/ re-elected?	Executive/legislative experience	Executive when elected	Elected or appointed
Wilson	Yes	2/0 (100%)	Yes (Governor)	Elected
F. D. Roosevelt	Yes	11/2 (85%)	Yes (Governor)	Elected
Eisenhower	Yes	Military (100%)	Yes (NATO Cmdr.)	Appointed
Reagan	Yes	8/0 (100%)	No (Private life)	n.a.
Clinton	Yes	14/0 (100%)	Yes (Governor)	Elected
Bush 43	Yes	6/0 (100%)	Yes (Governor)	Elected

Note: n.a. = not applicable.
Source: See Table 12.4.

Reagan.[7] As shown, Wilson had little governmental experience, having served just two years as governor of New Jersey. He profited from the split in the Republican Party in 1912, winning with just 42 per cent of the popular vote, with Progressive Party candidate Roosevelt coming in second with 27 per cent. Democrats won control of the House in 1910 and substantially increased their majority in 1912 (from 58 per cent to 67 per cent). Additionally, several Republicans ran as Progressives so that Republicans had but 29 per cent of the membership. Senate Republicans remained in the majority in 1910 but lost that status in 1912. Thus it was that a freshly reoriented Congress joined a new president committed to a progressive agenda. The election encouraged interpreting congruity between the presidential and congressional results.

Twice elected governor of New York, Roosevelt had earlier served for seven years as Assistant Secretary of the Navy. His huge win in 1932 was complemented by landslide wins for House and Senate Democrats. As was the case in 1910, Democrats had become the majority in the House two years before, in 1930. The Democratic House net gain in 1932 was the second greatest in history, resulting in a 72 per cent majority. Senate change was less dramatic, as befits the design of just one-third up for re-election. Still, Democrats in that chamber had a 61 per cent majority. Agenda congruity between Congress and the president has seldom been greater. The Great Depression was in its third year. It affected all elections and brought to Washington an anxiety for designing policy change.

Eisenhower's executive experience was almost entirely in the military. His command-level background brought him in frequent contact with Congress and made him highly knowledgeable about hierarchy. His sizable win in 1952 was not accompanied by huge increases for his party in Congress but House and Senate Republicans did garner bare majorities for just the second time since 1928 and 1930 respectively. There was substantially less reason to attribute congruity of presidential and congressional outcomes than was the case for Wilson and Roosevelt. The dominant issues were those of alleged corruption and ending the Korean War. Both were more presidential than congressional matters.

Reagan had retired to private life in 1975 following eight years serving as Governor of California. He sought the Republican nomination for president in 1976 and made a strong showing. In 1980 he was the oldest person to seek the presidency. As with Wilson and Roosevelt, the presidential and congressional results could be interpreted as congruous. Senate Republicans were in the majority for the first time in 26 years and though House Republicans remained in the minority, they had a net gain of 33 seats. The state of the economy was the principal issue and the new Congress came to the new presidency acknowledging the need to take action.

Clinton had the most elected executive experience of the six presidents listed in Table 12.6—two years as attorney general and twelve as governor. Yet his service was in the small state of Arkansas, ranked 33rd in population, compared with the high rankings of New York (Roosevelt), California (Reagan), and Texas (Bush 43). Like Wilson, Clinton benefited from a third party candidate that drew votes from an incumbent president. Yet he received only 43 per cent of the popular vote. House and Senate Democrats retained their majorities in the 1992 election but there was a net gain of just one Senate seat and a net loss of nine House seats. Thus it was not possible to identify anything like a congruent issue message from the presidential and congressional results. The principal issue was the state of the economy, though there was not the same urgency as in 1980. The new president's desire to enact reforms, most notably in health care and welfare, drove much of the agenda.

And that brings us to George W. Bush. By background he is among the most executive-oriented presidents in history. He served as governor of the second-ranked state in population. He is the son of a president who served in a number of executive positions, including as vice president. He worked with his father at different points. Yet however personally inclined toward an executive style of governing, Bush 43 had among the narrowest wins ever. And House and Senate Republicans had net losses while retaining majority control.

In summary, Bush 43 compares well in executive background with other presidents. Like the others, he was elected, and then re-elected; as with four of the five, he served as a governor; his service was exclusively executive; and his position prior to serving as president was elective. What differs is how Congress entered alongside the new president. In three cases (Wilson, FDR, and Reagan) the election results appeared congruent, thus encouraging cooperation with the new president. The results were less dramatic in the case of Eisenhower but the new president's landslide win in 1952 and the shift to majority status supported collaboration. The Clinton case was even less accommodating to interpreting congruent results, with Democrats having a net loss of nine House seats and gaining but one in the Senate. There was no landslide win for Clinton, yet it was an all-Democratic government for the first time in twelve years and expectations were high.[8]

Therefore, Bush 43 and the 107th Congress look most like Clinton and the 103rd Congress. In each case, Congress came to the new president with six years experience in working with a president of the opposite party. The new president won with a plurality of the vote, due in Clinton's case to a third candidate. And the president's party in each case had unimpressive congressional election results. Yet there are important differences too—mostly a result of the executive styles of the two presidents.

Governing Executively with Congress

Stephen Skowronek explains Bush 43's leadership style as *definitional*. As text for this label, Skowronek cites the foreword to Bush's book *A Charge to Keep*, where Bush repeats a political lesson he learned in his first campaign for the House of Representatives: "never allow others to define me."[9] This declaration of independence implies a determination to take charge of who one is, how one behaves, and what purposes political life serves. According to Skowronek: "This is a man who has pondered the fate of recent leaders and concluded that their success turned on their ability to define themselves and the others around them. This is a man who has come to believe that definitions effectively asserted can create their own reality."[10] Leadership by definition features steadfastness, perseverance, confidence, and direction. "By purging self-doubt and second guessing, the posture ultimately leaves the leader to scorn accountability and simply insist on the essential correctness of the decisions made."[11]

I accept this characterization of Bush's leadership rationale. But there is more to consider. One can almost envision a game of tag wherein leaders feign, dodge, race, and possibly hide in an effort to avoid being tagged by how others define their roles. One way to protect oneself is to create a shield that will simply not permit the tag. Presidents do have the advantage of their oneness. "The executive Power shall be vested in a President of the United States of America." (Art. II, Sect. 1) And so the president is the chief: chief executive and commander in chief. How others interpret the president's role is important to the extent that he incorporates their views into his definition of the job. Skowronek's general point is that Bush protects how presidential leadership is defined, thus is unlikely knowingly to permit others to influence his conceptions. My contention is that his definition is that of the pure executive, perhaps the purest since Eisenhower and among the most faithful in the history of the presidency. He serves as the chief executive first and foremost.

I contend further that a distinction can be made between chief executive and president. The former has a more structural or institutional interpretation of the separation of powers. The latter has a more political interpretation. Recall Neustadt's observation that: "The constitutional convention of 1787 was supposed to have created a government of 'separated powers.' It did nothing of the sort. Rather, it created a government of separated institutions *sharing* powers."[12] Neustadt even quotes Eisenhower, the military version of executive behavior, as stating: "I am part of the legislative process," referring primarily to his veto power.[13]

The evidence suggests Bush believes the constitutional convention did separate powers and that he is antithetical to the notion of sharing his powers with Congress. He has explained from time to time that he is not the Congress. His attitude appears to be classically separationist: I'll do my job. You do yours. Let's try not to do each other's. By the way, it is interesting that Bush has at this writing still not exercised what Eisenhower identified as his "part of the legislative process"—the veto.

Bush's understanding of and reliance on position explains much of how he exercises "leadership by definition." Neustadt's sources of presidential power are familiar: "the product of his vantage points in government, together with his reputation in the Washington community and his prestige outside."[14] As described elsewhere, Bush, upon entering the White House, could rely on neither reputation in Washington nor prestige outside. However the "vantage points in government" come with the designation of "president." But there is something more, a feature more subjective than the formal authority the Constitution, Congress, and custom give to the president. Qualities attributed to the presidency by the public and other power holders, such as national leadership, symbolic representation abroad, and moral suasion, can also serve as sources of power for presidents. Posturing is typically vital to demonstrating these qualities. I have bundled these features—vantage points plus the qualities of the office—in the term *position,* essentially the status of being president. George W. Bush capitalized on position from the day following the election forward and it has been his principal reliance in the exercise of presidential power since.[15] Accordingly, its loss or diminution would have serious effects for his presidency.

Dependence on position is compatible with a separationist orientation of leadership by definition. It is likely to be the most reliable anchor in the exercise of presidential power—reputation and prestige being more variable (also highly subjective, even if measurable). Dependence on position stresses separationism by defining power in institutional terms. Essentially it asserts: "I am the president and here is what that means." Both reputation and prestige invite attention to how others define presidential power, that is, how others judge standing, whether it be evaluations of capability by the Washington community or ratings of job performance by poll respondents. Emphasizing position also puts distance between the president and Congress by not incorporating the members into the definition of leadership.

Although it is true that a newly inaugurated President Bush had low ratings for reputation and prestige, the evidence suggests that he would have relied primarily on position even if his scores had been high on these other sources of power. In fact, his conception of chief executive preceded his 2001–2 rise in prestige as measured by polls, if not in reputation. As governor of Texas, Bush articulated this distinction between the legislature and the executive:

The legislative process is one of give-and-take, of agreement and disagreement. Their job is to figure out how to shape and mold legislation, to put together the pieces into a whole that can gather enough votes to pass.

My job is different. A Governor is a chief executive officer. I believe my job is to set its agenda, to articulate the vision, and to lead.... [T]he Governor has the power of the bully pulpit, the ability to communicate with the public to articulate a message, an idea, an agenda. A Governor sets a tone.... A strong person can make a powerful difference.[16]

It is relevant too that his reflections on leadership in an interview with Bob Woodward following 9/11 stressed a strong executive orientation:

I think my job is to stay ahead of the moment...be the strategic thinker that you're supposed to be.

One of my jobs is to be provocative...to provoke people.

I like clarity [in lines of responsibility].

The president has to be the calcium in the backbone. If I weaken, the whole team weakens.[17]

There is little, if any, evidence that Bush relied on poll ratings as a source of power even as his numbers were setting new records or equally on congressional evaluations of his reputation.[18] Rather he appears to believe that influence will follow from status, not measures of personal qualities. On the other hand, he places substantial trust in how he has achieved status through election. Here is how he evaluated his being re-elected governor in 1998:

Politics is not about the past or rewarding office holders for a job well done [so much for the effect of yesterday's polls]. Voters want to know a candidate's view for the future. I had earned political capital by doing in office what I said I would do during my first campaign. Now was the time to spend that capital on a bold agenda for change and reform in the second term.[19]

Bush used almost these same words upon his re-election as president: "I earned capital in the campaign, political capital, and now I intend to spend it. It is my style."[20] For Bush, elections are authenticating events for status or position. Once over, presidents then serve as the chief executive. By this perspective, little more needs to be said in regard to presidential power.

An ultra-separationist view of the presidency ("you do your job; I'll do mine") logically invites accountability whether or not the president feels accountable (see Skowronek above). Why? There are several reasons: there is but one president; the executive branch is, for the most part, organized hierarchically; Congress is bicameral and has no single leader; and the legislative portion of lawmaking tends to obscure accountability. It is normally the case, therefore, that presidents are held accountable, whether or not they feel accountable or have authored or endorsed a law or decision. But the pure executive as president asks for even more than the ordinary liability. How can a bare popular and Electoral College win be considered "political capital?" Because it returned the president to his position, and he is but one person. The result is very different from winning a congressional election in which the losers retain 49 per cent of House seats and 44 per cent of Senate seats (as in 2004).

Events too can have the effect of concentrating responsibility, especially the case with wars and natural disasters. Few turn first to Congress at the time of an attack on the homeland, as with 9/11, or a calamity of historical proportions, as with the Katrina hurricane. As it has happened, the Bush presidency has experienced a number of such events. Thus, in a sense, President Bush has defined his job as a person in charge and events have directed accountability his way.

Lawmaking with Chief Executive Bush

Analyzing how the 107th and subsequent congresses have met and interacted with chief executive Bush requires stepping back to what the membership had experienced in the years prior to 2001. What shaped their views of the executive? How might they be expected to fit a new president into their ongoing policy and political life?

The Republicans were starting their fourth Congress as the majority party in 2001. The three previous congresses—the 104th, 105th, and 106th—each had special features. The 104th witnessed an aggressive effort by Speaker Newt Gingrich to lead the separated system as he mounted an effort to force President Clinton to accept a Republican budget. By all accounts, Clinton won that battle. Against all odds, this contretemps was then followed in 1996 with an outpouring of major legislation—eleven laws enacted by Mayhew's count, third most for a single year in the post-World War II period.

The 105th Congress continued the impressive production of agreements between the Democratic president and Republican Congress with a historic balanced budget settlement in 1997. By the end of the year, it appeared to most analysts that President Clinton had mastered the difficult and delicate politics of leading an opposition party Congress. He was said by one analyst to hold "the upper hand as the 1998 legislative and political battles begin." A Democratic political strategist declared that he was "in the catbird seat." His 1998 State of the Union Address "will make him the defining center of political dialogue for the next two years."[21] Another analyst identified Clinton as entering a third phase of his presidency. The first was activist, the second was reactive, and the third "will be activist with less attitude." "He is already proposing programs that force the Republicans to react to him."[22] The press reported that the president wanted to dispel the notion that he was a lame duck. Accordingly there was a flurry of announcements of new initiatives to be set before Congress in the 1998 State of the Union Address.[23]

The president delivered the address as billed. It set forth an activist agenda for the last three years of the Clinton presidency, at least one year of which was guaranteed to be with a Republican Congress. Democratic expectations in advance were that the program would aid in their recapturing the Congress in 1998. As it happened, however, the revelations regarding the president's affair with Monica Lewinsky preceded the State of the Union Address. Thus, most judgments were about how well he delivered the speech under trying conditions, not how well crafted was the program as an agenda for the remainder of his presidency.

The Lewinsky revelations may have dramatically altered how viewers would analyze the 1998 Address, but the text itself remained a well-prepared, poll-tested, and adroitly expressed list of issues. Would Congress ignore the Lewinsky matter and proceed to enact the legislation requested by the president? Or would there be parallel tracks, with little or no overlap? Answering those questions requires separate analysis. Suffice it to state that the production of the major legislation requested by President Clinton was mostly not forthcoming. By Mayhew's count, there were but ten major laws enacted in 1998–2001, just three or four of which could be attributed to the requests made in 1998. The annual average of major laws enacted was halved, from six, 1993–8, to three, 1998–2001. In fact, many of the 1998 requests were repeated in Clinton's 2000 State of the Union Address, again with limited effect. The production of three major laws in Clinton's last year was the smallest for any postwar president in his final year since Eisenhower in 1960.

Interpretations differ in regard to who was to blame for the slowdown in legislative production in spite of a commendable outline of the national agenda in the 1998 State of the Union Address. What is not in dispute is the rise of bitter partisanship that led to an impeachment and trial of the president. The acquittal of the president was vindication with a price, making him even less effective than lame duck status would have otherwise. And the House and Senate Republican leaders who were instrumental earlier in forging cross-party agreements were no longer in Congress: Dole having run for president in 1996 and Gingrich having resigned in 1998.

The failure to act comprehensively on the 1998 agenda did not, however, cancel its relevance. Congress worked on many of the issues during the last three years. And the basic outline of the 1998 Address came to influence the 2000 campaign. John F. Harris asked these questions in regard to the 2000 State of the Union Address: "Was this a governing agenda...? Or was it a political platform [for 2000]...? The answer is both."[24] Presidential candidates Gore and Bush were likely to propose different solutions but there was general agreement on the agenda, as well as coincidence of items with those listed by Clinton in 1998.

A review of the issues cited by Clinton in 1998 and those named by Gore and Bush in their acceptance speeches in 2000 shows substantial overlap. Gore went to some lengths to establish his own identity: "But now we turn the page and write a new chapter... This election is not an award for past performance." Yet of the issues he listed, nearly half were mentioned in Clinton's 1998 State of the Union Address. Bush too repeated many of those same issues. In fact, there was agreement between the two candidates that Social Security, tax cuts, education (including Head Start), trade, health care, medicare, crime, and racial issues—all included in Clinton's Address— were priorities. They also both mentioned matters not specifically cited by Clinton but related to his agenda: prescription drugs, family values, and abortion.

There were also differences. Gore stressed other Clinton 1998 priorities that Bush did not—welfare, child care, campaign finance reform, pollution, global warming, medical research, and the internet. Bush listed tax code reform and drug use, and paid substantially more attention to the military. And each had special proposals to offer that were not cited by Clinton: after-school care, a patients' bill of rights, mental illness, home nursing care, and a victims' bill of rights for Gore; private retirement accounts, reduction of nuclear weapons, home purchase plan, charitable donations for Bush.

To summarize, this review portrays the political and policy experiences of the 107th Congress as they met on 3 January 2001. What had been developing as a productive model of competitive partisanship between a Democratic president and Republican Congress shifted dramatically in the aftermath of the Lewinsky affair and the report to Congress by Independent Counsel Kenneth Starr. Forecasts of President Clinton's mastery of the agenda at the start of 1998 were not overstated. He had demonstrated a capacity to identify and define issues. He also had shown an ability to propose programs judged to be worth consideration by Republicans and to respond to Republican initiatives. Politics and partisanship were intense but had been productive in 1996 and 1997.

That working relationship was replaced in 1998 with bitter confrontations over a nonpolicy constitutional matter of impeachment. Meanwhile, House and Senate Republicans experienced their own leadership predicaments when Dole ran for the presidency in 1996 and Gingrich resigned in 1998. Congressional committees continued to work on what was generally conceded to be the national agenda but impeachment politics made it virtually impossible to get the cross-party agreements necessary for passage of legislation. Further, the slight gains realized by Democrats in the 1998 congressional elections encouraged them to prepare for winning back the Congress in 2000, presumably to work with President Gore.

Consequently, members of Congress began the 107th Congress well schooled in major issues by virtue of their articulation by Clinton in 1998 and his two subsequent State of the Union Addresses and their own treatment of these issues over time, as well as in the 105th and 106th Congresses. The extraordinary partisan conflict associated with the 2000 presidential election and further net losses by congressional Republicans contributed to an intensely competitive mood as the new Congress met and the new president was inaugurated.

Under the circumstances, many recommended that President Bush preside over a sort of coalition government. That was unlikely to happen given his pure executive style, and it did not happen. Most congressional Republicans would have opposed any such move. And so a form of competitive partisanship ensued, one in which House Republicans used all the advantages of the majority (and then some) to press forward with the president's program, and Senate Republicans struggled to produce majorities against a strong minority. It did not take long for that Senate minority to become the majority (with James Jefford's switch from Republican to Independent), thus further complicating the lawmaking process.

Congress Reacts to Chief Executive Bush

Elsewhere I have identified five forms of partisan interaction as related to lawmaking: straight or noncompetitive partisanship, competitive partisanship, competitive bipartisanship, bipartisanship, and cross-partisanship.[25] The range is associated with incentives of party leaders in building majorities—essentially from one-party rule to variations in inter-party majority building. The latter are briefly defined as follows:

- Competitive: both parties actively competing in preparing alternatives that are seriously considered by both.

- Competitive bi: joint participation of both parties from the start, with each having competitive positions throughout.

- Bi: the form reserved for essentially nonpartisan cooperation throughout, primarily exhibited in crises.

- Cross: majority party reliance on a segment of the minority party known to be favorable to a proposal (as with trade pacts for Republicans or environmental issues for Democrats). Note: competitive partisanship may ultimately produce a cross-partisan majority.

The incentives during Bush's first term and beyond were mixed, perhaps as varied as for any president in recent memory. Elections, leadership styles, extraordinary events, and possibly historical and institutional circumstances were critical determinants. Differences between the House and Senate helped to explain the varied pattern of partisan interaction. Republican party leaders in the House sought to employ straight partisanship with one of the smallest majorities in history. Senate Republican leaders, on the other hand, won a tie in 2000, which they subsequently lost when Senator James Jeffords changed his affiliation in late May from Republican to Independent. Straight partisanship was not an option in that chamber, even when Republicans won back majority status in 2002.

What were the incentives in each chamber? And why would House Republicans even attempt straight partisanship with so small a working majority? The responses to these questions surely must consider the status of the House Republican Party in the post-World War II period. It was a minority party for 40 years and served as the majority for only 4 years out of 64 from 1930 to 1994. Senate Republicans broke their minority status in 1980 and had six years in the majority. Republican presidents were not only frequently elected in the postwar era but several (Eisenhower, Nixon, Reagan, and Bush 41) won by handsome margins. The so-called "Gingrich Revolution" was a reaction not only to permanent minority status but, as well, to the institutional and political factors that preserved that position.

Conditions were different for Senate Republicans. They had recently served in the majority, and even as a minority they had prerogatives not available to House Republicans. Senate rules and customs are more accommodating to the minority, notably those rules related to debate. Never was there a reference to a "Dole Revolution" during the 1994 election, and, in fact, relations between Dole and Gingrich were often strained.

Therefore, after having served as a majority during six years of tense relations with a Democratic president, House Republican leaders were ready for the first time in nearly 50 years to work with a president of their own party. Many analysts advised President Bush to work cooperatively with Democrats as he assumed office. Some even spoke of the situation as an opportunity for him. And he had campaigned as a "uniter, not a divider." But having retained their majority, if somewhat reduced, House Republicans were not prepared to serve as part of a coalition government. They were anxious to win and prepared to achieve the discipline required given their small margin.

The combination of a clear majority in the House and assurances by party leaders that discipline would produce winning votes encouraged the president to rely on a strategy of getting the most legislation possible in that chamber, knowing that compromises would be required in the Senate. There were costs to this strategy. Often the bills sent over to the Senate were partisan in two ways: they represented most of what the president wanted and efforts by House Democrats to modify the legislation were often thwarted, frequently by the Republican leadership relying on strong-arm tactics and questionable use of House rules.[26]

Thus it was that an anxious and combative House Republican majority met chief executive Bush. Senate Republicans were preoccupied at first with managing under an unusual agreement with Senate Democrats and later with losing majority status. These developments reinforced the determination of House Republicans to maintain discipline. For his part, the new president had prepared an ambitious agenda. Having had one of the least convincing wins in history may well have spurred him to continue campaigning, this time for his program. It was a technique he would continue to employ in what George C. Edwards III refers to as *Governing by Campaigning*: "George W. Bush has tried to lead a revolution in public policy. He has broken from the incremental, fiscally prudent, and moderate approaches that characterized the presidencies of both his father and Bill Clinton. Instead, he has boldly re-examined and challenged the basic tenets of decades of foreign, economic, and domestic policy."[27]

A budget surplus by the end of the Clinton presidency provided the rationale for substantial tax cuts—the prime proposal for the new president. Few, if any, requests would be more positively received by congressional Republicans. But, as Edwards records, Bush's proposals were not limited to a preferred Republican agenda, for example, sweeping education reform, grants for faith-based organizations, Social Security reform, a prescription drug plan, fast-track trade authority, and reordering of military preparedness. Many of these initiatives when combined with tax cuts and crisis-related spending were bound to expand government and bring back deficits.

Table 12.7 categorizes the principal partisan strategies during the Bush presidency. Those during the 107th Congress are of special interest because of the changing political and policy circumstances. At the start, a forthright president relied on the leadership and unity of House Republicans who passed his tax cuts with nearly perfect support scores. Compromises in the Senate attracted a dozen Democrats, thus setting in place a revenue-reduction effect that limited future non-defense-related proposals (not unlike similar effects of Reagan's tax cuts in 1981).

Democratic ascendancy to majority status in the Senate in late May denied Bush his control of the agenda in that chamber. David Frum referred to the "summer of our discontent" filled with "stalemate, stumbles, and defeats."[28] A preferred Senate Democratic agenda item, a patients' bill of rights, passed both houses and was presumably on its way to final disposition when members returned from their August recess. However, the terrorist attacks on September 11 recast the agenda for both the president and Congress.

The bipartisanship recommended by so many following the swearing-in of the 107th Congress and the inauguration of President Bush was finally realized. The stimulus, however, was not leaders' reaction to the narrow margins produced by the 2000 election. Rather it was an unprecedented attack on the homeland. Near perfect bipartisan unity was achieved on many of the security- and defense-related issues, most notably the Use of Force Resolution and the Patriot Act. During this time (September 11 until the end of the year), an effort by the president and House Republicans to enact certain of the original domestic agenda—energy, trade authority, economic stimulus—was thwarted by Senate Democrats. September 11 may have led to cross-party unity in Congress in regard to national security threats but it

Table 12.7. Partisan patterns of lawmaking, 2001–2006

Period	House	Senate	Examples
107th Congress			
Jan.–June 01	straight	competitive/cross	tax cuts
June–9/11 01	competitive/straight	competitive/cross	patients' rights
9/11–Dec. 01	bi	bi	use of force, Patriot Act
Jan.–Dec. 02	bi/competitive bi (nat. sec.)	bi/competitive bi (nat. sec.)	homeland sec.; Iraq Resolution
	straight/competitive (domestic)	competitive/cross (domestic)	energy, trade, campaign reform
108th Congress			
Jan. 03–Dec. 04	straight	competitive/cross	pres. drugs, tax cuts, intelligence overhaul
109th Congress			
Jan.–Dec. 05	straight/competitive	competitive/cross	energy, tort reform, Patriot Act renewal

Source: Compiled by the author. Examples taken primarily from Mayhew's updated list of major legislation at: ⟨http://pantheon.yale.edu/~dmayhew/⟩, accessed 21 November 2006.

did not change the party splits for other domestic issues. Pre-9/11 partisan strategies were re-employed on these other issues, and much of the original Bush agenda was not passed until Republicans recaptured the Senate in 2002.

Virtually from that point (the immediate post-9/11 months) forward, the 107th and subsequent Congresses settled into a two-track process: bipartisanship or substantial cross-partisanship on national security and defense issues; straight partisanship in the House, and competitive or cross-partisanship in the Senate on more domestic-related matters. The shift to a Republican Senate in 2002 returned agenda management to that side but the narrow margin gave Democrats power to thwart passage of legislation or to force compromises. As shown in Table 12.7, major legislation was enacted during the 108th and 109th Congresses, with much of the deliberation and negotiation protracted. The pattern continued of House passage, typically with straight partisanship enabled by strong party unity, followed by extended consideration and occasional filibustering in the Senate.

One rather remarkable lawmaking feat was accomplished in 2002—passage of a campaign finance reform law. Sponsored by cross-partisan coalitions in each house, this legislation was not a Bush priority, although he had finally acknowledged it as an issue in the 2000 campaign. In the end, changes in the House to increase hard money contribution limits convinced the president to sign the bill. Here was a case of legislation often touted as a priority by

Democrats, and listed as such by Clinton in his 1998 State of the Union Address, finally set in place during a Republican administration.

Judicial appointments are essentially a case of Senate-presidential relations. Mayhew has shown that split-party government can produce major legislation as frequently as one-party government. But appointments are not bills. Once made, it is not possible to negotiate for 50, 60, or 70 per cent of a nominee. The Senate confirms an overwhelming majority of appointments, but the process has become progressively more contentious, especially for the Courts of Appeal and the Supreme Court. Having lost majority status in 2002, Senate Democrats began to employ the filibuster in killing certain appointments. Republicans countered with a threat to alter the cloture rule for judicial appointments. A deal was struck when seven Democrats agreed not to support a filibuster except in extraordinary circumstances and seven Republicans agreed not to support the rule change. The arrangement did not reduce the rancor that had come to characterize certain appointments but Democrats subsequently did not filibuster any appointments, including two for the Supreme Court.

Comparing Presidencies

It would be useful at this point to compare the congresses of the Bush 43 presidency with analogous congresses in the post-World War II era. The following exercise identifies eleven orienting conditions for Bush 43, then checks to what extent the other seven newly elected presidents in the post-World War II period experienced similar circumstances. These conditions are:

Presidential
- The narrow and controversial win by the president.
- President with a pure executive style.
- An activist presidential agenda.
- Active congressional role for the vice president.

Congressional
- President's party having been the majority in Congress with an opposite party president.
- President's party has net loss of seats.
- Narrow margins.
- Heightened party unity in Congress.
- Preparatory work on principal agenda issues.

Events
- Subsequent events substantially altering the agenda.
- Subsequent events reinforcing the executive style of the president.

Table 12.8. Comparing newly elected presidents by Bush 43 conditions, post-World War II era

Conditions	Newly elected presidents						
	DDE	JFK	RMN	JEC	RWR	GHWB	WJC
Presidential							
Close win		x	x	x			x—
Ex. style	x		x—	x	x	x	x—
Agenda		x		x	x		x
V. President		x		x			x
Congressional							
Been majority		x		x			x
Net loss		x				x	x
Narrow margins	x						
Partisanship							x
Preparations		x	x—				x—
Events							
Alter agenda	x—	x—	x—	x—			x
Enhance ex. style							
TOTAL	3	7	3	7	3	2	8

Note: x— = to a lesser extent.

Source: Compiled by author.

Table 12.8 displays the results. As shown, the three Democratic presidents, Kennedy, Carter, and Clinton, come closest to meeting the Bush 43 conditions. No one of the four Republican cases met more than three of the eleven, with Bush's father meeting the fewest—an executive style and a small net loss of congressional seats.

There were interesting similarities in each of the three Democratic cases but some crucial differences as well. Like Bush, Kennedy had a very narrow win, an activist agenda, and a vice president, Lyndon Johnson, who had vast experience as a leader in Congress. Further, the Democrats had been serving a Republican president as the majority for six years, four of which by narrow margins in the Senate. Their huge win in 1958 provided substantial House and Senate majorities that encouraged preparations for an active agenda should a Democrat win in 1960. On the other hand, Kennedy was a legislator, as was his vice president. He had large working majorities in Congress that were increased even more for his successor. Partisanship was muted by the role of the Southern Democrat–Republican coalition on certain issues. Finally, the principal agenda-shifting event was the assassination of the president that did not alter as much as intensify action on the existing set of issues.

The Carter case met the presidential conditions—a close win, a mostly executive, if rather eccentric, style, an active agenda, and a vice president prepared to work with Congress. As with Kennedy, Carter too could depend on large Democratic majorities in Congress, primarily due to the huge win in 1974, the so-called "Watergate babies." The more important issue was the extent to which Carter's style would permit his taking advantage of these numbers. Partisanship continued to be influenced by the large number of Southern Democrats, though the shift of seats from Democrat to Republican was occurring in the south. Congressional Democrats were preparing for an all-Democratic government in 1976 but not exactly for the agenda proposed by Carter. And the agenda-shifting events included the president's assessment of his administration's failings (resulting in self-examination at Camp David) and a hostage crisis.

The Clinton case has several matches among the eleven conditions but, taken together, they do not provide much of a model for the Bush 43 case. Clinton's win was close only in the sense of his having won a plurality, not a majority, of the popular vote. He won a substantially higher percentage of the two-party vote than did Bush. His exclusively executive background did not lead to as pure an executive style as for Bush. His approach was much more malleable, even ad hoc; his organizational concept amorphous; and discipline lax. Yet, like Bush, he had an activist's agenda and his vice president had the congressional experience that Clinton lacked.

Among the congressional conditions, Clinton had substantial, if not over-whelming Democratic majorities in Congress (for which he could claim little or no credit). The congressional Democrats had six years of majority status with an opposition party president (just like the congressional Republicans for Bush). Partisanship intensified throughout—beginning with the 103rd Congress and escalating with the Republican takeover of Congress in 1994. The shift in southern congressional seats from Democrat to Republican con-tinued apace, thus providing less and less basis for predictable cross-party coalitions. Preparations among congressional Democrats for a government takeover in 1992 were less obvious than was a determination to thwart the program of Bush 41. It was less certain too than in 2000 that Democrats had a coordinated agenda. And, as described earlier, the agenda-altering event was mostly personal, having to do with the president's behavior and not an international or homeland crisis.

Where does that leave us? It is commonplace to take note of the differences among presidents. That variation is said by some to be at the root of the difficulty in generalizing or theorizing about presidential power. The mix of political and policy conditions for any one presidential term looks very different from that of another. It is apparent from this review that even where there are similarities, closer examination reveals that the circumstances are not replicable or that the combinations produce dissimilar effects. Thus, for example, in the case of Clinton (who scored highest on the eleven conditions) the agenda-altering event helped to explain the increased partisanship but did not, as was the case for Bush 43, reinforce executive style (at least not to the same extent or certainly in the same way).[29] Further, it was true that the congressional Democrats for Clinton and congressional Republicans for Bush met their new presidents having just served for six years with opposition party presidents. Yet the Democrats were still considered virtually to own the Congress, having had 38 consecutive years as a majority in the House and 32 out of 38 years in the Senate. The Republicans in 2000, on the other hand, had just completed their first six-year span of majority control of both houses since 1928. As noted previously, they (especially the House Republicans) were ready to make waves in working with a president of their own party.

Where Table 12.8 shows substantial differences, as with the four Republicans, one is left with little basis beyond party to judge how Bush's fellow Republican presidents might have managed under the conditions he faced. Comparisons are made, of course. Reagan and Bush both began with tax-cut packages but the battle for Reagan was in the Democratic House, for Bush in the 50–50 Senate. The father–son comparisons, too, attract commentators. As shown in Table 12.8, however, the conditions are too dissimilar to permit anything more than speculation regarding the behavior of the father under the conditions experienced by the son.[30]

One feature that this comparative exercise illustrates is that certain longer-stretch developments—greater partisanship, activist agendas, split-party control, narrow margins, executive styles, emergence of terrorism to influence the agenda, and globalization—have helped to reshape the politics of congressional–presidential relations. So if there is no one neatly packaged comparative presidency, still there is evidence of what was developing to shape congressional–presidential interaction in the post-World War II period. If the Bush 43 presidency is not the culmination of these developments, it surely is a reflection of their conflation.

Legislative Product

Judging what is a major legislative action is an uncommonly difficult endeavor for all of the reasons identified by the scholar who made the effort, David Mayhew, and by his critics. Not all major laws are created equal. Some are more equal than others; what is major today may look less so as time passes, the opposite for what was judged as less important today (a fault Mayhew sought to remedy with his "second sweep"); proposals for major issues that fail in a split-party Congress may then pass in a one-party Congress; attributing passage of a major law to one Congress may ignore the preparatory work done in earlier congresses; unilateral actions by the president (such as executive orders) also have the effect of law and are not counted; Congress tends to be treated as a single institution when counting end-point production rather than bicamerally; what is major today, in fact, may be legislation to

Table 12.9. Production of major legislation, Congresses during first terms, elected presidents, 1953–2005 (ranked from most to least)

President	Number (by year)	Total (mean)	Major, major (by year)
Nixon	6-16-5-11	38 (9.5)	0-0-0-0 = 0
Kennedy	9-6-6-7*	28 (7.0)	0-0-1-3 = 4
Bush 43	7-10-6-4	27 (6.8)	3-5-1-0 = 9
Clinton	7-4-4-11	26 (6.5)	2-0-0-2 = 4
Carter	7-5-3-7	22 (5.5)	1-0-0-0 = 1
Bush 41	2-3-7-5	17 (4.3)	0-1-0-0 = 1
Reagan	2-7-3-4	16 (4.0)	2-0-0-0 = 2
Eisenhower	1-8-2-4	15 (3.8)	0-0-0-0 = 0

* Johnson was president in the fourth year.

Source: Compiled by the author from data in D. Mayhew, *Divided We Govern: Control, Lawmaking, and Investigations, 1946–1990* (New Haven: Yale University Press, 1991), 52–73 and ⟨http://pantheon.yale.edu/~dmayhew/⟩, accessed 21 November 2006.

correct the faults of what was major in the past; and counting what comes out of Congress ignores the potentially major impact of failing to act (in other words, lawmaking on an issue is inevitably assigned a plus, not acting a minus).

To be fair to Mayhew, he was not attempting to resolve all the difficulties, even those that he acknowledged. He simply set about confirming his doubts that divided government in a separated system would necessarily result in gridlock any more than unified government. He went about his task by establishing a replicable two-sweep method for judging what is or is not major legislation. So, conceding the problems noted above, where does Bush 43 stand in relationship to other postwar newly elected presidents? Might one expect low productivity from a narrow-margin Congress (both houses) and a chief executive oriented president whose legitimacy is being questioned?

Table 12.9 provides some answers, based on Mayhew's analysis.[31] Included are the first-term numbers for elected, as distinct from takeover, presidents (one exception: Johnson's numbers are included for 1964, what would have been Kennedy's fourth year). As shown, Congresses for Bush 43 ranked third, just slightly behind Kennedy and slightly ahead of Clinton. Mayhew also takes note of legislation that was judged by end-of-year analysts as especially consequential, sort of "major, major." Congresses during Bush 43's first term lead in this category, having twice as many major, major laws passed, several dealing with terrorism issues, than during the other presidencies in Table 12.9.[32]

The bicameral point, different production numbers if done for each chamber, is especially well illustrated in the Bush 43 first term. As noted previously, House rules and party discipline resulted in a major portion of the Bush agenda passing, sometimes twice, only to be stalled in the Senate. It is worth doing a two-chamber analysis of postwar presidencies to supplement research by Sarah Binder on bicameral deadlock.[33] Also to be encouraged is research on the substance and cycling of legislation. Note, for example, that congresses during Nixon's first term enacted the most legislation, by some measure. Yet none of the actions was deemed "major, major." The explanation may be that so much of the legislation was designed to correct or adjust prior legislation rather than to enact new initiatives.

Conclusions

At this writing, congressional–presidential relations in the Bush 43 presidency are strained. The Twenty-Second Amendment helps to explain why. The certainty of a presidency coming to a close clashes with the ambition of the exiting president to have an impact, or, more prosaically, simply to meet responsibilities. President Bush began his second term with one of the most far-reaching agendas of recent decades, but did so with weak electoral standing. The issues—Social Security, tax code, immigration, and health care reform—are among the most partisanly divisive in the domestic agenda. Meanwhile events drew even more than the usual accountability to the chief executive—continued turmoil in Iraq, a terrorist organization winning the election in Palestine, more evidence of prisoner abuse, natural disasters of historic magnitude, complex homeland security issues (notably the matter of an Arab country's state-owned company managing east coast ports), and an unfortunate Supreme Court appointment that had to be withdrawn. Virtually all of these happenings negatively affected Bush's job approval ratings. They were executive, not legislative matters but cumulatively they had an effect too on Capitol Hill Republicans who were having their own leadership problems.

Historians warn us against drawing definitive conclusions about a presidency still in progress, and rightly so. For many of the reasons that it is difficult to designate what is a major law, so too is it hard to estimate the ultimate outcome and impact of extant policies and political developments. So let's stick with what is known, based on this review.

1. President Bush is one of the most executive-oriented presidents in history.
2. Executive-oriented presidents are prone to exercise "leadership by definition," which, in a separated system, can overstress separation and fail to take full advantage of the leeway it offers.
3. Crises tend to enhance an executive orientation. The Bush presidency has had more than its share of crises.
4. The Congressional Republicans had six years experience as the majority party when President Bush was inaugurated in 2001.

5. The Bush agenda in 2001 had antecedents in the Clinton State of the Union Address of 1998. It resonated with congressional Republicans who had worked on many of the issues in the 106th Congress.

6. The Republicans in Congress were prepared to cooperate with a president of their own party and, accordingly, welcomed much of his activist agenda.

7. The Republican House was in a better position than the Senate to act on Bush's priorities and did so with speed and efficiency prior to the indictment and eventual resignation of majority leader Tom DeLay (Texas).

8. The Senate Republicans were at a disadvantage from the start, made worse by the switch of James Jeffords (Vermont) from Republican to Independent and circumstances that led to a change in floor leadership from Trent Lott (Mississippi) to Bill Frist (Tennessee).

9. House and Senate Republicans had reason to be encouraged by the status of the Bush presidency following rare net increases in seats in the 2002 midterm elections and accompanying the president's re-election in 2004.

10. The 107th and 108th Congresses were among the most productive of major legislation in the postwar era, and the most productive of "major, major" legislation.

11. President Bush's second term agenda, as set forth in his 2005 State of the Union Address, further challenged congressional Republicans with partisanly divisive issues that were also controversial among Republicans.

One final note. I have stressed historical comparisons throughout the chapter, searching for analogous cases of congressional–presidential relations to those in 2001–5. The exercises have typically produced more that is different than is the same. Whether concentrating on the president or Congress, the results lead one to conclude that the Bush 43 presidency and the 107th and 108th Congresses are special in ways that make a difference. President Bush is on the far edge of an executive-legislative continuum of leadership styles. Likewise he moved into the job with significantly less electoral and political standing than most presidents, yet is among the most activist and resolute in agenda setting and separationist in pursuing his program. His penchant for governing executively has been enhanced by crises that ordinarily call more for presidential than congressional response and action. Failure to share and to implicate members of Congress or take advantage of their experience has invited sole accountability and its attendant criticism when things do not go well.

Congress too has had some exceptional characteristics during the Bush years. The margins have been narrow in both houses, the Senate had unprecedented political and organizational arrangements in the 107th Congress (a tie followed by a switch in majority control), Republicans experienced six years in the majority prior to Bush's inauguration, and Republican party margins were increased in both the midterm and presidential elections. Legislative production was high, with demands from chief executive Bush unrelenting.

How Congress will relate to chief executive Bush during the remaining 30-plus months of his service will be intriguing to observe. A president dependent primarily on position, less so on reputation and prestige, is especially vulnerable to a status ending term limitation. Perhaps Bush will try to be more legislative in style, developing greater sensitivity to how it is that Congress can be helpful even in the policy formulation stages of lawmaking. There is, however, little in Bush's experience as president to indicate how he might make those adjustments. Yet the 2006 congressional elections resulted in Democratic majorities in the House and Senate, substantially altering the president's power to designate and manage the agenda. Once again an election has provided lessons for governing in a separated powers system.

Notes

1. There are several works that equate the branches, some even that seek to correct the heavy emphasis on presidential dominance. A small sample: Nelson W. Polsby, *Congress and the Presidency*, 4th edn. (New York: Prentice-Hall, 1986); Michael Foley and John E. Owens, *Congress and the Presidency: Institutional Politics in a Separated System* (Manchester: Manchester University Press, 1996); George C. Edwards III, *At the Margins: Presidential Leadership of Congress* (New Haven: Yale University Press, 1989); and John R. Bond and Richard Fleisher, *The President in the Legislative Arena* (Chicago: University of Chicago Press, 1990). Others with special emphasis on correcting the notion of presidential dominance include Lawrence H. Chamberlain, *The President, Congress, and Legislation* (New York: Columbia University Press, 1946) and Mark A. Peterson, *Legislating Together: The White House and Capitol Hill from Eisenhower to Reagan* (Cambridge, Mass.: Harvard University Press, 1990).

2. For treatment of why this might be so, see Walter Dean Burnham, "The Legacy of George Bush: Travails of an Understudy," in Gerald M. Pomper (ed.), *The Election of 1992* (Chatham, NJ: Chatham House, 1993), ch. 1.

3. For details, see Charles O. Jones, "Ronald Reagan and the U. S. Congress: Visible Hand Politics," in Charles O. Jones (ed.), *The Reagan Legacy: Promise and Performance* (Chatham, NJ: Chatham House, 1988), ch. 2.

4. The new majority leader, Mike Mansfield (D-Montana) put the question to his colleagues. They voted in favor but word got out that there was opposition and Johnson did not so serve. Robert Dalleck, *Flawed Giant: Lyndon Johnson and His Times, 1961–1973* (New York: Oxford University Press, 1998), 8.

5. These descriptions draw from the author's policy brief for The Brookings Institution and a paper for an American Enterprise Institute symposium: "Bush and Kerry: Questions About Governing Style," Policy Brief 134 (The Brookings Institution, June 2004) and "Governing Executively: The Paradoxical Style of George W. Bush," forthcoming in a book edited by John Fortier.

6. One, Ford, was an appointed vice president.

7. Taft, Hoover, and Bush 41 also had either all or mostly executive backgrounds, yet they were primarily in appointive positions (Bush 41 was an exception, being elected as vice president) and none was re-elected.

8. See e.g. James L. Sundquist (ed.), *Beyond Gridlock? Prospects for the Clinton Years—and After* (Washington, DC: Brookings Institution, 1993).

9. George W. Bush, *A Charge to Keep* (New York: William Morrow, 1999), p. ix.

10. Stephen Skowronek, "Leadership by Definition: First Term Reflections on George W. Bush's Political Stance," *Perspectives on Politics* (December 2005), 819.

11. Ibid. 820.

12. Richard E. Neustadt, *Presidential Power and the Modern Presidents* (New York: Free Press, 1990), 29. Emphasis his.

13. Ibid.

14. Ibid. 150.

15. For details see Charles O. Jones, "Capitalizing on Position in a Perfect Tie," in Fred I. Greenstein (ed.), *The George W. Bush Presidency: An Early Assessment* (Baltimore: Johns Hopkins University Press, 2003), ch. 7.

16. Bush, *A Charge to Keep*, 118–19.

17. Bob Woodward, *Bush at War* (New York: Simon & Schuster, 2002), 136, 144, 244, 259. Similar qualities are illustrated in Woodward's subsequent book, *Plan of Attack* (New York: Simon & Schuster, 2004).

18. That is not to suggest polls were not taken or were ignored by political advisers in developing strategies. It is, rather, to suggest that Bush himself is less attentive to or knowledgeable of polls and their potential effects. Clinton, by contrast, was very much a student of polls, with a keen sense of how to read them in the context of ongoing policy and political debates. See his discussion in *My Life* (New York: Alfred A. Knopf, 2004), ch. 28, and that of Dick Morris, *Behind the Oval Office* (New York: Random House, 1997), 338, where Morris notes that Clinton viewed polls "as a way of conducting an extensive dialogue with the public."

19. Bush, *A Charge to Keep*, 218.

20. Quoted in Mike Allen, "Confident Bush Vows to Move Aggressively," *Washington Post*, 5 November 2004, A1.

21. Albert R. Hunt, "Clinton in the Catbird Seat," *Wall Street Journal*, 8 January 1998, A9.

22. E. J. Dionne, Jr., "Get Ready for Clinton's Third Act," *Washington Post*, 11 January 1998, C1.

23. See e.g. Peter Baker and John F. Harris, "To Boost his Presidency and Party, Clinton Leaps Into the Policy Void," *Washington Post*, 11 January 1998, A1.

24. John F. Harris, "After a Detour, a Return to Activist Agenda," *Washington Post*, 28 January 2000, A1.

25. Charles O. Jones, *The Presidency in a Separated System,* 2nd edn. (Washington, DC: Brookings Institution, 2005), 25–31.

26. Norman J. Ornstein and Thomas E. Mann cite a number of abuses of House rules, including violations of the regular order. *The Broken Branch.* New York: Oxford University Press, 2006.

27. George C. Edwards III, *Governing by Campaigning: The Politics of the Bush Presidency* (New York: Longman, 2006), ch. 1.

28. David Frum, *The Right Man: The Surprise Presidency of George W. Bush* (New York: Random House, 2003), 104.

29. At least not in the case of the Lewinsky affair. One could argue that the failure of the health care reform package had an effect on the agenda, which in turn led Clinton to issue more executive orders.

30. Closest, perhaps, would be the Gulf War for Bush 41 and the wars in Afghanistan and Iraq for Bush 43. Yet even in those cases there were fundamental differences in regard to the triggering events, the role of the United Nations, the congressional resolutions, and the objectives.

31. The data are drawn from David R. Mayhew, *Divided We Govern: Party Control, Lawmaking, and Investigations, 1946–1990* (New Haven: Yale University Press, 1991), 52–73; and his updates from ⟨http://pantheon.yale.edu/~dmayhew/⟩, accessed 21 November 2006. The latter are based primarily on his first sweep counting.

32. In an email (2 April 2003), Mayhew acknowledged problems in identifying major, major laws for the 106th and 107th Congresses.

33. Sarah A. Binder, *Stalemate: Causes and Consequences of Legislative Gridlock* (Washington, DC: Brookings Institution, 2000), 70–1.

13

Policy Histories and Partisan Leadership in Presidential Studies: The Case of Social Security

Fiona Ross

Subfields of political science differ in their evaluation of the scope for leadership and the magnitude of constraint deriving from formal structures, institutional histories, and extant policy regimes. Presidential scholars focus heavily on the role of political agency, taking the goals of its key actor, the president, as their point of departure and asking why various aspects of their leadership so often fail. Over the years, the field has generated a distinctive set of variables to understand the constraints and opportunities for presidential leadership, ranging from the partisan and ideological composition of Congress, presidential approval ratings, individual skill and character, and the power, intensity, and institutional position of potential veto players (Bond and Fleisher 1990; Edwards 1976, 1983, 1989, 2006; King 1996; Mezey 1989; Peterson 1990). The influence of contextual forces has also been effectively theorized in timing and sequencing analyses of the presidency (Skowronek 1997). Though scholars often disagree about the specific and precise impact of some of these variables, such as divided government (see Edwards, Barrett, and Peake 1997; Howell et al. 2000; Mayhew 1991), we have a defined group of explanations that most analysts accept as relevant to the leadership equation.

Historical and comparative institutional analyses often start from a starkly different premise. They ask: is the existing policy path or regime so locked in that the capacity for leadership is anything other than incremental? Some variants of historical institutionalism and path dependence theory, such as increasing returns, theorize that extant paths can be fundamentally restructured only through the disruptive impact of an unpredictable exogenous shock (see Pierson 2000; but also see Mahoney 2000; Thelen 2002). In these structuralist accounts, the capacity for actor-generated change is marginal in the absence of path disruption by an external event. These analyses start from the premise that policy regimes are not simply "dependent variables" that can be moved under conditions of unified government, through skilled tactical leadership or by a president enjoying high approval ratings. The policy regime itself has causal significance in conditioning the opportunities for leadership, with short-term political and institutional variables exerting their influence once a regime is ripe for reform.

Employing the case of Old Age, Survivors, and Disability Insurance (Social Security) reform during the administration of George W. Bush, this chapter illustrates why we should take the properties of the policy regime seriously in conceptualizing the scope for leadership. We know that landmark legislation is less likely to pass than routine laws, that popular and well-defended programmes are harder to reform than unpopular ones, and that fragmented programmatic structures help leaders "obfuscate" and avoid blame in a way that mature, monolithic ones do not (Pierson 1994). All these factors combine to render Social Security reform a huge political undertaking. We also know that attempted reform of programmes such as Social Security trigger voters' negativity biases (see Lau 1985). We need to pay more attention, however, to how a sequence of path-reinforcing moves reflects and conditions the opportunities for reform; endogenously generated change often follows a pattern of programmatic de-institutionalization and delegitimization.

The history of Social Security, for example, reveals a path that has been heavily locked in through a sequence of enlarging and replicating decisions across time. Consistent with path dependence theory, the only episode of significant restructuring in the history of the programme occurred at the very beginning of the path before the pension system had distributed benefits. Subsequent adjustments to the programme have reinforced the extant regime. Never has Social Security been modified in response to ideology for the purposes of retrenchment. Indeed, endogenously driven change in deeply institutionalized programmes usually requires a shared sense that the status quo has failed beyond remediation and that virtually anything is preferable to existing arrangements, particularly in power-sharing, consensus-dependent systems. To arrive at this scenario we typically witness an incremental weakening of the policy regime across time; rarely does it follow a sequence of path-reinforcing moves. Although the anticipation of future returns is impaired in the case of Social Security, support for the status quo remains robust and the moral panic that had engulfed Aid to Families with Dependent Children (AFDC) by 1994, two years before reform, is absent. Without a shared conception of policy failure and sequence of programmatic erosion, structural change to Social Security, with its single, uniform structure and vibrant vested interests, was unlikely irrespective of majorities in Congress or presidential commitment.

Path-centred explanations of this type speak to the underlying ripeness of a policy regime for reform. Of course, the pitfalls of path dependence theory, notably institutional and historical determinism, are well documented (Crouch and Farrell 2002; Schwartz 2002). Though presidential skill tends to matter "at the margins" (Edwards 1989) and our most compelling explanations for presidential success in the legislative arena are congressional-centred (Bond and Fleisher 1990), there are systematic asymmetries in the scope for presidential leadership that derive from the historically-shaped images of the parties and patterns of issue-ownership.[1] The Democrats "own" Social Security. Voters disproportionately trust them by significant margins to handle the programme, and they do not trust the Republicans to do so. Low levels of political trust exert a downward pressure on presidential approval ratings, in turn depressing levels of trust further (Hetherington and Globetti 2006, 237). Impaired approval ratings, of course, reduce all lawmakers' strategic interests in supporting the president's agenda (Edwards 1976, 1983, 2006).

This chapter seeks to illustrate the importance of both structural constraints deriving from the established trajectory of the policy regime itself and the relevance of the partisan character of key actors in understanding the scope for significant leadership. Institutionally embedded paths can be moved endogenously but change is usually subsequent to a pattern of path-erosion and conditional upon high levels of trust in the agents of change. Even when the returns generated by the extant path are impaired, the capacity for transformative leadership is often limited to actors who own the issue at hand.

Combining these points, I argue that presidential scholars can improve their predictive capacity significantly by factoring the properties of the path and issue-ownership by key actors into their analyses: both factors would have generated the very clear prediction that partial privatization of Social Security by the Bush Administration would fail. Conversely, an analysis based on the standard short-term political and institutional variables of unified government, presidential commitment, speed, and focus very early in a new administration mistakenly inspired some confidence that George W. Bush enjoyed a window of opportunity for reform.

Social Security Reform and the Bush Presidency

Though domestic agendas have shrunk over time, partly in response to falling revenues and rising deficits, the scope of George W. Bush's first-term agenda was limited even by the standards of his father and Ronald Reagan.[2] Social Security reform was, in part, an inheritance from the Clinton Administration and an issue in the 2000 election campaign, although it was clear from the Clinton experience that generating agreement on reform would be difficult given the diversity of plans emerging from the Social Security Advisory Council and the breadth of opposition (see Arnold 1998).[3] To the extent that the president chose to reform Social Security, the story is one of political miscalculation bred of overconfidence, an unwarranted faith in spin-control, and ideological insulation.

Inspired and informed by a conservative court led by think tanks such as the Cato Institute, an enthusiast of privatizing Social Security from 1983, the president had ambitions to be a "director of change" in the domestic arena and, based on his advisers' analysis of the opportunities for reform, the administration severely over-estimated its capacity to restructure one of America's most popular and successful entitlements (Edwards 1989; see Reedy 1970). Tom DeLay, House majority leader at the time, opined; "the Republican Party is a permanent majority for the future of this country . . . we are going to be able to lead this country in the direction we've been dreaming of for years."[4] Reflecting this sense of confidence, Karl Rove's assistant declared that private accounts would constitute "one of the most significant conservative governing achievements ever" (cited in Jacobs 2006: 298). The administration showed no appreciation of the constraints set by the institutionalization of the programme or the limitations of their partisan mode of leadership.

On the contrary, sensing a political realignment with their increased majorities in Congress, and perceiving private accounts to be a winning issue among younger Americans, many Republicans felt empowered, wrongly, to dismantle another major New Deal entitlement following the landmark retrenchment of Aid to Families with Dependent Children (AFDC). Of course, the lesson to be learnt from the termination of AFDC was not that the time was ripe to dismantle New Deal programmes. It was that under competing retrenchment agendas, a deeply unpopular status quo, a temporarily surging caseload, and a focused, unified Republican Congress working with a Democratic president who could rally opponents and mollify potential veto players (who, unlike the AARP, were already weak), far-reaching reform of a heavily fragmented programme was just barely achievable—and even then after two presidential vetoes and significant compromise. The parallels between welfare overhaul and pension reform were modest.

The administration placed great faith in the appeal of the president's vision of an "ownership society", framed as a conservative successor to crumbling New Deal entitlements. By the president's own admission, private accounts would have a "net neutral effect" on solvency. Yet, as history showed, this was the only legitimate basis for significant reform.[5] Social Security is a near-universal programme, covering 90 per cent of Americans and providing benefits to over 48 million recipients. It is the main means of survival for two-thirds of the elderly. It is responsible for lifting 46.8 per cent of its aged beneficiaries out of poverty.[6] For over 30 per cent of the aged, Social Security is their only source of income. Through its Survivors and Disability components, Social Security is America's most successful child poverty programme, save the Earned Income Tax Credit, and the premier program in alleviating the depth of poverty. It is particularly beneficial in lifting women, African Americans, and Latinos out of poverty (Spriggs 2005). Most Americans remain deeply committed to the concept of guaranteed benefits. Unlike welfare reform, they are not concerned about any adverse affects of benefits on the behaviour or the moral choices of the disabled and elderly and support for the existing structure of the programme remains robust. Majorities agree that Social Security generates strong returns. The so-called 'crisis' of the programme concerns its long-term capacity to continue yielding such strong returns well into the future; it is not one of policy failure.

Thus, without any mandate to reform one of America's most popular entitlements, the president created a 'bi-partisan' commission to generate reform options by December 2001. As a prerequisite for membership, however, appointees had to accept the validity of private accounts, as well as ensure that current and near recipients would not be affected by the changes and that the programme would achieve solvency.[7] No further action emerged during Bush's first term, although the president reaffirmed his commitment to partial privatization during the 2002 elections without any obvious electoral backlash.[8] In March 2004, the Social Security Board of Trustees, in many respects a policy advocate for reform, again emphasized the significance of the demographic pressures weighing down upon the programme. In the wake of increased Republican victories in both Houses of Congress following the November elections, President Bush, in his 2005 State of the Union address, prioritized the creation of private accounts as the principal domestic initiative of his second term.

What followed was a spectacularly unsuccessful investment of political capital by the administration to promote private accounts to the American people in the hopes of raising support among the many wavering members of Congress.[9] The naive faith that the administration placed in the power of communications, and even particular phrases such as "choice" and "owner-ship" to change public opinion on a deeply institutionalized and legitimate programme that had relevance to over 90 per cent of Americans was startling (Jacobs 2006: 299; see also Edwards 2003, 2005, 2006; Edwards and Brown 1996; Jerit 2006).

During the administration's 60-day-60-stop campaign, delivered through town hall meetings with sympathetic audiences, Americans grew somewhat more hostile to the president's proposal than before he had "gone public." The president's initial approval ratings were possibly too low to support a public strategy (see Kernell 1997) and partisan divisions further lowered the administration's capacity for spin-control.[10] A combined strategy of partisan polarization and going public, particularly with comparatively weak approval ratings and on an issue where the Democrats enjoyed greater trust and support, was, unsurprisingly, a losing one (see Edwards 2003, 2006; Hetherington and Globetti 2006).[11] It flagged failure and focused blame.

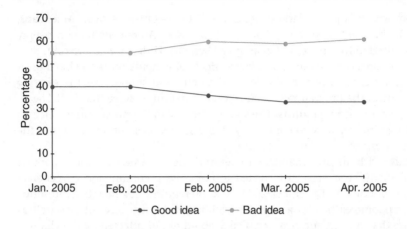

Source: In Gallup/CNN/*USA Today* polls reported in Bowman (2005, 20) in response to the question: "As you may know, one idea to address concerns with the Social Security system would allow people who retire in future decades to invest some of their Social Security taxes in the stock market and bonds, but would reduce the guaranteed benefits they get when they retire. Do you think this is a good idea or bad idea?"

Figure 13.1. Support for private accounts

Figure 13.1 charts support for private accounts between January and April 2005 when the president took his case to the American people. Clear and stable majorities reported that personal accounts were a bad idea, finishing at around 60 per cent by April 2005. With opponents of personal accounts outnumbering supporters by a ratio of 2 : 1 at the close of the president's campaign, it is unsurprising that few legislators wanted to work on reform. Equally revealing is that when polls mentioned the president's name, support for private accounts sunk even further (Bowman 2005, 18).

This loss of support sent unambiguous signals to members of Congress that they had few strategic reasons to support the president: if Bush continued to push forward with private accounts he could count on support only from members of his party who were ideologically committed to partial privatization, and even these Republicans divided about the optimality of competing alternatives. By governing "from the 'right-in' rather than the 'center-out' ", a strategy mimicked by Republican leaders in the House (Price 2004a, 3),[12] Bush appeared to be attempting to replicate Reagan's strategy of stretching his agenda in order to give himself ample room for compromise. For this partisan strategy to deliver success, however, moderate and electorally insecure Republicans in the Senate needed strong strategic reasons to support the president, incentives that were manifestly absent in the case of Social Security reform.

Aside from the heavy institutionalization and robust legitimacy of Social Security, the increasing polarization of the parties and the ideological distance between moderate and conservative Republicans itself made compromise difficult (Binder 2005). Many, including Tom DeLay, were furious when Bush signalled his willingness to consider raising the $90,000 cap on payroll taxes in February 2005. Divisions within congressional Republicans, not an anomaly following a second electoral victory for their president, were exaggerated by the vice president's announcement that he would not seek the party nomination for the 2008 race. Moreover, as it grew increasingly clear that Social Security reform would have to be an exercise in cross-party blame-avoidance not Republican credit claiming, a lesson that was very clear from the history of reform, many of the president's partisans in Congress wisely feared the political costs of proceeding in the absence of bipartisan support—something that was unachievable on partial privatization.

The limitations of the president's bully pulpit strategy were underscored by the huge financial investment supporting his efforts. Estimates suggest that in excess of $50 million, raised through interest groups and potential beneficiaries such as the Conservative Club for Growth, the Alliance for Worker Retirement Security, the US Chamber of Commerce, the Business Roundtable, USA Next, the securities industry, and Wall Street, was spent to promote private accounts.[13] Prior to the administration's 60-day campaign, the Club for Growth targeted the districts of ambivalent Republican representatives with commercials plugging the virtues of private accounts. In response to AARP commercials opposing "carve outs",[14] USA Next was reported to be investing at least $10 million on a campaign against the AARP and Progress for America a further $20 million on cable television adverts. Total spending estimates for the administration's Social Security campaign exceeded $100 million.[15] Yet the polls continued to show that statements by the AARP were trusted more than those of any other actor in the Social Security debate, enjoying a 52 per cent "trust" rating (Bowman 2005, 40). The president also launched a campaign within his administration. The *New York Times* reported that internal Social Security Administration documents required officials to promote the idea that the programme was in imminent crisis and the Treasury Department set up a Social Security "war room".[16]

In response to his poor and falling poll ratings on Social Security, President Bush held a televised news conference on 28 April in which he launched the idea of progressive indexing. Under this proposal, benefits for poorer recipients would be linked to wages and those for wealthier Americans would be indexed to inflation.[17] The initiative was intended to address the solvency of the programme through hidden benefits cuts, as well as increasing Democratic support for reform. More importantly, by dividing recipients in this way, the administration could take an incremental step towards changing the structure of Social Security by differentiating between beneficiaries and fostering a sense of welfare.[18] The president's proposal was opposed by a unified coalition of Democrats, unions, and the AARP, who argued that comparatively limited changes would secure the solvency of the programme and that structural changes were both unnecessary and incurred much larger problems. It was also unpopular among the American people (see Edwards 2006, 261).

Less than two weeks before the close of the administration's 60-day tour, scheduled to conclude on 1 May, 64 per cent of Americans "disapproved" of the president's handling of Social Security, more than double the 31 per cent who approved.[19] Regardless of ideological preferences, Republicans had few strategic reasons to support personal accounts and Democrats many strategic reasons to oppose them. The president's persistence risked antagonizing electorally insecure Republicans further. Even his ardent supporters in Congress began talking about tactical errors, particularly the decoupling of personal accounts from the solvency of the programme. Yet the core dilemma for George Bush in addressing the solvency of Social Security was that in so doing he would reinforce the existing regime as Ronald Reagan had done in 1983. Moreover, conservative Republicans now refused to move on the issue without a commitment to private accounts.

By late spring of 2005, Social Security reform appeared to be over. The hardening of public opposition against personal accounts exacerbated divisions between Senate Republicans regarding the merits of "carve outs" versus "add ons" and the importance of solvency versus structural reform. The ideological distance between conservative and moderate Republicans, and the institutional dominance of conservatives, made reaching intra-party and cross-party agreements difficult even before the president's sagging polling figures were factored into the equation. In an interview with PBS on 16 April 2005, Senate Finance Committee Chairman Senator Chuck Grassley of Iowa accepted; "You know, none of the 535 members of Congress, including all 100 Senators really want to deal with Social Security."[20] Senator Max Baucus (D-MO), ranking member of Senate Finance, likewise admitted the Democratic opposition was close to impenetrable; "there's total unity. I've never seen anything like it, I mean, it's astounding."

By early summer, leading Republicans were publicly admitting not only that Social Security reform was unlikely to emerge in 2005, but that the prospects for any action in 2006, an election year, were remote.[21] Strategically and of necessity, personal accounts plummeted down the list of Congressional priorities, quickly superseded by the Central America Free Trade Agreement (CAFTA) as the president's leading priority. Bill Thomas, chairman of Ways and Means, explained; "the issue is dealing with more time-sensitive legislation first."[22] In May, Roy Blunt, House majority whip, excluded Social Security from his list of priority legislation scheduled for action after Memorial Day.[23] More pressing issues ranged from replacing Justice Sandra Day O'Connor on the

Supreme Court to dealing with hurricane Katrina. Despite further negotiations in Congress over the summer of 2005 on various options, reform was clearly over (see Edwards 2006).

In his January 2006 State of the Union address, Bush paid just passing attention to Social Security. Despite the fact that he never sent Congress specific legislation on private accounts or progressive indexing, the president quickly blamed lawmakers for his failure to deliver reform in 2005. Again, the president advocated the creation of a bi-partisan commission to investigate the magnitude of the demographic time bomb, promising that it would present "bi-partisan solutions."[24] Yet in February 2006, Bush inserted his partial privatization plan and progressive indexation initiative into the 2007 budget proposal. Although the president seemed to have understood that reform would have to be an exercise in blame avoidance rather than credit claiming, he showed little appreciation that a more inclusive approach was an essential ingredient of this strategy (although bi-partisanship on partial privatization remained unattainable).

The failure of the Bush Administration to enact Social Security reform drives home the point that going public, an investment of political capital, forceful allies, and a very well funded promotional campaign, together with majorities in both Houses of Congress, are inadequate predictors of major change in salient and popular programmes. The president made additional tactical errors. His failure to submit a specific plan to Congress gave legislators plenty of reasons to avoid the issue and the administration's huge investment of money and political capital did more to help the Democrats' cause than the president's (something that was readily predictable when we consider the impact of issue-ownership). Not only did George Bush raise the salience of an issue "owned" by his opponents, by stipulating such an early and unlikely date for the completion of reform in May 2005, he advertised the failure of his defining domestic initiative very early in his term. Unable to generate support for his number one priority, despite unified government and a huge amount of effort, the significance of this early defeat threatened to overshadow the remainder of his administration.[25]

Yet political errors are superficial explanations for the failure of the Bush Administration to restructure Social Security. Although the standard variables of unified government, presidential commitment, period in the legislative term, and a broader sense of realignment suggested a favourable context for reform, the properties of the regime indicated that Social Security was strongly resistant to partial privatization at this point in time and by this leader. Consistent with path dependence theory, the historical trajectory of Social Security was at one of its strongest points in time. Irrespective of (weak) indicators of a Republican realignment and political opportunities for a new conservative agenda, the regime was not receptive to partial privatization.

Path-Centred Explanations: "Reform-Ready" Regimes

Presidential scholars treat the policy area under reform as a dependent variable. Historical institutionalists, by contrast, begin with the assumption that policy paths have causal significance and that the properties of the regime itself are integral to the capacity for path-breaking change, as well as the shape that new branching points will take. Policy trajectories are shaped over time through sequences of repeated moves. These positive feedback processes replicate and reinforce the regime. Programmes that are ripe for change typically demonstrate a gradual weakening of their intellectual and structural foundation across time (see Peters, Pierre, and King 2005). When AFDC was dismantled in 1996, for example, it had been under threat since at least the 1960s (see King 1992, 1995, 1999). There was a 20-year "incubation period" during which the ideational and institutional foundations for change were established and repeated decisions undermined and fragmented the programme (see Polsby 1984).

We have at least two signals of when programmes are amenable to restructuring or "reform-ready". The first indicator is a *de-institutionalization* or incremental erosion of the programme over time, wrought through a series of undermining decisions and actions. Rarely does sweeping reform immediately follow an uninterrupted sequence of programmatic entrenchment. The second indicator is a *delegitimization* of the path in terms of a pervasive sense that the extant regime has ceased to generate returns and that the status quo has become a contributory cause of the policy problem rather than a solution. The presence of either signal does not mean that reform will be straightforward. Political and institutional barriers to change remain high, as was evident in the case of welfare reform. In their absence, however, significant restructuring of large entitlements is unlikely.

The Path of Social Security: Reinforcing the Status Quo

The history of Social Security comes close to a textbook case of path dependence theory. The programme was created at an exogenously induced critical juncture and then reinforced through a steady sequence of path-replicating moves. For the first twenty years of its life, policymakers repeatedly, at least every two years and on twenty-five occasions, increased the reach of the programme, locking-in the existing regime institutionally and greatly improving its legitimacy (Arnold 1998, 215; Derthick 1979; Tynes 1996).[26] In times of stress, specifically near-term crises in the solvency of the programme, the dominant approach to reform has been a bi-partisan one aimed at securing the future of the programme, in turn eliminating the rationale for significant change. Indeed, the historical trajectory of Social Security provides a classic case of on-path remediation through a broad political consensus bred of good institutional returns (see Pierson 2000). Table 13.1 shows that every major Social Security reform has been a bi-partisan effort, reflecting the legitimacy of the programme and illustrative of the political mechanisms through which endogenous change can be delivered in deeply institutionalized paths.

Since the founding of the path, the only episode of significant structural change occurred before the programme was institutionalized and enjoyed broad legitimacy. The 1935 Act originally prescribed for an advanced funding system. By 1939, the programme was transitioning to a pay-as-you-go system, fast-forwarding eligibility by two years from 1942 to 1940. The institutional choice of a pay-as-you-go structure heightened the obstacles to reform by creating a double-payment dilemma. At the same time, Social Security was extended beyond the individual worker to cover dependents of both retired and deceased workers, increasing the number of Americans with a material and emotional stake in the programme.

From this point on, Social Security grew institutionally and in legitimacy through a steady flow of legislation. President Truman and Congress enacted the 1950 Social Security Amendments, increasing coverage to a much wider range of workers.[27] The 1950 Amendments secured the future worth, viability, and legitimacy of the programme by introducing the first Cost of Living Adjustments (COLAS). In 1956 Social Security was broadened further to include disability insurance for workers between the ages of 50 and 64. Coverage was extended to their dependents in 1958 and, two years later in 1960 the age specification for disability benefits was abolished. By 1967, spouses of deceased disabled beneficiaries were added to the programme once they reached the age of 50, albeit under stricter definitions of disability (see Derthick 1979). Together, the expansions enacted between 1950 and 1960 led to a four-and-a-half-fold increase in the number of beneficiaries.[28]

One of the most significant adjustments to Social Security in terms of locking in and depoliticizing the programme came in 1972 with the automatic indexation of benefit levels to the CPI. At this point, Social Security became a self-sustaining programme (see Arnold 1998, 216). After gaining this independence from politics, the chief rationale for reform concerned the solvency of the programme and only then in the face of near-term crisis. The 1977 reforms, securing the future of Social Security, emerged after two years of negotiation in Congress in response to the Trustees' report of 1975 that predicted a benefit shortfall as early as 1979.[29] In 1983, only dire actuarial predictions, suggesting that the trust fund would be unable to cover full benefits within a matter of months, generated the sense of urgency needed to reform the programme, and then again only after two years of bi-partisan negotiation. Consistent with path-dependence theorists' conceptualization of

Table 13.1. Congressional vote totals by party on major social security amendments

Amendment	House/Senate	Vote	Democrats	Republicans
1935	H	Yes	288	77
		No	13	18
		Not voting	18	6
	S	Yes	60	15
		No	1	5
		Not voting	8	4
1939	H	Yes	215	142
		No	0	2
		Not voting	40	22
	S	Yes	45	10
		No	2	6
		Not Voting	22	9
1950	H	Yes	231	138
		No	0	1
		Not voting	25	30
	S	Yes	46	35
		No	0	2
		Not voting	8	5
1956	H	Yes	203	169
		No	8	23
		Not voting		
	S	Yes	45	45
		No		
		Not voting		
1967	H	Yes	223	167
		No	2	1
		Not voting (13)		
	S	Yes	36	26
		No	11	3
		Not voting		
1972	H	Yes	191	107
		No	8	27
		Not voting	53	42
	S	Yes	41	35
		No	2	1
		Not voting	11	8
1977	H	Yes	170	16
		No	53	109
		Not voting	59	20
	S	Yes	38	17
		No	7	14
		Not voting	15	6
1983	H	Yes	158	81
		No	55	47
		Not voting	50	38
	S	Yes	26	32
		No	6	8
		Not voting	14	14
1996	H	Yes	100	227
		No	97	3
		Not voting	2	3
	S	Yes	25	53
		No	21	0
		Not voting	1	0

Note: 1996 Amendments were part of a much larger welfare reform bill that terminated the federal entitlement AFDC and thus incurred stronger partisan opposition from many Democrats.

Source: ⟨http://www.ssa.gov/history/tally(year).html⟩, accessed 21 November 2006 (replace "year" with appropriate year). Data for years 1956 and 1972 from Solomon (1986). Breakdown of non-voting by party not available for the 1956 and 1967 amendments.

the scope for endogenous change, the sole motivation for reform was one of on-path remediation to secure the future of the existing regime.

Of importance, members of both parties shared the blame for the politically contentious solutions needed to shore up the system. The fact that they were willing to do so was indicative of the legitimacy and efficiency of the existing path. Among the gamut of provisions included in the rescue effort was a rise in payroll taxes, an increase in the full retirement age from 65 to 67 across time for future retirees, and a degree of taxation of benefits for wealthier individuals (see Light 1995). These reforms forestalled a crisis for a further half century. They also signalled a long-term commitment to Social Security by requiring Federal civilian and non-profit workers to enroll in the programme, as well as barring state and local governments from exiting the system.

Likewise, in 1995 President Clinton and Congress reaffirmed the importance of the programme when they elevated the Social Security Administration to the status of an independent agency. While marginal retrenchments to Disability and Supplemental Security Income (SSI) were enacted as part of welfare restructuring in 1996, the pension programme itself was untouched and the Balanced Budget Act of 1997 reinstated SSI to specified groups of non-citizens.[30]

In summation, the historical trajectory of Social Security is a textbook case of path dependence theory. Here we find a sequence of path-creation through an exogenous shock, following by structural change at the outset of the path before the new regime became institutionalized through increasing returns, followed by a 70-year history of positive feedback processes during which the regime was reinforced and inefficiencies were remediated. The path of Social Security showed no signs of incremental de-institutionalization or a linear pattern of delegitimization across time. Of course, deeply entrenched programmes can change significantly in times of crisis and 'shocks' may invite policy makers to re-evaluate the costs and benefits of continuing down an established path. In the case of Social Security, however, unanticipated actuarial predications provided the political momentum to secure the programme and reinforce its viability. They served to replicate the status quo, not disrupt it. Crisis conditions do not lend themselves to ideologically driven structural change; rather they require a quick pragmatic response to solve an imminent problem. Moreover, unlike calculations on welfare, Social Security facilitates a politics of pragmatism: costs and benefits are comparatively amenable to statistical evaluation and, as yet, they have not generated inferences about the impact of benefits on behaviour.[31]

Although the past need not determine the future, a 70-year sequence of path-reinforcing and remediating moves is a clear indicator that Social Security was not ripe for landmark reform. The notable absence of any de-institutionalization and path erosion should have cautioned the Bush Administration that the barriers to restructuring would exceed the standard short-term challenges of policy leadership and that their limited political capital was severely inadequate to restructure such an institutionally sturdy programme. The second signal of a reform-ready regime, a delegitimization of the path, was also absent in the case of Social Security.

Anything but Social Security?

Before established regimes are amenable to significant restructuring they must often go through a period of delegitimization. Voters' negativity biases are well documented in political research (Lau 1985) and a pervasive sense that the status quo has failed is often needed to overcome the public's dispro-portionate reaction to losses, particularly in systems with a plethora of veto points and frequent elections. By the time President Clinton and Congress reformed AFDC, a majority of Americans had reached the point of "anything but welfare."

American attitudes were a very long way from "anything but Social Security" and, unlike opinions on welfare, there was absolutely no evidence to suggest that they perceived Social Security to be a source of poverty rather than a solution. Although Americans recognized solvency as a problem (with most predicting a shortfall within about 20 years), the majority did not believe that the programme was in crisis. The policy challenge, as Americans' perceived it, was one of remediating the extant path in order to maintain guaranteed benefits at their current level.

A Gallup/CNN/*USA Today* poll has asked Americans across time: "Which of these statements do you think best describes the Social Security system today—the Social Security system is in a state of crisis, it has major problems, or it does not have any problems?" The results are charted in Fig. 13.2.

A very clear majority of Americans believed, and had done for some time, that Social Security had "major problems." However, only a small minority believed that the programme was in crisis, fewer voters than believed it has just minor problems. These attitudes were not unexpected when we consider the quantifiable successes of the programme and the fact that, even by the Trustees' conservative estimates, the fund would not be exhausted until 2041 (and not until 2052 by the Congressional Budget Office's calculation). The actuaries' assessments showed the programme to be at one of the strongest points in its history owing to a combination of the 1983 rescue, immigration, and solid growth (Weller and Rasell 2000).

The legitimacy of Social Security is not just determined by the public's perception of its current performance. It is also affected by its anticipation of future returns. Americans' anticipation of future returns was impaired in the case of Social Security, producing notable differences in the attitudes of retirees and workers. Up to a third of workers expected Social Security to make a significant contribution to their income in retirement. By

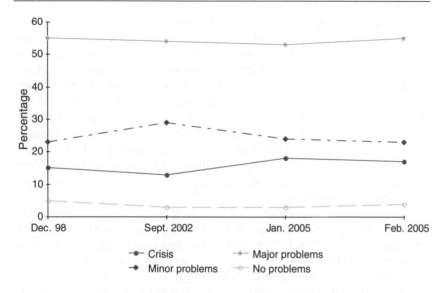

Source: Gallup/CNN/*USA Today* data reported in Bowman (2005, 11).

Figure 13.2. The state of social security, 1998–2005

contrast, Social Security constituted the main source of income for approximately 45 per cent of retired Americans in 2005. Most working Americans (53–57 per cent) envisioned Social Security as being a relevant but comparatively minor part of their retirement income. However, only 12–19 per cent believed the programme would be irrelevant to their future[32] and when asked the broader question, "do you expect to receive Social Security benefits after you retire?", a very stable 60–3 per cent of workers answered in the affirmative.[33]

Of importance, there had not been a steady decline in the legitimacy of Social Security across time nor was there a unique window for change in the sense of temporarily low support for the programme in 2005. Public confidence in the future of the programme was higher in 2005 than in 1981 when Congress and the president went to work on securing the regime for decades to come. In 1981 under a third of Americans had "a great deal" or "fair" amount of confidence that the fund could pay full benefits in 2000 and almost two-thirds had "little or no confidence at all" (Bowman 2005, 7). Yet such is the legitimacy of Social Security that even when public anticipation of future returns is impaired, Americans supported the difficult decisions necessary to secure the path into the future and they unambiguously rejected the risk of path-breaking change. In January 2005, just 13 per cent of respondents thought Social Security needed a complete overhaul, similar numbers to those saying that the programme was fine as it stands (11 per cent). A plurality of 43 per cent recommended minor changes and less than a third (31 per cent) thought major reforms were required.[34] When pollsters presented Americans with reform options in February 2005, a massive 86 per cent opposed "cutting guaranteed benefits for future retirees."[35] There was even greater support for increasing Social Security taxes (53 per cent) and cutting benefits (38 per cent).[36] Given that the president's plan would have cut guaranteed benefits, it is unsurprising that by June 2005, under a third of Americans thought that Bush's proposal would stabilize the long-term future of Social Security.[37] Opponents of private accounts also held disproportionately intense opinions on this score: a plurality of 38 per cent were "strongly opposed", against just 13 per cent who were "strongly in favour".[38]

As with other institutionalized and legitimate programmes, the president's scope for moving public opinion on Social Security was weak (Edwards 2003, 2006; Edwards and Brown 1996; Jerit 2006). Again, this is predictable when we conceive of the regime as causally prior to short-term political variables in conditioning the opportunities for change. The notable absence of de-institutionalization or delegitimization of Social Security across time or even temporarily in 2005, should have sent very clear signals to the administration that even a hugely expensive public relations campaign would not move opinion. The standing properties of Social Security mattered more in shaping the opportunities for change than presidential communication efforts.

In summary, presidential policy leadership is notoriously difficult for a whole range of political and institutional reasons. In the case of Social Security, the leadership challenge was exacerbated by the fact that the existing regime was not ripe for partial privatization. The history of Social Security reveals a path that had been continually strengthened across time. All significant changes to the programme had been on-path in the sense that they had remediated near-term inefficiencies and secured its future. The bi-partisan effort supporting these reforms illustrated the legitimacy of the regime as well as a lack of consensus concerning the superiority of alternative paths. This sequence of repeated moves had not given way to a pattern of gradual retrenchments or programmatic fragmentation across time in the way that characterized the last two decades of AFDC's life. The programme had not suffered from a broad delegitimization in the way that Americans perceived welfare as a source of poverty and moral degeneracy at the point of reform. In short, the properties of the regime itself are causally prior to presidential politicking in understanding the capacity for path-breaking change and in the case of Social Security George Bush's agenda required him to go into combat against an institutionally reinforced and deeply legitimate programme that had a strong status quo bias.

Partisan Asymmetries in Presidential Leadership

Historical institutionalism and path-dependence theory in particular are notoriously susceptible to the dangers of institutional determinism. Our conceptualization of the impact of political agency in presidential studies remains dominated by attempts to capture the impact of the skills and character of the individual office holder. There may be less personal and unpredictable ways of conceptualizing the impact of the actor. The single most systematic way of differentiating presidents' leadership capacity on salient issues is in terms of their partisanship, and not simply in terms of the effect ideology exerts on their policy preferences. Parties have historically developed images that connect them with specific issues in the public mind. Issue-ownership often comes about during periods of critical realignment, such as the New Deal for the Democrats (Trilling 1976). Parties own the issues in which they have the greatest interest, on which they have delivered the preferred outcome previously and on which they are trusted to deliver the preferred outcome in the future (see Budge 2001, 82; Budge and Bara 2001, 62).

Cognitive psychologists have documented how respondents' reaction varies to identical pieces of information when disseminated by different speakers owing to fluctuations in levels of trust and perceived knowledge (Druckman 1998, 2001). Because voters are subject to time, energy, and interest constraints, as well as cognitive limitations, they take cues from actors whom they trust. Actors who enjoy higher levels of trust, as Druckman has shown, have a higher capacity to frame policy problems. Presidential trust, in turn, positively correlates with higher approval ratings, increasing political capital among other Washington actors (Hetherington and Globetti 2006; Rivers and Rose 1985).

Figure 13.3 indicates that voters' trust in the Democrats to handle Social Security is robust between 1981 and 2005. There is not a single instance of the Republicans winning the confidence of voters on the issue and the Democratic lead is significant across time.[39]

More specific questions, with more precise prompts, reinforce this asymmetry in political trust. Figure 13.4 reveals a huge lead for the Democrats in Congress over either President Bush or Congressional Republicans, showing a 2:1 margin of trust in the Democrats' favour between January and May 2005 when the president took his case to the American people. Although the Democrats' lead has not broken the 50 per cent barrier during the recent reform effort on this more specific question, the partisan advantage typically exceeds 20 percentage points.

The Democrats strong partisan advantage on Social Security helps explain Bush's low approval ratings on reform (see Hetherington and Globetti 2006).

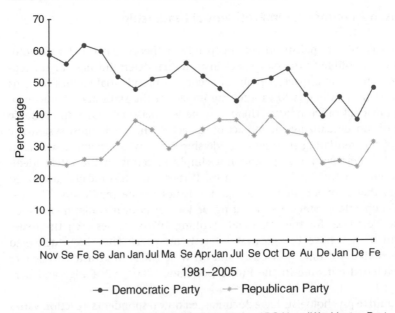

Percentage

70
60
50
40
30
20
10
0

Nov Se Fe Se Jan Jan Jul Ma Se Apr Jan Jul Se Oct De Au De Jan De Fe

1981–2005

—●— Democratic Party   —✳— Republican Party

Data: Between November 1981 and August 2003 the *ABC News/Washington Post* question asked, "Which political party, the Democrats or the Republicans, do you trust to do a better job of protecting the Social Security system? The data from December 2003 to December 2004 come from NBC/*Wall Street Journal* polls that ask, "When it comes to the following issues, which party do you think would do a better job: the Democratic Party, the Republican Party, both about the same, or neither ... deal with Social Security." The data for February 2005 are from a CBS/*New York Times* poll which asked, "Regardless of how you usually vote, do you think the Republican Party or the Democratic Party is more likely to make the right decisions about Social Security?" All polls recorded in Bowman (2005, 35–6).

Figure 13.3. Best US party on social security

The president's already weak approval ratings probably magnified these affects. Figure 13.5 charts President Bush's approval rating on Social Security, in isolation of other actors, from June 2001 to June 2005. As we would expect, the president enjoyed a temporary post-9/11 boost in his approval ratings that lasts for the following two years, with a minor blip a year after 9/11. After April 2003, however, his disapproval ratings again exceeded his positive polling figures. By spring 2005, when Bush was attempting reform, just one-third of Americans approved of the way he was handling Social Security.[40] Indeed, by the end of February, the president was receiving lower ratings on Social Security than on any other issue. Almost two-thirds of Americans, a significant 62 per cent, feared that he would "go too far" in reforming the programme (see Bowman 2005, 35).

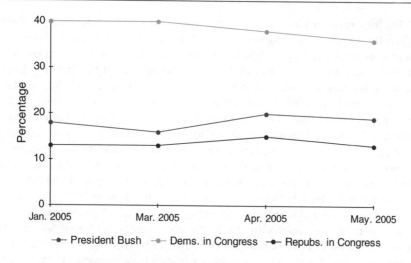

Source: Westhill Partners/Hotline, "Who do you trust the most to protect Social Security ... President Bush, or Democrats in Congress, or the Republicans in Congress?"

Figure 13.4. Trust to protect social security, January–May 2005

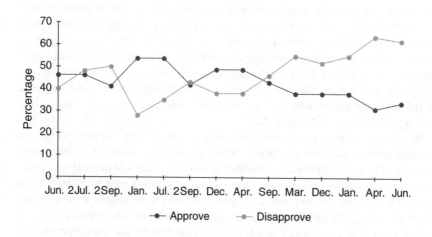

Source: ABC News/Washington Post survey: "Do you approve or disapprove of the way President Bush is handling Social Security?" reported in Bowman (2005, 37).

Figure 13.5. Presidential approval: social security

437

The impact of a leadership asymmetry on Social Security was starkly evident when the Democrats changed their policy frames. In opposition to President Bush's plans for partial privatization, Congressional Democrats switched their rhetoric from the "crisis" to "challenge" of Social Security in January 2005. Between January and February 2005, the number of Americans believing that Social Security required "major changes" within two years dropped by 11 percentage points from 49 per cent to 38 per cent (CNN/USA Today/Gallup, February 2005). By February 2005, a CBS News/New York Times poll reported that just 15 per cent of Americans agreed that Social Security was in crisis.[41] Likewise, as Democratic lawmakers emphasized the privatization aspects of the president's plan, growing numbers of Americans began to report that Bush's real objective was to terminate Social Security. By May 2005, 49 per cent of Americans claimed that Bush was trying to dismantle the programme.[42]

This partisan asymmetry in the leadership capacity on Social Security is one reason why a bi-partisan approach to reform is particularly important for Republican presidents and why a *politics of polarization* was so likely to fail. Democratic involvement is critical to assuring voters of the safety of change and bringing along wavering lawmakers.

The partisan disadvantage that Republican presidents labor under in seeking to restructure Social Security is reinforced by asymmetrical reactions among lawmakers that extend beyond the impact of public opinion. We have long known that labour unions react unequally to reforms by parties of the left and right (Garrett and Lange 1989). We also find a similar dynamic among legislators. The strongest opponents of Social Security reform, Democratic lawmakers and their interest group network, have clear strategic and ideological incentives to block path-breaking reform by a Republic president. Conversely, while they may not welcome restructuring by a Democratic president, some liberals will support their leader for strategic and partisan reasons. Many Democrats, for example, who supported the Welfare Reform Act in 1996 routinely referred to workfare as 'slavefare' just eight years earlier during passage of the Family Support Act.[43]

In short, partisan issue-ownership adds a predictable dimension to our understanding of how key actors affect policy leadership. The impact of partisanship is not limited to whether presidents share ideological and party bonds with congressional majorities. Historically developed partisan images produce asymmetries in trust and approval ratings on salient issues. Public trust in the agents of change is particularly important when leaders seek to break institutionalized and popular paths. In light of the partisan asymmetries on Social Security, it was unsurprising that George W. Bush could not move public opinion in support of partial privatization and that going public for two months would harden opposition to his plans. A highly partisan approach to reform by a Republican administration is only feasible in the case of very strong congressional majorities, particularly in the Senate. Even then, the risks remain high in terms of political exposure and legitimacy; as Arnold (1998, 223) states, "[m]ost legislators are unwilling to forfeit their careers to advance even a very good idea."

Conclusion: Understanding Social Policy Leadership

The short-term variables known to condition opportunities for presidential leadership might reasonably have generated the prediction that partial privatization of Social Security could be achieved in 2005. A re-elected president, enjoying increased majorities in both Houses of Congress, who hit the ground running and achieved big wins very early in his first administration through speed, focus, and presidential commitment, might well have been expected to deliver similar successes in the initial days of his second administration. Although the president's approval ratings were comparatively poor on entering his second term and he faced unified opponents, notably the AARP and a cohesive Democratic opposition, he had floated the issue of partial privatization in the 2000, 2002, and 2004 elections and increased his political support each time.

Of course, all path-breaking reform is loaded to fail. George Bush also made a number of political miscalculations. He exacerbated Democratic opposition and divided members of his own party by specifying a narrow set of reform alternatives. He should have framed his reforms as a rescue mission, diffused blame, and hidden costs (see Arnold 1998). Paul Pierson (1994, 19) identifies three such strategies that leaders may use to lessen opposition to pension reform: "obfuscation, division and compensation." President Bush attempted none of these. Instead he went public and partisan.

These errors, however, do not alone explain the failure of the Bush Administration to deliver significant Social Security reform. The persisting institutionalization and legitimacy of Social Security are far more important explanations. Established regimes can be changed endogenously but usually after a period of de-institutionalization and delegitimization. Social Security showed no signs of weakening across time. On the contrary, it remained a near-universal insurance system covering 90 per cent of the population that had been strengthened over time through a series of difficult decisions. No major reforms to the programme had ever been enacted without bipartisan support and all had been targeted at rescuing the system in response to a near-term crisis. Never had Social Security reform been driven by an ideological desire to alter its ethos or principles and there was absolutely no overriding feeling even among younger Americans of "anything but Social Security". Most Americans remained committed to a system of guaranteed benefits and were, to varying extents, willing to accept painful measures to secure this end.

439

In terms of the path of Social Security, the opportunities for leadership were not there to be exploited and the Bush Administration's sense of optimism based on their immediate political capital was unwarranted.[44] Their failed initiative, of course, also adds to the path, incubating the idea of privatization beyond the world of conservative think tanks (see King 1996).[45]

Likewise, in terms of the role of political actors, moving institutionally entrenched and legitimate programmes requires voters and organized interests to place considerable trust in the agents of change, particularly when they are planning radically to reform a long-standing, popular, and successful programme in favour of an unknown system that risks leaving clients considerably poorer. The concept of issue-ownership helps explain why parties assume an unequal risk in reforming social programmes: voters do not react with neutrality to political issues and they have significantly less trust in Republican leadership on social policy. Trust, in turn, affects approval ratings and the strategic interests of lawmakers. Asymmetries in public reactions to social policy reforms by the Republicans and Democrats are reinforced at the institutional level.

To conclude, an analysis of the path and partisan politics of Social Security generates less optimistic predictions regarding the opportunities for presidential leadership than might be drawn from one based solely on our standard set of variables. In no sense does this imply that these factors are unimportant to the leadership equation. Rather it suggests that we should also think seriously about the properties of the regime and the characteristics of the actors seeking its reform. Our analysis generates three broad propositions for students of presidential leadership:

1. Presidents severely exaggerate their leadership capacity when they ignore history and focus on their immediate political environment. History shows that their political capital is rarely as great as it momentarily seems. These dangers are magnified when presidents surround themselves by a court of like-minded ideologues, as did the Bush Administration (Reedy 1970).

2. Presidents should not attempt to bring about significant change in paths that have not already shown some signs of erosion in terms of their institutional foundations and legitimacy. Instead they should opt for an incremental strategy of programmatic fragmentation and differentiation between beneficiaries.

3. Presidents should *not* prioritize issues where their opponents enjoy higher levels of credibility, trust, and approval ratings, particularly on a thin agenda. When presidents use the bully pulpit to promote issues they do not own, they advantage their opponents, raising their political authority and credibility. Domestic legacies are best made up of many, limited issues (Aberbach and Rockman 1999).

References

Aberbach, Joel D., and Rockman, Bert A. 1999. "Hard Times for Presidential Leadership? (And How Would We Know?)." *Presidential Studies Quarterly* 29 (4): 757–77.

Arnold, Douglas R. 1998. "The Politics of Reforming Social Security." *Political Science Quarterly* 113 (2): 213–40.

Binder, Sarah A. 2005. "The Disappearing Political Center," in James P. Pfiffner and Roger H. Davidson (eds.), *Understanding the Presidency*, 3rd edn. London: Pearson Longman.

Bond, Jon R., and Fleisher, Richard. 1990. *The President in the Legislative Arena*. Chicago: University of Chicago Press.

Bowman, Karlyn. 2005. "Attitudes About Social Security Reform." *AEI Public Opinion Survey*, 1–58.

Budge, Ian. 2001. "Theory and Measurement of Party Policy Positions," in Ian Budge, Hans-Dieter Klingermann, Andrea Volkens, Judith Bara, and Eric Tanenbaum (eds.), *Mapping Policy Preferences: Estimates for Parties, Electors and Governments 1945–1998*. Oxford: Oxford University Press.

___and Bara, Judith. 2001. "Manifesto-Based Research: A Critical Review," in Ian Budge, Hans-Dieter Klingermann, Andrea Volkens, Judith Bara, and Eric Tanenbaum (eds.), *Mapping Policy Preferences: Estimates for Parties, Electors and Governments 1945–1998*. Oxford: Oxford University Press.

Crouch, Colin, and Farrell, Henry. 2002. "Breaking the Path of Institutional Development? Alternatives to the New Determinism." *MPIFG Discussion Paper*.

Derthick, Martha. 1979. *Policymaking for Social Security*. Washington, DC: Brookings Press.

Druckman, James N. 1998. "Source Credibility and Framing Effects," presented at the 1998 Annual Meeting of the American Political Science Association, Boston, 3–6 September.

___2001. "On the Limits of Framing Effects: Who Can Frame?" *Journal of Politics* 63 (4): 1041–66.

Edwards, George C., III. 1976. "Presidential Influence in the House: Public Prestige as a Source of Presidential Power." *American Political Science Review* 70 (1): 101–13.

___1983. *The Public Presidency: The Pursuit of Popular Support*. New York: St Martin's.

___1989. *At the Margins: Presidential Leadership of Congress*. New Haven: Yale University Press.

___2003. *On Deaf Ears: The Limits of the Bully Pulpit*. New York: Yale University Press.

___2005. "The Presidential Pulpit: Bully or Baloney?" in James P. Pfiffner and Roger H. Davidson (eds.), *Understanding the Presidency* 3rd edition. London: Pearson Longman.

___2006. *Governing by Campaigning: The Politics of the Bush Presidency*. New York: Pearson Longman.

___and Brown, B. Dan. 1996. "Who Influences Whom? The President, Congress and the Media." *American Political Science Review* 93 (2): 327–44.

___Barrett, Andrew, and Peake, Jeffrey S. 1997. "The Legislative Impact of Divided Government." *American Journal of Political Science* 41 (2): 545–63.

Garrett, G., and Lange, P. 1989. "Government Partisanship and Economic Performance: When and How Does 'Who Governs' Matter?" *Journal of Politics* 51: 676–93.

Hetherington, Marc J., and Globetti, Suzanne. 2006. "The Presidency and Political Trust," in Michael Nelson (ed.), *The Presidency and the Political System*. 8th edn. Washington, DC: CQ Press.

Howell, William; Adler, Scott; Cameron, Charles; and Riemann, Charles. 2000. "Divided Government and the Legislative Productivity of Congress, 1945–94." *Legislative Studies Quarterly*, 25 (2): 285–312.

Jacobs, Lawrence A. 2006. "The Presidency and the Press: The Paradox of the White House Communications War," in Michael Nelson (ed.), *The Presidency and the Political System*. 8th edn. Washington DC: CQ Press.

Jerit, Jennifer. 2006. "Reform, Rescue, or Run out of Money? Problem Definition in the Social Security Reform Debate." *Harvard International Journal of Press/Politics* 11 (1): 9–28.

Kernell, Samuel. 1997. *Going Public: New Strategies of Presidential Leadership*, 3rd edn. Washington, DC: CQ Press.

King, Desmond. 1992. "The Establishment of Work-Welfare Programs in Britain and the USA," in Sven Steinmo, Kathleen Thelen, and Frank Longstreth (eds.), *Structuring Politics: Historical Institutionalism in Comparative Analysis*. Cambridge: Cambridge University Press.

——1995. *Actively Seeking Work? The Politics of Unemployment and Welfare Policy in the United States and Britain*. Chicago: University of Chicago Press.

——1996. "Sectionalism and Policy Formation in the United States: President Carter's Welfare Initiatives." *British Journal of Political Science* 26 (3): 337–67.

——1999. *In the Name of Liberalism: Illiberal Social Policy in the United States and Britain*. Oxford: Oxford University Press.

Lau, Richard. 1985. "Two Explanations for Negativity Effects in Political Behavior." *American Journal of Political Science* 29 (1): 119–38.

Light, Paul C. 1995. *Still Artful Work: The Continuing Politics of Social Security Reform*. New York: McGraw-Hill.

——2000. "Domestic Policy Making." *Presidential Studies Quarterly*, 30 (1): 109–32.

——2004. "Fact Sheet on the President's Domestic Agenda." ⟨http://www.brookings.edu/views/papers/Light/20041012.pdf⟩, accessed 21 November 2006.

Mahoney, James. 2000. "Path dependence in Historical Sociology." *Theory and Society* 29 (4): 507–48.

Maltese, John A. 1992. *Spin Control: The White House Office of Communications and the Management of Presidential News*. Chapel Hill: University of North Carolina Press.

Mayhew, David. 1991. *Divided We Govern: Party Control, Lawmaking, and Investigations, 1946–1990*. New Haven: Yale University Press.

Mezey, M. 1989. *Congress, the President and Public Policy*. Boulder: Westview.

Peters, B. Guy; Pierre, Jon, and King, Desmond. 2005. "The Politics of Path Dependency: Political Conflict in Historical Institutionalism." *Journal of Politics* 67 (4): 1275–300.

Peterson, Mark A. 1990. *Legislating Together: The White House and Capitol Hill from Eisenhower to Reagan*. Cambridge, Mass.: Harvard University Press.

Petrocik, Jon R. 1996. "Issue-Ownership in Presidential Elections, with a 1980 Case Study." *American Journal of Political Science* 40 (3): 825–50.

Pierson, Paul. 1994. *Dismantling the Welfare State? Reagan, Thatcher, and the Politics of Retrenchment.* Cambridge: Cambridge University Press.

—— 2000. "Increasing Returns, Path Dependence, and the Study of Politics". *American Political Science Review* 94 (2): 251–67.

Polsby, Nelson W. 1984. *Political Innovation in America: The Politics of Policy Innovation.* New Haven: Yale University Press.

Price, David E. 2004*a*. "House Democrats under Republican Rule: Reflections on the Limits of Partisanship", paper given at the Miller Center of Public Affairs, University of Virginia, 16 January.

Reedy, George. 1970. *The Twilight of the Presidency.* New York: New American Library.

Rivers, Douglas, and Rose, Nancy L. 1985. "Passing the President's Program: Public Opinion and Presidential Influence in Congress." *American Journal of Political Science* 29 (2): 183–96.

Schwartz, Herman. 2002. "Down the Wrong Path: Path Dependence, Markets, and Increasing Returns." Typescript, University of Virginia.

Skowronek, Stephen. 1997. *The Politics Presidents Make: Leadership from John Adams to Bill Clinton.* Cambridge, Mass.: Harvard University Press.

Solomon, Carmen D. 1986. "Major Decisions in the House and Senate Chambers on Social Security: 19354985." *Congressional Research Service Report for Congress,* EPW, 86–193, 29 December.

Spriggs, William E. 2005. "'Pulling a Fast One? The Facts about Social Security." *The Crisis* (March/April): 17–21, ⟨http://www.epinet.org/issueguides/socialsecurity/spriggs.naacp.crisis.20050304.pdf⟩, accessed 21 November 2006.

Thelen, Kathleen. 2002. "How Institutions Evolve: Insights from Comparative Historical Analysis," in James Mahoney and Dieter Rueschemeyer (eds.), *Comparative Historical Analysis in the Social Sciences: Innovations in Theory and Methods.* Cambridge: Cambridge University Press.

Trilling, Richard J. 1976. *Party Image and Electoral Behaviour.* New York: Wiley.

Tynes, Sheryl. 1996. *Turning Points in Social Security: From "Cruel Hoax" to "Sacred Entitlement."* Stanford, CA: Stanford University Press.

Weaver, Kent. R. 2003. "The Politics of Public Pension Reform." *CRR WP 2003–06.*

Weller, Christian, and Rasell, Edie. 2000. "Getting Better all the Time: Social Security's Ever-Improving Future," ⟨www.epinet.org/content.cfm/socialsecurity⟩, accessed 21 November 2006.

Notes

1. The concept of issue ownership is an outgrowth of the party image literature (see Trilling 1976). See also Petrocik (1996).
2. The administration's massive $670 billion tax-cutting package, enacted as part of the Economic Growth and Tax Relief Reconciliation Act of 2001 (EGTRRA), placed clear budgetary constraints upon the president's ability to innovate. A Center on Budget and Policy Priorities report revealed that in 2004 federal tax revenues constituted the same proportion of the economy as they did in 1959. ⟨http://www.cbpp.org/2-4-05bud-pr.htm⟩, accessed 21 November 2006. See also Light (2000, 2004).

3. Although President Clinton explicitly framed Social Security as in "crisis", as with earlier presidencies, no detailed reform agenda was forthcoming (see Weaver, 2003). The only legislative action to emerge during his presidency was the non-contentious PL 106-182, signed in April 2000, repealing the earnings test for Americans between ages 65–9.

4. Quoted in *The Economist*, "A Pretty Sticky first 100 days," 7 May 2005, 47–89. DeLay's optimism was reminiscent of that of Carter officials regarding the opportunities for welfare reform. King (1996, 337) recounts how two of Carter's aides sent a memo to the president claiming "We believe you have an historic opportunity to establish new ideals for social and economic justice that will set the pattern in this country for the next several decades."

5. Center on Budget and Policy Priorities ⟨http://www.cbpp.org/2-2-05socsec4.htm⟩, accessed 21 November 2006. According to the president's plan, Americans under the age of 55 years would be able to divert up to 4 per cent of their payroll taxes to accounts that would fluctuate with the vagaries of the stock market. Government would administer the account at a cost and regulate the annuity.

6. Figures from the Center on Budget and Public Priorities ⟨http://www.cbpp.org/2-2-05socsec4.htm⟩; Economic Policy Institute ⟨http://www.epinet.org/⟩, both accessed 21 November 2006.

7. The president initially framed his plan in terms of *private* investment accounts. As public opinion began to harden against the idea and the reference became a liability, Bush and his aides changed their frames to *personal* accounts. See Edwards (2006) for a good discussion of this change of frames.

8. In the 108th Congress the Republicans regained a majority of 51 seats in the Senate, increasing this bare majority to 55 seats in the 109th Congress. In the House, they improved their majority, gaining 229 seats, increasing this lead further to 231 in the 109th Congress.

9. Edwards (2006, 252) offers a detailed discussion of this effort. He describes the initiative as "perhaps the most extensive public relations campaign in the history of the presidency on behalf of reforming Social Security."

10. Kernell suggests that the success of a "going public" strategy is contingent upon already sound approval ratings: unpopular presidents run the risk of weakening support for their message and are better advised to distance themselves from their initiatives. Party conflict increases media negativity towards the president, in turn depressing his approval ratings (Jacobs 2006).

11. Hetherington and Globetti (2006, 235) note that Bush is the only president since polling began to be granted a second term with approval ratings below the 50 per cent barrier.

12. Party voting has been as high in the House as during the Truman administration (Price 2004a, 4). A highly partisan mode of leadership, however, is a far less rational strategy in an era with a de-aligned electorate, and particularly so with regard to restructuring a salient and popular entitlement.

13. ⟨http://www.alternet.org/columnists/story/20916⟩. *The Washington Post* claimed that Wall Street would benefit to the tune of $240 billion in fees in the initial 12 years alone through their management of personal accounts. See "Paycheck Economics," Economic Policy Institute, ⟨http://www.epinet.org/content/cmf/paycheck_pesum1⟩. Both websites accessed 21 November 2006.

14. In a public statement of opposition to private accounts, the AARP's leadership complained that Bush's "new system could require as much as $2 trillion or more in benefit cuts, new taxes, or more debt" (cited in Jacobs 2006, 302).
15. *New York Times*, 21 February 2005. See also ⟨http://www.prwatch.org/node/3343⟩. This is a similar amount to that spent on adverts by interest groups during President's Clinton's health care initiative. See *The Economist*, 12 March 2005, 53.
16. *The Economist*, "Candidate Bush Returns," 12 March 2005, 53. See Maltese (1992) on the role of internal unity in promoting the president's message.
17. Edwards (2006) offers an illuminating account of the difficulties the administration had in scheduling this event, illustrating the challenges that presidents confront in reaching the public.
18. See Allan Sloan, *Washington Post*, 21 April 2006.
19. *ABC News/Washington Post* survey reported in Bowman (2005, 37).
20. ⟨http://www.pbs.org/newshour/bb/social_security/jan-june05/ss_4-26.html⟩, accessed 21 November 2006.
21. See Edwards (2006) for a detailed discussion of congressional reactions.
22. ⟨http://www.foxnews.com/story/0,2933,162474,00.html⟩, accessed 21 November 2006.
23. ⟨http://www.hillnews.com/thehill/export/TheHill/News/Frontpage/060105/social.html⟩, accessed 21 November 2006.
24. January 2006 State of the Union address: ⟨http://www/whitehouse.gov/news/releases/2006/01/20060131-10.html⟩, accessed 21 November 2006.
25. See Rivers and Rose (1985). The president's approval ratings subsequently plummeted. By May 2006, standing at 31 per cent, they were the lowest since he assumed office and the third lowest for any president in the past half century. While these ratings were primarily a function of Iraq, the economy, and immigration, some Republicans had already begun to distance themselves from the president during his campaign to reform Social Security. "Polls Give Bush Worst Marks Yet on Major Issues," *New York Times*, 10 May 2006, 1.
26. Derthick (1979) offers an insightful account of these changes that Arnold draws upon in reviewing the history of the programme.
27. See Derthick (1979) and Tynes (1996) for an analysis of these reforms.
28. ⟨http://www.ssa.gov/history/briefhistory3.html⟩, accessed 21 November 2006.
29. See King (1996) on the difficulties sectionalism played in forging coalitions during the Carter administration over and above institutional and relational variables.
30. For example, disability primarily induced by alcoholism and drug addiction was excluded from coverage, eligibility criteria for disabled children were tightened, and legal non-citizen immigrants had their rights to SSI curtailed.
31. Perhaps the only mild exception has been with regard to definitions of disability. However, these concerns have been long-standing and are not indicative of a broader moralizing about the negative incentives deriving from benefits.
32. Gallup/CNN/*USA Today poll* reported in Bowman (2005, 3).
33. Fox News/Opinion Dynamics polls taken between May 2002 and December 2004 reported in Bowman (2005, 8). Question wording can make a large difference to responses on Social Security. Questions that emphasize the crisis of the programme produce more negative responses than open-ended prompts.

34. NBC/*Wall Street Journal* poll reported in Bowman (2005, 15).
35. *Washington Post*/Kaiser/Harvard poll February 2005 reported ibid. 29.
36. Gallup/CNN/*USA Today* poll reported ibid. 31.
37. An ABC News/*Washington Post* survey reported ibid. 47.
38. February 2005 National Public Radio poll reported ibid. 45.
39. The Democrats' absolute level of trust on handling Social Security has declined across time. Hetherington and Globetti (2006) argue that the public's increased distrust in government more generally impairs their trust in political leadership on particular issues. Because the Democrats are associated with using government to further their policy ends, they have been disproportionately hurt by the broader decline in trust in government.
40. *CBS News* polls actually put the President's approval ratings as low as a quarter.
41. ⟨PollingReport.com/social.htm⟩, accessed 21 November 2006.
42. In May 2005 a Harris Interactive poll asked, "Do you think that President Bush's real agenda is to save and strengthen Social Security or to dismantle Social Security as we know it?" Poll cited in Bowman (2005, 40).
43. *Congressional Quarterly*, 20 April 1996, 1025.
44. King (1996) makes this point very effectively with respect to Carter's failed welfare reforms in contrast to Reagan's Family Support Act (see King 1992).
45. King (1996) describes how the failed welfare reforms of the Carter administration, with their emphasis on welfare and work, created the conditions for the Reagan Administration's Family Support Act. See also King (1992).

Index

Index

Index

Index